UNDERSTANDING SECURED TRANSACTIONS SECOND EDITION

William H. Lawrence

University of San Diego
School of Law

William H. Henning

University of Missouri-Columbia
School of Law

R. Wilson Freyermuth

University of Missouri-Columbia
School of Law

LEGAL TEXT SERIES

LEXIS Publishing™

LEXIS®-NEXIS® • MARTINDALE-HUBBELL®
MATTHEW BENDER® • MICHIE™ • SHEPARD'S®

QUESTIONS ABOUT THIS PUBLICATION?

For questions about the **Editorial Content** appearing in these volumes or reprint permission, please call:

Michael Bruno, J.D., at .... 1-800-252-9257 Ext. 2518
Michael Starvaggi, J.D., at .... 1-800-252-9257 Ext. 2302
Outside the United States and Canada please call .... (212) 448-2000

For assistance with replacement pages, shipments, billing or other customer service matters, please call:

Customer Services Department at .... (800) 833-9844
Outside the United States and Canada, please call .... (518) 487-3000
Fax number .... (518) 487-3584

For information on other Matthew Bender publications, please call
Your account manager or .... (800) 223-1940
Outside the United States and Canada, please call .... (518) 487-3000

ISBN 0–8205–4060–9

2000 Reprint

Editorial Offices
2 Park Avenue, New York, NY 10016-5675 (212) 448-2000
201 Mission St., San Francisco, CA 94105-1831 (415) 908-3200
701 East Water Street, Charlottesville, VA 22902-7587 (804) 972-7600
www.lexis.com

(Matthew Bender & Co., Inc.)   (Pub.587)

For my son, Marcus, with love

W.H.L.

For my wife, Jeannie,
who is still my sweetheart after all these years

W.H.H.

For my wife, Shari, with love and gratitude

R.W.F.

PREFACE

Like the other books in the *Understanding* series, this book is designed as a student text. Our approach is to aid students' understanding of secured transactions by informing them about both the law and the nature of the underlying transactions.

The primary sources of law are Article 9 of the Uniform Commercial Code and selected provisions of the Bankruptcy Reform Act. Beyond a focus on the text of the statutes, an analysis of their underlying rationales is critical to a true understanding of the codified provisions. The Official Comments to the UCC and the Historical and Revision Notes to the Bankruptcy Reform Act are helpful, but often lack sufficient insights or clarity to provide adequate guidance. Learning the essence of each statutory section in isolation is difficult but insufficient; students must also learn to interrelate multiple sections in a sophisticated manner to solve problems.

When the first edition of this book was published, the 1972 text of Article 9, as amended from time to time, was in effect in all fifty states. In 1998, the UCC's sponsoring bodies, the National Conference of Commissioners on Uniform State Laws and the American Law Institute, adopted a revised version of Article 9. The revision represents a comprehensive modernization and reformulation of the law governing secured transactions. The 1998 text is not in effect in any state as of the publication date of this book, but it can be expected to replace the 1972 text entirely over the course of the next few years. Promulgation of the 1998 text was the event that sparked our efforts to revise this book. Our goal is to present our readers with a thoroughgoing analysis of both the 1972 and 1998 texts, and to that end we have weaved the discussion of the revision into our treatment of current law.

We have also taken steps — both textual and visual — to avoid confusion. The text consistently alerts the reader to the law under discussion: The existing version of Article 9 is referred to as the 1972 text or version, or current law; its counterpart is called the 1998 text or version, Revised Article 9, or the revision. Further, each reference to a specific section number within the revision is preceded by the letter "R." Thus, a reference to section 9-301 means the 1972 version while section R9-301 refers to the revision. **Perhaps most importantly, our discussion of the revision is presented in bold-face type to avoid any possibility of confusion.** The discussion of the 1972 text and the cases interpreting it are presented in the traditional light-face type.

The law of secured transactions reflects business practices with which many students are unfamiliar. An understanding of the essential aspects of the transactions themselves is crucial for any student who seeks to comprehend the law that governs them. This book explains different types of secured transactions. For example, it describes the structure and use of financing arrangements that are made possible through such techniques as asset-based securitization, mortgage warehouse lending, terminal and field warehousing, financing of accounts, factoring of accounts, and floor planning, as well as other methods. The discussion of each financing arrangement is integrated into the place in the text in which the relevant substantive concepts are covered.

Much of the practice in the area of secured transactions involves preventative law, in which the practitioner advises the client on alternative methods of structuring transactions and the risks associated with each option. The book integrates and develops significant aspects of these considerations, going beyond the text of the UCC by explaining the practical constraints that ultimately shape decision-making in this field.

The organization of the subject matter of the text is largely based upon the traditional five-part approach to the law of secured transactions: scope, creation, perfection, priorities, and default. This organizational scheme is strongly emphasized by designating each of these five concepts a separate Part, which is the basic subdivision of the Table of Contents. In addition, the book contains a sixth Part that explains the rules that will govern the transition from the 1972 text to the 1998 revision.

Entries in the Table of Contents include a descriptive word or phrase, along with the basic section number of the UCC (both versions) and the Bankruptcy Reform Act. The Table of Contents does not include all of the sections that might be relevant, but only the most fundamental provisions relating to the topics indicated in the Table of Contents. This approach should aid students using the book as a supplemental text by enabling them to find the relevant discussion based on either the subject or the basic statutory section numbers. The Index and the Table of Statutes and Authorities enable a more detailed search.

ACKNOWLEDGMENTS

ACKNOWLEDGMENTS

Professor Lawrence gratefully acknowledges the support provided by a summer research grant from the University of San Diego.

Professor Henning gratefully acknowledges the extraordinary assistance of Cheryl Poelling, who has helped him in so many ways and on so many projects. He is also grateful for the generosity of John K. Hulston, an outstanding Missouri attorney and author whose generous financial support was instrumental to the successful completion of this book.

Professor Freyermuth gratefully acknowledges the generosity of John K. Hulston, W. Dudley and Elizabeth McCarter, and Charles H. Rehm, whose financial support facilitated his contributions to this book.

March 1999

William H. Lawrence
William H. Henning
R. Wilson Freyermuth

TABLE OF CONTENTS

PART I: SCOPE

[A] The Security Concept
[B] An Organizational Overview of Article 9

CHAPTER 1
TRANSACTIONS WITHIN ARTICLE 9

PART II: ATTACHMENT OF SECURITY INTERESTS

CHAPTER 2
CREATION AND ENFORCEABILITY OF SECURITY INTERESTS

CHAPTER 3
ONGOING FINANCING RELATIONSHIPS

PART III: PERFECTION OF SECURITY INTERESTS

CHAPTER 4
PERFECTION IN GENERAL

CHAPTER 5
PERFECTION BY FILING

CHAPTER 6
PERFECTION BY POSSESSION AND CONTROL

CHAPTER 7
AUTOMATIC PERFECTION

CHAPTER 8
TEMPORARY PERFECTION AND PERFECTION OF PROCEEDS

CHAPTER 9
MULTI-STATE TRANSACTIONS

PART IV: PRIORITIES

CHAPTER 10
AMONG SECURED CREDITORS

CHAPTER 11
PURCHASERS (OTHER THAN SECURED PARTIES) VERSUS PERFECTED SECURED PARTIES

CHAPTER 12
THE FARM PRODUCTS RULE

CHAPTER 13
CREDITORS WITH LIENS ARISING BY OPERATION OF LAW

CHAPTER 14
PURCHASERS (OTHER THAN SECURED PARTIES), LIEN CREDITORS, AND OTHER CLAIMANTS VERSUS UNPERFECTED SECURED PARTIES

CHAPTER 15
FIXTURES, ACCESSIONS AND PRODUCTS

PART V: DEFAULT

CHAPTER 17
DEFAULT AND ITS CONSEQUENCES

CHAPTER 18
THE FORECLOSURE PROCESS

CHAPTER 19
THE CONSEQUENCES OF CREDITOR MISBEHAVIOR

CHAPTER 20
THE TRANSITION TO REVISED ARTICLE 9

TABLE OF CASES

TABLE OF STATUTES

INDEX

PART I:

SCOPE

SYNOPSIS

[A]   The Security Concept

The concept of a secured obligation arose to encourage lending, and thus promote commercial activity, by reducing the risk borne by lenders. Absent security, a borrower's mere promise to repay borrowed money, albeit legally enforceable, might not suffice to induce a prospective lender to proceed with a transaction; and even if the lender agreed to proceed the interest rate would inevitably reflect the level of risk. Similarly, a seller might be reluctant to give a prospective buyer current possession of property based solely on the buyer's promise to make installment payments. Lenders and credit sellers inevitably, whether secured or not, run the risk that their obligor will prove unable or unwilling to make the agreed payments. An unsecured creditor of either type who wishes to enforce its rights following such a breach must proceed through judicial action. The process can be long and expensive, requiring a lawsuit to reduce the claim to judgment, and then perhaps an execution on the judgment. To execute on a judgment, the successful litigant must procure a writ of execution, which the sheriff will attempt to execute by levying on property of the debtor. Exemption provisions may shield some or all of the debtor's property from the execution process. For property that is reached, the sheriff will conduct an auction sale, which generally yields low prices, and distribute the proceeds to the creditor in satisfaction of the judgment. The expense and delay associated with these procedures leaves lenders and sellers reluctant to rely solely upon their rights under debt or sales law.

Lenders and credit sellers can enhance their positions in several ways. They can, for example, insist that their obligor obtain a promise from a third person to act as surety and repay the obligation in the event of default. They can also insist that their obligor grant them an interest in real or personal property as security. This latter technique gives the creditor a special property interest in the identified property. One of the great advantages of this enhanced position is that, in the event of default, the creditor can proceed directly against the security without having first to reduce the claim to judgment. Costs and delays in enforcing the rights of secured creditors thus can be reduced significantly.

Although mortgage financing and secured financing are analogous operations, with respect to real and personal property, respectively, they are governed by separate bodies of law. The focus of this book is on secured personal-property financing, with Article 9 of the Uniform Commercial Code (U.C.C.) as the predominant applicable law. There are overlaps that will be discussed in this book, the most important being the treatment of fixtures.[1]

In Article 9 terminology, the creditor's special property interest is called a "security interest,"[2] . and it is created through the consent of the debtor. Absent a security interest, a creditor has no property interest in any particular asset of its debtor. An unsecured seller of goods does not retain a property interest even in the goods sold;[3] in the event of a breach, the seller's basic remedy is its Article 2 claim for the unpaid balance of the purchase price.[4] Acquiring a consensual security interest adds the rights available to secured parties under Article 9.

Although a security interest gives a secured party a property interest in identified assets of the debtor, the interest is unique. Two primary features of the property interest define its essential nature. First, the secured party does not have any right to proceed against the property unless the debtor is in default.[5] Because the secured party's property interest does not allow it to proceed against the property in the absence of debtor default, such action would constitute conversion. Second, even following a default, the secured creditor's disposition of the collateral is only for the purpose of satisfying the outstanding indebtedness of the debtor. Generally, the secured creditor will sell the collateral and apply the proceeds against the amount of the debt still owed.[6] . The secured creditor cannot retain any surplus realized upon the sale, but rather must account for it to the debtor.[7] Security is thus designed to allow a lender or credit seller to proceed, after default and without judicial process, directly against specific assets of the debtor to satisfy the outstanding indebtedness.

[B]   An Organizational Overview of Article 9

The content of Article 9 is organized around five major conceptual areas: the scope of Article 9; attachment of security interests; perfection of security interests; priorities in collateral; and default. These concepts are so logical and basic that the text of this book is also structured around them; they constitute the subjects of the first five Parts of this book. A sixth Part deals with the transition to the revised Article 9.

---

[1] For discussion of fixtures, *see* Chapter 15 *infra. See also* § 1.07[C] *infra* (discussion of secondary financing of obligations secured by interests in real estate).

[2] U.C.C. § 1-201(37)

[3] A "sale" involves the passage of title to goods for a price. U.C.C. § 2-106(1). Unless the seller and buyer agree otherwise, the goods belong to the buyer and the seller receives in exchange only a legally enforceable right to the purchase price. U.C.C. §§ 2-607(1), 2-709(1).

[4] A credit seller may also have a right to reclaim the goods themselves from the buyer, but such rights are extremely limited. The seller must ascertain that the buyer received the goods while insolvent, and even then the seller generally must notify the buyer of its intent to reclaim them within ten days following their receipt. *See* U.C.C. § 2-702.

[5] "Unless otherwise agreed a secured party has *on default* the right to take possession of the collateral." U.C.C. § 9-503(emphasis supplied). **Revised Artcle 9 is similar.** § **R9-609(a)(1).** For discussion of this provision, *see* § 17.02 *infra.*

[6] U.C.C. §§ 9-504(1), **R9-615(a)**

[7] U.C.C. §§ 9-504(2), **R9-615(d)(1).** For discussion of the disposition of collateral after default, *see* § 18.02 *infra.*

Scope questions focus on identification of the transactions to which Article 9 applies. Although, generally, the applicability of Article 9 is eminently apparent, the issue has proved to be one of the most litigated areas under the U.C.C. Certain transactions may be labeled as something other than a security interest by the parties (*e.g.*, a lease or consignment) yet be the functional equivalent of an Article 9 secured transaction and thus within its scope.[8] In addition, certain outright sales transactions also fall within the scope of Article 9.[9]

"Attachment" of a security interest addresses how security interests are created. The process is contractual, because security interests are consensual in nature and thus must be created by agreement. The essential requirements are quite simple, although troublesome questions inevitably arise in some specific contexts. Enforceability of the agreement is also relevant through the inclusion in Article 9 of a statute-of-frauds provision.

Although the Article 9 relationship between a secured party and a debtor is established through the contract embodied in their security agreement, the secured party should also be concerned about the prospect of competing third-party claims to the collateral. In particular, courts are sympathetic with third parties who enter into relationships with the debtor on the mistaken belief that the debtor holds unencumbered ownership of the assets in its possession. This problem is sometimes referred to as an "ostensible ownership" problem. To enhance their position against such claimants, secured parties must ordinarily "perfect" their security interests, generally by taking steps that will publicize their interests. The most effective mechanism for overcoming the ostensible ownership problem is for the secured party to take possession of the collateral, and thus possession is an accepted method of perfection for assets capable of being physically possessed. Possession is often impractical, however, and the most commonly used alternative method of perfection is the public filing of a financing statement.[10] Perfection issues focus on the applicable methods of perfection and the policy choices that the drafters made in devising the perfection process.

When the interests of claimants conflict with respect to particular property, the law must have rules by which it can prioritize the competing interests. When one of the competing claimants is a secured party, most of these priority rules are contained in Article 9. Federal bankruptcy law is also important with respect to secured claims that are asserted in a bankruptcy proceeding. Some of the third-party claimants with whom a secured party might have to compete include a bankruptcy trustee, another secured party, an unsecured creditor who causes the sheriff to levy on the collateral, a person who buys or leases the collateral from the debtor, a person who stores or repairs the collateral and thereby acquires a claim to it based on state law other than Article 9, a governmental entity asserting a statutory claim to the collateral to satisfy an unpaid tax obligation, and a person other than the debtor with an interest in real estate that is the location for a fixture that is collateral. This by no means exhausts the list of potential claimants.

"Default" is a pivotal concept because it opens the opportunity for the secured party to enforce its security interest against the collateral. The enforcement phase of a

---

[8] *See* § 1.03[B] *infra*.

[9] *See* § 1.06 *infra*.

[10] There are several other methods of perfection, discussed generally in Chapter 4 *infra*.

transaction is sometimes referred to as the "foreclosure process." The issues associated with default include a determination of the events that constitute a default, the rights and duties of the parties following a default, the method chosen for the disposition of the collateral, and the provisions dealing with misbehavior by the secured party.

[C] The 1998 Revision

The Uniform Commercial Code is the product of a partnership between two organizations: The National Conference of Commissioners on Uniform State Laws (NCCUSL) and the American Law Institute (ALI). Once an Official Text has been approved by these sponsors, it is introduced in the legislatures of the states and ultimately becomes law only when it has been adopted through the appropriate legislative process. The 1962 Official Text was the first to be widely enacted. The 1962 version of Article 9 represented a radical departure from antecedent security devices,[11] and it was extensively revised in 1972. Although occasionally amended to conform with revisions to other articles, the 1972 Official Text is, as of the time of publication of this book, in effect in all fifty states and the District of Columbia.

The Permanent Editorial Board (PEB) is a standing committee within NCCUSL which oversees the development of the Uniform Commercial Code. In 1990, the PEB commissioned a study group to examine whether Article 9 should again be revised. On December 1, 1992 the study committee issued a report specifying certain areas in need of change and recommending that a drafting committee be appointed to begin the revision process. A thoroughly revised Article 9 was approved by its sponsors in 1998, and the text of the Code containing the revision is properly referred to as the 1998 Official Text. It is not yet the law anywhere, but if past is indeed prologue it can be expected over the next few years to thoroughly supplant the 1972 text.[12]

The 1998 Official Text retains the basic conceptual structure delineated in the preceding subsection, but it is a thoroughgoing revision. Indeed, even the section numbers that have become familiar to the cognoscenti and that were retained when the 1972 text supplanted that of 1962 have been changed. This book continues its comprehensive coverage of the 1972 text but also contains a detailed analysis of the revision. To avoid confusion, the existing version of Article 9 will be referred to as the 1972 text or version, and its counterpart will be referred to as the 1998 text or version, Revised Article 9, or sometimes just as the revision. Discussion of the 1972 text will be provided in light-faced type, **with the analysis of the revision presented in bold-faced type.** In the footnotes, references to the revision will be preceded by the letter "R." Thus, a reference to section 9-203 means the original version of that section, and a reference to section R9-203 means the revised version.

---

[11] *See* § 1.02 *infra.*

[12] The sponsoring organizations are recommending that the legislatures adopting the 1998 revisions select a deferred effective date of July 1, 2001. This will permit a large number of states to switch to the new version at the same time, decreasing the confusion that inevitably surrounds such a major change.

CHAPTER 1

TRANSACTIONS WITHIN ARTICLE 9

SYNOPSIS

§ 1.01 The Pre-Code Disarray of Secured Transactions Law

The law governing the use of personal property as collateral prior to the promulgation of the U.C.C. was inefficient, unduly complicated, and inadequate. It consisted of a patchwork quilt of common-law rules and statutes governing each of the security devices that a state might choose to recognize. Some of the traditional security devices included the pledge (where the lender took possession of the collateral pending default or repayment), chattel mortgage (where the debtor retained possession pending default), conditional sale (where purchased goods were delivered to the buyer but the seller retained title pending payment), trust receipt (a three-party arrangement by which a lender financed a dealer's acquisition of new inventory from a supplier), and factor's lien (where the debtor obtained financing on the strength of its existing inventory).[1]

Because each security device was the subject of a separate rule or statute, differences in formal requirements were common. For example, failure to file public notice of a chattel mortgage generally voided the mortgage against all third parties, whereas filing was not needed for a conditional sale, or at most was required only in order to prevail

---

[1] Other devices, usually authorized by statute, permitted the use of accounts receivable as collateral, facilitated the establishment of corporate trust indentures, authorized the use of field warehouses, etc. A laundry list of pre-Code security devices is provided in U.C.C. § 9-102(2).

over lien creditors.[2] States maintained multiple filing systems to accommodate the different security devices, and inconsistencies in formalities, rights, and filing requirements abounded. Most of the differences could not be traced to functional justifications. Errors attributable to the undue complexity of the overall system were frequent and had a serious impact on affected parties.

Despite the multiplicity of security devices, the overall system was inadequate. The economy constantly evolves, thereby necessitating the creation of new types of transactions that are responsive to unique business conditions. Some desirable secured financing transactions could not go forward because they did not fall squarely within the parameters of any of the existing security devices. For example, despite increased interest in using inventory and intangibles as collateral, lenders struggled for years to develop devices that would be effective for these kinds of assets. These problems were eventually solved in some states by the addition of new, statutorily-sanctioned security devices, but ultimately this approach proved unpalatable as each device added new wrinkles to an already overly-complex system. The state of the law imposed unacceptable delay, cost, and uncertainty.

§ 1.02 The Unitary Approach of Article 9 §§ 9-102, R9-109(a)(1)

The promulgation of Article 9 of the U.C.C. represented a significant milestone in the law of secured financing. Article 9 provides the basis for a single, comprehensive statutory framework for the governance of secured transactions in personal property and fixtures. The objective of the drafters is stated succinctly in the Comments: "The aim of this Article is to provide a simple and unified structure within which the immense variety of present-day secured financing transactions can go forward with less cost and with greater certainty."[3]

Article 9 achieves this objective through its unitary approach to drafting. It does not abolish the previously existing security devices.[4] Even today, the use of terms like "pledge" and "conditional sale" is quite common. The prior statutes governing these forms of security interests have been repealed, however, and the provisions of Article 9 now govern them. Unless specifically excluded,[5] Article 9 applies to all secured transactions in personal property and fixtures. Neither the form of the transaction nor the terminology used by the parties is controlling. In other words, all transactions in which the parties intend to create security interests in personal property or fixtures are swept into the scope of Article 9.[6]

In addition to overcoming the disarray associated with prior secured financing law, the enactment of Article 9 with its comprehensive, unitary approach has facilitated the use of new financing methods. The benefits of such flexibility are touted as among the basic objectives of Article 9. The Comments state:

---

[2] U.C.C. § 9-101 Cmt.

[3] U.C.C. § 9-101 Cmt.

[4] U.C.C. § 9-102(2) and Cmt. 1.

[5] See § 1.07 infra.

[6] U.C.C. §§ 9-102(1)(a), **R9-109(a).**

The Article's flexibility and simplified formalities should make it possible for new forms of secured financing, as they develop, to fit comfortably under its provisions, thus avoiding the necessity, so apparent in recent years, of year by year passing new statutes and tinkering with the old ones to allow legitimate business transactions to go forward.[7]

The simplification achieved by Article 9's unitary approach is readily demonstrated through the terms used to describe secured transactions and their participants. Irrespective of the nature of the transaction or the terminology employed by the parties, Article 9 applies a consistent set of terms. The underlying "security agreement"[8] creates a "security interest"[9] in favor of the "secured party."[10] The property that is subject to the security interest is the "collateral."[11] In the pre-revision Code, the person who owes the payment or other performance of the obligation secured is the "debtor."[12]

Revised Article 9 resolves some ambiguities in the basic terminology. In the 1972 version the term "debtor" can mean either the obligor, the owner of the collateral, or both, depending on the context.[13] For example, suppose that A needs to borrow money but has insufficient collateral. A's friend, B, allows A to use her car as collateral but refuses to become personally obligated for A's debt. Under the 1972 text, the term "debtor" may refer to A, B, or both. For example, Section 9-504(2) provides that after foreclosure the debtor is liable for any deficiency but is entitled to any surplus. As applied to a deficiency, the term refers to A alone since B is not personally obligated to pay the debt. As applied to a surplus, however, the same term refers to B. It is B's car, and if it brings more than enough to pay the debt the equity must be returned to the owner.[14]

Use of the same term to refer to different parties creates confusion, and the revision separates the concepts. In the revision the term "debtor" refers to a person having property rights in the collateral[15] and the term "obligor" refers to a person obligated on the debt.[16] In a transaction in which one person becomes obligated and provides the collateral, that person will be both a debtor and an obligor. In the above hypothetical, A would be an obligor and B would be a debtor. If the above

---

[7] U.C.C. § 9-101, Comment.

[8] U.C.C. §§ 9-105(1)(l), **R9-102(a)(73)**. Security agreements are discussed extensively in Chapter 2.

[9] U.C.C. § 1-201(37). This term has undergone recent revision. It is discussed extensively in the next subsection of the text.

[10] U.C.C. §§ 9-105(1)(m), **R9-102(a)(72)**.

[11] U.C.C. §§ 9-105(1)(c), **R9-102(a)(12)**. For discussion of the different classifications of collateral, *see* §§ 1.04 and 1.10[A] *infra*.

[12] U.C.C. §§ 9-105(1)(d), **R9-102(a)(28)**.

[13] U.C.C. § 9-105(1)(d). The word "owner" does not fully capture the concept. § R9-102(a)(28) more appropriately describes a debtor as "a person having an interest, other than a security interest or other lien, in the collateral . . . "

[14] *See also* U.C.C. § 9-112(enumerating rights and duties when owner of collateral is nonobligor).

[15] U.C.C. § **R9-102(a)(28)**.

[16] U.C.C. § **R9-102(a)(59)**.

transaction qualified as a "consumer transaction,"[17] A would be a "consumer obligor"[18] and B would be a "consumer debtor."[19]

Revised Article 9 also contains certain provisions that apply to parties who are secondarily obligated, such as sureties,[20] and such parties are known as "secondary obligors."[21] If, in our prior example, B had not only provided the car as collateral but had also incurred personal liability for the debt by co-signing A's promissory note for accommodation[22] or by signing a separate guaranty agreement, A would be an obligor and B would be both a debtor and a secondary obligor. For another example, assume that A borrows money and uses his car as collateral. To accommodate A, B co-signs A's note and also grants a security interest in her car as collateral for her obligation as co-signer. If the secured party enforces its security interest in A's car, A is the debtor and an obligor, and B is a secondary obligor. If the secured party enforces its security interest in B's car, A is an obligor but not a debtor. B is the debtor and a secondary obligor.

Finally, in certain situations collateral is transferred from the original debtor to a new debtor who takes subject to the security interest.[23] To differentiate between the parties in such a transaction, revised Article 9 refers to the transferor as the "original debtor"[24] and the transferee as the "new debtor."[25]

§ 1.03   General Applicability of Article 9

[A]   Consensual Security Interests §§ 9-102(2), R9-109(a)(1)

The scope of Article 9 is directed primarily toward a discrete type of encumbrance. It "applies to security interests created by contract"[26] in personal property or fixtures.[27]

---

[17] See U.C.C. § R9-102(a)(26) and discussion in § 1.04[A][1] *infra*. The revision contains a number of protective provisions applicable to consumer transactions.

[18] U.C.C. § R9-102(a)(25).

[19] U.C.C. § R9-102(a)(22).

[20] For example, most of the rights and duties with regard to the foreclosure process affect only secondary obligors. *See, e.g.*, U.C.C. § R9-611(c)(requiring secured party to send notice of disposition to secondary obligors but not obligors).

[21] U.C.C. § R9-102(a)(71).

[22] See U.C.C. § 3-419(a)(accommodation party is one who, without benefitting directly, signs a negotiable instrument in order to accommodate another party to the instrument). An accommodation party's obligation might be stated in primary (*i.e.*, unconditional) terms, but such a party would have a right of recourse against the party accommodated (§ 3-419(e)) and thus would qualify as a secondary obligor.

[23] See, e.g., U.C.C. § R9-508(dealing with the effectiveness of a financing statement filed in the name of the original debtor after a new debtor has become bound by the security agreement).

[24] U.C.C. § R9-102(a)(60)(original debtor is "a person that, as debtor, entered into a security agreement to which a new debtor has become bound under Section 9-203(d)").

[25] Revision § R9-102(a)(56)(new debtor is "a person that becomes bound as debtor under Section 9-203(d) by a security agreement previously entered into by another person.").

[26] U.C.C. §§ 9-102(2), R9-109(a)(1)

[27] U.C.C. §§ 9-102(1)(a), R9-109(a)(1).

"Security interest" is defined broadly in Article 1 as "an interest in personal property or fixtures which secures payment or performance of an obligation."[28] Article 9 thus applies to consensual encumbrances, as distinct from encumbrances that arise by operation of law, such as judicial, common-law, or statutory liens. Excluding certain designated exceptions,[29] Article 9 governs all consensual security interests in personal property and fixtures.

The scope of Article 9 is based on substance rather than form. The 1972 version states that it applies "to any transaction (regardless of its form) which is intended to create a security interest in personal property or fixtures...."[30] Unfortunately, the reference to the intent of the parties has led to undue confusion.[31] With parties sometimes disposed to disguise the true nature of their transactions, courts cannot accept their expressions of intention as controlling and simply pursue their underlying subjective intentions to ascertain the appropriate legal characterization of any given transaction.[32] The Comments to the 1972 version indicate that the parties' intent is to be inferred either from their understanding as to the nature of the transaction or from its effect.[33]

[B] The Revised Definition of "Security Interest" § 1-201(37)

[1] Distinguishing Leases

One of the primary areas of difficulty with the intent standard has been in trying to distinguish secured transactions from leases of goods. With the promulgation of Article 2A on leases of personal property, the drafters extensively amended the Article 1 definition of security interest to address this problem. The previous definition,[34] which relied on intent, was replaced with tests that focus on the transaction's true economic nature.[35]

The essential characteristics of secured transactions and leases are easy to distinguish. A credit seller who retains a security interest in goods delivered to a buyer passes title

---

[28] U.C.C. § 1-201(37).

[29] *See* § 1.07 *infra.*

[30] U.C.C. § 9-102(1)(a).

[31] **U.C.C. § R9-109(a)(1) deletes any reference to intent, referring instead to "a transaction, regardless of its form, that creates a security interest in personal property or fixtures by contract." § R9-109 Cmt. 2 indicates that no change in substance is intended.**

[32] "It is clear enough that 'intended' in [the § 1-201(37) definition of security interest] has nothing to do with the subjective intention of the parties, or either of them." G. Gilmore, *Security Interests in Personal Property* § 11.2 (1965).

[33] "Transactions in the form of consignments or leases are subject to this Article if the understanding of the parties or the effect of the arrangement shows that a security interest was intended." U.C.C. § 9-102 Cmt. 1. **The revision avoids the confusion generated by the word "intended" by defining its basic scope in terms of "a transaction, regardless of its form, *that creates* a security interest in personal property or fixtures by contract." § R9-109(a)(1)(emphasis supplied).**

[34] U.C.C. § 1-201(37)(1987).

[35] U.C.C. § 1-201(37) Cmt. 37.

to the goods.[36] The retained security interest gives the seller the right to repossess the goods in the event of default by the buyer.[37] Upon repossession, the seller/secured party must dispose of the goods[38] and apply the proceeds to the outstanding indebtedness.[39] Any surplus proceeds belong to the buyer/debtor.[40]

A lessor also retains an interest in goods delivered to another, in this case a lessee. Like a secured party, a lessor can repossess the goods following a default.[41] Unlike the secured party, however, the lessor is not required to dispose of the goods following repossession.[42] The lessor owns the residual interest and at the end of the lease term has no obligation to the lessee with regard to that interest.

Distinguishing leases and secured transactions in actual practice has proved difficult and has led to some of the most pervasive litigation under the Code.[43] The similarity of some of the attributes of these two transactions contributes to the problem. An even more significant factor is that, for a variety of reasons related to taxes, accounting or bankruptcy, parties sometimes disguise a secured transaction as a lease. For example, suppose a dealer delivers a piece of equipment to a user pursuant to a written contract binding the user to make 24 equal monthly payments of $1,000 each. The writing, which refers to the transaction as a "lease," the installments as "lease payments," and the parties as "lessor" and "lessee," provides that the user will have the option to purchase the equipment for $10 at the end of the "lease term," even though the parties anticipate that it will have significantly more value at that time. Since any rational economic actor will exercise the option and become the owner, the transaction is the economic equivalent of a sale. Further, the "lessor's" right to repossess the "leased property" in the event of default operates as a security device. The Code directs the courts to look through the parties' terminology and sweeps the security aspects of the transaction into Article 9.[44] This means that the "lessor" will have to follow Article 9's disposition rules after repossession and will have to perfect its interest under Article 9 (usually by a public filing[45]) to obtain priority against third parties that might acquire a competing interest

---

[36] A sale by definition involves the passage of title. U.C.C. § 2-106(1). Even if the seller and buyer agree that the seller will retain title to the goods pending full payment (sometimes called a "conditional sale"), the seller's interest is limited to a reservation of a security interest. § 2-401(1). *See also* § 9-113.

[37] U.C.C. §§ 9-503, **R9-609(a)**.

[38] U.C.C. §§ 9-504(1), **R9-610(a)**.

[39] U.C.C. §§ 9-504(1), **R9-615(a)**. This assumes that strict foreclosure is not used. The different methods for disposing of collateral after default are discussed in § 18.02 *infra*.

[40] U.C.C. §§ 9-504(2), **R9-615(d)(1)**.

[41] U.C.C. § 2A-525(2).

[42] U.C.C. § 2A-527.

[43] *See* the extensive case law citations in W. Lawrence & J. Minan, *The Law of Personal Property Leasing* 2-6 to 2-21 (1993).

[44] U.C.C. §§ 9-102(2), **R9-109(a)(1)**.

[45] Article 9 permits a lessor who is concerned that a court might conclude that a transaction called a lease is in fact a disguised security interest to make a protective filing, using the terms "lessor" and "lessee" instead of "secured party" and "debtor." Such a filing, standing alone, is not an admission that the transaction is not a true lease. U.C.C. §§ 9-409, **R9-505(a)**. This provision

in the goods.[46]

Inadequate legal standards have played a significant role in blurring the boundaries. The original definition of "security interest" in the 1972 text included a sentence directed toward distinguishing leases and secured transactions[47] which proved woefully inadequate.[48] The revised definition of "security interest" that accompanied the promulgation of Article 2A in 1990 is extremely long and complex, but it does provide an effective definition based on functional considerations. Rather than continuing the predecessor definition's unworkable central standard relying on the parties' intent, the new definition focuses on the economics of the transaction. The basic economic reality of a lease is that the lessor has retained a meaningful residual interest. The new definition thus is directed toward determining whether the terms of the transaction actually compensate the purported lessor for the residual interest, as well as for the use of the goods during the lease term.

A transaction creates a security interest as a matter of law if: 1) the lessee does not have a right to terminate the lease before its stated expiration date,[49] and 2) any one of several enumerated factors is present. When the lessee has a right to terminate the lease, the lessor retains a meaningful residual interest unless the right cannot be exercised until the lessor has been fully compensated for the economic value of the goods. A right of termination thus precludes a transaction from being categorized as a security interest as matter of law.

Assuming no right of termination, a transaction creates a security interest if any of the factors enumerated in the second part of the test is present. One of these factors is that the original term of the lease equals or exceeds the remaining economic life of the goods. The economic reality of such a transaction is that the purported lessor has not retained a meaningful residual interest in the goods, but rather has sold the goods and retained a security interest in them against the outstanding obligation to pay rent. Since the lessee is obligated to compensate the lessor for the full economic value of the goods, the transaction is a security interest as a matter of law.

The practical effect is precisely the same if a lessee who cannot terminate the lease is bound to renew it to the end of the economic life of the goods, or is bound to become the owner of the goods. The lessee is contractually obligated to pay for the remaining economic life of the goods, leaving no meaningful residual in the purported lessor. These factors, therefore, are also included in the revised definition as sufficient to satisfy the second part of the test.

The remaining factors stated in the second part of the test address the role of options. They cover the circumstances in which a lessee, upon compliance with the terms of the

---

also applies to certain consignment and consignment-like transactions, a related topic that is discussed in the next subsection.

[46] With one exception for leased goods that become fixtures (U.C.C. § 2A-309), a true lessor need not make a public filing to protect its residual interest. U.C.C. § 2A-301.

[47] U.C.C. § 1-201(37)(last sentence)(original version).

[48] For a critique of the inadequacies of the original definition, see W. Lawrence & J. Minan, *The Law of Personal Property Leasing* 2-15 to 2-21 (1993).

[49] U.C.C. § 1-201(37)(2nd para.).

lease, has the option to become the owner of the goods or to renew the lease for the remaining economic life of the goods. If the lessee can exercise either option for no additional consideration or for only nominal consideration, the transaction is not a true lease but is rather a security interest. The purported rental payments in such a transaction obviously compensate the lessor not only for the lessee's use of the goods during the lease term but also for the residual value that remains in the goods following the lease term.

Despite the labels applied by the parties to the transaction, the economic reality is that a lessor willing to allow the lessee to retain the goods for nominal or even no additional consideration has not retained any meaningful residual interest. Conversely, the lessor has retained the requisite interest for a true lease when the lessee must pay more than nominal additional consideration in order to exercise an option to purchase the goods or to renew the lease until the end of the economic life of the goods.

[2] Distinguishing Consignments

In some trades it is quite common for a supplier to send goods to a retailer on consignment, with the understanding that the retailer will make an effort to sell the goods. If successful, the retailer retains a percentage of the sales price and remits the remainder of the sales proceeds to the supplier. Until and unless the consigned goods are sold, title remains with the supplier/consignor and does not pass to the retailer/consignee. Goods that the retailer cannot sell are returned to the supplier, with no further obligation on the part of the retailer. The consignment approach, which has the legal characteristics of a bailment with an authority in the bailee to sell, serves to entice the retailer to attempt sales of merchandise that the retailer would not purchase outright. It can also serve as a type of inventory financing because the retailer's inventory is maintained through the capital of the consignor.

At common law consignors could reacquire consigned goods free of the interests of creditors of the consignee, even if the consignor did nothing to provide public notice of its interest in the consigned goods, thereby creating an ostensible-ownership problem.[50] This approach meant that a dishonest consignee could hold itself out as the true owner of the consigned goods and thereby deceive a lender into advancing funds against their value.[51]

---

[50] Ostensible-ownership problems arise whenever goods in one party's possession are subject to an interest asserted by another. Third parties, believing that the party in possession has unencumbered title, may acquire an interest in the goods, thereby creating a priority contest. Often, but not always, the outcome turns on whether the third party has the attributes of a bona fide purchaser for value. *See, e.g.,* U.C.C. § 2-403(1). Public filing provisions are designed to solve the ostensible-ownership problem by giving notice of interests that would otherwise be hidden.

[51] A consignment is a type of bailment, meaning a transaction in which goods are placed in the rightful possession of one who is not their owner. R. Brown, *The Law of Personal Property* § 10.1 (W. Raushenbush 3d ed. 1975). There are numerous types of bailments, and the rules governing the rights of third parties who are misled by the bailee's ostensible ownership vary with the context. *See* § 2.02[C] *infra.*

[a]   The 1972 Text

Under the 1972 version of the U.C.C., the definition of "security interest" draws a distinction concerning consignments. It provides that "[u]nless a consignment is intended as security, reservation of title thereunder is not a 'security interest,' but a consignment in any event is subject to the provisions on consignment sales (section 2-326)."[52] This provision refers to three types of transactions: A consignment intended as security, a consignment not intended as security (true consignment), and a consignment-like sale (sale or return). True consignments are subject to section 2-326 governing consignment sales, and for present purposes the analysis of these two transactions is identical.[53]

If the risk of nonsale falls on the consignee (*e.g.*, the consignee must pay for the goods if they are not sold within a certain period of time), a transaction that is called a consignment by the parties is the economic equivalent of a credit sale of the goods to the consignee with title retained by the consignor as a security device. Consignments that are intended as security devices are within the scope of Article 9 in the same manner as "leases" that are in fact disguised security interests.[54] In such cases, a repossessing "consignor" must follow Article 9's disposition rules. Further, public filing of an Article 9 financing statement is required to protect the "consignor's" interest against third parties who assert competing claims to goods in the possession of the "consignee." Despite the parties' labels, the consignor is in reality a seller who has retained an Article 9 security interest in the goods and the consignee is an Article 9 debtor.[55]

Article 2 regulates two types of sales transactions that are similar to consignments: the "sale on approval" and the "sale or return."[56] A sale on approval occurs when goods are delivered to a buyer primarily for that buyer's use but may be returned by the buyer, and a sale or return occurs when goods are delivered to a buyer primarily for resale but may be returned. Analogizing to the common law of consignments, Article 2 provides that the goods are not subject to the claims of the buyer's creditors when there is a sale on approval,[57] but it adopts the opposite approach for a sale or return.[58] Even though Article 9 does not apply directly to a sale or return because it is not a disguised security interest, the practical effect of Article 2's approach is to require the filing of an Article 9 financing statement. Section 2-326 provides for three alternative methods to address the ostensible-ownership problem created by a sale or return.[59] One method is to comply

---

[52] U.C.C. § 1-201(37)(1st para.).

[53] There are differences in the treatment of a true consignment and a sale or return, but such differences are beyond the scope of this work. For example, a sale or return is subject to Section 2-327 (dealing directly with exercise of the return option and indirectly with passage of the risk of loss) while a true consignment is not.

[54] *See* preceding section for a discussion of the attributes of a secured-sale transaction.

[55] *Cf.* U.C.C. § 2-401(1)(in a sale transaction, reservation of title by seller is limited in effect to a security interest); § 9-102(2)(conditional sale subject to Article 9).

[56] U.C.C. § 2-326(1).

[57] U.C.C. § 2-326(2).

[58] U.C.C. § 2-326(2), (3).

[59] U.C.C. § 2-326(3).

with an applicable law that allows signs installed at the buyer's business location to evidence a consignment-like interest. This option is not generally available, however, because most states have not enacted such laws.[60] The second method is to establish that the buyer is generally known by its creditors to be substantially engaged in selling the goods of others. Strict judicial construction concerning the "generally known" element has created an extremely difficult burden-of-proof problem.[61] As a practical matter, the only viable, certain option is the third method, which requires compliance with the filing provisions of Article 9.

The filing of an Article 9 financing statement fulfills the section 2-326 public-notice requirement but does not convert the sale or return into an Article 9 security interest.[62] The filing is sufficient under Article 2's rules to defeat the claims of creditors of the buyer generally. Article 9 has a special section that deals specifically with the priority rights of the sale-or-return seller[63] who is required to file for protection under section 2-326[64] as against an Article 9 secured party with a prior-perfected security interest in the buyer's inventory.[65] That section provides that the seller will attain priority over the competing secured party only if its filing is made before the goods are delivered to the buyer and the seller gives written notice of its interest to the competing secured party, also before delivering the goods.[66] This provision protects the seller in the same way that another provision protects Article 9 purchase-money inventory financers against prior-perfected general inventory financers.[67]

---

[60] Liebowitz v. Voiello, 107 F.2d 914 (2d Cir. 1939) (the only case in which compliance with a sign law provided insulation against a creditor).

[61] United Agri-Products Fin. Serv., Inc. v. O's Gold Seed Co., 733 P.2d 252, 3 U.C.C. Rep. Serv. 2d 562 (Wyo. 1987) (burden not met by fact that all seed companies in area worked through consignments).

[62] The most important distinction is that a sale-or-return seller who gets the goods back from the buyer owns them and need not subject them to a foreclosure process. This is also the case when a consignor in a true consignment recovers the goods from the consignee.

[63] U.C.C. § 9-114. The section uses consignment rather than sale-or-return terminology, and a literalist might argue that it applies only to true consignments and not sale-or-return transactions. Since the two transactions are virtually identical for purposes of commercial financing, such a narrow interpretation makes no sense.

[64] A sale-or-return seller who can establish priority over creditors under U.C.C. § 2-326(3)(a)(reliance on a sign law) or § 2-326(3)(c)(establishing that the buyer is generally known by its creditors to be substantially engaged in selling the goods of others) can obtain priority over all creditors, including prior-perfected general inventory financers, without making an Article 9 filing.

[65] The general inventory financer's security agreement with the consignee will inevitably contain an after-acquired property clause, and thus its security interest will attach to the consigned goods as they are acquired by the consignee.

[66] U.C.C. § 9-114. The seller will need to perform a search of the filing system to identify any competing secured party and the notice, which must be in writing and must identify the goods by item or type, must be received by the secured party before the goods are delivered to the buyer. Once the proper steps have been taken, the seller can engage in subsequent transactions involving the same kinds of goods for five years without the need for a new filing or a new notice.

[67] See U.C.C. § 9-312(3). For the details and policies of this priority scheme, see § 10.04[B] infra.

rules governing sale-or-return transactions also apply to true consign-
rue consignment the consignor retains title to the goods, but title retention
is not a security device since the risk of nonsale remains on the consignor. Put another
way, the consignor does not retain title to protect against the risk that it will not be paid
the purchase price since the consignee is not obligated to pay that price. The main
difference between a true consignment and a sale or return is that title technically passes
to the buyer when the goods are delivered in a sale or return subject to revesting in the
seller if the return option is exercised. Since the goods are subject to the claims of the
consignee's creditors, the consignor will want to make a protective filing under section
2-326. The rationale for the filing is identical to the sale-or-return seller's rationale for
making an Article 9 filing.

A sale-or-return seller or true consignor filing under Article 9 can take advantage of
section 9-408, which permits a filing using the terms "consignor" and "consignee" rather
than "secured party" and "debtor."[69] The section specifies that the filing itself does not
constitute evidence that the transaction was intended to create a security interest. The
filing meets the requirements of section 2-326, and if for other reasons it is determined
that a security interest was in fact created, the filing is sufficient to perfect that interest.
The bottom line is that notwithstanding the theoretical intricacies, the distinctions in this
area are largely irrelevant. Whether a transaction is a consignment intended as security,
a true consignment, or a sale or return, the party delivering the goods should make an
Article 9 filing using the terms "consignor" and "consignee" to obtain priority over the
consignee's creditors generally and should both file and give notice before delivering
the goods to defeat a prior-perfected inventory financer.

[B]   The 1998 Text

Revised Article 9 makes an attempt to unify this troubling area by bringing most
consignment-like transactions that might be relevant to secured financing within
its scope.[70] The term "consignment" for Article 9 purposes is defined[71] as a
transaction in which goods are delivered to a merchant for the purpose of sale and
the merchant "(i) deals in goods of that kind under a name other than that of the
person making delivery; (ii) is not an auctioneer; and (iii) is not generally known
by its creditors to be substantially engaged in selling the goods of others." Further
limiting the definition are requirements that each delivery have an aggregate value
of $1,000 or more, that the goods not be consumer goods immediately before delivery
to the merchant, and that the transaction not be a disguised security interest.[72]

The revision defines a "consignor"[73] as the one who delivers the goods to the
merchant, who is defined as a "consignee,"[74] and the consignor's interest in the

---

68 U.C.C. § 1-201(37). A true consignment is analogous to a sale or return, not a sale on approval.

69 Protective filings are also discussed at note 45 *supra* in the context of leases that might be
viewed as disguised security interests.

70 U.C.C. § R9-109(a)(4).

71 U.C.C. § R9-102(a)(20).

72 Disguised security interests are still within the scope of Article 9 and there is no change
in their treatment under the revision. U.C.C. § R9-109(a)(1).

73 U.C.C. § R9-102(a)(21).

74 U.C.C. § R9-102(a)(19).

goods is a security interest[75] in inventory that is deemed to be purchase-money in nature.[76] The consignor's interest is subject to the claims of creditors of the consignee,[77] but it can protect that interest by using the methods available to any other Article 9 secured party.[78] These steps include filing to defeat the consignee's creditors generally, and making certain that the filing occurs and notice is given before the goods are delivered to the consignee in order to defeat a prior-perfected general inventory financer. Many sale-or-return transactions, even though not true consignments under current law, will be swept into this definition and will be governed by Article 9 rather than Article 2.

As discussed above, true consignments and sale-or-return transactions have features that are inconsistent with an ordinary Article 9 security interest, most notably the fact that, once recovered from the consignee or buyer, the goods belong to the consignor or seller. Revised Article 9 makes it clear that a consignor in a transaction within its definition of consignment need not go through a foreclosure process.[79] By contrast, an ordinary Article 9 foreclosure is necessary for a consignment that is a disguised security interest.

The revision does not wholly unify this area. In effect, there will be three kinds of consignments: 1) disguised security interests governed by the revision, 2) transactions that are within the scope of the revision because they are within its new definition of consignment, and 3) all other consignment-like transactions. If a transaction in the third category qualifies as a sale on approval, Article 2 will continue to govern and place the goods beyond the reach of the buyer's creditors. If it qualifies as a sale or return but is not within the definition of consignment in Revised Article 9, because the aggregate value of the goods at the time of delivery to the consignee is less than $1,000, because the consignee is generally known by its creditors to be substantially engaged in selling the goods of others, or because the consignor is a consumer, Article 2 will continue to govern and subject the goods to the claims of the buyer's creditors. However, a conforming amendment to Article 2 will delete current section 2-326(3), creating a risk that courts will inappropriately subordinate the seller's interest to the claims of the buyer's creditors. If a transaction in the third category qualifies as a true consignment, no provision of the Code will apply. Presumably, such transactions will be governed once again by the common law, which insulates the consignor from the claims of creditors.

§ 1.04   Classifications of Collateral

Any form of personal property can be used to secure an obligation, provided that the creditor is willing to accept it as collateral. Different forms of personal property, however, pose distinct issues within the context of secured financing. The functional distinctions

---

[75] U.C.C. § R1-201(37)(conforming amendment).

[76] U.C.C. § R9-103(d).

[77] U.C.C. § R9-319(a).

[78] U.C.C. § R9-319(b).

[79] U.C.C. § R9-601(g)(exempting transactions defined as consignments from default provisions).

(Matthew Bender & Co., Inc.)

within Article 9 are most often based on the type of personal property involved. The classification of personal property is thus frequently critical with respect to the application of numerous provisions in Article 9.[80]

Most personal property fits, sometimes uncomfortably, into one of three distinct, broad categories: Goods, indispensable paper, and intangibles. Goods and intangibles represent opposite ends of a scale based on tangible characteristics. The term "goods" refers to assets which are movable at the time the security interest attaches to them, with the specific exclusion of any of the property belonging to the indispensable paper and intangibles categories.[81] Essentially, a good is a form of personal property whose value is a function of its own physical (tangible) characteristics.

Intangibles are, as the term implies, completely intangible. They consist of choses in action, like accounts receivable, rights arising from contract, and other miscellaneous rights, such as licenses, patents, trademarks, and copyrights. Although records of these rights may be maintained in various forms, the business and legal communities do not recognize such records as the physical embodiment of the underlying rights. Intangibility means that the rights can be enforced by an assignee even if the assignee does not obtain possession of whatever records may happen to exist.

The category of indispensable paper fits between the other two categories, reflecting aspects of each. "Indispensable paper" includes instruments, negotiable documents and chattel paper.[82] These forms of personal property consist of rights that are reified, meaning that they are embodied (made real) in a writing. The writing is tangible and moveable, but its value is not based on the value of the paper itself. Its value is instead based on the reified rights that are tied to the paper. A promissory note or a check, for example, has value because it evidences a right to enforce an obligation to pay money. Because the writing is recognized as the single embodiment of the right, physically

---

[80] The Comments to the 1972 text provide a very helpful index. They are organized by each type of collateral and list all of the Article 9 sections that state special provisions with respect to each type. U.C.C. § 9-102 Cmt. 5.

[81] U.C.C. §§ 9-105(1)(h), **R9-102(a)(44)**. In the 1972 text, the term also includes fixtures and "standing timber which is to be cut and removed under a conveyance or contract for sale, the unborn young of animals, and growing crops" but does not include "minerals or the like (including oil and gas) before extraction." § 9-105(1)(h). This definition is similar to the Article 2 definition (§ 2-105(1)) except that under Article 2 unextracted minerals qualify as goods if they are to be severed by the seller before delivery to the buyer. U.C.C. § 2-107(1).

Revised Article 9 adds two new subcategories of goods, "manufactured homes" (§ R9-102(a)(53)) and "as-extracted collateral" (§ R9-102(a)(6)). Both subcategories are discussed in § 1.10[A] *infra.* **The term "goods" has also been expanded to include embedded software, discussed in § 1.04[A]** *infra.*

[82] Chattel paper fits somewhere between indispensable paper and intangibles. Enforcement rights can be transferred by assignment without transfer of the paper itself, but the paper has certain characteristics of negotiability. Chattel paper is sufficiently similar to other types of indispensable paper that it is placed in that category for purposes of this discussion.

Investment property is another type of collateral that cannot be neatly categorized. Certain rights within this category are represented by indispensable paper while other rights are intangible. Investment property is discussed in § 1.04[E] *infra.* *See also* § 14.03 *infra.*

transferring the paper itself is the way to transfer the right to enforce the payment obligation. For this reason, the paper is referred to as "indispensable."[83]

The forms of personal property that comprise the indispensable paper category also possess another important attribute-negotiability. As a rule rights are derivative in nature, meaning that the rights of a transferee of property in a voluntary transaction are coextensive with the rights of the transferor. This rule finds expression in the law governing assignments, where the assignee is said to "stand in the shoes" of the assignor.[84] This simply means that the assignee cannot enforce the assigned rights if the assignor could not have done so. The significance of property's being negotiable is that its transfer can invoke an exception to the derivative-rights rule. Under the right circumstances, a bona-fide purchaser for value of negotiable property can receive rights greater than those of the transferor. The classic illustration with regard to indispensable paper is found in Article 3, which provides that a transferee of a negotiable instrument who qualifies as a holder in due course (a specialized type of bona-fide purchaser for value) takes the instrument free from claims of ownership and defenses that would be good against the transferor. The negotiability of personal property is most significant in secured financing with respect to prioritizing competing claims to the property.[85]

Classification of collateral has numerous consequences, but one of the most important relates to the use of generic descriptions. If, for example, a generic description like "all farm products" is used in a security agreement, the security interest will attach to all assets that are within that category at the moment the security interest first attaches to any asset.[86] Subsequently acquired assets that fall within that category will also be covered if an after-acquired property clause is included in the agreement, as will existing assets in other categories whose classification later changes to farm products.[87] Assets that are farm products at the time of attachment continue to be subject to the security interest if their classification later changes,[88] but an asset that is not a farm product at the time of attachment and does not fall into that category at a later date cannot be subject to the security interest. Coverage of such an asset requires an expanded description.

Classification drives perfection as well. Under the 1972 text, many states have filing systems that require that financing statements covering consumer goods and certain farm-related assets be filed in the county of the debtor's residence, while financing statements

---

[83] See U.C.C. § 9-106 Cmt.

[84] It also underlies the common-law rule that precludes a thief of goods from transferring good title to anyone, even a bona-fide purchaser for value. Of course, there are exceptions to this rule where the owner voluntarily gives a bad actor possession of the goods, thereby creating an appearance of ownership. In such cases, the law often clothes the bad actor with voidable title, meaning that good title can be passed to a bona-fide purchaser for value. See, e.g., U.C.C. § 2-403(1). The voidable-title doctrine can best be understood as a rule of negotiability applicable to goods.

[85] See § 11.03[D] infra.

[86] Attachment is discussed in Chapter 2 infra.

[87] After-acquired property clauses are discussed in § 3.02 infra.

[88] The new category would be a proceed of the old category. Attachment to proceeds is discussed in § 2.04[B] infra.

covering other assets must be filed in a central-filing system, usually maintained by the secretary of state. Further, certain assets cannot be perfected by filing (*i.e.*, instruments), while other assets must be so perfected (i.e., accounts and general intangibles). As with generic descriptions, if a secured party properly files taking into consideration an asset's classification at the time of filing, its perfected status is not disrupted by the fact that the asset later changes to another category.[89]

The following material describes the types of assets that fall within the Code's various categories. Most of the discussion concerning foreclosure, perfection and priorities appears in other chapters.

[A]   Goods §§ 9-105(1)(h), R9-102(a)(44)

Article 9 establishes four basic classifications of goods: consumer goods, farm products, inventory, and equipment. The proper classification of goods may change over time, depending upon changes in their use.[90] For example, goods held as inventory by a dealer might be sold and used as consumer goods in the buyer's home and then later used as equipment in the buyer's office.[91] The classifications are mutually exclusive, however, so that at any given point in time the goods can fit into only one of the classifications.[92]

There is an important distinction between mixed usage and permanent changes in use. The drafters recognized that sometimes a use (or intended use) of the goods will not be exclusive. In cases of mixed use, the primary use predominates for classification purposes. For example, if the goods are used most of the time for personal reasons and only occasionally in the owner's business, the goods are continuously classified as consumer goods.[93] As indicated above, though, a permanent change in the pattern of usage throws the goods into another category.

Revised Article 9 creates two new subcategories of goods, "manufactured homes" and "as-extracted collateral." These subcategories are discussed elsewhere in this chapter.[94] The term "goods" also includes what might be called "embedded" software.[95] For example, a software program that is embedded in a car's mechanisms is considered part of the car. A person who buys the car is not asked to agree to a separate licensing agreement in order to use the embedded software,

---

[89] U.C.C. § 9-401(3).

[90] *In re* Elie, 11 B.R. 24, 31 U.C.C. Rep. Serv. 687 (Bankr. D. Mass. 1981) (primary factor is principal use to which goods are put).

[91] First Nat'l Bank of Thomasboro v. Lachenmyer, 146 Ill. App. 3d 1035, 497 N.E.2d 844, 2 U.C.C. Rep. Serv. 2d 703 (1986) (airplane originally purchased in pursuit of hobby was later used for business purposes).

[92] North Ridge Farms, Inc. v. Trimble, 37 U.C.C. Rep. Serv. 1280 (Ky. Ct. App. 1983). *See also,* U.C.C. § 9-109 Cmt. 2.

[93] Commercial Credit Equip. Corp. v. Carter, 83 Wash. 2d 136, 516 P.2d 767, 13 U.C.C. Rep. Serv. 1212 (1973) (occasional use of airplane in new employment did not affect its classification as consumer goods).

[94] *See* § 1.10[A] *infra.*

[95] U.C.C. § R9-102(a)(44).

and a secured party financing the purchase need not take a separate security interest in such software. On the other hand, the buyer of a computer is subjected to a licensing agreement as a condition of using the nonembedded software that comes loaded in the computer. A secured party financing the purchase of such a computer should consider taking a security interest in both the computer and the software. Nonembedded software is a general intangible.[96]

[1] Consumer Goods §§ 9-109(1), R9-102(a)(23)

Goods are classified as consumer goods if they are "used or bought for use primarily for personal, family, or household purposes."[97] Actual use for these purposes is generally controlling. Note, however, that goods that are purchased for personal or household uses qualify as consumer goods at that time even though they have not actually been placed into such service.[98]

The 1972 text of Article 9 has a few protective provisions that apply only when the collateral is consumer goods.[99] In addition, many states have enacted consumer protection laws that either preempt or supplement the Code's provisions,[100] and the Federal Trade Commission has adopted a rule that makes it a deceptive trade practice for a lender to take a nonpossessory, nonpurchase-money security interest in many types of consumer goods.[101]

Revised Article 9 provides more extensive protection for consumers than does the current Code. It creates two categories of consumer transactions and provides regulatory rules applicable to each. The broader category is "consumer transactions."[102] A consumer transaction is one in which an individual incurs a consumer debt (i.e., an obligation primarily for personal, family or household purposes) and the collateral is held primarily for consumer purposes. For example, a consumer transaction might involve an individual borrowing to pay medical expenses and granting a security interest in investment property that was acquired for personal purposes. "Consumer-goods transactions"[103] are a subset of consumer transactions.

---

[96] See § R9-102(75)(defining "software"); see also note 160 infra (discussing expanded definition of chattel paper).

[97] U.C.C. §§ 9-109(1), R9-102(a)(23). In re Elia, 18 B.R. 89, 33 U.C.C. Rep. Serv. 750 (Bankr. W.D. Pa. 1982) (hospital beds purchased for personal use); In re Nicolosi, 4 U.C.C. Rep. Serv. 111 (Bankr. S.D. Ohio 1966) (purchase of engagement ring as gift to fiancee does not mean it was not for purchaser's own "personal, family, or household purposes").

[98] In re Pettit, 18 B.R. 8, 33 U.C.C. Rep. Serv. 1762 (Bankr. E.D. Ark. 1981) (debtor unambiguously represented to seller/secured party that goods were purchased for personal, family, or household purposes).

[99] See, e.g., U.C.C. § 9-505(1)(secured party generally precluded from using strict foreclosure when collateral is consumer goods and sixty percent of obligation has been paid).

[100] See U.C.C. §§ 9-201, 9-203(4), R9-201(b).

[101] 16 C.F.R. Pt. 444. A parallel rule, Regulation AA, has been adopted by the Federal Reserve Board. 12 C.F.R. Pt. 227. See discussion in §§ 3.02[B] and 7.01[B] infra.

[102] U.C.C. § R9-102(a)(26).

[103] U.C.C. § R9-102(a)(24).

A consumer-goods transaction is one in which an individual incurs a consumer debt and secures it with consumer goods or consumer goods and software (*e.g.*, a computer with an integrated operating system).[104]

[2] Farm Products §§ 9-109(3), R9-102(a)(34)

Under the 1972 text, farm products consist of crops, livestock or supplies used or produced in a farming operation, but only if they are in the possession of a person engaged in such an operation.[105] Goods that constitute crops and livestock can be readily determined, but an issue can arise as to whether they were produced in a farming operation.[106] Vegetables grown in a family garden by a farmer are unlikely to qualify. By contrast, farming operations can be undertaken by someone who has a separate career or livelihood.[107] Seed and fertilizer held in stock to produce a farm crop are examples of goods that would qualify as supplies, as is gasoline held in an underground tank installed on a farm and used to run farm machinery. Note that the tank itself would be a fixture and the machinery would be equipment.

A potentially difficult line-drawing problem arises because crops and livestock often are processed. The 1972 definition provides only general guidance on this issue by providing an alternative means to satisfy the first part of the farm products definition. Goods meet this aspect if they are "products of crops or livestock in their unmanufactured states."[108] The courts must determine whether the goods have been subjected to a manufacturing operation (and thus become inventory), or whether they simply have been processed in a way that falls short of "manufacturing.'[109] To illustrate, grapes harvested from a vintner's land would be farm products, but bottled wine would be inventory.

Obviously, this particular characterization can present close questions on which reasonable persons might differ. An attorney's advice to a client on this issue should reflect the practical considerations involved. For example, the characterization might determine where to file a financing statement that is necessary for the maximum

---

[104] **The revision distinguishes between embedded and nonembedded software. See § 1.04[A]** *supra.*

[105] U.C.C. §§ 9-109(3). **The revision, discussed** *infra* **this subsection, deletes the words "used or produced" and the express requirement of possession, referring instead to goods "with respect to which the debtor is engaged in a farming operation." § R9-102(a)(34).**

[106] Morgan County Feeders, Inc. v. McCormick, 836 P.2d 1051, 18 U.C.C. Rep. Serv. 2d 632 (Colo. Ct. App. 1992) (stipulating that longhorn cattle used for recreational cattle drives were not farm products); *In re* Creel, 118 B.R. 372, 13 U.C.C. Rep. Serv. 2d 943 (Bankr. D. S.C. 1988) (commercial logging not considered farming operation). "Animals in a herd of livestock are covered whether they are acquired by purchase or result from natural increase." U.C.C. § 9-109 Cmt. 4.

[107] *In re* Blease, 24 U.C.C. Rep. Serv. 450 (Bankr. D. N.J. 1978) (veterinarian who owned and operated two farms qualified).

[108] U.C.C. § 9-109(3). **The revision is in accord. § R9-102(a)(34)(D).** The 1972 text gives as examples "ginned cotton, wool-clip, maple syrup, milk, and eggs." **The revision omits the examples.**

[109] *In re* K.L. Smith Enters., Ltd., 2 B.R. 280, 28 U.C.C. Rep. Serv. 534 (Bankr. D. Colo. 1980) (highly mechanized process of washing, candling, spraying with oil, and packing eggs for shipment did not constitute manufacturing process).

protection of the secured party's interests.[110] In many states following the 1972 text, the filing would be in a state central-filing office if the goods are inventory, whereas the filing would be local if the goods are farm products. The costs of filing are quite low, so the best advice would be to use both categories (farm products and inventory) in describing the goods in both the security agreement and the financing statement and then to file in both places in order to avoid the risk that a court might later disagree with either characterization.

The 1972 text also requires that for goods to qualify as farm products they must be "in the possession of a debtor engaged in raising, fattening, grazing, or other farming operations."[111] Once the goods leave the possession of the farming debtor, they lose their characterization as farm products.[112] Their subsequent characterization will depend upon the use to which the goods are then applied.[113] For example, cattle on a rancher's land are a farm product, but the same cattle held for sale in a commission merchant's barn are inventory. Again, the prudent secured party will describe the collateral using both categories and will file in the proper location for each category.

Revised Article 9 does not expressly require that the goods be in a farmer's possession, but it is not clear that possession has become irrelevant. The category is limited to goods "with respect to which the debtor is engaged in a farming operation"[114] and "farming operation" is defined as "raising, cultivating, propagating, fattening, grazing, or any other farming, livestock, or aquaculture operation."[115] Once the goods are no longer part of the debtor's farming operation, they cease to be farm products. For example, if cattle have been turned over to a commission merchant for sale, it can be argued that they are no longer part of the debtor's farming operation. Nevertheless, the statute is sufficiently broad that a court might conclude that the sales phase is still part of the debtor's farming operation and that the cattle qualify as farm products.

The revision is clearer than the 1972 text in articulating that assets such as crops grown on trees, vines and bushes, and aquatic goods produced in aquaculture operations (*e.g.*, fish, kelp), fall within the farm-products category.[116]

---

[110] *See* Chapter 5 *infra.*

[111] U.C.C. § 9-109(3). *In re* Charolais Breeding Ranches, Ltd., 20 U.C.C. Rep. Serv. 193 (Bankr. W.D. Wis. 1976) (operator of breeding ranch which dealt with cattle under programs to provide tax benefits to investors was engaged in farming operations); Baker Production Credit Ass'n v. Long Creek Meat Co., Inc., 266 Or. 643, 513 P.2d 1129, 13 U.C.C. Rep. Serv. 531 (1973) (debtor who bought cattle, fed and fattened them, and sold them for slaughter was engaged in farming operations).

[112] U.C.C. § 9-109 Cmt. 4.

[113] First Nat'l Bank of Elkhart County v. Smoker, 153 Ind. App. 71, 286 N.E.2d 203, 11 U.C.C. Rep. Serv. 10 (1972) (cattle became inventory upon transfer of possession from farmer to packer).

[114] U.C.C. § R9-102(a)(34).

[115] U.C.C. § R9-102(a)(35).

[116] U.C.C. §§ R9-102(34), (35).

(Matthew Bender & Co., Inc.)

[3] Inventory §§ 9-109(4), R9-102(a)(48)

Some aspects of the Article 9 definition of "inventory" correlate precisely with a layperson's understanding of the term: As stated in the 1972 text, goods are inventory "if they are held by a person who holds them for sale or lease or to be furnished under contracts of service or if he has so furnished them, or if they are raw materials, or work in process."[117] This part of the definition is the principal test of inventory, and it is implicit that these transactions occur within the ordinary course of business.[118] Thus, if a company occasionally sold its used machinery when it needed to be replaced, such sales would be insufficient to characterize the machinery as inventory.[119]

The Article 9 concept of inventory is in some respects both broader and narrower than the layperson's understanding. It is broader because it includes materials used or consumed in a business.[120] Thus, a stockpile of packaging material used by a company to ship its manufactured goods and the coal used to fire its generators would be characterized as inventory under Article 9. These types of goods are inventory even if they are not held for sale or any other type of transfer to another party.

The concept of inventory is also narrower for Article 9 purposes because particular goods that satisfy the definition of "farm products" are expressly excluded from the Article 9 definition of inventory.[121] Thus, chickens and eggs that are raised for sale by a debtor who is engaged in farming operations will be classified as farm products.[122]

[4] Equipment §§ 9-109(2), R9-102(a)(33)

Part of the definition of "equipment" in the 1972 text is very simplistic in that it is drawn in contrast to the definition of "consumer goods." Thus, goods are equipment "if

---

[117] U.C.C. § 9-109(4). **The revision uses almost identical language but clarifies that, from the perspective of the secured party financing the lessor, goods remain inventory after they have been leased. § R9-102(a)(48).** *See, e.g.,* Litwiller Mach. & Mfg., Inc. v. NBD Alpena Bank, 184 Mich. App. 369, 457 N.W.2d 163, 12 U.C.C. Rep. Serv. 2d 538 (1990) (components supplied for assembly constituted work in progress); In re Brower, 104 B.R. 226, 11 U.C.C. Rep. Serv. 2d 233 (Bankr. N.D. 1988)(cattle leased to farmers for milk production); Graves Constr. Co., Inc. v. Rockingham Nat'l Bank, 220 Va. 844, 263 S.E.2d 408, 28 U.C.C. Rep. Serv. 588 (1980)(electrical supplies furnished under contract between subcontractor and prime contractor); *In re* Beacon Light Marina Yacht Club, Inc., 125 B.R. 154, 14 U.C.C. Rep. Serv. 2d 1230 (Bankr. W.D. Va. 1990) (boats used by yacht club to sell "time-share" interests to club members involved no passage of title to participants and thus were not inventory because not held for sale).

[118] U.C.C. § 9-109 Cmt. 3. Nichols Motorcycle Supply, Inc. v. Regency Kawasaki, Inc., 295 S.C. 138, 367 S.E.2d 438, 6 U.C.C. Rep. Serv. 2d 823 (S.C. Ct. App. 1988) (bulk transfer of goods is transfer not in ordinary course of business).

[119] The machinery is equipment under U.C.C. § 9-109(2). *See* § 1.04[A][4] *infra. In re* Benton Trucking Serv., Inc., 21 B.R. 574, 34 U.C.C. Rep. Serv. 332 (Bankr. E.D. Mich. 1982).

[120] U.C.C. §§ 9-109(4), **R9-102(a)(48)(D).**

[121] U.C.C. §§ 9-109(3), **R9-102(a)(48).** First State Bank v. Producers Livestock Marketing Ass'n Non-Stock Co-op., 200 Neb. 12, 261 N.W.2d 854, 23 U.C.C. Rep. Serv. 500 (1978).

[122] *See In re* Northeast Chick Servs., Inc., 43 B.R. 326, 39 U.C.C. Rep. Serv. 1034 (Bankr. D. Mass. 1984). Under the 1972 text, the debtor would have to retain possession for the goods to be farm products.

they are used or bought for use primarily in business (including farming or a profession)."[123] Goods classified as equipment are used or bought for use for business purposes, rather than for personal, family or household purposes.[124] "Business usage" is defined broadly to include professional use and farming use. A dentist's implements and a farmer's machinery are thereby included as equipment.[125]

The equipment category in both the 1972 and 1998 texts is a residual classification. **Indeed, the revision defines equipment solely in residual terms.** This means that the category includes all goods that are not within the definitions of inventory, farm products or consumer goods.[126] Suppose, for example, that an individual who is the sole proprietor of a business buys a pick-up truck to make deliveries. The truck is also used as a family vehicle. If the business use predominates, the truck is equipment. If the family use predominates it is a consumer good. If a court finds that the buyer's mixed business and pleasure motives are evenly balanced, there would be no "primary" use, and the truck would drop into the equipment category by default.

That part of the definition of "inventory" that includes materials used or consumed in a business should be analyzed with respect to the definition of equipment. Both a truck and a stored supply of fuel might eventually be consumed in a business. Nevertheless, the truck will be classified as equipment and the fuel as inventory. The Comments to the 1972 text provide the following basis of distinction: "In general it may be said that goods used in a business are equipment when they are fixed assets or have, as identifiable units, a relatively long period of use; but are inventory, even though not held for sale, if they are used up or consumed in a short period of time in the production of some end product."[127] As a rule of thumb, goods that are used up are inventory, while goods that are used again are equipment.

Cases involving use periods that are not clearly either long or short obviously pose close characterization questions.[128] As in other close cases, the best advice is to describe the collateral using both categories and to file a financing statement in the offices that are appropriate for each category.

---

[123] U.C.C. § 9-109(2). The definition also classifies goods as equipment if they are used or bought for use primarily "by a debtor who is a non-profit organization or a governmental subdivision or agency."

[124] Strevell-Paterson Fin. Co. v. May, 77 N.M. 331, 422 P.2d 366, 3 U.C.C. Rep. Serv. 1094 (1967) (guitar and amplifier used to perform in night clubs are equipment rather than consumer goods).

[125] Central Nat'l Bank of Greencastle, Ind. v. Wonderland Realty Corp., 38 Mich. App. 76, 195 N.W.2d 768, 10 U.C.C. Rep. Serv. 1117 (1972) (farm tractors).

[126] U.C.C. §§ 9-109(2), **R9-102(a)(33)**. *In re* Rex Group, Inc., 80 B.R. 774, 5 U.C.C. Rep. Serv. 2d 712 (Bankr. E.D. Va. 1987) (horses used for breeding, training, showing, and racing rather than held for sale are equipment).

[127] U.C.C. § 9-109 Cmt. 3.

[128] Morgan County Feeders, Inc. v. McCormick, 836 P.2d 1051, 18 U.C.C. Rep. Serv. 2d 632 (Colo. Ct. App. 1992) (longhorn cattle used for recreational cattle drives held to have relatively long period of use compared to rodeo calves and feeder cattle).

[B] Indispensable Paper

[1] Documents §§ 9-105(1)(f), R9-102(a)(30)

Article 9 defines "document" to mean either a document of title (a term that is defined in the general definitions of Article 1 (Section 1-201)) or a receipt of the kind that is described in Section 7-201(2).[129] The essence of this form of property is contained in Article 1: "[A]ny... document which in the regular course of business or financing is treated as adequately evidencing that the person in possession of it is entitled to receive, hold, and dispose of the document and the goods it covers."[130] The most common forms of documents of title are bills of lading issued by a carrier upon shipment of goods and warehouse receipts issued by a warehouse upon storage of goods.[131]

A document of title operates as a receipt for goods placed in the custody of a bailee[132] and the document also controls access to those goods. In other words, the bailee will not release the goods to anyone who cannot present a document in proper form. A negotiable document also represents title to the goods that it covers. That is, an interest in the goods can be created by transferring the document to the party acquiring the interest even though the goods remain in the custody of the bailee.[133] Even though an interest has been conveyed by transfer, the bailee need not (and should not) release the goods unless the transferee is a "person entitled under the document."[134] Both negotiable and

---

[129] U.C.C. §§ 9-105(1)(f), **R9-102(a)(30)**.

[130] U.C.C. § 1-201(15).

[131] U.C.C. § 1-201(15). *See also* U.C.C. §§ 1-201(45)(warehouse receipt defined) and 1-201(6)(bill of lading defined).

[132] "To be a document of title a document must purport to be issued by or addressed to a bailee and purport to cover goods in the bailee's possession which are either identified or are fungible portions of an identified mass." U.C.C. § 1-201(15). "Bailee" is defined in U.C.C. § 7-102(1)(a).

[133] A transferee to whom a negotiable document is "duly negotiated" acquires title to both the document and the underlying goods. U.C.C. §§ 7-502(1)(a), (b). Due negotiation is defined in § 7-501(4). At the core of the concept is a requirement that the transferee have the characteristics of a bona-fide purchaser for value.

A transferee of a nonnegotiable document acquires the title and rights which his transferor had or had actual authority to convey (as does a transferee of a negotiable document who does not take by due negotiation). U.C.C. § 7-504(1). In other words, the transferee derivatively acquires the transferor's title (with whatever defects may exist), but the document does not represent complete title.

[134] A "person entitled under the document" means the holder of a negotiable document or the named consignee under a nonnegotiable document (or delivery order issued pursuant to a nonnegotiable document). U.C.C. § 7-403(4). A person becomes a holder of a negotiable document when it is negotiated to that person. If the document runs to bearer, it can be negotiated by delivery alone, but if it runs to the order of a named person negotiation requires delivery plus the indorsement of that person. U.C.C. §§ 7-501(2), (1). A nonnegotiable document will inevitably name a consignee (without additional words of order). That consignee is entitled under the document. If the named consignee wants another person to obtain possession, the nonnegotiable document can be surrendered to the bailee in exchange for a new document running to the other person, or the named consignee can issue written instructions directing the bailee to release all or a portion of the goods to the other person. § 7-403(4).

nonnegotiable documents play important roles in secured financing, and those roles are discussed later in this book. [135]

[2]　Instruments §§ 9-105(1)(i), R9-102(a)(47), (65)

An instrument is either a negotiable instrument (defined in section 3-104) or any other writing evidencing a right to be paid money which is a type of writing that is, in the ordinary course of business, transferred by delivery with any necessary indorsement or assignment. [136] The definition thus recognizes two basic categories of instruments: Those that are negotiable, and those that are technically nonnegotiable but that the marketplace imbues with some of the key attributes of negotiability. Instruments in the latter category are sometimes called "quasi-negotiable."

A negotiable instrument, governed by Article 3, is essentially a written promise or order to pay a fixed amount of money that is in negotiable form. [137] The most common forms of negotiable instruments are checks, promissory notes, and certificates of deposit. [138] The value of commercial paper is based on the obligation to pay money that the paper represents. This form of indispensable paper thus can be referred to as "money paper."

The second category of instrument has created difficult line-drawing issues. [139] Conceptually, these instruments could have been categorized as intangibles, because the right to payment is not reified. On the other hand, the market treats some nonnegotiable instruments as if they were negotiable for certain purposes, including transferring rights to payment through delivery of the writings themselves. Because these practices affect

---

[135] See §§ 6.02[B][1](terminal warehousing), 6.02[C](goods in transit), and 6.02[B][2](field warehousing) infra.

[136] U.C.C. §§ 9-105(1)(i), R9-102(a)(47). A writing that evidences a right to payment of money and is a security interest or a lease is excluded from the definition of instrument because it is chattel paper. See § 1.04[B][3] infra. Prior versions of the Code classified certificated securities as instruments, but the 1995 Official Text defines such securities as part of the broader class of investment property. See § 1.04[E] infra.

[137] U.C.C. § 3-104(a). To be negotiable, an instrument must be payable to bearer or order. U.C.C. § 3-104(a)(1).

[138] Certificates of deposit are discussed in § 1.07[H] infra.

[139] Cases in which nonnegotiable writings were held not to be instruments include Capitran Inc. v. Great W. Bank, 872 P.2d 1370, 22 U.C.C. Rep. Serv. 2d 1191 (Colo. Ct. App. 1994) ("vacation membership" contracts); In re Newman, 993 F.2d 90, 20 U.C.C. Rep. Serv. 2d 1377 (5th Cir. 1993) (annuity contract); In re Brendle's Stores, Inc., 22 U.C.C. Rep. Serv. 2d 450 (M.D. N.C. 1993) (credit card receivables); In re Air Fla. Sys. Inc., 49 B.R. 321, 41 U.C.C. Rep. Serv. 197 (Bankr. S.D. Fla. 1985) (airline tickets); In re Blankinship-Cooper, Inc., 43 B.R. 231, 39 U.C.C. Rep. Serv. 1008 (Bankr. N.D. Tex. 1984) (quarter horse's registration certificate).

Cases in which nonnegotiable writings have qualified as instruments include Army Nat'l Bank v. Equity Developers, Inc., 245 Kan. 3, 774 P.2d 919, 9 U.C.C. Rep. Serv. 2d 722 (1989) (nonnegotiable mortgage note); Berkowitz v. Chavo Int'l, Inc., 74 N.Y.2d 144, 544 N.Y.S.2d 569, 542 N.E.2d 1086, 9 U.C.C. Rep. Serv. 2d 4 (1989) (nonnegotiable promissory note); First Nat'l Bank in Grand Prairie v. Lone Star Life Ins. Co., 524 S.W.2d 525, 17 U.C.C. Rep. Serv. 835 (Tex. Civ. Ct. App. 1975) (nonnegotiable certificate of deposit).

secured financing with respect to written obligations to pay money, characterizing them as instruments is a functional classification.[140]

Revised Article 9 recognizes "promissory notes" as a subset of instruments.[141] In essence, a promissory note is an instrument that is neither a draft nor a certificate of deposit. Current Article 9 does not govern sales of instruments; revised Article 9 governs sales of promissory notes but not other instruments.[142] In a loan transaction, a security interest in all instruments will cover promissory notes. The category thus has no real significance outside the sale context.

[3] Chattel Paper §§ 9-105(1)(b), R9-102(a)(11), (78), (31)

The 1972 text defines "chattel paper" as follows:

"Chattel paper" means a writing or writings which evidence both a monetary obligation and a security interest in or a lease of specific goods, but a charter or other contract involving the use or hire of a vessel is not chattel paper. When a transaction is evidenced both by such a security agreement or a lease and by an instrument or a series of instruments, the group of writings taken together constitutes chattel paper.[143] Chattel paper is thus a writing or group of writings that include a payment obligation either as part of or together with a security agreement or a lease.

One common pattern involving chattel paper arises when a merchant sells goods to a consumer on a secured basis, retaining a purchase-money security interest. Typically, this transaction will be accomplished with one writing,[144] usually called a "retail installment contract," which combines features of a promissory note and a security agreement.[145] That is, the buyer's payment obligation and the merchant's security interest are both covered in the writing. Title to the goods has passed to the buyer as part of the sale,[146] but the merchant has retained an Article 9 security interest that it can foreclose if the buyer defaults. In effect, the merchant has traded the goods for a set of intangible

---

[140] This characterization does not mean that these nonnegotiable instruments will be treated like negotiable instruments for all aspects of Article 9. The major differences will be in priorities because holder-in-due-course status is available only with negotiable instruments. *See* § 11.03[C] *infra*.

[141] U.C.C. § **R9-102(a)(65).**

[142] *See* **discussion in** § **1.06** *infra*.

[143] U.C.C. § 9-105(1)(b). U.C.C. § **R9-102(a)(11), discussed in this subsection** *infra*, **retains the same basic concept.**

[144] The buyer need not be a consumer, nor do the payment and security aspects of the transaction have to be in one writing. Two writings consisting of a promissory note and a security agreement will be taken together and treated as chattel paper. U.C.C. §§ 9-105(b), **R9-102(a)(11).**

[145] It is possible for a writing that includes both a monetary obligation and a security interest to qualify as a negotiable instrument under Article 3 (although most retail installment contracts contain provisions that render them nonnegotiable). U.C.C. § 3-104(a)(3). Such a writing would not qualify as an instrument for Article 9 purposes, however. U.C.C. §§ 9-105(1)(i) and **R9-102(a)(47)** specify that an instrument cannot be a writing that itself qualifies as a security agreement or lease.

[146] U.C.C. § 2-106(1). Even if the writing states that the seller is to retain title pending final payment, the seller's interest is limited to a security interest. U.C.C. § 2-401(1).

rights: The right to enforce the buyer's payment obligation (through litigation, if necessary), and the right to use Article 9's mechanisms to foreclose on the goods if that payment obligation is not fulfilled.

The writing executed by the buyer is chattel paper, but this term has no significance if the merchant does not make use of the paper in a secondary financing arrangement. That is, if no third party acquires an interest in the paper, the merchant simply has a garden-variety security interest in the buyer's goods. If, however, the merchant uses the chattel paper as collateral for a loan from a bank,[147] the bank's collateral is the chattel paper itself rather than the goods sold by the merchant. The easiest way to understand this is to visualize a two-tier arrangement in which one security agreement (the merchant/buyer agreement) serves as collateral for another security agreement (the merchant/bank agreement). The collateral in the merchant/buyer transaction is consumer goods; the collateral in the merchant/bank transaction is chattel paper. If the merchant defaults, the bank will foreclose on the chattel paper. Foreclosure entitles the bank to enforce the rights that, absent default, could have been enforced by the merchant. The Code has a provision that allows the bank to force the buyer to begin making the installment payments to it.[148] That provision permits an assignee[149] of chattel paper to notify the obligor (referred to in this context as the "account debtor"[150]) and thereby divert the payments from the merchant to itself. The bank is in the same position with regard to the buyer's goods as the merchant, however, and cannot foreclose on them unless the buyer goes into default.

Chattel paper also arises when goods are leased. A written lease agreement almost invariably includes the payment obligation of the lessee.[151] If the lessor borrows money from a bank on the security of the lease, the lease is chattel paper.[152] If the lessor defaults, the bank can enforce the payment obligations created by the lease using the mechanism discussed in the preceding paragraph. If the lessee in turn defaults, the bank can recover the leased goods.[153] The bank would not be obligated to go through a foreclosure process

---

[147] Article 9 is also triggered if the merchant sells the chattel paper outright. Article 9's treatment of sales of chattel paper is discussed in § 1.06 *infra*.

[148] U.C.C. §§ 9-318(3), **R9-406(a)**.

[149] The merchant/bank security agreement operates as a conditional assignment to the bank of the merchant's rights in the paper. It is conditional in that, unless otherwise agreed, the bank cannot enforce its rights as assignee unless the merchant defaults.

[150] The term includes an obligor on an account, chattel paper or general intangible. U.C.C. §§ 9-105(1)(a), **R9-102(a)(3)**.

[151] *In re* ICS Cybernetics, Inc., 123 B.R., 467, 17 U.C.C. Rep. Serv. 2d 609, *aff'd w.o. op.*, 123 B.R. 480(N.D.N.Y. 1990), dealt with multiple writings. Because the master agreement provided for payment of "the monthly rent set forth in [the] equipment schedules" and did not specify the basic lease terms, the court held that the equipment schedules alone constituted chattel paper. *Compare* this case *with In re* Funding Sys. Asset Management Corp., 111 B.R. 500, 11 U.C.C. Rep. Serv. 2d 205 (Bankr. W.D. Pa. 1990) (chattel paper consisted of twelve equipment schedules, which contained monetary obligations, and master leases, which contained lease terms).

[152] *In re* Keneco Fin. Group, Inc., 131 B.R. 90, 16 U.C.C. Rep. Serv. 2d 219 (Bankr. N.D. Ill. 1991) (equipment leases). Charters of vessels are excluded because they constitute accounts. U.C.C. §§ 9-105 Cmt. 3, **R9-102(a)(2)**.

[153] U.C.C. § 2A-525(2). Article 2A governs the relationship between lessor and lessee.

since the lessor's rights, which the bank is asserting derivatively, include ownership of the residual interest in the leased goods.

Note that transactions using chattel paper based on an underlying lease or an underlying security agreement are comparable because the paper in both instances includes a payment obligation that is tied to specific goods against which the obligee can proceed in the event of default on payment.[154] These rights that the paper represents with respect to the goods are the feature distinguishing chattel paper from other forms of personal property that include an obligation to pay money (*i.e.*, instruments and accounts).[155] These goods-oriented rights pose some unique issues when chattel paper is used to secure financing. These issues thus justify identifying such writings as a separate category of personal property for Article 9 purposes. Thus, even if the monetary obligation is evidenced by a separate writing that, standing alone, qualifies as an instrument, it is treated as part of the chattel paper.

Chattel paper has the same basic characteristics under Revised Article 9[156] but can be broken down into "tangible chattel paper"[157] and "electronic chattel paper."[158] The latter term adapts Article 9 to the growing practice among some secured lenders of representing such interests in a purely electronic form. The revision also clarifies that its provisions will govern what might be called "hybrid" chattel paper, meaning obligations relating to software[159] created in integrated transactions in which goods are sold or leased and the software is used in the goods.[160]

---

[154] Note that the problems that can arise in determining whether an agreement is a true lease or a security interest in the form of a disguised lease, discussed in § 1.03[B][1] *supra*, are not important in this context because both leases and security agreements are included within the meaning of chattel paper.

[155] Berkowitz v. Chavo Int'l, Inc., 74 N.Y.2d 144, 544 N.Y.2d 569, 542 N.E.2d 1086, 9 U.C.C. Rep. Serv. 2d 4 (1989) (written purchase agreement was not chattel paper because it did not create a security interest in the goods sold under it); *In re* Padgett, 49 B.R. 212, 41 U.C.C. Rep. Serv. 1020 (Bankr. W.D. Ky. 1985) (monetary obligation alone not sufficient to create chattel paper).

[156] U.C.C. § R9-102(a)(11).

[157] U.C.C. § R9-102(a)(78).

[158] U.C.C. § R9-102(a)(31). **The revision permits a security interest in electronic chattel paper to be perfected either by filing (§ R9-312(a)) or by control (§§ R9-314(a), R9-105).** *See* **discussion of control of electronic chattel paper in § 6.04[B]** *infra* **and priority of purchasers of electronic chattel paper in § 11.03[C]** *infra.*

[159] **Software is defined as "a computer program, any informational content included in the program, and any supporting information provided in connection with a transaction relating to the computer program or informational content." U.C.C. § R9-102(a)(75). Certain software that is embedded in goods is treated as part of the goods.** *See* **discussion in § 1.04[A]** *supra.*

[160] U.C.C. § R9-102(a)(11). **A secured party (including a seller) financing the sale of a computer that is loaded with software should take a security interest in both the computer (a good) and the software (a general intangible). When used in a secondary financing transaction, the total secured obligation qualifies as chattel paper.** *See also* **§ 1.04[A]** *supra* **(discussing software "embedded" in goods); and note 193** *infra* **(discussing § R9-408(a), which partially negates the effect of limitations on assignability in general intangibles).**

[C] Intangibles

Intangible rights that do not qualify as "indispensable paper" (*i.e.*, instruments, documents, or chattel paper) are treated separately because they are not in writing or, even if they are, they are not dealt with as though they are negotiable.[161] These distinctions have practical ramifications for secured financing that make separate categories necessary for purposes of Article 9. These intangibles are themselves further subdivided into two classifications of collateral: accounts and general intangibles.

[1] Accounts §§ 9-106, R9-102(a)(2), (46)

An "account" is defined in the 1972 text to mean "any right to payment for goods sold or leased or for services rendered which is not evidenced by an instrument or chattel paper, whether or not it has been earned by performance."[162] An account is closely related to an instrument and to chattel paper in that all three categories include an obligation to pay money. They are mutually exclusive, however, and the definition of account excludes any payment obligation that qualifies for either of the other two classes.[163] Another similarity between accounts and chattel paper is that outright sales of each are within the scope of Article 9.[164]

The term "account" does not cover all remaining obligations for payment.[165] Under the 1972 text, the payment obligation must stem from the sale or lease of goods[166] or the performance of services.[167] In short, an account is "the ordinary commercial account

---

[161] U.C.C. § 9-106, Comment.

[162] U.C.C. § 9-106. The following types of collateral have been found to qualify as accounts under Article 9: *In re* Rankin, 102 B.R. 439, 9 U.C.C. Rep. Serv. 2d 301 (Bankr. W.D. Pa. 1989) (right to receive lifetime payments from insurance company in exchange for services performed); *In re* Air Fla. Sys. Inc., 49 B.R. 321, 41 U.C.C. Rep. Serv. 197 (Bankr. S.D. Fla. 1985)(airline ticket sales); Sun Bank, N.A. v. Parkland Design & Dev. Corp., 466 So. 2d 1089, 40 U.C.C. Rep. Serv. 636 (Fla. Ct. App. 1985) (earned real estate commission); Matthews v. Arctic Tire, Inc., 262 A.2d 831, 7 U.C.C. Rep. Serv. 369 (R.I. 1970) (payment rights from sale of inventory).

[163] General Elec. Capitol Corp. v. Deere Credit Servs., Inc., 799 F. Supp. 832, 19 U.C.C. Rep Serv. 2d 933 (S.D. Ohio 1992) (account cannot be evidenced by chattel paper); *In re* Clover Leaf Dairy, 79 B.R. 499, 5 U.C.C. Rep. Serv. 2d 446 (Bankr. M.D. Fla. 1987) (account cannot be evidenced by an instrument).

[164] *See* § 1.06 *infra*. **The scope of the revision is expanded to govern sales of instruments that qualify as promissory notes and general intangibles that qualify as payment intangibles.** *Id.*

[165] **The definition in the revision, discussed in this subsection** *infra*, **is much broader than that contained in the 1972 text.**

[166] If the lease is in writing and includes the payment obligation, it is chattel paper. *See* § 1.04[B][3] *supra*.

[167] The following have all been held not to constitute accounts for purposes of Article 9: *In re* Parker Steel Co., 149 B.R. 834, 21 U.C.C. Rep. Serv. 2d 118 (Bankr. N.D. Ohio 1992) (checking account); *In re* Koppinger, 113 B.R. 588, 12 U.C.C. Rep. Serv. 2d 534 (Bankr. N.D. 1990) (funds set aside by debtor for state fuel taxes); *In re* D.J. Maltese, Inc., 42 B.R. 589, 39 U.C.C. Rep. Serv. 657 (Bankr. E.D. Mich. 1984) (contract for sale of realty); Northwestern State Bank of Luverne v. Barclays Am. Business Credit, Inc., 354 N.W.2d 460, 38 U.C.C. Rep. Serv. 1739 (Minn.

receivable."[168] A payment obligation that is not an account, instrument, or chattel paper falls within the class of general intangibles. For example, a vendor's right to payment under an installment land contract has been categorized as a general intangible rather than an account because the right to payment stems from the sale of land rather than goods.[169]

Prior to the 1972 revisions to Article 9, accounts were further subdivided depending upon whether or not the right to the payment of money had been earned by performance. When the right had not yet been earned, the personal property was classified as a contract right. For example, suppose a painting contractor needing a loan was owed $5,000 for a completed job and had a contract to paint a building the next week for another $5,000. The completed job would be called an account and the pending job would be called a contract right. The contract right could not be enforced by the contractor or an assignee until it had been earned by performance, however, at which point it would have become an account.[170] Article 9 had no substantive provisions that differentiated between accounts and contract rights, and the 1972 revisions simplified the matter by folding the definition of contract rights into the definition of accounts.

It can sometimes be difficult to understand the value of an intangible right like an account. Suppose, using the illustration in the preceding paragraph, the painting contractor uses the described accounts (one earned, the other unearned) as collateral for a loan from a bank. The security agreement executed by the contractor (the Article 9 debtor) will have the effect of assigning to the bank the contractor's collection rights. The assignment will typically be conditional, meaning that the contractor will be allowed to collect the accounts until he or she defaults to the bank.[171] Upon default, the bank is entitled to notify the account debtors[172] that the rights to be paid have been assigned and that payment is to be made to the bank.[173] The term "account debtor" is used to describe

---

Ct. App. 1984) (workmen's compensation insurance premium refund); Merchants Nat'l Bank of Mobile v. Ching, 681 F.2d 1383, 34 U.C.C. Rep. Serv. 270 (11th Cir. 1982) (claim for damages resulting from breach of contract).

[168] U.C.C. § 9-106 Cmt.

[169] Mastro v. Witt, 39 F.3d 238, 24 U.C.C. Rep. Serv. 2d 1041 (9th Cir. 1994). **The definition of accounts is expanded in the revision to encompass the right to payment for any property sold, including land. U.C.C. § R9-102(a)(2).**

[170] The security interest would continue to attach to the payment obligation after this transformation because the account would be a proceed of the contract right.

[171] *See* U.C.C. §§ 9-205, **R9-205(a)** (permitting debtors to collect or compromise accounts, or to use, commingle or dispose of proceeds, without invalidating secured party's interest). This provision repeals the rule of Benedict v. Ratner, 268 U.S. 353 (1925)(invalidating security device as fraudulent conveyance because debtor given dominion over proceeds).

By agreement, the parties can provide for account debtors to make payment directly to the secured party prior to default, thereby reducing debtor's obligation. U.C.C. §§ 9-502(1), **R9-607(a)**.

[172] The bank can also sell its collection rights and use the proceeds to reduce the contractor's indebtedness to it. U.C.C. §§ 9-504(1), **R9-610(a)**. It will effectuate the sale through an unconditional assignment.

[173] U.C.C. §§ 9-318(3), **R9-406(a)**. The notification must reasonably identify the assigned rights. §§ 9-318(3), **R9-406(b)(1)**.

an obligor on an account, chattel paper or general intangible.[174] Upon receipt of this notification, the account debtor's payment obligation shifts to the secured party.[175] That is, the account debtor can no longer pay the contractor and obtain a discharge. Note that the secured party's rights are generally coextensive with the contractor's rights, meaning that any defense that the account debtor could assert against the debtor arising out of the transaction that gave rise to the account can also be asserted against the secured party.[176] Thus, neither the contractor nor the bank can collect the unearned account prior to the contractor's performance.[177] It is the secured party's collection rights that give value to the collateral.

Revised Article 9 expands the type of payment obligations that fall within the definition of account. Many of these obligations would be general intangibles under the 1972 text. Specifically included within the new definition are rights to payment:

(i) for property that has been or is to be sold, leased, licensed, assigned, or otherwise disposed of, (ii) for services rendered or to be rendered, (iii) for a policy of insurance issued or to be issued, (iv) for a secondary obligation incurred or to be incurred, (v) for energy provided or to be provided, (vi) for the use or hire of a vessel under a charter or other contract, (vii) arising out of the use of a credit or charge card or information contained on or for use with the card, or (viii) as winnings in a lottery or other game of chance operated or sponsored by a State, governmental unit of a State, or person licensed or authorized to operate the game by a State or governmental unit of a State.[178]

The revision also creates a new subset of accounts called health-care-insurance receivables.[179] The 1972 text excludes from its scope any transfer of an interest in a

---

[174] U.C.C. §§ 9-105(1)(a), **R9-102(a)(3).**

[175] The account debtor may request reasonable identification and continue to pay the debtor (assignor) until it is provided. U.C.C. §§ 9-318(3), **R9-406(c).**

[176] U.C.C. § 9-318(1). The account debtor can also assert any other defense or claim, including those arising out of unrelated transactions, that accrues before the account debtor receives notice of the assignment. **Revised Article 9 makes it clear that, as against an assignee, such claims and defenses cannot be used to justify an affirmative recovery. § R9-404(b).**

If the contract between the debtor and the account debtor contains a provision by which the account debtor waives defenses against assignees, the secured party can collect the account free of most defenses, but only if it acquired the account for value, in good faith and without notice of the defense. U.C.C. §§ 9-206, **R9-403(b).**

By contrast, a term in the contract between the debtor and the account debtor that prohibits assignment is ineffective. U.C.C. §§ 9-318(4), **R9-401(b).** This free-assignability provision is broader than either the common-law or Article 2 rule limiting the effect of non-assignability clauses in cases outside the scope of Article 9. *See, e.g.,* U.C.C. § 2-210.

[177] Until fully earned by performance, any modification of (or substitution for) the contract entered into by the debtor and the account debtor in good faith and in a commercially reasonable manner is binding on the secured party. U.C.C. §§ 9-318(2), **R9-405.**

[178] U.C.C. § **R9-102(a)(2). The definition excludes payment obligations that fall within the definitions of other collateral categories (*e.g.,* instruments, chattel paper, commercial tort claims, etc.).**

[179] U.C.C. § **R9-102(a)(46). A health-care-insurance receivable is "an interest in or claim under a policy of insurance which is a right to payment of a monetary obligation for health-care goods or services provided."**

policy of insurance.[180] **The revision narrows this exclusion [181] and thereby facilitates commerce by making it easier for health-care providers to sell or borrow against their rights to their patients' health-insurance proceeds.[182]**

[2] General Intangibles §§ 9-106, R9-102(a)(42), (61)

Article 9 defines "general intangibles" in residual terms, meaning any personal property that does not fall within one of the other categories.[183] General intangibles thus include any form of personal property that might be used as collateral and that is not covered by any of the other Article 9 classifications of collateral nor specifically excluded from the coverage of Article 9. It is a residual classification. Just a few examples of personal property that have been categorized by the courts as general intangibles include patent rights,[184] trademark rights,[185] tax refunds,[186] refunds for overpayments to an employee pension plan,[187] claims for breach of contract,[188] liquor licenses,[189] FCC licenses,[190] and state water permits.[191]

Why is a general intangible of value as collateral? To illustrate, a patent represents a federally guaranteed right to exclusive exploitation of an invention for seventeen

---

[180] U.C.C. § 9-104(g). *See* § 1.07[G] *infra.*

[181] U.C.C. § R9-109(d)(8).

[182] There are some differences between the revision's treatment of accounts generally and its treatment of health-care-insurance receivables. U.C.C. § R9-404(e), for example, excludes health-care-insurance receivables from the general rules governing the rights of account debtors to assert claims and defenses against assignees. The rationale is that the obligation of an insurer (the account debtor in this context) is governed by other law. For similar reasons, § R9-405(d) excludes health-care-insurance receivables from the general rules governing the effects of modifications against assignees, and § R9-406(e) excludes health-care-insurance receivables from other aspects of the assignment rules, such as the obligation to pay an assignee after receiving notification.

Health-care-insurance receivables are subject to § R9-408(a), which invalidates an anti-assignment clause to the extent that it prohibits assignment or makes assignment an event of default between the account debtor (insurer) and the debtor (insured), but that section specifies that the account debtor need not honor the assignment if the anti-assignment clause would be effective under other law. § R9-408(d). *See also* discussion of § R9-408 as applied to general intangibles in note 193 *infra.*

[183] U.C.C. §§ 9-106, R9-102(a)(42).

[184] *In re* Emergency Beacon Corp., 23 U.C.C. Rep. Serv. 766 (S.D.N.Y. 1977).

[185] *In re* Roman Cleanser Co., 43 B.R. 940, 39 U.C.C. Rep. Serv. 1770 (Bankr. E.D. Mich. 1984), *aff'd* 802 F.2d 207, 2 U.C.C. Rep. Serv. 2d 269 (6th Cir. 1986).

[186] *In re* Metric Metals Int'l, Inc., 20 B.R. 633, 33 U.C.C. Rep. Serv. 1495 (S.D. N.Y. 1981).

[187] *In re* Long Chevrolet, Inc., 79 B.R. 759, 5 U.C.C. Rep. Serv. 2d 462 (N.D. Ill. 1987).

[188] Merchants Nat'l Bank of Mobile v. Ching, 681 F.2d 1383, 34 U.C.C. Rep. Serv. 270 (11th Cir. 1982).

[189] Queen of the N., Inc. v. LeGrue, 582 P.2d 144, 24 U.C.C. Rep. Serv. 1301 (Alaska 1978).

[190] *In re* Ridgely Communications, Inc., 139 B.R. 374, 17 U.C.C. Rep. Serv. 2d 877 (Bankr. Md. 1992).

[191] Lake Region Credit Union v. Crystal Pure Water, Inc., 502 N.W.2d 524, 21 U.C.C. Rep. Serv. 2d 774 (N.D. 1993).

years.[192] The patent holder can produce and sell the invention, or license another to do so. A secured party with a security interest in the patent can sell the patent, including the patent-holder's exploitation rights, at foreclosure in the event of default. Likewise, a secured party with a security interest in a government-issued license can sell the license at foreclosure in the event of default.[193] Often the license is the single most valuable asset owned by a business.

Although one would not ordinarily anticipate any difficulties in characterizing property as either goods or general intangibles, courts, on occasion, have been faced with the necessity of distinguishing the two. In *United States v. Antenna Sys., Inc.*,[194] the court held that the blueprints, drawings, and technical data produced by a company's engineering staff constituted general intangibles rather than goods. It reasoned that, even though this property had been reduced to a tangible form, it was in reality a visual reproduction of engineering concepts and ideas. Similarly, the court found that the written bids, proposals, and cost estimates that various departments of the company had preserved over the year, and that could be drawn upon in preparing future bids, were general intangibles.

Revised Article 9 continues to define general intangibles as a residual category but clarifies that a security interest in software falls within the category.[195] It also creates a new subset of general intangibles called payment intangibles. A payment intangible is "a general intangible under which the account debtor's principal

---

[192] Although Article 9 applies to most aspects of a secured transaction involving a patent, the federal patent statute (35 U.S.C. § 261) preempts its perfection rules. *See* discussion of federal preemption in § 1.07[A] *infra*.

[193] Some government licenses are regulated by statutes or rules that make them nontransferable and, therefore, worthless as collateral. *See, e.g.,* Brown v. Baker, 688 P.2d 943, 39 U.C.C. Rep. Serv. 1105 (Alaska 1984)(state statute invalidated security interest in limited-entry fishing permits). Many licenses are transferable, although typically the issuing governmental agency must approve of the transferee. This simply means that the foreclosing secured party must locate a qualifying buyer.

A similar problem arises with franchise agreements. Some franchise agreements can be assigned if the franchisor approves of the transferee while others are by their terms nonassignable. **In this context, Revised Article 9 contains a provision that makes any legal rule or franchise agreement ineffective to the extent that it either impairs the creation, attachment, or perfection of a security interest or causes any of those events to constitute a default. U.C.C. §§ R9-408(a), (c). However, to the extent that such limitations are generally effective outside Article 9, the affected governmental agency or franchisor need not recognize the security interest or the rights of a foreclosure-sale transferee. § R9-408(d). Put another way, a debtor can grant a valid security interest in an otherwise nontransferable license without suffering any penalties, but that does not mean that it will have value in the event of default. A secured party with an interest in a franchise agreement can do no more than ask the franchisor to waive the anti-assignment clause. Perhaps the most important effect of these provisions is that they may provide a basis for increasing the value of secured claims in bankruptcy. *See* discussion in § 16.02[C] *infra*.**

[194] 251 F. Supp. 1013, 3 U.C.C. Rep. Serv. 258 (D.N.H. 1966).

[195] **U.C.C. § R9-102(a)(42). Software is defined in § R9-102(a)(75). Certain software that is embedded in goods becomes part of the goods themselves.** *See* discussion in § 1.04[A] *supra*.

obligation is a monetary obligation."[196] Sales of general intangibles are not within the scope of the 1972 text. The revision governs sales of payment intangibles but not sales of other general intangibles.[197] In a loan transaction, a security interest in all general intangibles will cover payment intangibles, and thus the category has no real significance outside the sale context.[198]

[D] A Comparison of Accounts, Instruments, and Chattel Paper

Assume that a farm-implement dealer sells a tractor to a farmer. The farmer might pay cash for the tractor but it is more likely that the farmer would prefer a credit transaction, and the dealer might feel compelled to comply in order to close the deal. The dealer will then receive one of three forms of personal property that will be created in the noncash sale: An account, an instrument in the form of a promissory note, or chattel paper. Distinctions among these three forms of property can be explained by comparing them in the context of this simple hypothetical.

If the dealer sells the tractor to the farmer on an open account, the dealer acquires an Article 2 contract right to payment by the buyer, in accordance with the terms of the contract.[199] In the event that the buyer breaches, the dealer does not have a right to retake the tractor.[200] The dealer must sue the farmer for breach.[201] If the suit is successful and the farmer does not pay the judgment, the dealer must then have the sheriff execute on the judgment by seizing available assets of the farmer, selling them, and remitting proceeds of the sale to pay off the judgment. In the suit for breach, however, the farmer would be able to assert any applicable defenses, such as breach of a warranty of quality with respect to the tractor.

If the dealer takes a promissory note for the farmer's payment obligation, the dealer will acquire Article 3 rights on the note, in addition to the Article 2 rights on the sale. The major significance of the additional Article 3 rights of the dealer/payee who retains the note are the procedural advantages that would be available in litigating against the farmer. The dealer would have to sue to enforce the payment obligation on the note, but Article 3 provisions make the case easier to prove.[202] The farmer could still assert any available contract defenses on the sales transaction with the dealer.

If the dealer sells the tractor on secured credit and takes back chattel paper from the farmer, the dealer will acquire both Article 2 rights on the sales contract and Article 9 rights on the security agreement that is part of the chattel paper.[203] Since the dealer

---

[196] U.C.C. § R9-102(a)(61).

[197] U.C.C. § R9-109(a)(3).

[198] Sales of payment intangibles are discussed in § 1.06 *infra*.

[199] U.C.C. § 2-301.

[200] The sale passes title to the buyer (U.C.C. § 2-106(1)), and the dealer receives an enforceable promise in exchange.

[201] The dealer's cause of action in this context is predicated on U.C.C. § 2-607(1), which makes the buyer liable for the contract price once the tractor has been accepted.

[202] U.C.C. § 3-308.

[203] If the chattel paper consists of two writings, a negotiable promissory note and a security agreement, the dealer will also have Article 3 rights, meaning that it can use the procedural advantages of Article 3 if it brings an action to enforce the payment obligation.

sold the tractor to the farmer, the lease aspect of chattel paper is not applicable to this hypothetical. If the farmer defaults on the payment obligation, the dealer can repossess the tractor, sell it, and use the sale proceeds to satisfy the outstanding indebtedness. The dealer thus could protect its interests without having to reduce its claim to judgment through a lawsuit.

Selling the tractor on any of these noncash bases creates a problem for the dealer. The dealer must replenish its inventory of tractors, and, if the dealer's supplier does not sell to the dealer on credit or consignment, the dealer must pay cash for replacement inventory. Payment for the tractor sold to the farmer, however, will be made only over a term of several months. Confronted with this cash-flow problem, the dealer is likely to seek its own inventory financing, and it probably would be interested in securing that financing with the property it has received from the farmer. Thus the dealer might wish to borrow from a bank and give the bank a security interest in the account, the note, or the chattel paper received from the farmer.[204]

Further aspects of these three forms of personal property can be illustrated by comparing them in a secured transaction between the dealer and a bank. Note carefully, however, that the hypothetical now involves the dealer offering as collateral for its loan from the bank the personal property (meaning the set of rights) that was created in the dealer's favor by the sale of the tractor to the farmer. In Article 9 terminology, the bank will be the secured party, the dealer will be the debtor, and the personal property acquired from the farmer will be the collateral. The essence of each of the forms of personal property under comparison involves an obligation by the farmer to pay money.

Assume that the bank accepts the open account as collateral and that the dealer defaults. The bank can then require the payments the farmer makes on the account to be made to the bank to satisfy the dealer's indebtedness, or it can sell the account outright at a foreclosure sale and use the proceeds to satisfy the dealer's indebtedness.[205] Because the enforcement rights of the bank and any subsequent purchaser of the account are predicated on the farmer's Article 2 obligation to pay the price of the tractor, they are subject to defenses that the farmer could have asserted against the dealer had the account not been assigned (the merchandise risk). For example, the tractor might be defective in breach of an Article 2 warranty of quality.[206] The bank and any subsequent purchaser

---

[204] Often the dealer will borrow on the strength of its inventory and the account, note or chattel paper would be a proceed of the inventory-financer's security interest. *See* discussion of proceeds in § 2.04 *infra*.

The dealer can also generate revenue by selling the account, chattel paper or instrument. Sales of accounts and chattel paper are governed by Article 9 and are discussed in § 1.06 *infra*. Sales of instruments are beyond the scope of the 1972 text **but sales of promissory notes, a subset of instruments discussed in § 1.06 *infra* are within the scope of the revision. U.C.C. § R9-109(a)(3).**

[205] *See* § 1.04[C][1] *supra* for a discussion of the mechanics by which the bank will assert its collection rights.

[206] The bank and any subsequent purchaser of the account can enforce it free from such defenses if the contract between the dealer and the farmer contains an enforceable waiver-of-defenses clause. U.C.C. §§ 9-318(1) and 9-206, **R9-404(a) and R9-403(b).** In consumer purchases of goods, a Federal Trade Commission rule makes it an unfair or deceptive act for a seller to take a contract

of the account also run the risk that the farmer might become insolvent (the credit risk). Because of these risks, lenders significantly discount the value of accounts when lending against them.

The position of the bank will be significantly improved if the dealer acquired the farmer's payment obligation in the form of a negotiable note. The bank will then be much less concerned about the underlying transaction between the dealer and the farmer because of the enhanced rights that it will obtain under Article 3. As with the account, if the dealer defaults on its debt to the bank, the bank can either apply the farmer's payments on the note to the dealer's debt or it can sell the note in satisfaction of the dealer's debt. The enhanced position of the bank or its successor results in the event that the farmer stops paying on the note. Unlike the dealer, the bank did not deal with the farmer. Provided that the bank qualifies as a holder-in-due-course, which is essentially nothing more than a particular type of bona-fide purchaser for value, the bank (and any of its subsequent transferees) will take free of most contract defenses of the farmer.[207] The elimination of the risk that the account debtor will prove unwilling to pay, combined with the procedural advantages afforded in suing on the note, render the payment obligation of the farmer more readily marketable.

If chattel paper is created by the underlying sales transaction, the bank will again have a form of property that represents the farmer's Article 2 payment obligation.[208] Further, with the inclusion of the security interest in the tractor, if both the dealer and the farmer default on their payment obligations, the bank as assignee will be able to enforce the dealer's right to foreclose on the tractor.

---

that does not contain a notice preserving the consumer's defenses against assignees. The FTC rule applies whether the consumer buyer's payment obligation takes the form of an account, an instrument, or chattel paper. Trade Regulation Rule Concerning Preservation of Consumer Claims and Defenses, 16 C.F.R. § 433. **U.C.C. §§ R9-403(d) and R9-404(d) provide that in a consumer transaction a record that** *should* **contain the required FTC notice will be treated as if it** *did* **contain the notice.**

[207] U.C.C. §§ 3-302(a)(2), 3-305(b).

[208] If the chattel paper is a package that includes both a negotiable instrument and a security agreement, the bank's rights and duties are governed by Articles 3 and 9 to the extent they are consistent. In case of a conflict, Article 9 governs. U.C.C. § 3-102(b). The discharge rule is an example of a conflict between Article 3 and the 1972 text of Article 9. The bank is subject to an Article 9 rule that grants account debtors a discharge to the extent of payments made to the assignor before receiving notice of an assignment. §§ 9-318(3). Article 3's rule is otherwise. § 3-602(a)(no discharge for payment made to a person not entitled to enforce the instrument). **§ R9-102(a)(3) changes this result by providing that the term "account debtor" does not include a person obligated on a negotiable instrument even if the instrument is part of chattel paper.**

Although the rule is found in Article 9, a bank enforcing a negotiable instrument that is part of chattel paper can have rights similar to those enjoyed by an Article 3 holder in due course. U.C.C. §§ 9-318(1) and 9-206, **R9-404(a) and R9-403(b)**. It can obtain similar protection with chattel paper that does not include a negotiable instrument, but only if the contract between the debtor and the account debtor contains an enforceable waiver-of-defenses clause. *Id. See also* n. 205 *supra* (waiver-of-defense clause for accounts).

As this hypothetical demonstrates, the greatest bundle of property rights in a non-cash sale is created when the seller takes chattel paper. Legal rights alone, however, do not drive all business transactions. Transactional costs are higher with respect to the creation and transfer of notes and chattel paper. These costs may outweigh the enhanced rights provided, particularly when relatively small amounts of debt are involved. Alternative methods of risk assessment may also lessen the need for additional rights. The rights themselves may not be very workable in some transactions. The right to foreclose on the underlying collateral when chattel paper is involved may not be viable if the property is difficult to resell or if an entity like a bank is not well-suited to undertake its sale. Practical aspects of the choices involved in structuring the transaction with respect to accounts, notes, or chattel paper, are developed in subsequent discussions in this text.[209]

[E] Investment Property §§ 9-115, R9-102(a)(49)

"Investment property" is a broad category of intangible assets that qualify for one or more of the following categories: Securities (both certificated and uncertificated), security entitlements, securities accounts, commodity contracts, and commodity accounts.[210] Certain of these assets function like indispensable paper while others do not. Accordingly, it is best to deal with investment property as a separate category altogether.

Although investment property is an Article 9 term, it relies to a certain extent on Article 8. As will be explained below, Article 8 deals with securities held directly by an individual and with financial assets, including securities, held through a securities intermediary, like a broker. Investments in commodities are beyond the scope of Article 8, and Article 9 is self-contained with respect to security interests in such investments.

A security is an obligation of an issuer or a share or other interest in an issuer or its property that is, or is of a type, commonly dealt with in the securities markets, or is a medium for investment that by its terms expressly provides that it is within the scope of Article 8.[211] A certificated security is a security that is represented by a certificate.[212] The most common forms of certificated securities are stock and bond certificates.[213] The represented rights are commonly transferred by physical delivery of the certificate,[214] and thus a certificated security is a form of indispensable paper.

An uncertificated security, sometimes called a book-entry security, is a security for which there is no certificate.[215] The security holder's interest is represented by a notation

---

[209] *See, e.g.,* § 3.04 *infra.*

[210] U.C.C. §§ 9-115(1)(f), **R9-102(a)(49)**.

[211] U.C.C. § 8-102(a)(15). An asset need not actually be dealt with in the securities markets as long as it is of a type that is traded. Thus, a stock certificate representing an ownership interest in a closely held corporation is a security even though the stock is not publicly traded.

[212] U.C.C. § 8-102(a)(4).

[213] *In re* H.J. Otten Co., Inc., 8 B.R. 781, 31 U.C.C. Rep. Serv. 702 (W.D.N.Y. 1981) (municipal bonds included); Traverse v. Liberty Bank & Trust Co, 5 U.C.C. Rep. Serv. 535 (Mass. Super. Ct. 1967) (convertible debentures included).

[214] *See* U.C.C. §§ 8-104(a)(1)(describing how a person acquires an interest in a security), 8-302 (describing the rights acquired by a purchaser of a security), and 8-301(a)(defining delivery in the context of certificated securities).

[215] U.C.C. § 8-102(a)(18).

in books or records maintained by or on behalf of the issuer. Uncertificated securities are typically transferred by making appropriate changes in these records.[216] For example, mutual funds do not ordinarily issue certificates to their shareholders but instead show shareholder interests as notations in their records. An uncertificated security cannot function as an indispensable writing.

The term "security" includes both certificated and uncertificated securities,[217] and it is primarily used when there is a direct relationship between the investor and the issuer.[218] Most assets held indirectly through a broker are called "security entitle-ments,"[219] which are defined in terms of "financial assets." A financial asset may be a security, but the term also includes investment vehicles that are not securities but that are either of a type commonly traded on financial markets or are a recognized medium for investment.[220] Article 8 contains a section that further differentiates between financial assets that are securities and those that are not.[221] A financial asset that is not a security and is held directly by the debtor is not investment property and is almost certainly a general intangible. A financial asset held by a broker is almost always a security entitlement whether or not it qualifies as a security, and is therefore investment property.[222]

Assume, for example, that an investor owns 100 shares of ABC Corp. If the investor is in possession of a certificate showing this interest, the asset is called a certificated security. If there is no certificate but the books of ABC Corp. reflect the investor's interest, the asset is called an uncertificated security. If the investor indirectly holds 100 shares of ABC Corp. through a broker, the asset is a security entitlement. A securities account consists of all security entitlements held in a particular account by a broker.[223]

Now assume that the same investor directly owns an interest in a limited liability company. Unless the terms that define the interest specify that it is a security governed by Article 8, the interest is a financial asset but not a security.[224] It does not qualify as investment property and is instead a general intangible. If, however, a broker holds the financial asset for the investor, it is a security entitlement and investment property.

---

216 *See* U.C.C. §§ 8-104(a)(1)(describing how a person acquires an interest in a security), 8-302 (describing the rights acquired by a purchaser of a security), and 8-301(b)(defining delivery in the context of uncertificated securities).

217 U.C.C. § 8-102(a)(15)(i).

218 U.C.C. § 9-115 Cmt. 1.

219 U.C.C. § 8-102(a)(17). The investor is called an "entitlement holder." § 8-102(a)(7).

220 U.C.C. § 8-102(a)(9). The term also includes any other asset that is held in a securities account and that the broker and customer have agreed will be treated as a financial asset.

221 U.C.C. § 8-103.

222 It is possible for a financial asset held through a broker to be treated as if it were held directly by the debtor. *See* § 8-501(d)(financial asset registered in the name of, payable to the order of, or specially indorsed to the debtor and not indorsed by the debtor to the broker or in blank). If such a financial asset is a security, it is investment property. If it is not a security, it is a general intangible.

223 U.C.C. § 8-501(a). Attachment of a security interest to a securities account carries with it automatic attachment to each security entitlement within the account. §§ 9-115(2), **R9-203(h).**

224 U.C.C. § 8-103(c). Partnership interests are treated similarly.

The treatment of investments in commodity contracts is similar to that for security entitlements and securities accounts. A commodity account is an account maintained by a commodity intermediary (dealer) on behalf of an investor.[225] A commodity contract is a commodity futures contract or option that is traded on a commodities market.[226] Commodity contracts are functionally identical to security entitlements. A commodity account includes all the commodity contracts in an account maintained by a dealer and is functionally identical to a securities account.[227]

A security agreement that describes the collateral as "all investment property" will cover every asset within each category. The parties can also carve up the assets: The security agreement might, for example, cover "all securities," giving the secured party an interest in all certificated and uncertificated securities held directly by the debtor and all financial assets that are securities held through a broker. The secured party would not have a security interest in other financial assets held through a broker, nor would its interest attach to any commodity contract or commodity account. On the other hand, a security agreement that covers "all security entitlements" will reach each financial asset held through a broker but will not reach securities held directly by the debtor, nor will it reach commodity contracts or commodity accounts. A security agreement that describes the collateral as a particular securities account attaches to all security entitlements within the account, and a security agreement that describes the collateral as a particular commodity account attaches to all commodity contracts within the account.[228] Of course, the parties need not select a generic category. If the debtor holds a stock certificate representing an interest in a closely held corporation, the description in the agreement can be tailored to that asset. Likewise, if the parties want to use a particular security entitlement without using all the assets in a particular account they are free to do so.[229]

§ 1.05 Purchase-Money Security Interests §§ 9-107, R9-103

Although most distinctions in Article 9 are based on the classification of collateral involved in a transaction, the nature of the transaction itself can also be relevant.[230] One form of secured transaction does not involve a purchase of the collateral. The debtor

---

[225] U.C.C. §§ 9-115(1)(a), **R9-102(a)(14)**. The investor is called a "commodity customer." §§ 9-115(1)(c), **R9-102(a)(16)**.

[226] U.C.C. §§ 9-115(1)(b), **R9-102(a)(15)**.

[227] U.C.C. §§ 9-115(1)(a). Attachment of a security interest to a commodity account carries with it automatic attachment to each commodity contract within the account. §§ 9-115(2), **R9-203(i)**.

[228] U.C.C.§§ 9-115(3), (2).

[229] U.C.C. §§ 9-115(3) and **R9-108(d)** validate generic descriptions that use investment property or any of its subcategories, as well as specific descriptions of the underlying asset. Further, §§ 9-115(3) and **R9-108(b)** permit the description to identify the collateral by category, by quantity, by a computational or allocational formula or procedure, or by any other method, if the identity of the collateral is objectively determinable. **In a consumer transaction under the revision, however, a description of a security entitlement, securities account or commodity account only by one of the defined categories is insufficient. § R9-108(d).**

[230] For example, a purchase-money security interest, which is described in this section, can enable a creditor to acquire special rights in priority contests.

simply grants a security interest in personal property in which the debtor already has an interest. For example, a consumer debtor might grant a security interest in her car or a business debtor might grant a security interest in its existing equipment.

Secured transactions often also play a significant role in the purchase of goods. Many buyers cannot afford to pay the full purchase price at the time of entering a sales contract, or they choose for a variety of reasons not to do so. One solution that facilitates these transactions is an installment sales contract. The buyer is allowed to take immediate possession of the goods upon paying a modest down payment and agreeing to pay the balance in a series of monthly payments. Obviously, the total payment obligation includes additional financing charges.

The seller faces risks that often will make such a transaction unpalatable. If the seller does not receive the promised installments, its options are essentially limited to bringing an action for the unpaid balance. The seller has extremely narrow rights to recover the goods themselves in the event that the buyer does not pay or becomes insolvent.[231] Under Article 2 governing the sales transaction, title to the goods passes to the buyer.[232] This risk exposure is too great for many sellers to assume.

An alternative is for the seller and the buyer to enter into a conditional sales contract. In this type of contract, the seller essentially extends title to the goods to the buyer, but the title is conditioned. The condition is that the buyer fulfill all of its continuing obligations with respect to installment payments and the care and maintenance of the goods. In the event that the buyer defaults, the seller can then proceed against the goods themselves.[233] The conditional-sales aspect of the transaction is created by a security agreement between the parties.

The term "conditional sales contract" actually predates Article 9. Under Article 9, the seller's interest is a "purchase-money security interest."[234] The transaction just described is one of the two types of such interests: A security interest is purchase-money in nature to the extent that it is retained by a seller to secure all or part of the price.[235] The collateral

---

[231] The seller must ascertain that the buyer received the goods on credit while insolvent and, even then, the seller generally must give notice of its intent to reclaim them within ten days of their receipt. *See* U.C.C. § 2-702.

[232] "Unless otherwise explicitly agreed title passes to the buyer at the time and place at which the seller completes his performance with reference to the physical delivery of the goods...." U.C.C. § 2-401(2). Although the seller in Evans Prods. Co. v. Jorgensen, 245 Or. 362, 421 P.2d 978, 3 U.C.C. Rep. Serv. 1099 (1966), had intended to reserve title until it was paid for the veneer that it delivered to a plywood manufacturer, the delivery passed title. As the subsequent discussion in the text explains, the only interest that the seller could have retained was a purchase-money security interest. The seller did not take the necessary steps to create such an interest in this case.

[233] "Any retention of reservation by the seller of the title (property) in goods shipped or delivered to the buyer is limited in effect to a reservation of a security interest." U.C.C. § 2-401(1).

[234] Burlington Nat'l Bank v. Strauss, 50 Wis. 2d 270, 184 N.W.2d 122, 8 U.C.C. Rep. Serv. 944 (1971) (defendant retained purchase-money security interest in cattle sold to debtor under conditional sales contract taken by defendant to secure sales price).

[235] U.C.C. §§ 9-107(a), **R9-103(a)(2)**. *In re* Cerasoli, 27 B.R. 51, 36 U.C.C Rep. Serv. 1743 (Bankr. M.D. Pa. 1983) (security interest taken by seller to secure price of furniture previously sold to debtor on credit qualified as purchase-money security interest). *But see In re* Carter, 169

that secures the debtor's obligation to the seller is simply the property that the buyer purchases from the seller.

Practical business considerations will preclude many of these types of transactions. Many retailers do not have sufficient capital to finance purchasers of their inventory. They must replenish their inventory stock, and, if their suppliers require payment on delivery, these retailers cannot wait for monthly installment payments to be made. Their business depends upon turning over inventory, not upon earning the time-price differential that is added to an installment-payment obligation.

These transactions can nevertheless go forward through the involvement of a bank or other financing entity. When strategic planning necessitates purchase-money secured financing, a transaction can be structured to qualify as the second type of purchase-money secured transaction. Such a security interest is created when it is taken by a person who makes an advance or incurs an obligation to enable the debtor to acquire the collateral.[236] These transactions are commonly referred to as "enabling loans" because the lender provides financing that enable the debtor to acquire the collateral.[237]

Care must be exercised to satisfy a statutory requirement that the value provided be in fact used to enable the debtor to acquire rights in the collateral.[238] A lender will find itself unsecured if the debtor squanders the loan proceeds and never acquires the described collateral. Even if the debtor acquires the collateral so that a security interest attaches, it will not be a purchase-money interest if the lender is unable to bear the burden of tracing its loan proceeds into the collateral. The lender can protect itself by making payment directly to the seller of the collateral or by issuing a check naming the seller and the debtor as joint payees.

Purchase-money secured parties operating under the 1972 text have also run into difficulty when they have refinanced their original loan. The refinancing can take many forms. For example, a financially-troubled debtor might ask that a purchase-money loan be restructured to reduce monthly payments. If the secured party cancels the old agreement and substitutes a new agreement reflecting new payment terms, a court might hold that there has been a new loan and that its proceeds were used to pay off the old loan, not to "enable the debtor to acquire the collateral."[239] Lenders can avoid this problem by making it clear that they are modifying, not canceling, the original loan.

B.R. 227, 25 U.C.C. Rep. Serv. 2d 239 (Bankr. M.D. Ga. 1993) (security interest taken in furniture five months after sale held not created to secure purchase price but rather to secure pre-existing balance of buyer's account with seller).

[236] U.C.C. §§ 9-107(b), **R9-103(a)(2)**.

[237] Chrysler Credit Corp. v. B.J.M., Jr., Inc., 834 F. Supp. 813, 22 U.C.C. Rep. Serv. 2d 379 (E.D. Pa. 1993), *aff'd*, 30 F.3d 1485 (3d Cir. 1994) (lender's financing was intended to permit dealer to acquire its inventory); Nauman v. First Nat'l Bank of Allen Park, 50 Mich. App. 41, 212 N.W.2d 760, 13 U.C.C. Rep. Serv. 1191 (1973) (bank made advances to customers to enable them to acquire rights in trailers).

[238] *Id. See* Mays v. Brighton Bank, 832 S.W.2d 347, 18 U.C.C. Rep. Serv. 2d 621 (Tenn. Ct. App. 1992) (question of fact as to whether loan given by bank was used to purchase trailer).

[239] U.C.C. § 9-107(b). *See In re* Matthews, 724 F.2d 798, 37 U.C.C. Rep. Serv. 1332 (9th Cir. 1984). *But see In re* Billings, 838 F.2d 405, 5 U.C.C. Rep. Serv. 1259 (10th Cir. 1988)(refinancing did not amount to new loan).

(Matthew Bender & Co., Inc.)

A related problem occurs when the security interest in acquired goods secures more than their purchase price. For example, a seller with a purchase-money security interest in one item might sell a second item to the debtor, also on a purchase-money basis. If the two loans are consolidated into one for which both items serve as collateral,[240] a court might apply the "transformation rule" and hold that the seller's combined security interest is not purchase-money as applied to either item. The rationale is that the security interest, as applied to each item, was not retained solely to secure "all or part of its price."[241] The problem can also arise when an enabling lender makes an advance to the debtor for a purpose other than the acquisition of collateral and combines the obligations, thus mixing purchase-money with nonpurchase money.

Some courts, relying on the "to the extent" language in section 9-107, have rejected the transformation rule and held a secured party's interest is purchase-money if it can prove the extent to which the outstanding loan balance at any given point in time retains its purchase-money character. Suppose, for example, a bank lends $15,000 to enable a debtor to acquire an item of collateral. When the principal balance has been reduced to $10,000, the bank agrees to refinance the loan by extending an additional $5,000. If the debtor goes into default shortly thereafter, the collateral will serve as security for the entire $15,000, but the security interest will be purchase-money in nature only to the extent of $10,000. If default occurs the next year, though, after a series of payments has been made, a secured party will be unable to prove the extent to which the loan retains its purchase-money character unless its agreement specifies how payments are to be allocated. The "dual-status" approach is more consistent with the language of the Code, but it is not a panacea.

Revised Article 9 adopts the dual-status approach for nonconsumer transactions.[242] It defines "purchase-money collateral" as "goods or software that secures a purchase-money obligation with respect to that collateral"[243] and "purchase-money obligation" as an obligation "incurred as all or part of the price of the collateral or for value given to enable the debtor to acquire rights in or the use of collateral if the value is in fact so used."[244] It then states that a security interest is purchase-money in nature "to the extent that the goods are purchase-money collateral with

---

240 This approach is called "cross-collateralization."

241 U.C.C. § 9-107(a). *See In re* Manuel, 507 F.2d 990, 16 U.C.C. Rep. Serv. 493 (5th Cir. 1975). The most extreme example of this approach is Southtrust Bank of Ala. v. Borg-Warner Acceptance Corp., 760 F.2d 1240, 40 U.C.C. Rep. Serv. 1601 (11th Cir. 1985), which held that a purchase-money inventory financer who relied on an after-acquired property clause in a single security agreement to cover multiple transactions had lost its purchase-money position through cross-collateralization. The opinion has been properly criticized for requiring a new security agreement for each of a series of virtually identical, wholly purchase-money, transactions. *Southtrust* is explicitly reversed in the revision. *See* **§ R9-103(b)(2).**

242 **U.C.C. § R9-103(f). The revision leaves the approach in consumer transactions to the courts but provides that the adoption of the dual-status rule for other transactions does not create an inference that the transformation rule should be adopted for consumer transactions. U.C.C. § R9-103(h).**

243 U.C.C. § R9-103(a)(1).

244 U.C.C. § R9-103(a)(2).

respect to that security interest."[245] The "to the extent" language is emphasized by providing that "[a] purchase-money security interest does not lose its status as such, even if (1) the purchase-money collateral also secures an obligation that is not a purchase-money obligation; (2) collateral that is not purchase-money collateral also secures the purchase money obligation; or (3) the purchase-money obligation has been renewed, refinanced, consolidated, or restructured."[246]

The revision also deals with the allocation-of-payments problem in nonconsumer transactions. It provides that payments are to be allocated according to any reasonable agreement of the parties, in the absence of reasonable agreement to any expressed intention of the obligor manifested at or before the time the payment is made, and in the absence of either reasonable agreement or manifested intention to unsecured obligations first and then to secured obligations in the order in which they were incurred.[247] The burden of establishing the extent to which a security interest is purchase-money in nature rests on the party claiming that status.[248]

There is a special provision protecting the purchase-money priority of secured parties who use cross-collateralization clauses in the context of inventory financing.[249] For example, suppose a credit seller retains a purchase-money security interest in an item as collateral for its price and for any other obligation of the buyer. The seller later sells another item to the buyer on the same terms, and the buyer resells the second item to a buyer in the ordinary course who takes it free from the seller's security interest.[250] Under the revision, the seller's security interest in the first item is still entirely purchase-money in nature even though that item now secures the price of both items. Without this special provision, the dual status approach would apply and the seller's security interest would only be partially purchase-money.

§ 1.06 Sales of Accounts, Chattel Paper, Payment Intangibles and Promissory Notes §§ 9-102(1)(b), R9-109(a)(3)

Most Article 9 transactions are loan transactions, and the security interest serves the function of providing collateral in the event of default. An ostensible-ownership problem arises when the secured party lacks possession of the collateral, but the public filing of a financing statement resolves that problem. The filing protects the secured party from most adverse claims to its collateral.

In real estate recording systems, any person with an interest in land, including mortgage lenders and buyers, records that interest in order to gain protection against adverse claimants. A buyer, for example, will record a deed so that the seller cannot fraudulently reconvey an interest in the property to a third party whose claim might defeat the buyer's interest. Buyers of most goods need not record their interests since the mere fact of

---

[245] U.C.C. § R9-103(b)(1).

[246] U.C.C. § R9-103(f).

[247] U.C.C. § R9-103(e).

[248] U.C.C. § R9-103(g).

[249] U.C.C. § R9-103(b)(2).

[250] The rights of a buyer in the ordinary course are discussed in § 11.03 *infra*.

possession is sufficient to put third parties on notice. Public recording is required, however, for certain types of goods. We are accustomed, for example, to title certificates evidencing ownership of motor vehicles, and buyers of aircraft must register with the Federal Aviation Administration to gain protection from adverse claimants.[251]

Recall that an account is a pure intangible, meaning that there is no indispensable paper that can be transferred in order to assign the right to payment represented by the account.[252] The owner of an account who wants to enforce the right to payment must wait until payment is due. If the owner wants to realize upon the account before that time, it can either conditionally assign the account as collateral for a loan or sell it via an unconditional assignment. In either case, the underlying mechanism by which the right to payment is transferred is assignment.

Assignment of accounts is most important in the context of merchants who sell some of their inventory on an installment plan. Because of the need to replenish inventory supplies and the desire to free the capital represented by the account, many merchants seek to finance against the value of their accounts. Various dynamics of the marketplace, which will be explained later,[253] tend to dictate whether the merchant can borrow against the accounts or must sell them outright. The driving force in both circumstances, however, is the need of the merchant to finance the acquisition of additional inventory.

In a loan transaction, the assignment is effectuated by an Article 9 security agreement, and the secured party (assignee) must file a financing statement to protect its security interest in the event the owner fraudulently assigns the account a second time. The intangible nature of the collateral facilitates reassignment by a fraudulent owner, and the filing puts third parties on notice of the secured party's interest and establishes priority should a third party take an assignment anyway. The same problems can arise when an account is sold by an unconditional assignment. The drafters of the 1972 text wanted a mechanism that would encourage the buyer of an account to make a public filing in order to warn third parties who might either buy or lend against the same account. Their resolution was to expand the scope of Article 9 to cover "any sale of accounts or chattel paper."[254] The 1972 text does not govern the sale of any other type of asset. **The revision adds sales of payment intangibles (a subset of general intangibles) and promissory notes (a subset of instruments) to the scope of Article 9.[255]**

The rationale for bringing sales of these assets into Article 9 is to encourage assignees to give public notice by filing financing statements. The mechanism employed by the drafters of both the 1972 text **and the revision** to achieve that goal is awkward and

---

251 49 U.S.C. § 1403.

252 *See* discussion in §§ 1.04[C][1] and [D] *supra.*

253 *See* § 3.04 *infra.*

254 U.C.C. § 9-102(1)(b). Chattel paper is included because rights represented by chattel paper can be assigned without transferring the paper, thus creating an ostensible-ownership problem. Chattel paper has characteristics of both pure intangibles and indispensable paper, and the Code permits a secured party to perfect either by filing a financing statement or by taking possession of the paper. U.C.C. §§ 9-304(1), 9-305. For reasons discussed in § 6.01 *infra*, perfection by possession is more secure.

255 U.C.C. § R9-109(a)(3).

confusing. The Code defines a "security interest" to include the interest of a buyer of accounts or chattel paper,[256] "secured party" to include a buyer of such assets,[257] and "debtor" to include a seller of such assets.[258] Since a buyer of accounts or chattel paper is a secured party with a security interest, it needs to file a financing statement to protect its interest. Under the normal Code priority rule governing contests between secured parties,[259] a buyer of accounts who fails to file will lose to a subsequent buyer or secured lender who does file.

This mechanism has accomplished the drafters' goal, but calling a buyer's interest a security interest when there is no loan and therefore no security inevitably has consequences. For example, the sales agreement between the buyer and seller is a "security agreement"[260] and to be enforceable must meet the formalities required of any security agreement.[261] Also, since there is no real security the Code's foreclosure procedures had to be drafted so that they do not apply to sales of accounts and chattel paper. For example, if a lender acquires a security interest in accounts to secure a loan, following default it must adhere to Article 9's provisions governing foreclosure. Most importantly, it is subject to the duty of commercial reasonableness in either collecting the accounts[262] or selling (reassigning) them at a foreclosure sale.[263] If the foreclosure brings a surplus it must be turned over to the debtor, and if proper procedures have been followed the debtor **(the obligor in the revision)** is liable for any remaining deficiency.[264] If, however, a buyer of accounts acquires a security interest that does not secure an indebtedness, foreclosure makes no sense. The buyer has bought the entire interest and can keep whatever is collected on the accounts or generated by their resale. Because there will typically be neither a surplus nor a deficiency,[265] it should not matter whether the buyer's collection or resale efforts are commercially reasonable. To effectuate this functional distinction, relevant sections of the 1972 text differentiate between security interests that secure an indebtedness and those that do not.[266] **The revision achieves**

---

[256] U.C.C. § 1-201(37). **This section has been amended, in conformity with the revision, to include the interest of a buyer of a payment intangible or promissory note.**

[257] U.C.C. §§ 9-105(1)(d), **R9-102(a)(72)(D).**

[258] U.C.C. §§ 9-105(1)(d), **R9-102(a)(28)(B).**

[259] U.C.C. §§ 9-312(5)(a), **R9-322(a)(1).**

[260] U.C.C. §§ 9-105(1)(l), **R9-102(a)(73).**

[261] U.C.C. §§ 9-203, **R9-203.**

[262] U.C.C. §§ 9-502(2), **R9-607(c).**

[263] U.C.C. §§ 9-504(3), **R9-610(b).**

[264] U.C.C. §§ 9-504(2), **R9-615(d).**

[265] The parties sometimes agree that the seller of accounts or chattel paper will make up any deficiency if collections do not bring a projected amount and/or the seller will be liable for any surplus if they exceed a projected amount. These consensual risk-allocation mechanisms are enforceable. U.C.C. §§ 9-502(2), 9-504(2), **R9-607(c)(2).**

[266] *See, e.g.,* U.C.C. §§ 9-502(2), 9-504(2). For business reasons, a sale may be structured in such a way that the buyer of accounts or chattel paper will have a right of recourse against the seller if collection efforts fail. This may, for example, be tied to uncollectibility that results when the account debtor asserts a defense arising from the underlying transaction. If there is a right of recourse, the buyer of the account or chattel paper must make commercially reasonable collection efforts as a condition to exercising the right. § 9-502(2).

(Matthew Bender & Co., Inc.)

the same result through a somewhat cleaner drafting technique.[267]

At least one court was thoroughly fooled by Article 9's terminology. It concluded that since an account buyer's interest was limited to a security interest, Article 9 precluded the seller from transferring outright ownership of the account. Accordingly, it held that the account was still owned by the seller and was part of the seller's bankruptcy estate.[268] Of course, the decision is wrong,[269] but using "security interest" to describe a buyer's interest invites such confusion.

As mentioned above, the scope of revised Article 9 has been expanded to include sales of payment intangibles[270] and promissory notes.[271] The primary rationale for the inclusion of payment intangibles is related to a financing device called "securitization." Securitization occurs when receivables (rights to the payment of money) are used as collateral for securities. For example, a credit card company that needs immediate funds can create a trust vehicle and then sell (*i.e.*, assign outright) a portion of its accounts[272] to the vehicle.[273] The company then raises capital through the sale to investors of shares in the trust, sometimes called "asset-backed securities." Securitization allows receivables to be separately packaged and sold. The credit card company might, for example, create one vehicle for accounts generated during January and another for its February accounts.

Investors in the vehicle must be certain that the vehicle's interest in the accounts is protected against adverse claimants, primarily a trustee in the event the credit

---

[267] U.C.C. § R9-601(f) states that, except as set forth in § R9-607(c), the Code imposes no duties on a buyer of accounts, chattel paper, payment intangibles or promissory notes. § R9-607(c) requires commercially reasonable collection efforts if the buyer is entitled to charge back uncollected assets against the seller or otherwise has a right of recourse.

[268] Octagon Gas Sys., Inc. v. Rimmer, 995 F.2d 948, 20 U.C.C. Rep. Serv. 2d 1330 (10th Cir. 1993), *cert. denied*, 510 U.S. 993 (1993).

[269] P.E.B. Commentary No. 14 (June 10, 1994) disapproves of *Octagon Gas* and cites with approval Major's Furniture Mart v. Castle Credit Corp., 602 F.2d 538, 26 U.C.C. Rep. Serv. 1319 (3d Cir. 1979). The Permanent Editorial Board (P.E.B.) is a standing committee of the National Conference of Commissioners on Uniform State Laws that oversees the development of the Uniform Commercial Code. One of the responsibilities of the P.E.B. is to provide commentaries that clarify issues that have troubled the courts.

[270] U.C.C. § R9-109(a)(3). A payment intangible is a general intangible in which the account debtor's principle obligation is to pay money. § R9-102(a)(61). *See* discussion in § 1.04[C][2] *supra*.

[271] U.C.C. § R9-109(a)(3). The term refers to instruments other than drafts and certificates of deposit. § R9-102(a)(65).

[272] Under the 1972 text, credit-card receivables (a credit card company's right to payment from its cardholders) are probably general intangibles. *See, e.g., In re* Brendle's Stores, Inc., 165 B.R. 811, 22 U.C.C. Rep. Serv. 2d 450 (M.D.N.C. 1993); *but see* First United Bank v. Philmont Corp., 533 So. 2d 449, 7 U.C.C. Rep. Serv. 2d 1550 (Miss. 1988)(classifying credit-card receivables as instruments). Under the revision, they are clearly accounts. U.C.C. § R9-102(a)(2)(vii).

[273] The transaction can also be structured as a secured loan from the vehicle to the credit card company with the accounts serving as collateral.

card company seeks protection in bankruptcy. Because the sale of accounts to the vehicle is within the scope of Article 9, this simply means that the vehicle must file a financing statement. Under the revised Code, most of the assets used for securitization purposes will fall within the expanded definition of accounts, but the line between accounts and general intangibles has always been quite thin. Because of the variety of assets that can qualify as general intangibles, the sale of such assets is not within the scope of either current Article 9 or the revision. However, sales of payment intangibles have been brought within the scope of the revision to protect securitizations. Should a court decide that an asset backing a securitized offering is a general intangible rather than an account, Article 9 still governs. Sales of payment intangibles are automatically perfected,[274] so no action is required by the vehicle to guard against this risk.

Similar reasoning underlies the decision to cover sales of promissory notes.[275] As new forms of financing evolve, a court might some day decide that the asset backing a securitized offering is an instrument rather than an account or general intangible.[276] To guard against this risk, the "promissory note" subcategory was created.[277] Sales of promissory notes are governed by Article 9 and, as with payment intangibles, the buyer's interest is automatically perfected.[278]

§ 1.07   Exclusions from Article 9 §§ 9-104, R9-109(c)

Some types of transactions fit the definition of a security interest and would otherwise clearly be within the general scope of Article 9, except that the drafters have chosen

---

[274] U.C.C. § R9-309(3). The automatic perfection approach was adopted because of problems arising from loan participation arrangements. Mortgage lenders often sell fractional interests in their notes and mortgages, and these interests qualify as payment intangibles under the revision. Filing of financing statements is not customary in such arrangements, and the rationale for adopting automatic perfection is to prevent the necessity of such filings under the revision. Buyers of loan participations should be wary, however. A number of courts have held that participation arrangements characterized as "sales" by the parties are in fact disguised security transactions. See, e.g., In re Coronet Capital Co., 142 B.R. 78 (Bankr. S.D.N.Y. 1992)(discussing factors indicative of disguised security transaction). Automatic perfection applies to outright sales of payment intangibles but not to their use as collateral for loans. A precautionary filing is suggested to protect against a court holding that the "buyer" is really a lender.

[275] The securitization problem drove the decision to include sales of promissory notes, but the provision governs all such sales, including sales of notes secured by mortgages on land (discussed in § 1.07[C] infra).

[276] See note 272 supra (case law under 1972 text splits as to whether credit-card receivables are instruments or general intangibles).

[277] Promissory notes can be negotiable or nonnegotiable. Article 9's treatment of nonnegotiable notes is discussed in § 1.04[B][2] supra.

[278] U.C.C. § R9-309(4). Notwithstanding automatic perfection, which will suffice in bankruptcy, the buyer should take possession of the instrument to preclude the seller from fraudulently reconveying the instrument to a holder in due course of a negotiable instrument or a good faith purchaser for value of a nonnegotiable instrument. See discussion in § 8.01[A] infra. Further, if the instrument is negotiable, the buyer should have it indorsed by the seller so that the buyer can become a holder in due course.

to exclude them from the scope of the Article. A variety of policies supports these exclusions. The excluded transactions and the reasons for their exclusion are summarized below.

[A] Federal Statutes

The first exclusion is based on the principle of federal preemption. Article 9 does not apply to a security interest that is subject to a federal statute to the extent that such statute governs the rights of the parties.[279] A number of federal statutes govern security interests in a variety of kinds of personal property.[280] None of these statutes, however, are comprehensive in their regulation of secured financing. Because the exclusion applies only "to the extent" of federal preemption, Article 9 can be applied to any additional aspects of transactions not within the jurisdiction of the federal statutes.[281] For example, the Federal Aviation Act of 1958 establishes a federal recording system for security interests in aircraft, but most courts have determined that priority issues are decided under Article 9 because the Aviation Act does not address them.[282]

Some of the most complex issues of federal preemption occur in the area of intellectual property. Patent rights, trademark rights, and copyrights are general intangibles under Article 9, but assignments of such rights are the subject of federal law. Under patent law, for example, assignments are void as against any purchaser and mortgagee without notice of the assignment unless a notice is recorded with the federal patent office.[283] Filing a financing statement is thus ineffective to protect a secured party from someone who buys the patent from the debtor or who lends against it and properly records in the federal system.[284] The scope of federal recording systems vary, and a lawyer must carefully consider the relevant statutes and cases in determining the extent to which Article 9 is preempted.[285]

---

[279] U.C.C. §§ 9-104(a), **R9-109(c)(1)**.

[280] 15 U.S.C. § 1060 (trademarks); 17 U.S.C. § 205 (copyrights); 35 U.S.C. § 261 (patents); 46 U.S.C. §§ 911-961(ship mortgages); 49 U.S.C. § 1403 (aircraft); 49 U.S.C. § 11304(railroad rolling stock).

[281] Despite the clear intent of the drafters, not every court has understood that the preemption is only partial. *See, e.g., In re* Peregrine Entertainment, Ltd., 116 B.R. 194, 11 U.C.C. Rep. Serv. 2d 1025 (C.D. Cal. 1990)(copyrights). **The revision clarifies that Article 9 defers to federal law only when, and to the limited extent that, it must. U.C.C. § R9-109(c)(1) and § R9-109 Cmt. 8.**

[282] Carolina Aircraft Corp. v. Commerce Trust Co., 289 So. 2d 37, 14 U.C.C. Rep. Serv. 505 (Fla. Dist. Ct. App. 1974) (repairman's lien priority under § 9-310); Suburban Trust & Sav. Bank v. Campbell, 250 N.E.2d 118, 6 U.C.C. Rep. Serv. 964 (Ohio Ct. App. 1969) (buyer in ordinary course prevails under § 9-307(1)).

[283] 35 U.S.C. § 261. If the notice is filed within three months of the assignment it is retroactively effective to the date of the assignment. *Id.*

[284] Since patent law does not require recordation to defeat lien creditors, an Article 9 financing statement may be sufficient for that purpose. *See, e.g.,* City Bank & Trust Co. v. Otto Fabric, Inc., 83 B.R. 780, 5 U.C.C. Rep. Serv. 2d 1459 (D. Kan. 1988). Federal recordation should also defeat a lien creditor, though, so a state filing is not necessary.

[285] For example, the Lanham Act, which governs trademarks, provides that an unrecorded as-

[B] Landlord and Statutory Liens

Article 9 does not apply to a landlord's lien[286] or to a lien given by statute or common-law rule "for services or materials."[287] These exclusions simply reiterate the intention to limit the scope of Article 9 to consensual security interests. *Any* lien that attaches to personal property or fixtures can fit within the Article 1 definition of a security interest: "An interest in personal property or fixtures which secures payment or performance of an obligation."[288] Article 9, however, applies *only* to security interests created by contract.[289] Article 9, thus, does not apply to liens that arise by operation of law, either through statutory provisions or through the common law.[290] This means that no security agreement is necessary for the creation of such a lien and the lienor need not follow Article 9's rules governing foreclosure.

Even though Article 9 does not apply to liens that arise by operation of law, section 9-310 nevertheless governs the priority of certain of these lien interests against a security interest in the property to which the lien has attached.[291] Section 9-310 of the 1972 text **and Section 9-333 of the revision** generally grant priority for such lienors who, in the ordinary course of business, furnish services or materials with respect to goods.[292] For example, an auto-body repair shop might be granted a statutory lien covering body restoration work performed on an automobile that had been in a collision. The priority applies only to possessory lien interests, however. Article 9 does not provide a rule that governs priority between a secured party and a nonpossessory lien interest that arises by operation of law. Article 9 also does not provide a rule that governs priority between a secured party and a landlord's lienor, even one in possession of the goods, since a landlord by definition provides land rather than services or materials.

The court in *Leger Mill Co. v. Kleen-Leen, Inc.*[293] understood the proper application of the exception with respect to liens for services and materials. An Oklahoma statutory

---

signment is void as against subsequent purchasers but does not mention mortgagees. 15 U.S.C. § 1060. A mortgagee is a type of purchaser at common law, a distinction accepted by the Code (definition of purchaser includes any party, including a secured party, whose interest is acquired in a consensual transaction (U.C.C. §§ 1-201(33), (32)). However, since patent law expressly refers to mortgagees, the exclusion of that term from trademark law may place security assignments of trademark rights entirely beyond the scope of federal law. For that reason, lenders with security interests in trademarks should file a financing statement under state law and record their interests under federal law. *See, e.g., In re* Chattanooga Choo-Choo Co., 98 B.R. 792, 8 U.C.C. Rep. Serv. 2d 795 (Bankr. E.D. Tenn. 1989).

[286] U.C.C. §§ 9-104(b), **R9-109(d)(1)(except agricultural liens, discussed in this subsection** *infra*).

[287] U.C.C. §§ 9-104(c), **R9-109(d)(2) (excluding agricultural liens)**.

[288] U.C.C. § 1-201(37).

[289] U.C.C. § 9-102(2), **R9-109(a)(1)**.

[290] *In re* Tacoma Aviation Ctr., Inc., 23 B.R. 326, 35 U.C.C. Rep. Serv. 298 (Bankr. W.D. Wash. 1982) (statutory mechanic's lien excluded); Universal C.I.T. Credit Corp. v. Congressional Motors, Inc., 228 A.2d 463, 4 U.C.C. Rep. Serv. 152 (Md. 1967) (common-law landlord's lien excluded).

[291] U.C.C. §§ 9-104(c), **R9-109(d)(2)**.

[292] This priority is discussed in § 13.01 *infra*.

[293] 563 P.2d 132, 21 U.C.C. Rep. Serv. 896 (Okla. 1977).

feeder's lien did not provide a pig feeder with priority over a prior perfected Article 9 security interest in the animals because the feeder did not have possession of the animals when it tried to enforce the lien. The court did not conclude by negative implication, however, that the secured party should prevail. Rather, the court concluded that the nonpossessory lien fell within the exclusion provision and that the priority determination was outside the scope of Article 9. [294]

The scope of revised Article 9 has been expanded to govern perfection and priority of "agricultural liens." [295] **An agricultural lien is a nonpossessory statutory lien on farm products that is not a security interest (*i.e.*, is not consensual) and that secures payment to a person who in the ordinary course of business furnishes goods or services, or leases real property, to assist with a debtor's farming operation.** [296] **An example of an agricultural lien would be the pig feeder's lien in *Leger Mill*. The revision would not cover the creation of the lien, which is still governed by state law, but to obtain priority the pig feeder would have to file a financing statement covering the affected farm products under Article 9.** [297]

[C] Real Estate Interests

Article 9 also does not apply to the creation or transfer of real-estate interests, including liens on real estate and leases or the rents due thereunder. [298] Like the exclusion on landlords' liens, this exclusion simply reiterates the general scope provision that Article 9 applies to contractual transactions creating security interests in personal property or fixtures. [299] Security in realty is excluded. Mortgages are governed by state real estate law. Fixtures, however, are governed by both real-estate law and by Article 9. [300]

Article 9 explicitly applies to certain secondary financing transactions involving real estate. The relevant provision states as follows: "The application of this Article to a security interest in a secured obligation is not affected by the fact that the obligation is itself secured by a transaction or interest to which this Article does not apply." [301] In other words, even though the creation of a mortgage on land is beyond its scope, Article 9 applies to a security interest in a mortgage-backed debt. If a credit buyer of land executes

---

[294] The court ultimately found priority for the secured party, but it reached that result by shaping a common-law rule. The court might alternatively have granted priority to the secured party under Article 9's "default" priority provision found in U.C.C. §§ 9-201, **R9-201**. *See* § 14.02 *infra*.

[295] U.C.C. § **R9-109(a)(2)**. *See* § 13.02 *infra*.

[296] U.C.C. § **R9-102(a)(5)**.

[297] *See* U.C.C. § **R9-308(b)**(agricultural lien perfected when it becomes effective and proper step has been taken); § **R9-310(a)**(proper step for perfecting agricultural lien is filing financing statement); § **R9-509(a)(2)**(person holding agricultural lien entitled to file financing statement); and § **R9-322** (agricultural lienor treated like secured party for priority purposes, except that statute creating agricultural lien can provide that it takes priority over all secured parties if it is perfected (§ **R9-322(g)**).

[298] U.C.C. §§ 9-104(j), **R9-109(d)(11)**.

[299] U.C.C. § 9-102(1)(a).

[300] The nature of fixtures and the relationship between real estate law and Article 9 are covered in Chapter 15 *infra*.

[301] U.C.C. §§ 9-102(3), **R9-109(b)**.

a note that embodies the payment obligation and secures it with a mortgage, the transaction is beyond the scope of Article 9.[302] If the note-holder uses the note and mortgage to secure a subsequent loan, Article 9 governs that transaction. The primary collateral is the note, which qualifies as an instrument.[303] The lender also takes an assignment of the mortgage, giving it foreclosure rights in the event both its borrower and the note's maker (the buyer of the land) default on their payment obligations.

The foregoing analysis does not resolve all the issues in what has become an unjustifiably complex area. Article 9 clearly applies, but does real-estate law also apply since the assignment of the mortgage is a transfer of an interest in real property? If only Article 9 applies, the secured party need only perfect its security interest in the note,[304] but if real-estate law also applies it must record its mortgage assignment in the real-estate records. The courts ought not apply both real-estate law and the U.C.C. to a particular transaction, and the secured party's primary interest in the note dictates that the Code govern. Nevertheless, a prudent lender operating under the 1972 text[305] should consider recording its assignment as a precaution.

A related problem arises when a vendor sells land pursuant to an installment land contract, sometimes called a contract for deed. Instead of taking back a note and mortgage, the vendor retains title to the land until the last installment is paid. This transaction is outside the scope of Article 9, but what if the vendor uses the stream of payments as collateral for a loan? The secondary financing transaction is within the scope of Article 9.[306] The collateral is a general intangible under the 1972 text[307] **and an account under the revision.**[308] Real estate law ought not apply to the secondary transaction, but a prudent lender operating under the 1972 text[309] should nevertheless record its assignment of the installment land contract.[310]

---

[302] If the note is negotiable it is governed by Article 3. The mortgage is governed by local real estate law.

[303] *See* U.C.C. § 9-102 Cmt. 4. The note will probably be an instrument even if it is not negotiable. *See* U.C.C. §§ 9-105(1)(i) and **R9-102(a)(47)**, discussed in § 1.04[B][2] *supra*.

[304] Security interests in instruments must ordinarily be perfected by possession under the 1972 text. U.C.C. § 9-304(1). **They can be perfected by either possession or filing under the revision. §§ R9-312(a)(filing), R9-313(a)(possession). Automatic perfection is available when promissory notes have been sold, a topic that is discussed in § 1.06** *supra.*

[305] **This issue·under the revision is discussed in this subsection** *infra.*

[306] Not all courts have so held. *See, e.g., In re* Shuster, 784 F.2d 883, 42 U.C.C. Rep. Serv. 1433 (8th Cir. 1986)(third party tracing title to land would not check U.C.C. filings). The decision is wrong. The vendor's title-retention scheme is a security device, rendering the underlying transaction a secured obligation within the meaning of U.C.C. §§ 9-102(3) and **R9-109(b)**.

[307] *In re* Southworth, 22 B.R. 376, 34 U.C.C. Rep. Serv. 1372 (Bankr. D. Kan. 1982). The right to payment is not an account because it is a right to payment for land, not goods or services. Perfection of a security interest in a general intangible under the 1972 text must be accomplished by filing a financing statement. U.C.C. § 9-302(1).

[308] **U.C.C. § R9-102(a)(2). Perfection of a security interest in an account under the revision must ordinarily be accomplished by filing a financing statement. U.C.C. § R9-310(a).**

[309] **This issue under the revision is discussed in this subsection** *infra.*

[310] *In re* Southworth, 22 B.R. 376, 34 U.C.C. Rep. Serv. 1372 (Bankr. D. Kan. 1982), held

Revised Article 9 attempts to resolve some of the foregoing issues by providing that a security interest in a secured obligation automatically attaches to the interest that secures the obligation.[311] In other words, a security interest in a note secured by a mortgage automatically attaches to the secured party's interest in the mortgage, and a security interest in a vendor's interest in an installment land contract also attaches to the secured party's interest in the underlying land. Moreover, perfection of the security interest in the payment obligation also perfects the underlying security interest.[312] Thus, the revision brings the entire transaction within the scope of Article 9, thereby excluding real-estate law. In the note-and-mortgage situation, the secured party need only perfect as to the note.[313] Recall that revised Article 9 classifies the secured party's interest in an installment land contract as an account rather than a general intangible, and the secured party should only have to perfect as to the account. Note that revised Article 9 also applies to the outright sale of both accounts and promissory notes.[314]

[D] Wage Claim Assignments

Article 9 does not apply to a transfer of a claim for wages, salary, or other employee compensation.[315] An agreement to assign future wages as collateral to secure a loan would certainly be contractual and otherwise within the scope of Article 9. These assignments are expressly excluded because they "present important social problems whose solution should be a matter of local regulation."[316] Many states have enacted regulations that either prohibit or significantly limit wage assignments. These regulations are designed to protect wage earners from financially overburdening themselves and their families.[317]

---

that such a transaction is within the scope of both Article 9 and real estate law. Thus, the lender was required to both file a UCC financing statement for the general intangible aspect of the transaction and record its assignment for the real estate aspect.

[311] U.C.C. § R9-203(g).

[312] U.C.C. § R9-308(e). Although the intent is to preempt real-estate law, a legislative note appended to revised § R9-308 suggests that each state legislature should provide further clarification by enacting an amendment to the state's real-estate recording act expressly providing that perfection under Article 9 is sufficient.

[313] The secured party should also have a negotiable note indorsed to it so that it can become a holder-in-due course under Article 3, and it should make certain that the original mortgagee properly recorded the mortgage.

[314] See discussion in § 1.06 supra.

[315] U.C.C. §§ 9-104(d), R9-109(d)(3). See Massachusetts Mutual Life Ins. Co. v. Central Penn. Nat'l Bank, 372 F. Supp. 1027, 14 U.C.C. Rep. Serv. 212 (E.D. Pa. 1974), aff'd mem., 510 F.2d 970 (3d Cir. 1975) (agent for insurance company held to be more like independent contractor than employee, so that renewal commissions were not employee compensation).

[316] U.C.C. § 9-104 Cmt. 4.

[317] See In re Gwynn, 82 B.R. 121, 5 U.C.C. Rep. Serv. 2d 1136 (Bankr. S.D. Cal. 1988) (California statutory prohibition against wage assignments absent permission of wage earner's spouse).

[E] Government Transfers

Transfers by a government or government agency are excluded from the 1972 text of Article 9.[318] For example, a government body could borrow money and provide collateral in the form of charges to be received for water, electricity, or sewer service. The government transfers are excluded because they generally are governed by special provisions of law.[319]

Revised Article 9 significantly narrows this exception. The revision applies to a government-created security interest unless preempted by a state statute that expressly governs the creation, perfection, priority or enforcement of the interest.[320] In other words, government transfers are within the scope of the revision unless another state statute expressly takes them out. The revision also defines a new category of transactions called "public-finance transactions."[321] A public-finance transaction is a secured transaction in which the obligation is represented by debt securities (*e.g.*, bonds, indentures, certificates of participation) with an initial stated maturity of at least twenty years issued by a state or governmental unit of a state. The primary importance of the category is that a financing statement perfecting a security interest in the collateral securing the debt securities in a public-finance transaction can be made effective for a period of thirty years.[322]

[F] Transfers Irrelevant to Commercial Finance

Article 9 essentially is concerned with commercial financing. The primary transaction involves a person consenting to put up personal property or fixtures as collateral to secure a debt. Outright sales of accounts and chattel paper (**and, in the revision, payment intangibles and promissory notes**) are also motivated primarily by commercial finance considerations, and thus are also brought within the scope of Article 9. Certain transfers which fit within these two transactional models, however, have little or nothing to do with commercial financing. They are, therefore, excluded from the scope of Article 9.

[1] Specified Transfers of Accounts and Chattel Paper

Several types of transfers of accounts and chattel paper (**and, under the revision, payment intangibles and promissory notes**) are irrelevant to commercial financing interests and, thus, are excluded from Article 9.[323] These transfers are: (1) the sale of any such asset as part of a sale of the business out of which it arose; (2) the assignment of any such asset for the purpose of collection; (3) a transfer of a right to payment under a contract to an assignee who is also to do the performance under the contract; and (4) a transfer of a single account (**or, under the revision, payment intangible or promissory**

---

[318] U.C.C. § 9-104(e).

[319] U.C.C. § 9-104 Cmt. 5.

[320] U.C.C. § **R9-109**(c)(2).

[321] U.C.C. § **R9-102**(a)(67).

[322] U.C.C. § **R9-515(b).**

[323] U.C.C. §§ 9-104(f), **R9-109(d)(4)-(7).**

note) to an assignee in whole or partial satisfaction of a preexisting debt.[324] These exclusions enable transferees like collection agencies and delegates to take an assignment without having to comply with the Article 9 perfection provisions to protect their interests against other parties who deal with the assignor.

[2] Judgment Rights and Tort Claims

Article 9 does not apply to "a right represented by a judgment."[325] If a party obtains a judgment and then assigns the right to collect that judgment as collateral to secure a loan, the assignee will not be required to file a financing statement with respect to the assignment because the assignment is expressly exempt from the application of Article 9.[326] An assignee should be cautious, however. Except for claims arising in tort, an assignment covering rights which might arise from litigation that has not yet commenced or has not yet reached the judgment stage will be within the scope of Article 9.[327]

The exclusion from Article 9 does not include "a judgment taken on a right to payment that was collateral."[328] A security interest, for example, might cover an instrument or an account. If the obligation to pay that is represented by such collateral is reduced to judgment, an assignment of that judgment right is not excluded from Article 9. The judgment right is a proceed of the original collateral.

The 1972 text does not apply to "a transfer in whole or in part of any claim arising out of tort."[329] This exclusion would encompass an assignment as collateral of any potential recovery for a claim sounding in tort. This treatment stands in stark contrast to the assignment of contract claims as collateral, which is clearly covered by Article 9. Once a claim is reduced to judgment, be it a claim in tort or contract or otherwise, the exclusion with respect to judgments would apply. If a tort claim is settled, however, the settlement agreement is a general intangible within the scope of Article 9.[330]

Revised Article 9 permits a security interest in a "commercial tort claim,"[331] meaning a claim that arises out of the borrower's business or profession. If the borrower is an individual rather than an organization, the tort claim must not include a claim for death or personal injury. Special limitations regulate the use of commercial tort claims as collateral: They must be described with specificity in

---

[324] *See* Bramble Transp., Inc. v. Sam Senter Sales, Inc., 294 A.2d 97, 10 U.C.C. Rep. Serv. 939 (Del. Super. Ct. 1971), *aff'd* 294 A.2d 104, 10 U.C.C. Rep. Serv. 939 (Del. 1972) (transfer under collection-only exclusion requires transfer after accounts are in default).

[325] U.C.C. §§ 9-104(h), **R9-109(d)(9)**.

[326] Sun Bank, N.A. v. Parkland Design and Dev. Corp., 466 So. 2d 1089, 40 U.C.C. Rep. Serv. 636 (Fla. Dist. Ct. App. 1985).

[327] Estate of Hill, 557 P.2d 1367, 20 U.C.C. Rep. Serv. 1319 (Or. Ct. App. 1976). **Commercial tort claims are within the scope of the revision. U.C.C. § R9-109(d)(12).**

[328] U.C.C. §§ 9-104(h), **R9-109(d)(9)**.

[329] U.C.C. § 9-104(k). *In re* Monroe Cty. Housing Corp., 29 B.R. 686, 36 U.C.C. Rep. Serv. 1734 (Bankr. S.D. Fla. 1983).

[330] **The settlement agreement would be a general intangible under the 1972 text and a payment intangible, a subset of general intangible, under the revision.**

[331] U.C.C. §§ **R9-109(d)(12), R9-102(a)(13)**.

the security agreement,[332] which means that a security interest cannot attach to a commercial tort claim pursuant to an after-acquired property clause.[333]

[3] Rights to Set-off

Another express exclusion from Article 9 includes any right of set-off.[334] Clearly, this exclusion exempts banks from having to obtain written agreements or file financing statements in order to preserve their set-off rights. Subject to certain limitations that are beyond the scope of this work, a bank that is not paid money which is due and owing to it by one of its depositors can simply set-off the money owed by reducing the depositor's account balance. The case law under the 1972 text has been inconsistent with respect to determining priority between a secured party who claims money in the debtor's bank account as proceeds of its security interest and the bank that asserts a set-off right to the money.[335] **The revision contains a specific provision resolving the issue.**[336]

[G] Insurance Assignments

The 1972 text also excludes "a transfer of an interest or claim in or under any policy of insurance."[337] It thus does not apply to a security assignment of the cash surrender value of a life insurance policy or of an insured's right to recover unearned premiums following cancellation.[338]

The exclusion, however, does not encompass all transactions related to insurance. An assignment of renewal commissions earned by an insurance agent is covered by Article 9.[339] The exclusion also specifically indicates that it does not extend to proceeds or to priorities in proceeds. Payments made because of a casualty to insured collateral are within the scope of Article 9 and can be reached by a secured party as proceeds of the collateral.[340]

---

[332] U.C.C. § R9-108(e)(1).

[333] U.C.C. § R9-204(b)(2).

[334] U.C.C. §§ 9-104(i), R9-109(d)(10).

[335] Citizens Nat'l Bank of Whitney County v. Mid-States Dev. Co., Inc., 177 Ind. App. 548, 380 N.E.2d 1243, 24 U.C.C. Rep. Serv. 1321 (1978) (exclusion does not apply, meaning that secured party prevails under residual priority rule of U.C.C. § 9-201); Associates Discount Corp. v. Fidelity Union Trust Co., 268 A.2d 330, 7 U.C.C. Rep. Serv. 1350 (N.J. Super. Ct. 1970) (priorities issues excluded altogether).

[336] **U.C.C. § R9-340 (bank with right of set-off generally prevails as against secured party with interest in deposit account).** *See* **§ 14.04** *infra.*

[337] U.C.C. § 9-104(g).

[338] *In re* Duke Roofing Co., 47 B.R. 990, 40 U.C.C. Rep. Serv. 1431 (E.D. Mich. 1985).

[339] *In re* Rankin, 102 B.R. 439, 9 U.C.C. Rep. Serv. 2d 301 (Bankr. W.D. Pa. 1989). The right to renewal commissions is probably a general intangible since the right arises from a sale of an insurance policy rather than a sale goods, although an argument for the account category can be made since the agent provides services for the insured. **Revised Article 9 clearly classifies the right as an account. U.C.C. § R9-102(a)(2)(iii).**

[340] Brown v. First Nat'l Bank, 617 F.2d 581, 28 U.C.C. Rep. Serv. 609 (10th Cir. 1980). An assignment of insurance payments that is made after the casualty occurs would be excluded because it would not constitute proceeds of the collateral. For discussion of the Article 9 concept of proceeds, *see* § 2.04 *infra.*

The reasons given for the insurance transfer exclusion are that "[s]uch transactions are often quite special, do not fit easily under a general commercial statute and are adequately covered by existing law."[341] The exclusion from Article 9 does not mean that insurance interests are not transferable. Most states allow parties to enter security assignments as long as the policy does not prohibit them. Such interests are perfected in most states by directly notifying the insurer of the assignment.

Revised Article 9 narrows the insurance exclusion by creating a new subset of accounts called health-care-insurance receivables. This category is discussed in the context of accounts generally.[342]

[H] Deposit Accounts

The same reasons stated above with respect to the insurance transfer exclusion are advanced by the 1972 version of Article 9 as the reasons for excluding a transfer of an interest in any deposit account.[343] The 1972 text thus does not govern a transaction in which a checking account or a savings account[344] is provided as original collateral to secure a loan.[345] Like the insurance-transfer exclusion, the deposit-accounts exclusion includes a proviso that brings within the scope of the 1972 text deposit accounts that constitute proceeds from the disposition of other collateral.[346]

The definition of "deposit account" in the 1972 text specifically excludes certificates of deposit.[347] What is meant by this exclusion, though, is a certificate of deposit that qualifies as an instrument.[348] To be an instrument, the certificate must do more than merely acknowledge a bank's obligation to repay deposited funds. It must also contain a promise to do so.[349] Both negotiable and nonnegotiable certificates can be instruments,[350] but not every asset called a "certificate of deposit" by a bank is an instrument. For example, banks sometimes label accounts "book-entry certificates of deposit." When funds are deposited to a book-entry certificate, the depositor is given a receipt for the deposit, but there is no indispensable writing in which the bank promises to make repayment. The contract between the customer and the bank governs the customer's right to the deposited funds. Book-entry certificates are deposit accounts and are outside the scope of Article 9.

---

[341] U.C.C. § 9-104 Cmt. 7.

[342] *See* § 1.04[C][1] *supra.*

[343] U.C.C. § 9-104(1) and Cmt. 7. The drafters may also have been influenced by the fact that a custodial bank may not need a security interest because of its right of set-off.

[344] The term includes "a demand, time, savings, passbook or like account maintained with a bank, savings and loan association, credit union or like organization, other than an account evidenced by a certificate of deposit." U.C.C. § 9-105(1)(e). **The definition in the revision is substantially the same. § R9-102(a)(29).**

[345] Walton v. Piqua State Bank, 204 Kan. 741, 466 P.2d 316, 7 U.C.C. Rep. Serv. 1067 (1970).

[346] *See* § 2.04[A] *infra.*

[347] U.C.C. § 9-105(1)(e).

[348] **The revision is explicit on this point. U.C.C. § R9-102(a)(29).**

[349] U.C.C. §§ 9-105(1)(i), **R9-102(a)(47)**, 3-104(j).

[350] *See* § 1.04[B][2] *supra* for a discussion of nonnegotiable instruments.

The exclusion of deposit accounts from the scope of the 1972 text does not mean that they cannot be used as collateral for a loan. It simply means that security assignments of deposit accounts are governed by non-Code law. Most states recognize what are called "common-law pledges" of deposit accounts, at least when the account is maintained at the lending bank.[351] The rules governing the creation and perfection of common-law pledges, and the priority rights of the pledgee (lender), vary from state to state.

Revised Article 9 narrows this exclusion, bringing deposit accounts within its scope except where the transaction qualifies as a "consumer transaction."[352] This approach eliminates the confusing state laws governing common-law pledges and provides lenders with clear rules for creating and perfecting security interests in, and resolving priority disputes regarding, these assets. Security interests can be created in deposit accounts maintained at banks other than the lender, and they are not invalidated merely because the debtor has access to the funds in the account.[353]

§ 1.08   Relationship Between Article 9 and Other Articles

Although Article 9 is the primary source for determining the existence and effect of security interests, it is by no means the only source. It is just one article within the U.C.C., and it must be viewed in relation to the other articles.

Article 2 has a number of rules that intersect with Article 9. When a seller and buyer of goods agree that the seller will retain title pending payment of the purchase price, Article 2 limits the effect of the term to the reservation of a security interest.[354] When a lender extends funds on the strength of goods being bought by the borrower, Article 2 determines when the borrower/buyer has sufficient rights in the goods for a security interest to attach to them.[355] When a buyer in possession of goods rightfully rejects or justifiably revokes acceptance of them, Article 2 grants the buyer a security interest in the goods as collateral for any payments made on the price and for certain expenses.[356]

---

[351] *See, e.g., In re* A&B Homes, Ltd., 98 B.R. 243, 9 U.C.C. Rep. Serv. 2d 748 (Bankr. E.D. 1989).

[352] **U.C.C. § R9-109(d)(13). In consumer transactions, discussed in § 1.04[A][1]** *supra* **and 1.10[B]** *infra,* **deposit accounts remain beyond Article 9's scope except for proceeds and priorities in proceeds.**

[353] **U.C.C. § R9-104(b). Although the debtor's access does not invalidate the security interest, it may create a choateness problem that would subordinate the interest to the federal government making a claim under the Tax Lien Act (26 U.S.C. § 6321 et seq.) or the federal claims priority statute (31 U.S.C. § 3713(a), usually referred to by its Revised Statute designation, R.S. § 3466). Choateness is discussed in § 13.03** *infra.*

[354] U.C.C. § 2-401(1).

[355] The buyer acquires a special property interest in the goods when they are identified to the contract for sale. U.C.C. § 2-501(1). Issues involving rights in the collateral are discussed in § 2.02[C] *infra.*

[356] U.C.C. § 2-711(3). U.C.C. §§ 9-113 and **R9-110** intersect with security interests arising solely by force of Article 2 or Article 2A. They provide that the provisions of Article 9 govern such security interests generally, but so long as the debtor does not obtain possession of the goods no security agreement is necessary to make the interest enforceable, no filing is necessary to perfect it, and the rights of the secured party upon default are governed by the rules of Article 2 or Article 2A.

Article 2 even contains priority rules protecting bona fide purchasers for value that can be utilized by secured parties.[357]

Article 2A also contains provisions that intersect with Article 9. For example, a lessee in possession of goods who rightfully rejects or justifiably revokes acceptance of them has a security interest in them for any lease payments made and for certain expenses.[358] It also contains provisions governing the priority rights of secured parties with interests in both the lessor's and lessee's rights in the goods.[359]

Article 4, which deals with bank deposits and collections, provides that a collecting bank (usually a depositary bank) that has given its customer access to funds represented by a deposited item such as a check before the item clears the payor bank has a security interest in the item and its proceeds.[360] The security interest is subject to Article 9 but no security agreement is necessary to make it enforceable, no filing is necessary to perfect it, and it has priority over conflicting security interests.[361]

Under Article 5, the beneficiary of a letter of credit can assign its right to the proceeds[362] of the letter, either outright or as collateral for a loan.[363] A present security assignment of such a right creates a security interest within the scope of Article 9 if the letter of credit is written.[364] Security assignments of such letter-of-credit rights are not within the scope of current Article 9 unless the letter is written.

---

357 U.C.C. §§ 1-201(33), (32)(defining "purchaser" to include party with consensual lien). For an example of the operation of the priority rule, *see In re* Samuels & Co., 510 F.2d 139, 16 U.C.C. Rep. Serv. 577 (5th Cir. 1975), *rev'd* 526 F.2d 1238 (5th Cir. 1975), *cert. denied* 429 U.S. 834 (1976)(secured party with security interest in debtor's inventory qualified as bona fide purchaser for value under § 2-403(1), thus defeating reclamation rights of unpaid seller).

358 U.C.C. § 2A-508(5). *See also* discussion in note 356 *supra*.

359 U.C.C. § 2A-307.

360 U.C.C. § 4-210(a). Receipt of a final settlement for the item is a realization upon the security interest. § 4-210(c). The statutory grant of a security interest has ramifications for Article 3 as well as Article 9because the collecting bank is deemed to have given value for holder-in-due-course purposes to the extent that it has a security interest. U.C.C. § 4-211.

361 U.C.C. § 4-210(c).

362 U.C.C. § 5-114(a)defines the term "proceeds of a letter of credit" to mean value given by the issuer or any nominated person under the letter.

363 U.C.C. § 5-114(b). Article 5 differentiates between assignments of the beneficiary's right to the proceeds of the letter and transfers of the beneficiary's right to draw or demand performance under the letter. Transactions in the latter category are analogous to novations in which a new beneficiary is substituted for the original beneficiary. *See* U.C.C. § 5-112 and Comment 2. Because of this distinction, Article 5 provides that an issuer (or nominated person) need not recognize an assignment of the proceeds of the letter until it consents to the assignment. In other words, the secured party with a security interest in the proceeds cannot enforce the beneficiary rights as against a nonconsenting issuer. § 5-114(c).

364 U.C.C. § 9-104(m)excludes from the scope of Article 9 all other transfers of interests in letters of credit. **Revised Article 9 eliminates this exclusion and creates a new category, "letter-of-credit right." § R9-102(a)(51). A letter-of-credit right is a right to payment and performance under any letter, written or otherwise, but the term does not include the right of a beneficiary to demand payment or performance. This maintains the distinction between the right to proceeds of a letter and the right to demand payment, discussed in the preceding note.**

Article 6, like Article 2, contains a priority rule that can be exploited by secured parties. If a bulk transferee fails to give proper notice of the transfer, unsecured creditors who were entitled to notice can reach the transferred goods in the hands of the transferee. Their claims, however, are cut off by a bona fide purchaser for value from the transferee, including a secured party.[365]

Article 7 contains rules that govern warehouse receipts and bills of lading. Article 9 deals with security interests in such documents and the goods they represent.[366]

Article 8 governs transfers of securities held directly by investors and certain financial assets held indirectly through financial intermediaries such as brokers. Security interests in such assets are governed in part by Article 8 and in part by Article 9 and are described in detail elsewhere in this book.[367]

In sum, understanding secured transactions law requires more than an understanding of Article 9. It requires that Article 9's rules be placed in the context of a unified code.

§ 1.09 Nonuniform Adoptions

As part of the Uniform Commercial Code, Article 9 is a statutory model that has no force of law until it is enacted by an appropriate legislative body. Congress has never enacted any of the Code as federal law. State legislatures, rather, have been the enacting bodies.

Although one of the underlying objectives of the Uniform Commercial Code is uniformity of law among the various jurisdictions,[368] state legislatures can, and frequently do, deviate from the Code model. The greatest variations have occurred in Article 9. This pattern no doubt is influenced by the tradition of perceiving many types of secured transactions as matters of particular local significance. Differences in the economic base of various states also influence the tendency toward nonuniform Article 9 adoptions. As a result, readers of this text should be mindful of the fact that this text discusses the uniform provisions of the promulgated version of Article 9 and that variations from those provisions in particular jurisdictions are more likely than with respect to other Code articles.

§ 1.10 An Overview of Revised Article 9: Changes in Scope and Terminology

Revised Article 9 retains its predecessor's conceptual framework but greatly expands its scope. It also introduces a host of new terms and redefines many familiar terms. This section catalogs these changes. For the most part, the transactional effects of these changes are discussed elsewhere, but having them listed and briefly discussed in one section may prove useful to the reader.

---

[365] U.C.C. § 6-110(2)(1987 Official Text). In 1989, the National Conference of Commissioners on Uniform State Laws recommended that the states repeal Article 6 or, in the alternative, adopt a revised version. Revised Article 6 reduces creditors' claims against the transferee to money claims. § 6-107 (1989 Official Text). Since creditors have no claim to goods in the transferee's hands, there is no need for a rule protecting bona fide purchasers for value from the transferee.

[366] *See* § 1.04[B] *supra.*

[367] *See* § 1.04[E] *supra.*

[368] U.C.C. § 1-102(2)(c).

[A]   Changes in the Collateral-Classification Scheme

Revised Article 9 creates new categories of collateral, sometimes by narrowing or eliminating the exclusions found in current law, and redefines some of the existing categories. The major changes in this area are as follows:

Accounts. The definition of the term "account" has been expanded to include a wide variety of payment rights that might have qualified as general intangibles under the 1972 text.[369]

Health-care-insurance receivables. A new subset of accounts, "health-care-insurance receivables,"[370] has been created, thus narrowing the 1972 text's exclusion of transfers of interests in insurance policies.[371] A health-care-insurance receivable is a right under an insurance policy to be paid for health-care goods or services. Even though a health-care-insurance receivable is an account, it is subject to certain special rules that are not applicable to accounts generally.[372]

Promissory notes. A new subset of instruments, "promissory notes," has been created.[373] A promissory note is an instrument that is neither a draft nor a certificate of deposit. The new category is necessary to facilitate a decision to expand the scope of Article 9 to cover outright sales of promissory notes but not other instruments.[374] The 1972 text does not govern sales of any instruments.

Payment intangibles. A new subset of general intangibles, "payment intangibles,"[375] has been created. A payment intangible is a general intangible under which the principal obligation of the account debtor is the payment of money. The new category is necessary to facilitate a decision to expand the scope of Article 9 to cover outright sales of payment intangibles but not other general intangibles.[376] The 1972 text does not govern sales of any general intangibles.

Chattel paper. The revision makes two changes with regard to chattel paper. It clarifies that its provisions will govern what might be called "hybrid" chattel paper, meaning obligations relating to software[377] created in integrated transactions in which goods are sold or leased and the software is used in the goods.[378] It also creates a new subset called "electronic chattel paper,"[379] meaning chattel paper that consists of information stored in an electronic medium. Electronic chattel paper

---

[369] U.C.C. § R9-102(a)(2). *See* § 1.04[C][1] *supra.*

[370] U.C.C. § R9-102(a)(46).

[371] *See* § 1.07[G] *supra.*

[372] *See* § 1.04[C][1] *supra.*

[373] U.C.C. § R9-102(a)(65).

[374] *See* §§ 1.04[B][2], 1.06 *supra.*

[375] U.C.C. § R9-102(a)(61).

[376] *See* §§ 1.04[C][2], 1.06 *supra.*

[377] U.C.C. § R9-102(a)(75)(defining software). Certain software that is embedded in goods is treated as part of the goods. *See* § 1.04[A] *supra.*

[378] U.C.C. § R9-102(a)(11). *See* § 1.04[B][3] *supra.*

[379] U.C.C. § R9-102(a)(31).

differs from "tangible chattel paper"[380] in that a security interest in electronic chattel paper can be perfected by control.[381]

Commercial tort claims. The revision creates a new category of collateral, "commercial tort claims,"[382] thus narrowing the 1972 text's exclusion of transfers of interests in tort claims.[383] A commercial tort claim is a claim that arises out of the borrower's business or profession, but it does not include a claim for personal injury to or death of an individual. Commercial tort claims must be described with specificity in the security agreement, meaning that after-acquired property clauses cannot be used to reach assets within this category.[384]

Deposit accounts. The 1972 text excludes a security interest in a deposit account except to the extent that proceeds can be traced into the account.[385] The revision will permit a security in a deposit account as original collateral unless the transaction qualifies as a consumer transaction, thus narrowing the exclusion.[386]

Letter-of-credit rights. The 1972 text excludes a security interest in a right to the proceeds of a letter of credit unless the letter is written.[387] The revision creates a new category, "letter-of-credit right," which is expansively defined to include a right to the proceeds of any letter of credit.[388] The definition continues the distinction between a right to the proceeds of a letter of credit and a right to draw against the letter.[389]

Supporting obligations. The revision uses a new term, "supporting obligation,"[390] which means a letter-of-credit right or other secondary obligation (such as a guaranty) that supports payment or performance under an account, chattel paper, document, general intangible, instrument or investment property. A security interest in a supported obligation automatically attaches to the supporting obligation,[391] and perfection of the security interest in the supported obligation also perfects the security interest in the supporting obligation.[392] If, for example, a secured party has a perfected security interest in a negotiable promissory note (an instrument) that is supported by a standby letter of credit, it automatically has a perfected security interest in the underlying letter-of-credit rights.

---

[380] U.C.C. § R9-102(a)(78).

[381] Perfection by control is discussed in § 6.04 *infra*.

[382] U.C.C. § R9-102(a)(13).

[383] *See* § 1.07[F][2] *supra*.

[384] After-acquired property clauses are discussed in § 3.02 *infra*.

[385] *See* § 2.04[B] *supra*.

[386] *Id.*

[387] *See* text accompanying notes 362-364 *supra*.

[388] U.C.C. § R9-102(a)(51).

[389] *Id.*

[390] U.C.C. § R9-102(a)(77).

[391] U.C.C. § R9-203(f).

[392] U.C.C. § R9-308(d).

Accessions. The 1972 text takes a curious approach with accessions. For attachment purposes, Article 9 defers to the common law, which generally limits accessions to assets that are integral to the functioning of the greater whole. However, it contains a priority rule that applies whenever a security interest attaches to goods that are "installed in or affixed to other goods" whether such goods qualify as accessions under the common law or not.[393] Revised Article 9 defines accessions for all purposes as "goods that are physically united with other goods in such a manner that the identity of the original goods is not lost."[394] This unifies the category for both attachment and priority purposes.

Fixtures. The 1972 text leaves the definition of fixtures to the real estate law of the state.[395] The revision is consistent, referring to fixtures as "goods that have become so related to particular real property that an interest in them arises under real property law."[396]

As-extracted collateral. This is less a new category than a drafting convention. That is, its use makes the revision cleaner in that it obviates the necessity to use a long and cumbersome phrase to describe certain collateral. Oil, gas and other minerals that have not been extracted from the ground are real property and Article 9 does not apply to their use as collateral. If they have been fully extracted before the debtor acquires an interest in them they are goods and Article 9 applies, but they are not as-extracted collateral. If, for example, a manufacturer grants a security interest in a pile of coal that it acquired to fire its furnaces, the coal is inventory. As-extracted collateral refers to a security interest in oil, gas or other minerals that is created by a debtor who has an interest in the minerals before extraction and that attaches to them as they are extracted,[397] that is, as they pass from real estate to goods. The term also includes accounts arising out of the sale at the wellhead or minehead of minerals in which the debtor had an interest prior to extraction.[398] The category's primary importance relates to the method of perfection. For example, a security interest in as-extracted collateral is perfected by filing a financing statement in the real estate records,[399] whereas a security interest in fully extracted minerals is perfected by filing in the Article 9 filing system.[400]

Manufactured homes. The revision contains a new collateral category, "manufactured home,"[401] which means a transportable structure that has certain design characteristics. The characteristics are derived from standards established by the federal Manufactured Housing Act.[402] This definition is used in conjunction with

---

[393] U.C.C. § 9-314(1). *See* § 15.05 *infra.*

[394] U.C.C. § R9-102(a)(1).

[395] U.C.C. § 9-313(1)(a). Fixtures are discussed in § 15.01 *infra.*

[396] U.C.C. § R9-102(a)(41).

[397] U.C.C. § R9-102(a)(6).

[398] *Id.*

[399] U.C.C. § R9-501(a)(1)(A).

[400] U.C.C. § R9-501(a)(2).

[401] U.C.C. § R9-102(a)(53).

[402] 42 U.S.C. §§ 5401 *et seq.*

a "manufactured-home transaction,"[403] meaning a secured transaction that creates a purchase-money security interest in a manufactured home that is either not inventory or in which a manufactured home that is not inventory serves as the primary collateral. These terms have primary importance with regard to perfection and priority issues. For example, a financing statement covering a manufactured-home transaction can be made effective for thirty years.[404] Also, there is a special priority rule for manufactured homes that have become fixtures and are perfected under state certificate of title laws.[405] The fact that an asset is a manufactured home for purposes of a manufactured-home transaction does not prevent it from also being a consumer good for purposes of a consumer-goods transaction.

[B] Expansion or Clarification of Transactions Subject to Article 9

Revised Article 9 creates certain new categories of transactions for which it provides special rules. An example is the manufactured-home transaction discussed in the preceding section. In other instances, the revision clarifies the rules governing transactions that are within the scope of current law. The most important categories are:

Secondary financing of real-estate related transactions. The revision continues the 1972 text's governance of payment obligations secured by interests in real estate.[406] It brings needed clarity to this area by providing that a security interest in the payment obligation automatically attaches to the underlying real estate rights,[407] and that perfection of the interest in the payment obligation perfects the interest in the underlying real estate rights.[408]

Consignments. The revision expands the scope of Article 9 by bringing most commercially valuable consignment-like transactions within its scope. It does so through a new definition of the term "consignment,"[409] which includes some transactions that are not actually consignments but have features similar to consignments. This entire area is highly intricate, and the reader is referred to the discussion elsewhere in this chapter.[410]

Agricultural liens. The revision expands the scope of Article 9 in that it governs certain aspects of "agricultural liens."[411] An agricultural lien is a nonpossessory statutory or common-law lien on farm products that supports payment or performance of an obligation for farm inputs (goods or services furnished by a person in the ordinary course of business in connection with the debtor's farming operation)

---

[403] U.C.C. § R9-102(a)(54).

[404] U.C.C. § R9-515(b).

[405] U.C.C. § R9-334(e)(4). See discussions of certificate of title laws in § 9.06 *infra* and fixtures in § 15.01 *infra*.

[406] U.C.C. § R9-109(b). *See* § 1.07[C] *supra*.

[407] U.C.C. § R9-203(g).

[408] U.C.C. § R9-308(e).

[409] U.C.C. § R9-102(a)(20).

[410] *See* § 1.03[B][2] *supra*.

[411] U.C.C. § R9-102(a)(5).

(Matthew Bender & Co., Inc.)

or rent on real property leased in connection with the debtor's farming operation. Such liens continue to be created by non-Code state law, but they must be perfected under Article 9's rules if the lienor is to have priority against adverse interests.[412] For priority purposes, an agricultural lienor is treated as a secured party.[413]

Consumer transactions (including consumer-goods transactions). The revision creates two categories of consumer transactions and provides regulatory rules applicable to each. The broader category is "consumer transactions."[414] A consumer transaction is one in which an individual incurs a consumer debt (*i.e.,* an obligation primarily for personal, family or household purposes) and the collateral is held primarily for consumer purposes.[415] The collateral need not be consumer goods. For example, a personal loan might be secured by investment property. If the collateral is consumer goods or consumer goods and software (*e.g.,* a computer with an integrated operating system), the transaction is also a "consumer-goods transaction."[416] Consumer-goods transactions are a subset of consumer transactions.

Public-finance transactions. The revision creates a new category of transactions called "public-finance transactions."[417] A public-finance transaction is a secured transaction in which the obligation is represented by debt securities (*e.g.,* bonds, indentures, certificates of participation) with an initial stated maturity of at least twenty years issued by a state or governmental unit of a state. The primary importance of the category is that a financing statement perfecting a security interest in the collateral securing the debt securities in a public-finance transaction can be made effective for a period of thirty years.[418]

[C] New and Redefined Terms

The revision introduces a variety of new terms and redefines many existing terms. Most of these changes are relatively minor and are discussed elsewhere. A handful are critical to a basic understanding of the revision and are briefly referenced in this subsection.

Parties to the transaction. The 1972 text refers only to the secured party and the debtor, although the latter term is flexible and can mean the party obligated to the secured party, the owner of the collateral, or both depending on the context.[419] The revision refers to the party obligated as the obligor,[420] the owner (or other party with property rights in the collateral) as the debtor,[421] and a surety as a secondary

---

412 *See* § 13.02 *supra.*

413 U.C.C. § R9-102(a)(72)(B).

414 U.C.C. § R9-102(a)(26).

415 *See* § 1.04[A][1] *supra.*

416 U.C.C. § R9-102(a)(24).

417 U.C.C. § R9-102(a)(67).

418 U.C.C. § R9-515(b).

419 U.C.C. § 9-105(1)(d).

420 U.C.C. § R9-102(a)(59).

421 U.C.C. § R9-102(a)(28).

obligor.[422] When collateral is transferred from the original debtor to a new person who takes it subject to a security interest, the transferor is called the "original debtor"[423] and the transferee is called the "new debtor."[424] The use of these terms in context is discussed elsewhere.

Record. The revision uses "record" rather than "writing" to make it clear that effective communications can use an electronic format. A record consists of "information that is inscribed on a tangible medium or which is stored in an electronic or other medium and is retrievable in perceivable form."[425]

Authenticate. In order to accommodate electronic communications, records will be authenticated rather than signed. The term "authenticate"[426] includes anything that would be a signature in the Article 1 definition[427] and also includes encryption of a record. The definition makes it clear that one can authenticate a record for the following purposes depending upon the intent of the authenticating party: 1) to identify the authenticating party; 2) to adopt or accept a record or a term; or 3) to establish the authenticity of a record or term.

Good faith. The 1972 text relies on Article 1's definition of good faith, which is purely subjective.[428] The revision adopts a definition that has both subjective and objective components and is consistent with the definition used in the more recent revisions of other Articles[429] (except Article 5).[430] The new definition is "honesty in fact and the observance of reasonable commercial standards of fair dealing."[431]

---

[422] U.C.C. § R9-102(a)(71).

[423] U.C.C. § R9-102(a)(60).

[424] U.C.C. § R9-102(a)(56).

[425] U.C.C. § R9-102(a)(69).

[426] U.C.C. § R9-102(a)(7).

[427] U.C.C. § 1-201(39)defines "signed" to include "any symbol executed or adopted with present intention to authenticate a writing."

[428] U.C.C. § 1-201(19).

[429] *See, e.g.,* U.C.C. § 3-103(a)(4).

[430] U.C.C. § 5-102(a)(7).

[431] U.C.C. § R9-102(a)(43).

PART II:

ATTACHMENT OF SECURITY INTERESTS

CHAPTER 2

CREATION AND ENFORCEABILITY OF SECURITY INTERESTS

SYNOPSIS

---

§ 2.01 Overview: The Concept of Attachment

A security agreement is a specialized type of contract entered into between the secured party and the debtor. Through this contract, the debtor creates a security interest in personal property or fixtures that runs in favor of the secured party. The consensual nature of the transaction, which is necessary to bring it within the scope of Article 9, is satisfied through the voluntary association of the parties that underlies any contract.[1]

Three prerequisites underlie the creation of an enforceable security interest: a security agreement, value given by the secured party, and the debtor having rights in the collateral.[2] In addition, Article 9 contains a statute-of-frauds provision.[3] When all of these elements have been satisfied, the security interest "attaches."[4]

The term "attachment" goes to the essence of contracts of this type. An Article 9 security interest cannot exist as an abstract or generalized concept. Rather, it creates a property interest in specific collateral that has been identified by the parties. There is no such thing as an Article 9 security interest in just any of the property owned by the debtor that might be sufficient to satisfy the outstanding indebtedness.

Unless another provision of Article 9 yields a contrary result, the terms of a security agreement are effective between the parties to the agreement, against purchasers of the collateral,[5] and against creditors who acquire an interest in the collateral.[6] When third parties are involved, there are many exceptions to this general rule. With respect to the secured party and the debtor, there are but a few exceptions. Certain clauses in their agreement might be unenforceable,[7] and a secured party's failure to comply with the default procedures dictated in Article 9 might cause a loss of rights against the debtor.[8] The relationship between the secured party and the debtor is, however, established through their security agreement, which follows the general principles of freedom of contract.

It is important at the outset to differentiate between the concepts of attachment and perfection. Once a security interest attaches, it is enforceable against the debtor.[9] This means that the secured party may proceed to foreclose upon the collateral in the event of default. Perfection is irrelevant to a dispute between the secured party and the debtor. Perfection, which is best understood as a method for giving public notice of a security interest, becomes important only in the context of a dispute between the secured party and a third party asserting rights in the collateral.[10]

§ 2.02   Creation of an Enforceable Security Interest — §§ 9-203, R9-203

An Article 9 security interest attaches only if the parties enter into a security agreement.[11] Unless the secured party takes possession or control of the collateral, the

---

[1] U.C.C. §§ 9-102(2), **R9-109(a)(1)**. *See* § 1.03[A] *supra*.

[2] U.C.C. §§ 9-203(1), **R9-203(b)**.

[3] U.C.C. §§ 9-203(1)(a), **R9-203(b)(3)**.

[4] U.C.C. §§ 9-203(2), **R9-203(a)**.

[5] The term "purchasers" is broadly defined to include any party who acquires an interest in the collateral through a voluntary transaction (*e.g.,* buyers, lessees, donees, licensees, etc.). U.C.C. §§ 1-201(33), (32).

[6] U.C.C. §§ 9-201, **R9-201(a)**.

[7] U.C.C. §§ 9-501(3), **R9-602**.

[8] *See* § 19.02[A] *infra*.

[9] U.C.C. §§ 9-203(2), **R9-203(a)**.

[10] *See* § 4.01 *infra*.

[11] U.C.C. §§ 9-203(1)(a), **R9-203(b)(3)**.

1972 text requires that the debtor sign a security agreement that contains a description of the collateral. **The 1998 revision adopts the same concept but uses media-neutral terminology to require that the debtor "authenticate" the security agreement.** [12] **In some instances, the agreement must also describe any land that may be affected.** [13]

The requirement that a debtor sign **or authenticate** a security agreement serves as a statute of frauds, [14] providing probative evidence that an asserted security interest rests on a real transaction between the parties. The agreement must be signed **or authenticated** by the party against whom the security interest is to be enforced, the debtor. The security interest cannot be enforced unless Article 9's statute of frauds has been satisfied. [15]

Consistent with the approach to the statute of frauds in Article 2, [16] Article 9 provides an exception to the signature **or authentication** requirement. The security agreement is enforceable, even in the absence of a signed writing **or authenticated record,** if the secured party has possession or control of the collateral pursuant to agreement. [17] The secured party's possession or control provides corroborative evidence to support its assertion that the parties entered into a security agreement.

In addition to the requirement that there be a security agreement and that a statute-of-frauds provision be satisfied, attachment requires that value be given by the secured party and that the debtor have rights in the collateral. The requirements for attachment can occur in any order. When the last of the requirements occurs, the security interest attaches unless the parties explicitly postpone the time for attachment. [18]

[A]   Security Agreement — §§ 9-203(1)(a), R9-203(b)(3)

Article 9 defines "security agreement" as an agreement that "creates or provides for a security interest." [19] The term "agreement" is itself defined as "the bargain of the parties in fact as found in their language or by implication from other circumstances including course of dealing or usage of trade or course of performance as provided in this Act." [20] All that is required is that the parties enter into a contractual relationship that falls within the scope of Article 9; it is not necessary that they contract with reference to Article 9. [21] A legally operative writing might describe particular goods yet evidence a transaction

---

[12] **U.C.C. § R9-203(b)(3)(A). Authentication includes a signature on a writing but also covers encryption of a record. § R9-102(a)(7).**

[13] *See* discussion in § 2.02[A][3] *infra.*

[14] "The formal requisite of a writing stated in this section is not only a condition to the enforceability of a security interest against third parties, it is in the nature of a Statute of Frauds." U.C.C. § 9-203 Cmt .5; Tate v. Gallagher, 116 N.H. 165, 355 A.2d 417, 19 U.C.C. Rep. Serv. 281 (1976).

[15] *In re* R. & L. Cartage & Sons, Inc., 118 B.R. 646, 13 U.C.C. Rep. Serv. 2d 543 (Bankr. N.D. Ind. 1990) (oral agreement with debtor not sufficient for enforceable security interest).

[16] U.C.C. § 2-201(3).

[17] U.C.C. §§ 9-203(1)(a), **R9-203(b)(3)(B)-(D).**

[18] U.C.C. §§ 9-203(2), **R9-203(a).**

[19] U.C.C. §§ 9-105(1)(*l*), **R9-102(a)(73).**

[20] U.C.C. § 1-201(3).

[21] It is not even necessary that they knowingly intend a security arrangement. The 1972 text

for their sale, lease, or bailment, or it might be completely ambiguous with respect to the type of transaction intended. A writing in the latter category cannot operate as a security agreement absent a finding that it creates a security interest.

Some courts have been too rigid in construing the agreement requirement. They have injected into the Article 9 realm a degree of formalism generally associated with real-property conveyances by requiring that the parties use formal granting language (e.g., "I hereby grant to the secured party a security interest").[22] A security agreement is not a formal conveyancing document. Although the prerequisites for attachment are sometimes referred to as the "formalities" for the creation of a security interest, they are both simple in nature and easily satisfied. No formalistic or magic words are required.

A comparison of the bankruptcy referee's findings and the appellate court's decision in *In re Amex-Protein Development Corp.*[23] is illustrative. The parties intended to create a security interest in property sold as collateral for a promissory note signed by the buyer. The note contained the following language: "This note is secured by a Security Interest in subject personal property as per invoices."[24] The referee held that the note was insufficient to constitute a security agreement because the quoted language was merely passive and informative, not active or creative. The Ninth Circuit properly found the referee's construction too restrictive and held that the language was sufficient in that it demonstrated that the parties had agreed that the note would be secured.[25]

Article 9 does not require the existence of a writing designated "Security Agreement." In a nonpossessory arrangement, it does require that the debtor sign a security agreement that contains a description of the collateral, but a number of courts have been willing to consider multiple sources to locate these elements. In *Amex-Protein*, for example, the requisite intent to contract and the signature were found in the note, and the collateral description was found in the invoices. In *In re Bollinger Corp.*,[26] a promissory note indicated that it was secured by a security agreement to be delivered by the debtor to the secured party, but the referenced agreement was never in fact delivered.[27] By itself,

---

is misleading on this point, providing that Article 9 applies "to any transaction (regardless of its form) which is intended to create a security interest." U.C.C. § 9-102(1)(a). The parties must intend a contractual relationship, but they need not intend that it create a security interest. For example, a transaction intended by the parties as a lease of goods may come within the scope of Article 9 by operation of law. *See* §§ 9-102(2) and 1-201(37). *See also* § 1.03[B][1] *supra.* **The revision more accurately indicates that Article 9 governs "a transaction, regardless of its form, that creates a security interest." § R9-109(a)(1).**

[22] *In re* Modafferi, 45 B.R. 370, 40 U.C.C. Rep. Serv. 268 (Bankr. S.D.N.Y. 1985); Mitchell v. Shepherd Mall State Bank, 458 F.2d 700, 10 U.C.C. Rep. Serv. 737 (10th Cir. 1972).

[23] 504 F.2d 1056, 15 U.C.C. Rep. Serv. 286 (9th Cir. 1974).

[24] 504 F.2d at 1057, 15 U.C.C. Rep. Serv. at 287.

[25] *See also* Simplot v. William C. Owens, MD, PA, 805 P.2d 449 (Idaho 1990) (note stating "SECURITY: 1956 GMC bus" sufficient when accompanied by debtor's indorsement and delivery of certificate of title to bus).

[26] 614 F.2d 924 (3d Cir. 1980).

[27] Reference to a nonexistent writing can be fatal. *See, e.g.,* Wilmot v. Central Okla. Gravel Corp., 629 P.2d 1350, 29 U.C.C. Rep. Serv. 1650 (Okla. Ct. App. 1980) (note stated that it was secured by a security agreement bearing the same date, but no such agreement existed).

S. A. is way to enforce creditor's interest against debtor.

the note did not suffice as a security agreement because it did not show present intent to contract. Likewise, although there was a financing statement describing the collateral and signed by the debtor, the financing statement by itself could not constitute a security agreement.[28] The court, however, read the note and financing statement in conjunction with a series of correspondence between the parties (subsequent to the execution of the note) in which they clarified whether the debtor could substitute or replace collateral in the ordinary course of its business. Although the court never even found the type of passive language relied upon by the *Amex-Protein* court, it concluded that the correspondence made no sense if the parties had not intended that their transaction be secured. Summarizing *Bollinger*, the signature was found on both the note and the financing statement, the description was found in the financing statement, and the present intent to contract was found in an inference based on correspondence exchanged during a course of performance. *Same argument that both used together okay.*

Occasionally, parties adopt a final writing that categorizes their transaction as something other than a secured transaction, but one of the parties may later attempt to prove that their real intent was to create a security interest. For example, a writing might indicate that one party has delivered goods to another as part of a credit sales transaction. After paying the stipulated "price," the "seller" may argue that the goods were actually delivered to the "buyer" as security for an obligation that has now been satisfied. In other words, the argument is that the seller is in reality an Article 9 debtor, and the buyer is a secured party with a possessory security interest in the goods. Traditionally, parties have been allowed to introduce extrinsic evidence to the effect that a bill of sale that is absolute on its face was actually given as security. The Code provisions are not intended to change this right.[29] Establishing that the transaction was in fact for security entitles the "seller" (debtor) to a return of the asset upon complete satisfaction of the obligation.

In contrast, Article 9 rejects the principle of equitable mortgage, under which a creditor can enforce a real estate security arrangement that does not comply with the requisite formalities by presenting clear and convincing evidence of intent.[30] Even courts that are willing to find an Article 9 security agreement in a collage of documents must locate a writing that is signed by the debtor, a written description of the collateral, and evidence of present intent to contract. Lenders who cannot satisfy these minimal formalities cannot use extrinsic evidence to establish their secured status.

[1] Signed or Authenticated by the Debtor

Unless the secured party has taken possession or control of the collateral, the 1972 text requires that the debtor sign a writing in order for attachment to occur. The Code

---

[28] A financing statement can be filed before a security agreement is made (U.C.C. §§ 9-402(1), R9-502(d)), and there are numerous decisions holding that a financing statement standing alone does not constitute a security agreement. *See, e.g.,* American Card Co. v. HMH Co., 196 A.2d 150, 1 U.C.C. Rep. Serv. 447 (R.I. 1963). *But see* Gibson County Farm Bureau Co-op Ass'n. v. Greer, 643 N.E.2d 313, 25 U.C.C. Rep. Serv. 2d 954 (Ind. 1994) (extrinsic evidence admissible to show that debtor intended to grant a security interest to secured party whose only writing was a signed financing statement). *See also* § 5.02[D] *infra.*

[29] U.C.C. § 9-203 Cmt. 4.

[30] U.C.C. § 9-203 Cmt. 5.

defines "signed" broadly to include "any symbol executed or adopted by a party with present intention to authenticate a writing."[31] The Comments explain the definition as follows:

> The inclusion of authentication in the definition of "signed" is to make clear that as the term is used in this Act a complete signature is not necessary. Authentication may be printed, stamped or written; it may be by initials or by thumbprint. It may be on any part of the document and in appropriate cases may be found in a billhead or letterhead.[32]

The critical issue is not the form of the signature, but whether the requisite intent to authenticate is present.

The 1998 revision uses the media-neutral term "record" rather than writing. The term includes writings and electronic information that is "retrievable in perceivable form."[33] It also uses the term "authenticate" rather than "sign." Authenticate means either to sign (as defined above)[34] or "to execute or otherwise adopt a symbol, or encrypt or similarly process a record in whole or in part, with the present intent of the authenticating person to identify the person and adopt or accept a record."[35] As with a signature, the critical issue is the intent of the authenticating party.

The Code states that the "debtor" must sign the writing, but under the 1972 text use of this term can inject a degree of uncertainty. Depending on the context, the term "debtor" may mean: 1) the person who owes payment or performance of the secured obligation (even though that person may neither own nor have rights in the collateral), 2) the person who owns (or at least has rights in[36]) the collateral, or 3) both.[37] Because the attachment provisions deal with the creation of a property right in the secured party, the term "debtor" as used in that context must refer to a party who has rights in the collateral. For example, suppose that A needs to borrow money but has insufficient collateral. A's friend, B, allows A to use her car as collateral but refuses to become personally obligated for the debt. Because A has permission to use B's car, A has sufficient rights in the collateral to grant the security interest.[38] Thus, A should qualify as a "debtor" whose signature will satisfy the statutory requirement. B also qualifies as a "debtor" because she owns the car. If the secured party obtains only A's signature, it must prove that B authorized the use of the car as collateral. If it obtains only B's signature, the writing requirement is satisfied and the secured party need not prove

---

[31] U.C.C. § 1-201(39).

[32] U.C.C. § 1-201 Cmt. 39.

[33] U.C.C. § R9-102(a)(69).

[34] U.C.C. § R9-102(a)(7)(A).

[35] U.C.C. § R9-102(a)(7)(B).

[36] The word "owner" as used in U.C.C. § 9-105(1)(d) is inapt. The term "debtor" must of necessity include a person whose rights in the collateral amount to less than full ownership. **§ R9-102(a)(28)(A), discussed *infra* this subsection, uses the more accurate phrase "person having an interest, other than a security interest or lien, in the collateral, whether or not the person is an obligor . . ."**

[37] U.C.C. § 9-105(1)(d). *See* § 1.02 *supra*.

[38] *See* § 2.02[C] *infra*.

authorization. A prudent secured party will want to obtain the signature of every party with an interest in the collateral, not because Article 9 requires all signatures but because the signatures are proof of authorization.[39]

The 1998 revision resolves the uncertainty by using "debtor" to mean a person having an interest (other than a security interest or lien) in the collateral[40] and "obligor" to mean a person who owes payment or performance of the obligation.[41] If the same person provides the collateral and incurs the obligation, that person will be both a debtor and an obligor. In the example above, however, A would be the obligor and B would be the debtor. Even though A has "rights" in the collateral as that term is used in the 1972 Code, the Comments to the revision indicate that A does not have a property interest in the collateral and therefore does not qualify as a debtor.[42] Because it is the debtor that must authenticate the security agreement,[43] A's signature will not suffice. B must authenticate the agreement for attachment to occur. If A had used some of his property as collateral and also been given permission to use B's car, A would be the debtor with regard to the collateral that he contributed.[44]

When the debtor is a business entity like a corporation or a partnership, the signature **or authentication** must be made by a representative acting with actual or apparent authority. Extrinsic evidence can be used to bind the business entity if the security agreement does not identify it.[45]

[2] Description of the Collateral

[a] The 1972 Text — § 9-110

Under the 1972 text, a written security agreement must contain "a description of the collateral and in addition, when the security interest covers crops growing or to be grown or timber to be cut, a description of the land concerned."[46] The description is the means by which to identify the property to which the security interest attaches. Because a security interest cannot attach indiscriminately to a debtor's assets,[47] the specific property that is affected must be identified. A description is not necessary when the secured party takes

---

[39] It is common practice for the obligated party to sign the security agreement and for other parties with an interest in the collateral to sign a separate agreement, called either an hypothecation agreement or a waiver, evidencing their consent.

[40] U.C.C. § R9-102(a)(28).

[41] U.C.C. § R9-102(a)(59).

[42] U.C.C. § R9-102, Cmt. 2(a), Example 3.

[43] U.C.C. § R9-203(b)(3)(A).

[44] U.C.C. § R9-102, Cmt. 2(a), Example 4.

[45] *In re* Mid-Atlantic Piping Prods. of Charlotte, Inc., 24 B.R. 314, 35 U.C.C. Rep. Serv. 618 (Bankr. W.D.N.C. 1982).

[46] U.C.C. § 9-203(1)(a).

[47] *See* § 2.01 *supra.*

possession or control of the collateral pursuant to agreement because the secured party's possession or control provides the identification. [48]

The description in a security agreement delineates the assets of the debtor that are subject to the security interest. [49] If the debtor defaults and the secured party ascertains that it is under-collateralized (meaning that the value of the collateral is not sufficient to satisfy the balance of the debtor's outstanding indebtedness), the secured party might be inclined to try to extend the reach of its security interest. The collateral, however, consists only of the property that is encompassed within the description. [50]

The sufficiency of the description is determined according to the following standard: "[A]ny description of personal property or real estate is sufficient whether or not it is specific if it reasonably identifies what is described." [51] This standard is an explicit direction to analyze descriptions under a functional test. The objective is to be able to identify the property that comprises the collateral with a reasonable degree of certainty.

The court's opinion in *In re Drane* [52] provides some valuable insights into the application of this standard. The secured party filed proof of its claim in a bankruptcy proceeding in which it claimed a perfected security interest in specified furniture. A part of the description of the collateral was as follows: "1-2 pc. Living room suite, wine." [53] The bankruptcy referee determined that this type of description was insufficient because such a two-piece suite could consist of any of a variety of combinations of pieces of furniture commonly used in a living room, such as two chairs, a chair and a couch, or a chair and a couch that could converted into a bed. The referee's position was essentially that a description must be sufficient on its face to identify the property that is subject to the security interest.

The United States District Court appropriately rejected this position. Relying on precedent, the court stressed that the written description can be aided by extrinsic evidence. The relevant evidence in *Drane* was that the debtor had possession of only one living-room suite, and it consisted of two pieces that were wine-colored. Because of this extrinsic evidence, the written description satisfied the standard in that it reasonably identified the collateral. [54]

---

[48] *In re* Airwest Int'l, 70 B.R. 914, 3 U.C.C. Rep. Serv. 2d 1936 (Bankr. D. Haw. 1987) (sufficiency of description of two certificates of deposit in written security agreement was irrelevant because certificates had been pledged and were in possession of secured party).

[49] Personal Thrift Plan of Perry, Inc. v. Georgia Power Co., 242 Ga. 388, 249 S.E.2d 72, 25 U.C.C. Rep. Serv. 310 (1978) (descriptions in security agreement have purpose of avoiding disputes over identity of collateral).

[50] *In re* Levitz Ins. Agency, Inc., 152 B.R. 693, 19 U.C.C. Rep. Serv. 2d 1177 (Bankr. D. Mass. 1992) (description in security agreement as "customer list" did not extend to cover accounts).

[51] U.C.C. § 9-110. There is a separate description requirement for investment property. § 9-115(3).

[52] 202 F. Supp. 221, 1 U.C.C. Rep. Serv. 436 (W.D. Ky. 1962).

[53] 202 F. Supp. at 221, 1 U.C.C. Rep. Serv. at 436.

[54] *See also In re* Simplified Data Processing Sys., 55 B.R. 77, 42 U.C.C. Rep. Serv. 1441 (Bankr. E.D.N.Y. 1985) (description of collateral as "Prime 550" and "Prime 650" computer was upheld because the debtor had only one Prime 550 and one Prime 650 system).

Drane by no means stands for the proposition that a nonspecific description of goods will always pass muster. The description could very well have failed if the debtor had owned two separate living room suites consisting of two wine-colored pieces each, or if the debtor had owned a single, wine-colored living-room suite consisting of three pieces. In either case, the evidence of the living room furniture in the debtor's possession would not facilitate the identification of which two pieces of furniture were intended to serve as collateral.[55]

In *Drane*, the collateral description was ambiguous, and the parol evidence rule does not preclude the use of extrinsic evidence to resolve ambiguities. The parol evidence rule was successfully (although incorrectly) invoked to defeat a creditor's claim in *In re Martin Grinding & Machine Works, Inc.*[56] In that case, the parties apparently intended that a loan be secured by equipment, fixtures, inventory, and accounts. The security agreement inadvertently omitted inventory and accounts, but they were included in descriptions in an SBA authorization, the debtor's corporate resolution authorizing the transaction, and the financing statement signed by the debtor. The description in the security agreement was unambiguous, and the court held that this precluded the introduction of extrinsic evidence. The court's analysis of the parol evidence rule is not convincing. The court did not discuss whether the security agreement was intended as a complete integration of the parties' agreement;[57] a writing that is merely a partial integration can be supplemented by evidence of consistent additional terms. Nothing in the security agreement was inconsistent with the addition of inventory and accounts as collateral categories. Moreover, the court failed to consider the fact that evidence from contemporaneous writings is not excluded by the parol evidence rule.[58] All such writings should be read together to determine the intent of the parties. The court's policy rationale, which is that third parties will be misled by the description in the security agreement, cannot withstand scrutiny. The primary function of the security agreement is to identify the assets that the parties have agreed will serve as collateral, and it is the financing statement that provides notice to third parties. Nevertheless, *Martin Grinding* sounds a cautionary note for lenders.

Although not required, a detailed description of collateral can often help identify collateral with great precision, lessening the problems that flow from ambiguities. Increased specificity can also, however, lead to errors. Including a serial number, for example, enhances the specificity of the description[59] but increases the chances of a

---

[55] *See* Raash v. Tri-County Trust Co., 712 S.W.2d 5, 2 U.C.C. Rep. Serv. 2d 294 (Mo. Ct. App. 1986) (description of hogs only by number and breed is insufficient when debtor owns other hogs of same breed); Pontchartrain State Bank v. Poulson, 684 F.2d 704, 34 U.C.C. Rep. Serv. 693 (10th Cir. 1982) ("various equipment totaling $158,600.00 located at Haskel County, Oklahoma" failed as description because it did not enable identification of specific equipment covered).

[56] 793 F.2d 592, 1 U.C.C. Rep. Serv. 2d 1329 (7th Cir. 1986).

[57] *See In re* Maddox, 92 B.R. 707, 9 U.C.C. Rep. Serv. 2d 333 (Bankr. W.D. Tex. 1988) (*Martin Grinding* analysis not applicable because security agreement was not found in a completely integrated writing).

[58] *Cf.* U.C.C. § 2-202.

[59] *In re* Richman, 181 B.R. 260, 26 U.C.C. Rep. Serv. 2d 506 (Bankr. D. Md. 1995) (description

mistake by misstating the numbers. The measure of acceptable error depends on the reasonableness of the description in light of the error and the total circumstances of the case.

The transposition of two digits in a serial number is not likely to be fatal to the description,[60] whereas a number that does not correspond at all with the number on the collateral poses a greater problem. Even a description containing a noncorresponding serial number was upheld, however, when the court determined that the rest of the description of a tractor and its make and model corresponded to the only tractor that the debtor owned.[61] Other courts, however, have not been as lenient.[62]

Increased specificity can also increase the risk of debtor deceit. For example, specificity is enhanced by indicating the location of the collateral or features like its color. Identification issues can arise, however, if the collateral is relocated or painted a different color.[63] For example, the secured creditor in *American Indian Agricultural Credit Consortium, Inc. v. Fort Pierre Livestock, Inc.*[64] was fortunate that the court upheld its description even though the collateral did not fit part of the description. The cattle subject to the security interest were described as the ones that were branded "-W on their right ribs, with an orange ear tag right ear." The court upheld the description with respect to the cattle with the "-W" brand alone, contending that the reference to the ear tag was simply surplus identification that could not be relied upon because of the ease with which they could be removed. All courts would not be this liberal, which suggests the importance of devising descriptions that can withstand the tests of time, debtor manipulation and judicial vagaries.

Although broad, generic descriptions might be perceived as potentially more vulnerable to attack on grounds of sufficiency, such descriptions are often the most precise. A description reading "all of the equipment and fixtures" of the debtor has the virtues of

---

as "all amounts on deposit in brokerage firm account no. 6282588026038 upheld); Personal Thrift Plan of Perry, Inc. v. Georgia Power Co., 242 Ga. 388, 249 S.E.2d 72, 25 U.C.C. Rep. Serv. 310 (1978) (use of model and serial numbers to identify consumer appliances).

[60] Dick Hatfield Chevrolet, Inc. v. Bob Watson Motors, Inc., 10 Kan. App. 2d 350, 699 P.2d 566, 40 U.C.C. Rep. Serv. 1876 (1985) (inadvertent addition of extra digit to serial number of pickup truck held not to affect sufficiency of description), *rev'd on other grounds*, 238 Kan. 41 708 P.2d 494, 42 U.C.C. Rep. Serv. 144 (1985).

[61] Appleway Leasing, Inc. v. Wilkin, 39 Or. App. 43, 591 P.2d 382, 26 U.C.C. Rep. Serv. 209 (1979). *See also In re* Vintage Press, Inc., 552 F.2d 1145, 21 U.C.C. Rep. Serv. 1197 (5th Cir. 1977) (erroneous serial number of offset press was not fatal because rest of description was sufficient to identify collateral).

[62] *In re* Eldridge, 10 B.R. 835, 36 U.C.C. Rep. Serv. 1422 (Bankr. E.D. Mich. 1981) (mistake in last four digits of vehicle information number was fatal to description); *In re* Bolinger, 3 B.R. 186, 28 U.C.C. Rep. Serv. 1119 (Bankr. E.D. Mich. 1980) (correct serial number listed but Pontiac automobile was described as a Chevrolet).

[63] *In re* Freeman, 33 B.R. 234, 37 U.C.C. Rep. Serv. 268 (Bankr. C.D. Cal. 1983) (description of collateral as "all furniture and fixtures and inventory of debtor now or at any time located or installed" at a specified location held inadequate to cover inventory kept at a different location).

[64] 379 N.W.2d 318, 42 U.C.C. Rep. Serv. 1443 (S.D. 1985).

being both inclusive and precise.[65] It is certainly more efficient, and ultimately likely to be more accurate, than using a description that attempts to state every separate item of the debtor's equipment and fixtures. Generic descriptions are the only means by which after-acquired property clauses can be drafted.[66]

Broad descriptions pose a concern that differs from reasonable identification of the collateral. The broadest possible description would be "all personal property and fixtures" of the debtor. Although some courts have upheld such "supergeneric" descriptions,[67] the attitude of other courts renders their use risky.[68] Many courts maintain an attitude that a single creditor should not be able to encumber all of the assets of a debtor. They are therefore inclined to strike such broad descriptions as dragnet clauses that are unconscionable or violative of public policy. Such a mindset reflects a judicial tendency toward policing against creditor overreaching that runs counter to the fundamental principle of freedom of contract.[69] It also ignores the reality that, even with this broad description in the security agreement, other mechanisms exist for secured financing that prevent a debtor from being tied exclusively to financing from the original secured party.[70] Irrespective of the soundness of this judicial attitude, however, the practical reality of its existence serves as a warning against the use of supergeneric descriptions.

Although generic descriptions that identify a category of collateral are generally upheld, further caution should be exercised with respect to some categories. The most obvious category for concern is consumer goods. A court is most likely to be sensitive to potential creditor overreaching in the context of transactions with consumers. Taking a security interest in "all consumer goods" of the debtor, particularly if the secured party is significantly over-collateralized, may invite a court to impose aspects of consumer protection into its deliberations.[71] Many states have consumer-protection statutes that limit the secured party's ability to encumber an entire class of consumer goods,[72] and both the Federal Trade Commission and the Federal Reserve Board have adopted

---

[65] Credit Alliance Corp. v. Trigg, 41 U.C.C. Rep. Serv. 208 (S.D. Miss. 1985) (description of collateral as "all ... equipment" belonging to the debtor was sufficient to include a bulldozer used in the debtor's business).

[66] After-acquired property clauses are discussed in § 3.02 infra.

[67] In re Legal Data Sys., Inc., 135 B.R. 199, 16 U.C.C. Rep. Serv. 2d 519 (Bankr. D. Mass. 1991) (all of debtor's "properties, assets, and rights of every kind and nature"); Federal Deposit Ins. Corp. v. Hill, 13 Mass. App. 514, 434 N.E.2d 1029, 33 U.C.C. Rep. Serv. 1510 (1982) (description as "all personal property" upheld).

[68] In re Wolsky, 68 B.R. 526, 2 U.C.C. Rep. Serv. 2d 1689 (Bankr. D.N.D. 1986) ("all property of every kind and description in which the Debtor has or may acquire any interest" held insufficient).

[69] United States v. First Nat'l Bank in Ogallala, Neb., 470 F.2d 944, 11 U.C.C. Rep. Serv. 1048 (8th Cir. 1973) (description requirement is not intended to limit amount of collateral creditor can secure).

[70] See § 3.02[B] infra.

[71] For some limitations on the scope of a security interest in consumer goods, see U.C.C. § 9-204(2) and the discussion at § 3.02[B] infra.

[72] See, e.g., § 408.560(4), R.S.Mo. (precluding some security interests in consumer goods identified only as a general class, such as "household goods" or "furniture").

regulations that preclude certain nonpurchase-money, nonpossessory security interests in household goods.[73]

The use of generic categories can also raise ambiguity issues. One concern is whether the parties to the transaction used the term in accordance with its Article 9 meaning.[74] For example, a creditor of a manufacturing concern with a large stockpile of finished gymnasium apparatuses might describe the collateral as "all of the debtor's equipment," whereas Article 9 would characterize the finished products as inventory. The courts should seek to ascertain the intentions of the parties;[75] the risk, however, is that a court will simply apply the Code classifications to terms of the description that echo the categories included in Article 9.[76] For this reason, secured creditors often describe their collateral in multiple, overlapping categories.

[b] The 1998 Text — § R9-108

The 1998 revision continues the description requirement for nonpossession and noncontrol situations, meaning those transactions in which an authenticated record is required. It continues the basic "reasonably identifies" test for the sufficiency of a description,[77] but it adds examples of descriptions that are sufficient and others that are not. Examples of reasonable descriptions include those that identify the collateral by specific listing, category, type of collateral defined in the Code (with exceptions), quantity, or computational or allocational formula or procedure. Any other method may be used if it renders the identity of the collateral objectively determinable.[78]

With regard to specific listings, the case authority discussed in the preceding subsection should continue to be relevant. The term "category" must refer to something other than one of the types of collateral defined in the Code because such types are separately mentioned in the statute. Examples of a category would be "machinery" or "furniture." A category might also use one of the Code's types (e.g., "equipment") but not utilize the Code's definition for that type. As suggested in the preceding subsection, the use of a category is dangerous in that it opens the door to ambiguity.

There is a special description rule for investment property.[79] Much of the terminology in this area comes from Article 8 and is unfamiliar to most lenders,[80] and

---

[73] 16 C.F.R. Pt. 444 (FTC); 12 C.F.R. Pt. 227 (FRB). *See* § 3.02[B] *infra.*

[74] Many security agreements make it clear that the categories are being used in a manner consistent with their Article 9 definitions.

[75] Because of the notice function they serve, the courts should construe descriptions in financing statements in accordance with the Code definitions. For discussion of the description requirement in financing statements, *see* § 5.02[A][4] *infra.*

[76] K.L. Smith Enters. v. United Bank, 2 B.R. 280, 28 U.C.C. Rep. Serv. 534 (Bankr. D. Colo. 1980) (description of inventory of debtor farmer's egg business held not to include eggs).

[77] U.C.C. § R9-108(a).

[78] U.C.C. § R9-108(b). This list is derived from § 9-115(3), which deals only with investment property.

[79] U.C.C. § R9-108(d).

[80] *See* § 1.04[E] *supra.*

the special rule is designed to minimize the damage when the wrong term is selected.[81] With certain exceptions for consumer transactions that are discussed in the next paragraph, a description of a security entitlement, securities account or commodity account is sufficient if it uses those terms, the term "investment property," or if it describes the underlying financial asset or commodity contract. The special rule invites the courts to accept extrinsic evidence to ascertain the intent of the parties even though their description uses a term that appears facially to be unambiguous.

Supergeneric descriptions (e.g., "all assets of the debtor") are expressly disapproved in the security agreement,[82] although they are sufficient as a matter of law in a financing statement.[83] Nevertheless, a secured party can achieve virtually the same result by separately listing each Code type. The result is not precisely the same because there are a few situations in which a description by type will not suffice. Commercial tort claims[84] must be separately described[85] and, in a consumer transaction,[86] the same is true for consumer goods, security entitlements, securities accounts and commodity accounts.[87]

[3] Description of the Land

Under the 1972 text, when the collateral is crops growing or to be grown, or timber to be cut, the security agreement must, in addition to a description of the collateral, contain a description of the land on which the collateral is or will be growing.[88] **The 1998 revision deletes the land-description requirement for crops.**[89] The description need only reasonably identify the land,[90] meaning that a legal description is not required. A street address or rural route number will suffice, and even more casual designations like Dale Wilson farm located on Lancaster Road, four miles from Danville, Ky." have been upheld.[91] There are risks in using such casual descriptions. For example, Dale Wilson might own two separate farms on Lancaster Road, each approximately four miles from Danville, thereby creating an ambiguity. As with collateral descriptions, extrinsic evidence should be admissible to resolve ambiguities.[92]

---

[81] U.C.C. § R9-108 Cmt. 4.

[82] U.C.C. § R9-108(c).

[83] U.C.C. § R9-504(2).

[84] U.C.C. § R9-102(a)(13), discussed in § 1.07[F][2] *supra.*

[85] U.C.C. § R9-108(e)(1).

[86] U.C.C. § R9-102(a)(26), discussed in § 1.04[A][1] *supra.*

[87] U.C.C. § R9-108(e)(2).

[88] U.C.C. § 9-203(1)(a).

[89] U.C.C. § R9-203(b)(3)(A). **Farmers often lease different land from year to year, and the requirement has proven burdensome in that it necessitates frequent amendment of the security agreement.**

[90] U.C.C. § 9-110.

[91] Bank of Danville v. Farmers Nat'l Bank, 602 S.W.2d 160, 29 U.C.C. Rep. Serv. 1020 (Ky. 1980).

[92] *See* § 2.02[A][2] *supra.*

The land-description requirement for security agreements must be contrasted with a similar requirement for financing statements.[93] If a secured party with an interest in timber to be grown places a land description in its security agreement but not in its financing statement, its interest attaches but is unperfected. If a secured party fails to place a land description in either, its interest does not even attach. If it places a land description in the financing statement but not in the security agreement, the court must decide whether to read the documents together so as to cure the defect in the agreement.[94]

[B] Value — §§ 9-203(1)(b), R9-203(b)(1), 1-201(44)

A security interest does not attach until the creditor gives value.[95] One way that a creditor can give value is to provide consideration. The U.C.C. provides that "a person gives 'value' for rights if he acquires them . . . generally, in return for any consideration sufficient to support a simple contract."[96]

The common-law's bargain theory of consideration, particularly as manifested by the preexisting duty rule, is too restrictive for many commercial transactions. The U.C.C. thus expands the concept of value to include the acquisition of rights "as security for or in total or partial satisfaction of a pre-existing claim."[97] A creditor can give value by taking a security interest based upon an existing legally enforceable obligation.[98] For example, the court in *Hillman's Equipment, Inc. v. Central Realty, Inc.*[99] recognized that the debt incurred for the purchase price of restaurant equipment constituted value even though the security agreement with respect to the equipment was not executed until after the purchase. In *Ford Motor Credit Co. v. State Bank & Trust Co.*,[100] a finance

---

[93] U.C.C. §§ 9-402(1) (crops growing or to be grown), 9-402(5) (timber to be cut), **R9-502(b) (timber to be cut).** The 1972 text's land-description requirement for crops is governed by the functional standard of § 9-110. **Neither security agreements nor financing statements need a land description for crops under the 1998 text.** In the case of timber to be cut, most states have adopted optional language in the 1972 text requiring a legal description. **The 1998 text continues to provide this option.** In addition to timber to be cut, § 9-402(5) imposes a land-description requirement for minerals or the like, accounts arising out of the sale of minerals or the like at the wellhead or minehead, and fixture filings. **§ R9-502(b) is to the same effect.** Neither the 1972 text **nor the 1998 revision** contain a land-description requirement for security agreements covering this latter group of assets.

[94] *See* § 2.02[A][2] *supra.*

[95] U.C.C. §§ 9-203(1)(b), **R9-203(b)(1).**

[96] U.C.C. § 1-201(44)(d); Trinity Holdings, Inc. v. Firestone Bank, 24 U.C.C. Rep. Serv. 2d 1263 (W.D. Pa. 1994) (forbearance to commence collection on two delinquent loans).

[97] U.C.C. § 1-201(44)(b). **The 1998 revision adopts the more restrictive meaning of value in § 3-303(a) when the issue involves the right of an assignee to enforce an account debtor's agreement not to assert defenses. U.C.C. § R9-403(a).**

[98] Chicago Limousine Serv., Inc. v. Hartigan Cadillac, Inc., 191 Ill. App. 3d 886, 548 N.E.2d 386, 10 U.C.C. Rep. Serv. 2d 1418 (1989) (preexisting indebtedness owed to lender by debtor constituted value with respect to subsequently-acquired limousines), *rev'd on other grounds*, 139 Ill.2d 216, 564 N.E.2d 797, 13 U.C.C. Rep. Serv. 2d 306 (1990).

[99] 144 Ind. App. 18, 242 N.E.2d 522, 5 U.C.C. Rep. Serv. 1160 (1968), *rev'd on other grounds*, 253 Ind. 48, 246 N.E.2d 383 (1969).

[100] 571 So. 2d 937, 13 U.C.C. Rep. Serv. 2d 548 (Miss. 1990).

company gave value by taking a security interest in all of a car dealer's inventory only after the dealer failed to pay for the new cars that it had financed.

The pre-existing claim aspect of value is particularly important with after-acquired property clauses.[101] For example, suppose the debtor signs a security agreement granting the secured party a security interest in all equipment, including after-acquired equipment, in exchange for a loan. Later, the debtor acquires a new piece of equipment. For the security interest to attach to that piece, all the prerequisites for attachment must be met. The requirement that there be agreement is satisfied by the after-acquired property clause. The debtor's signature satisfies the statute of frauds, and the description requirement is satisfied by the reference to equipment in conjunction with the after-acquired property clause. The value requirement is satisfied because the security interest in the new piece of equipment is taken as security for a pre-existing claim. The security interest attaches at the moment the debtor acquires rights in the new piece.

The U.C.C. definition of value includes another alternative that is directly relevant to secured financing. It provides that a person gives "value" for rights if he acquires them in "return for a binding commitment to extend credit or for the extension of immediately available credit whether or not drawn upon and whether or not a charge-back is provided for in the event of difficulties in collection."[102] Under this provision, value is given at the time that an executory promise to extend credit becomes binding.[103] For example, a merchant and a bank might agree to a revolving line of credit pursuant to which the merchant is entitled on demand to draw up to a prescribed amount of money, and the merchant might sign a security agreement granting the bank a security interest in its inventory. Even though no funds have yet been requested, value has been given and the security interest can attach if the other elements are present. Of course, the merchant will not have any repayment obligation until it draws against the line of credit, and until that occurs there will be no occasion for the secured party to foreclose on the inventory.[104] Nevertheless, it is in the secured party's interest for attachment to occur at the earliest possible moment.

Article 9 requires that the secured party give value but not that the party who provides the collateral receive it. In *In re Valle Feed of Farmington, Inc.*,[105] the assets of a corporation were used as security for a loan from a bank to the corporation's only shareholders. The security interest was supported by value even though it did not flow to the corporation.

---

[101] After-acquired property clauses are discussed in § 3.02 *infra*.

[102] U.C.C. § 1-201(44)(a); *see* Pittsburgh Tube Co. v. Tri-Bend, Inc., 185 Mich. App. 581, 463 N.W.2d 161, 14 U.C.C. Rep. Serv. 2d 230 (1990) (extension of credit by agreeing to receive payment over five years).

[103] *In re* Air Vt., Inc., 45 B.R. 817, 39 U.C.C. Rep. Serv. 1534 (D. Vt. 1984) (value given by binding commitment to extend credit even though money not transferred to debtor until six days later).

[104] It is possible (but unlikely) for the merchant to breach the agreement with the bank before drawing against the credit line, and any obligation to pay damages to the bank would be secured by the inventory.

[105] 80 B.R. 150, 5 U.C.C. Rep. Serv. 2d 1499 (Bankr. E.D. Mo. 1987).

Rights in the Collateral — §§ 9-203(1)(c), R9-203(b)(2)

The debtor must have rights in the collateral before a security interest can attach.[106] This requirement is inherent because, in an enforceable secured transaction, the debtor transfers a property interest in a specific asset to the secured party. The interest that the secured party receives is controlled by the extent to which the debtor has transferable rights in the asset. Put another way, a security interest does not attach to the described asset; it attaches to the debtor's rights in the asset.

The common conceptualization of property rights as consisting of a bundle of sticks is helpful in understanding when a debtor has sufficient rights in an asset to grant an enforceable Article 9 security interest. Full ownership of an asset includes, *inter alia*, the rights to possess and use the asset. All or some of the owner's rights can be transferred by way of sale, lease, or license. A person with transferable rights can grant an enforceable security interest in those rights. In the full-ownership situation, the security interest attaches to the full panoply of rights, and upon default the secured party can take possession of the asset[107] and convey full ownership to a purchaser through a foreclosure disposition, most often a sale.[108] At the other extreme, a thief with mere possession of goods does not have transferable rights and thus cannot create an enforceable security interest in them.[109] Cases can fall between these two extremes: A debtor may have transferable rights that amount to something less than the full panoply of rights represented by full ownership.[110]

The foregoing analysis is nothing more than a particularized application of the doctrine of derivative rights. Under that doctrine, rights that are transferred are derivative in nature, and a transferee's rights are coextensive with those of the transferor.[111] A debtor with only limited rights in an asset can convey no more than the extent of its own interest. The limitations on the debtor's rights also constitute limitations on the interest taken by the secured party and on the interest that can be conveyed to a foreclosure-sale buyer. Recall that the "collateral" to which the security interest attaches is not the asset itself; it is the sum total of the debtor's transferable rights with respect to the asset.

---

[106] U.C.C. §§ 9-203(1)(c), **R9-203(b)(2)**. **The 1998 text clarifies that the debtor must have either rights or the power to transfer rights.**

[107] U.C.C. §§ 9-503, **R9-609**.

[108] U.C.C. §§ 9-504(4), **R9-617(a)** (disposition after default transfers all of the debtor's rights in the collateral).

[109] *See, e.g.,* First S. Ins. Co. v. Ocean State Bank, 562 So. 2d 798, 11 U.C.C. Rep. Serv. 2d 1255 (Fla. Ct. App. 1990). A thief of a negotiable instrument that qualifies as bearer paper has the power to transfer full ownership to a secured party who qualifies as a holder in due course. U.C.C. § 3-302(e).

[110] State Bank of Young Am. v. Vidmar Iron Works, Inc., 292 N.W.2d 244, 28 U.C.C. Rep. Serv. 1133 (Minn. 1980) (debtor's rights in the collateral consisted of statutory lien for services provided on goods owned by third party).

[111] The doctrine of derivative title underlies the common expression that an assignee "stands in the shoes" of the assignor. *See* U.C.C. §§ 9-318(1), **R9-404(a)** for a statement of this doctrine in the context of Article 9.

The limits on a debtor's ability to create a security interest in goods leased by it provide a good illustration.[112] A lessee does not acquire any of the residual interest in the leased goods, and therefore cannot create a security interest that will effectively encumber that interest.[113] The lessee does, however, acquire the right to the exclusive use and enjoyment of the goods for the duration of the lease term, and those property rights can be used as the basis for a security interest.[114] If the debtor (lessee) were to default, the secured party could not dislodge the lessor's residual interest in the goods, but the secured party could proceed against the debtor's remaining leasehold interest.[115] In practical terms, this means that through foreclosure the secured party could convey to a purchaser the right to the exclusive use and enjoyment of the goods for the remainder of the debtor's lease (subject, of course, to any obligation to pay rent under the terms of the lease contract).[116]

Similarly, a secured party that takes a security interest in a joint tenant's interest in an asset cannot thereby dislodge the interest of the other joint tenant. At foreclosure, the secured party can convey only the rights to which its security interest attached, and the purchaser at foreclosure becomes a tenant-in-common[117] with the nonobligated owner.

A buyer of goods often will grant a security interest in the purchased goods either to the seller or to a lender who provides the financing that is used to acquire the goods.[118] Under Article 2, the buyer acquires an insurable interest and a special property interest when the goods are "identified" to the contract. Identification is an Article 2 concept which essentially signifies the earliest point in time at which the actual goods that the seller will deliver to the buyer are designated.[119] For example, if a seller with a contract to deliver 100 units of a specific model of television has 1,000 of those units in its warehouse, identification occurs at the moment that 100 of the units are selected as the

---

[112] Provisions on the transferability of leasehold interests in goods are included in Article 2A. *See* U.C.C. § 2A-303. For assistance in working through the thicket posed by this section, *see* W. Lawrence & J. Minan, *The Law of Personal Property Leasing* 8-4 to 8-13 (1993).

[113] *In re* Holiday Airlines Corp., 647 F.2d 977, 31 U.C.C. Rep. Serv. 1172 (9th Cir. 1981).

[114] A lease agreement can make any transfer of any interest in the goods by lessee, including the creation of a security interest, a default under the lease. U.C.C. § 2A-303(5). Combined with the lessor's right to cancel the lease contract upon default, the lessor can effectively limit the viability of the leasehold interest as desirable collateral. *See* U.C.C. §§ 2A-523(1)(a),(3)(a); 2A-303(3).

[115] Towe Farms, Inc. v. Central Iowa Prod. Credit Ass'n, 528 F. Supp. 500, 32 U.C.C. Rep. Serv. 1431 (S.D. Iowa 1981).

[116] United States v. PS Hotel Corp., 404 F. Supp. 1188, 18 U.C.C. Rep. Serv. 770 (E.D. Mo. 1975), *aff'd*, 527 F.2d 500, 18 U.C.C. Rep. Serv. 775 (8th Cir. 1975). The foreclosure-sale purchaser is not personally obligated to pay rent, but a failure to pay will give the lessor the right to cancel the lease and repossess the goods.

[117] It is a tenancy in common because the unity of title has been severed. As a tenant in common, the foreclosure-sale buyer can sue for partition, in which the asset is sold and the proceeds distributed according to the interests of the co-tenants.

[118] These transactions typically create purchase-money security interests. U.C.C. §§ 9-107, **R9-103**. *See* § 1.05 *supra*.

[119] U.C.C. §§ 2-401(1), 2-501(1).

units that will be sent. The buyer's special property interest provides a sufficient quantum of rights for attachment to occur.[120]

The significance of attachment upon identification can easily be overstated. Because identification creates an insurable interest, a secured party could reach insurance proceeds[121] if the buyer's interest was insured and the goods were lost or damaged. The secured party could not defeat the seller, however, if the buyer were to breach its purchase-contract obligation before taking delivery of the goods. Such a breach would entitle the seller to cancel the contract, thereby ending the debtor's rights in the goods.[122] Because the rights of the secured party are coextensive with the rights of the debtor, they would also be extinguished.[123]

A secured party's rights expand as additional parties with rights in the collateral consent to have their rights encumbered. For example, if both the lessee and the lessor consent to the security interest, the secured party's interest attaches cumulatively to the full ownership interest. The same result obtains if each joint tenant consents to the security interest. Consent to use a person's property rights as collateral does not automatically render that person liable for the underlying indebtedness. Consistent with suretyship principles, the value given by the secured party can run to the party obligated to pay the indebtedness.[124]

Even a person who has not actually consented to a security interest may be estopped to deny its effectiveness. The effect of estoppel is equivalent to that of consent in that the estopped person cannot contest the secured party's contention that the security interest attached to that person's rights in the collateral. Estoppel can result from either a common-law rule or a statute and is inevitably based on the estopped person's actions in clothing the debtor with indicia of ownership.[125] In this regard, the analysis is similar to that which underlies the doctrine of voidable title.[126]

---

[120] Kendrick v. Headwaters Prod. Credit Ass'n, 523 A.2d 395, 3 U.C.C. Rep. Serv. 2d 1551 (Pa. Super. Ct. 1987).

[121] For discussion of the concept of proceeds under Article 9, *see* § 2.03 *infra*.

[122] U.C.C. § 2-703(f).

[123] These limitations generally should not be a problem for purchase-money secured parties. If the seller retains the security interest in the goods sold, the seller will simply retain title to those goods following a default by the buyer/debtor. If the purchase-money secured party is a lender who loans the money for the buyer/debtor to obtain the goods, the lender should protect itself by loaning the money in a form that will go directly to the seller of the goods. A seller that is paid will lack the grounds to retain title to the goods.

[124] *In re* Terminal Moving & Storage Co., 631 F.2d 547, 29 U.C.C. Rep. Serv. 679 (8th Cir. 1980).

[125] First Nat'l Bank v. Kisaare, 22 Okla. 545, 98 P. 433 (1908).

[126] Indeed, the doctrine of voidable title can be directly relevant. Under U.C.C. § 2-403(1), a person with voidable title has power to transfer full title to a bona fide purchaser for value. The term "purchaser" includes, *inter alia*, secured parties. §§ 1-201(33), (32). Thus, a person with voidable title has the power to grant a security interest that attaches to the true owner's rights to a secured party who gives value and lacks notice of the true owner's interest. § 2-403(1) not only gives the person with voidable title the power to grant the security interest, it provides a priority rule in favor of the secured party. *See, e.g., In re* Samuels & Co., 526 F.2d 1238, 18 U.C.C. Rep.

Many of the estoppel cases arise in the context of a bailment, meaning a transaction in which the owner of goods (the bailor) places them in the rightful possession of another (the bailee).[127] In giving up possession, the bailor clothes the bailee with the appearance of ownership, and the question arises whether the grant of a security interest by the bailee should cause the security interest to attach by estoppel to the bailor's rights.

Perhaps the simplest type of bailment is one in which the bailor has turned the property over to the bailee for storage or carriage but has not given the bailee permission to use the goods while they are in the bailee's possession. At common law, such a bailee does not have even voidable title and therefore lacks the power to convey good title even to a bona fide purchaser for value.[128] Because such a bailee cannot alienate the bailor's rights, a security agreement executed by the bailee cannot cause a security interest to attach to the bailor's rights. There are numerous cases holding that such a bailee lacks sufficient rights to grant a security interest in the bailed goods.[129]

At the other extreme lies a consignment in which the consignor (the bailor) authorizes the consignee (the bailee) to sell the goods. For example, suppose a manufacturer of goods consigns them to a merchant in the business of selling such goods with the understanding that they can be returned if they are not sold. Because a third party would naturally believe that the goods were part of the consignee's inventory and could be misled more easily than a third party dealing with a bailee for storage or carriage, the case for estoppel is especially strong. Indeed, the U.C.C. explicitly makes the consigned goods subject to the claims of creditors of the consignee[130] — estoppel by statute — but provides a mechanism for the consignor to give public notice to third parties and thereby preserve a priority position vis-a-vis the goods.[131] A security interest created by the consignee will attach to the consignor's rights in the goods.

Another example of statutory estoppel comes from Article 2, which governs the rights of third parties when there is a bailment that qualifies as an "entrustment."[132] In an entrustment the owner of goods delivers (or acquiesces in the delivery of) goods to a merchant who deals in goods of that kind. The merchant has the statutory power to convey the entruster's title to a buyer in the ordinary course of business. The classic example is the watch owner who delivers a watch to a jeweler for repair and the jeweler negligently or fraudulently places the watch in its inventory and sells it to an ordinary buyer off

---

Serv. 545 (5th Cir.), *cert. denied*, 429 U.S. 834 (1976) (secured inventory financer of cattle buyer prevailed as bona fide purchaser for value over cash seller of cattle's reclamation rights when buyer's checks to seller bounced).

[127] R. Brown, *The Law of Personal Property* § 10.1 (W. Raushenbush 3d ed. 1975).

[128] E. Goddard, *The Law of Bailments and Carriers* § 29 (2d ed. 1908); Smith v. Clews, 114 N.Y. 190, 21 N.E. 160 (1889).

[129] *See, e.g.,* Evergreen Me. Corp. v. Six Consignments of Frozen Scallops, 4 F.3d 90, 21 U.C.C. Rep. Serv. 2d 502 (1st Cir. 1993).

[130] U.C.C. §§ 1-201(37), 2-326(2). The intersection between the law of consignments and Article 9 is discussed in detail in § 1.03[B][2] *supra.*

[131] U.C.C. §§ 2-326(3), 9-408, 9-114. **For a discussion of the 1998 text's approach to the consignment problem,** *see* **§ 1.03[B][2][b]** *supra.*

[132] *See* U.C.C. §§ 2-403(3),(2).

the street. The sale transfers the enruster's title to the buyer. Because the entrustment statute protects only buyers in the ordinary course, it cannot be used by a secured party to whom the jeweler has granted a security interest. Under the general common-law rule governing bailments, the jeweler lacks sufficient rights to grant an enforceable security interest in the watch. The fact that a secured party cannot prevail over the owner under either Article 2's entrustment rule or the general common-law rule does not end the analysis. In any bailment situation, including an entrustment, the bailor may, in addition to placing the goods in the hands of the bailee, have used language or engaged in conduct that led the secured party to believe that the bailee had the power to transfer full ownership. In such a case, general estoppel principles would come into play and cause the security interest to attach to the bailor's interest.[133]

Kinetics Technology International Corp. v. Fourth National Bank[134] is an example of common-law estoppel in a bailment context. In that case the plaintiff delivered certain goods that it owned to a manufacturer, whose job was to add components to the goods and create a finished product that was to be returned to the plaintiff. The Tenth Circuit Court of Appeals ultimately subjected the plaintiff's ownership interest in those goods still in the manufacturer's hands to a security interest that the manufacturer had granted to the defendant. The court's rationale was that the plaintiff was in effect a type of lender, one who loaned goods rather than money to enable the manufacturer to produce the finished product. Had the plaintiff loaned money to enable the manufacturer to acquire the goods, it could have taken a security interest in the goods and filed a financing statement to protect its interest. The financing statement would have warned the defendant of the plaintiff's interest. Even though it supplied the goods directly, the plaintiff should have used the mechanisms of Article 9 to take and perfect a security interest in them. Other courts in similar circumstances have reached the same result by holding that the goods in question were actually sold to the manufacturer and that the attempt to retain title amounted to nothing more than a security interest.[135] As owner, the manufacturer would clearly have sufficient rights to grant a security interest to a third party, and as a secured party the supplier could protect itself from such a third party by filing a financing statement.[136]

§ 2.03 Proceeds

Debtors sometimes dispose of the collateral that remains in their possession. The disposal might be authorized by the secured party, as commonly occurs when the secured party expects the debtor to sell financed inventory in order to acquire the money to repay the loan, or it might be without the awareness of the secured party and in violation of

---

[133] U.C.C. § 1-103 (unless displaced, principles of law and equity supplement the Code). *Cf.* Tumber v. Automation Design and Mfg. Corp., 130 N.J. Super. 5, 324 A.2d 602 (1974) (one who does not qualify as a buyer in the ordinary course may nevertheless utilize common-law estoppel principles).

[134] 705 F.2d 396, 36 U.C.C. Rep. Serv. 292 (10th Cir. 1983). *See also In re* Pubs, Inc., 618 F.2d 432, 28 U.C.C. Rep. Serv. 297 (7th Cir. 1980) (closely held corporation estopped when two key officers used its assets as collateral for a personal loan).

[135] U.C.C. § 2-401(1).

[136] *See, e.g.*, Morton Booth Co. v. Tiara Furniture, Inc., 564 P.2d 210 (Okla. 1977).

a prohibition in the security agreement. Either way, the secured party is likely to be interested in pursuing the proceeds that the debtor receives from the disposition of the collateral. The discussion below explains the concept and classification of proceeds, and describes how a security interest attaches to proceeds. Problems involving perfection and priority of the security interest are discussed elsewhere in the text. [137]

[A] Defined — §§ 9-306(1), R9-102(a)(64)

The 1972 text defines a "proceed" as an asset that is acquired upon the "sale, exchange, collection or other disposition" of collateral. [138] When collateral is disposed of in any manner, whatever replaces it is a proceed. If a proceed is later disposed of, any asset that is then acquired also qualifies as a proceed. [139] This secondary disposition results in "proceeds of proceeds." [140]

Proceeds can take almost any form. Cases have found proceeds to consist of cash, [141] checks, [142] promissory notes, [143] all payments of principal and interest on promissory notes, [144] used cars accepted as trade-ins on sales of automobile inventory, [145] shares of stock received in the sale of partnership assets, [146] and a new certificate of deposit resulting from rolling over two other certificates. [147] In contrast, calves are not proceeds of the cattle that give birth to them because they do not in any sense replace those cattle. [148]

Determining the meaning of "disposition" has proved contentious. Because the terms "sale," "exchange" and "collection" refer to types of transactions in which title to

---

[137] See discussions in §§ 8.02 (perfection) and 10.05 (priority) infra.

[138] U.C.C. § 9-306(1). **The revision is consistent but more detailed. § R9-102(a)(64).**

[139] U.C.C. § 9-306(1). **The revision is consistent, defining collateral to include proceeds. § R9-102(a)(12)(A).**

[140] Central Prod. Credit Ass'n v. Hans, 189 Ill. App. 3d 889, 545 N.E.2d 1063, 11 U.C.C. Rep. Serv. 2d 696 (1989) (proceeds of crop were withdrawn to purchase investments, which were then sold and proceeds deposited in account); Bank of Kan. v. Hutchinson Health Serv., Inc., 12 Kan. App. 2d 87, 735 P.2d 256, 3 U.C.C. Rep. Serv. 2d 1537 (1987) (cash from check received in payment of account).

[141] Bank of Kan. v. Hutchinson Health Serv., Inc., 12 Kan. App. 2d 87, 735 P.2d 256, 3 U.C.C. Rep. Serv. 2d 1537 (1987).

[142] Farms Assocs., Inc. v. South Side Bank, 93 Ill. App. 3d 766, 417 N.E.2d 818, 30 U.C.C. Rep. Serv. 1729 (1981).

[143] In re Guil-Park Farms, Inc. v. South Side Bank, 90 B.R. 180, 7 U.C.C. Rep. Serv. 2d 1675 (Bankr. W.D.N.C. 1988).

[144] In re Charter First Mortg., Inc., 56 B.R. 838, 2 U.C.C. Rep. Serv. 2d 1409 (Bankr. D. Or. 1985).

[145] Chrysler Credit Corp. v. Knebel Chevrolet-Buick, Inc., 976 F.2d 1012, 20 U.C.C. Rep. Serv. 2d 645 (7th Cir. 1992).

[146] In re Guaranteed Muffler Supply Co., Inc., 1 B.R. 324, 27 U.C.C. Rep. Serv. 1217 (Bankr. N.D. Ga. 1979).

[147] In re Airwest Int'l, 70 B.R. 914, 3 U.C.C. Rep. Serv. 2d 1936 (Bankr. D. Haw. 1987).

[148] Citizens Sav. Bank, Hawkeye, Iowa v. Miller, 515 N.W.2d 7, 24 U.C.C. Rep. Serv. 2d 1032 (Iowa 1994).

collateral is surrendered or rights to payment are satisfied, some courts have adopted a "passage-of-title" approach that denies proceeds status to an asset unless the debtor either parts with title to the original collateral or releases the right to payment that constitutes the original collateral. This approach fails to recognize that the economic value of an asset can be replaced in multiple ways that do not involve a transfer of title.[149] Any reasonable secured party is concerned with the loss of value rather than the location of title,[150] and thus the passage-of-title approach frustrates the *ex ante* bargain of the parties.[151]

Under the 1962 version of Article 9, a majority of courts applied the passage-of-title approach and held that casualty insurance payments arising out of damage to insured collateral did not qualify as proceeds because there was no disposition of the original collateral.[152] The 1972 text expressly overruled this line of cases by providing that casualty insurance payments are proceeds except to the extent that they are payable to a party other than the secured party or the debtor.[153] **The 1998 text follows (and even expands upon) this approach.**[154]

Adoption of the 1972 text resolved the insurance issue but did not end the courts' reliance on conceptions of title. For example, the original collateral in *In re Hastie*[155] consisted of 248 shares of stock in a bank holding company, and the dispute was over cash dividends that had been paid on account of the stock. The Tenth Circuit Court of Appeals concluded that the dividends were not proceeds because the debtor did not give up title to the stock in order to obtain them. The *Hastie* approach was reversed by a conforming amendment to section 9-306(1) that was adopted at the time Article 8 was extensively revised in 1994.[156]

---

[149] *See generally* Freyermuth, *Rethinking Proceeds: The History, Misinterpretation and Revision of U.C.C. Section 9:306*, 69 Tulane L. Rev. 645 (1995).

[150] Indeed, a title-based approach is inconsistent with Article 9's basic theory that the location of title is immaterial. *See* U.C.C. §§ 9-202, **R9-202**.

[151] The rule that a security interest shifts automatically to proceeds is a default rule, and the primary justification for any default rule is that it represents the *ex ante* expectations of reasonable contracting parties.

[152] *See, e.g.,* Universal C.I.T. Credit Corp. v. Prudential Inv. Corp., 101 R.I. 287, 222 A.2d 571, 3 U.C.C. Rep. Serv. 696 (1966).

[153] U.C.C. §§ 9-306(1) (defining proceeds), 9-104(g) (narrowing the exclusion from Article 9 so that transfers of insurance interests that constitute proceeds are within its scope). A prudent secured party should insist on becoming the named loss payee under the debtor's casualty insurance policy.

[154] **U.C.C. § R9-102(64)(D). Included as proceeds are "insurance payable by reason of the loss or nonconformity of, defects or infringement of rights in, or damage to, the collateral." The revision also includes as proceeds tort claims against noninsurors "arising out of the loss, nonconformity, or interference with the use of, defects or infringement of rights in, or damage to, the collateral." This corresponds with a narrowing of the exclusion from Article 9 for claims arising in tort. § R9-109(d)(12).**

[155] 2 F.3d 1042, 21 U.C.C. Rep. Serv. 2d 212 (10th Cir. 1993).

[156] "Any payments or distributions made with respect to investment property collateral are proceeds." **The 1998 text is consistent. U.C.C. § R9-102(a)(64)(B).**

Despite the partial fixes for insurance payments and dividends, analogous problems remain under pre-revision text. For example, most courts have held that rental payments arising from a lease of collateral are not proceeds because a lease does not involve the passage of title.[157] Such decisions defy economic reality. Leased property depreciates in value as it ages and is used, and the rental payments, which reflect that depreciation, are direct economic substitutes for the collateral's lost value. The Comments to the pre-revision text have been amended to disapprove of these holdings,[158] **and the 1998 text overrules them by including as proceeds "whatever is acquired upon the sale, lease, license, exchange, or other disposition of collateral."[159]**

Neither the 1972 text nor the revision deal directly with "nonexistent collateral" cases. Suppose, for example, that a secured party acquires a security interest in the debtor's crops. The parties anticipate at the time that the debtor will plant crops annually, but subsequently the debtor enrolls in a federal program that pays a subsidy to farmers who permit their land to go fallow. The subsidy is a direct economic substitute for a crop that never existed and therefore ought to qualify as a proceed, but most courts facing this issue have held otherwise.[160] The 1972 text's treatment of insurance payments, the 1994 amendment dealing with dividends, and the tenor of the 1998 text reflect a value-based approach to proceeds that honors the *ex ante* expectations of the parties. Courts considering nonexistent collateral cases[161] should carefully consider the implications of this approach.

Article 9 distinguishes for some perfection and priority purposes between cash and noncash proceeds. Cash proceeds[162] include assets like money, checks and deposit accounts.[163] The definition is open-ended so that an asset that is a cash equivalent, like

---

[157] *See, e.g., In re* Cleary Bros. Constr. Co., 9 B.R. 40, 30 U.C.C. Rep. Serv. 1444 (Bankr. S.D. Fla. 1980).

[158] U.C.C. § 9-306, Cmt. 6, authorized by P.E.B. Commentary No. 9 (June 25, 1992). The holdings are also inconsistent with the value-based approach to the boundary between leases and secured transactions adopted at the time Article 2A was first promulgated. *See* § 1-201(37) and discussion in § 1.03[B] *supra*.

[159] **U.C.C. § R9-102(a)(64)(A).**

[160] *See, e.g., In re* Schmaling, 783 F.2d 680, 42 U.C.C. Rep. Serv. 1074 (7th Cir. 1986) (federal Payment-in-Kind, or PIK, program). *Contra* Sweetwater Production Credit Ass'n v. O'Briant, 764 S.W.2d 230, 7 U.C.C. Rep. Serv. 2d 1247 (Tex. 1988).

[161] Another example of nonexistent collateral arises in the context of business interruption insurance. A secured creditor may claim that the debtor's insurance claim is a proceed of accounts or general intangibles that would have existed but for the interruption of the business. Cases dealing with this issue include *In re* Investment and Tax Servs., 148 B.R. 571, 19 U.C.C. Rep. Serv. 2d 905 (Bankr. D. Minn. 1992) (business interruption insurance not a proceed); and MNC Commercial Corp. v. Rouse,No. 91-0615-CV-W-2, 1992 U.S. Dist. Lexis 22166 (W.D. Mo. 1992) (business interruption insurance qualifies as proceed).

[162] U.C.C. §§ 9-306(1), **R9-102(a)(9).**

[163] "Deposit account" is defined in U.C.C. §§ 9-105(1)(e), **R9-102(a)(29).** A transfer of an interest in a deposit account is outside the scope of the 1972 text except to the extent the interest represents proceeds from the disposition of collateral. U.C.C. §§ 9-104(l), 9-306(1). **This exclusion was narrowed in the 1998 text so that Article 9 governs the creation of security interests in deposit accounts except in consumer transactions. § R9-109(d)(13).** *See* § 1.07[H] *supra*.

a money-market account that is a financial asset in a securities account, is covered.[164] All other proceeds are noncash proceeds.[165] For example, suppose a secured party has a security interest in the debtor's inventory. If the debtor sells the inventory for cash or a check, the proceeds are cash proceeds. If the debtor takes a used item in trade or sells the inventory on credit, the proceeds are noncash proceeds.[166] If the debtor takes a check for the inventory and later deposits it to a bank account, the bank's obligation to repay the deposited funds is a proceed of a proceed (and therefore qualifies as a proceed), and because it is a deposit account it is a cash proceed. If the money is later withdrawn from the account and used to buy a piano, the money is a cash proceed and the piano is a noncash proceed.

[B] Attachment — §§ 9-203(3), 9-306(2), R9-203(f), R9-315(a)(2), R9-315(b)

The attachment concept applies automatically to proceeds. The section on attachment provides that a security interest in collateral attaches automatically to proceeds as soon as they come into existence even if the security agreement is silent on the matter.[167] A corresponding provision then limits attachment to proceeds that are identifiable.[168] Identification means that the proceeds can be traced back to the collateral from which they sprang, and the cases place the burden of tracing on the secured party.[169] The fact that the secured party can look to the proceeds to satisfy the indebtedness does not mean that its interest in the original collateral was severed by the disposition. A secured party who consents to disposition of the collateral free from its security interest is limited to the identifiable proceeds from the disposition.[170] When the disposition occurs without such consent, the secured party's interest attaches to the identifiable proceeds and, unless a provision of Article 9 provides to the contrary, continues in the original collateral.[171] This allows the secured party to look to two sources for satisfaction.

An inevitable issue that the courts have had to address is the impact on identification when cash proceeds are deposited to a deposit account. Depositing proceeds from the disposition of collateral into a deposit account that contains only proceeds permits easy

---

[164] U.C.C. § R9-102, Cmt. 13(e).

[165] U.C.C. §§ 9-306(1), R9-102(a)(58).

[166] The buyer's obligation would qualify as an account. U.C.C. §§ 9-106, R9-102(a)(2). An account is a noncash proceed, while a deposit account is a cash proceed.

[167] U.C.C. §§ 9-203(3), R9-203(f). The cited provision from the 1972 text makes explicit that the parties can agree that a security interest will not attach to proceeds. **The cited provision from the 1998 text is silent on this issue, but such an agreement would be enforceable under general contract principles. See § R9-201(a).**

[168] U.C.C. §§ 9-306(2), R9-315(a)(2).

[169] See, e.g., Universal C.I.T. v. Farmers Bank, 358 F. Supp. 317, 13 U.C.C. Rep. Serv. 109 (E.D. Mo. 1973).

[170] U.C.C. § 9-306(2), R9-315(a)(1). For a detailed discussion of when transferees take free of a security interest, see § 11.01 infra.

[171] U.C.C. § 9-306(2); Dry Canyon Farms, Inc. v. United State Nat'l Bank of Or., 84 Or. App. 686, 735 P.2d 620, 4 U.C.C. Rep. Serv. 2d 277 (1987) (security interest continues in proceeds, whether or not secured party authorizes disposition). For a discussion of a secured party's continuing interest in the collateral disposed of by a debtor, see §§ 11.01, 11.02 infra.

identification [172] but is not required. Commingling funds, on the other hand, raises problems. Because the 1972 text does not specifically provide for the identification of proceeds that are commingled with other funds in a deposit account, [173] the courts have turned to tracing concepts developed in the law of trusts. [174] The courts uniformly follow the "lowest intermediate balance" test, which is based on the following assumptions: 1) as a debtor spends funds from an account, it spends the proceeds of a security interest last; [175] and 2) the amount that can constitute identifiable proceeds is not increased by a later deposit of nonproceed funds into the account unless the parties intend that the later deposit restore the proceeds balance. [176] For example, suppose a secured party has a security interest in the debtor's inventory and permits the debtor to deposit cash proceeds into its general checking account. On Day 1, the debtor has a balance of $10,000 in the account, none of which represents proceeds. On Day 2, the debtor deposits $5,000 in cash proceeds, resulting in an overall balance of $15,000 and a proceeds balance of $5,000. The next day, the debtor withdraws and dissipates $4,000. [177] This reduces the overall balance to $11,000, but applying the first assumption leaves the proceeds balance at $5,000. On Day 3, the debtor withdraws an additional $7,000 and buys a piece of equipment. The overall balance is $4,000, all of which is proceeds. In addition, the secured party has an interest in the equipment to the extent of $1,000 (the amount of proceeds

---

[172] *In re* Cullen, 71 B.R. 274, 3 U.C.C. Rep. Serv. 2d 815 (Bankr. W.D. Wis. 1987).

[173] Some pre-Code courts invalidated security arrangements as fraudulent if the debtor was allowed to exercise dominion over proceeds. *See, e.g.,* Benedict v. Ratner, 268 U.S. 353 (1925). U.C.C. § 9-205 reverses this result.

[174] Bank of Kan. v. Hutchinson Health Serv., Inc., 12 Kan. App. 2d 87, 735 P.2d 256, 3 U.C.C. Rep. Serv. 2d 1537 (1987). The tracing concept is not limited to deposits into the debtor's account. Frike v. Valley Prod. Credit Ass'n, 778 S.W.2d 829, 10 U.C.C. Rep. Serv. 2d 1454 (Mo. Ct. App. 1989) (secured party traced deposit of sale proceeds into business account of debtor's business partner); Farns Assoc., Inc. v. South Side Bank, 93 Ill. App. 3d 766, 417 N.E.2d 818 (1981) (prior-perfected secured party traced proceeds by showing that bank received checks representing proceeds directly from account debtor and then cashed the checks).

[175] *Ex parte* Alabama Mobile Homes, Inc., 468 So. 2d 156, 40 U.C.C. Rep. Serv. 1898 (Ala. 1985).

[176] The deposit of new proceeds is distinguishable. In Central Prod. Credit Ass'n v. Hans, 189 Ill. App. 3d 889, 545 N.E.2d 1063, 11 U.C.C. Rep. Serv. 2d 696 (1989), identifiable proceeds that had been deposited in an account were withdrawn to purchase investments. When those investments were sold, their proceeds were deposited into the same account. Because the second deposit also constituted identifiable proceeds, that deposit increased the balance of proceeds in the account.

[177] U.C.C. § 9-306, Cmt. 2(c) addresses what happens when money is paid out of an account into which proceeds have been deposited:

> Where cash proceeds are covered into the debtor's checking account and paid out in the operation of the debtor's business, recipients of the funds of course take free of any claim which the secured party may have in them as proceeds. What has been said relates to payments and transfers in ordinary course.

Payments in ordinary course thus terminate a secured party's claim to cash proceeds. *See, e.g.,* J.I. Case Credit Corp. v. First Nat'l Bank of Madison Cty., 991 F.2d 1272, 20 U.C.C. Rep. Serv. 2d 1091 (7th Cir. 1993).

that went toward the purchase). On Day 4, the debtor deposits $15,000, none of which is proceeds. The overall balance is $19,000, but applying the second assumption leaves the proceeds balance at $4,000. In other words, the proceeds balance is the lowest balance between the time proceeds are first withdrawn and the time the account balance is later restored as a result of nonproceed deposits — *i.e.*, the lowest intermediate balance. If the debtor deposits $6,000 in new proceeds on Day 5, the overall balance will rise to $25,000 and the proceeds balance will rise to $10,000. **The 1998 text ratifies the use of tracing principles to identify commingled proceeds that are not goods.** [178]

The 1972 text indicates that the security interest "continues in any identifiable proceeds including collections received by the debtor." [179] Controversy has developed as to whether the clause "received by the debtor" modifies only collections or, instead, all identifiable proceeds. [180] The intent of the drafters, however, is quite clear. The unmistakable position stated in the Comments is: "This section states a secured party's right to the proceeds *received by a debtor* on disposition of collateral . . ." [181] In other words, the phrase applies to all proceeds and is not limited to collections.

The case of *Beneficial Finance Co. v. Colonial Trading Co.* [182] demonstrates the proper application of this provision. The plaintiff in that case held a perfected security interest in the debtors' household furnishings, which were improperly sold to the defendant. The defendant, who took the furnishings subject to the plaintiff's security interest, later sold them at public auction. The secured party sued the defendant to recover the unpaid balance of the loan and to reach the proceeds of the auction. The court denied a recovery. When goods are sold to a buyer subject to a security interest, the secured party has the option of replevying any goods that remain in the buyer's possession or suing the buyer in tort for conversion. The reach against the buyer does not extend to an action based on the original debt, nor can the secured party reach the proceeds of the buyer's resale because such proceeds are not received by the debtor. The court gave the plaintiff leave to amend its complaint to allege conversion.

The 1998 revision deletes any reference to the party who must receive the proceeds. The Comments to the revision indicate that all that is important is that the proceeds be traceable to the original collateral. [183]

---

[178] U.C.C. § R9-315(b)(2). **When goods, including goods that are proceeds, are commingled in such a way that their separate identity is lost, a security interest ceases to attach to them and instead attaches to the product or mass into which they have been subsumed. §§ R9-315(b)(1), R9-336.** The 1972 text, although not explicitly drafted with regard to proceeds, contains a similar rule for commingled goods generally. § 9-315.

[179] U.C.C. § 9-306(2).

[180] For cases indicating that the clause modifies all proceeds, *see In re* Halmar Distribs., Inc., 12 U.C.C. Rep. Serv. 2d 1 (Bankr. D. Mass. 1990); First Interstate Bank v. Arizona Agrochemical Co., 2 U.C.C. Rep. Serv. 2d 711 (Colo. Ct. App. 1986). For cases stating that only the term "collections" is modified, *see* Leasing Serv. Corp. v. Seafirst Bank, 1 U.C.C. Rep. 2d 548 (W.D. Wash. 1986); *In re* San Juan Packers, Inc., 696 F.2d 707 (9th Cir. 1983).

[181] U.C.C. § 9-306, Cmt. 1 (emphasis supplied).

[182] 43 Pa. D & C.2d 131, 4 U.C.C. Rep. Serv. 672 (Cty. Ct. 1967).

[183] U.C.C. § R9-102 Cmt. 13(d).

§ 2.04 Attachment to Underlying Obligations in Revised Article 9 — §§ R9-203(f), R9-203(g)

Revised Article 9 contains special attachment rules that apply to: 1) obligations that support payment or performance of collateral; and 2) property, including real estate, that secures a right to payment or performance that is within the scope of Article 9.

Section R9-203(f) provides that attachment of a security interest to collateral causes the security interest also to attach to any "supporting obligation" for the collateral. A supporting obligation is a letter-of-credit right or other type of secondary obligation, such as a guaranty, that supports payment or performance under a supported obligation that is itself within the scope of Article 9.[184] A supported obligation might be an account, chattel paper, document, general intangible, instrument or investment property. A security interest that attaches to a supported obligation automatically attaches to any supporting obligation.[185] For example, suppose a secured party has a security interest in a negotiable promissory note (an instrument) that is supported by a standby letter of credit. The security interest automatically attaches to the letter-of-credit right[186] even though there is no reference to the right in the security agreement.[187]

Section R9-203(g) contains a similar attachment rule for property that secures a right to payment or performance. For example, suppose the secured party lends money and takes a security interest in a note that is secured by a mortgage on real estate. Even though the initial acquisition of the mortgage by the payee of the note was outside the scope of Article 9, the secondary financing transaction in which the note and mortgage are used as collateral is within its scope. The security interest automatically attaches to the mortgage when it attaches to the note.[188] This area presents complex issues that overlap with aspects of real-estate law and is discussed in detail in connection with the revision's scope provisions.[189]

---

[184] U.C.C. § R9-102(a)(77).

[185] U.C.C. § R9-203(f). Moreover, perfection of the security interest in the supported obligation also perfects the security interest in the supporting obligation. § R9-308(d).

[186] U.C.C. § R9-102(a)(51) defines "letter-of-credit right." See § 1.10[A] supra.

[187] Moreover, the interest in the letter-of-credit right is perfected even though an interest in such a right must ordinarily be perfected by control. U.C.C. § R9-312(b)(2).

[188] U.C.C. § R9-308(e). Moreover, perfection of the interest in the note automatically perfects the interest in the mortgage. Although the drafters' intent in adopting these provisions is to preempt real estate law, a legislative note appended to § R9-308 suggests that each state legislature should provide further clarification by enacting an amendment to the state's real estate recording act expressly providing that perfection under Article 9 is sufficient for all purposes.

[189] See § 1.07[C] supra.

CHAPTER 3

ONGOING FINANCING RELATIONSHIPS

SYNOPSIS

§ 3.01   Facilitating Clauses

The parties to some financing arrangements do not view their initial security agreement as a static, one-shot transaction. Rather, they anticipate at least the potential for a dynamic, ongoing financing relationship. They foresee that additional funds will be advanced or that further property of the debtor will become encumbered as collateral.

The parties to such a transaction would be burdened considerably if they had to formalize all subsequent modifications and additions to their agreement. The transactional costs associated with a requirement that they enter into a new security agreement each time additional funds are advanced by the secured party, or each time the debtor acquires more property to be added to the pool of collateral, would be a drawback. Requiring new agreements would also slow the processing of some transactions, as well as increase the chances of overlooking some necessary formality. The parties would be better served if they could incorporate their long-term intent into their initial security agreement.

Consider the following hypothetical: Secured Party (SP) finances all of Debtor's (D) inventory in a retail furniture outlet and takes a security interest in all of D's inventory.

D will pay its obligation to SP with proceeds that it derives from making retail sales. The parties envision a long-term financing arrangement under which SP will finance D's acquisitions of inventory for many years to come. Each future extension of credit will be secured by D's entire stock of inventory, and SP's security interest will attach to new inventory as D acquires it.

Article 9 includes provisions that greatly facilitate such transactions. It enables parties to include clauses in their security agreement that will implement their intentions with respect to the continuing nature of their financing arrangement. The use of an after-acquired property clause or a future advances clause, or both, enables the parties to craft their transaction with efficiency.

Although both an after-acquired property clause and a future advances clause refer to events that are to transpire in the future, they cover very distinct concepts and should not be confused. An after-acquired property clause concerns assets that will serve as collateral for the obligation. It reflects the parties' understanding that the security interest will attach to property of the type described which the debtor acquires subsequent to the effective date of the security agreement. In the hypothetical stated above, if the security agreement contains an after-acquired property clause, SP will acquire a security interest not only in all of D's existing inventory, but in any additional inventory as D subsequently acquires it.

A future advances clause, on the other hand, concerns the money or other value that is advanced by the secured party. In the hypothetical, if the security agreement contains a future-advances clause, D's inventory will be encumbered as collateral to the extent of the initial loan and all future loans. Article 9 thus validates "floating liens" — that is, liens that expand the pool of collateral as new assets are acquired and that expand the obligation as new value is advanced.[1]

Historically, this approach generated considerable judicial hostility.[2] This aversion was premised "on a feeling, often inarticulate in the opinions, that a commercial borrower should not be allowed to encumber all his assets present and future, and that for the protection not only of the borrower but of his other creditors a cushion of free assets should be preserved."[3] This judicial resistance reached its zenith in the United States Supreme Court opinion of *Benedict v. Ratner.*[4] The Court there struck down as a fraudulent conveyance an assignment of present and future accounts receivable. The debtor's unfettered dominion and control over the collateral and the proceeds from its disposition was held to be fraudulent against other creditors of the debtor.

The effect of rulings like *Benedict* was simply to impose expensive formalities on the ongoing financing of accounts and inventory. For example, "it was thought necessary for the debtor to make daily remittances to the lender of all collections received, even though the amount remitted is immediately returned to the debtor in order to keep the

---

[1] Article 9 security interests also "float" in the sense that they attach automatically to proceeds. *See* § 2.04[B] *supra.*

[2] *See generally* 1 G. Gilmore, *Security Interests in Personal Property* §§ 2.2-2.5, 11.6-11.7 (1965).

[3] U.C.C. § 9-204, Cmt. 2.

[4] 268 U.S. 353 (1925).

loan at an agreed level."[5] Many states overcame the policing requirements that constituted the substance of the *Benedict* rule by enacting laws that countered its effect.[6]

Article 9 includes a provision that effectively repeals *Benedict*. It provides:

A security interest is not invalid or fraudulent against creditors by reason of liberty in the debtor to use, commingle or dispose of all or part of the collateral (including returned or repossessed goods) or to collect or compromise accounts or chattel paper, or to accept the return of goods or to make repossessions, or to use, commingle or dispose of proceeds, or by reason of the failure of the secured party to require the debtor to account for proceeds or replace collateral.[7] A lender with a nonpossessory security interest might, as a practical matter, be quite concerned with policing the activities of its debtor with respect to collateral and proceeds received upon disposition of collateral. The extent of policing measures now, however, is determined by business rather than legal considerations.[8]

§ 3.02   After-Acquired Property — §§ 9-204(1), (2), R9-204(a), (b)

[A]   General Applicability

Article 9 explicitly validates the use of after-acquired property clauses.[9] Such clauses are common with regard to all types of commercial loans, but they are most important with "revolving" forms of collateral like inventory and accounts. By their nature, these forms of collateral will dissipate over a period of time. Inventory will be sold to buyers in the ordinary course who will take it free from the security interest,[10] and accounts will be collected.

If a secured lender continues to loan additional money against inventory or accounts, it must have its interest attach to additional inventory or accounts as they are acquired by the debtor or its collateral will ultimately disappear. An after-acquired property clause extends the scope of the security interest to cover the property acquired later by the debtor.[11] Without such a clause, a secured party would have to enter into a new security agreement with respect to each of the debtor's new acquisitions of inventory or accounts. In the absence of both an after-acquired property clause and a new security agreement, the secured party would be effectively unsecured with respect to all new property acquisitions.[12]

---

[5] U.C.C. § 9-205 Cmt. 1.

[6] U.C.C. § 9-205 Cmt. 1. *Benedict v. Ratner* was based on New York law, rather than the federal law of bankruptcy.

[7] U.C.C. §§ 9-205, **R9-205**.

[8] U.C.C. § 9-205 Cmt. 5.

[9] U.C.C. §§ 9-204(1), **R9-204(a)**.

[10] *See* § 11.03 *infra*.

[11] The case of *In re* Travelers Petroleum, Inc., 86 B.R. 246, 6 U.C.C. Rep. Serv. 2d 911 (Bankr. W.D. Okla. 1987), shows how an after-acquired property clause also can later bring some of the debtor's existing property within the scope of the security agreement. Trucks that were being used by the debtor as equipment later became inventory, and subject to the after-acquired property clause, when they were leased.

[12] New assets might qualify as proceeds, but tracing requirements would make their identification as such problematic. *See* § 2.04[B] *supra*.

An after-acquired property clause is, in essence, part of the description of the collateral in the security agreement. Rather than covering only property like the debtor's existing inventory or accounts, the collateral is described to include also any property of the type specified that is subsequently acquired by the debtor.[13] This arrangement creates a floating lien on a shifting pool of assets.[14]

How can a security interest attach to after-acquired property? When the parties initially enter into their security agreement, the debtor does not yet have rights in such property. Indeed, the property may not even yet exist. Because of the debtor's lack of rights, the security interest cannot yet attach.[15] Attachment occurs immediately upon the debtor's acquisition of rights in the collateral, however.[16] The after-acquired property clause provides the necessary agreement in advance,[17] and the value initially given by the secured party is sufficient to support extension of the security interest to the newly-acquired assets.[18]

A question that has been litigated several times is whether, in the absence of an explicit clause, a security agreement covering all of a particular category extends to after-acquired property within the category. For example, suppose a security agreement describes the collateral as "inventory" or "all inventory." Does this description mean "existing inventory" or "existing and future" inventory. A judicial finding that the term is ambiguous opens the door to extrinsic evidence to explain the parties' intent. When a bank lends against a revolving type of asset like inventory or accounts, it can introduce evidence of a course of dealing,[19] usage of trade[20] or course of performance[21] to support its

---

[13] Parker Roofing Co. v. Pacific First Fed. Sav. Bank, 59 Wash. App. 151, 796 P.2d 732, 13 U.C.C. Rep. Serv. 2d 501 (1990) ("general intangibles...now or hereafter owned"); In the Matter of Penn Housing Corp., 367 F. Supp. 661, 13 U.C.C. Rep. Serv. 947 (W.D. Pa. 1973) ("inventory present and after-acquired" and "all present and future accounts receivable submitted, including new accounts receivable whenever acquired"); South Cty. Sand & Gravel Co., Inc. v. Bituminous Pavers Co., 106 R.I. 178, 256 A.2d 514, 6 U.C.C. Rep. Serv. 901 (R.I. 1969) (all of debtor's accounts receivable "now existing and hereafter arising").

[14] U.C.C. § 9-204 Cmt. 2.

[15] *See* U.C.C. § 9-203(1)(c) and § 2.02[C] *supra*. Valley Nat'l Bank of Arizona v. Flagstaff Dairy, 116 Ariz. 513, 570 P.2d 200, 22 U.C.C. Rep. Serv. 787 (Ariz. Ct. App. 1977) (security interest cannot attach in after-acquired property until debtor acquires rights in it).

[16] Babson Credit Plan, Inc. v. Cordele Prod. Credit Ass'n, 146 Ga. App. 266, 246 S.E.2d 354, 24 U.C.C. Rep. Serv. 437 (1978). With respect to accounts, the interest in after-acquired property attaches when the accounts are created. Shaw Mudge & Co. v. Sher-Mart Mfg. Co., Inc., 132 N.J. Super. 517, 334 A.2d 357, 16 U.C.C. Rep. Serv. 847 (1975).

[17] "This section follows Section 9-203, the section requiring a written security agreement, and its purpose is to make clear that confirmatory agreements are not necessary where the basic agreement has the clauses mentioned." U.C.C. § 9-204 Cmt. 5.

[18] Barry v. Bank of N.H., N.A., 113 N.H. 158, 304 A.2d 879, 12 U.C.C. Rep. Serv. 732 (1973); In the Matter of King-Porter Co., Inc., 446 F.2d 722, 9 U.C.C. Rep. Serv. 339 (5th Cir. 1971). "[A] person gives 'value' for rights if he acquires them...as security for or in total or partial satisfaction of a pre-existing claim." U.C.C. § 1-201(44)(b).

[19] U.C.C. § 1-205(3).

[20] U.C.C. § 1-205(2).

[21] *Cf.* U.C.C. § 2-208(1).

argument for an expansive interpretation. Suppose, however, an individual sells a business enterprise to another on credit and retains a security interest in "all inventory." Because the secured party is not providing ongoing financing, there is less likely to be convincing extrinsic evidence supporting an expansive interpretation. [22] The most plausible meaning is that the parties intended that the security interest attach only to the inventory delivered to the buyer as part of the sale of the business.

Although the courts generally have been permissive with ordinary-course financers of inventory and accounts, [23] there are decisions to the contrary. [24] The secured party's argument for implicit coverage of after-acquired assets is much weaker when the collateral is not of a revolving type. [25] The ease of avoiding the issue in litigation should provide ample motivation to use specific language referring to after-acquired property in any security agreement that contemplates the inclusion of such assets. [26]

[B] Exceptions

Both the 1972 and 1998 versions of Article 9 include a limitation on the reach of after-acquired property clauses in the context of consumer goods. The limitation precludes a security interest created by such a clause from attaching to consumer goods given as additional collateral unless the debtor acquires rights in them within ten days after the secured party gives value. [27] For example, suppose a secured party makes a loan and takes a security interest in a consumer's furniture pursuant to a security agreement that includes an after-acquired property clause. The security interest will not attach to furniture that the debtor acquires six months later, unless the secured party extends additional value and the debtor grants a new security interest in the new furniture. [28]

Secured parties need to be careful with respect to after-acquired property clauses for consumer goods. Assume that the secured party in the illustration as it was initially presented were to act in reliance upon its after-acquired property clause following default by the debtor. If, in addition to the furniture that it financed, the secured party were to seize the furniture that the debtor acquired six months later, it could incur liability for the tort of conversion. [29]

---

[22] *See* Stoumbos v. Kilimnik, 988 F.2d 949, 20 U.C.C. Rep. Serv.2d 333 (9th Cir. 1993).

[23] Kubota Tractor Corp. v. Citizens & S. Nat'l Bank, 198 Ga. App. 830, 403 S.E.2d 218, 14 U.C.C. Rep. Serv. 2d 1247 (1991); *In re* Shenandoah Warehouse Co., 202 B.R. 871, 32 U.C.C. Rep. Serv.2d 573 (W.D. Va. 1996).

[24] Wollenberg v. Phoenix Leasing Inc., 182 Ariz. 4, 893 P.2d 4, 24 U.C.C. Rep. Serv. 2d 770 (Ct. App. 1994) (accounts); *In re* Balcain Equip. Co., Inc., 80 B.R. 461, 5 U.C.C. Rep. Serv. 2d 766 (Bankr. C.D. Ill. 1987) (inventory).

[25] *See, e.g.,* Dowell v. D.R. Kincaid Chair Co., 125 N.C. App. 557, 481 S.E.2d 670, 31 U.C.C. Rep. Serv. 2d 987 (1997), where the court refused to imply an after-acquired property clause for a security agreement covering equipment.

[26] U.C.C. § 9-204, Cmt. 5 indicates that neither after-acquired property clauses nor future advances clauses need be included in a financing statement.

[27] U.C.C. §§ 9-204(2), **R9-204(b)(1).**

[28] *In re* Harris, 23 U.C.C. Rep. Serv. 220 (Bankr. N.D. Ga. 1977) (clause giving secured party security interest in replacement household consumer goods was ineffective to give security interest in such goods acquired more than ten days after the loan).

[29] For discussion of conversion liability, *see* § 19.01[B] *infra.*

The secured party must also be concerned about compliance with applicable state and federal consumer protection laws.[30] For example, a Federal Trade Commission rule makes it an unfair trade practice for a lender or a retail installment seller to take from a consumer a nonpossessory security interest in household goods other than a purchase-money security interest.[31] The Federal Reserve Board has adopted a parallel rule that applies the same constraint on financial institutions.[32] Under the rules, "household goods" are defined to include clothing, furniture, appliances, one radio and one television set, linens, china, crockery, kitchenware, and personal effects (including wedding rings). Lenders are prohibited from taking nonpossessory, nonpurchase-money security interests in these items.

Another limitation can be found in the federal Truth-in-Lending Act and Regulation Z, which require that the property to which a security interest relates be clearly identified.[33] The Federal Reserve Board has interpreted the statute and regulation to mean that a creditor cannot claim that it has a security interest in all after-acquired property of the debtor in transactions to which the Act applies.[34] That interpretation has been upheld in a number of court opinions.[35]

The limitation on the effectiveness of after-acquired property clauses does not apply to consumer goods that qualify as accessions. An accession is an item of personalty that is attached to another item of personalty but retains its separate identity, meaning that it can be removed and sold separately.[36] If a secured party takes a security interest in a consumer debtor's car, a clause in the security agreement extending the security interest to after-acquired accessions is fully enforceable. Thus, the secured party's interest will attach to assets like replacement tires and batteries whenever they are acquired and installed in the car.

Revised Article 9 contains an additional limitation for consumer transactions [37] that applies to both existing and after-acquired collateral. A description only by one of the following Code categories is insufficient as a matter of law: consumer goods, a security entitlement, a securities account or a commodity account.[38] Thus, in

---

[30] Article 9's rules are explicitly subordinated to such laws. U.C.C. §§ 9-201, 9-203(4), **R9-201(b).**

[31] 16 C.F.R. § 444.2(a)(4).

[32] 12 C.F.R. 227.13(d)(Regulation AA). The Federal Reserve Board is required to promulgate deceptive trade practice rules that are substantially similar to designated rules prescribed by the FTC. This approach ensures that the limitations imposed by the FTC will also govern banks, savings and loans, and federal credit unions.

[33] 15 U.S.C. § 1638(a)(9)(1994); 12 C.F.R. §§ 226.8(b)(5), 226.18(m)(1995).

[34] Public Loan Co., Inc. v. Hyde, 47 N.Y.2d 182, 390 N.E.2d 1162, 4117 N.Y.S.2d 238, 26 U.C.C. Rep. Serv. 781 (N.Y. 1979).

[35] *In re* McCausland, 63 B.R. 665, 1 U.C.C. Rep. Serv. 2d 1372 (Bankr. E.D. Pa. 1986); Smith v. No. 2 Galesburg Crown Fin. Corp., 615 F.2d 407, 53 A.L.R. Fed. 406, 28 U.C.C. Rep. Serv. 212 (7th Cir. 1980).

[36] Accessions are discussed generally in § 15.05 *infra.*

[37] *See* § 2.02[A][2][b] *supra.*

[38] **U.C.C. § R9-108(e)(2).**

a consumer transaction a security agreement covering "all present or after-acquired consumer goods" would not attach to any collateral, including consumer goods owned by the debtor at the time value is given and those acquired within ten days thereafter. The revision leaves open the possibility that a description using a category not defined in the Code (e.g., "all present or after-acquired watercraft") might suffice. Even though such a description is not *per se* insufficient under the Code, it might be invalidated under other law; and the reach of its after-acquired aspect is limited to watercraft acquired within the ten-day limit.

The revision also contains limitations that preclude the use of generic descriptions by Code type to security interests in existing or after-acquired commercial tort claims. [39]

§ 3.03   Future Advances — §§ 9-204(3), R9-204(c)

Both the 1972 and 1998 versions of Article 9 validate the use of clauses that provide that the collateral will serve as security for advances or other value that might be extended in the future, whether such advances are obligatory or discretionary. [40] The Code uses the phrase "pursuant to commitment" to refer to advances or other value that the secured party is required to extend under the terms of the security agreement. [41] An advance can be pursuant to commitment even though an event such as default has occurred that would permit the secured party to be relieved of its obligation.

A future advances clause precludes the necessity of the parties entering into another security agreement every time that the secured party advances more money to the debtor. Through the clause, the debtor in essence agrees to grant a security interest in the designated collateral to the extent not only of the original advance by the secured party, but also of any subsequent advances. [42] The future advances clause is an efficient means to extend a secured party's status with each new advance.

A secured party who advances more money to the same debtor under a security agreement that lacks a future advances clause will be an unsecured creditor with respect to the new advance unless the parties enter into a new security agreement to cover the new advance. [43] In the absence of either a future advances clause or a new security

---

[39] U.C.C. §§ R9-108(e)(1)(descriptions generally), R9-204(b)(2)(after-acquired property clauses). *See* discussion of commercial tort claims generally in § 1.07[F][2] *supra.*

[40] U.C.C. §§ 9-204(3), R9-204(c).

[41] U.C.C. §§ 9-105(k), R9-102(a)(68). As between the debtor and the secured party, whether an advance is obligatory or discretionary is irrelevant. In certain circumstances, a secured party's priority rights are enhanced for obligatory advances. *See* § 10.02 *infra.*

[42] Farmers Nat'l Bank v. Shirey, 126 Idaho 63, 878 P.2d 762, 25 U.C.C. Rep. Serv. 2d 566 (1994) (security agreement provided that security interest "is to secure payment and performance of the liabilities and obligations of Debtor to Secured Party of every kind and description... due or to become due, now existing or hereafter arising").

[43] Idaho Bank & Trust Co. v. Cargill, Inc., 105 Idaho App. 83, 665 P.2d 1093, 36 U.C.C. Rep. Serv. 691 (1983) (in the absence of future advances clause, such advances are not within scope of security agreement). The lender can become secured with respect to a subsequent additional advance by entering into a new security agreement with the debtor. Thorp Fin. Corp. of Wisconsin v. Ken Hodgins & Sons, 73 Mich. App. 428, 251 N.W.2d 614, 21 U.C.C. Rep. Serv. 881 (1977). A future advances clause simply precludes the necessity of entering into the second agreement.

agreement, there is no agreement by the debtor to allow a security interest to attach to the collateral to cover the new advance. A new security agreement provides the necessary debtor consent at the time of the advance; a future advances clause provides it at the time of the original agreement.

Issues sometimes arise concerning the scope of a future advances clause. The parties might include a clause with broad language yet nevertheless intend a much narrower scope. For example, the security agreement in *In re* Eshleman [44] contained a clause which provided that the debtor's automobile "shall secure Debtor's obligations to pay the note of the Debtor of even date herewith...(and) all other liabilities of Debtor to Lender, now existing or hereinafter incurred...." [45] A year and a half later, the secured party loaned the debtor more money and took a security interest in inventory, equipment, and accounts. The secured party forgot to perfect the second security interest and was therefore subordinated to a bankruptcy trustee with respect to the newly acquired collateral. [46] The bankruptcy referee refused to allow the secured party's claim that the automobile served as security for the second loan. He determined that the money advanced in the second loan "was so unrelated to the earlier loan transaction... as to negate the inference that the debtor consented to its inclusion." [47] The *Eshleman* court seems justified in finding that the parties never intended a security interest in a consumer good to cover funds advanced under a separate security agreement for collateral of a commercial nature.

Traditional judicial hostility has continued to assert itself in construing future advances clauses. Broad-sweeping clauses were derisively labeled "dragnet clauses," and courts routinely refused to enforce them. Remnants of that judicial attitude, in the guise of the "same-class rule," have survived the adoption of Article 9. Under this rule, a clause describing future advances in general terms is enforceable only if the later advances are of the same class as the initial obligation; [48] otherwise, the advance is not considered to have been related to the financing that was contemplated by the parties when they entered into the security agreement. [49] The decision in *In re* Eshleman discussed above reflects the same-class rule. The rule has considerable modern force.

Given the currency of the same-class rule, secured parties are well-advised to draft their future advances clauses with care. [50] A broad, general clause is simply an invitation for a court to strike the clause with respect to future, unrelated financing. To increase

---

[44] 10 U.C.C. Rep. Serv. 750 (Bankr. E.D. Pa. 1972).

[45] 10 U.C.C. Rep. Serv. at 751.

[46] Perfection was necessary because new collateral was taken. A new act of perfection is not necessary merely because a future advance has been made.

[47] 10 U.C.C. Rep. Serv. at 753.

[48] *In re* Smith & West Constr., Inc., 28 B.R. 682, 36 U.C.C. Rep. Serv. 989 (Bankr. D. Or. 1983) (all loans were of a commercial nature related to debtor's construction business).

[49] *In re* Blair, 26 B.R. 228, 36 U.C.C. Rep. Serv. 985 (Bankr. W.D. Tenn. 1982) (two personal loans on vehicles were sufficiently related, but business loan was not); Community Bank v. Jones, 566 P.2d 470, 22 U.C.C. Rep. Serv. 168 (Or. 1977) (dragnet clause in inventory loan held not to cover subsequent overdrafts).

[50] *In re* Johnson, 105 B.R. 661, 10 U.C.C. Rep. Serv. 2d 1002 (D. Kan. 1989) (dragnet clauses are to be scrutinized carefully and strictly construed).

the chances that it will be upheld, the clause should express an intent to include unrelated financing.

The future advances clause upheld in *In re* Dorsey Elec. Co.[51] is illustrative. It provided for the inclusion of "all other indebtedness of every kind and nature, direct and indirect... whether or not the same shall be similar or dissimilar or related or unrelated to the primary indebtedness."[52] A clause that shows an intent to include unrelated financing is a good response to the same-class rule because the rule is based on the premise that, when the future advance is not of the same class as the initial obligation, the consent of the debtor cannot be inferred.[53]

§ 3.04 Financing Inventory and Accounts

Some of the most sophisticated financing transactions involve inventory, accounts, and their proceeds. These are the assets that are expected to turn over on a regular basis.[54] As a result, they are the most likely candidates for financing transactions that will utilize after-acquired property and future advances clauses. These transactions thus can be creatively tailored to meet the specific needs of the parties with respect to their ongoing financing relationship.

Three financing patterns have become common: 1) factoring of accounts; 2) general financing of inventory, accounts or both; and (3) floor planning of inventory. Some of the parameters of these common financing patterns are discussed below.

[A] Factoring of Accounts

Factoring of accounts is the outright purchase of accounts from a dealer by a financing agency. It does not involve a secured loan from the financing agency; rather, the accounts are sold by the dealer. The customers on the accounts (the account debtors)[55] are notified that their accounts have been sold and that they are to make payments to the factor when due.[56] The financing agency typically purchases the accounts without recourse, meaning

---

[51] 344 F. Supp. 1171 (E.D. Ark. 1972).

[52] 344 F. Supp. at 1175.

[53] Pellegrini v. Nat'l Bank of Wash., 28 U.C.C. Rep. Serv. 209 (D.C. Super. Ct. 1980).

[54] Inventory will be sold to buyers in the ordinary course, who will take it free of even a perfected security interest. *See* § 11.03[A][1] *infra*. The obligation to pay money that is at the core of an account is satisfied as the account is paid.

[55] An "account debtor" is a person obligated on an account, chattel paper or a general intangible. U.C.C. §§ 9-105(1)(a), **R9-102(a)(3). The revision clarifies that a person obligated on an instrument is not an account debtor, even if the instrument is part of chattel paper.**

[56] Although notification of the account debtor is typical, the parties are free to structure the transaction so that the dealer continues to collect the accounts as agent for the factor. If the dealer fails to remit the collections, the factor will be unable to recover from the account debtors for payments made to the dealer. An account debtor is credited for payments made to the assignor prior to receiving notice that the account has been assigned and that payments are to be made to the assignee. U.C.C. §§ 9-318(3), **R9-406(a). The revision requires that the notice be authenticated by either the assignor or assignee.**

that, if an account debtor does not pay the account when it becomes due, the financing agency cannot recover from the dealer that sold the account.[57]

Even though factoring of accounts does not involve a secured loan, the transaction nevertheless falls within the scope of Article 9. For reasons that have already been discussed and will be expanded on in the current discussion, Article 9 applies to outright sales of accounts.[58] The factor's interest is called a security interest even though the accounts do not serve as security for an obligation,[59] and the agreement between the parties is a security agreement. Accordingly, the factor must be certain that the Article 9 formalities are observed. This means that the factor must reduce the agreement with the dealer to a writing **or record** that describes the accounts and is signed **or authenticated** by the dealer.[60] In addition, the factor needs to perfect its agreement by filing a financing statement in the appropriate office.[61]

Factoring of accounts is a service that enables a dealer to contract separately to have another party conduct the activities related to extending credit to the dealer's customers and assuming the risk that accompanies those activities. The typical factor engages in investigations of the creditworthiness of customers, establishes available credit lines for those customers, does the bookkeeping with respect to accounts, sends the billing statements, and undertakes collection of the accounts. Each account is purchased by the factor at the time that the dealer provides its customers with goods or services. Because the accounts are purchased without recourse, the factor also assumes the risk of any credit losses.

In exchange for assuming these duties for the dealer and the risks that they entail, the factor is compensated in accordance with the factoring agreement. The amount is negotiated between the parties, but is based on a percentage of the accounts purchased, such as between of one and two percent. The higher or lower amount will reflect matters such as the number of accounts that have to be handled, the average value of each account, and projected volume and expected losses.

The factoring business is highly specialized and requires careful assessment of all relevant criteria. Keeping compensation lower creates a competitive advantage to attract business, but miscalculations can have disastrous consequences for a factor. Factoring allows the dealer to eliminate a credit department in its business, thereby saving costs that can be used to pay the factor's compensation. Economies of scale and modern credit information networks that utilize computers enable factors to provide efficient and effective service.

---

[57] Many factoring agreements provide for a right of recourse where the account debtor's failure to pay is predicated on a defect in the goods or services.

[58] Sales of both accounts and chattel paper fall within the scope of Article 9. **The revision also governs sales of promissory notes and payment intangibles.** See **U.C.C. §§ 9-102(1)(b), R9-109(a)(3). The rationale for inclusion and some aspects of the mechanics of such transactions are discussed in § 1.06** supra.

[59] U.C.C. § 1-201(37).

[60] U.C.C. §§ 9-203(1)(a), **R9-203(b)(3)(A). The revision's use of "record" and "authenticate" rather than "writing" and "signed" is discussed in § 1.10[C]** supra.

[61] Perfection of security interests in accounts by filing a financing statement is discussed in § 5.04[B] infra.

Some dealers will not be able to wait until the accounts become due before they receive payment from the factor. Their capital needs can preclude their ability to delay turning the accounts. These dealers can negotiate an advance from the financing agency against some or all of the sales price of the accounts. These advances are relatively expensive, as in three percent or more over the prime rate.

[B] Financing Against Inventory and Accounts

A dealer who needs money immediately can sell its accounts to a factor or use them as collateral for a loan. When accounts are used as collateral, the dealer commonly collects the accounts and remits the proceeds to the lender to reduce the outstanding indebtedness. That is, account debtors will not be instructed to pay the lender directly unless the dealer goes into default.[62] The dealer also typically bears the entire risk of nonpayment. The secured party's loan must be repaid, and nonpayment by an account debtor will not discharge any part of the indebtedness. By way of contrast, account debtors are typically instructed to pay factors directly, and the factor bears some or all of the risk of nonpayment.[63]

A dealer's inventory can also be used as collateral. Lenders do not generally consider inventory to be a particularly desirable form of collateral because of certain practical difficulties. Lenders often insist that a percentage of the proceeds of each sale be remitted to reduce the outstanding indebtedness, but desperate dealers can easily sell "out of trust," diverting proceeds for use in their day-to-day operations. Other problems materialize only after repossession. If a dealer defaults because it could not sell its inventory, there is no reason to believe that a secured lender will fare any better. Problems such as obsolescence and erroneous judgment concerning consumer tastes can leave the lender greatly undersecured, notwithstanding the high costs associated with the inventory's acquisition. Even if the inventory has good value, the secured lender faces the necessity of making a forced sale of a large volume of merchandise. As a result, the value of the inventory often diminishes considerably following default.

Because of these problems and risks, many secured lenders pursue conservative strategies when lending against inventory. Lenders are usually unwilling to advance more than a small percentage of the value of the dealer's inventory. In other words, lenders typically require very high loan-to-value ratios. For example, a lender may be willing to advance only 25% to 40% of the inventory's value. A 40% loan-to-value ratio means that for every dollar of inventory acquired by the dealer, the lender is willing to advance only 40 cents.

Because the amounts available for financing against inventory are so low, most parties seek alternatives. One approach is to utilize warehousing arrangements to reduce the risks associated with inventory financing.[64] Another approach is to floor plan inventory when it consists of big-ticket items.[65]

---

[62] The security agreement can provide for account debtors to be instructed to pay the secured party prior to default. Payments received by the secured party reduce the outstanding indebtedness. *See* U.C.C. §§ 9-502(1), **R9-607(a)**(secured party may notify account debtors to pay it pursuant to agreement and, in any event, on default).

[63] *See* § 3.04[A] *supra.*

[64] For a discussion of warehousing arrangements, *see* § 6.02[B] *infra.*

[65] For a discussion of floor planning, *see* § 3.04[C] *infra.*

Inventory financing is often used in conjunction with accounts financing or factoring.[66] Accounts are generally more attractive than inventory as collateral. Accounts arise when the dealer's inventory has been sold to a willing buyer, eliminating concerns about the dealer's ability to sell goods and the realistic value of those goods. A lender often will be better able to assess the value of a dealer's accounts than to predict the value of inventory in a forced-sale context. In the event of the dealer's default, the lender generally is better equipped to proceed against a dealer's accounts than against the bulk of the dealer's inventory.

These advantages are reflected in the marketplace. If a dealer produces quality accounts, a secured lender might be willing to advance as much as 85% of their face value. As an accommodation to the nature of a given dealer's business, such as seasonal build-ups of merchandise, a secured lender might be willing to finance the dealer's acquisition of inventory in conjunction with financing the accounts that it generates.

Accounts financing provides a dealer with great flexibility. The dealer can borrow more money against new accounts as they are generated. It can use the proceeds of accounts that it collects to repay the borrowed funds. Most agreements provide a dealer with an assured line of credit upon which it can draw as needed. The limit to the credit is established by the percentage of collateralization that is agreed upon in the security agreement. The pricing can be fairly high, as much as six or seven percent over the prime rate. The advantage, however, is that the dealer has to pay that amount only on the outstanding balance. The dealer can reduce its capital costs by keeping its balance low. It has the credit line, however, to take advantage of business opportunities that require liquidity.

Accounts financing poses significant risks of fraud. A dealer who encounters severe cash-flow difficulties may be tempted to use an accounts-financing arrangement as a means to obtain additional cash. Because the dealer is entitled to borrow based on the volume of accounts generated in its business, the dealer might be inclined to falsify some accounts in the hope that it can borrow and repay the additional funds without the secured lender's learning of its dishonest activity. Falsification of accounts is tempting because they are so easy to fabricate.

Commercial finance companies that lend against accounts have developed mechanisms to detect fraud in order to minimize losses. They often seek verifications from the identified clients of the dealer to ascertain whether they really ordered and received the stated goods or services. They also typically insist that payments to the dealer be remitted to the lender without a change in form. One example of this practice is a "lock box" arrangement in which account debtors are instructed to send checks payable to the dealer to a particular post office box. The account debtor believes that the dealer is being paid, but in fact the post office box is controlled by the lender. The security agreement authorizes the lender to collect the checks, thereby reducing the indebtedness. Secured lenders also make unannounced inspections of the dealer's books and records, utilizing personnel who are specially trained to detect signs of fraudulent accounts. They must

---

66 Indeed, a security interest in inventory attaches automatically to the accounts that are proceeds of that inventory. Proceeds are discussed generally in § 2.04 *supra*. Priorities in accounts that are proceeds of inventory are discussed in § 10.04 *infra*.

carefully control their personnel in order to minimize the risk of collusion between inspectors and dealers.

Because controls against the risk of fraud impose higher costs on accounts financers, accounts financing is economically feasible only when a dealer has a very high volume of accounts. Depending upon the nature of the business and the types of accounts generated, it is not unusual to require a volume of between $500,000 and $1 million in outstanding accounts at any given time. Dealers with smaller volumes who need advances against accounts will be relegated to factoring their accounts and drawing some of the payment price as an advance. The choice between accounts financing and factoring of accounts thus often is not determined by the dealer but rather by the market forces that impose restrictions based on volume of business. Factoring can be a good source of immediate cash, but it does not provide the flexibility that is available with accounts financing.

[C] Floor Planning Inventory

One of the most attractive forms of inventory financing is commonly used when a dealer's inventory consists of big-ticket items, such as automobiles, construction equipment, or mobile homes. The suppliers of such items generally do not deliver goods on consignment or even extend much credit to dealers. They tend to insist that dealers pay at least most of the price in cash. Because most dealers do not have that kind of liquidity, they need to finance the acquisition of their inventories. Floor planning is the predominant method.

Floor planning consists of a two-part transaction. In the first part, the lender provides the funds to pay all or most of the dealer's costs in acquiring big-ticket items and takes back a purchase-money security interest that attaches to each item. The purchase-money status of the lender will enable it to prevail with respect to the goods it finances against any prior secured party with an interest in the dealer's inventory. For example, the dealer might have secured an operating loan from another lender with a blanket lien on all its assets, including inventory.[67]

The second part of floor planning concerns the dealer's retail transactions. Most buyers of big-ticket items cannot afford to pay cash and thus must finance their purchase. The dealer could sell to the buyer on an unsecured basis, thereby generating an account. Given the amounts involved, however, a secured sale that involves the creation of chattel paper is much more likely. Chattel paper is created when the buyer issues a promissory note to the dealer for the unpaid purchase price, together with a written security agreement granting the dealer a security interest in the item purchased.[68]

The availability of the security interest is valuable for big-ticket items, like automobiles, because the value of the item and the existence of established markets for used goods of that type mean that the item can be readily converted into cash if repossession becomes necessary. Of course, a dealer who was too strapped for cash to purchase its inventory

---

[67] For a discussion of priority in this context, *see* § 10.05[B] *infra*.

[68] Chattel paper, discussed in § 1.04[B][3] *supra*, can also consist of a single writing, sometimes called a "retail installment sales contract," that combines the payment obligation and security interest.

without outside financing is not going to be in a position to carry the paper of its customers who will be paying on the chattel paper over a period of several years. The solution is to sell the chattel paper to the secured lender.[69]

The retail side can be the most attractive aspect of floor planning to the lender. The finance charge included in the chattel paper often is quite high, which enables the buyer of the chattel paper to realize a good return. The floor planning arrangement thus often entails two aspects: The secured lender finances the dealer's acquisition of inventory at a relatively attractive rate of interest as the means to assure itself of acquiring the dealer's chattel paper with its high interest rate. The two aspects are often linked so that the dealer is obligated to sell all of its chattel paper to the secured lender.

---

[69] Sales of chattel paper, like sales of accounts, are within the scope of Article 9. *See* generally § 1.06 *supra*. The similar practice of factoring accounts is discussed in § 3.04[A] *supra*. The parties to a sale of chattel paper often agree that the dealer will buy the paper back if the account debtor goes into default, thereby shifting to the dealer the costs associated with foreclosing on the underlying big-ticket item.

PART III:

PERFECTION OF SECURITY INTERESTS

CHAPTER 4

PERFECTION IN GENERAL

SYNOPSIS

§ 4.01 Purpose

A creditor or seller who acquires a security interest in some of a debtor's property may subsequently learn that other parties claim a competing interest in the same property. Competing claims can be asserted by an array of potential claimants, including *inter alia* a purchaser (other than a secured party), another secured party, or a lien creditor (*e.g.*, a trustee in bankruptcy). The assertion of competing claims raises issues concerning priorities in rank-ordering the claims, and these issues are covered in Part IV of this book. The concern in this Part of the book is to explain the steps that a secured party can undertake to enhance its position with respect to other potential competing claimants.

These steps are referred to as "perfection" of a security interest. Attachment of a security interest simply establishes the relationship between the secured party and the debtor and gives the secured party a special property interest in the collateral.[1] Perfection

---

[1] Farmers' State Bank of Palestine v. Yealick, 69 Ill. App. 3d 353, 387 N.E.2d 399, 26 U.C.C. Rep. Serv. 509 (1979) (even unperfected security interest is enforceable against a debtor).

is relevant only to the secured party's position vis-a-vis third-party claims to the collateral. Perfection has no bearing on the relationship between the debtor and the secured party, and an unperfected secured party has the right to enforce its security interest if the debtor defaults.[2] By perfecting the security interest, a secured party can reduce the risk that a third-party claimant can successfully assert a superior claim to the collateral.

Although perfection may be accomplished by a variety of methods, the general principle underlying the perfection concept is simple. Because a security interest is created by a contract between the secured party and the debtor, its existence might be known only to the two principals. Perfection generally requires that the secured party take designated steps that are deemed to be sufficient to publicize its interest to other parties that might have an interest in the same property. This notice is intended to overcome, at least in part, problems of "ostensible" ownership.[3] A prospective buyer of the collateral, for example, has an obvious interest in knowing whether the offered property is subject to an outstanding security interest, just as a subsequent lender would want to know of a prior security interest in the same collateral.

Perfection, thus, entails the steps that are necessary for a secured party to provide adequate public notice of the existence of its security interest. Although the rules concerning priorities will not enable an attorney to guarantee to a client that perfection will assure the client priority against all potential competing claimants, perfection will substantially improve the priority position of the client.

§ 4.02   The Alternative Methods of Perfection — §§ 9-302, R9-310

Article 9 identifies eight different methods by which secured parties can perfect their security interests. The various alternatives are all described, with applicable cross-references to other sections, in section 9-302 of the 1972 text **and R9-310 of the revision**. The availability of any given method of perfection depends upon the kind of property used for the collateral and, sometimes, upon the nature of the transaction.

[A]   Filing a Financing Statement

Article 9's default rule requires that a financing statement be filed to perfect all security interests **and, in the revision, agricultural liens**.[4] All other methods of perfection are considered to be exceptions to this general rule.[5]

A financing statement is a simple form that is filed in the appropriate public filing office to enable interested parties to obtain sufficient information concerning a security interest in personal property of the debtor. It is analogous to the public filing of a deed to show a mortgage interest in real property, except that most financing statements are

---

[2] Doyle v. Northrop Corp., 455 F. Supp. 1318, 25 U.C.C. Rep. Serv. 932 (D.N.J. 1978) (unnecessary in action between debtor and secured party to determine sufficiency of financing statement to perfect security interest because perfection only determines priority among competing claimants and is irrelevant to validity of security interest).

[3] Ostensible-ownership problems are discussed in context throughout the book. For an overview *see* § 1.02[B][2][a] n. 62 *supra*.

[4] U.C.C. §§ 9-302(1); **R9-310(a)**.

[5] U.C.C. §§ 9-302 Cmt. 1, **R9-310, Cmt 2.**

filed in a distinct filing system and are considerably simpler than a real estate filing. The requirements, policies, and issues with respect to perfection by filing financing statements are covered extensively in Chapter 5 *infra*.

[B] Possession

A secured party generally is entitled to perfect a security interest in goods or in any form of indispensable paper by taking actual or constructive possession of the collateral.[6] With respect to some types of indispensable paper, perfection by possession is the only available method, other than short periods of temporary perfection.[7] The issues, policies, and approaches of perfection by possession are discussed in Chapter 6 *infra*.

[C] Automatic Perfection

In a few circumstances, a secured party will not be required to take any steps beyond attachment of the security interest for it to be deemed perfected. In these instances, perfection occurs automatically upon attachment.[8] The policy justifications and implications for exempting the applicable transactions from any additional steps for perfection are explored in Chapter 7 *infra*.

[D] Temporary Perfection

Article 9 also allows automatic perfection in certain additional, specified circumstances, but in these categories of cases, the perfection has only a limited duration.[9] Temporary perfection is possible in designated circumstances involving instruments, certificated securities, negotiable documents, and goods in the possession of a bailee other than one who has issued a negotiable document for them.[10] Temporary perfection is also recognized with respect to specified cases involving proceeds.[11] The details of temporary perfection are spelled out in Chapter 8 *infra*.

[E] Perfecting Under Federal Law

Federal law includes some requirements concerning methods of perfecting a security interest.[12] For example, the Federal Aviation Act requires a security interest in an airplane to be perfected by filing with the Federal Aviation Administration.[13] Bowing to inevitable

---

[6] U.C.C. §§ 9-302(1)(a); 9-305; **R9-310(b)(6), R9-313.** The concept of indispensable paper is discussed in § 1.04[B] *supra*.

[7] In the 1972 Code, the affected collateral is money or instruments (other than certificated securities or instruments which constitute part of chattel paper). U.C.C. § 9-304(1). **Under the revision, a security interest in instruments can be perfected by permissive filing. § R9-312(a). A security interest in money can only be perfected by possession. § R9-312(b)(3).**

[8] U.C.C. §§ 9-302(1)(c),(d),(e),(f),(g); **R9-310(b)(2); R9-309.**

[9] U.C.C. §§ 9-302(1)(b); **R9-310(b)(5),(9).**

[10] U.C.C. §§ 9-304(4),(5); **R9-312(e),(f),(g).**

[11] U.C.C. §§ 9-306(3); **R9-315(d)(3).** When certain conditions are satisfied, the temporary perfection automatically extends beyond the applicable period, thereby constituting a form of automatic perfection.

[12] Federal preemption is discussed generally in § 1.07[A] *supra.*

[13] 49 U.S.C. § 1403.

principles of federal preemption, Article 9 recognizes that filing a financing statement is not required and cannot even be effective to perfect a security interest if a federal statute or treaty establishes a national or international registration, a national or international certificate of title, or otherwise requires a different filing location from that which is specified in Article 9.[14]

[F] State Certificate-of-Title Statutes

All states have enacted separate certificate-of-title statutes that cover motor vehicles and that may cover additional related goods, such as trailers, boats, and tractors. In addition to establishing paper titles to the designated goods, these state statutes also provide that a security interest in the property can be noted on the title itself. In some, but not all states, such notation on the certificate of title is the exclusive method of perfecting a security interest in the designated classes of goods.

To achieve consistency between these state statutes and each state's enactment of the U.C.C., Article 9recognizes that the filing of a financing statement is neither required nor effective to perfect a security interest in collateral covered by a state certificate-of-title statute.[15] The nuances posed by certificate-of-title statutes are detailed in Chapter 9 *infra.*[16]

[G] Control

Under the current text of Article 9 **and the revision**, the primary method for perfecting a security interest in investment property is control.[17] **The revision extends the concept to deposit accounts, letter-of-credit rights and electronic chattel paper.**[18] **The specifics on perfection by control are covered in Chapter 6** *infra.*

[H] Delivery

Both current Article 9 **and the revision** permit a security interest in a certificated security in registered form to be perfected by delivery to the secured party even though the indorsement that is necessary for the secured party to take control is missing.[19] Delivery is nothing more than possession of the security certificate, but the term is used in order to conform to the usage of Article 8.[20]

§ 4.03 When Perfection Occurs — §§ 9-303(1), R9-308(a)

A security interest becomes perfected when it has attached and when any additional steps set out in the Code have been taken.[21] Satisfaction of mechanical steps required

---

[14] U.C.C. §§ 9-302(3)(a); **R9-310(b)(3); R9-311(a)(1).**

[15] U.C.C. §§ 9-302(3)(b); **R9-310(b)(3); R9-311(a)(2),(3).**

[16] *See* § 9.05 *infra.*

[17] U.C.C. § 9-115, **R9-314(a), R9-106.**

[18] *See* U.C.C. §§ **R9-314(a) and R9-104 (deposit accounts), R9-107 (letter-of-credit rights), R9-105 (electronic chattel paper).**

[19] U.C.C. § 9-115(6), **R9-313(a).**

[20] U.C.C. § 8-301(a)(1)(delivery requires possession of the security certificate).

[21] U.C.C. §§ 9-303(1), **R9-308(a).**

for perfection is not alone sufficient; the security interest must also attach.[22] It simply makes no sense to talk in terms of perfecting an interest that does not exist.[23] The Code makes it clear that the steps to attachment and to perfection can be completed in any order by providing that, if the applicable steps required for perfection are completed prior to attachment, perfection is delayed until the security interest attaches.[24] In essence, perfection occurs at the first point in time at which all of the requirements for both attachment and perfection are satisfied.

Because of practical aspects of achieving priority that will be explained later,[25] a prospective secured party will sometimes want to complete the applicable steps for perfection before the security interest attaches. For example, when it appears that the parties are about to reach a final agreement, a lender might insist that, before proceeding any further, the prospective debtor must sign a financing statement that will then be filed in the appropriate office. Although all of the necessary steps for perfection by filing might have then been completed, the security interest would not attach, and actual perfection would not occur, until completion of the requirements for attachment. The debtor thus might not sign the security agreement or the secured party might not give value until after the filing of the financing statement is completed. The order of completion of each requirement does not matter,[26] but completion of all of the requirements for both attachment and perfection is required before there is a perfected security interest.

The opportunity to complete the mechanical steps of perfection prior to attachment is also significant in the context of an after-acquired property clause. The security interest in any applicable property subsequently acquired by the debtor cannot attach until the debtor obtains rights in the property.[27] The secured party, nevertheless, can file a financing statement with respect to the original collateral and, so long as the description in the financing statement is sufficient to describe the collateral subsequently acquired by the debtor, the single filing will be sufficient to satisfy the steps of perfection by filing for both the original collateral and all after-acquired collateral.[28] The secured party then

---

[22] In *In re* Browning, 66 B.R. 79, 2 U.C.C. Rep. Serv. 2d 724 (S.D. Ill. 1986), a financing statement filed in 1983 described the collateral as the debtor's crops to be grown during 1983 through 1987. Perfection did not result immediately in the later crops, because perfection requires attachment, and attachment requires the debtor to have rights in the collateral.

[23] Bradley v. K&E Inv., Inc., 847 S.W.2d 915, 22 U.C.C. Rep. Serv. 2d 915 (Mo. Ct. App. 1993) (lender that failed to obtain executed agreement that met U.C.C. § 9-203's requirements for security agreement could not have perfected security interest in cars of debtor).

[24] U.C.C. §§ 9-303(1), **R9-308(a).**

[25] *See* §§ 5.03, 10.01 *infra.*

[26] NBD-Sandusky Bank v. Ritter, 437 Mich. 354, 471 N.W.2d 340, 15 U.C.C. Rep. Serv. 2d 260 (1991) (order of applicable steps is not determinative for perfection).

[27] *See* § 2.02[C] *supra.*

[28] A previously filed financing statement, however, is insufficient to perfect an interest in after-acquired property when there is no security agreement. J.I. Case Credit Corp. v. Foos, 717 P.2d 1064, 11 Kan. App. 2d 185, 717 P.2d 1064, 1 U.C.C. Rep. Serv. 2d 250 (1986).

will have perfected secured status as to all after-acquired collateral, just as soon as the debtor obtains rights in each unit of collateral. [29]

§ 4.04 Continuity of Perfection — §§ 9-303(2), R9-308(c)

Article 9 allows a security interest to be perfected by one method and thereafter remain continuously perfected through the process of tacking other methods of perfection. When different but nevertheless appropriate methods of perfection are subsequently used, the security interest is deemed to be continuously perfected from the date of the original perfection, *provided* that the interest was not allowed to become unperfected during any interim period. [30] A gap during which the interest was unperfected cannot be bridged by tacking, so that subsequent perfection would date only from the time that perfection was accomplished after the gap. Allowing a gap to occur endangers the interests of a secured party because the general rules of priority are based on the principle of first-in-time, first-in-right. A secured party will thus want to be able to establish rights based on the earliest point in time.

A simple example illustrates the application of the continuity-of-perfection provision. Assume that, on March 1st, a secured party takes a security interest in the debtor's stamp collection and perfects the interest by taking possession of the collection. On September 1st the parties agree that the collection will be returned to the debtor so that the debtor can remount several of the stamps. The secured party determines to perfect the interest further by filing a financing statement, which it accomplishes on September 1st. If the financing statement is filed before the secured party relinquishes possession of the collection, the security interest will be continuously perfected from March 1st. [31] If the collection is returned to the debtor prior to the filing, however, an intervening period will result during which the security interest was unperfected. The perfected, secured status thus would date back only until September 1st, the date of filing. [32] The secured party would thus be vulnerable to any competing interest that arose between March 1st and September 1st, a result that could have been avoided by maintaining continuity of perfection.

---

[29] Bank of the West v. Commercial Credit Fin. Servs., Inc., 852 F.2d 1162, 6 U.C.C. Rep. Serv. 2d 602 (9th Cir. 1988) (bank acquired perfected security interest in debtor's after-acquired inventory, accounts, and proceeds at time transfer of the assets took effect because financing statement covering a security interest in such collateral was already on file).

An originally filed financing statement will also support future advances against the same collateral, even though the interest does not attach with respect to the future advance until the secured party gives the new value associated with it. Thorp Fin. Corp. of Wis. v. Ken Hodgins & Sons, 73 Mich. App. 428, 251 N.W.2d 614, 21 U.C.C. Rep. Serv. 881 (1977).

[30] U.C.C. §§ 9-303(2), **R9-308(c)**.

[31] The reverse sequence of perfecting methods was effectively used in First Interstate Bank of Ariz. N.A. v. Interfund Corp., 924 F.2d 588, 14 U.C.C. Rep. Serv. 2d 247 (5th Cir. 1991). A security interest in a horse farm's chattel paper that was perfected originally by filing and subsequently by possession was deemed to be continuously perfected.

[32] *See In re* Stewart, 74 B.R. 350, 4 U.C.C. Rep. Serv. 2d 271 (M.D. Ga. 1987) (secured party became unperfected upon releasing possession of diamond ring back to debtor because execution of document to effect that debtor held ring in trust for secured party was not adequate method of subsequent perfection).

CHAPTER 5

PERFECTION BY FILING

SYNOPSIS

§ 5.01   General Method — §§ 9-302(1), R9-310(a)

Filing a financing statement is the Code's preferred method of perfection. By filing a written form that includes certain required information in a designated public office, a secured party publicly announces its security interest to any third parties who are concerned enough to search the public files. The filing of a financing statement for purposes of perfecting a security interest is thus analogous to the public recording of a mortgage to indicate an encumbrance on real estate. Third parties considering a transaction with the debtor involving property capable of being perfected by filing should first examine the filing records for a financing statement evidencing someone else's interest in that property.

Article 9 provides, as a default rule, that a financing statement must be filed for perfection to occur.[1] There are numerous situations in which alternative methods of perfection may be used,[2] but all are stated as exceptions to the default rule. Part 4 of current Article 9 **and Part 5 of the revision** are devoted to the filing process. Their provisions are explained and analyzed in this chapter.

§ 5.02   What to File

[A]   Requirements — §§ 9-402(1), R9-502(a)

In the 1972 text the formal requisites of a financing statement are stated in section 9-402. A financing statement is sufficient if it includes:

- The names of the debtor and the secured party;
- The signature of the debtor;
- An address of the secured party from which information concerning the transaction can be obtained;
- A mailing address of the debtor; and
- A description of the collateral.[3]

A financing statement that covers crops that are growing or are to be grown must also include a description of the real estate where the crops are or will be planted. Because financing statements covering crops are filed in the chattel records rather than the real estate records, a legal description of the land (*i.e.*, a "metes-and-bounds" description) is not required — an informal description that reasonably identifies the land is sufficient.

Real estate descriptions are also required when a financing statement covers timber to be cut, minerals or the like (including oil and gas) and accounts resulting from sales

---

[1] U.C.C.§§ 9-302(1), **R9-310(a). In the revision, agricultural liens are also perfected by filing. § R9-310(a).**

[2] See generally Chapter 4 *supra.*

[3] U.C.C. § 9-402(1).

of minerals or the like at the wellhead or minehead, and fixtures.[4] With these types of collateral, the financing statement must indicate that it is to be filed in the real estate records,[5] and the Code gives the states the option of requiring a full legal description.[6] If the debtor does not have an interest of record in the real property (*e.g.*, when the debtor is a lessee), the financing statement must also provide the name of a record owner.[7] Security interests in fixtures can also be perfected by the recording of a real estate mortgage if the mortgage indicates the collateral covered and otherwise satisfies the requirements for a financing statement.[8]

To be sufficient to perfect a security interest under the revision, an initial financing statement[9] must include:

- The name of the debtor;
- The name of the secured party or a representative of the secured party;
- An indication of the collateral covered; and
- A real property description for as-extracted collateral, timber to be cut, and fixtures.[10]

An initial financing statement that does not contain this minimal information is ineffective to perfect a security interest, even if it is accepted by the filing office. The following information is also required for an initial financing statement[11] but is not necessary for it to be legally sufficient:

- A mailing address for the debtor;
- A mailing address for the secured party;
- Whether the debtor is an individual or an organization; and

---

[4] U.C.C. § 9-402(1). Real estate descriptions are also required for security agreements covering crops growing or to be grown and timber to be cut. U.C.C. § 9-203(1)(a). *See* § 2.02[A][3] *supra*. If a financing statement omits a required real estate description, the secured party is unperfected. If a security agreement omits such a description, attachment does not occur and there is no interest to perfect.

[5] U.C.C. § 9-402(5).

[6] *Id.*

[7] *Id.*

[8] U.C.C. § 9-402(6)(when mortgage effective as fixture filing).

[9] In the revision "financing statement" means a record composed of an initial financing statement and any subsequent filings related thereto (*e.g.*, continuation statements, termination statements). U.C.C. § R9-102(a)(39).

[10] U.C.C. §§ R9-502(a), (b). Note that the revision deletes the land-description requirement for crops. § R9-502(b). *See also* § 2.02[A][3] *supra*. The revision's approach to the sufficiency of real estate descriptions is identical to that taken by the 1972 Code. *See also* § R9-502(c) (mortgage effective as financing statement).

[11] Requirements for other records presented for filing, and the filing office's responsibilities with regard to such records, are discussed in § 5.06 *infra*.

- If the debtor is an organization: 1) the type of organization, 2) the jurisdiction of organization, and 3) an organizational identification number (or an indication that the debtor has no such number).[12]

The filing office must refuse to accept a record that is an initial financing statement if it does not contain this information.[13] Further, a filing that is properly refused is not effective to perfect a security interest.[14] If, however, the filing office inadvertently accepts a financing statement that contains the minimum required information but omits an additional required item, the security interest is perfected.[15] A filing office may not refuse to accept a filing because it does not contain requested information that is not on the above list.[16] For example, a filing office might ask for the social security number of an individual debtor, but it cannot refuse to accept a financing statement that omits the number.

The simplicity of the financing statement in both current Article 9 and the revision stands in sharp contrast to the typical security agreement. Terms that are significant in a security agreement — such as the extent of indebtedness, the terms for payment, events of default and covenants regarding the use of the collateral — simply have no place in a financing statement.[17] Both versions of Article 9 provide a simple form which, if completed properly, will be sufficient as a matter of law.[18]

[1] Names — §§ 9-402(7), R9-503(a)-(c)

The names of the parties play significant roles in the filing system. The filing officer places financing statements into the public files according to the name of the debtor.[19] The debtor's name is a logical basis upon which to index the files because an individual

---

[12] U.C.C. § R9-516(b)(4)(5). The requirements that relate to the debtor are included to aid the searcher in excluding records that are revealed in a search but do not pertain to the debtor in question, and to aid in identifying the proper jurisdiction for filing.

[13] U.C.C. §§ R9-520(a), R9-516(b). The filing office must also refuse to accept an initial financing statement that does not contain the name of the debtor, the name of the secured party of record (or its representative), or a sufficient description of real property when such a description is required. Id. The filing office may not refuse to accept an initial financing statement that fails to indicate the collateral. Id.

[14] U.C.C. § R9-516(b) ("[f]iling does not occur with respect to a record that a filing office refuses to accept" for a proper reason). A record that is refused for a reason not listed in § R9-516(b) is effective "except as against a purchaser of the collateral which gives value in reasonable reliance upon the absence of the record from the files." § R9-516(d). See § 5.05 infra.

[15] U.C.C. § R9-520(c).

[16] U.C.C. § R9-520(a).

[17] The 1972 text permits the security agreement to be filed as a financing statement if it contains all the required information. U.C.C. § 9-402(1). The revision eliminates this option.

[18] U.C.C. §§ 9-402(3), R9-521.

[19] Both versions of Article 9 require that filings be indexed in the name of the debtor. U.C.C. §§ 9-403(4), R9-519(c).

who searches the files is interested in ascertaining whether a particular person[20] has previously granted a security interest that would conflict with the searcher's proposed transaction. The search, thus, will be based on the debtor's name. If the debtor's name is incorrect, the search may not reveal the financing statement and could thus mislead the searcher. The effect of errors and changes in the debtor's name is discussed later.[21]

The 1972 version of Article 9 addresses a potential ambiguity concerning the proper identification of the debtor. Section 9-402(7) provides that "[a] financing statement sufficiently shows the name of the debtor if it gives the individual, partnership or corporate name of the debtor, whether or not it adds other trade names or names of partners."[22] Thus, a prudent secured party should state the individual name of a debtor that operates as a sole proprietor, although trade names under which the debtor conducts business can also be added.

The reason for this approach is that the business of a sole proprietor is not considered to be a separate legal entity. For example, a court held that a secured party whose financing statement gave the debtor's name as "D.B.A. [Doing Business As] The Tape Shack, Allan W. Jones, owner and Richard Jones" was unperfected;[23] if the inclusion of the trade name was desired,[24] the debtor's name should have been stated as "Allen W. Jones, D.B.A. The Tape Shack, and Richard Jones." Individual names should not be used when the debtor is a corporation.[25] They should not ordinarily be used when the debtor is a partnership, although some informal partnerships have no legal name and can only be identified through the names of all of the partners.

Although most courts have held filings which use only the trade name ineffective,[26] some courts have ruled the other way.[27] They have construed the word "sufficiently"

---

[20] "Person" includes an individual or organization. U.C.C. § 1-201(30). "Organization" includes, *inter alia*, corporations, partnerships, associations, governmental entities, trusts and estates. § 1-201(28).

[21] *See* § 5.02[C].

[22] U.C.C. § 9-402(7).

[23] *In re* Jones, 11 U.C.C. Rep. Serv. 249 (Bankr. W.D. Mich. 1972).

[24] Cross-filing under trade names can be useful because it might enable a searcher who does not know the rules to stumble across the filing, thus preventing a later dispute.

[25] *See, e.g., In re* LFT, Ltd., 36 B.R. 411, 37 U.C.C. Rep. Serv. 1766 (Bankr. D. Haw. 1984) (the debtor's correct name was "My Place or Yours, Inc."; filing under name "Rick Storm & Rob Niebling dba My Place or Yours" was ineffective). *See also In re* McCauley's Reprographics, Inc., 638 F.2d 117, 30 U.C.C. Rep Serv. 801 (9th Cir. 1981) (corporation designated as partnership).

[26] *In re* Covey, 66 B.R. 459, 2 U.C.C. Rep. Serv. 2d 1716 (Bankr. D.N.H. 1986) (trade name of "RBF" inadequate to perfect when individual's name was George R. Covey); Pearson v. Salina Coffee House, Inc., 61 B.R. 538, 1 U.C.C. Rep. Serv. 2d 584 (D. Kan. 1986), *aff'd,* 831 F.2d 1531, 4 U.C.C. Rep. Serv. 2d 1225 (10th Cir. 1987) (filing under trade name of "Hilton Inn" not valid for partnership named "Beacon Realty Investment Co.).

[27] Peoples Nat'l Bank v. Uhlenhake, 712 P.2d 75, 42 U.C.C. Rep. Serv. 1839 (Okla. Ct. App. 1985) (filing under trade name "Bud's Construction Company" upheld even though debtor's actual name was "L.E. Uhlenhake"); *In re* McBee, 714 F.2d 1316, 36 U.C.C. Rep. Serv. 1473 (5th Cir. 1983) (filing under trade name "Oak Hill Gun Shop" held valid).

in section 9-402(7) to authorize the deletion of a trade name, but not to preclude the effectiveness of a filing that does not give an individual's name but instead uses a trade name that has broad recognition among creditors.

The Comments to the 1972 text resolve any ambiguity in the language chosen by the drafters or in the underlying policy objectives:

> In the case of individuals, it [§ 9-402(7)] contemplates filing only in the individual name, not in a trade name. In the case of partnerships it contemplates filing in the partnership name, not in the names of any of the partners, and not in any other trade names. Trade names are deemed to be too uncertain and too likely not to be known to the secured party or person searching the record, to form the basis for a filing system. However, provision is made in Section 9-403(5) for indexing in a trade name if the secured party so desires. [28]

The drafters strove for a degree of certainty in the notice-filing system. Relying on the extent of perceived recognition of a particular trade name as the standard of acceptability for filing under that name injects vagueness that the drafters sought to avoid.

The revision provides more explicit guidance on the name of the debtor for a financing statement. If the debtor is a "registered organization," meaning an organization organized under a state or federal law that requires the maintenance of a public record indicating the organization's existence, [29] the financing statement must reflect the name shown on those records. [30] The revision also has rules for decedents' estates [31] and trusts. [32]

The general rule for other debtors is that, if the debtor has a name, the financing statement sufficiently provides the name of the debtor "only if it provides the individual or organizational name of the debtor." [33] Section 1-201(28) defines "organization" broadly to include both legal entities and associations that lack entity status. If the debtor does not have a name, the financing statement sufficiently provides the name of the debtor "only if it provides the names of the partners, members, associates, or other persons comprising the debtor." [34] The text is now

---

[28] U.C.C. § 9-402 Cmt. 7.

[29] U.C.C. § R9-102(a)(70).

[30] U.C.C. § R9-503(a)(1) refers to the debtor's name as shown on the records in the jurisdiction of organization. This means "the jurisdiction under whose law the organization is organized." U.C.C. § R9-102(a)(50).

[31] U.C.C. § R9-503(a)(2) (name of decedent and indication that debtor is an estate).

[32] U.C.C. § R9-503(a)(3) (name as shown in organic documents or, if no name is shown, settlor's name, additional information to distinguish debtor from similar trusts, and information showing that debtor is a trust).

[33] U.C.C. § R9-503(a)(4)(A). Thus, if an organization has a name, even though it is not a separate legal entity, the name of the organization is to be used. U.C.C. § R9-503 Cmt. 2.

[34] U.C.C. § R9-503(a)(4)(B). Thus, if the organization that is the debtor does not have a name, the names of the individuals or other entities that make up the organization should be used. U.C.C. § R9-503 Cmt. 2.

explicit that a financing statement that includes only a trade name does not sufficiently name the debtor.[35] It also explicitly provides that a financing statement is not rendered ineffective merely because it omits either: 1) a trade name, or 2) except as set out above for debtors without a name, the names of partners, members, associates or the like.[36]

[2] Signature

The requirement in the 1972 text that a financing statement include the signature of the debtor seems to be compelled by two related considerations. First, the mandate of the signature means that the debtor must cooperate before an effective filing can be made. This participation guards against creditor overreaching. It provides a control against a secured party who otherwise might overstate the scope of assets that are encumbered by a security agreement.[37]

The signature requirement also serves a verification function. Because the debtor must participate at least to the extent of signing the financing statement, the effective financing statement at least reflects voluntary dealings between the parties with respect to the described collateral. This participation guards against the creation of a false impression that the debtor has willingly allowed an encumbrance upon his or her assets.

Under some designated exceptional circumstances, the signature of the secured party rather than the debtor on the financing statement can be effective to perfect a security interest.[38] The circumstances which permit the substitute signature by the secured party all arise once financing has commenced between the parties, which means that the cooperation of the debtor existed at one point but might no longer be forthcoming. Because the secured party's ability to perfect under these circumstances should not be held hostage by a recalcitrant debtor, the secured party is entitled to provide the signature.

The situation differs for an amendment of a financing statement, which can affect the interests of both parties. In order to preclude one party from adversely affecting the interests of the other, an amendment can be accomplished only by filing a writing signed by both the secured party and the debtor.[39] An amendment that is merely a release of collateral, however, can be signed by the secured party alone.[40]

---

[35] U.C.C. § R9-503(c).

[36] U.C.C. § R9-503(b). A financing statement is also not rendered ineffective merely because it fails to indicate the representative capacity of the secured party or a representative of the secured party. § R9-503(d).

[37] The potential of a tort action for slander of title also operates to control overreaching.

[38] U.C.C. § 9-402(2). The situations involve changes in location of the collateral or of the debtor that trigger new filing requirements under the interstate filing rules (see § 5.04[C] infra), proceeds when the security interest in the original collateral was perfected (see § 8.02 infra), collateral as to which the filing has lapsed (see § 5.06 infra), and collateral acquired after a change in the debtor's name or identity (see § 5.02[C][2] infra). Because the requirement of the debtor's signature is eliminated in the revision, the exceptions in § 9-402(2) are not necessary.

[39] U.C.C. § 9-402(4).

[40] U.C.C. § 9-406.

A signature under the U.C.C. is not a highly formalistic requirement. The term "signed" is defined to include "any symbol executed or adopted by a party with present intention to authenticate a writing."[41] The Comments show that the definition is intended to be taken literally; they stress that a variety of forms can be acceptable (including printed, stamped, written, initials only, or a thumbprint), and that "[T]he question always is whether the symbol was executed or adopted by the party with present intention to authenticate the writing."[42] The few cases that nevertheless insist upon a higher degree of formalism are simply wrong.[43]

The requirement of the debtor's signature on an initial financing statement was eliminated in the revision to facilitate paperless, electronic filings.[44] The control and verification objectives are satisfied through alternative methods. The debtor must authorize the filing of an initial financing statement or of an amendment that adds either collateral or a new debtor to the initial financing statement.[45] Merely by authenticating a security agreement, the debtor authorizes the filing of an initial financing statement and any amendment that covers collateral described in the security agreement.[46] An amendment that adds collateral not covered in the security agreement or adds a new debtor must be authorized in an authenticated record.[47] Any person who files an unauthorized initial financing statement or amendment can be held liable for damages and a statutory penalty of $500.[48] Furthermore, a filing is effective only to the extent that it was authorized.[49] Thus, if the debtor authorizes filing with respect to inventory, but the secured party files for inventory and equipment, the filing is effective only as to inventory.[50]

[3] Addresses

Appropriate addresses of both parties are required by the 1972 text for an effective financing statement. For the debtor, a mailing address is required. The inclusion of this address can aid in determining the identity of the debtor. Someone searching the files generally should know the debtor's address as well as its name. This additional information can help in distinguishing between debtors of the same name and in

---

[41] U.C.C. § 1-201(39). *See* discussion of 1972 text's comparable signature requirement for security agreements in § 2.02[A][1] *supra.*

[42] U.C.C. § 1-201 Cmt. 39.

[43] *In re* Carlstrom, 3 U.C.C. Rep. Serv. 766 (Bankr. D. Me. 1966) (signature must be sufficient to provide evidentiary value); *In re* Kane, 1 U.C.C. Rep. Serv. 582 (Bankr. E.D. Pa. 1962) (signature must be manually written by the signer on applicable document).

[44] **U.C.C. § R9-502 Cmt. 3.**

[45] **U.C.C. § R9-509(a).**

[46] **U.C.C. § R9-509(b). Authentication includes both signing a writing and encrypting a record. U.C.C. § R9-102(a)(7). *See* § 2.02[A][1] *supra.***

[47] **U.C.C. § R9-509(a). Only the secured party need authorize the filing of an amendment that releases collateral. § R9-509(c). Releases are discussed in § 5.06[B] *infra.***

[48] **U.C.C. § R9-625(e)(3). Damages are described in § R9-625(b).**

[49] **U.C.C. § R9-510(a).**

[50] **U.C.C. § R9-510 Cmt. 2.**

overcoming the misleading effect of filings that contain errors in the statement of the debtor's name.

The 1972 text states that a financing statement must provide an address of the secured party "from which information concerning the security interest may be obtained."[51] This reference assumes that a searcher who finds a filed financing statement will be able to gain useful information directly from the secured party, but in fact very few secured parties are willing to reveal confidential information to searchers without permission from the debtor. Under the current Code, the address is of primary use if the searcher wants to send a notice to the secured party.[52] Of course, a searcher will not want to rely exclusively on explanations provided by the debtor, and the Code provides a mechanism by which the debtor can confirm information regarding its transaction with the secured party of record.[53] A prudent searcher will require the debtor to obtain information through the use of this mechanism.

The addresses of the parties are also required by revised Article 9 but are not necessary for an initial financing statement to be legally sufficient to perfect a security interest.[54] Nevertheless, the filing office must refuse to accept an initial financing statement that omits addresses, and a filing is not effective if it is properly refused by the filing office.[55] The revision, however, recognizes the limited function served by the address requirement. A secured party's address is significant primarily as the place to which others can send any required notifications. A notification sent to the address provided will satisfy the requirement, even if the address is in error.[56] The secured party will also be deemed to have received such a notification.[57]

[4] Description

A financing statement governed by the 1972 text must contain "a statement indicating the types, or describing the items, of collateral."[58] The test for determining the sufficiency of a property description required under that version of Article 9 is stated in section 9-110: "[A]ny description of personal property or real estate is sufficient whether or not it is specific if it reasonably identifies what is described."[59] The drafters clearly intended

---

[51] U.C.C. § 9-402(1).

[52] Notices to secured parties of record are important when the searcher takes a purchase-money security interest in inventory (*see* § 10.04[B] *infra*) and when the searcher wants to establish its rights in the event of foreclosure (*see* § 18.02[B] *infra*). *See also* the discussion of function of the secured party's address in the revision *infra* this subsection.

[53] U.C.C. § 9-208. *See also* §§ **R9-210, R9-102(a)(4).** These mechanisms are discussed in § 5.02[B][2] *infra*.

[54] *Cf.* **U.C.C. § R9-502(a) (contents required for sufficient financing statement).**

[55] *See* § 5.02[A] *supra*.

[56] **U.C.C. § R9-516 Cmt. 5.** *See also* **U.C.C. § R9-102(a)(74) (defining "sends").**

[57] **U.C.C. § R9-516 Cmt. 5.** *See also* **U.C.C. § 1-201(26)(defining "notifies").**

[58] U.C.C. § 9-402(1).

[59] **The revision continues this general provision on the sufficiency of a description, but adds further detail. *See* U.C.C. § R9-108 and the discussion of that section at § 2.02[A][2] *supra*.**

a more liberal, functional approach to descriptions than the fanatical "serial number" test that often characterized earlier chattel mortgage cases.[60]

The functional approach to description sufficiency is stressed in the Comments: "The test of sufficiency of a description laid down by this section is that the description do the job assigned to it—that it make possible the identification of the thing described."[61] This test suggests that a wider degree of latitude should apply to a description in a financing statement as compared to a description in a security agreement because of the different purposes served by each writing.[62] A greater degree of precision is necessary in a security agreement because it establishes the intent of the parties regarding the specific assets that will be subject to the security interest.[63] As in other contractual contexts, ambiguities are often resolved against the drafter. A financing statement, in contrast, serves merely to notify interested third parties that the debtor has dealt with the named secured party concerning the property described. The financing statement is not intended to reveal the ultimate details of those dealings, but rather to alert the searcher to investigate those dealings before proceeding with any proposed, potentially conflicting transaction with the debtor.[64] The purpose of the financing statement thus can be satisfied with a more general description of the collateral.[65]

Descriptions in security agreements and in financing statements must, nevertheless, both be sufficient in order to fulfill their respective functions. For example, if a security agreement describes the collateral as "inventory and accounts," but the financing statement indicates only "accounts," perfection does not extend to the security interest in inventory.[66] A third party who read the financing statement would have notice of only the narrower description.[67] Conversely, had the security agreement indicated only

---

[60] U.C.C. § 9-110 Cmt. *See* discussion of description requirement for security agreements in § 2.02[A][2] *supra.*

[61] U.C.C. § 9-110 Cmt.

[62] *In re* F.R. of N.D., Inc., 54 B.R. 645, 41 U.C.C. Rep. Serv. 265 (Bankr. D.N.D. 1985). An occasional court has improperly reversed this order. *In* re Cilek, 115 B.R. 974, 11 U.C.C Rep. Serv. 2d 937 (Bankr. W.D. Wis. 1990) (financing statement must be more specific because it provides notice to third parties).

[63] World Wide Tracers, Inc. v. Metropolitan Protection, Inc., 384 N.W.2d 442, 42 U.C.C. Rep. Serv. 1573 (Minn. 1986).

[64] U.C.C. § 9-402 Cmt. 2; Kubota Tractor Corp. v. Citizens & Southern Nat'l Bank, 198 Ga. App. 830, 403 S.E.2d 218, 14 U.C.C. Rep. Serv. 2d 1247 (1991). *See* § 5.02[B] *infra.*

[65] DeKalb Bank v. Klotz, 151 Ill. App. 3d 638, 502 N.E.2d 1256, 3 U.C.C. Rep. Serv. 2d 1214 (1986) ("livestock" was adequate description for debtor's cattle); *In re* Alexander, 39 B.R. 110, 38 U.C.C. Rep. Serv. 674 (Bankr D.N.D. 1984) ("farm and other equipment" reasonably identified possible interest in debtor's farm machinery).

[66] *In re* Katz, 563 F.2d 766, 22 U.C.C. Rep. Serv. 1282 (5th Cir. 1977). *See also In re* Coody, 59 B.R. 164, 1 U.C.C. Rep. Serv. 2d 581 (Bankr. M.D. Ga. 1986) (financing statement that listed only four of five lots described in security agreement left secured party perfected only with respect to crops grown on those four lots); *In re* American Home Furnishings Corp., 48 B.R. 905, 4 U.C.C. Rep. Serv. 631 (Bankr. W.D. Wash. 1985) (inclusion in security agreement of intangibles held broad enough to cover tax refund, but omission from financing statement left the interest unperfected).

[67] *In re* Marta Cooperative, Inc., 74 Misc. 2d 612, 344 N.Y.S.2d 676, 12 U.C.C. Rep. Serv. 955 (N.Y. Co. Ct. 1973).

"accounts" and the financing statement stated "inventory and accounts," the security interest would cover only the accounts.[68] The security interest, of course, is the contract that creates the security interest.[69]

An interest in after-acquired property need not be indicated in the financing statement's description of the collateral. An after-acquired property clause may be included in a security agreement to eliminate the necessity for the debtor and secured party to enter subsequent security agreements each time the debtor acquires additional property that fits the description of the collateral.[70] For as long as a financing statement is effective, however, it functions without regard to the time at which the debtor acquires the collateral. The financing statement can be filed even before any security agreement has been entered into,[71] which means that it could be filed even before the debtor has any rights in the initial collateral. A prudent searcher who encounters a filed financing statement will inquire to determine the property that is subject to an effective security agreement. Nevertheless, despite unequivocally clear drafters' statements to the contrary[72] and the vast bulk of conforming case law,[73] an occasional court decision refuses to recognize perfection of after-acquired property because the description in the financing statement did not include an after-acquired property clause.[74]

In a series of decisions similar to a line of cases striking down overly-broad descriptions in security agreements, the courts often have been unwilling to uphold broad descriptions in financing statements, particularly "supergeneric" descriptions that encompass all of a debtor's personal property.[75] Ironically, the 1972 text provides more support for

---

[68] The issue turns on whether the court will admit extrinsic evidence to supplement the description in the security agreement. *See* discussion in § 2.02[A][2][a] *supra* of *In re* Martin Grinding & Machine Works, Inc., 793 F.2d 592, 1 U.C.C. Rep. Serv. 2d 1329 (7th Cir. 1986) (inclusion of inventory and accounts receivable in the financing statement description does not expand scope of security interest when those categories of property were inadvertently omitted from the security agreement's description of collateral). *See also* Landen v. Production Credit Ass'n of the Midlands, 737 P.2d 1325, 4 U.C.C. Rep Serv. 2d 240 (Wyo. 1987) (narrower description of "cattle" in the security agreement controlled over the description in the financing statement of "livestock" to exclude a security interest in the debtor's horses).

[69] *In re* Marta Cooperative, Inc., 74 Misc. 2d 612, 344 N.Y.S.2d 676, 12 U.C.C. Rep. Serv. 955 (N.Y. Co. Ct. 1973).

[70] U.C.C. § 9-204(1). "The references to after-acquired property clauses and future advance clauses in Section 9-204 are limited to security agreements." U.C.C. § 9-204 Cmt. 5.

[71] U.C.C. § 9-402(1). *See* § 5.03 *infra*.

[72] "There is no need to refer to after-acquired property or future advances in the financing statement." U.C.C. § 9-402 Cmt. 5.

[73] *In re* Brace, 163 B.R. 274, 22 U.C.C. Rep. Serv. 2d 1184 (Bankr. W.D. Pa. 1994); American Nat'l Bank & Trust Co. of Sapula v. National Cash Register Co., 473 P.2d 234, 7 U.C.C. Rep. Serv. 1097 (Okla. 1970).

[74] *In re* Young, 42 B.R. 939, 39 U.C.C. Rep. Serv. 1041 (Bankr. E.D. Pa. 1984).

[75] *In re* Boogie Enters., Inc., 866 F.2d 1172, 7 U.C.C. Rep. Serv. 2d 1662 (9th Cir. 1989) (description of "personal property" lacks required specificity); *In re* Grey, 29 B.R. 286, 36 U.C.C. Rep. Serv. 724 (Bankr. D. Kan. 1983) (description "all personal property" held insufficient to perfect an interest in grain).

invalidating such a description in a financing statement than for invalidating a comparable description in a written security agreement.[76] The provision respecting financing-statement descriptions requires "a statement indicating the types, or describing the items, of collateral."[77] Many courts simply conclude that descriptions which are broader than "types" of personal property do not comply with this requirement.[78]

The broadest description a prudent secured party operating under the 1972 text should ever employ in a financing statement is one that lists one or more of the categories of collateral defined in Article 9.[79] If the secured party wants a blanket lien on all assets, then all the categories (including fixtures and accessions) should be used.[80] Even using these categories can be risky. Courts are likely, of course, to apply the Article 9 definitions to these terms.[81] A secured creditor, thus, must be careful to ascertain that the correct categories are used to encompass specific assets that are intended to be included.[82] Unstated concerns about overreaching by consumer and farm creditors have also apparently influenced some courts to find broad descriptions of consumer goods or farm-related collateral to be insufficient, even when used in a financing statement.[83] The notice function that financing statements are intended to serve[84] discredits these latter holdings.

Section R9-504 of the revision addresses the identification of collateral in financing statements. It recognizes that a description that is sufficient for a security agreement is also sufficient for a financing statement.[85] In addition, however, the revision specifically authorizes "an indication that the financing statement covers all assets

---

[76] For discussion of the courts' approach to supergeneric descriptions in security agreements, *see* § 2.02[A][2] *supra.*

[77] U.C.C. § 9-402(1).

[78] *In re* Volpe Enters., Inc., 42 B.R. 90, 39 U.C.C. Rep. Serv. 662 (Bankr. S.D. Fla. 1984).

[79] *See* U.C.C. §§ 9-105(1)(b),(f),(j); 9-106; 9-109; *In re* H. L. Bennett Co., 588 F.2d 389, 25 U.C.C. Rep. Serv. 284 (3d Cir. 1978).

[80] An Ohio case demonstrates how an all-inclusive listing of these categories can allow a creditor extensive reach. The court allowed the secured party to repossess the entire assets of the debtor company under a description of collateral that included "all goods, equipment, machinery, furnishings and other personal property, all inventory, merchandise, raw materials, work in process and supplies, all accounts, general intangibles, chattel paper, instruments, and other forms of obligations and receivables." Frayer Seed, Inc. v. Century 21 Fertilizer & Farm Chems., Inc., 51 Ohio App. 3d 158, 555 N.E.2d 654, 11 U.C.C. Rep. Serv. 2d 1320 (1988).

[81] *In re* Dillard Ford, Inc., 940 F.2d 1507, 15 U.C.C. Rep. Serv. 2d 1072 (11th Cir. 1991) (general intangibles).

[82] *See* Sannerud v. First Nat'l Bank of Sheridan, Wyo., 708 P.2d 1236, 42 U.C.C. Rep. Serv. 751 (Wyo. 1985) (description as "equity" was insufficient to cover any tangible personal property of the debtor).

[83] *In re* Werth, 443 F. Supp. 738, 23 U.C.C. Rep. Serv. 489 (Bankr. D. Kan. 1977) (financing statement description of "all equipment now owned or hereafter acquired by debtor" held insufficient to perfect security interest in items of farm equipment specifically identified in security agreement).

[84] See § 5.02[B] *infra.*

[85] *See* **U.C.C. § R9-108 and the discussion of that section at § 2.02[A][2][b]** *supra.*

or all personal property."[86] Such a supergeneric description will not suffice for purposes of a security agreement, however.[87]

Under the 1972 text, a financing statement must also include a description of the real estate involved when the collateral is crops that are growing or are to be grown.[88] Although a legal description of the land is not required, the description must nevertheless be sufficient for its reasonable identification. Descriptions that have passed judicial scrutiny include the following: "Dale Wilson farm located on Lancaster Road, four miles from Danville, Ky.,"[89] and "all crops growing or to be grown on real estate located in Jasper County, Missouri, approximately 15 miles northwest of Carthage, Missouri."[90] The following descriptions, however, have been held inadequate: "land owned or leased by debtor in Cherokee County, Kansas,"[91] "land owned or leased by the undersigned debtor situated at various locations,"[92] and "Roy Peeler Farm located in Cross County, Arkansas."[93]

The revision eliminates the requirement that a financing statement covering crops growing or to be grown must contain a real estate description.[94] The comments to the revision state that the drafters considered such a requirement to be unwise.[95] Farmers frequently lease different land from year to year, and the requirement has proven burdensome in that it necessitates the filing of frequent amendments.

[B] Notice Filing

[1] The Function of Notice

The filing of an effective financing statement does not indicate as much as an uninitiated searcher is likely to assume. It does not show, for example, that the parties have even entered into a security agreement. Article 9 specifically provides that "[a] financing statement may be filed before a security agreement is made or a security interest otherwise attaches."[96] For reasons that will be developed in a later chapter,[97] prudent

---

[86] U.C.C. § R9-504(2).

[87] U.C.C. § R9-108(c).

[88] U.C.C. § 9-402(1). A similar requirement for security agreements is discussed in § 2.02[A][3] *supra.*

[89] Bank of Danville v. Farmers Nat'l Bank, 602 S.W.2d 160, 29 U.C.C. Rep. Serv. 1020 (Ky. 1980).

[90] United States v. Newcomb, 682 F.2d 758, 33 U.C.C. Rep. Serv. 1748 (8th Cir. 1982).

[91] Chanute Prod. Credit Ass'n v. Weir Grain Supply, Inc., 210 Kan. 181, 499 P.2d 517, 10 U.C.C. Rep. Serv. 1351 (Kan. 1972).

[92] *In re* Schwab, 613 F.2d 1279, 28 U.C.C. Rep. Serv. 1123 (5th Cir. 1980).

[93] *In re* Peeler, 145 B.R. 973, 18 U.C.C. Rep. Serv. 2d 1244 (Bankr. E.D. Ark. 1992).

[94] *Cf.* U.C.C. § R9-502(b) (real estate description required only for timber to be cut, as-extracted collateral, and fixtures). The revision also eliminates the related requirement for security agreements covering crops. *Cf.* § R9-203(b)(3)(A) (real estate description required only for timber to be cut).

[95] U.C.C. § R9-502 Cmt. 4.

[96] U.C.C. §§ 9-402(1), R9-502(d). For discussion of the desirability of pursuing this option, *see* §§ 5.03, 10.01 *infra.*

[97] *See* § 10.01 *infra.*

secured parties commonly insist upon "pre-filing;" that is, filing a completed financing statement before making a commitment to give the value necessary for the creation of a security interest. At most, therefore, a filed financing statement indicates only that there *might* be a security interest affecting the indicated property.[98] The function that the filing system is designed to serve is strikingly modest.

The drafters have adopted a system of "notice filing" that had been used previously in the Uniform Trust Receipts Act.[99] The function of notice filing is described quite ably in the Comments to the 1972 text:

> What is required to be filed is not, as under chattel mortgage and conditional sales acts, the security agreement itself, but only a simple notice which may be filed before the security interest attaches or thereafter. The notice itself indicates merely that the secured party who has filed may have a security interest in the collateral described. Further inquiry from the parties concerned will be necessary to disclose the complete state of affairs.[100]

Once placed on notice of the possible existence of a security interest, the searcher can protect itself through further inquiry.[101] A financing statement simply cannot be relied upon to reveal all of the information needed by a prudent searcher.

[2] Requests for Information — §§ 9-208, R9-210, R9-625(f),(g)

A searcher should not, of course, rely totally upon the debtor's explanation of the secured party's interest. The searcher who contacts the secured party for information directly, however, is likely to be rebuffed.[102] Accordingly, the searcher should ask the debtor to employ a Code mechanism that enables the debtor to verify its position vis-a-vis the secured party. Under the 1972 text, the debtor is entitled to submit to the secured party a statement indicating what the debtor believes to be the covered collateral.[103] The secured party must then send a written correction or approval within two weeks.[104] A secured party who fails to comply is liable to the debtor for any damages caused by the failure.[105] Further, as against a party misled by its failure to comply, a secured party

---

[98] Chase Bank of Fla., N.A. v. Muscarella, 582 So. 2d 1196, 14 U.C.C. Rep. Serv. 2d 1274 (Fla. Ct. App. 1991).

[99] U.C.C. § 9-402 Cmt. 2.

[100] *Id.*

[101] *In re* Wak Ltd., Inc., 147 B.R. 607, 19 U.C.C. Rep. Serv. 2d 915 (Bankr. S.D. Fla. 1992) (description directed reader to specific lease). The requirement that the financing statement include at least a statement indicating the collateral is designed to spare every prospective creditor from the need to make further inquiry of every party who has filed a financing statement against the debtor. *In re* Kirk Kabinets, Inc., 15 U.C.C. Rep. Serv. 746 (Bankr. M.D. Ga. 1974).

[102] Secured lenders, particularly banks, are often subject to confidentiality requirements. **Comment 3 to U.C.C. § R9-210, reflecting this fact, states that "the secured party should not be under a duty to disclose any details of the debtor's financial affairs to any casual inquirer or competitor who may inquire."**

[103] U.C.C. § 9-208(1). A statement may also be submitted indicating what the debtor "believes to be the aggregate amount of unpaid indebtedness as of a specific date." *Id.*

[104] U.C.C. § 9-208(2).

[105] *Id.*

is estopped to claim a security interest beyond the collateral shown on a list submitted by the debtor in good faith.[106]

The revision also permits the debtor to make a request[107] of the secured party. The debtor is entitled to submit an authenticated record requesting a list of the collateral,[108] a statement of account,[109] or an "accounting."[110] A secured party must respond to the request within fourteen days after its receipt.[111] A secured party that fails to comply with its duty to respond is liable to the debtor for $500 and for any damages caused by its failure.[112] As against a party misled by its failure to respond to a request for a list of collateral, the secured party may claim an interest only as shown in the debtor's list.[113]

[C] Effect of Errors and Changes

[1] Errors — §§ 9-402(8), R9-506(a)

Errors are inevitable whenever parties are required to prepare even a simple writing. The Code provides a standard for resolving the effect of errors that appear on filed financing statements: A financing statement that substantially complies with Article 9's requirements is effective even though it contains minor errors that are not "seriously misleading."[114] The objective of the drafters is clear from the comments to the 1972 text: The provision "is in line with the policy of this Article to simplify formal requisites and filing requirements and is designed to discourage the fanatical and impossibly refined reading of such statutory requirements in which courts have occasionally indulged themselves."[115]

The effect of errors is a matter of degree. The purpose of a filed financing statement is to provide notice that apprises interested parties that a particular person might have granted a security interest in particular property. If the filing, despite some error, is reasonably sufficient to place such parties on notice, the error should not be considered

---

[106] *Id.*

[107] U.C.C. § R9-210(a)(1) (defining "request").

[108] U.C.C. § R9-210(a)(3) (request to approve or correct a list stating collateral and reasonably identifying the transaction or relationship that is the subject of the request).

[109] U.C.C. § R9-210(a)(4) (request to approve or correct a statement of the aggregate unpaid balance as of a specified date and reasonably identifying the transaction or relationship that is the subject of the request).

[110] U.C.C. § R9-210(a)(2) (request must reasonably identify the transaction or relationship that is the subject of the request). An accounting is a record authenticated by the secured party that indicates the aggregate unpaid secured obligations (as of a date not more than 35 days before or after the date of the record) and identifies the components of the obligation in reasonable detail. U.C.C. § R9-102(a)(4).

[111] U.C.C. § R9-210(b). A secured party who is a consignor or a buyer of accounts, chattel paper, payment intangibles or promissory notes need not respond. *Id.*

[112] U.C.C. § R9-625(f).

[113] U.C.C. § R9-625(g).

[114] U.C.C. §§ 9-402(8), R9-506(a).

[115] U.C.C. § 9-402 Cmt. 9.

fatal. The savings provision that permits effectiveness for financing statements that contain minor errors places a greater degree of responsibility on searchers. While even minor errors might tend to mislead, searchers have grounds to complain only when they have been seriously misled. **For example, the Comments to the 1998 text suggest that searchers will rarely be seriously misled by an error in the secured party's name.** [116]

The application of this "no harm, no foul" standard can be illustrated with respect to errors in the debtor's name. Any error that is so significant as to cause the financing statement to be filed in such a way that it is not likely to be found at all by a reasonably prudent searcher will not pass muster. [117] If the financing statement is likely to be found notwithstanding the error, the issue is whether the error would seriously mislead the searcher as to the collateral covered by the statement or as to whether the person named as debtor on the statement is the same as the person whose record is being investigated.

For example, a filing made under the debtor's name shown on the financing statement as "Arnold, Jack" was not effective to perfect because the debtor's correct name was Herschel I. Arnold. [118] The court concluded that a reasonably prudent searcher could not be expected to find this financing statement in conducting a search for the debtor. In contrast, a financing statement naming the debtor as "Excel Department Stores" rather than the correct name of "Excel Stores, Inc." was held to be sufficiently accurate that it should have been located by the filing officer and should not thereafter have misled the searcher. [119]

The same basic standard is applied in determining whether the use of a trade name in lieu of the proper designation of the debtor's individual, partnership, or corporate name should nevertheless suffice as not seriously misleading. [120] Many courts will save the trade name filing when that name and the debtor's correct name are substantially similar. [121] These decisions are debatable in that they do not consider whether the search protocol adopted by the relevant filing office would have revealed the erroneous financing statement during a search using the correct name. The concern again is that a searcher using the correct name should be advised of the existence of the filed statement and should

---

[116] U.C.C. § R9-506 Cmt. 2.

[117] Whether a filing is likely to be found by a prudent searcher is an issue of fact that turns largely on the search protocol adopted by the particular filing office. Searchers today do not typically access the files themselves, although such a practice may develop as the files become more computerized. Instead, the searcher submits a request and relies on the filing office to provide information within the parameters of the request. *See* U.C.C. §§ 9-407(optional provision on obtaining information from filing officer), **R9-523.**

[118] *In re* Arnold, 21 U.C.C. Rep. Serv. 1479 (W.D. Mich. 1977). *See also In re* Leichter, 471 F.2d 785, 11 U.C.C. Rep. Serv. 673 (2d Cir. 1972) (financing statement stating the debtor's name as "Landman Dry Cleaners" was ineffective when debtor's name was Leichter).

[119] *In re* Excel Stores, Inc., 341 F.2d 961, 2 U.C.C. Rep. Serv. 316 (2d Cir. 1965). *See also In re* A & T Kwik-N-Handi, Inc., 12 U.C.C. Rep. Serv. 765 (Bankr. M.D. Ga. 1973) (omission of "Inc." from correctly-indexed financing statement was not fatal).

[120] The trade name is not the correct name to use for the debtor. *See* § 5.02[A][1] *supra.*

[121] *In re* Maples, 33 B.R. 14, 37 U.C.C. Rep. Serv. 351 (Bankr. W.D. Mo. 1983) (trade name was "Maples Machine Shop and Welding" and the individual proprietors were Loren and Grace Maples).

then be able to recognize that it applies to the person whose record is being searched. Computerized filing systems have raised new concerns with respect to the determination of whether an error in the debtor's name is seriously misleading. Even a slight error has been held to be seriously misleading when the computerized search logic utilized by the filing office can make only an exact match. [122]

Courts must, of course, consider whether reasonable prudence requires the searcher to look for names that are substantially similar to the debtor's correct name. In *In re Thriftway Auto Supply, Inc.*, [123] the correct corporate name was "Thriftway Auto Supply, Inc." but the secured party filed under the trade name "Thriftway Auto Stores." The bankruptcy court upheld the filing as valid against a subsequent creditor who ran a computerized search based on the corporate name and did not find the filed financing statement. It believed that the searcher should have conducted a search using the broader roots of the debtor's name. By searching under "Thriftway" or "Thriftway Auto," the subsequent creditor would have found the prior filing. Increased computerization of filing systems surely will generate more cases concerning the reasonableness of search requests. Outcomes will likely be determined in part by the search capabilities of the system itself. [124]

Because of the critical role that a debtor's name plays in the indexing of a financing statement, the revision expands on the legal standard for determining the effect of an error in stating the debtor's name. The default rule is that a financing statement that fails to provide the debtor's name as required in section R9-503(a) is seriously misleading. [125] An exception, however, provides that the failure of the secured party to comply with that section does not render the financing statement seriously misleading if a search under the correct name using the standard search logic of the filing office would nevertheless disclose the financing statement. [126] This rule will result in considerable differences among jurisdictions in the near-term future, as the search standard still varies considerably among filing offices with computerized systems. The rule, however, properly allocates to the filer the risk of mistake.

Even if an error in the preparation of a financing statement is considered to be a minor error that is not seriously misleading, a court will not necessarily uphold the effectiveness of the filing. In the 1972 text the standard for effectiveness of such filings applies only

---

[122] *In re* Wardcorp, Inc., 133 B.R. 210, 16 U.C.C. Rep. Serv. 2d 1242 (Bankr. S.D. Ind. 1990) (correct name was "Wardcorp, Inc." but filing was under "Ward Corporation, Inc."); *In re* McGovern Auto Specialty, Inc., 51 B.R. 511, 41 U.C.C. Rep. Serv. 1101 (Bankr. E.D. Pa. 1985) (correct name was "McGovern Auto Specialty, Inc." but filing was under "McGovern Auto & Truck Parts, Inc.").

[123] 156 B.R. 300, 21 U.C.C. Rep. Serv. 2d 377 (Bankr. W.D. Okla. 1993).

[124] In a questionable outcome, the court in *In re* Esparza, 118 Wash. 2d 251, 821 P.2d 1216, 16 U.C.C. Rep. Serv. 2d 1217 (1992), upheld a filing under "Esparsa" for a debtor named "Esparza" on the grounds that the pronunciation of the two names is similar. Unless the computer is programmed to match similar sounding names, the reasoning of the decision does not seem justified.

[125] U.C.C § R9-506(b). **For discussion of the requirements of § R9-503(a), *see* § 5.02[A][1] *supra*.**

[126] U.C.C. § R9-506(c).

to a "financing statement substantially complying with the requirements of [section 9-402]." [127] This requirement is likely to be violated if any of the formal requisites of a financing statement is completely omitted. [128] For example, a financing statement that does not include the signature of the debtor should fail, even if searchers are not misled because the correct name of the debtor is included. [129] The signature requirement serves verification and control functions that go beyond mere identification of the purported debtor. [130] Although the drafters clearly sought to free the law of secured transactions from the restrictive procedural requirements that plagued prior law, they did consider the basic requirements for a financing statement to be indispensable. [131] They predictably would have had little patience for the complete omission of one of the few requisites for such a simple form. **By contrast, the revision's savings provision explicitly extends to both errors and omissions.** [132]

The revision also provides a nonjudicial method for a debtor to correct a financing statement that contains errors or that was wrongfully filed. [133] **The debtor can file a record that indicates that it is a correction statement and states the debtor's basis for believing that there is an error or a wrongful filing. The correction statement must also indicate any way in which the financing statement can be amended to eliminate the error. The correction statement becomes part of the financing statement** [134] **but does not negate its effectiveness.** [135]

The seriously-misleading standard in the 1972 text applies explicitly only to financing statements. [136] **In the revision, "financing statement" includes "any filed record relating to the initial financing statement"** [137] **and the first record filed is referred to as the initial financing statement. Through this mechanism, the seriously-misleading standard is made applicable to initial financing statements, amendments, continuation statements, termination statements and the like.**

---

[127] U.C.C. § 9-402(8).

[128] The total omission of a description of the collateral has not been upheld. Most cases have treated similarly the omission of the debtor's or the secured party's address. *In re* L & K Transp. Co., 8 B.R. 921, 30 U.C.C. Rep. Serv. 1745 (D. Mass. 1981) (debtor's address omitted). *But see* Rooney v. Mason, 394 F.2d 250, 5 U.C.C. Rep. Serv. 308 (10th Cir. 1968) (despite omission of both addresses, filing was upheld because addresses were readily available and known by virtually all creditors). The omission of a secured party's name has been held fatal. *In re* Copper King Inn, Inc., 918 F.2d 1404, 12 U.C.C. Rep. Serv. 2d 1155 (9th Cir. 1990).

[129] *In re* Joyce, 52 B.R. 45, 41 U.C.C. Rep. Serv. 1031 (Bankr. S.D. Ohio 1985) (financing statement not signed by wife as one of joint debtors was not effective).

[130] *See* § 5.02[A][1] *supra.*

[131] The title to section 9-402 is, in part, "Formal Requisites of Financing Statement."

[132] **U.C.C. § R9-506(a).**

[133] **U.C.C. § R9-518.**

[134] **U.C.C. § R9-102(a)(39).**

[135] **U.C.C. § R9-518(c).**

[136] The term "financing statement" in the 1972 text explicitly includes only the original financing statement and any amendments. U.C.C. § 9-402(4).

[137] **U.C.C. § R9-102(a)(39).**

[2] Name Changes and Transfers of Collateral — §§ 9-402(7), R9-507, R9-508

Even if a financing statement does not include any errors in its preparation, changes might occur after filing that can mislead subsequent searchers. The general rule under the 1972 text is that such changes do not render a properly completed, properly filed financing statement ineffective.[138] There is an exception, however, for changes in the debtor's name, identity or corporate structure. Section 9-402(7) provides:

> Where the debtor so changes his name or in the case of an organization its name, identity or corporate structure that a filed financing statement becomes seriously misleading, the filing is not effective to perfect a security interest in collateral acquired by the debtor more than four months after the change, unless a new appropriate financing statement is filed before the expiration of that time.[139]

A change in the name of the debtor has a limited impact on the effectiveness of a properly prepared financing statement.[140] The original filing continues to perfect the security interest with respect to all of the collateral acquired by the debtor prior to the change. Furthermore, the original filing remains effective to perfect the security interest in collateral acquired during the four months following the change, even if the secured party does not file a new financing statement under the debtor's new name.[141] Thus, the secured party needs to file a financing statement under the debtor's new name only to perfect its security interest in collateral acquired by the debtor more than four months following the change,[142] and then only if the name change has rendered the original financing statement "seriously misleading."[143] This four-month grace period allows the

---

[138] *See* U.C.C. §§ 9-401(3), **R9-507(b)**, discussed in § 5.04[C] *infra.*

[139] U.C.C. § 9-402(7). An amendment to a financing statement, *see* U.C.C. § 9-402(4), has been held to qualify as a "new appropriate financing statement" for purposes of § 9-402(7). Pennsylvania Record Outlet, Inc. v. Mellon Bank, 894 F.2d 631, 10 U.C.C. Rep. Serv. 2d 673 (3d Cir. 1990).

[140] The change in the debtor's name refers to the name of the individual, the partnership, or the corporation, as required in Article 9. *See* U.C.C. § 9-402(7). A change in the trade name of a debtor will not trigger the name-change provision when the secured party has filed under the proper name. *In re* Miraglia, 11 B.R. 77, 31 U.C.C. Rep. Serv. 1196 (Bankr. W.D.N.Y. 1981) (debtor's change of trade name from "Louie's Deli" to "Pizza Pit" held irrelevant because financing statement was in name of individual proprietor).

[141] Fleet Factors Corp. v. Bandolene Indus. Corp., 86 N.Y.2d 519, 658 N.E.2d 202, 634 N.Y.S. 2d 425, 27 U.C.C. Rep. Serv. 2d 1105 (1995) (amended financing statement not required with respect to assets acquired by debtor six weeks after changing its name).

[142] *In re* Cohuta Mills, Inc., 108 B.R. 815, 11 U.C.C. Rep. Serv. 2d 338 (N.D. Ga. 1989) (failure to file in name of new corporation within four months of its creation left secured party unperfected with respect to all collateral acquired after the grace period).

[143] U.C.C. § 9-402(7). This standard is identical to the standard for determination of the effect of errors in the initial preparation of financing statements. *See, e.g.,* Union Nat'l Bank of Chandler v. Bancfirst (Seminole), 871 P.2d 422, 22 U.C.C. Rep. Serv. 2d 347 (Okla. 1993) (change from "Webb Metals, Inc." to "Webb Expanded, Inc." in corporate restructuring held not seriously misleading because names are linguistically similar); First Agri. Servs., Inc. v. Kahl, 129 Wis.2d 464, 385 N.W.2d 191, 42 U.C.C. Rep. Serv. 1583 (Ct. App. 1986) (financing statement listing debtor as "Gary and Dale Kahl" held seriously misleading when debtors began operating their farm as a partnership under the name "Kahl Farms" and filing officer had separate indexes for individual and organizational debtors).

secured party to check on the debtor's name and identity on a periodic basis without having to monitor the debtor constantly.

Assume, for example, that a bank has a perfected security interest in all the debtor's present and after-acquired inventory. On June 1, the debtor's name changes in a manner that renders the bank's financing statement seriously misleading. The bank does not refile under the new name during the four-month grace period. On October 1, a finance company takes a competing security interest in the debtor's inventory. Despite its failure to refile, the bank will be perfected, and will thus have priority over the finance company,[144] as to all inventory on hand at the time of the name change and all inventory acquired during the next four months. It will be unperfected and subordinate to the finance company as to all inventory acquired after the expiration of the grace period. If the bank refiles under the new name *after* the expiration of the grace period, it will be perfected as to new inventory acquired thereafter but will remain subordinate to the finance company as to that new inventory.

The practical implications for parties conducting searches of financing statements are that it behooves them to know any prior names the debtor may have used. Otherwise, a search under the debtor's current name may not reveal an effective financing statement. Because many secured parties do not look to after-acquired property for their collateralization, their interests will be unaffected by changes in the debtor's name. This is true even though their financing statements can seriously mislead subsequent searchers. The secured parties who most commonly look to after-acquired property, and who thus should be the most concerned with the refiling requirement, are financers against inventory or accounts.

Like the 1972 text, the general rule in the revision is that a financing statement is not rendered ineffective if the information becomes inaccurate and even seriously misleading after filing.[145] An exception for name changes reflects the same basic approach as that taken in section 9-402(7) of the 1972 text.[146] Thus, the initial filing continues to perfect with respect to the original collateral and after-acquired collateral acquired by the debtor within four months after the name change. If the name change would be seriously misleading,[147] an amendment must be filed within four months after the change in order for the financing statement to be effective to perfect a security interest in collateral acquired more than four months after the name change. The prior Article 9 provision is clarified by providing that the amendment will be sufficient if it either provides the debtor's new correct name or otherwise renders the financing statement not seriously misleading.[148]

---

[144] Priority contests between secured parties are discussed in detail in Chapter 10.

[145] **U.C.C. § R9-507(b). For the consequences of filing a financing statement that contains incorrect information at the time that it is filed, *see* U.C.C. § R9-338 and the discussion at § 5.02[C][1] *supra.***

[146] U.C.C. § R9-507(c).

[147] **The standard used for "seriously misleading" is the standard provided in U.C.C. § R9-506.** *See* § 5.02[C][1] *supra.*

[148] U.C.C. § R9-507(c)(2).

The reference in section 9-402(7) to changes in identity or corporate structure has generated a great deal of confusion because it overlaps with a related issue. When the debtor transfers collateral subject to a perfected security interest, does it remain subject to the security interest and, if so, does that interest remain perfected? The general rule on continuation, expressed in section 9-306(2) of the 1972 text, is that a security interest, whether or not perfected, continues in collateral notwithstanding its disposition by the debtor unless the secured party authorized the disposition or a provision of Article 9 dictates a contrary result. The general rule on perfection of such an interest, expressed in section 9-402(7), is that a filed financing statement remains effective notwithstanding a transfer by the debtor. This rule follows even though the secured party knows of or consents to the transfer.[149]

For example, suppose Bank takes and perfects by filing a security interest in Debtor's present and after-acquired equipment. Debtor later sells an item of equipment to Buyer. Bank consents to the sale on condition that its security interest remain enforceable against the item. Bank does not refile in the name of Buyer. Buyer later resells the equipment to Purchaser. In a subsequent priority contest, Bank's original filing in Debtor's name perfects its interest as against Purchaser. Note one other consequence of Debtor's transfer to Buyer. If Buyer acquires more equipment after it buys the item from Debtor, the new equipment will not be subject to Bank's security interest. The reason for this result is that Buyer is not bound by the after-acquired property clause agreed to by Debtor.

The interpretive problems inherent in the 1972 text are well illustrated by *In re Scott*,[150] where a bank properly perfected a security interest in the present and after-acquired inventory of Shannon and Patricia Scott by filing in their individual names. The Scotts subsequently incorporated as "K.C. of Camden, Inc." and transferred all their business-related assets, including inventory, to the corporation. Subsequently the corporation granted a security interest to a finance company, which properly filed under the corporate name. If the establishment of the corporation was the equivalent of a name change and the corporation was bound by the after-acquired property clause in the bank's security agreement, the bank's filing in the Scotts' names would have perfected it as to all inventory on hand at the time of the transfer to the corporation and all inventory acquired by the corporation during the next four months. The bank would have an unperfected security interest in inventory acquired by the corporation after the expiration of the four-month grace period. If, in contrast, the corporation was a new entity not bound by the bank's after-acquired property clause, the bank would have a perfected security interest in all inventory transferred by the Scotts but would not have *any* security interest in inventory acquired by the corporation.

The court in *Scott* concluded that the incorporation had produced a new entity that was not bound by the bank's agreement with the Scotts. In other words, the court concluded that the transfer from the Scotts to the corporation fell within the third sentence

---

[149] The apparent discrepancy between U.C.C. §§ 9-306(2) and 9-402(7) with regard to consent by the secured party is discussed in § 11.02 *infra.* In short, § 9-306(2) refers to consent to transfer the collateral *free from* the security interest, while § 9-402(7) refers to consent to transfer the collateral *subject to* the security interest.

[150] 113 B.R. 516, 11 U.C.C. Rep. Serv. 2d 670 (Bankr. W.D. Ark. 1990).

of section 9-402(7). Other courts have concluded that the incorporation of a sole proprietorship creates an entity that is the alter-ego of its predecessor and that the secured party's interests are governed by the second sentence of section 9-402(7).[151]

The uncertainty created by section 9-402(7) is resolved in the 1998 text. The revision continues the rule that a filed financing statement remains effective with respect to collateral transferred by the debtor even if the secured party knows of or consents to the transfer.[152] Whether the transferee is bound by the terms of the existing security agreement turns on whether it is a "new debtor." A new debtor[153] is a person that is bound by the terms of the security agreement entered into by the original debtor.[154] Whether a transferee is a new debtor is determined by section R9-203(d), which states:

A person becomes bound as debtor by a security agreement entered into by another person if, by operation of law other than this article or by contract: 1) the security agreement becomes effective to create a security interest in the person's property; or 2) the person becomes generally obligated for the obligations of the other person, including the obligation secured under the security agreement, and acquires or succeeds to all or substantially all of the assets of the other person.

Whether a person becomes bound as a new debtor is thus determined by law other than Article 9, primarily the law of contracts and business organizations. For example, if the corporation in *Scott* had agreed to assume the contractual obligations of the Scotts, it would have qualified as a new debtor. The same result often obtains under the laws governing the merger of corporate entities. If a person becomes bound as a new debtor, a new security agreement is not necessary to make the terms of the original agreement enforceable against it. Finally, if the difference between the name of the original debtor and the name of the new debtor is sufficient to render a filing seriously misleading, the filing is effective as to the collateral transferred[155] and any new collateral acquired during the four months after the new debtor becomes bound.[156] The secured party is unperfected, however, as to new collateral acquired after the expiration of the four-month grace period unless it files an initial financing statement in the name of the new debtor.[157]

[D] Single Writing for Two Functions

Many secured transactions entered into under the 1972 text use two separate writings: 1) a written security agreement that meets the requirements of section 9-203(1)(a) for

---

[151] *See, e.g.*, Bank of the West. v. Commercial Credit Fin. Servs., Inc., 852 F.2d 1162, 6 U.C.C. Rep. Serv. 602 (9th Cir. 1988).

[152] U.C.C. § R9-507(a).

[153] U.C.C. § R9-102(a)(56).

[154] U.C.C. § R9-102(a)(60).

[155] U.C.C. §§ R9-508(c), R9-507(a).

[156] U.C.C. § R9-508(b)(1).

[157] U.C.C. § R9-508(b)(2).

attachment and statute-of-frauds purposes,[158] and 2) a financing statement that complies with section 9-402.[159] Security agreements are often lengthy because they include provisions that go far beyond the minimum requirements for attachment. A filed financing statement, in contrast, is generally a simple form that follows the model provided in section 9-402(3). The use of the simple form for a financing statement usually is efficient. The limited basic information that is required facilitates the practice of filing a financing statement even before creation of the security interest. Filing fees that are based on the number of pages and whether or not the financing statement is in a standard prescribed form also create an incentive to keep filings simple.

The question sometimes arises whether one of these writings can serve both functions. The 1972 text provides a clear answer to at least part of this question. It provides that "[a] copy of the security agreement is sufficient as a financing statement if it contains the information required in section 9-402(1) and is signed by the debtor."[160] The only information required for a financing statement that is not also mandated in a written security agreement is the names of the parties, the address of the secured party, and the mailing address of the debtor. If the security agreement is drafted to include this additional information, the security agreement itself can be filed to serve as the financing statement.

Substantial litigation has resulted because the 1972 text does not explicitly state that the converse approach to the single-writing issue can also be effective. The question that is not answered directly is whether a financing statement that meets the requirements of section 9-402(1) can also serve as an enforceable security agreement.

The court's decision in *Evans v. Everett*[161] is instructive. The *Evans* court stated that "[a] financing statement which does no more than meet the requirements of section 9-402 will *not* create a security interest in the debtor's property."[162] The court considered the basic financing statement to be insufficient because it did not create or provide for a security interest. The financing statement before the court, however, contained more than the basic requirements of section 9-402, stating that it *"covers the following type of collateral: (all crops now growing or to be planted on 5 specified farms) same securing note for advanced money to produce crops for the year 1969."*[163] This additional language was held sufficient to show that the debtor provided for a security interest in the plaintiff.[164]

---

[158] *See* § 2.02 *supra.*

[159] *See* § 5.02[A] *supra.*

[160] U.C.C. § 9-402(1). **This provision is deleted in the revision to Article 9 as both unnecessary and unwise. U.C.C. § R9-502 Cmt. 4.**

[161] 279 N.C. 352, 183 S.E.2d 109, 9 U.C.C. Rep. Serv. 769 (1971).

[162] 183 S.E.2d at 113, 9 U.C.C. Rep. Serv. at 774 (emphasis supplied).

[163] 183 S.E.2d at 114, 9 U.C.C. Rep. Serv. at 775 (emphasis supplied). The debtor had also signed a promissory note that contained a statement that it "is secured by Uniform Commercial Code financing statement of North Carolina." *Id.*

[164] The courts have been virtually unanimous in holding that a financing statement that does not create or provide for a security interest cannot qualify as a security agreement. *See, e.g., In re* Arctic Air, Inc., 202 B.R. 533, 31 U.C.C. Rep. Serv. 2d 233 (Bankr. D.R.I. 1996). Prof. Grant Gilmore, a principal drafter of the original version of Article 9, disagreed, arguing that "nothing

Although the 1972 text does not state explicitly that a financing statement that satisfies the requirements of section 9-402 can also serve as a security agreement, such a result is implicit. As noted above, the 1972 text does provide that a security agreement can be filed as a financing statement if it includes all of the information required for a financing statement.[165] Conversely, an effective financing statement that creates or provides for a security interest qualifies *a fortiori* as an enforceable security agreement because it complies with section 9-203(1)(a). Such a financing statement is effective as a security agreement even if it is not filed.

§ 5.03 When to File — §§ 9-402(1), R9-502(d)

One caveat on the timing of filing is readily apparent. A secured party perfects to enhance its position versus other potential, competing claimants against the debtor's property. It is, therefore, in the secured party's interest to file sooner rather than later because, as a general proposition, the secured party will defeat most claimants whose interests arise after perfection, but will be subordinate to most preceding claims. This ranking of competing claimants is the concept of priorities, which is covered in great detail in subsequent chapters. Nevertheless, the basic importance of perfecting promptly is easy to grasp. Delay in perfection simply leaves the secured party vulnerable to competing interests that arise during the period of delay.

A logical assumption is that parties would first create a security interest through a written security agreement and the secured party would then perfect that interest by filing a financing statement. The logic stems from the fact that you cannot perfect an interest that has not yet attached.[166] As is often the case with Article 9, however, inherent logic is not always reliable.

A specific rule of priority affects the issue of the timing of perfection in another, less obvious way. This rule affords a significant priority advantage to a secured party who files a financing statement even before taking the security interest.[167] The explanation of this advantage and the other priority rules would be premature at this point in the discussion, and is therefore reserved for proper development in a subsequent chapter.[168]

For now, the focus is simply on the question of when to file a financing statement. Based upon recognition of the potential priority advantage, Article 9 specifically authorizes early filing: "A financing statement may be filed before a security agreement is made or a security interest otherwise attaches."[169] Knowing about the priority advantage and the risks that it can help eliminate, lenders often require a prospective

---

in § 9-203 requires that the 'security agreement' contain a granting clause." 1 G. Gilmore, *Security Interests in Personal Property*, § 11.4, at 347 (1965). For a case that relies on Prof. Gilmore's analysis to conclude that a financing statement qualifies as a security agreement if extrinsic evidence shows that the parties so intended, *see* Gibson County Farm Bureau Co-op Ass'n v. Greer, 643 N.E.2d 313, 25 U.C.C. Rep. Serv. 2d 954 (Ind. 1994). *See also* § 2.02[A] *supra.*

[165] U.C.C. § 9-402(1).

[166] U.C.C. § 9-303(1). *See* § 3.03 *supra.*

[167] U.C.C. §§ 9-312(5), **R9-322(a)(1)**.

[168] See § 10.01 *infra.*

[169] U.C.C. §§9-402(1), **R9-502(d)**.

debtor to sign a financing statement as a precondition to continuing the negotiations on the secured transaction. The lender then promptly files the signed financing statement in order to optimize its position.

§ 5.04 Where to File — §§ 9-401, R9-501

[A] Central versus Local Filing

A financing statement must be filed in the appropriate office to be effective. Interested parties are likely to search the files only in the office designated in Article 9 as the place for financing statements covering particular types of collateral to be filed. A filing in any other office simply cannot meet the notice function which perfection by filing is intended to advance.[170]

Because Article 9 is state law, its provisions that designate the office in which to file refer to offices within the borders of the state.[171] Some secured transactions can involve contacts with more than one state, however, when the collateral or the debtor move from one state to another. Multiple-state contacts can raise a choice-of-law issue that is addressed by other Article 9 provisions that determine the state in which to file initially and the effect of subsequent moves to another state.[172] The choice-of-law provisions are explained in a subsequent chapter.[173] The focus now is on the choices that confront a secured party who wants to file a financing statement once the appropriate state has been determined.

The choice is between filing at the local level or at the state level.[174] Historically, states have differed on the geographical unit for filing purposes. The desirability of central versus local filing often depends on the perspective of the party conducting a search. The Comments to the 1972 text include a good illustration of when central filing is advantageous:

> Consider for example the national distributor who wishes to have current information about the credit standing of the thousands of persons he sells to on credit. The more completely the files are centralized on a state-wide basis, the easier and cheaper it becomes to procure credit information; the more the files are scattered in local filing units, the more burdensome and costly.[175]

For financing conducted on the local level, however, it has been assumed that the local availability of the files facilitated searches. The validity of that proposition was doubtful in 1972, and it is clearly outdated today. With the advent of computerized systems capable of handling massive quantities of information, it is inevitable that there will be more and more movement toward centralized filing. Some states already permit electronic filing

---

[170] See § 5.02[B] supra.

[171] This point is made clear in the revision. U.C.C. § R9-501(a).

[172] See U.C.C. §§ 9-103; R9-301 – R9-307.

[173] See Chapter 9 infra.

[174] The revision eliminates this distinction. See § 5.04[B][1] infra.

[175] U.C.C. § 9-401 Cmt. 1.

in a centralized data bank, and others are moving in that direction.[176] **The 1998 text recognizes this trend and provides for local filing only when the collateral is closely associated with real property.** The trend ultimately may culminate with a single national (or international) system in which searchers can search a single data bank from their desks and filers can make effective filings with the push of a button.

[B] Alternatives

Although uniformity among the state enactments of the Code was one of the objectives of the drafters,[177] they could not attain it with respect to the choices between central and local filing. The previously existing approaches varied considerably among the states, and local officials often were reluctant to lose their influence over transactions which they traditionally handled and from which they received income in the form of filing fees. Rather than risk the unwillingness of states to enact Article 9, the drafters of the 1972 text prepared three alternatives from which the states could choose and deferred to local policies to determine the choice between central and local filing.[178]

The Alternatives are set forth in section 9-401. Each progression from the First Alternative involves incorporating the previous alternative and drawing additional distinctions. Each alternative also allows the states to determine the specific governmental offices in which the filing system will be located. Local filing generally is tied to an office in the county courthouse. Central filing is predominantly in the office of the Secretary of State.

A filing made in an improper place (or in less than all the required places) can still have some limited effectiveness, provided it is made in good faith.[179] The appropriateness of local or central filing is based on the type of collateral involved. Even though a filing is ineffective with respect to some of the described collateral, it is nevertheless effective for any collateral for which the filing is appropriate. Furthermore, the Code has an estoppel-based rule that renders a filed financing statement effective against any person who has knowledge of its contents.[180]

Knowledge of the filing of a financing statement is not enough for notice by estoppel.[181] Actual knowledge[182] of the *contents* of the financing statement is required.

---

[176] For a detailed survey as of 1991, *see* Report of the PEB Study Group, Uniform Commercial Code Article 9, Appendix B (Report of the Filing System Task Force). A significant increase in electronic filing has been realized since the report was issued.

[177] U.C.C. § 1-102(2)(c).

[178] U.C.C. § 9-401 Cmt. 1.

[179] U.C.C. § 9-401(2).

[180] First Nat'l Bank of Glasgow v. First Security Bank of Mont., N.A., 222 Mont. 118, 721 P.2d 1270, 1 U.C.C. Rep. Serv. 2d 1745 (1986) (debtor informed subsequent bank about earlier transaction with another bank); State of Mo. v. Kerr, 509 S.W.2d 61, 14 U.C.C. Rep. Serv. 844 (Mo. 1974) (holding that, prior to filing tax lien, local sales tax representative had knowledge of contents of filed financing statement).

[181] Citizens State Bank v. Peoples Bank, 475 N.E.2d 324, 40 U.C.C. Rep. Serv. 1549 (Ind. Ct. App. 1985) (defendant's awareness that plaintiff claimed security interest in collateral held not sufficient).

For example, suppose a bank in a state that has adopted the Second Alternative incorrectly files as to inventory in a local office in the county of the debtor's residence.[183] Suppose further that a searcher contemplating a security interest in the debtor's inventory learns of the local filing but does not obtain a copy of the financing statement. The searcher is justified in concluding that the filing does not cover inventory and ought not be estopped. If, however, the searcher knows of the contents of the local filing and is therefore aware of the bank's error, it would be unjust for it to be allowed to take advantage of the error.

The revision eliminates the alternatives available to the states on the places in which to file a financing statement. The provision on filing offices follows the approach provided in the First Alternative to the 1972 text and is discussed further in the ensuing subsection.

[1]   First Alternative

Under the First Alternative, central filing encompasses the vast bulk of Article 9 filings. The alternative contains a residual provision that requires all filings, other than the relatively infrequent transactions otherwise specified, to be made centrally.[184] The specified transactions that are excluded from central filing are based on the types of collateral involved. The following categories of collateral are excluded: 1) timber to be cut; 2) minerals or the like (including gas and oil); 3) accounts resulting from the sale of minerals or the like (including gas and oil) at the wellhead or minehead; and 4) "fixture filings" as to goods that are or are to become fixtures.[185]

For convenience, the excluded categories can be designated as real-estate-related collateral. Each of the categories of collateral is closely related to real estate and to interests associated with affected real estate. For example, whether the security interest is in minerals to be extracted from the ground or in accounts that arise immediately upon their extraction, a secured party's claim to such collateral will very likely conflict with third-party claims to an interest in those same minerals and accounts through a real property interest. These categories are excluded from the predominant central-filing approach of the First Alternative because of their strong nexus to affected real estate.

Filings for transactions involving the four categories of real-estate-related collateral are made locally. The filing is in "the office where a mortgage on the real estate would be filed or recorded."[186] In other words, the filing for these categories is made in the office where real estate mortgages and liens are recorded. That office is most likely to be in the county in which the affected real property is located. A separate filing system for personal property is not maintained locally under the First Alternative. Because of

---

[182] U.C.C. § 1-201(25)("knowledge" means actual knowledge). *See also In re* Mistura, Inc., 705 F.2d 1496, 36 U.C.C. Rep. Serv. 329 (9th Cir. 1983) (Arizona courts would follow lines of cases requiring actual knowledge).

[183] Under the Second Alternative, inventory filings are made centrally and consumer-goods filings are made locally.

[184] U.C.C. § 9-401(1)(b)(1st Alt.) ("in all other cases").

[185] U.C.C. § 9-401(1)(a)(lst Alt.). Fixture filings are discussed in § 15.02 *infra.*

[186] U.C.C. § 9-401(1)(a)(1st Alt.).

the high probability of competing real estate claimants with respect to a secured transaction utilizing real-estate-related collateral, the filing with respect to such collateral is consolidated in the real estate filing system to provide effective and comprehensive notice to parties with concerns about any affected real estate interests.

The revision follows the approach of the First Alternative. The office designated for filing or recording a mortgage on real property is the appropriate office in which to file with respect to timber to be cut or as-extracted collateral, as well as for a fixture filing for goods that are or are to become fixtures.[187] In all other cases, central filing is required.[188]

The elimination of most local filing is based on the greater ease in modern-day transactions of attaining access to centrally filed records. Increased use of electronic technologies means that many records can be accessed from distant locations. Private companies also provide search services that are fast and efficient by obtaining filing information from official records and by maintaining their own filing systems.[189] The revision represents the loss of a significant source of revenue to local government offices that have relied upon these fees. Predictably, they may be active in resisting such extensive central filing.

[2]   Second Alternative

The final two subsections of the 1972 text's Second Alternative state word-for-word the same bifurcation as in the First Alternative.[190] The difference, however, is that the scope of the Second Alternative's central-filing residual provision is narrowed by the addition of a further designation of security interests that must be filed locally in a filing system separate from the real estate recordation system. To distinguish it from the real estate filing system, this additional local system is often referred to as the "chattel-filing system."

The Second Alternative designates property to be filed in this chattel-filing system based on the type of collateral described in the financing statement. The types of collateral subject to this local filing are: 1) equipment used in farming operations;[191] 2) farm

---

[187] U.C.C. § R9-501(a)(1).

[188] U.C.C. § R9-501(a)(2).

[189] U.C.C. § R9-523(f).

[190] U.C.C. § 9-401(1)(b),(c)(2d Alt.).

[191] The courts have devised three tests to determine when goods qualify as "equipment used in farming operations." Konkel v. Golden Plains Credit Union, 778 P.2d 660, 9 U.C.C. Rep. Serv. 2d 278 (Colo. 1989). The "intended use test" focuses on the use that the debtor intends for the goods at the time of attachment. *In re* Butcher, 43 B.R. 513, 39 U.C.C. Rep. Serv. 345 (Bankr. E.D. Tenn. 1984) (intention to syndicate stallion as investment marketing scheme did not constitute farming operation). The "actual use test" is based upon the actual use to which the goods are applied. *In re* Rahberg Farms, Inc., 8 B.R. 244, 31 U.C.C. Rep. Serv. 332 (Bankr. W.D. Wis. 1981) (although capable of being used in farming operations, skid loader was used by debtor in logging and trucking activities unrelated to farming operations). This test has the disadvantage of not being applicable until the debtor has made some use of the collateral. The "normal use test" identifies equipment that is normally used for farming, irrespective of whether the debtor is a farmer or of the actual use of the equipment. Sequoia Mach., Inc. v. Jarrett, 410 F.2d 1116, 6 U.C.C. Rep. Serv. 476

products;[192] 3) accounts or general intangibles that arise from or are related to the sale of farm products by a farmer;[193] and 4) consumer goods.[194]

These categories of collateral are specified for local filing because, in most instances, the financing that they secure is effected locally.[195] Most farm-related financing is through a local bank or the local office of a federal lender. Consumer financing is also conducted locally. Transactions in which the debtor goes outside of the local county to obtain financing for these types of collateral have been relatively rare.[196] States that have adopted local financing for these forms of collateral have predicated their choice on the convenience associated with having the files available locally.[197]

When local filing is required, the secured party must be careful to select the correct local office. The general rule stated in the Second Alternative is that the proper place to file is in the county of the debtor's residence.[198] In the event that the debtor is not a resident of the state but the Code's choice-of-law rules dictate filing within the state, local filing is to be in the county where the goods are kept. For local filing purposes, the residency of a corporate debtor or other organizational debtor is considered to be its place of business, and if it has more than one place of business, its chief executive office.[199]

When the collateral consists of crops growing or to be grown, a filing must also be made in the office of the county in which the land is located.[200] This further requirement for crops will require filing in two counties only when the land used to grow the crops is in one county and the debtor's residence is in another county. Note that the local filing with respect to crops is in the chattel-filing system, not in the real estate records.[201]

(9th Cir. 1969) (combines used by custom harvester who was not farmer and owned no land but rather harvested crops for a fee were classified as equipment used in farming operations because they were useable only to harvest grain). The courts have held consistently that equipment used in logging operations does not constitute equipment used in farming operations. Belgrade State Bank v. Elder, 157 Mont. 1, 482 P.2d 135, 8 U.C.C. Rep. Serv. 1359 (1971).

[192] Swift & Co. v. Jamestown Nat'l Bank, 426 F.2d 1099, 7 U.C.C. Rep. Serv. 788 (8th Cir. 1970) (central filing ineffective because local filing was required).

[193] Arizona Ammonia of Tucson, Inc. v. Mission Bank, 152 Ariz. 361, 732 P.2d 591, 2 U.C.C. Rep. Serv. 2d 1722 (Ct. App. 1986).

[194] U.C.C. § 9-401(1)(a)(2d Alt.).

[195] U.C.C. § 9-401 Cmt. 1; In re Roy, 21 U.C.C. Rep. Serv. 325 (Bankr. N.D. Ala. 1977) (local filing to perfect security interest in consumer goods is based on convenience).

[196] The local filing option is available for "states where it is felt wise to preserve local filing for transactions of essentially local interest." U.C.C. § 9-401 Cmt. 3.

[197] U.C.C. § 9-401 Cmt. 1.

[198] Wolinsky v. Bradford Nat'l Bank, 34 B.R. 702, 37 U.C.C. Rep. Serv. 609 (D. Vt. 1983) (residence defined as place in which debtor is living at time of filing).

[199] U.C.C. § 9-401(6); Farmers Bank v. First-Citizens Nat'l Bank, 39 U.C.C. Rep. Serv. 355 (Tenn. Ct. App. 1983) (filing in county where individual partners personally resided held ineffective).

[200] Lawhon Farm Supply, Inc. v. Hayes, 316 Ark. 69, 870 S.W.2d 729, 23 U.C.C. Rep. Serv. 2d 290 (1994) (attempt to perfect ineffectual because filings were not made in both locations).

[201] In re Hill, 83 B.R. 522, 6 U.C.C. Rep. Serv. 2d 193 (Bankr. E.D. Tenn. 1988) (recording of mortgage is not perfection as to crops).

The drafters followed pre-Code law, thereby continuing filing in locations where creditors would normally conduct a search.[202]

[3] Third Alternative

The Third Alternative is exactly like the Second Alternative, except that a dual filing requirement is added to the residual provision. In addition to filing centrally under the residual provision, the secured party often is also required to make an additional local filing.[203] The secured party must make this additional local filing in the office of the debtor's place of business if the debtor has a place of business in only one county in the state.[204] If the debtor does not have any place of business in the state but resides in the state, the additional filing is required in the county in which the debtor resides.

The dual-filing requirement is intended to make centrally-filed financing statements also available at the local level, at least in circumstances in which the dual filing would not be a significant additional burden. The additional filings could become more difficult if the debtor maintained several places of business throughout the state. The local filing thus is required only in the designated circumstances, which means that only one local filing would be required in addition to the central filing.[205] When the debtor maintains places of business in more than one county, no local filing is required.

The courts have had to wrestle with the issue of what constitutes a place of business for the purpose of the dual filing requirement.[206] Most courts have adopted a notoriety test: the existence of the business location must have gained a general notoriety before it is sufficient to be considered under the dual-filing provision.[207] Thus, for example, if a debtor conducted substantial record-keeping functions within the privacy of his or

---

[202] U.C.C. § 9-401 Cmt. 3.

[203] U.C.C. § 9-401(1)(c)(3d Alt.).

[204] *In re* Hot Shots Burgers & Fries, Inc., 169 B.R. 920, 24 U.C.C. Rep. Serv. 2d 1289 (Bankr. E.D. Ark. 1994) (central filing only required because debtor had places of business in more than one county).

[205] Chrysler Credit Corp. v. B.J.M., Jr., Inc., 834 F. Supp. 813, 22 U.C.C. Rep. Serv. 2d 379 (E.D. Pa. 1993) (lender properly filed by filing centrally and in county where debtor had its only place of business).

[206] Three different tests have evolved. *In re* Yale Mining Corp., 39 B.R. 201, 38 U.C.C. Rep. Serv. 1387 (Bankr. W.D. Va. 1984). One test addresses the quantity of work accomplished at a specific location. *In re* L & K Transp. Co., Inc., 8 B.R. 921, 30 U.C.C. Rep. Serv. 1745 (Bankr. D. Mass. 1981) (offices and garage in one location, but debtor's residence also a place of business because debtor billed from there). The second test is based on notoriety of the business place. *In re* Sterling Wood Prods., Inc., 34 B.R. 183, 37 U.C.C. Rep. Serv. 981 (Bankr. E.D.N.Y. 1983) (location of subsidiary in another county not sufficient to establish that potential creditors had knowledge that subsidiary might also be debtor's place of business). The third test focuses on whether the debtor conducts manufacturing and commercial activities at a particular location. *In re* P.S. Prods. Corp., 7 U.C.C. Rep. Serv. 411 (E.D.N.Y. 1970), *aff'd*, 435 F.2d 781, 8 U.C.C. Rep. Serv. 389 (2d Cir. 1970) (sole place of business was county in which all manufacturing and commercial activities were conducted despite leasing post office box and listing in telephone directory in another county).

[207] *In re* Sterling Wood Prods., Inc., 34 B.R. 183, 37 U.C.C. Rep. Serv. 981 (E.D. N.Y. 1983).

her home, the home location would not be considered a place of business in the absence of public notoriety concerning these activities.[208]

[C] Effect of Changes After Filing

One of the complications posed by a local filing requirement is that, in addition to having to select the correct county in which to file, the basis for selecting the county can change after an initial filing. The drafters, faced with determining the impact of such a change on the effectiveness of the filing, promulgated two alternative provisions in response.

One approach, followed by most states, is to leave the effectiveness of the initial filing unaffected by the subsequent changes. Section 9-401(3) provides:

A filing which is made in the proper place in this state continues effective even though the debtor's residence or place of business or the location of the collateral or its use, whichever controlled the original filing, is thereafter changed.

A person who searches the files needs to be aware of this provision because it affects the conclusions that can be safely drawn from the search results. Assume that a secured party takes a security interest in goods that the debtor is using as consumer goods and that the secured party properly files in the county of the debtor's residence in a state that has adopted the Second or Third Alternative to section 9-401(1). The debtor might later begin using the goods as equipment in its nonfarming business and might try to get a second lender to loan money against the goods. The second lender's search of only the central files will not reveal the local filing that is still effective. Any lender concerned that the use of collateral has changed should check both the local and central files.[209] Similarly, a prospective lender should be concerned about other potential changes that might mislead it in a search. If a prospective debtor has recently established a new residence and wants to use collateral that requires local filing, the lender should ascertain where the prior residence was and check the files in that county.[210]

The main lesson here is that a prospective lender cannot rely upon current circumstances of debtor residency, location of goods, place of business, or use of collateral because the circumstances that dictated the place of initial filing may have changed. A search based solely on existing circumstances can be seriously misleading. A lender who searches based only on current circumstances and concludes, after not finding a filed financing statement, that a security interest has not been perfected with respect to a prospective debtor may nonetheless be subject to an effective filing in another location.

---

[208] *In re* McQuaide, 5 U.C.C. Rep. Serv. 802 (Bankr. D. Vt. 1968), *aff'd*, 6 U.C.C. Rep. Serv. 419 (D. Vt. 1969).

[209] *In re* Barnes, 11 U.C.C. Rep. Serv. 670 (Bankr. D. Me. 1972) (proper filing with respect to truck purchased and used as consumer goods continued effective even though debtor later used truck in his business).

[210] *In re* Howard's Appliance Corp., 91 B.R. 204, 7 U.C.C. Rep. Serv. 2d 263 (Bankr. E.D.N.Y. 1988) (change of place of business within state did not affect validity of original filing); *In re* Gildner, 6 U.C.C. Rep. Serv. 973 (Bankr. W.D. Mich. 1969) (debtor's change of address did not affect perfection).

(Matthew Bender & Co., Inc.)

Continuing the effectiveness of a filing even after a change in the factors that affect the proper location for the filing is premised on the idea that a secured party who initially complies with filing requirements should not be required to monitor the debtor's activities in order to remain perfected. Changes that a debtor does not reveal to subsequent lenders can mislead those lenders not sophisticated enough to understand the limited conclusions which can be safely drawn from not finding a financing statement during any given search. This approach to changes after an initial filing, however, allocates the risk from unrevealed changes to subsequent parties who rely upon searches of the files.[211] It does not really alleviate the burden of monitoring, however, since an interstate (as opposed to intrastate) movement of the collateral or the debtor may trigger a filing requirement in another state.[212]

Because some legislatures do not like this policy, the drafters of Article 9 provided an alternative approach in subsection (3) to section 9-401. It states:

> A filing which is made in the proper county continues effective for four months after a change to another county of the debtor's residence or place of business or the location of the collateral, whichever controlled the original filing. It becomes ineffective thereafter unless a copy of the financing statement signed by the secured party is filed in the new county within said period.[213]

The alternative approach places more responsibility on a secured party to overcome misleading appearances that can result in the filing systems after filings that are initially correct. It essentially allows the secured party a four-month grace period during which the original filing remains effective, even after a change by the debtor that makes the filing misleading.[214] This grace period is based on the practical realization that secured parties generally cannot constantly monitor their debtors' activities for these types of changes. It compromises on four months as the appropriate period of time for a secured lender to detect these changes and to file again in the new county.[215] Because, at the expiration of the four-month period, the original filing lapses,[216] a secured party who

---

[211] *In re* Page, 6 U.C.C. Rep. Serv. 250 (Bankr. W.D. Ky. 1968) (filing made in proper place continues effective even after subsequent change in factors that determine place for filing).

[212] Interstate perfection problems are discussed in Chapter 9 *infra.*

[213] Note that a change in the use of the collateral does not require filing again in the new county: "A change in the use of the collateral does not impair the effectiveness of the original filing." U.C.C. § 9-401(3)(Alt.).

[214] *In re* Nardulli & Sons Co., Inc., 66 B.R. 871, 2 U.C.C. Rep. Serv. 2d 1107 (Bankr. W.D. Pa. 1986) (secured party should stay advised with respect to location of debtor's business in order to reperfect during grace period if office is moved).

[215] The four-month period is comparable to the grace period provided in U.C.C. § 9-103(1)(d)with respect to changes involving more than one state, and to the grace period provided in U.C.C. § 9-402(7)for name changes. For discussion of these provisions, *see* §§ 9.04[C], 9.05[C] *infra* and § 5.02[C][2] *supra.*

[216] *In re* B & L Coal Co., Inc., 20 B.R. 864, 33 U.C.C. Rep. Serv. 1558 (Bankr. W.D. Pa. 1982).

wants continuous perfection without a gap must file in the new county within this time period.[217]

The provisions of section 9-401(3) apply to changes made after an effective initial filing that perfects the security interest. If the initial filing is not effective, the security interest obviously is unperfected. A secured party can, of course, file in the proper location and perfect its interest as of the date of the filing. In addition, a subsequent change can render the original filing effective, as when the debtor moves to the county in which the secured party erroneously filed.

Some courts have misconstrued the effect of a subsequent change which should make the initial filing effective. They have held that a security interest that is unperfected because a filing was made in the wrong location cannot later become perfected by subsequent changes that make the initial filing location correct.[218] These courts reason that the proper location for filing is determined as of the time that the security interest attaches. Their decisions fail to recognize that a security interest can be perfected at any time after a security interest attaches. Filing in the wrong location leaves the security interest unperfected. If a change occurs later, with respect to the applicable factor that determines the place to file, such as the location of the debtor's residence, so that the place for proper filing becomes the same place in which a financing statement has already been filed, the security interest becomes perfected as of the date of the change. Refusing to recognize the effectiveness of the filing upon the appropriate change would require the secured party to make a redundant second filing in the same filing office.

Because the revision of Article 9 deletes local chattel filing as an option of a proper place in which to file a financing statement,[219] rules concerning the effect of a change that affects whether filing should be in the local or central system become unnecessary. Thus, the provisions discussed under this subsection are deleted in the revision.

§ 5.05   When Filing is Effective — §§ 9-403, R9-516, R9-517

Filing under the 1972 text of Article 9 occurs upon the completion of two events: 1) presentation of a financing statement[220] for filing, and 2) tender of the filing fee or acceptance of the financing statement by the filing officer.[221] Thus, effective filing does

---

[217] In re Armstrong, 7 U.C.C. Rep. Serv. 781 (Bankr. W.D. Okla. 1970) (even if secured party is not aware of change, the security interest becomes unperfected if reperfection is not effected within four months of the change). "The security interest may also be perfected in the new county after the expiration of the four-month period; in such case perfection dates from the time of perfection in the new county." U.C.C. § 9-401(3)(Alt.).

[218] In re Chagrin Valley Dental Assocs., 58 B.R. 912, 1 U.C.C. Rep. Serv. 2d 305 (Bankr. N.D. Ohio 1986) (relocation of debtor business to county in which filing was erroneously made did not make original filing effective).

[219] See § 5.04[B][1] supra.

[220] The term "financing statement" explicitly covers only original financing statements and any amendments. U.C.C. § 9-402(4). Other filings should be effective under the same rule, applied by analogy.

[221] U.C.C. § 9-403(1).

not depend upon completion of the ministerial task of entering the financing statement into its correct location within the files or even of indexing the financing statement. Actual indexing and entry into the files is done by governmental filing officers. Because secured parties cannot complete these tasks, they are not responsible for either their implementation or the errors of filing officers. Filing is effective from the moment that the secured party finishes its required action.

The events for the effectiveness of a filing under the 1998 text are essentially the same as those under the 1972 text, except that the revision refers to "communication of a record" rather than "presentation of a financing statement."[222] "Communicate" is defined broadly to include, in addition to sending a written record or other tangible record, transmitting the record by a means prescribed by the rules adopted by the filing office.[223] "Send" is defined to mean depositing in the mail or delivering for transmission.[224] The approach is designed to maximize the opportunities for filing offices to use any technology to transmit the filing data, including electronic, voice, and optical.

The revision goes beyond the prior version of Article 9 by providing in section 9-516(b) an exclusive list of the reasons for a filing officer to reject a record.[225] Refusal to accept for any of these reasons means that filing of the record does not occur.[226] Justifiable reasons to refuse to accept a record include, among others, the following: communication by any method that is not authorized; failure to tender the amount of the filing fee; in an initial financing statement, omission of a name for the debtor, omission of a required description of the real property to which the initial financing statement relates, omission of a name and mailing address for the secured party of record, omission of a mailing address for the debtor, and omission of required information for a debtor that is an organization;[227] in an amendment (including a continuation statement or termination statement) or correction statement, failure to identify the initial financing statement by file number.[228]

---

[222] U.C.C. § R9-516(a). The provision explicitly covers the effectiveness of the filing of any record, thus including assignments, termination statements, continuation statements and the like.

[223] U.C.C. § R9-102(a)(18).

[224] U.C.C. § R9-102(a)(74).

[225] U.C.C. §§ R9-516(b), R9-520(a) ("filing office . . . may refuse to accept a record for filing only for a reason set forth in Section R9-516(b)"). This provision was deemed necessary because of problems in some states with filing offices rejecting filings for insufficient reasons.

[226] U.C.C. § R9-516(b).

[227] See also § 5.02[A] supra on required contents for initial financing statements. Many of the grounds for rejection are predicated on the omission of required information.

[228] This latter requirement implements the revision's "open drawer" policy with respect to filings. The filing office must have the capability to retrieve the financing statement by the name of the debtor or by the file number assigned to the initial financing statement, and it must maintain the capability to associate and retrieve together an initial financing statement and any other filed record that relates to the initial financing statement. U.C.C. § R9-519(f)(Alt. A). Alternative B to this section requires that local recording offices maintain the same capability with regard to real-estate-related filings.

The list in section R9-516(b) serves not only to establish the exclusive grounds for which a filing officer *may* reject a record for filing; the filing officer *must* reject a record for those reasons.[229] It must then communicate the reason for the rejection to the person that presented the record.[230] If the filing officer rejects a record for a reason that is not within the statutory grounds, the filing is effective "except as against a purchaser of the collateral which gives value in reasonable reliance upon the absence of the record from the files."[231] The rationale for the exception is that rejections for invalid reasons should be rare given the severe restrictions on the filing office's discretion, and in any event the gap in the record caused by an invalid rejection should be short-lived because the reason for the rejection must be promptly communicated to the secured party. If the filing officer inadvertently accepts an initial financing statement that it should have rejected and the initial financing statement complies with the minimum requirements set forth in sections R9-502(a) and (b),[232] the initial financing statement is effective to perfect the security interest.

Because a filing may be legally effective before the ministerial act of inputting the information into the system occurs, a gap may exist between the time of perfection and the time a searcher can reasonably learn of the fact of perfection. Anyone who conducts a search during this interim will be misled by the failure of the search to show a recent filing that is nevertheless effective. Contributing further to a searcher's concern is the fact that filings are backlogged as much as six weeks in some jurisdictions.[233] A searcher is additionally vulnerable to effective financing statements that are not found because the filing officer has somehow lost or misfiled them.

As between a searcher and the party who presents a financing statement for filing, the latter would appear to be in the better position to initiate action that might alleviate the misleading appearances that can result from filing errors. Knowing that its financing statement has been presented, the filing party could initiate a search for its own financing statement to determine whether it was properly filed. Imposition of a search obligation on the filing party would, however, shift a significant risk to that party since the timing of effective filing can be crucial in deciding the outcome of a priority dispute.[234] The

---

[229] U.C.C. § R9-520(a).

[230] U.C.C. § R9-520(b) (communication of reason for rejection must be according to filing-office rules but in no event more than two days after filing office receives record).

[231] U.C.C. § R9-516(d).

[232] The minimum requirements for an effective financing statement are set forth in § 5.02[A] *supra*. If the financing statement contains the minimum information but should have been rejected because it failed to give information required by U.C.C. § R9-516(b)(5) (*e.g.*, information necessary to determine the proper state of filing for an organization), the financing statement is effective generally but the interest of the secured party is subordinated to certain secured parties and other purchasers who are misled. § R9-338, This section also applies when the information required by § R9-516(b)(5) is supplied but is incorrect.

[233] The backlog is attributable to the dramatic increase in filings in recent years. With significant problems in many sectors of the economy, lenders have been more careful to protect their interests by using secured financing and carefully perfecting their interests. Many filing offices were understaffed to begin with, and budgetary constraints generally precluded adding staff to deal with the increased workloads.

[234] Recognizing the critical role of time of filing, the drafters of Article 9 required filing officers

drafters have chosen not to impose upon the filer the burden of confirming that the filing has been properly handled by the filing officer.[235]

Because much of the onus of the practical difficulties in the filing system is borne by parties who conduct searches, those parties should be aware of how to protect their interests as much as possible. For example, they should be aware of the extent of the backlog in filings in the particular jurisdictions in which they conduct searches. A prospective secured party can then, as a condition to actually committing itself to a secured transaction with the debtor, insist upon waiting for that time period to pass after it files its own financing statement. If that period seems unreasonably long, the prospective lender must then make a business judgment as to whether it is willing to risk the existence of an effective financing statement filed before its own that does not yet appear. In any event, a commercially significant backlog in filings creates an incentive to file financing statements early in the negotiating stages with prospective debtors in order to protect oneself against competing filings that might arise during at least part of the backlog.

The 1972 text does not deal with the backlog problem at all. **The revision addresses the problem through two approaches. First, the filing office is required to respond to a search request no later than two business days after receiving it.[236] The information provided by the filing office must be current based on a date no earlier than three business days before receipt of the request.[237] The effect is that filing offices must index records within two business days of their receipt. Because filing offices sometimes cannot or will not comply with such time requirements, the drafters have included another provision aimed at surmounting the backlog problem. A filing office or the appropriate official must offer to sell or license to the public on a nonexclusive basis copies of all records filed with it.[238] The copies are provided in bulk in every medium available to the filing office, and they must be available at least weekly. This provision facilitates access to the records by private companies that maintain parallel filing systems. If the official filing office fails in meeting its mandate to file financing statements in the time prescribed, searchers can rely on any such privately-maintained systems.**

A secured party which finds itself in a priority battle with someone who filed earlier should scrutinize the earlier filing for compliance with the requirements for effectiveness. One basis for a challenge to the effectiveness of the earlier filing under the 1972 text is the requirement to present the financing statement for filing. The court in *Peoples Nat'l*

---

to mark the time of filing on each financing statement. U.C.C. §§ 9-403(4), **R9-519(a)(2), R9-523.** The 1972 text refers to the "date and hour" of filing. **The revision refers to the "date and time" of filing, with no specific requirement on how to determine the time. This determination is to be made by rules adopted by each filing office. U.C.C. § R9-519, Cmt. 4.**

[235] U.C.C. §§ 9-403(1), **R9-519(a), R9-517.**

[236] U.C.C. § **R9-523(e).**

[237] U.C.C. § **R9-523(c)(1). Revised section 9-526 imposes requirements on the appropriate governmental official or agency to adopt and publish rules consistent with revised Article 9. Delays beyond the prescribed time limits are excusable for circumstances beyond the control of the filing office, provided that it exercises reasonable diligence under the circumstances. U.C.C. § R9-524.**

[238] U.C.C. § **R9-523(f).**

Bank of Rockland County v. Weiner,[239] for example, held that some positive proof that a financing statement was received by a filing officer is required to establish presentation. Simply mailing the financing statement to the appropriate office is not enough.[240] The best evidence that the filing officer received the financing statement is a signed receipt for the payment or a copy of the stamped financing statement.[241] The canceled check used to initiate payment of the filing fee is also good evidence. Absent such evidence, a certified mail receipt showing that a cover letter and the financing statement were received by the filing officer has been held sufficient.[242] **As indicated above in this subsection, the revision requires the communication of the financing statement to the filing office rather than its presentation.[243] This reverses the requirement that a financing statement must be received by the filing office to be effective.**

The effectiveness of a filing can also be challenged based on the requirement to tender the filing fee. In *In re Fidler*,[244] a bank was held to be unperfected because it tendered an insufficient check for filing fees, even though the filing office delayed in returning the check for nearly two years. A challenge based on the filing fee is likely to have limited utility, however, because acceptance of the financing statement by the filing officer also constitutes filing.[245] In a matter related to the filing-fee requirement, some jurisdictions levy a tax on U.C.C. filings, but vary with respect to the effect that nonpayment has on effectiveness of the filing.[246]

A secured party that cannot challenge the effectiveness of a prior-filed financing statement might be able to hold another entity responsible for any resulting losses. Cases have held filing officers liable for losses to searchers caused by their errors.[247] The claims lie in negligence, however, and governmental immunity may be available under state tort law.[248] A common response in jurisdictions in which filing officers remain

---

[239] 514 N.Y.S.2d 772, 129 A.D.2d 782, 3 U.C.C. Rep. Serv. 2d 1615 (N.Y. Sup. Ct. 1987).

[240] A presumption that materials sent by mail will be delivered does not meet the Article 9 need to establish the time of filing.

[241] An optional provision of Article 9 requires the filing officer, upon request, to note on a copy of the financing statement the file number and the date and hour of the filing of the original and to return the copy to the filer, if the filer furnishes the copy with the original. U.C.C. § 9-407(1). Most states have enacted this provision.

[242] *In re* Flagstaff Food Serv. Corp., 16 B.R. 132, 32 U.C.C. Rep. Serv. 1666 (Bankr. S.D.N.Y. 1981).

[243] **U.C.C. § R9-516(a).**

[244] 24 U.C.C. Rep. Serv. 465 (Bankr. D. Or. 1978).

[245] U.C.C. §§ 9-403(1), **R9-516(b)(2), R9-520(a),(c) (filing officer required to reject a record if an amount sufficient to cover the filing fee is not tendered, but such a filed financing statement is nevertheless effective).**

[246] *Compare* American City Bank of Tullahoma v. Western Auto Supply Co., 631 S.W.2d 410, 32 U.C.C. Rep. Serv. 1251 (Tenn. Ct. App. 1981) (security interest not perfected to extent that tax had not been paid), *with* Associates Commercial Corp. v. Sel-O-Rak Corp., 746 F.2d 1441, 39 U.C.C. Rep. Serv. 1529 (llth Cir. 1984) (perfection not withheld until tax is paid).

[247] Hudleasco, Inc. v. State, 90 Misc. 2d 1057, 396 N.Y.S.2d 1002, 22 U.C.C. Rep. Serv. 545 (Ct. Cl. 1977) (error by filing officer in certifying absence of prior financing statement).

[248] After the Kansas Supreme Court, in Borg-Warner Acceptance Corp. v. Secretary of State,

potentially subject to claims for loss is for the officers to reduce their risk by offering very little assistance to searchers. In addition to filing officers, abstract companies hired to conduct a search have been sued for negligence.[249]

An abstract company and an attorney have also been held liable to a secured lender for breach of their duty of care in ascertaining that the financing statement was properly filed. The court in *Peoples Nat'l Bank of Rockland County v.* Weiner[250] granted summary judgment to the secured lender because the defendants could not provide any positive evidence that the financing statement that the abstract company mailed was ever received by the filing officer. Because mailing the financing statement is not sufficient to constitute presentation to the filing office under the 1972 text, the agents' duties extended to obtaining proof that the statement was received.

§ 5.06 Lapse and Termination of Filing

[A] Lapse of Initial Financing Statement — §§ 9-403(2), R9-515(a)

The general rule under both versions of Article 9 is that a financing statement is effective for five years after filing.[251] Unless continued through the mechanisms that will be discussed below, the effectiveness of the financing statement lapses at the end of this five-year period.[252] Lapse provides a means to keep the filing system from being cluttered with financing statements that are unlikely to have further commercial relevance. Note that the five-year period runs from the date of filing of the financing statement, not the date of attachment of the security interest. Even though a filing made before attachment does not result in perfection,[253] the effective period during which the filing perfects a subsequently attached interest is measured from the date of filing.

Under the 1972 text, the filing office can remove lapsed statements from the files and destroy them immediately if a photographic record is maintained, or, in other cases, after

---

240 Kan. 598, 731 P.2d 301, 2 U.C.C. Rep. Serv. 2d 1725 (1987), upheld negligence liability of the secretary of state for several certificates that failed to disclose a prior filing, the Kansas legislature amended Article 9 to grant immunity to filing officers in conducting searches.

[249] Chemical Bank v. Title Servs., Inc., 708 F. Supp. 245, 9 U.C.C. Rep. Serv. 2d 402 (D. Minn. 1989) (title abstractor found not negligent for failing to conduct search under various misspellings of debtor's name).

[250] 514 N.Y.S.2d 772, 129 A.D.2d 782, 3 U.C.C. Rep. Serv. 2d 1615 (N.Y. Sup. Ct. 1987).

[251] U.C.C. §§ 9-403(2), **R9-515(a)**. Both the 1972 text and the revision provide that a mortgage can be effective as a fixture filing if it contains all the information required of a fixture filing, and in such cases the mortgage is effective until it "is released or satisfied of record or its effectiveness otherwise terminates" as to the realty. §§ 9-403(6), **R9-515(g)**. There are also provisions in both versions of the Code that permit a filing as to the assets of a transmitting utility to be made centrally even though the filing covers fixtures. The rationale is that the fixtures are typically located in numerous counties, rendering local filings impractical. A filing as to a transmitting utility is effective until a termination statement is filed. §§ 9-403(6), **R9-515(f)**. **Under the revision, a special 30-year period is available for public-finance transactions and manufactured-home transactions. § R9-515(b).**

[252] U.C.C. §§ **R9-403(2), R9-515(c)**.

[253] U.C.C. §§ 9-303(1), **R9-308(a)**.

a year following lapse.[254] Similarly, the revision permits the filing office to destroy any written record immediately upon lapse[255] but requires that it maintain a record of the information for at least one year thereafter.[256]

[B] Continuation Statements — §§ 9-403(3), R9-515(c)-(e)

Obviously, some secured transactions will extend beyond five years, and the secured lenders in these transactions will be concerned about being continuously perfected beyond the five-year period of effectiveness. The solution for these lenders is to file a continuation statement. A timely continuation statement prevents the effectiveness of the filed financing statement from lapsing.[257]

A continuation statement is a simple form filed by a secured party to provide notice that the effectiveness of a financing statement is being extended. The 1972 text requires that it "be signed by the secured party, identify the original statement by file number and state that the original statement is still effective."[258] A filing fee also must be paid.[259] The filing officer is directed to annex a continuation statement to the related financing statement in such a manner that the financing statement will be preserved for the effective period of continuation.[260]

In the revision the required contents are set forth in the definition of "continuation statement." The term refers to an amendment of a financing statement which: "(A) identifies, by its file number, the initial financing statement to which it relates; and (B) indicates that it is a continuation statement for, or that it is filed to continue the effectiveness of, the identified financing statement."[261] The signature requirement is eliminated, as authorization of the secured party is all that is necessary.[262]

---

[254] U.C.C. § 9-403(3).

[255] U.C.C. § R9-522(b).

[256] U.C.C. § R9-522(a).

[257] U.C.C. §§ 9-403(3), R9-515(c). The courts have disagreed on the necessity of filing a continuation statement after a secured party has commenced litigation. *Compare* Hassell v. First Pa. Bank, N.A., 41 N.C. App. 296, 254 S.E.2d 768, 26 U.C.C. Rep. Serv. 1380 (1979) (secured party held to be unperfected despite having obtained judgment against debtor prior to expiration of five-year period) *with* Chrysler Credit Corp. v. United States, 24 U.C.C. Rep. Serv. 794 (E.D. Va. 1978) (filing of litigation tolled any obligation of plaintiff to defendant to file continuation statement because defendant was clearly aware of plaintiff's security interest).

[258] U.C.C. § 9-403(3); Nat'l Bank of Fulton City v. Haupricht Bros., Inc., 55 Ohio App. 3d 249, 564 N.E.2d 101, 14 U.C.C. Rep. Serv. 2d 215 (1988) (filing that failed to meet these requirements was not effective as continuation statement). If a security interest is assigned, it makes sense to record the assignment. U.C.C. § 9-405(1). Otherwise, the assignor will continue as the secured party of record and a continuation statement signed by the assignee will have to be accompanied by a separate written statement of assignment signed by the secured party of record. U.C.C. § 9-403(3). The revision still allows the assignment of a security interest of record in two ways: naming the assignee in the initial financing statement or making a subsequent filing. U.C.C. § R9-514.

[259] U.C.C. §§ 9-403(5), R9-525.

[260] U.C.C. § 9-403(3).

[261] U.C.C. § R9-102(a)(27).

[262] U.C.C. § R9-509(d)(1).

The filing office is required to index all filed records that relate to an initial financing statement, including continuation statements, in a way that associates the related records to the initial financing statement.[263]

A continuation statement can be filed any time during the six months that precede lapse of the financing statement.[264] A timely filing that contains the correct information extends the effectiveness of the financing statement for an additional period of five years.[265] The additional five years are measured not from the date of filing of the continuation statement, but rather from the date that the five-year period under the original filing ends.[266] A secured party who desires to extend the effectiveness of a financing statement even further can file additional continuation statements during the six-month period that precedes lapse *ad infinitum.*[267]

Under the 1972 text, a special rule can apply in cases in which insolvency proceedings are commenced. A security interest that has been perfected by filing[268] will continue perfected for the duration of the insolvency proceeding and for sixty days after termination of the proceedings, even if a five-year period upon which filing is based expires before that time.[269] This provision reflects bankruptcy cases that excuse a secured party from refiling during bankruptcy proceedings. The secured party need not refile because the filing of the petition in bankruptcy fixes the rights of prepetition creditors and the trustee in bankruptcy.[270] A 60-day grace period for refiling follows the termination of bankruptcy proceedings so that secured parties that rely upon the bankruptcy stay will not inadvertently lose their perfected status.[271]

This tolling provision is deleted in the revision. Section 362(b)(3) of the Bankruptcy Code has been amended to allow a secured party to maintain its perfected status with respect to its collateral by filing a continutation statement without first obtaining relief from the automatic stay.[272] A secured party now must take care to be certain that its filed financing statement does not lapse during the pendency of its debtor's bankruptcy proceedings.

---

263 U.C.C. § R9-519(c).

264 U.C.C. §§ 9-403(3), **R9-515(d). Under the revision, a filing office is required to reject a continuation statement that is not filed within this six-month period. U.C.C. §§ R9-520(a), R9-516(b)(7). Any continuation statement that nevertheless is accepted for filing outside of this time frame is ineffective. U.C.C. § R9-510(c).**

265 U.C.C. §§ 9-403(3), **R9-515(e).**

266 *Id. See also In re* Davison, 29 B.R. 987, 36 U.C.C. Rep. Serv. 717 (Bankr. W.D. Mo. 1983).

267 U.C.C. §§ 9-403(3), **R9-515(e).** *See also* United States v. Branch Banking & Trust Co., 11 U.C.C. Rep. Serv. 2d 351 (E.D.N.C. 1990).

268 U.C.C. § 9-403(2).

269 *In re* Laninga, 51 B.R. 199, 41 U.C.C. Rep. Serv. 1126 (N.D. Ill. 1985) (this provision could not be used to continue perfection of secured party whose financing statement lapsed prior to filing of debtor's petition in bankruptcy).

270 *In re* Delia Bros., Inc., 29 U.C.C. Rep. Serv. 1446 (S.D.N.Y. 1980). The continuation notice is thus irrelevant to these parties because they have knowledge of the perfected interest on the date of filing. *In re* Laninga, 51 B.R 199, 41 U.C.C. Rep. Serv. 1126 (N.D. Ill. 1985).

271 *In re* Laninga, 51 B.R. 199, 41 U.C.C. Rep. Serv. 1126 (Bankr. N.D. Ill. 1985).

272 U.C.C. § **R9-515 Cmt. 4.**

Unless it is perfected through some means other than filing,[273] a security interest becomes unperfected prospectively upon lapse.[274] Under the 1972 text, the security interest is also "deemed to have been unperfected as against a person who became a purchaser or lien creditor before lapse."[275] Even though the filing is effective and the security interest is thus perfected when the interest of a purchaser or lien creditor arises, this "retroactive invalidation" provision will cause the unperfected status of the secured party to relate back in the case of a later priority dispute with the purchaser or lien creditor.[276] In other words, a secured party which allows its filing to lapse will be treated as if it had never filed at all. This approach is followed to avoid the possibility of circular priority that existed under some prior statutes.[277] **The revision adopts the retroactive-invalidation rule for security interests and agricultural liens but limits its applicability to purchasers for value.[278] In other words, a secured party who allows its financing statement to lapse will find itself unperfected prospectively and will be deemed unperfected as against a purchaser for value whose interest arose before lapse, but it will retain its perfected status as against a lien creditor.[279]**

The array of competing claimants that fall within the scope of the retroactive-invalidation rule is broader than initially appears. The term "purchaser" is defined very broadly under the Code to include a buyer, secured party, and any other party who acquires an interest in property through a voluntary transfer.[280] For example, suppose SP-1 takes and perfects by filing a security interest in Debtor's equipment. A year later, SP-2 does likewise. If a priority dispute comes to trial before SP-1's financing statement lapses, SP-1 will have priority.[281] If SP-1 permits its filing to lapse, however, SP-2 will gain the upper hand. Even if SP-1 files a new financing statement after lapse, it cannot repair the gap in perfection caused by lapse. The new filing will only operate to perfect SP-1 prospectively for five years.

---

[273] See Chapter 4 *supra.*

[274] U.C.C. §§ 9-403(2), **R9-515(c)**; State Bank of Harland v. Arndt, 129 Wisc.2d 411, 385 N.W.2d 219, 42 U.C.C. Rep. Serv. 1850 (Ct. App. 1986).

[275] U.C.C. § 9-403(2).

[276] In *re* Hilyard Drilling Co., Inc., 60 B.R. 500, 2 U.C.C. Rep. Serv. 2d 370 (Bankr. W.D. Ark. 1986) (upon lapse, prior-perfected secured party became junior to competing security interest that had been perfected during five-year period of effective filing of prior-perfected secured party); General Elec. Credit Corp. v. Isaacs, 90 Wash. 2d 234, 581 P.2d 1032, 24 U.C.C. Rep. Serv. 1001 (1978) (lapse left secured company vulnerable to federal tax lien that had been filed during period of protection).

[277] See U.C.C. § 9-403 Cmt. 3. *Compare* U.C.C. § 9-103(1)(d), discussed at § 9.04[C] *infra.*

[278] U.C.C. § R9-515(c).

[279] **The primary effect of this change is to protect the secured party whose debtor files for bankruptcy prior to lapse from the bankruptcy trustee. Priority contests between secured parties and lien creditors, including bankruptcy trustees, are discussed in § 14.02 *infra.***

[280] "Purchaser" is defined to mean "a person who takes by purchase." U.C.C. § 1-201(33). The term "purchase" is, in turn, defined to include "taking by sale, discount, negotiation, mortgage, pledge, lien, issue or re-issue, gift or any other voluntary transaction creating an interest in property." U.C.C. § 1-201(32).

[281] Priority rules governing competing security interests are discussed in detail in Chapter 10 *infra.*

[C] Termination Statements and Releases of Collateral — §§ 9-404, 9-406, R9-513, R9-509

A debtor will encounter significant difficulty in obtaining secured financing against any property that is described as collateral on a filed financing statement. The reasons for this reluctance on the part of prudent lenders are covered in a subsequent chapter.[282] The mere existence of this potential difficulty is sufficient for present purposes, however, to suggest that a debtor who pays off the debt and has no further financing relationship with a secured party will desire to terminate the effectiveness of the filed financing statement without waiting for lapse to accomplish that objective.

The solution for such a debtor is the termination statement.[283] The general rule governing termination statements in the 1972 text provides that the debtor can make written demand on the secured party to provide the debtor with such a statement, provided that "there is no outstanding secured obligation and no commitment to make advances, incur obligations or otherwise give value."[284] The termination statement must be signed by the secured party, must identify the financing statement being terminated by file number, and must state, in effect, that the secured party no longer claims a security interest under the financing statement. The debtor can then present the termination statement and the required fee to the filing officer.[285] The filing officer must note the termination statement in the index, and can remove the financing statement from the files immediately if it is on microfilm or photographic record, or, in the absence of such records, within a year after receipt of the termination statement.[286] The filed termination statement thus serves to end the effectiveness of the financing statement earlier than would occur through lapse.[287]

If the secured party fails to provide a termination statement to the debtor within ten days after a proper demand, the secured party incurs two forms of liability.[288] First, a civil penalty of $100 automatically applies in favor of the debtor.[289] Second, the secured party is liable for any losses to the debtor caused by the secured party's failure to comply.

---

[282] *See* § 10.02 *infra.* For a case in which a subsequent creditor did not concern itself with a prior-filed financing statement on a debt that had been paid in full but found itself ultimately in a subordinate position, *see* Provident Fin. Co. v. Beneficial Fin. Co., 36 N.C. App. 401, 245 S.E.2d 510, 24 U.C.C. Rep. Serv. 1332 (1978).

[283] U.C.C. §§ 9-404, **R9-513.**

[284] U.C.C. § 9-404(1).

[285] U.C.C. § 9-404(2),(3).

[286] U.C.C. § 9-404(2).

[287] J.I. Case Credit Corp. v. Foos, 11 Kan. App. 2d 185, 717 P.2d 1064, 1 U.C.C. Rep. 2d 250 (1986) (filing of termination statement under erroneous belief that debtor had paid in full was nevertheless effective to terminate perfection).

[288] U.C.C. § 9-404(1). **Under the revision, the secured party has 20 days in which to respond to an authenticated demand from a debtor by either sending a termination statement to the debtor or filing a termination statement in the filing office. U.C.C. § R9-513(c). The liability for failure to do so is the same as that imposed for filing an unauthorized financing statement or amendment. U.C.C. § R9-625(e).**

[289] Household Fin. Corp. of Atlanta v. Raven, 136 Ga. App. 424, 221 S.E.2d 488, 18 U.C.C. Rep. Serv. 540 (1975).

Although a secured party does not ordinarily have a duty to provide a termination statement absent a demand from the debtor,[290] an exception applies with respect to a financing statement that covers consumer goods. Under this exception, the secured party must file a properly executed termination statement within one month after the outstanding secured obligation is extinguished even without a demand by the debtor.[291] A written demand by the debtor reduces the time period to ten days. Note that in the case of consumer goods, the secured party must actually file the financing statement. As in other cases, a secured party who fails to comply with its duties is liable for a $100 penalty plus damages.

The revision follows the same general approach as the 1972 text except that the compliance period following an authenticated demand is increased from ten to twenty days.[292] If the secured party[293] fails to file (in the case of consumer goods) or send (in other cases) a required termination statement, a termination statement can be filed without the secured party's authorization.[294] The filed termination statement is effective, however, "only if the debtor authorizes the filing and the termination statement indicates that the debtor authorized it to be filed."[295] A secured party who fails properly to perform its duties is liable for a $500 fine plus damages.[296]

Under the revision a termination statement is treated as an amendment which "(A) identifies, by its file number, the initial financing statement to which it relates; and (B) indicates either that it is a termination statement or that the identified financing statement is no longer effective."[297] As with continuation statements and

---

[290] Full payment of all outstanding indebtedness does not terminate the effectiveness of a filed financing statement. *In re* Bishop, 52 B.R. 470, 41 U.C.C. Rep. Serv. 1491 (Bankr. D.N.D. 1985). Absent the required demand from the debtor, a secured party is not under a duty to prepare or file a termination statement. Texas Kenworth Corp. v. First Nat'l Bank of Bethany, 564 P.2d 222, 21 U.C.C. Rep. Serv. 1512 (Okla. 1977).

[291] U.C.C. §§ 9-404(1), R9-513(a). Under the revision, the filing must be made within 20 days after the secured party receives an authenticated demand from the debtor, if it would be earlier than the one-month period. U.C.C. § R9-513(b).

[292] The revision clarifies that a demand is proper if the debtor did not authorize the filing of the initial financing statement. U.C.C. §§ R9-513(a)(2) (consumer goods), R9-513(c)(4)(other cases). In cases not involving consumer goods, it also permits a debtor to make an authenticated demand for a termination statement if the financing statement covers accounts or chattel paper on which the person obligated is discharged, or the financing statement covers goods on consignment that are not in the debtor's possession. U.C.C. §§ R9-513(c)(2) (accounts or chattel paper), R9-513(c)(3) (goods on consignment).

[293] If a secured party who has assigned its security interest receives an authenticated demand, it must cause the secured party of record to perform its duties with regard to termination statements. U.C.C. §§ R9-513(c). In the case of consumer goods, it must do so even without an authenticated demand. § R9-513(a).

[294] U.C.C. § R9-509(d)(2).

[295] *Id.*

[296] U.C.C. §§ R9-625(b) (damages), R9-625(e)(4) (penalty).

[297] U.C.C. § R9-102(a)(79).

all other records that relate to an initial financing statement, the filing office must index a termination statement in a way that associates it to the initial financing statement.[298]

Instead of filing a termination statement, a secured party can release some or all of the collateral described in its financing statement through a release. In addition to the secured party's signature, the 1972 text requires that a statement of release include "a description of the collateral being released, the name and address of the debtor, the name and address of the secured party, and the file number of the financing statement."[299] The release is effective upon presentation of the statement to the filing office, with the required fee.[300]

Under the revision, a release is accomplished through an amendment to the initial financing statement. As with other amendments, including termination statements and continuation statements, a release must identify the initial financing statement by file number[301] **and must be filed in a manner that relates it to the initial financing statement.**[302] **An amendment that adds collateral or a debtor must be authorized by the debtor in an authenticated record,**[303] **but an amendment that operates as a release of collateral need only be authorized by the secured party.**[304]

As the case law demonstrates, secured parties who intend a partial release of collateral should be careful that they do not inadvertently create a termination statement instead. In one bankruptcy decision, the assignee of a bank's security interest asserted that a statement filed by the bank had been intended only as a partial release.[305] The court held that reforming the statement, which indicated that it was a "termination" statement, would materially mislead subsequent searchers who relied on the public record. The statement was thus held to have terminated perfection.

The error by the secured bank was clear in another case, decided by the Fourth Circuit.[306] The bank erroneously checked a box on the form that it filed which indicated that the filing was a "termination statement" rather than a "partial release of collateral." The description portion of the form showed that the bank intended to release only two specific items of collateral, whereas its security interest was in nearly all of the debtor's

---

[298] U.C.C. § R9-519(c).

[299] U.C.C. § 9-406.

[300] Filed statements are not the exclusive means to effectuate a release. Oral releases are also effective. *Cf.* U.C.C. § 9-406 Cmt. *In re* Belize Airways Ltd., 7 B.R. 604, 31 U.C.C. Rep. Serv. 730 (Bankr. S.D. Fla. 1980).

[301] U.C.C. § R9-512(a)(1).

[302] U.C.C. § R9-519(c).

[303] U.C.C. § R9-509(a)(1).

[304] U.C.C. § R9-509(d)(1).

[305] *In re* Silvernail Mirror & Glass, Inc., 142 B.R. 987, 18 U.C.C. Rep. Serv. 2d 322 (Bankr. M.D. Fla. 1992).

[306] *In re* Kitchin Equip. Co. of Va., Inc., 960 F.2d 1242, 17 U.C.C. Rep. Serv. 2d 322 (4th Cir. 1992).

assets. The court, nevertheless, held that, by checking the box, the bank created an effective termination statement.[307]

---

[307] *Id. See also In re* Pacific Trencher & Equip., Inc., 735 F.2d 362, 38 U.C.C. Rep. Serv. 1121 (9th Cir. 1984).

CHAPTER 6

PERFECTION BY POSSESSION AND CONTROL

SYNOPSIS

---

§ 6.01 Possession: When Permissible and When Mandatory — §§ 9-305, 9-304(1), R9-313, R9-312

[A] Historical

The Code's approach to perfection by possession is illuminated by the problems surrounding nineteenth-century secured financing. Common-law judges in the first half of that century refused to enforce "chattel mortgages" in which the debtor retained possession of the collateral. The perceived problem was ostensible ownership — the arrangement could mislead third parties into believing that the debtor had unfettered ownership of the collateral. Courts were concerned that another creditor might be induced to make an ill-advised loan because the debtor's apparent ownership of the collateral would lead the creditor to miscalculate the debtor's net worth. As a result, nonpossessory security arrangements were routinely voided by the courts, which classified them as fraudulent conveyances.[1] Because the arrangements were avoided, creditors were precluded from foreclosing on their collateral, even when no third party was misled.

The ostensible ownership problem was curtailed when the debtor surrendered possession of the collateral to the creditor.[2] This arrangement, called a "pledge" at common law,[3] provided sufficient notice to third parties to overcome judicial concerns about fraud.[4] The pledge, however, was not sufficient to meet the needs of the marketplace. It was simply impractical for borrowers to surrender possession of assets that they used in the ordinary course of their business affairs.

Responding to these needs, state legislatures began to pass statutes, called chattel mortgage recording acts, permitting nonpossessory security interests conditioned on creditors placing notices describing their interests in the public records. The legislatures saw filing as a satisfactory substitute for possession, but the courts remained hostile. They required the description of the collateral in the filing to be very specific, and any mistake, such as transposing digits within a serial number, could lead the court to invalidate the arrangement as fraudulent. Of course, a failure to file at all led to the same result.

The Code's approach to filing and possession is radically at odds with this history. Filing is the norm,[5] and possession is the substitute.[6] The Code facilitates the primacy of filing by dramatically reducing the formal requirements for an effective financing

---

[1] *See, e.g.,* Clow v. Woods, 5 Sergeant & Rawle 275, 9 Am. Dec. 346 (Pa. 1819). This line of cases can be traced to Twyne's Case, 76 Eng. Rep. 809, 3 Coke 80 (Star Ch. 1601).

[2] Although pledges were routinely enforced at common law, it is worth noting that the pledge does not entirely remove the ostensible ownership problem. Third parties can still be misled about the nature of the creditor's interest in the pledged collateral.

[3] *See* Restatement of Security § 1 (1941) (a pledge constitutes bailment to secure an obligation). The origins of the pledge can be traced to all of the ancient nations. A. Dobie, *Handbook on the Law of Bailments and Carriers* § 70 at 173-74 (1914).

[4] An extensive array of citations to pre-Code authorities on the law of the pledge have been collected in R. Hillman, J. McDonnell, & S. Nickles, *Common Law and Equity Under the Uniform Commercial Code* ¶ 23.01 (1985).

[5] U.C.C. §§ 9-302(1), **R9-310(a)**(filing mandatory absent provision to the contrary).

[6] U.C.C. §§ 9-302(1)(a), **R9-310(b)(6)**(possession available as alternative to filing).

statement. Serial number specificity is no longer required, and the description of the collateral is sufficient if it "reasonably identifies what is described."[7] **The 1998 text even validates financing statements that use supergeneric descriptions like "all assets" or "all personal property."**[8] The Code also makes it clear that a security interest is not fraudulent merely because the debtor retains control of the collateral.[9] Thus, even an unperfected nonpossessory security interest can be enforced against the debtor.[10]

The provisions authorizing or mandating possession as a method of perfection are the modern counterpart to the pledge and provide an alternative to the Code's filing rule.[11] Although the term "pledge" is still commonly used, it is in the process of being supplanted by the more precise phrase "possessory security interest."

[B] Permissive

Section 9-305 of the 1972 text specifies all of the following forms of collateral as appropriate for possessory perfection: goods, instruments, money, negotiable documents, or chattel paper.[12] In addition, a security interest in a right to the proceeds of a written letter of credit can be perfected by taking possession of the letter.[13] The listing in Section 9-305 includes goods and virtually all the kinds of personal property that can be reduced to the form of an indispensable paper.[14] The only kinds of personal property that are omitted are accounts and general intangibles.[15] With minor exceptions,[16] security interests in these kinds of personal property can be perfected only by filing a financing statement.[17] **The 1998 text is essentially the same, although possession of chattel**

---

[7] U.C.C. §§ 9-110, **R9-108(a)**. In addition, minor errors in a financing statement that do not seriously mislead searchers are to be ignored by the courts. U.C.C. §§ 9-402(8), **R9-506(a)**. *See* § 5.02[C][1] *supra.*

[8] U.C.C. § **R9-504(2)**.

[9] U.C.C. §§ 9-205, **R9-205(a)(1)(A)**. *See* § 3.01 *supra.*

[10] The adverse consequence of nonfiling is the potential loss of priority to third parties. *See* Introduction to Part IV *infra.*

[11] U.C.C. §§ 9-305, **R9-313**.

[12] The Minnesota Court of Appeals clearly erred in State of Minnesota v. 14,000 Dollars, 345 N.W.2d 277, 38 U.C.C. Rep. Serv. 1007 (Minn. Ct. App. 1984) when it held that a security interest cannot be taken in money, because U.C.C. § 9-305explicitly recognizes that such an interest can be perfected.

[13] U.C.C. § 9-305.

[14] Certificated securities, a kind of indispensable paper, are dealt with in U.C.C. § 9-115, which governs all types of investment property. For a discussion of perfection of security interests in investment property, *see* § 6.04 *infra.*

[15] Nonnegotiable documents are typically ignored and secured parties take and perfect their security interests in the goods covered by such documents. The use of nonnegotiable documents in commercial financing transactions is discussed in § 6.02[B][2] *infra.*

[16] U.C.C. §§ 9-302(1)(c)(beneficial interests in trusts or decedent's estates), (e)(purchase-money security interests in consumer goods), (g)(isolated assignments of accounts), 9-304(3)(nonnegotiable documents).

[17] *In re* Holiday Intervals, Inc., 931 F.2d 500, 14 U.C.C. Rep. Serv. 2d 562 (8th Cir. 1991) (installment contracts for purchase price of real estate were general intangibles and thus could not be perfected by possession).

paper is limited to tangible chattel paper [18] and letter-of-credit rights are dropped from the list. [19]

Perfection by possession is limited to assets that are embodied in a single physical form. Perfection by possession requires an ability to take physical possession of something that is tangible and that allows the secured party to control the disposition of the collateral without the further involvement of the debtor. The right to payment created by an account cannot satisfy this requirement. [20] The tangible forms that indicate the existence of an account — ledger entries, invoices, written contracts, or other records — are not recognized as the exclusive physical embodiment of the right to be paid. Such tangible forms have evidentiary value, but the right to be paid can be enforced by an assignee who has not taken physical possession of them. Similarly, no indispensable writing represents the rights that constitute general intangibles.

Negotiable instruments and negotiable documents, by contrast, are writings that do exclusively represent the rights indicated thereon. Thus, the right to enforce payment of an obligation represented by a negotiable instrument is normally transferred by delivering the writing to the transferee. [21] Similarly, title to goods represented by a negotiable document is normally transferred by delivery of the document. [22] The nonnegotiable writings that fall within the Code's definition of "instrument" [23] are generally treated as the single physical embodiment of the right to be paid. They are similar to negotiable instruments in this respect and might be considered "quasi-negotiable."

Possession can serve as a reliable means of perfection only if it provides notice comparable to that achieved by filing. [24] If a debtor seeks to induce subsequent parties to enter into a transaction with respect to pledged collateral, those parties should be alert enough to inquire why a third party has possession of the debtor's property. Adequate notice through possession is only workable with respect to those kinds of property that the legal and business communities recognize as being comprised of a complete physical embodiment.

Failure to take possession of the complete physical embodiment of the collateral cost a bank perfection of its security interest, worth more than $5 million, in *In re* Funding

---

[18] **Electronic chattel paper is perfected by control. U.C.C. §§ R9-314(a), R9-105.**

[19] **Control is the mandatory method of perfection for letter-of-credit rights. U.C.C. §§ R9-314(a), R9-107.**

[20] *In re* Sanelco, 7 U.C.C. Rep. Serv. 65 (Bankr. M.D. Fla. 1969) (account receivable is not capable of possessory security interest).

[21] U.C.C. §§ 3-203(b)(transfer requires delivery), 1-201(14)(delivery requires voluntary transfer of possession), 3-203(b)(transfer vests in the transferee any enforcement rights of the transferor).

[22] U.C.C. § 7-502(1)(b). The use of negotiable documents in commercial financing transactions is discussed in §§ 6.02[B][1] and 6.02[C] *infra.*

[23] U.C.C. §§ 9-105(1)(i), **R9-102(a)(47).**

[24] The court in Hutchison v. C.I.T. Corp., 726 F.2d 300, 37 U.C.C. Rep. Serv. 1760 (6th Cir. 1984), stressed that, for the purpose of notice to third parties, possession must be unequivocal, absolute and notorious. A night watchman on the property where the equipment serving as collateral was located said that he would keep an eye on the equipment for the secured party. The court easily found that such an arrangement was insufficient to provide any notice to interested third parties and thus did not constitute perfection.

Systems Asset Management Corp.[25] The collateral consisted of chattel paper made up of a note and leases of underlying equipment. The leases had been prepared in duplicate originals (original ink signatures without any designation of one as the original). The secured party took possession of one set of originals, but left another set in the possession of the debtor. The court properly noted that a subsequent lender would not be placed on notice if the debtor decided to offer the duplicate originals as collateral. **The Comments to revised Article 9 suggest that problems arising from the use of duplicate originals are easily solved, noting that the parties may "by designation on the chattel paper identify only one counterpart as the original chattel paper for purposes of taking possession."[26]**

[C] Mandatory

Article 9 draws some further refinements with respect to perfection of security interests in indispensable paper. Section 9-304(1) of the 1972 text recognizes that perfection by filing is an appropriate alternative for security interests in chattel paper and negotiable documents.[27] This provision really adds nothing that cannot be gleaned from sections 9-302(1) and 9-305. The rest of the provision, however, creates an exception to the general rule that filing a financing statement perfects a security interest. It provides that "[a] security interest in money or instruments (other than instruments which constitute part of chattel paper) can be perfected only by the secured party's taking possession, except for designated methods of temporary automatic perfection."[28] As a consequence of section 9-304(1), filing as an effective method to perfect a security interest in money[29] or "money paper" (instruments)[30] is precluded.

Perfection by filing is eliminated under the 1972 text with respect to money and instruments because of the underlying policy of "currency" that seeks to promote the free transferability of these forms of personal property. Promissory notes need to be freely

---

[25] 111 B.R. 500, 11 U.C.C. Rep. Serv. 2d 205 (Bankr. W.D. Pa. 1990).

[26] **U.C.C. § R9-330 Cmt. 4.**

[27] Although filing perfects security interests in chattel paper and negotiable documents, possession is safer. A secured party who leaves such collateral in the debtor's possession runs the risk that it will be conveyed to a good-faith purchaser for value who will take priority over the secured party's interest. U.C.C. §§ 9-308(chattel paper), 9-309(negotiable document). **The 1998 text is in accord. U.C.C. §§ R9-330(a)(chattel paper), R9-331(a)(negotiable document).**

[28] The U.C.C. defines "money" as "a medium of exchange authorized or adopted by a domestic or foreign government." U.C.C. § 1-201(24). The court ruled appropriately in In the Matter of Midas Coin Co., 264 F. Supp. 193, 4 U.C.C. Rep. Serv. 220 (E.D. Mo. 1967), *aff'd sub nom.* Zuke v. St. John's Community Bank, 387 F.2d 118, 4 U.C.C. Rep. Serv. 908 (8th Cir. 1968), that a coin collection used as collateral constituted goods and not money. As a collector's item, the coins were no longer used as a medium of exchange, and perfection by filing based on their being goods was appropriate.

[29] *In re* S&J Holding Corp., 4 B.R. 621, 39 U.C.C. Rep. Serv. 668 (Bankr. S.D. Fla. 1980) (perfected security interest in business' video games did not extend to coins used to play the games because creditor did not have possession of them prior to debtor's bankruptcy).

[30] In the Matter of Staff Mortgage & Inv. Co., 550 F.2d 1228, 21 U.C.C. Rep. Serv. 887 (9th Cir. 1977) (filing under Article 9 or in the real estate records cannot perfect a security interest in note secured by real estate).

alienable, and that goal would be undermined by a system that required potential transferees to consult the Article 9 filing records to determine if a prior party holds a perfected security interest. **The 1998 text continues to promote the free alienability of instruments, but in a much different way. The revision contains a permissive filing provision for instruments,** [31] **leaving money as the only asset in the mandatory-possession category.** [32] **The permissive-filing provision must be read in conjunction with section R9-330(d), which grants priority over a security interest perfected by filing to a purchaser for value who acquires possession of an instrument in good faith and without knowledge of the security interest.** [33] **Such good-faith transferees for value can rely on appearances and need not worry about consulting the Article 9 filing system. Filing protects the secured party from nonreliance lien creditors like the bankruptcy trustee.** [34]

§ 6.02 Possessory Security Arrangements in Specific Types of Personal Property

Even though Article 9 recognizes possession as a permitted method of perfection for security interests in an expansive array of collateral, practical considerations narrow considerably the circumstances in which a secured party realistically can take delivery of the debtor's property. For example, a manufacturer that gives its equipment to a creditor will not have the machinery it needs to produce its products. The same problem exists for a consumer who needs to use at home collateral consisting of appliances or furniture. Any collateral that the debtor must use is not well-suited to a possessory security interest. Another practical problem results when the goods comprising the collateral have great bulk. For example, a bank simply cannot store a debtor's pile of coal or its stockpiled inventory of finished goods in the bank lobby or even in the bank vault. Although more appropriate facilities could be arranged, the transactional costs associated with storage and transport would be prohibitively high. In addition to the other problems associated with taking delivery, a secured party in possession of collateral incurs an obligation to "use reasonable care in the custody and preservation of collateral" in its possession. [35]

The secured lending community has responded to these practical problems in two distinct ways. One approach is to confine possessory secured lending to transactions in

---

[31] U.C.C. § R9-312(a).

[32] U.C.C. § R9-312(b)(3).

[33] *See also* §§ R9-331(a), (c)(filing under Article 9 does not constitute notice of a claim to a negotiable instrument that would preclude a third party from asserting the rights of a holder in due course under Article 3).

[34] U.C.C. § R9-201(a).

[35] U.C.C. §§ 9-207(1), **R9-207(a).** First Nat'l Bank of Thomasboro v. Lachenmyer, 131 Ill. App. 3d 914, 476 N.E.2d 755, 41 U.C.C. Rep. Serv. 234 (1985) (debtor allowed to set off damages to property in bank's possession). The provisions establishing the secured party's duties apply when possession of the collateral is taken following default by the debtor, as well as when possession is taken as a pledge to perfect a security interest. For discussion of the default context, *see* Chapter 17 *infra.* **Revised Article 9 also has special rules establishing the rights and duties of a secured party who has perfected by control, a method that is similar to possession and is discussed in § 6.04 *infra.* §§ R9-207(c), R9-208.**

which the lender can easily manage receipt and custody of the collateral. The other approach is to use documents as a means to facilitate possessory security interests in goods. The basic patterns of these practices are explained below.

[A] Pledges of Valuables and Indispensable Paper

Secured lenders can realistically take delivery and maintain a possessory security interest in a relatively narrow range of goods. For an entity like a bank, the goods must be valuables, like jewelry, that the bank can simply store in its vault. Pawn brokers have more expanded facilities for dealing with goods, but they also generally limit their transactions to distinct items rather than bulky transfers. Some of the items against which loans are extended become the inventory of the pawn broker's shop.

Much possessory secured financing uses indispensable paper as the collateral. Financing institutions can easily take a pledge of paper — like promissory notes or chattel paper — that represents an obligation to pay money. Deprived of possession of the paper, the debtor cannot transfer it to create a bona-fide-purchaser type of status in a subsequent transferee.[36] Possession not only perfects the security interest and eliminates the risk of bona-fide purchasers, it facilitates collection in the event of debtor default.[37] The secured creditor does incur the additional responsibility in the case of a possessory security interest in an instrument or chattel paper of "taking necessary steps to preserve rights against prior parties unless otherwise agreed."[38] The rights and responsibilities with respect to these types of paper are well within the expertise of most financial institutions, however, and thus do not constitute barriers to the effective use of possessory security interests.[39]

Negotiable documents are another form of indispensable paper that is ideal for a possessory security interest. The document controls access and title to specified goods, thereby facilitating a possessory security interest in the goods without having to deal

---

[36] Article 9 contains a series of rules that protect good-faith purchasers for value who acquire possession of paper collateral that is subject to a perfected security interest. Purchasers must satisfy slightly different requirements to obtain priority depending upon the circumstances. *See, e.g.*, U.C.C. §§ 9-308, **R9-330** (chattel paper and instruments).

[37] For example, only a "person entitled to enforce" a negotiable instrument can collect it. That status typically requires physical possession of the instrument. U.C.C. § 3-301.

[38] U.C.C. §§ 9-207(1), **R9-207(a)**. For example, persons who indorse negotiable instruments may be discharged by lack of timely notice of dishonor. U.C.C. § 3-503(a). Courts generally have found secured parties liable for failure to make a favorable conversion of pledged debentures into common stock. Traverse v. Liberty Bank & Trust Co., 5 U.C.C. Rep. Serv. 535 (Mass. Super. Ct. 1967). Although secured parties are clearly responsible for the physical care of pledged stock, almost without exception, they have not been found responsible to sell the stock in a declining market. Tepper v. Chase Manhattan Bank, NA, 376 So. 2d 35, 27 U.C.C. Rep. Serv. 1104 (Fla. Dist. Ct. App. 1979).

[39] Possession is permissive for chattel paper but mandatory (except for temporary automatic perfection) for instruments under the 1972 text. **It is permissive for both chattel paper and instruments under the 1998 text.** *See* § 6.01[B] *supra.* Possession is preferred over filing because it eliminates bona-fide-purchase risks and facilitates foreclosure. Filing is sufficient, however, to defeat lien creditors like the bankruptcy trustee. U.C.C. §§ 9-201, **R9-201(a)**.

directly with them. The secured creditor deals instead with the paper, a medium that the secured creditor readily understands and can properly maintain in its regular course of business. The role of the pledge of negotiable documents in possessory secured financing is discussed below in the contexts of terminal warehousing and goods in transit.[40] Bear in mind that possession is permissive and that a security interest in a negotiable document can also be perfected by filing a financing statement. Possession is preferred, however, because it eliminates the risk that the document will be "duly negotiated" to a holder who will gain priority over the secured party[41] and it facilitates disposition of the goods in the event of debtor default. Despite the superiority of possession, filing is sufficient to defeat lien creditors like the bankruptcy trustee.[42]

A secured party cannot perfect a security interest in an asset subject to a state certificate-of-title law by taking possession of the certificate.[43] A certificate of title is issued by the state as a fraud-prevention mechanism. It is not issued by a possessor of the goods to represent title for purposes of further transfers of rights in the goods, and it does not qualify as a document under Article 9.[44]

[B] Goods in Storage or Manufacture

Raw materials or finished goods which are either being stored by a manufacturer or used in the manufacturing process typically represent a considerable capital investment by the manufacturer. Consequently, many manufacturers are interested in using these goods as collateral to facilitate financing of their operations. A prospective lender might be willing to finance on a secured basis but, nevertheless, balk at relying upon perfection by filing. Proper filing would certainly perfect the security interest, but it would not provide the same protection against debtor dishonesty as would secured-party possession of the collateral. The challenge to the financing community was to develop mechanisms by which the creditor could attain protection comparable to a possessory security interest without having to receive delivery of the underlying goods.

[1] Terminal Warehousing — §§ 9-304(2), R9-312(c)

Terminal warehousing is used to store goods. The name is derived from the fact that many terminal warehouses are located on railroad terminals in order to facilitate the ultimate shipment of the large quantity of goods stored. The warehouse company is responsible for the care and custody of the goods placed in its charge.[45] It usually issues a negotiable document to the party that deposits goods for storage.

Negotiable documents can be envisioned as "goods paper." The Comments to the 1972 text stress that Article 9, like Article 7 on negotiable documents, "takes the position that,

---

[40] *See* §§ 6.02[B][1] and 6.02[C] *infra.*

[41] U.C.C. §§ 9-309, **R9-331(a)**. A holder to whom a negotiable document is duly negotiated is the Article 7 equivalent of a bona-fide purchaser for value. § 7-501(4).

[42] U.C.C. §§ 9-201, **R9-201(a)**.

[43] McDonald v. Peoples Automobile Loan & Fin. Corp. of Athens, Inc., 115 Ga. App. 483, 154 S.E.2d 886, 4 U.C.C. Rep. Serv. 49 (1967).

[44] Nationwide Mut. Ins. Co. v. Hayes, 276 N.C. 620, 174 S.E.2d 511, 7 U.C.C. Rep. Serv. 1105 (1970).

[45] U.C.C. § 7-204.

so long as a negotiable document covering goods is outstanding, title to the goods is, so to say, locked up in the document and the proper way of dealing with such goods is through the document."[46]

A farmer who harvests wheat thus might transport the wheat to a grain elevator so that it can be properly dried and stored. The elevator operator will give the farmer a negotiable document for the quantity of the grade of wheat that was delivered. The farmer then can sell the wheat to a willing buyer by simply delivering the negotiable document. In fact, the document might pass through the hands of several buyers until ultimately a buyer like a cereal manufacturer wants to take delivery of the wheat. This can be accomplished only by surrendering the document to the elevator operator.[47] In the interim, use of a negotiable document facilitates the marketing of the wheat without having to move the wheat itself because the document is the exclusive representation of title to the wheat.

A negotiable document can also be used to facilitate secured financing. The relevant provision in Article 9 states that while goods are in the possession of a bailee who has issued a negotiable document for them, a security interest in the goods is perfected "by perfecting a security interest in the document."[48] The motivating interest of the creditor is in the goods, because the goods dictate the value of the collateral. When goods have been warehoused under a negotiable document, however, the document controls title to the goods, so that a prudent secured lender will deal with such goods only through the document. This fusion of title to the goods into the document facilitates secured lending because the lender can confidently control access to the goods by taking both a security interest in the document and possession of the document.

The pledge of the negotiable document furthermore perfects the lender's interest.[49] The lender controls access to the goods because the warehouse will not release the goods without surrender of the negotiable document. When the debtor pays the outstanding indebtedness, the lender will return the document to the debtor so that the debtor can either sell it or acquire possession of the goods for use in its own operations. In the event of default by the debtor, the secured party can sell the document in satisfaction of the outstanding indebtedness.[50]

Most goods will have an existence both prior to and after being warehoused. During these prior and subsequent periods, the goods obviously are not in the possession of someone who has issued a negotiable document for them. Accordingly, buyers or lenders who wish to deal with the goods during these periods cannot deal with them through a document, but rather must deal with the goods themselves.

---

[46] U.C.C. § 9-304 Cmt. 2. *See* U.C.C. § 7-502(1)(holder to whom negotiable document of title is duly negotiated receives title to the document, title to the goods, and obligation of the issuer to hold or deliver the goods).

[47] The issuer of the negotiable document must deliver the goods to the holder of the document. U.C.C. § 7-403(1), (4).

[48] U.C.C. §§ 9-304(2), **R9-312(c)(1)**.

[49] U.C.C. § 9-305, **R9-313(a)**.

[50] After default, the secured party can proceed against either the documents or the goods covered thereby. U.C.C. §§ 9-501(1), **R9-601(a)(2)**.

Assume that goods are in the debtor's possession during Year 1, in the possession of a warehouse that issues a negotiable document for them during Year 2, and back in the debtor's possession during Year 3. Any security interest taken and perfected in the goods during Years 1 and 3 must be in the goods themselves. A secured party who takes a security interest in the goods during Year 1 and files a financing statement describing them need not reperfect as to the document in order to protect its interests during Year 2.[51]

A secured party who takes a security interest during Year 2, however, should deal with the goods through the negotiable document. In other words, the security agreement should describe the document for attachment purposes, and the security interest should be perfected by filing a financing statement describing the document or taking possession of it. What is the consequence to a lender who takes a security interest in the goods rather than the document during Year 2 and perfects by filing a financing statement covering the goods? The Code subordinates such a lender's interest to that of another secured party, either earlier or later in time, who takes and perfects a security interest in the document.[52] This is an exception to the general rule that rank-orders perfected security interests on the principle of "first-in-time, first-in-right."[53] The lender would, however, have a perfected security interest in the goods that would defeat any subsequent secured party who dealt with the goods rather than the document. It would also defeat lien creditors, most notably the bankruptcy trustee.

When Year 2 ends, the document will have to be surrendered in order to facilitate the debtors regaining possession of the goods.[54] Once the document is surrendered to the bailee in exchange for possession of the goods, it ceases to exist. If the secured party has, in addition to taking and perfecting its security interest in the document, previously filed a financing statement describing the goods, it will continue its perfected status without interruption. If it filed a financing statement covering the document but not the goods, the goods are a proceed of the document and the secured party's interest remains continuously perfected.[55] Relying on its proceeds interest is dangerous, however, because the secured party will have to identify the proceeds if it wishes to foreclose on them. Identification is difficult under any circumstances, and virtually impossible with fungible goods. If the secured party perfected its security interest in the document by possession and did not file as to the goods, the goods still qualify as proceeds (if they can be identified), but the secured party's interest in them becomes unperfected 10 days after

---

[51] Article 7 is consistent. Absent specified entrustment or acquiescence, "[a] document of title confers no right in goods against a person who before issuance of the document had a legal interest or a perfected security interest in them." U.C.C. § 7-503(1).

[52] U.C.C. §§ 9-304(2), **R9-312(c)(2)**.

[53] For discussion of the general rule of priority, *see* § 10.01 *infra.*

[54] The secured party will be temporarily perfected without either filing or possession for a short time after it surrenders the document to the debtor. U.C.C. §§ 9-304(5)(a)(21 days), **R9-312(f)(20 days)**.

[55] This observation assumes that a financing statement covering the goods as the original collateral would have been filed in the same office or offices where the financing statement covering the document was filed. It may not be true as to farm products under the 1972 text. Perfection as to proceeds is discussed in § 8.02 *infra.*

their receipt by the debtor unless the secured party files a financing statement describing them.[56] Accordingly, the best practical advice to a secured party acquiring a security interest during the period when goods are subject to a negotiable document is not only to take a possessory security interest in the document but also to file a financing statement describing the goods. This will eliminate the need to take further action after the document is finally surrendered.[57]

[2] Field Warehousing — §§ 9-304(3), R9-312(d)

Whereas a terminal warehouse is used to store goods, a field warehouse is not created for storage and is simply a method of facilitating secured financing. It facilitates a possessory secured interest by placing the goods in the actual possession and control of the secured party's agent, who acts as a warehouseman on the premises of the debtor. The transactional costs associated with a possessory interest in bulky goods are reduced sharply because the warehouse is created around the goods while they are located on the debtor's premises, eliminating any need to move them back and forth between the secured party and the debtor.

A field warehouse can be a very simple creation.[58] Assume that the debtor has a large stock of finished inventory, like Christmas ornaments, that will be delivered to retail merchants for resale during the holiday season. The secured party would like to take possession of the inventory until the debtor needs it but does not want to pay moving and storage costs. A field warehouse is an ideal solution. The key to the creation of the field warehouse is to exclude the debtor's access to the goods, both physically and legally. The warehouse can be created physically merely by enclosing the area around the finished goods with temporary walls of chicken wire with access through a padlocked door. The debtor and secured party should also enter into a simple lease whereby the portion of the debtor's premises that comprises the warehouse is leased to the secured party.

The secured party is likely to be too busy to be bothered with actually operating the field warehouse, so it commonly appoints an agent to perform that task.[59] The agent often will issue nonnegotiable warehouse receipts to the secured party for the goods that are located within the warehouse. These nonnegotiable documents, unlike the negotiable variety, are not used in commercial transactions to represent title to the goods.[60] Like

---

[56] Id.

[57] As long as a financing statement is being filed anyway, it is useful to include a description of the document along with the description of the goods. This provides perfected status in the event the document is surrendered and the debtor retains possession of it beyond the period of temporary perfection.

[58] For a description of a typical field warehouse, see Scott v. Lawrence Warehouse Co., 227 Or. 78, 360 P.2d 610 (1961).

[59] The agent, while frequently an employee of the debtor, must be made responsible to the secured party, and not to the debtor. U.C.C. § 9-305, Comment 2.

[60] A transferee of a nonnegotiable document acquires only whatever title and rights the transferor has or has power to transfer (U.C.C. § 7-504(1)), not complete title. Thus, there is no practice by secured parties of taking security interests in nonnegotiable documents (as opposed to the goods they represent), and Article 9's perfection rules (discussed infra this subsection) focus on the goods rather than the document.

their negotiable counterparts, however, they serve as a receipt for goods that have been delivered to the bailee and stored in the warehouse, and they establish a contractual relationship between the bailor and the warehouse company.

Nonnegotiable warehouse receipts play a role in satisfying the notice requirement for perfection of a security interest in the underlying goods. Article 9 provides three perfection alternatives for a security interest in goods covered by a nonnegotiable document: 1) issuance of a document in the name of the secured party; 2) the bailee's receipt of notification of the secured party's interest; and 3) filing as to the goods.[61] The field-warehouse agent will typically use the first alternative, issuing warehouse receipts for the goods in the name of the secured party. This makes the secured party the "person entitled under the document,"[62] giving it control over the disposition of the goods.[63]

If the debtor seeks to enter into subsequent transactions concerning the goods with other parties, those parties will be alerted to the prior interest upon finding that the debtor cannot open the lock on the field warehouse to gain access to the goods on its premises. Upon consulting with the only person who can gain access, the field-warehouse agent, the interested parties will learn of the secured party's prior perfected security interest in the goods. The notice function of perfection can also be advanced by placing signs outside the warehouse indicating that the goods contained within are subject to a security interest and providing the name and telephone number of the agent for purposes of any interested inquiries.

Secured lenders using a field warehouse are well-advised to take the additional step of filing with respect to the goods. Then, if any aspect of the field-warehousing arrangement is challenged for the purpose of defeating perfection by possession, the secured party can easily prove perfection by filing. The advantage of the field warehousing arrangement, however, is that it facilitates a secured financing agreement if the lender is unwilling to finance against goods that remain within the control and custody of the debtor.[64]

Sometimes, a field warehouse can be incredibly simple and not require much of the field-warehouse agent. For example, a large cask of whiskey might need to age for several years without being disturbed. Debtor access can be denied by having the field-warehouse agent padlock the spigot. Notice to interested parties can be facilitated by posting signs on the cask, indicating that the goods have been pledged to the secured party and providing the name and address of the field-warehouse agent from whom further information can be obtained. The agent need not be on the premises very often, but visits should be frequent enough to determine that the posted signs have not been removed and the padlocked access has not been tampered with.

---

[61] U.C.C. §§ 9-304(3), **R9-312(d)**.

[62] U.C.C. § 7-403(4). "Person entitled to enforce" in the case of a nonnegotiable document means "the person to whom delivery is to be made by the terms of or pursuant to written instructions under" the document. *Id.*

[63] U.C.C. § 7-403(1)(bailee must deliver the goods to a person entitled under the document).

[64] An article that focuses extensively on the control aspects of field warehousing and on the requirement of possession in this context is Skilton, *Field Warehousing as a Financing Device*, 1961 Wisc. L. Rev. 221 (Part I), 403 (Part II).

More sophisticated field warehouses can also be established. Rather than locking up a completed seasonal inventory for several months, the parties might create a more fluid arrangement whereby the debtor can remove some of the finished goods as sales of those goods are executed and store additional finished goods as they are manufactured. The field-warehouse agent would issue nonnegotiable documents in the name of the secured party as goods are received into the warehouse. The secured party could then prepare delivery instructions to the agent concerning the release of collateral to the debtor.[65] The precise arrangements would depend upon the terms negotiated between the secured party and the debtor. One possibility is that the agent would be instructed to release any goods requested by the debtor but always to retain within the warehouse finished goods whose value totals a particular amount (called in the industry a "loan-to-collateral ratio").[66]

The bailee's compliance with written instructions leaves the lender with a perfected security interest in goods whose value is considered sufficient to cover the indebtedness incurred by the debtor. If the debtor continues to borrow more money against an established credit line or makes payments that reduce the extent of indebtedness, new delivery instructions from the secured party to the field-warehouse agent can change the amount of collateral required to be maintained within the warehouse.

Another possibility is to create two field warehouses, one for raw materials used in the debtor's manufacturing operations and the other for finished goods produced, and to prepare delivery instructions that tie the two warehouses together. The field warehouse agent could be instructed, for example, that for every ten units of raw materials released to the debtor, three units of finished goods must be received. Extending field warehouses to the raw materials facilitates secured financing of those goods as well, allowing an enhanced borrowing position for the debtor.

The consequences of becoming too lax in establishing a field warehouse are illustrated in *Whitney National Bank of New Orleans v. Sandoz.*[67] A bank took a security interest in the debtor canning company's inventory of canned goods that it purportedly perfected by possession through a field-warehouse arrangement. Parts of the debtor's plants were leased to the warehouse company, which issued warehouse receipts for the goods. The debtor, however, retained possession of the leased spaces and complete access to its inventory.[68] The court found that the transaction was a sham and that the bankruptcy

---

[65] The debtor becomes the person entitled to enforce the document to the extent of the secured party's written instructions (U.C.C. § 7-403(4)), and the bailee is then obligated to deliver the designated goods to the debtor. § 7-403(1).

[66] Ribaudo v. Citizens Nat'l Bank of Orlando, 261 F.2d 929 (5th Cir. 1958) (warehousing company instructed by bank to retain in its custody warehoused merchandise worth 133 1/3% of $50,000 loaned, or $66,666.67).

[67] 362 F.2d 605 (1966).

[68] The potential risk exposure associated with poorly-maintained field warehouses is illustrated in the extreme by one of the biggest business-fraud cases ever. Several banks in the United States and Britain extended loans for $150 million based on warehouse receipts for vegetable oils supposedly located in Bayonne, New Jersey. The contents that were actually located there were over a billion pounds short. *See* Proctor & Gamble Distrib. Co. v. Lawrence American Field Warehousing Corp., 16 N.Y.2d 344, 266 N.Y.S.2d 785, 213 N.E.2d 873, 21 A.L.R.3d 1320, 3 U.C.C. Rep. Serv. 157 (1965); N. Miller, *The Great Salad Oil Swindle* (1965).

court had properly held that the warehouse receipts were invalid. The warehouse agent filled the function in name only, because the goods were not actually warehoused. The warehouse agent did not maintain exclusive possession and control over the goods, as even the debtor was allowed unfettered access to the goods. In the absence of any signs or markings on the warehouse or the goods, subsequent parties interested in dealing with the goods could have been easily deceived by the debtor.

The obvious lesson is that a field warehouse must exist in more than name only to provide perfection by possession. It must be operated in a manner sufficient to satisfy the notice function that underlies perfection of security interests.[69] Another lesson is that a proper filing as to the goods, while insufficient to protect against debtor defalcations, would have defeated the bankruptcy trustee.

An alternative method of protecting a secured lender against a debtor's improper use of the collateral has developed. Rather than creating a field warehouse and issuing warehouse receipts to the secured party, a bonded warehousing company issues a written certification of the value of the collateral on the debtor's premises. The company also contracts to comply with the secured party's delivery instructions concerning the collateral and to assume liability for any losses that result from not fulfilling its duties. A three-way agreement among the debtor, the secured party and the warehouse company authorizes policing and control by the warehouse company, and the secured party simply perfects by filing as to the goods. This approach to certified inventory control protects the secured party by passing the risk of debtor defalcation on to the warehousing company.[70]

[C] Goods in Transit

Sometimes a party will wish to arrange financing that will be secured by goods that are in transit. Assume a transaction in which an importer in the United States is purchasing several hundred tons of copper from Chile. The goods might take up to three weeks to

---

[69] Article 9 stresses the importance of proper maintenance of a field warehouse. U.C.C. §§ 9-205, **R9-205** allow the debtor to use and dispose of collateral without impairing the security interest's validity. *See* § 3.01 *supra*. The last sentence of § 9-205 provides that the section "does not relax the requirements of possession where perfection of a security interest depends upon possession of the collateral by the secured party or by a bailee." **§ R9-205(b) is consistent with regard to perfection and extends the principle to attachment and enforcement.** The relationship to field warehousing is explained in the Comments to the 1972 text:

> The last sentence is added to make clear that the section does not mean that the holder of an unfiled security interest, whose perfection depends on possession of the collateral by the secured party or by a bailee (such as a field warehouseman), can allow the debtor access to and control over the goods without thereby losing his perfected interest. The common law rules on the degree and extent of possession which are necessary to perfect a pledge interest or to constitute a valid filed warehouse are not relaxed by this or any other section of this Article.

§ 9-205 Cmt. 6.

[70] Descriptions of certified inventory control arrangements are provided in McGuire, *The Impact of the UCC on Field Warehousing*, 6 UCC L.J. 267, 280-82 (1974). The article further explains that warehouse companies also enter into accounts receivables programs in which they guarantee the validity of accounts and protect against debtor diversion of funds received on accounts.

arrive by ocean carrier at a U.S. port. The importer will then break down the shipment into domestic shipments that it will route to each of its pre-arranged buyers. An importer who must pay the seller shortly after the goods are shipped but will not be paid on its resale transactions until the copper is delivered to domestic buyers may need financing to cover the interim period.

The importer can enter into a transaction with a bank in this country under which the bank will issue a letter of credit to the exporter. [71] The bank will require that the importer execute a security agreement granting a security interest in the copper and in any documents covering the copper, and it will file a financing statement perfecting its security interest in the goods and documents. The letter of credit will require the bank to pay the exporter's drafts, provided that the appropriate papers are included with the draft. [72] One of the required papers will be a negotiable bill of lading, which will be issued by the carrier when the goods are shipped. [73] After shipment, the exporter will prepare a draft drawn on the bank demanding payment in the amount of the purchase price. It will then forward the draft and the negotiable bill of lading (together with other required papers [74]) through banking channels to the bank. The bank will receive possession of the bill of lading when it pays the draft. [75] Although the secured party's interest was perfected by its filed financing statement, possession of the bill of lading enhances its position. [76]

This type of transaction can be desirable from the perspectives of all of the parties. The exporter need not relinquish ownership or control of the goods until it is paid, because it will not deliver the bill of lading to the bank until its draft is paid. The bank, on the other hand, acquires control over the goods when it pays the draft. The importer is able to use the copper in transit as security to facilitate the transaction.

The bank, of course, will have to relinquish possession of the bill of lading for the goods to be released by the ocean carrier. It will then have a perfected nonpossessory

---

[71] A letter of credit is "an engagement by a bank or other person made at the request of a customer and of a kind within the scope of Article 5 of the U.C.C. that the issuer will honor drafts or other demands for payment upon compliance with the conditions specified in the credit." U.C.C. § 5-103(1)(a). The U.C.C. provisions on letters of credit are contained in Article 5.

[72] A draft is a negotiable instrument that includes an order to pay money. U.C.C. § 3-104(e).

[73] A bill of lading is "a document evidencing the receipt of goods for shipment issued by a person engaged in the business of transporting or forwarding goods, and includes an airbill." U.C.C. § 1-201(6). The U.C.C. provisions on bills of lading are provided in Article 7 on documents. For interstate shipments and exports, however, bills of lading are governed by the Federal Bills of Lading Act, 49U.S.C. App. §§ 81-124(1988), rather than the U.C.C..

[74] To assure itself that conforming goods have been shipped, the bank's letter of credit will probably require the seller to deliver certificates related to inspection of the goods. It will also require evidence of insurance, and papers showing compliance with the laws of the exporting and importing countries.

[75] The named consignee on the bill of lading, the exporter, will "negotiate" it to the bank by indorsing and physically delivering it. U.C.C. § 7-501(1). This gives the bank the status of holder, making it the person entitled to enforce the document. § 7-403(4). The carrier will only release the goods to a person entitled to enforce the document. § 7-403(1).

[76] See § 6.02[B][1] supra.

security interest in the importer's copper. The bank can further enhance its position by insisting that each buyer of copper provide the importer with a letter of credit.[77] As the copper is delivered to domestic shippers, new negotiable bills of lading will be issued. These can be negotiated to the secured party, who will then forward them to the issuing banks with drafts ordering payment to the secured party. Payments under the drafts will be applied to reduce the importer's indebtedness.

§ 6.03   The Concept of Possession — §§ 9-305, R9-313

[A]   Possession by the Secured Party

Section 9-305 of the 1972 text provides that "[a] security interest is perfected by possession from the time possession is taken without relation back and continues only so long as possession is retained."[78] The first part of this sentence rejects the common-law theory of the "equitable pledge." Under this theory, the taking of possession could relate back to the date of an original security agreement which included an agreement to take possession in the future.[79] Taking possession shortly before bankruptcy, however, may create a voidable preference under federal bankruptcy law.[80] To achieve consistency with this federal policy, relation back is eliminated for possessory security interests.[81] Perfection by possession applies only during the time that the secured party takes and retains possession of the collateral.[82] Perfection either prior to or after the period of

---

[77] The bank's security agreement can cover the importer's rights to the proceeds of the letters of credit as additional collateral. Letter-of-credit rights are discussed generally in § 1.10[A] *supra.* The 1972 text is limited to rights to the proceeds of a written letter of credit (U.C.C. § 9-104(m)), and perfection requires possession of the letter. §§ 9-305, 9-304(1). **The 1998 text governs "letter-of-credit rights," a term which includes a right to payment or performance under any letter of credit (§ R9-102(a)(51)). Letter-of-credit rights are perfected by control (§§ R9-314(a), R9-107), which requires that the issuer or its nominee consent to the security assignment. Without this consent, the secured party is not only unperfected but cannot require that the issuing bank honor the letter.** *See* § 1.08, nn. 362 and 363, *supra.*

[78] **The 1998 text is in accord. U.C.C. § R9-313(d)("perfection occurs no earlier than the time the secured party takes possession and continues only while the secured party retains possession").**

[79] U.C.C. § 9-305 Cmt. 3. When security interests in instruments, certificated securities and negotiable documents are given as collateral for new value, the Code provides for a short period of perfection without possession. §§ 9-304(4)(21 days), **R9-312(e)(20 days)**. This period of automatic perfection can be seen as a limited relation-back rule. There can also be automatic perfection for a short time after possession is relinquished when the collateral consists of negotiable documents, goods in the possession of a bailee other than one who has issued a negotiable document, instruments and certificated securities. §§ 9-304(5)(21 days), **R9-312(f), (g)(20 days)**. Temporary automatic perfection is discussed in §§ 8.01, 8.02 *infra.*

[80] Bankruptcy Code, 11U.S.C. § 547. *See* § 16.04[E] *infra.*

[81] *In re* Granite City Coop. Creamery Ass'n, Inc., 7 U.C.C. Rep. Serv. 1083 (Bankr. Vt. 1970).

[82] Possession need not be taken for the purpose of perfecting the security interest. An otherwise unperfected secured party that takes possession of collateral following a default by the debtor thereby perfects its security interest. *In re* Osborn, 389 F. Supp. 1137, 16 U.C.C. Rep. Serv. 827 (N.D. N.Y. 1975); Walter E. Heller & Co. v. Salerno, 168 Conn. 152, 362 A.2d 904, 16 U.C.C. Rep. Serv. 840 (1975). Obtaining a default judgment against the defendant in a replevin action

possession must be attained through tacking with other applicable methods of perfection. [83]

In *Transport Equipment Co. v. Guaranty State Bank*,[84] perfection by possession of the debtor's machinery occurred too late to protect the secured party against a second secured party who perfected by filing. Although representatives of the secured party arrived on the debtor's premises in the morning, they did not load the collateral onto trucks until the afternoon. The court held that possession occurred only upon the loading, and that the filing by the competing secured party earlier in the afternoon afforded it priority.

The purchase-money seller in *In re* Automated Bookbinding Services., Inc.,[85] lost perfection when it shipped the goods by carrier under a nonnegotiable bill of lading showing the buyer as the consignee. Possession terminated because the seller lost control of the goods in transit.

[B] Possession by Third Parties

A secured party is not required to obtain or retain possession personally, but rather may use an agent for purposes of possession.[86] In accordance with the principles of agency law, the agent acts on behalf of the principal, so that possession by the agent serves as possession by the secured party.[87] The key is to exclude the debtor from both possession and control of the collateral.[88] The Comments to the 1972 text succinctly state the necessary relationship: "Possession may be by the secured party himself or by an agent on his behalf: it is of course clear, however, that the debtor or a person controlled by him cannot qualify as such an agent for the secured party."[89] Retention of possession or control by the debtor facilitates the possibility that the debtor might use that possession or control for the purpose of deceiving subsequent parties. Possession by the secured party or by an agent controlled by the secured party advances the notice function that lies at the core of the concept of perfection.

Possession by the secured party or its agent is actual possession. A secured party can also attain constructive possession when personal property of the debtor is held by a bailee.[90] A bailee will hold the property because the debtor, not the secured party, placed

---

is not sufficient to perfect by possession because the right to take possession of the collateral is not the same as having actual possession of it. *In re* Walter Neilly & Co., Inc., 1 U.C.C. Rep. Serv. 364 (Bankr. W.D. Pa. 1961).

[83] U.C.C. §§ 9-305, **R9-308(c)**. *See also* § 4.04 *supra.*

[84] 518 F.2d 377, 17 U.C.C. Rep. Serv. 1 (10th Cir. 1975).

[85] 471 F.2d 546, 11 U.C.C. Rep. Serv. 897 (4th Cir. 1972).

[86] *In re* Bruce Farley Corp., 26 B.R. 164, 35 U.C.C. Rep. Serv. 1304 (Bankr. S.D. Cal. 1981).

[87] Restatement (Second) of Agency § 17 Cmt. a (1958) (delegated act done by representative has same legal effect as if done personally by the principal).

[88] *In re* Maryville Sav. & Loan Corp., 27 B.R. 701, 35 U.C.C. Rep. Serv. 983 (Bankr. E.D. Tenn. 1983) (collateral that remained in debtor's possession was not constructively delivered for purposes of perfection by possession).

[89] U.C.C. § 9-305 Cmt. 2.

[90] A bailment is a transaction in which goods are placed in the rightful possession of one who

the bailee in possession.[91] The 1972 text of Article 9 provides that "the secured party is deemed to have possession from the time the bailee receives notification of the secured party's interest."[92] A bailee's receipt of such notification makes the bailee legally accountable through an implied-in-law bailment with respect to the secured party's interest.[93] Even though the goods were bailed at the direction of the debtor, the accountability resulting from notification obligates the bailee to withhold possession from the debtor and to protect the interest of the secured party.[94] The notice function of perfection is advanced because the bailee must also reveal that secured party's interest to subsequent parties that inquire as to the nature of the bailment. Consequently, "receipt of notification of the secured party's interest by the bailee . . . is looked on as equivalent to taking possession by the secured party."[95]

Determining whether a third person is an agent or a bailee can occasionally be difficult. In *In re* Rolain,[96] for example, the collateral consisted of a promissory note issued to the debtor by a third party. The promissory note contained confidential information which the debtor had agreed not to release, and the secured party and debtor agreed that the note would be held by the debtor's attorney pursuant to an escrow agreement. The court did not have to decide whether the attorney was an agent of the secured party or a bailee since the attorney was at all times aware of the reason for his taking possession.

Courts have held notification to a bailee insufficient to perfect a security interest by constructive possession when the family or business relationship between the debtor and the bailee is so close that it substantially reduces the likelihood that the bailee will carry out its duty to the secured party by restricting the debtor's access to the collateral.[97]

---

is not their owner. R. Brown, *The Law of Personal Property* § 10.1 (W. Raushenbush 3d ed. 1975). For an excellent discussion of bailment law in this context, see R. Hillman, J. McDonnell, & S. Nickles, *Common Law and Equity Under the Uniform Commercial Code* ¶ 23.03 (1985).

[91] Situations in which the secured party delivers pledged collateral to a third party are discussed *infra* this subsection.

[92] Estate of Hinds, 10 Cal. App. 3d 1021, 89 Cal. Rptr. 341, 8 U.C.C. Rep. Serv. 3 (Cal. Ct. App. 1970) (notice to bailee holding stock certificates). "[T]his rule rejects the common law doctrine that it is necessary for the bailee to attorn to the secured party or acknowledge that he now holds on his behalf." U.C.C. § 9-305 Cmt. 2.

[93] Ingersoll-Rand Fin. Corp. v. Nunley, 671 F.2d 842, 33 U.C.C. Rep. Serv. 757 (4th Cir. 1982); Sumner v. Hamlet, 29 Mass. (12 Pick.) 76 (1831). *See* Restatement of Security § 8 (1941).

[94] *In re* Rolain, 823 F.2d 198, 4 U.C.C. Rep. Serv. 2d 5 (8th Cir. 1987) discussed *infra* this subsection.

[95] U.C.C. § 9-304 Cmt. 3. The discussion here focuses on bailees who have not issued documents of title against the goods. The receipt-of-notification method of perfection can also be used when a bailee has issued a nonnegotiable document. §§ 9-304(3), **R9-312(d)(2)**. The method does not apply when the bailee has issued a negotiable document because title to the bailed goods and the bailee's duties with respect to the goods are tied to control of the document. *Compare* §§ 9-304(2), **R9-312(c)** *with* §§ 9-304(3), **R9-312(d)**. The use of negotiable documents in commercial financing transactions is discussed in §§ 6.02[B][1] and 6.02[C], and the use of nonnegotiable documents is discussed in § 6.02[B][2] *infra*.

[96] 823 F.2d 198, 4 U.C.C. Rep. Serv. 2d 5 (8th Cir. 1987).

[97] **This limitation continues under the revision, notwithstanding its requirement (discussed**

Notification was thus not sufficient to perfect a security interest in goods that the debtor had stored in his father's garage.[98] Similarly, notification did not constitute perfection by possession of stock that the corporate debtor had bailed to the president of the corporation.[99] On the other hand, the attorney in *In re* Rolain was considered sufficiently independent to qualify as either an agent for the secured party for purposes of actual possession or as a bailee for purposes of constructive possession. This conclusion is entirely appropriate given the rules of professional conduct and the fact that attorneys are capable of understanding situations involving divided loyalties.

Revised Article 9 restricts the receipt-of-notification method for obtaining constructive possession to bailees who have issued nonnegotiable documents covering the goods.[100] In other situations, constructive possession under the revision requires that the bailee authenticate a record acknowledging that it holds, or as to future assets will hold, the collateral for the secured party's benefit.[101] This technique, which provides an escape for a bailee who does not wish to assume any duties toward a secured party, cannot be used when the bailee is a lessee of the collateral from the debtor in the ordinary course of the debtor's business.[102] This limitation represents a policy judgment that the lessee's possession of the goods in such circumstances is insufficient to provide adequate public notice of the secured party's interest.[103]

The revision makes it clear that a bailee is under no legal obligation to authenticate an acknowledgment;[104] and unless the bailee otherwise agrees or law outside Article 9 otherwise provides, the fact that the bailee has chosen to do so does not subject the bailee to any duty to the secured party or to any third party.[105] Although this provision makes it clear that revised Article 9 imposes no duties on the bailee, it should not be read to preclude application of the common-law rule shifting the bailee's duty to account for bailed assets from the debtor to the secured party. The point at which the shift occurs merely changes from receipt of notification to authentication of an acknowledgment. Any other interpretation would be inconsistent with the notice function that underlies perfection and would expose lenders to

---

infra this subsection) that the bailee authenticate a record acknowledging that it holds the collateral for the secured party's benefit. U.C.C. § R9-313, Cmt 3 states that "a court may determine that a third person in possession is so closely connected to or controlled by the debtor that the debtor has retained effective possession . . . ."

[98] *In re* Hill, 7 B.R. 433, 30 U.C.C. Rep. Serv. 1454 (Bankr. W.D. Okla. 1980).

[99] In the Matter of North Am. Builders, Inc., 320 F. Supp. 1229, 8 U.C.C. Rep. Serv. 1132 (D. Neb. 1970).

[100] U.C.C. §§ R9-312(d)(2); R9-312 Cmt. 7.

[101] U.C.C. § R9-313(c).

[102] The term "lessee in ordinary course of business" is defined in U.C.C. § 2A-103(1)(o).

[103] The revision rejects the reasoning of *In re* Atlantic Computer Sys., Inc., 135 B.R. 463, 16 U.C.C. Rep. Serv. 2d 1204 (Bankr. S.D.N.Y. 1992)(receipt of notification by lessee in ordinary course perfected security interest in leased goods). See U.C.C. § R9-313 Cmt. 7.

[104] U.C.C. § R9-313(f).

[105] U.C.C. § R9-313(g)(2). § R9-313(g)(1) makes the acknowledgment effective even if it violates the debtor's rights.

unacceptable risks. Because of the risk that the bailee will refuse to authenticate an acknowledgment, secured parties should take the precautionary step of filing a financing statement in order to ensure perfected status. In addition, secured parties contemplating the use of escrow agreements like the one in *In re Rolain* will have to exercise caution. If that case had been decided under the revision and the court had determined that the debtor's attorney was a bailee and not an agent for the secured party, the secured party would have lacked actual or constructive possession. As a precaution, a secured party that uses such a technique should obtain an acknowledgment authenticated by the escrowee.[106]

The authenticated-acknowledgment requirement might create problems in certain types of transactions. For example, it is common for a mortgage lender to pledge the notes and mortgages arising from its real estate loans to a commercial bank as collateral for a line of credit. Although the initial transactions that give rise to the notes and mortgages are governed by real estate law, the secondary-financing transaction in which the notes and mortgages are used as collateral is within the scope of Article 9.[107] The commercial bank that provides the line of credit is known as a mortgage warehouse lender. Typically, the instruments[108] will remain with the warehouse lender until there is a pool sufficient to justify selling them on the secondary mortgage market.[109] A secondary-market investor may wish to inspect the instruments before agreeing to purchase them, and this requires that they be forwarded by the warehouse lender.[110] A warehouse lender has an incentive to facilitate such sales since the proceeds can be used to pay down the line of credit, and the practice has developed of forwarding the instruments to prospective buyers under cover of letters advising of the security interest. This practice gives the warehouse lender constructive possession under the 1972 text. The Comments to the 1998 revision reflect a concern that requiring warehouse lenders to obtain an authenticated acknowledgment from each prospective buyer might be "unduly burdensome and disruptive of established practices."[111]

Because of this concern, the revision contains a special rule that applies to cases in which a secured party already in possession of collateral delivers it to a person other than the debtor or a lessee from the debtor in the ordinary course of the debtor's business.[112] In that context, delivery does not amount to a relinquishment

---

[106] The Comments suggest that an escrowee is an agent for both parties and that in the typical escrow arrangement "the debtor's relationship to the escrowee is not such as to constitute retention of possession by the debtor." U.C.C. § R9-313 Cmt. 3.

[107] Secondary-financing transactions collateralized by payment obligations backed by real-estate interests are discussed in § 1.07[C] *supra.*

[108] As used here, the term "instrument" refers to both the note and the mortgage.

[109] Sales of promissory notes are within the scope of revised Article 9 and are discussed in § 1.06 *supra.*

[110] This is a likely request only when the mortgage loan is on nonresidential real estate and hence is not written on the standard forms used for residential loans.

[111] U.C.C. § R9-313 Cmt. 9.

[112] The limitation for lessees from the debtor in the ordinary course of the debtor's business is discussed in the text accompanying nn. 102 and 103 *supra.*

of possession if the recipient is instructed before, or contemporaneously with, the delivery to hold possession for the secured party's benefit or to redeliver the collateral to the secured party.[113] Although drafted with the mortgage warehouse lender in mind, this rule is also applicable when the secured party itself borrows funds and "repledges" collateral delivered to it by a debtor as security for its own loan.[114]

[C] Symbolic or Constructive Delivery

Possession is a concept that arises in numerous legal contexts and has varied meanings within those contexts. The popular saying that "possession in nine points of the law" reflects the fundamental significance that possession historically has had in our legal culture. In numerous contexts, possession has evolved to encompass many forms of possession based on symbolic or constructive delivery.[115] Although some forms of such delivery are appropriate in the context of possession for purposes of perfecting an Article 9 security interest, their recognition for this purpose necessarily is substantially curtailed. Any form of possession must be sufficient to satisfy the public-notice function that underlies any appropriate method of perfection.

The case of *In re* Bialk[116] is illustrative. The secured party sought to take a pledge of medals and coins that the debtor had placed in a bank safe-deposit box. The debtor gave his only keys to the box to the secured party, who argued that delivery of the keys constituted symbolic delivery of the contents sufficient to constitute perfection by possession. The bankruptcy court disagreed, because the bank had not also been notified of the secured party's interest. The debtor could still have gained ready access to the locked goods even without the keys because the bank would have opened the box for him if he had stated that he lost his keys. Consequently, delivery of the keys to the secured party's possession was not sufficient notice to subsequent third parties because the debtor could still show them the goods without the keys.

§ 6.04　Perfection by Control

Control was first introduced as a method of perfection when Article 9 was amended to conform to the 1994 revisions to Article 8. At that time, it applied only to investment

---

[113] U.C.C. § R9-313(h). Unless the prospective purchaser otherwise agrees or law other than Article 9 otherwise provides, the purchaser does not owe any duty to the secured party or to a third party. § R9-313(i). This provision should not be read to preclude common-law rules imposing duties on bailees. *See* discussion *supra* this subsection.

[114] *See also* U.C.C. § R9-207(c)(3)(secured party may create security interest in collateral in its possession). A pledgee's possession is not interrupted even if delivery of pledged collateral to a lender violates the debtor's rights. U.C.C. § R9-313(i). However, unless the collateral is indispensable paper and the repledgee qualifies as a type of bona-fide purchaser for value under one of the Code's priority rules, the repledgee's rights in the collateral will be congruent with the rights of the original secured party (the pledgee). The problems associated with limited rights in collateral are discussed in § 2.02[C] *supra*.

[115] It is important to differentiate between constructive delivery of an asset to a secured party and constructive possession by a secured party. Constructive possession is discussed in the preceding subsection.

[116] 16 U.C.C. Rep. Serv. 519 (Bankr. W.D. Mich. 1974).

property. **The 1998 revision extends perfection by control to deposit accounts, electronic chattel paper and letter-of-credit rights.**

[A]   Investment Property — §§ 9-115, R9-314(a), R9-106

The Code's treatment of securities has evolved significantly over the past quarter-century. Prior to the revision of Article 8 and conforming amendments to Article 9 in 1977, the assumption was that certificates would be issued for investment securities. The owner of a certificated stock or bond could create a perfected secured interest in a lender by entering into a security agreement with the lender and giving the lender possession of the certificate. This type of asset was thus treated as indispensable paper, like an instrument.[117] Any interest that a debtor might have in an investment vehicle for which no certificate existed qualified as a general tangible.

The number of securities transactions increased so drastically during the 1960s that the industry looked for ways to reduce the amount of paperwork. One practice that developed was the issuance of certificates in "street name." Rather than issuing certificates to each individual investor, a corporation would issue only a few certificates in large amounts to stockbrokers, representing the ownership interests of each of the broker's customers. In other words, the broker held the certificate on behalf of multiple customers.

Today, it is unlikely that even the broker will hold a certificate. Under the indirect holding system that has developed in recent years, it is more common for a "jumbo certificate" to be held by a clearing corporation of which the broker is a member. Thus, the broker may own, for all its customers, 100,000 shares of a particular stock, and the books of the broker will reflect the ownership interests each of the broker's customers. The certificate itself will be held by a clearing corporation and may represent hundreds of thousand of shares. The books of the clearing corporation will show that the broker owns 100,000 of these shares.

Another practice is the issuance of uncertificated securities, which are also referred to as "book entry" securities. The corporation does not issue any certificate; rather, ownership and transfer are simply recorded through book or computer entries. When uncertificated securities are held through a broker, the customer's interest is shown through the broker's records and confirmations of purchase. Many government securities are issued in uncertificated form.

Perfection of a security interest in certificated securities held indirectly by a broker or other intermediary created problems. Filing was ineffectual since the securities were certificated; and to pledge them, the debtor would have to go to the trouble of obtaining a certificate from the broker (who, in turn, would often have to obtain it from a clearing corporation). Perfecting an interest in uncertificated securities was also problematic. Such securities were classified as general intangibles, and the only means of perfection was to file a financing statement. The securities industry, however, was not in the practice of searching financing statements because securities previously had all been certificated and filing was excluded as a method of perfection. Although the use of uncertificated securities might have forced a change in industry practices, the objective of lessening

---

[117] Certificated securities were defined as instruments for Article 9 purposes until the 1994 revision of Articles 8 and 9. *See* U.C.C. § 9-105(1)(i)(1978 Official Text).

paperwork that was a leading motivation for the introduction of uncertificated securities would have been undercut with the imposition of a different paperwork requirement for dealing with the U.C.C. filing system.

In an attempt to accommodate these changes in the securities industry, the U.C.C. was revised in 1977. These amendments, however, proved unsatisfactory, and the Code was revised again in 1994. These latter amendments created "investment property" as an umbrella category for most interests in investment vehicles. [118] Investment property consists of securities (whether held directly or indirectly and whether certificated or uncertificated), security entitlements, securities accounts, commodity contracts and commodity accounts. Many of the key provisions governing noncommodity-related investment property are found in Article 8. Commodity-related assets are beyond the scope of Article 8, and thus the provisions governing security interests in commodity contracts and commodity accounts are found exclusively in Article 9. **The 1998 revisions to Article 9 have left this area essentially unchanged.**

Control is the primary method for perfecting a security interest in investment property. [119] A secured party has control when it is has the power to control the disposition of the collateral. Filing is available as an alternative means of perfection [120] unless the debtor is a broker, [121] a securities intermediary [122] or a commodity intermediary. [123]

As applied to a certificated security, uncertificated security or security entitlement, control has the meaning that is specified in Article 8. [124] For a certificated security held directly by the debtor, control requires that the certificate be delivered to the secured party. [125] If the certificate is in bearer form, the secured party must gain actual or constructive possession. [126] If it is in registered form, meaning that it specifies the debtor as the person entitled to it, [127] the secured party must gain actual or constructive possession and must also either obtain the debtor's indorsement [128] or have the certificate registered in the secured party's name. [129] This latter method might occur, for example,

---

[118] The definitions and basic structure for investment property are discussed in detail in § 1.04[E] *supra*.

[119] U.C.C. §§ 9-115(4)(a)**R9-314, R9-106**.

[120] U.C.C. §§ 9-115(4)(b), **R9-312(a)**.

[121] A "broker" is a person defined as a broker or dealer under federal securities laws, including a bank acting in that capacity. U.C.C. § 8-102(a)(3).

[122] The term "securities intermediary" includes brokers and clearing corporations. U.C.C. § 8-102(a)(14).

[123] The term "commodity intermediary" includes persons registered under federal law as futures commission merchants and others who perform clearance or settlement services for certain boards of trade. U.C.C. §§ 9-115(1)(d), **R9-102(a)(17)**.

[124] U.C.C. §§ 9-115(1)(e), **R9-106(a)**.

[125] U.C.C. § 8-106(a), (b). "Delivery" as applied to certificated securities is defined in § 8-301(a).

[126] U.C.C. § 8-106(a), 8-301(a).

[127] U.C.C. § 8-102(a)(13)(i).

[128] U.C.C. §§ 8-106(b)(1), 8-301(a). Indorsements are governed by § 8-304.

[129] U.C.C. §§ 8-106(b)(2), 8-301(a).

by surrendering the certificate to its issuer and having it reissued showing the secured party as the entitled person.

Uncertificated securities held directly by the debtor can also be controlled through delivery,[130] but delivery has an unusual meaning in this context. It means that the issuer has registered the secured party (or another person acting on the secured party's behalf) on its books as the owner of the security.[131] Control can also be obtained without delivery, but only if the issuer agrees to comply with the secured party's orders without the further consent of the debtor.[132]

Security entitlements[133] are by definition held indirectly through a securities intermediary,[134] usually a broker, and a secured party can acquire control either by becoming the entitlement holder (meaning that the books of the broker are changed to reflect ownership by the secured party)[135] or by having the broker agree to comply with the secured party's orders without the further consent of the debtor.[136] With a commodity contract, the secured party, debtor and commodity intermediary (*e.g.*, dealer) must agree that any value on account of the contract will be distributed as directed by the secured party without the further consent of the debtor.[137] Securities and commodity accounts are controlled when the secured party has control of all security entitlements or commodity contracts.[138] Perfection as to the account carries with it perfection as to each security entitlement or commodity contract held within the account.[139]

Investors often obtain purchase-money financing from their brokers, who take security interests in the purchased financial assets.[140] A secured party that takes control of a financial asset held indirectly through a broker or other securities intermediary should obtain an agreement subordinating any security interest that the intermediary may have to that of the secured party. Otherwise, the intermediary will have priority over the secured party.[141]

As an alternative to control, Article 9 permits secured parties to perfect by filing an ordinary Article 9 financing statement. Permissive filing is sufficient to defeat lien creditors, including the bankruptcy trustee, but it exposes the secured party to significant risks.

---

[130] U.C.C. § 8-106(c)(1).

[131] U.C.C. § 8-301(b).

[132] U.C.C. § 8-106(c)(2).

[133] A "security entitlement" is defined in terms of financial assets, which may or may not be securities. U.C.C. § 8-102(a)(17). *See* discussion in § 1.04[E] *supra.*

[134] U.C.C. §§ 8-102(a)(17), (7).

[135] U.C.C. § 8-106(d)(1).

[136] U.C.C. § 8-106(d)(2).

[137] U.C.C. §§ 9-115(1)(e), **R9-106(b)(2)**.

[138] U.C.C. §§ 9-115(1)(e), **R9-106(c)**.

[139] U.C.C. §§ 9-115(1)(e), **R9-308(f)(security entitlements), R9-308(g)(commodity contracts)**.

[140] An intermediary has control of all security entitlements or commodity contracts entrusted to it. *See* U.C.C. §§ 9-115(1)(e)(commodity intermediary), 8-106(e) (securities intermediary).

[141] U.C.C. §§ 9-115(5)(c)(securities intermediary), (5)(d) (commodity intermediary), **R9-328(3),(4)**.

For example, a secured party that perfects by control takes priority over another secured party that perfects by filing, even if the filing predates control and the secured party with control knows of the other secured party's interest.[142] In addition, a security interest perfected by filing may be severed by a buyer that acquires bona-fide-purchaser type status.[143] The rule subordinating security interests perfected by filing to those perfected by control and to bona fide purchasers stems from the realities of the securities market, where it would be impractical for investors to check the Article 9 filing system.[144]

There is a special alternative perfection rule for certificated securities. If a certificated security in registered form is delivered to a secured party without indorsement by the debtor or registration in the name of the secured party, the security interest is perfected even though the secured party does not have control.[145] A security interest in a certificated security that is perfected by delivery alone has priority over a conflicting security interest perfected by a means other than control,[146] including filing a financing statement.[147]

[B] Deposit Accounts, Electronic Chattel Paper and Letter-of-Credit Rights — §§ R9-314(a), R9-104, R9-105, R9-107

The 1998 revision extends the concept of control beyond investment property. Security interests in deposit accounts, electronic chattel paper and letter-of-credit rights may also be perfected by control. Indeed, with certain limited exceptions, control is the exclusive method for deposit accounts[148] and letter-of-credit rights.[149] Filing is an alternative for electronic chattel paper.[150]

With deposit accounts, control is automatic, meaning it occurs upon attachment, if the secured party is the bank[151] where the account is maintained.[152] If the account is maintained at another bank, control requires either that the secured party become the customer with regard to the account[153] or that the secured party, debtor

---

[142] U.C.C. §§ 9-115(5)(a), **R9-328(1)**. If both secured parties perfect by filing, the normal first-to-file rule applies. §§ 9-115(5)(f), **R9-328(7)**.

[143] U.C.C. §§ 9-309, **R9-331(b)**, which defer to Article 8 for a description of protected purchasers. *See* § 8-303.

[144] U.C.C. § 9-115 Cmt. 5.

[145] U.C.C. §§ 9-115(6), **R9-313(a)**.

[146] Another secured party might gain control if a bailee to whom the certificated security was entrusted wrongfully surrendered possession of the certificate. A security interest perfected by delivery is subordinate to a security interest perfected by control.

[147] U.C.C. §§ 9-115(6), **R9-328(5)**.

[148] U.C.C. § **R9-312(b)(1)**.

[149] U.C.C. § **R9-312(b)(2)**.

[150] U.C.C. § **R9-312(a)**.

[151] **"Bank" is broadly defined to include, *inter alia*, savings and loan associations, credit unions and trust companies. U.C.C. § R9-102(a)(8).**

[152] U.C.C. § **R9-104(a)(1)**.

[153] U.C.C. § **R9-104(a)(3)**.

and bank agree that the bank will follow the secured party's orders without the further consent of the debtor.[154] A secured party that has satisfied one of the above requirements has control even though the debtor retains the right to direct the disposition of the deposited funds.[155] For example, suppose the secured party takes a security interest in a deposit account and enters into an agreement with the debtor and the bank that gives it control. This means that the bank must follow the secured party's orders. The parties also agree, however, that the bank must follow the debtor's instructions as well. What the secured party obtains is a perfected security interest in whatever remains in the account at the time default occurs. This flexibility also permits banks to take security interests in accounts maintained with them, leave the borrower free to use the funds, and take priority over a trustee if the debtor subsequently files for bankruptcy protection.[156] Article 8 contains a similar provision for uncertificated securities and security entitlements that are controlled through an agreement by which the issuer or securities intermediary agrees to comply with the secured party's orders.[157]

With letter-of-credit rights control requires that the issuer or any nominated person consent to the security assignment of the proceeds of the letter.[158] This approach can be traced to the distinction in the letter-of-credit area between a right to the proceeds of the letter and a right to draw against it.[159] Control of electronic chattel paper requires that the electronic record be stored in such a way that there is a single authoritative copy which identifies the secured party, and that the copy cannot be changed in any way without the secured party's participation.[160]

---

[154] U.C.C. § R9-104(a)(2). A bank is not under a duty to enter into a control agreement. § R9-342.

[155] U.C.C. § R9-104(b).

[156] Priority contests between a secured party and a bankruptcy trustee are discussed in § 16.02[C] *infra.*

[157] U.C.C. § 8-106(f).

[158] U.C.C. § R9-107. Consent may be pursuant to U.C.C. § 5-114(c) or any other applicable law or practice.

[159] *See* Chapter 1, note 389 *supra.*

[160] U.C.C. § R9-105.

CHAPTER 7

AUTOMATIC PERFECTION

In some transactions, the security interest is perfected as soon as it attaches. The secured party is not required to take any further action to perfect because perfection occurs automatically with attachment. Parties dealing with types of personal property that are eligible for automatic perfection need to be aware that a perfected security interest might exist despite the secret nature of the encumbrance on the property. The policy considerations that led the drafters to permit automatic perfection and some practical consequences of the provisions are discussed in this chapter. **The 1972 version of Article 9 provided for automatic perfection indirectly. The revision is explicit, stating that the listed security interests are perfected "when they attach."[1]**

SYNOPSIS

---

[1] U.C.C. § R9-309.

§ 7.01 Purchase-Money Security Interests in Consumer Goods — §§ 9-302(1)(d), R9-309(1)

[A] Application

The most important automatic perfection provision applies to purchase-money security interests in consumer goods.[2] As the comments indicate, this situation is the only permanent exception to the general filing requirement when goods subject to a security interest are left in the debtor's possession.[3] Thus, a seller of goods that are to be used for a consumer purpose is automatically perfected with respect to an interest retained in the goods to secure the unpaid purchase price. Similarly, a lender who provides an enabling loan to facilitate a debtor in acquiring consumer goods obtains an automatically perfected security interest in the purchased goods. **The revision also recognizes that purchase-money security interests in consumer goods are perfected upon attachment.**[4]

To qualify for automatic perfection under this provision, obviously, the goods must be consumer goods[5] and the transaction must create a purchase-money security interest.[6] An issue that has received considerable attention is the effect on automatic perfection of a secured party's reliance upon erroneous representations by the debtor concerning the projected use of the purchased goods. Some courts have upheld automatic perfection when the debtor has unequivocally indicated to the secured party that the goods will be used for personal, family or household purposes.[7] A bankruptcy court in Pennsylvania approved this result but added the qualification that the secured party not have reason to believe that the debtor would actually use the goods differently.[8] That court denied automatic perfection to the seller of a lawn tractor because the seller should have known that the buyer intended to use the tractor in its business after the buyer initially tried to obtain the tractor in its business name. The seller's designation of the loan application as "personal" and its insistence that the buyer use a personal charge card were irrelevant.[9]

---

[2] U.C.C. § 9-302(1)(d). *In re* Haus, 18 B.R. 413, 33 U.C.C. Rep. Serv. 694 (Bankr. D. S.C. 1982) (household appliances). Although perfection is automatic with respect to purchase-money security interests in consumer goods, secured parties who rely on automatic perfection incur a unique risk with respect to certain competing claimants. *See* U.C.C. § 9-307(2). For discussion of this priority issue *see* §§ 7.01[B] *infra* this chapter and 11.03 [A][2] *infra*.

[3] U.C.C. § 9-302 Cmt. 4. In other instances automatic perfection may extend indefinitely with respect to goods that constitute proceeds, but an appropriate filing is required with respect to the original collateral. U.C.C. §§ 9-306(3)(a), **R9-315(d)(1)**. *See* § 8.02[C] *infra*.

[4] **U.C.C. § R9-309(1).**

[5] For discussion of the concept of consumer goods, *see* § 1.04[A][1] *supra.*

[6] For discussion of the requirements for a purchase-money security interest, *see* § 1.05 *supra*.

[7] *In re* Pettit, 18 B.R. 8, 33 U.C.C. Rep. Serv. 1762 (Bankr. E.D. Ark. 1981); Franklin Inv. Co. v. Homburg, 252 A.2d 95, 6 U.C.C. Rep. Serv. 60 (D.C. App. 1969).

[8] *In re* Fiscante, 141 B.R. 303, 19 U.C.C. Rep. Serv. 2d 1188 (Bankr. W.D. Pa. 1992).

[9] Decisions permitting automatic perfection based on the debtor's representations are troubling. Automatic perfection creates an ostensible-ownership problem in that the debtor appears to third parties to have unfettered ownership of the goods. The normal steps required for perfection deal with the ostensible-ownership problem by giving notice of the security interest to the public. Courts

The most prevalent issue with respect to whether a transaction qualifies as a purchase-money security interest arises when the security agreement covers all items purchased previously or that are to be purchased in the future. A security interest retained by a seller is a purchase-money security interest to the extent that it secures all or part of the price of the collateral.[10] Trustees in bankruptcy have argued frequently in these cross-collateralization cases that a security interest in past and future purchases cannot qualify as a purchase-money security interest. That position has been upheld in several cases that refused to recognize automatic perfection.[11] **Revised Article 9 deals specifically with the problem of cross-collateralization, and the reader is referred to that discussion for further detail.**[12]

[B] Policy

A provision permitting automatic perfection authorizes the creation of a secret lien — a circumstance that Article 9, for the most part, studiously avoids. Several policy considerations underlie this radical departure from the norm. The Comments are not very helpful in explaining these policies; they only indicate that automatic perfection for purchase-money security interests in consumer goods follows the policy of jurisdictions that, under prior law, did not impose filing requirements in connection with security interests in consumer goods for conditional sales or bailment leases.[13] The pertinent Comment simply shows that automatic perfection in these transactions is consistent with prior law.

One reason for treating these transactions differently is the undesirable consequences that would result from requiring perfection by filing. These consumer transactions are so common that a filing requirement would over-burden the filing system. No one is well-served if the volume of filings renders use of the system unwieldy. A related consideration is that most of these consumer transactions involve a relatively low value. The transactional costs associated with preparing and filing financing statements would, thus, be proportionately higher on these transactions.

Astute lenders and buyers should be aware of the potential for automatic perfection of a purchase-money security interest for relatively new goods in the possession of a consumer. These parties can protect themselves by requiring satisfactory documentation from the consumer showing that the seller of the goods has been paid and the source of the funds for the payment -*i.e.*, that a new secured interest was not given to obtain the funds used to pay off the original seller.

---

should be reluctant to allow private understandings to have a deleterious effect on innocent third parties. On the other hand, it must be recognized that public notice does not fully resolve the problem of ostensible ownership, and courts appropriately are concerned about protecting lenders from misrepresentations by their borrowers. Cf. **U.C.C. § R9-628(c)(insulating secured party from liability where as a result of debtor's representation it reasonably believed that a transaction was not a consumer-goods transaction or was not a consumer transaction).**

[10] U.C.C. §§ 9-107(a), **R9-107(b)(1).**

[11] *In re* Manuel, 507 F.2d 990, 16 U.C.C. Rep Serv. 493 (5th Cir. 1975); *In re* Scott, 5 B.R. 37, 29 U.C.C. Rep. Serv. 1038 (Bankr. M.D. Pa. 1980).

[12] *See* § 1.05 *supra.*

[13] U.C.C. § 9-302 Cmt. 4.

Another buyer of the goods who also qualifies as a consumer is not expected to have the same degree of sophistication concerning automatic perfection. Reflecting this assessment, a special priority provision enables such a buyer to attain priority over the purchase-money secured party who relies upon automatic perfection.[14] Secured parties can avoid the risk posed by consumer buyers by taking the additional step of filing with respect to the goods.[15]

[C] Exceptions

The automatic perfection provision with respect to consumer goods in the 1972 text is subject to two stated exceptions. If the consumer goods become fixtures, a fixture filing is needed to attain the priorities that Article 9 provides with respect to most other realty interests, although automatic perfection will defeat lien creditors like a trustee in bankruptcy.[16] The other exception covers motor vehicles required to be registered. If the motor vehicle is subject under state law to a certificate-of-title requirement, perfection of a purchase-money security interest cannot be automatic, even if the vehicle is used for consumer purposes.[17]

The revision is comparable with respect to these provisions. A fixture filing is required for priority over most conflicting realty interests in fixtures. Consistent with the new choice-of-law provisions involving goods subject to certificate-of-title statutes,[18] the revision omits any reference to the registration of motor vehicles. It instead precludes automatic perfection for goods subject to any state statute that provides for a security interest to be indicated on a certificate-of-title as a condition or result of perfection, as well as goods subject to any federal statute, regulation, or treaty that preempts Article 9 with respect to perfection.[19]

An occasional court has sought to create exceptions to automatic perfection for types of consumer goods that are not consistent with the Code provision. In *In re Sprague*,[20] the bankruptcy referee in New York refused to characterize a mobile home as a consumer good, even though it had been purchased for household purposes. The referee reasoned that automatic perfection was not intended to apply to goods as large and expensive as mobile homes. Subsequent opinions in New York have not endorsed this reasoning but have rather refused to allow automatic perfection for mobile homes on the ground that

---

[14] U.C.C. §§ 9-307(2), **R9-320(b)**. For discussion of this provision, *see* § 11.03[A][2] *infra.*

[15] *Id.*

[16] Fixtures are discussed in Chapter 15 *infra. See also In re* Hinson, 77 B.R. 34, 5 U.C.C. Rep. Serv. 2d 233 (Bankr. M.D. N.C. 1987) (fixture filing required for windows and gutters attached to house); *In re* Weaver, 69 B.R. 554, 3 U.C.C. Rep. Serv. 2d 1231 (Bankr. W.D. Ky. 1987) (no automatic perfection for mobile home situated on permanent foundation).

[17] United States v. One 1987 Cadillac DeVille, VIN 1G6CD5184H4348815, 774 F. Supp. 221, 16 U.C.C. Rep. Serv. 2d 1194 (D. Del. 1991) (automobile); *In re* Radny, 12 U.C.C. Rep. Serv. 583 (Bankr. W.D. Mich. 1973)(mobile home).

[18] *See* § 9.03 *infra.*

[19] U.C.C. § **R9-309(1)**. *See also* §§ **R9-311(a)(2)(certificate-of-title statutes), R9-311(a)(1)(federal law).**

[20] 4 U.C.C. Rep. Serv. 702 (Bankr. N.D.N.Y. 1966).

a requirement to register mobile homes in New York places them within the express exception to automatic perfection.[21]

The court in *Union National Bank of Pittsburgh v. Northwest Marine, Inc.*[22] held that a 33-foot motorboat purchased for family purposes for $8,000 was not consumer goods for purposes of automatic perfection. The court reasoned that the concept of consumer goods envisions a "using up" or "wasting away" of the asset to the extent that a second institution would not be inclined to loan money against it. It thus found that the motorboat was a good of substantial magnitude compared to the "ordinary" concept of consumer goods. The court also reasoned that the boat was analogous to motor vehicles that are required to be registered. It concluded, therefore, that the secured lender which had provided the enabling loan was not automatically perfected.[23]

Judicial extension of the exception to automatic perfection for consumer goods is not appropriate. The drafters clearly did not include any limiting criteria based on the size or value of the consumer goods. Even if a limitation upon automatic perfection is considered desirable, the standard articulated by the courts is far too vague for practical application. Some state legislatures have narrowed the availability of automatic perfection for consumer goods by including a monetary limitation on the value of the affected goods.[24]

§ 7.02 Certain Assignments of Accounts and Intangibles

Article 9 recognizes automatic perfection for security interests in specified types of assets, including: an assignment of a beneficial interest in a decedent's estate and, in the 1972 version, a trust;[25] an assignment of accounts **or payment intangibles** that does not transfer a significant part of the assignor's outstanding accounts **or payment intangibles;**[26] and an assignment for the benefit of all the creditors of the transferor.[27]

---

[21] *In re* Vinarsky, 287 F. Supp. 446, 5 U.C.C. Rep. Serv. 1042 (N.D.N.Y. 1968) (definition of consumer goods not limited by size of chattel); *In re* Brown, 45 B.R. 766, 40 U.C.C. Rep. Serv. 684 (Bankr. N.D.N.Y. 1985) (registration required for mobile home, even though consumer goods).

[22] 27 U.C.C. Rep. Serv. 563 (Pa. Ct. Comm. Pl. 1979).

[23] The 1972 text excepts only motor vehicles from its automatic-perfection provision. U.C.C. § 9-302(1)(d). Some states have reconciled any ambiguity over whether a motorboat that must be registered falls within the exception to automatic perfection for consumer goods. Cal. Comm. Code § 9-302(1)(d)(automatic perfection not available for "boat required to be registered"); Mich. C.L. 440.9302(1)(d),M.S.A. § 19.9302(1)(d)(automatic perfection not available for "vehicle, mobile home, or watercraft, for which a certificate of title is required by the laws of this state"). **The revision resolves the ambiguity by referring generally to consumer goods subject to a certificate-of-title law. §§ R9-309(1), R9-311(b), (a).**

[24] The states with monetary limitations include Colorado ($250), Kansas ($2,500), Maine ($1000), and Wisconsin ($500).

[25] U.C.C. §§ 9-302(1)(a), **R9-309(13)(decedents' estates only). The collateral assignment of a beneficial interest in a trust is excluded from automatic perfection under the revision.** *See* § 7.02[A] *infra.*

[26] U.C.C. §§ 9-302(1)(e), **R9-309(2).**

[27] U.C.C. §§ 9-302(1)(g), **R9-309(12).**

The revision also provides for automatic perfection of the security interest that is created when a health-care-insurance receivable, a subset of accounts, is assigned to the provider of health-care goods or services.

The foregoing provisions must be read in conjunction with the Code's scope provision, which excludes certain transfers from the reach of Article 9 entirely. Excluded transactions include sales of accounts **or payment intangibles** that are transferred as part of a sale of the business in which they arose;[28] assignments of such assets for collection purposes;[29] and a single assignment of an account **or payment intangible** to an assignee in full or partial satisfaction of a preexisting debt.[30] The exclusions are discussed in detail elsewhere in this book.[31]

Article 9 also recognizes automatic perfection for security interests created under other articles of the Code, specifically security interests arising under Article 2 on sales or Article 2A on leases, and the security interest of a collecting bank under Article 4.[32] These security interests are unique to the transactions covered in those articles and thus are beyond the scope of this book.

[A] Assignment of a Beneficial Interest in a Trust or a Decedent's Estate — §§ 9-302(1)(c), R9-309(13)

The 1972 version of Article 9 eliminates the filing requirement for "a security interest created by an assignment of a beneficial interest in a trust or a decedent's estate."[33] A lending institution that takes an assignment of a debtor's interest in a family trust or anticipated inheritance as security for a loan would acquire a general intangible as collateral, which generally can only be perfected through a filed financing statement. The Article 9 exception, however, provides for automatic perfection upon attachment of the security interest.

The Official Comments to the 1972 text curiously provide that "[a]ssignments of interests in trusts and estates are not required to be filed because they are often not thought of as collateral comparable to the types dealt with by this Article."[34] The collateral certainly has an apparent relationship to commercial financing transactions; otherwise, the transactions would be excluded in their entirety from the scope of Article 9. Transactions based on this type of collateral also will generally involve a commercial lender. Why such professionals would not normally associate this type of intangible with Article 9 secured financing, yet understand that assignments of other intangibles require filing for perfection, is not readily apparent.

---

[28] U.C.C. § 9-104(f), **R9-109(d)(4)**.

[29] U.C.C. § 9-104(f), **R9-109(d)(5)**.

[30] U.C.C. § 9-104(f), **R9-109(d)(7)**.

[31] *See* § 1.07 *supra.*

[32] U.C.C. §§ 9-302(1)(f), **R9-309(6),(7)**. **The revision also provides for automatic perfection of a security interest of an issuer of a letter of credit (or that of a nominated person) arising under Article 5. § R9-309(8).** *See also* §§ 9-113, **R9-110.**

[33] U.C.C. § 9-302(1)(c).

[34] U.C.C. § 9-302 Cmt. 5.

Nearly all of the cases concerning this filing exception have involved the assignment of beneficial interests in Illinois land trusts. Illinois courts have held that a beneficial interest created in a land trust is an interest in personal property rather than in real estate.[35] Under the exception, an assignment of such an interest as collateral does not require filing in order to perfect the lender's security interest.[36] The extent of the litigation in Illinois courts with respect to assignments of land trusts provides vivid proof of the uncertainty created by this questionable exception to the filing requirement.

The revision continues to recognize automatic perfection for a security interest created by an assignment of a beneficial interest in a decedent's estate.[37] Filing, however, is required to perfect a security interest in a beneficial interest in a trust. The change with respect to these interests in trusts is explained by their more frequent use as collateral in commercial transactions.[38]

[B] Isolated Assignment of Accounts or Payment Intangibles — §§ 9-302(1)(e), R9-309(2)

Filing is not required for perfection with respect to an assignment of accounts which, by itself or together with other assignments to the same assignee, does not transfer a significant part of the outstanding accounts of the assignor.[39] **The revision expands this availability of automatic perfection to include comparably-situated payment intangibles.[40]** The Official Comments indicate that this exception is designed to save "casual or isolated" assignments from invalidation.[41] It was included in response to accounts receivable statutes that were commonly enacted prior to the Code and that encompassed "many assignments which no one would think of filing."[42] The Comments also caution, however, that anyone who regularly takes assignment of debtor accounts should file.[43] The Comments thus strongly suggest that automatic perfection with respect to assigned accounts should be construed as a narrow exception.

The only strong conclusion that can be drawn from the cases construing this exception is that the uncertainty generated ought to be more than sufficient to convince anyone aware of perfection concepts to attain perfection by filing rather than relying on automatic perfection. Courts have been inconsistent both in the criteria that they have advanced as relevant and their application of those criteria.

---

[35] Levine v. Pascal, 94 Ill. App. 2d 43, 236 N.E.2d 425, 5 U.C.C. Rep. Serv. 344 (1968). *Compare In re* Preston, 52 B.R. 296, 42 U.C.C. Rep. Serv. 607 (Bankr. M.D. Tenn. 1985) (intention of settlors of trust, expressed in trust agreement, for beneficial interest to be personal property, was controlling).

[36] *In re* Bugos, 34 B.R. 382, 37 B.R. Rep. Serv. 571 (N.D. Ind. 1983) (applying Illinois law); *In re* Cowsert, 14 B.R. 340, 32 U.C.C. Rep. Serv. 942 (Bankr. S.D. Fla. 1981) (applying Illinois law).

[37] **U.C.C. § R9-309(13).**

[38] **U.C.C. § R9-309 Cmt. 7.**

[39] U.C.C.§§ 9-302(1)(e), **R9-309(2).**

[40] *Id.*

[41] U.C.C. §§ 9-302 Cmt. 5, **R9-309 Cmt. 4.**

[42] *Id.*

[43] *Id.,* **R9-309 Cmt. 4.**

Some courts apply the "casual or isolated" test indicated in the Comments. Sometimes, the focal point has been the extent of business transacted, so that a one-shot transaction, even though for a considerable amount, has been held to be automatically perfected.[44] These courts tend to look at whether or not the assignee regularly accepts assignments of accounts.[45] The status of the assignee has also served as a central feature of the "casual or isolated test." The focus is whether or not the assignee regularly engages in commercial financing transactions, thereby precluding use of the exception by professional creditors.[46] Some courts have emphasized both of these factors as relevant.[47]

Other courts ignore the "casual or isolated" test in favor of focusing on a percentage test. Some of these courts look at the percentage of the assignor's accounts in determining whether they are a significant part,[48] whereas other courts address the percentage of the dollar value of total accounts that has been assigned.[49] Court focusing on the latter percentage have also been influenced by the amount involved.[50] Yet other courts have required that both a percentage test and the casual or isolated test be satisfied in order for automatic perfection to apply.[51]

---

[44] Architectural Woods, Inc. v. State of Wash., 88 Wash. 2d 406, 562 P.2d 248, 21 U.C.C. Rep. Serv. 1181 (1977) (assignment of $100,000, of an account for $144,953, held to be isolated). *See also In re* Fort Dodge Roofing Co., 50 B.R. 666, 41 U.C.C. Rep. Serv. 1839 (Bankr. N.D. Iowa 1985) (one-shot transaction).

[45] Daly v. Shrimplin, 610 P.2d 397, 29 U.C.C. Rep. Serv. 237 (Wyo. 1980) (no automatic perfection because assignees each regularly took assignments of accounts from this assignor).

[46] K.A.O.P. Co. v. Midway Nat'l Bank of St. Paul, 372 N.W.2d 774, 41 U.C.C. Rep. Serv. 1045 (Minn. Ct. App. 1985) (exception applicable only to assignee not regularly engaged in financing as a business).

[47] M.D. Hodges Enters., Inc. v. First Ga. Bank, 243 Ga. 664, 256 S.E.2d 350, 26 U.C.C. Rep. Serv. 1333 (1979)(exception not available because, as part of its business, plaintiff bank regularly loaned money and accepted accounts as security).

[48] *In re* Bougher, 8 U.C.C. Rep. Serv. 144 (Bankr. W.D. Mich. 1970) (no exception when assignor assigned all accounts due from his company, even though assignee was not a professional and did not regularly take assignments of accounts); *In re* Rankin 102 B.R. 439, 9 U.C.C. Rep. Serv. 2d 301 (Bankr. W.D. Pa. 1989)(exception not applicable because entire account was assigned and it was debtor's only account of substance).

[49] *In re* Crabtree Constr. Co., Inc., 87 B.R. 212, 6 U.C.C. Rep. Serv. 2d 1322 (Bankr. S.D. Fla. 1988) (transfer of 14% of debtor's overall accounts was not significant portion, even though transfer actually covered 25% of collectible accounts); *In re* Munro Builders, Inc., 20 U.C.C. Rep. Serv. 739 (Bankr. W.D. Mich. 1976) (40% of total accounts of bankrupt was significant part).

[50] Consolidated Film Indus. v. U.S., 547 F.2d 533, 20 U.C.C. Rep. Serv. 1360 (10th Cir. 1977) (size of transaction did not suggest casual transaction that would ordinarily be exempt); Miller v. Wells Fargo Bank Int'l Corp., 406 F. Supp. 452, 18 U.C.C. Rep. Serv. 489 (S.D.N.Y. 1975) (no exemption for assignment of just under 20% of debtor's total outstanding accounts, particularly in view of $1,000,000 absolute value of transaction).

[51] *In re* Tri-County Materials, Inc., 114 B.R. 160, 12 U.C.C. Rep Serv. 2d 869 (Bankr. C.D. Ill. 1990)(12% of outstanding accounts met percentage test, but formality and notice to account debtor meant it was not a casual transaction); H. & Val J. Rothschild, Inc. v. Northwestern Nat'l Bank of St. Paul, 309 Minn. 35, 242 N.W.2d 844, 19 U.C.C. Rep. Serv. 673 (1976) (assigned percentage exceeded one-third and bank was involved in business of interim financing, although it had not previously taken assignments of contract rights as security).

[C] Assignment for the Benefit of All Creditors — §§ 9-302(1)(g), R9-309(12)

Another exception from a filing requirement for perfection applies to "an assignment for the benefit of all the creditors of the transferor, and subsequent transfers by the assignee thereunder."[52] The Official Comments state that these assignments need not be filed "because they are not financing transactions and the debtor will not ordinarily be engaging in further credit transactions."[53] This policy justification suggests that, rather than providing for automatic perfection of these assignments, the transactions should be excluded in their entirety from the scope of Article 9.[54]

[D] Assignment of Health-Care-Insurance Receivables — § R9-309(5)

The revision expands automatic perfection to a security interest created by the assignment of health-care-insurance receivables, but only if the assignment is made to the person that provided the health-care goods or services.[55] The provider of the goods or services thus can take the transfer of the right to payment under the insurance policy without having to file a financing statement. An assignment of a health-care-insurance receivable to another entity, such as a financer, would require filing for perfection unless the assignment falls within the exception for isolated assignments of accounts.

§ 7.03 Certain Additional Sales — R9-309(3),(4)

The revision provides for automatic perfection of the security interest acquired by the buyer of payment intangibles[56] or promissory notes.[57] Payment intangibles is a subset of general intangibles, and promissory notes is a subset of instruments. This topic has no counterpart in the 1972 text, which does not govern sales of general intangibles or instruments. The payment intangible and promissory note categories were created so that their sale could be brought within the scope of Article 9 while leaving sales of other general intangibles and instruments outside its scope. The rationale for both the expansion in scope and the automatic-perfection rule is the protection of specialized financing arrangements like loan participations and securitizations, topics that are discussed elsewhere in this book.[58]

Article 9 does apply to the sale of accounts under both the 1972 and the 1998 versions. Consequently automatic perfection applies with respect to any of the assignments of accounts referred to above in § 7.02 whether the assignment is through sale of the accounts or through the granting of a security interest against the accounts. The expansion of the revision in section R9-309(2) to encompass an

---

[52] U.C.C. §§ 9-302(1)(g), R9-390(12).

[53] U.C.C. §§ 9-302 Cmt. 5., R9-309 Cmt. 8.

[54] *See* U.C.C. § 9-104 Cmt. 6 (transfers of accounts that are excluded from Article 9 because, by their nature, they have nothing to do with commercial financing transactions).

[55] U.C.C. § R9-309(5).

[56] U.C.C. § R9-309(3).

[57] U.C.C. § R9-309(4).

[58] *See* § 1.06 *supra.*

isolated assignment of payment intangibles also covers assignment as a sale or for security purposes. Section R9-309(3) on automatic perfection for the sale of a payment intangible overlaps with section R9-309(2) only to the extent of an isolated assignment by sale of payment intangibles. Section R9-309(3) will pick up any additional sales of payment intangibles, but section R9-309(2) is the exclusive coverage for an assignment as security of payment intangibles.

§ 7.04   Investment Property — §§ 9-116(2), 9-115(4)(c),(d), R9-309(10),(11)

Section 9-116 was added in 1994 to create special rules for security interests in investment property in order to provide certainty in the securities settlement system. One of those rules applies to the rights of persons who deliver financial assets in physical form to the buyer's securities custodian before the agreed-upon payment is received. [59] In accordance with the custom in the trade, the security is to be returned to the deliverer if payment is not forthcoming. [60] The added rule provides that the person making delivery has a security interest in the financial asset that secures the right to payment, no security agreement is required for attachment, and no filing is required for perfection. [61] **The revision continues the availability of automatic attachment and perfection in this context.** [62]

Section 9-115 was also added in 1994, in conjunction with the revision of Article 8 on investment securities. Automatic perfection provisions are included to facilitate secured financing arrangements for securities firms. [63] **These provisions are continued under the revision.** [64] In some transactions, the lender requires that securities maintained on a clearing corporation's books be transferred to the lender's account, resulting in perfection by control. [65] In other transactions the lender allows the debtor to retain the positions in its own accounts under an agreement-to-deliver arrangement. The debtor's books reflect the security and the debtor promises that the security will be transferred to the lender's account upon demand. [66] Perfection in these latter transactions occurs automatically when the debtor is a broker or securities intermediary. [67] Comparable automatic perfection is provided for a security interest in a commodity contract or a commodity account created by a commodity intermediary. [68] The availability of automatic perfection precludes the necessity for these parties to engage in their prior practice of indefinitely rolling over a new loan agreement every 21 days in order to continually qualify for temporary perfection in the absence of filing. [69]

---

[59] U.C.C. § 9-116(2).

[60] U.C.C. § 9-116 Cmt. 3.

[61] U.C.C. § 9-116(2).

[62] **U.C.C. §§ R9-206(c)(attachment), R9-309(9)(perfection).**

[63] U.C.C. § 9-115(4)(c),(d).

[64] **U.C.C. § R9-309(10),(11).**

[65] U.C.C. §§ 9-115 and Cmt. 6, **R9-309 and Cmt. 6.**

[66] *Id.*

[67] U.C.C. §§ 9-115(4)(c), **R9-309(10).**

[68] U.C.C. §§ 9-115(4)(d), **R9-309(11).** *See* U.C.C. § 9-115 Cmt. 8.

[69] U.C.C. §§ 9-115 Cmt. 6, **R9-309 Cmt. 6.**

CHAPTER 8

TEMPORARY PERFECTION AND PERFECTION OF PROCEEDS

In addition to the normal methods of perfection, Article 9 includes some circumstances in which a secured party can either acquire or retain temporary perfection. Although temporary perfection is a form of automatic perfection, it is distinguishable from the continuous automatic perfection discussed in Chapter 7. Temporary perfection is limited to periods of short duration—either twenty-one days or ten days under the 1972 text; **twenty days under the revision.**

SYNOPSIS

§ 8.01 Instruments, Certificated Securities, Documents and Bailed Goods — §§ 9-304(4)-(6), R9-312(e)-(h)

[A] Initial Perfection

Under the 1972 version, perfection with respect to instruments, certificated securities and negotiable documents can be automatically attained by a secured party for a period of 21 days. Section 9-304(4) provides:

> A security interest in instruments, certificated securities, or negotiable documents is perfected without filing or the taking of possession for a period of 21 days from the time it attaches to the extent that it arises for new value given under a written security agreement.

In other words, a secured party who gives new value is automatically perfected with respect to such assets for the first 21 days following the date of attachment. Prior to expiration of the 21-day grace period, a secured party must comply with another applicable method of perfection in order to remain continuously perfected without a gap. [1]

New value is defined indirectly in section 9-108, which deals primarily with whether a security interest in after-acquired collateral can be taken for new value. That section provides that "[w]here a secured party makes an advance, incurs an obligation, releases a perfected security interest, or otherwise gives new value" to be secured by after-acquired collateral, the security interest in the after-acquired collateral "shall be deemed to be taken for new value and not as security for an antecedent debt if the debtor acquires his rights in such collateral either in the ordinary course of his business or under a contract of purchase made pursuant to the security agreement within a reasonable time after new value is given." For example, suppose Bank makes a loan to Debtor to be secured by all existing and after-acquired instruments. Bank's security interest will be temporarily perfected upon attachment as to any after-acquired instruments that the debtor takes in the ordinary course of business. A new advance or other new value must be given for there to be temporary perfection as to instruments not acquired in the ordinary course of the debtor's business.

The revision continues the availability of temporary perfection as to instruments, certificated securities and negotiable documents but reduces the period of temporary perfection to twenty days. [2] This duration is used as a consistent time period that is generally applicable throughout revised Article 9. [3] Like the 1972 version, the period for temporary perfection runs from the date of attachment of the security interest. The revision is also consistent in requiring that the secured party give new value under an authenticated security agreement, but it contains an explicit definition of new value [4] and deletes section 9-108's provision permitting

---

[1] U.C.C. § 9-304(6).

[2] U.C.C. § R9-312(e).

[3] U.C.C. § R9-312 Cmt. 8.

[4] "New value" means (i) money, (ii) money's worth in property, services, or new credit, or (iii) release by a transferee of an interest in property previously transferred to the transferee. The term does not include an obligation substituted for another obligation." U.C.C. § R9-102(57).

after-acquired collateral to be deemed taken for new value.[5] Thus, a secured party cannot gain the protection of temporary perfection without making an advance or otherwise giving new value as each item of collateral is acquired by the debtor.

This type of temporary perfection (*i.e.*, initial perfection upon attachment) is available to permit flexibility in facilitating commercial transactions involving instruments, certificated securities, and negotiable documents. Sometimes the financing itself is short-term. For example, a commercial bank may provide a two-day loan to a mortgage lender secured by the lender's stockpile of instruments. Temporary perfection obviates the need for the bank to take possession of the collateral, the act necessary for permanent perfection under the 1972 text.

The need for temporary perfection has lessened significantly in recent years and will diminish further under the revision. Prior to the 1994 revision of Article 8 with its conforming amendments to Article 9, banks commonly made "day loans" to stockbrokers and relied on temporary perfection to protect their interests in certificated securities. At that time, permanent perfection of a security interest in such a security required possession and, as with instruments in the prior example, temporary perfection obviated the need for possession. Under the 1994 revisions, perfection of a security interest occurs automatically upon attachment if the debtor is a broker, securities intermediary or commodity intermediary.[6] This is continuous automatic perfection, unlimited by time.

Filing has long been available as a method of perfecting security interests in negotiable documents, and thus temporary perfection need only be used when it is inconvenient for the secured party to either file or take possession.[7] Beginning in 1994, permissive filing has been available to perfect security interests in all forms of investment property, including certificated securities,[8] **and the revision extends permissive filing to security interests in instruments. Once the revision takes effect, there will be no category of collateral for which this type of temporary possession is really necessary, although its existence will remain convenient for truly short-term transactions.**

Despite the convenience facilitated by the temporary-perfection rule, secured lenders must be aware of the basic risks inherent in relying upon such perfection. Of course, any lender who agrees to a security interest based on collateral that the debtor claims to own always runs the risk that the property does not exist or that the debtor either does not own it or has already encumbered it. In the case of negotiable instruments, certificated securities, and negotiable documents, however, a significant risk persists even after the security interest attaches and temporary perfection is attained for the short-term duration. Although the action would be wrongful, a debtor who retains possession of these forms of indispensable paper is still empowered to pass possession of the paper

---

[5] **The Comments indicate that the provision was "unnecessary, counterintuitive, and ineffective for its original purpose of sheltering after-acquired collateral from attack as a voidable preference in bankruptcy." U.C.C. § R9-102 Cmt. 21.**

[6] U.C.C. §§ 9-115(4)(c), (d), **R9-309(10), (11).** *See* § 7.04 *supra.*

[7] U.C.C. §§ 9-304(1), **R9-312(a).**

[8] U.C.C. §§ 9-115(4)(b), **R9-312(a).** Under the 1972 text, filing is not even effective if the debtor is a broker, securities intermediary or commodity intermediary, but this provision is meaningless since the security interest is perfected automatically. § 9-115(4)(c), (d).

to another secured lender or to a buyer. A subsequent transferee who gives value and takes the paper with the requisite bona fides will take priority over the earlier security interest, even though the earlier interest is perfected.[9]

The advantage of permissive filing can be illustrated with reference to negotiable documents. The filing will not be sufficient to overcome the loss of priority if the debtor left in possession of the negotiable document wrongfully transfers it to a bona-fide purchaser for value.[10] Filing addresses a different risk. A negotiable document represents title to goods and, during the period of temporary perfection, the debtor might surrender the document and obtain the goods from a carrier or a warehouse. In fact, the very purpose of relying upon temporary perfection might be to enable the debtor to acquire the goods for resale or other use. The advantage of filing is that it provides continuous perfection of the collateral, whether in the form of the document or the underlying goods.

In the absence of such a filing, the 1972 text is ambiguous with respect to continuous perfection when the negotiable document is surrendered by the debtor during the period of temporary perfection. The Comments state that "the 21 days applies only to the documents and to the goods obtained by surrender thereof,"[11] yet subsection (4) of section 9-304 is written solely in terms of the security interest in the negotiable document. The goods obtained would be proceeds of the surrendered negotiable document, but temporary perfection under the proceeds section would extend for only ten days unless the secured party were to take action within that time to perfect by possession or filing.[12] The uncertainties associated with determining the extent of temporary perfection once the negotiable document is surrendered, plus the possible need for assuring perfection in the affected goods thereafter, suggest that a prior filing is prudent. **This uncertainty is alleviated under the revision, which extends temporary perfection with respect to proceeds to twenty days.**[13] **As is explained in a subsequent section of this chapter, a variety of additional provisions in the revision also makes it more likely that a**

---

[9] U.C.C. §§ 9-309, **R9-331**. *See* § 11.03[C] *infra*. *In re* Kontaratos, 10 B.R. 956, 31 U.C.C. Rep. Serv. 1124 (Bankr. D. Me. 1981)(perfected security interest under § 9-304(4) in shares of stock held subordinate to subsequent security interest of bank to whom stock certificates were delivered as collateral).

[10] The only adequate protection against this risk is for the secured party to perfect by taking possession of the document, leaving the debtor unable to pass the possession that a subsequent transferee needs to attain priority over a prior-perfected secured party. The risk of wrongful transfer explains why most secured lenders rely on their own possession of the document for perfection, rather than filing a financing statement. *See* U.C.C. §§ 9-309, **R9-331(a),** (c), 7-501, 7-502, 1-201(20). The same analysis applies with respect to certificated securities **and, under the revision, instruments.**

[11] U.C.C. § 9-304 Cmt. 4.

[12] *See* U.C.C. § 9-306(3)(c) and § 8.02[A],[D] *infra.* The Tenth Circuit held in *In re* Reliance Equities, Inc., 966 F.2d 1338, 17 U.C.C. Rep. Serv. 2d 1316 (10th Cir. 1992), that the sale of promissory notes within the 21-day period of perfection under section 9-304(4) resulted in an automatically perfected security interest in the proceeds under section 9-306(3) for ten more days from the date of sale. Perfection ceased at the end of that period because the secured party did nothing during that time to further perfect its interest.

[13] *See* **U.C.C. § R9-315(d),(e) and § 8.02[A],[D]** *infra.*

security interest in proceeds will continue indefinitely beyond the twenty-day grace period. [14]

[B] Continuing Perfection

A temporary perfection period of 21 days is also provided in the 1972 version for certain circumstances in which the collateral is returned to the debtor. In addition to instruments, certificated securities and negotiable documents, this type of temporary perfection also applies to goods in the possession of a bailee who has not issued a negotiable document for them. Unlike initial temporary perfection, continuing temporary perfection is subject to limitations on the purposes for which the collateral is returned to the debtor.

Section 9-304(5) provides:

A security interest remains perfected for a period of 21 days without filing where a secured party having a perfected security interest in an instrument, a certificated security, a negotiable document or goods in possession of a bailee other than one who has issued a negotiable document therefor

(a) makes available to the debtor the goods or documents representing the goods for the purpose of ultimate sale or exchange or for the purpose of loading, unloading, storing, shipping, transshipping, manufacturing, processing or otherwise dealing with them in a manner preliminary to their sale or exchange, but priority between conflicting security interests in the goods is subject to subsection (3) of Section 9-312; or

(b) delivers the instrument or certificated security to the debtor for the purpose of ultimate sale or exchange or of presentation, collection, renewal or registration of transfer.

Thus, a secured party who is initially perfected by possession can remain continuously perfected, despite returning the collateral to the debtor for one of these purposes. The temporary perfection period runs from the date that the secured party makes the document or goods available, or delivers the instrument or certificated security, to the debtor. Perfection by a different means is required prior to expiration of the temporary perfection if the secured party wishes to remain continuously perfected. [15]

Continuing temporary perfection for any of these purposes is also available under the revision, [16] although the period of perfection is reduced to twenty days. The revision adds "enforcement" as one of the purposes for which certificated securities

---

[14] See § 8.02 infra.

[15] U.C.C. § 9-304(6). See U.C.C. § 9-303(2) and the illustration in Cmt. 2. In McIlroy Bank v. First Nat'l Bank of Fayetteville, 252 Ark. 558, 480 S.W.2d 127, 10 U.C.C. Rep. Serv. 1111 (1972), the bank was temporarily perfected when it returned a promissory note to its debtor for collection. When the debtor retained the note long after 21 days in order to obtain a judgment on it, the bank became unperfected.

[16] U.C.C. § R9-312(f)(negotiable documents and goods in the possession of a bailee that has not issued a negotiable document therefor); § R9-312(g)(instruments and certificated securities).

and instruments can be released to the debtor in order to qualify for temporary perfection. [17]

The revision and the 1972 version are consistent in additional respects for purposes of maintaining temporary perfection after surrendering possession of the designated collateral to the debtor. Unlike initial temporary perfection, new value is not required, but the collateral must be returned to advance one of the stated purposes. The security interest must be perfected by another method under Article 9 if continuous perfection beyond the duration of temporary perfection is desired. [18] Priority in a security interest in goods after a document that covers them is surrendered by the debtor is not governed by the provisions on continuing temporary perfection. [19]

Although continuing temporary perfection requires that the collateral be returned for one of the indicated purposes, the requirement is not very limiting because it covers nearly all of the legitimate purposes for returning such collateral. Case law has recognized the legitimacy of the return of a certificate of deposit so that it could be renewed by issuance of a new certificate, [20] the return of a negotiable bill of lading to acquire the goods from a carrier and store them, [21] and the return of a promissory note for purposes of collection. [22] Even the return of the collateral for the purpose of sale is recognized as legitimate, based on the rationale that the parties may envision debtor sale of the collateral as the means by which the debtor will acquire the assets to pay the secured debt.

The convenience associated with temporary perfection must be balanced against the enhanced risk that accompanies debtor reacquisition of the collateral. The debtor will then have the means to transfer the paper or in some instances the goods to a party who can achieve priority against even a perfected security interest. [23] The risks are described in more detail in the prior subsection dealing with initial temporary perfection. [24]

§ 8.02 Proceeds — §§ 9-306(3), R9-315(c)-(e)

[A] The Grace Period of Temporary Perfection

Article 9 provides that a secured party's interest in collateral attaches automatically to identifiable proceeds received by a debtor upon disposition of that collateral, [25] and it also determines when the secured party's interest in the proceeds is perfected. [26]

---

[17] U.C.C. § R9-312(g).

[18] U.C.C. §§ 9-304(6), R9-312(h). *See aslo* n. 15 *supra*.

[19] *See* U.C.C. §§ 9-312(3), R9-324 and § 10.03[B] *infra*.

[20] Wrightman v. American Nat'l Bank of Riverton, 610 P.2d 1001, 29 U.C.C. Rep. Serv. 251 (Wyo. 1980).

[21] Scallop Petroleum Co. v. Banque Trad-Credit Lyonnais S.A., 690 F. Supp. 184, 6 U.C.C. Rep. Serv. 2d 1573 (S.D.N.Y. 1988).

[22] McIlroy Bank v. First Nat'l Bank of Fayetteville, 252 Ark. 558, 480 S.W.2d 127, 10 U.C.C. Rep. Serv. 1111 (1972).

[23] *See* U.C.C. §§ 9-307(1), 9-309, R9-320(a), R9-321(c), R9-331. *See also* Chapter 11 *infra*.

[24] *See* § 8.01[A] *supra*.

[25] U.C.C. § 9-306(2), R9-315(a)(2). For discussion of automatic attachment of security interests to identifiable proceeds, *see* § 2.04[B] *supra*.

[26] U.C.C. §§ 9-306(3), R9-315(c)-(e). The effect of insolvency proceedings instituted by or against

"Proceeds" are whatever the debtor receives upon any disposition of the collateral.[27] Irrespective of whether the debtor's disposition of the collateral is authorized or is in violation of the security agreement, the security interest continues automatically in the proceeds so long as they can be identified.

In some types of financing, proceeds are expected and are enormously important to secured parties. In inventory financing, for example, secured parties are virtually certain to authorize sale or lease of the collateral. Their security interest is extinguished by such an authorized disposition,[28] and secured parties will then look for their continuing security to an interest in the proceeds from the disposition. Proceeds from inventory are likely to be in the form of cash, checks, notes, accounts, or chattel paper. Similarly, an accounts financer will be concerned with the proceeds received from payments on the accounts or the outright sale of the accounts.

Although a security interest extends automatically to identifiable proceeds, perfection may be necessary to protect the secured party's interest in the proceeds against other claimants. Perfection with respect to proceeds is covered in the 1972 text by section 9-306(3). The baseline rule is that "[t]he security interest in proceeds is a continuously perfected security interest if the interest in the original collateral was perfected but it ceases to be a perfected security interest and becomes unperfected ten days after receipt of the proceeds by the debtor unless [one of the additional enumerated conditions is satisfied]."[29] **The revision continues this basic approach. Perfection with respect to proceeds continues automatically if the security interest in the original collateral was perfected[30] but "becomes unperfected on the 21st day after the security interest attaches to the proceeds unless [one of the additional enumerated conditions is satisfied]."[31] The revision's extension of the grace period to twenty days is consistent with its approach of making twenty-day time periods generally applicable throughout Article 9.**

The secured party's goal is to have its security interest in proceeds continuously perfected so that its priority relates back to the initial perfection of its interest in the original collateral.[32] In every case, the Code grants temporary perfection for the duration

---

a debtor on a perfected secured party's right to proceeds is governed in the 1972 text by § 9-306(4). **This provision is deleted in the revision. A secured party's right to proceeds when the debtor enters into bankruptcy is not affected other than as provided in the Bankruptcy Code. U.C.C. § R9-315 Cmt. 8.**

[27] U.C.C. §§ 9-306(1), **R9-102(64).** For discussion of the concept of proceeds, *see* § 2.04[A] *supra.*

[28] U.C.C. § 9-306(2), **R9-315(a)(1).** For discussion of these provisions, *see* §§ 11.01, 11.02 *infra.*

[29] U.C.C. § 9-306(3). The legislatures of several states considered the ten-day grace period to be too short and thus have extended it for a longer period of time.

[30] **U.C.C. § R9-315(c).**

[31] **U.C.C. § R9-315(d).**

[32] Section 9-306(3) does not provide any continuous automatic perfection with respect to proceeds if the secured party was not perfected in the original collateral. *In re* Beacon Light Marina Yacht Club, Inc., 125 B.R. 154, 14 U.C.C. Rep. Serv. 2d 1230 (Bankr. W.D. Va. 1990)(secured party, which did not perfect its interest in boat by noting its interest on boat's certificate of title, did not have perfected security interest in proceeds from sale of boat). **The revision is comparable. U.C.C. § R9-315(c).**

of the grace period. If one of the conditions that does not require any further action by the secured party is satisfied, the perfection in the proceeds continues automatically beyond that period. In other words, temporary perfection becomes continuous automatic perfection. If none of these conditions are satisfied and the secured party does not during the grace period successfully undertake any action required to perfect its interest in the proceeds, that interest becomes unperfected. In this latter circumstance, the enumerated time duration serves as a grace period of temporary perfection in the proceeds during which the secured party must act to continue its priority.

[B] Continuous Automatic Perfection

The 1972 text includes a provision under which temporary perfection can become continuous automatic perfection when the proceeds are identifiable cash proceeds, but, unless the original collateral was investment property, the security interest in the original collateral must have been perfected by a filed financing statement.[33] "Cash proceeds," defined to include only "cash, checks, deposit accounts and the like,"[34] are essentially cash or property readily convertible to cash. The automatic extension of perfection with respect to money and checks is an exception to the general requirement that a security interest in money or instruments can be perfected only by possession.[35] **The revision expands continuous automatic perfection to identifiable cash proceeds of original collateral perfected by any method.**[36]

The exception for identifiable cash proceeds most commonly applies when the secured party has a perfected security interest in accounts and the cash proceeds are paid in satisfaction of an account,[37] and when the perfected security interest is in inventory and the cash proceeds are received on its sale.[38] One bankruptcy opinion correctly indicates that perfection was continuous and automatic with respect to identifiable cash proceeds from the sale of inventory in which the secured party had a perfected security interest, but not with respect to the proceeds of inventory in which the secured party did not have a perfected interest.[39] Another bankruptcy decision held that a filing for national registration with the FAA, which is required to perfect a security interest in an airplane, was equivalent to filing a financing statement under the 1972 text. Thus the secured party's interest in the cash proceeds generated when the airplane was sold was continuously and automatically perfected.[40]

---

[33] U.C.C. § 9-306(3)(b). Perfection of security interests in the identifiable cash proceeds of investment property is continuous and automatic without regard to the method of perfection. § 9-306(3)(c).

[34] U.C.C. § 9-306(1). **The definition in the revision is comparable. U.C.C. § R9-102(a)(9).**

[35] *See* U.C.C. § 9-304(1). **Under the revision a security interest in instruments may be perfected by filing. U.C.C. § R9-312(a).** *See* § 6.01[C] *supra.*

[36] U.C.C. § R9-315(d)(2).

[37] *In re* John Deskins Pic Pac, Inc., 59 B.R. 809, 1 U.C.C. Rep. Serv. 2d 1696 (Bankr. W.D. Va. 1986); Farns Assocs., Inc. v. South Side Bank, 93 Ill. App. 3d 766, 417 N.E.2d 818, 30 U.C.C. Rep. Serv. 1729 (1981).

[38] Dixie Prod. Credit Assn. v. Kent, 167 Ga. App. 714, 307 S.E.2d 277, 37 U.C.C. Rep. Serv. 595 (1983).

[39] *In re* Critiques, Inc., 29 B.R. 941, 36 U.C.C. Rep. Serv. 1778 (Bankr. D. Kan. 1983).

[40] *In re* Turner, 13 B.R. 15, 32 U.C.C. Rep. Serv. 1240 (Bankr. D. Neb. 1981).

The cash and cash-like nature of the property that constitutes "cash proceeds" suggests that great care is advisable in structuring a transaction in which a secured party desires continuous automatic perfection in the proceeds. Cash is easily dissipated, which may jeopardize the secured party's interest on the grounds that the cash proceeds are no longer identifiable.[41] A secured lender may be wise to require the debtor to segregate all cash proceeds it receives and deposit them into a special account to which the secured party can control access. The secured party can then make unannounced spot-checks to monitor the debtor's compliance with this requirement. A secured party also should not feel particularly secure even when perfected with respect to such highly negotiable proceeds. For example, a transferee of a check who qualifies as a holder-in-due-course will achieve priority in the check over even a prior-perfected secured party.[42]

[C] Same Filing Office

[1] The Basic Rule

Continuous perfection in proceeds beyond the grace period is sometimes also recognized with respect to noncash proceeds. Perfection continues under the 1972 version when "a filed financing statement covers the original collateral and the proceeds are collateral in which a security interest may be perfected by filing in the office or offices where the financing statement has been filed."[43] This provision does not require that the secured party file or have filed a financing statement that describes the proceeds. It is enough if the office in which a filing *would* be made to perfect an original interest in the assets that constitute the proceeds is the same office in which a filing covering the original collateral has *in fact* been made. The initial filing continues effective for the proceeds, even if the description of collateral on the financing statement does not describe the proceeds.[44] Although perfection continues beyond the grace period automatically in the sense that the secured party need take no additional steps with respect to the proceeds, the same-filing-office rule does not result in true automatic perfection. Perfection is predicated on the financing statement, and the secured party will become unperfected if the financing statement lapses.

Section 9-306(3) represents a compromise between the need for efficiency on the part of the secured party and the need for adequate notice on the part of the searcher. The basic idea is that there are certain common financing practices in which a searcher should recognize that a particular type of described collateral is likely to yield proceeds of a different type. The classic example is inventory and accounts. A searcher who is interested in buying or lending against a dealer's accounts should be aware that accounts typically

---

[41] *See* § 2.04[B] *supra.*

[42] U.C.C. § 9-309, **R9-331(a)**. Secured parties need to be aware that in several types of cases a transferee will take free of a perfected security interest. *See, e.g.,* §§ **R9-330(d)(purchaser of check), R9-331 (holder-in-due-course of check), R9-332 (transferee of money or funds from a deposit account).** *See generally* § 11.03[C] *infra.*

[43] U.C.C. § 9-306(3)(a).

[44] The proper office(s) for purposes of filings under the 1972 text is determined by U.C.C. §§ 9-401(1)(local versus central filing) and 9-103 (multistate transactions). *See* § 5.04[B] *supra* and Chapter 9 *infra.*

arise from the credit sale of inventory. Thus, a searcher who finds a financing statement describing an interest in the dealer's inventory is on notice that the secured party also claims the accounts that arise from the sale of the dealer's inventory. This explains why it is so important that the filing as to the original collateral be in the same office as that in which a filing would be made as to the proceeds. A searcher who looks in the proper office for accounts and does not find a financing statement describing inventory cannot draw the proper inference.

For example, assume that a secured party makes a proper central filing with respect to the inventory of a dealer in a state that does not have dual-filing requirements, the accounts at issue are generated from sales of inventory, the inventory is kept within the state, and the dealer is located in the state. The secured party will be continuously perfected as to the accounts, even though the filed financing statement describes the collateral only as inventory. [45] If the dealer had been located in another state, however, the filing would not have sufficed. Under the multistate filing rules in the 1972 text, an original security interest in accounts is perfected by filing in the state where the debtor is located, [46] while an original security interest in inventory held for sale is perfected by filing in the state where the collateral is located. [47] A searcher interested in the dealer's accounts would naturally search in the state where the dealer is located, would not find the financing statement covering the dealer's inventory, and thus would not be on notice. The secured party's perfected status would lapse at the end of the grace period.

In the type of common transaction for which the perfection rule was drafted, the filing office for the original collateral and that for the proceeds is almost invariably the same unless there is a multistate problem. That is not always true, particularly under the 1972 text with its local filing options. For example, assume that the state has adopted Alternative 2 to section 9-401(1), [48] the original collateral is equipment used in farming operations (for which perfection requires local filing), and the sale of this equipment results in an account. Continuous perfection is now not available because a financing statement with respect to such an account must be filed centrally. [49] The same result would apply if the proceeds took the form of a promissory note because under the 1972 text filing is not effective in any office to perfect an interest in an instrument. [50]

---

[45] *In re* Dinsmore Tire Ctr., Inc., 38 B.R. 943, 38 U.C.C. Rep. Serv. 1379 (Bankr. S.D. Fla. 1984). *See also In re* SMS, Inc., 15 B.R. 496, 32 U.C.C. Rep. Serv. 1631 (Bankr. D. Kan. 1981)(central filing was proper for credit memo and bank had filed there initially for inventory).

[46] *See* U.C.C. § 9-103(3) and § 9.05*infra*.

[47] *See* U.C.C. § 9-103(1) and § 9.04*infra*.

[48] The alternatives to U.C.C. § 9-401(1) are discussed in § 5.04 *supra*.

[49] By way of comparison, a bank's security interest in crops was properly perfected by local filing and continued automatically under U.C.C. § 9-306(3)when the crops were sold on credit because the state's version of § 9-401(1) also required local filing for accounts arising from the sale of farm products by a farmer. When checks and drafts were later received in payment of the accounts, the bank's interest remained continuously and automatically perfected in these proceeds under § 9-306(3)(b). Central Wash. Bank v. Mendelson-Zeller, 113 Wash. 2d 346, 779 P.2d 697, 9 U.C.C. Rep. Serv. 2d 1352 (1989).

[50] A promissory note is a noncash proceed, so continuous automatic perfection is not available under U.C.C. § 9-306(3)(b).

The revision continues the availability of continuous perfection for noncash proceeds when the office in which a financing statement would be filed with respect to the proceeds is the same office in which the secured party filed to perfect the security interest in the original collateral.[51] Changes that the revision makes concerning appropriate filing offices, however, greatly enhance the prospect for continuous perfection under this provision. The revision eliminates local filing except for certain limited filings in the real estate filing system, and it consistently designates the state where the debtor is located as the proper state in which to file for all nonpossessory security interests except for those same real-estate related assets.[52] With only one state in which to file and only one proper filing office within the state, there is little chance that an interest in proceeds would be perfected by filing in a different office than that in which a filing covering original collateral would be filed.[53] Thus filing for perfection of a security interest in inventory will inevitably be made in the same office in which filing would be made for virtually every type of noncash asset that might be generated as a proceed of the inventory. The change in the revision that recognizes filing as a method to perfect with respect to instruments[54] expands even further the number of cases for continuous perfection with respect to proceeds.

Because the same-filing-office rule is based on the predictability of certain types of proceeds in common financing transactions, it tends to break down in less common situations. For example, suppose the secured party files to perfect a security interest in farm products and the farmer then trades a cow to a neighbor for a valuable painting. Under every alternative filing option in the 1972 text, **and under the basic filing provisions of the revision,** filings as to consumer goods and filings as to farm products are made in the same office. Thus if the farmer later sells the painting to another neighbor, the secured party's interest will be continuously perfected and can be enforced against the neighbor. Such situations are, of course, relatively rare.

[2] The "Cash-Phase" Rule

The opportunity for continuous perfection with respect to noncash proceeds is more restricted when there is a "cash phase" between the original collateral and the noncash proceeds being claimed by the secured party, *i.e.*, after the original collateral is disposed of to produce cash proceeds which are in turn used to acquire noncash proceeds. The reason is that cash proceeds can be used to purchase a new asset of any type, and thus the predictability upon which the same-filing-office rule is predicated vanishes. For example, assume that a debtor sells the collateral for cash and then uses the cash to buy

---

[51] U.C.C. § R9-315(d)(1). Following the passage of the grace period of 20 days, a security interest in the proceeds that is perfected continuously and automatically will become unperfected when the effectiveness of the financing statement covering the original collateral lapses or is terminated. U.C.C. § R9-315(e).

[52] *See* U.C.C. § R9-501(a) and § 5.04[B] *supra.*

[53] *See* U.C.C. § R9-301(1) and § 9.03 *infra.*

[54] U.C.C. § R9-312(a).

goods. The goods are proceeds of the cash proceeds.[55] Even a sophisticated searcher could not trace the acquisition of the new proceeds through cash proceeds simply by examining the financing statement. Perfection in the proceeds will not extend beyond the grace period therefore, unless the description of the collateral in a financing statement filed in the proper office indicates the types of property which constitute the proceeds.

For example, if a farm debtor were to sell cattle that constitute collateral and use the cash proceeds to purchase additional cattle, the secured party's interest would remain continuously perfected in the new cattle, unless the financing statement's description of the collateral was too narrow or specific to encompass them. A purchase of a tractor with the cash proceeds, however, would surely leave the secured party outside the scope of the provision for continuous perfection. Similarly, a financing statement that describes the collateral as accounts will not perfect a security interest in new inventory acquired with cash proceeds from the sale of the accounts. The result would be otherwise if the financing statement also listed inventory as collateral.

The drafters of the revision correctly saw the cash-phase rule as superfluous.[56] If a secured party has perfected as to the original collateral under a filed financing statement that describes not only that collateral but the property that constitutes the proceeds as well, the security interest in the proceeds would attain perfection under the general rules pertaining to after-acquired collateral.[57] The revision requires these cases to be analyzed from this perspective. It makes the same-filing-office rule inapplicable to cases in which noncash proceeds are acquired with cash proceeds,[58] thereby achieving the same result as that produced by the cash-phase rule.

The facts in *Citicorp (USA), Inc. v. Davidson Lumber Co.*[59] demonstrate the application of continuous perfection in noncash proceeds that are acquired with cash proceeds. Two banks had security interests in general intangibles that had been perfected by filing. The debtor later received a federal tax refund of approximately $1.3 million, which it used, without the knowledge of the banks, to purchase a certificate of deposit. The right to a tax refund was a general intangible, and the check from the federal government was a cash proceed of that right. Transfer of the check in exchange for the certificate of deposit created noncash proceeds from the cash proceeds.[60] Even if the

---

[55] Proceeds include "whatever is received upon ... disposition of collateral *or proceeds.*" U.C.C. § 9-306(1)(emphasis provided). **The revision is consistent, defining collateral to include proceeds. U.C.C. § R9-102(a)(12)(A).**

[56] **U.C.C. § R9-315 Cmt. 5.**

[57] U.C.C. §§ 9-303(1), 9-204(1), 9-302(1), **R9-308(a), R9-204(a), R9-310(a). This result with respect to proceeds acquired by identifiable cash proceeds is affirmed through U.C.C. § R9-315(d)(3), discussed in § 8.02[D]** *infra.*

[58] **The section applies only when "the proceeds are not acquired with cash proceeds." U.C.C. § R9-315(d)(1)(C). When proceeds have been acquired with identifiable cash proceeds, section R9-315(d)(3) applies.**

[59] 718 F.2d 1030, 37 U.C.C. Rep. Serv. 324 (11th Cir. 1983).

[60] The characterization of the certificate of deposit was one of the primary issues litigated. The appellate court properly held that the CD was non-cash proceeds, thus precluding continuous automatic perfection under section 9-306(3)(b). The court followed prior decisions in holding that

banks had included CDs within the descriptions of collateral in their financing statements, they could not have achieved continuous perfection because under the 1972 text the filing of a financing statement is not effective in any office to perfect a security interest in instruments. The banks could have attained continuous perfection of their interests in the CD only by taking possession of the CD within the ten-day grace period.[61] The court properly rejected the policy argument of the banks that such a requirement was "preposterous" because it left them vulnerable to the actions of a debtor who secretly converted the collateral into a type of proceeds that required perfection by possession. The court noted that this argument simply raises concerns regarding creditors' need to implement adequate measures to police the actions of their debtors. It further noted that the banks could have protected themselves with respect to the tax refund that they knew was going to be paid by using the Federal Assignment of Claims Act.[62]

[D]   Timely General Perfection

If neither the identifiable-cash-proceeds option nor the same-filing-office option discussed above are available, continuous perfection will not extend beyond the grace period unless the secured party takes whatever steps are necessary to perfect with respect to the proceeds before the grace period expires.[63] A secured party might still achieve continuous perfection under this provision. **The revision's treatment of the cash-phase situation discussed in the preceding subsection is an example. If the debtor uses identifiable cash proceeds to acquire noncash proceeds, the secured party filed a financing statement to perfect its security interest in the original collateral, and the description in the financing statement is broad enough to cover the property that constitutes the noncash proceeds, no additional perfection steps would be required.**[64]

Whenever the general rules on perfection would require the secured party to take some action with respect to the proceeds (such as taking possession of the proceeds or filing a financing statement that describes the proceeds in the applicable office), however, the timely-general-perfection rule requires that the action be completed before the expiration of the grace period. A secured party that allows the grace period to expire becomes unperfected, and even though it can later perfect its interest in the proceeds, its priority date cannot relate back to the date on which it perfected as to the original collateral.

---

an instrument in the form of a certificate of deposit is more like a promissory note than like a check.

[61] U.C.C. § 9-306(3)(c). **Continuous perfection could have been attained under the revision through a filed financing statement with a description that was broad enough to cover the instrument. U.C.C. § R9-315(d)(3). Otherwise, the secured party would have to act before the expiration of the revision's twenty-day grace period to take necessary steps to perfect as to the instrument.** See § 8.02[D] infra.

[62] 31 U.S.C. § 203(1976), amended by 31 U.S.C. § 3727(1983). Under the Assignment of Claims Act, the federal government can be notified that a right to receive money has been assigned and that payment is to be made to the assignee.

[63] U.C.C. §§ 9-306(3)(c), **R9-315(d)(3).**

[64] Under the 1972 version, continuous perfection would occur under the cash-phase rule discussed in § 8.02[C][2] supra.

An occasional case involves a secured party who has succeeded in taking the timely action to achieve continuous perfection in proceeds. In *In re Airwest International,*[65] the bank used possession to perfect its interest in two certificates of deposit and, when the bank "rolled over" the certificates upon their maturity, to perfect its interest continuously in the resulting single new certificate. In *Wrightman v. American National Bank of Riverton,*[66] the bank, initially perfected by possession of an instrument in the form of a certificate of deposit, continued perfection under section 9-304(5) by returning the certificate to the owner for its renewal by issuance of a new certificate. The replacement certificate constituted proceeds of the first certificate, and the bank's interest in the proceeds continued perfected because the bank obtained possession of the new certificate before the expiration of section 9.304(5)'s period.

Secured parties have also become unperfected with respect to proceeds by reason of their failure to take timely steps to perfect their interest in those proceeds. In *Citicorp (USA), Inc. v. Davidson Lumber Co.,*[67] banks that were perfected by filing with respect to general intangibles did not take timely possession of a certificate of deposit purchased with a check that had been sent to the debtor in payment of an obligation that constituted one of the intangibles. In *Security Savings Bank of Marshalltown, Iowa v. United States,*[68] the bank had a security interest in a Chevrolet truck which it perfected properly by notation on the certificate of title. The bank agreed that the debtor could substitute a Ford truck for the collateral, but, because the bank did not provide for notation of its security interest on the Ford certificate of title within the grace period, continuous perfection was lost. Another case in which continuous perfection in a vehicle as proceeds was lost is *In re Charles E. Sutphin, Inc.*[69] The secured party properly perfected by filing with respect to farm vehicles that were part of the debtor's inventory. In exchange for two of those vehicles, the debtor received a tractor as proceeds. This tractor was not added to the debtor's inventory, but rather was placed in over-the-road service and thus was subject to a certificate-of-title requirement. A notation on the certificate of title was the only way to perfect an interest in such property. Because the secured party did not perfect within the grace period, its interest in the tractor became unperfected.

---

[65] 70 B.R. 914, 3 U.C.C. Rep. Serv. 2d 1936 (Bankr. D. Haw. 1987).

[66] 610 P.2d 1001, 29 U.C.C. Rep. Serv. 251 (Wyo. 1980).

[67] 718 F.2d 1030, 37 U.C.C. Rep. Serv. 324 (11th Cir. 1983).

[68] 440 F. Supp. 444, 22 U.C.C. Rep. Serv. 1260 (S.D. Iowa 1977).

[69] 44 B.R. 533, 39 U.C.C. Rep. Serv. 1499 (Bankr. W.D. Va. 1984).

CHAPTER 9

MULTISTATE TRANSACTIONS

---

§ 9.01 The Code's Basic Choice-of-Law Provision — § 1-105

The Code's basic choice-of-law provision, which is contained in Article 1 and is therefore applicable throughout the U.C.C., permits the parties to select the state whose laws will govern their transaction, so long as there is a reasonable relationship between the transaction and the selected state. Specifically, the Code provides:

Except as provided hereafter in this section, when a transaction bears a reasonable relation to this state and also to another state or nation the parties may agree that the law either of this state or of such other state or nation shall govern their rights and duties. Failing such agreement this Act applies to transactions bearing an appropriate relation to this state.[1]

The parties' right to choose the applicable law is consistent with the Code's basic freedom-of-contract philosophy, but it is not unlimited. The basic choice-of-law provision requires that the transaction bear a reasonable relationship to the selected state. More importantly, Article 9 contains a mandatory choice-of-law provision that governs perfection of security interests and the effects of perfection or nonperfection.[2] These restrictions are addressed below.

[A] The Reasonable Relationship Test

The Comments[3] indicate that the Code's "reasonable relationship" test is similar to the test created by the United States Supreme Court in *Seeman v. Philadelphia Warehouse Co.*,[4] but this cross-reference is not particularly helpful. In *Seeman,* the Court upheld a choice-of-law clause designating Pennsylvania because the lender was a Pennsylvania corporation that regularly conducted business within the state. The courts have routinely acceded to the parties' wishes when one of them (usually the creditor) resides or conducts business in the selected state.[5]

Even when neither party resides in the chosen state, the courts may find a sufficient nexus between the transaction and the state to uphold the choice. For example, in *Key Bank of Me. v. Dunbar,*[6] a choice-of-law clause selecting Maryland law was held to be reasonable because the collateral, a boat, was to be kept in that state. The courts have not required that the parties select the state that has the most significant contacts with the transaction, only that they select a state that has some legitimate contact with the transaction.

Only rarely has a choice-of-law agreement[7] been invalidated, and when this occurs, the result is obvious. In *Woco. v. Benjamin Franklin Corp.,*[8] for example, the parties

---

[1] U.C.C. § 1-105(1).

[2] The revisions also make it clear that Article 9 choice-of-law provisions govern priority of security interests. *See* **Article 9, Part 3, Subpart 1. Other relevant issues concerning secured transactions, including attachment, validity, characterization, and enforcement, are governed by the rules of § 1-105.** *See* **Prefatory Comment, Part 3, Article 9.**

[3] U.C.C. § 1-105 Cmt. 1.

[4] 274 U.S. 403, 47 S. Ct. 626, 71 L. Ed. 1123 (1927).

[5] *See, e.g., In re* Keene Corp., 188 B.R. 881, 28 U.C.C. Rep. Serv. 2d 651 (Bankr. S.D.N.Y. 1995) (selection of Illinois law upheld where debtor, a New York resident, granted secured party, an Illinois corporation, a security interest in book-entry Treasury securities).

[6] 28 U.C.C. Rep. Serv. 2d 398 (E.D. Pa. 1995), *aff'd,* 91 F.3d 124 (3d Cir. 1996).

[7] Section 1-105(1) requires that the parties "agree" on the law of a particular state, and "agreement" as defined in section 1-201(3) includes both the expressions of the parties and implications drawn from the surrounding facts. While most choice-of-law agreements are memorialized in a writing (and it is dangerous not to do so), a writing is not required. *See, e.g.,* Neville Chem. Co. v. Union Carbide Corp., 422 F.2d 1205 (3d Cir. 1970), *cert. denied,* 400 U.S. 826, 91 S. Ct. 51, 27 L. Ed. 2d 55 (1970) (court relies on fact that parties assumed Pennsylvania law would apply).

[8] 20 U.C.C. Rep. Serv. 1015 (D.N.H. 1976), *aff'd on other grounds,* 562 F.2d 1339 (1st Cir. 1977).

to a lease agreement selected California law, but the testimony failed to establish that either party resided or did business there, that the collateral was kept there, or that the contract was entered into there. The court properly applied New Hampshire law to resolve the dispute.

The fact that the 1972 version of Article 9 is in effect in all fifty states significantly dilutes the importance of the choice-of-law issue. Nevertheless, there are some significant differences among the states. Virtually every state has nonuniform amendments that make its version of Article 9 unique, and even the uniform provisions have been subjected to varying judicial interpretations. In most cases, a court will apply the parties' choice-of-law provision routinely, but in certain situations one party (usually the debtor) may argue that a compelling state policy requires the courts of that state to ignore an otherwise valid choice.

Suppose, for example, that the forum state has an anti-deficiency rule that penalizes secured parties who fail to follow the proper procedures for foreclosure, but the law of the chosen state allows the secured party to overcome a negative presumption and recover a deficiency. Courts faced with such arguments should defer to the parties' choice and resist the temptation to apply local law and, for the most part, they have done so.[9] **If the revision becomes effective in some states but not others,[10] the choice that the parties make will take on increased significance.**

It is generally understood that a court that applies the substantive law of another state will nevertheless apply the procedural law of the forum state. In *Nez v. Forney*,[11] for example, the parties had selected the law of Texas. The court held, however, that New Mexico's statute of limitations was procedural in nature and applied it.

[B]   The Appropriate Relationship Test

When the parties fail to designate the controlling law (or when their choice-of-law clause is not enforced), a particular state's version of the Code "applies to transactions bearing an appropriate relation to this state."[12] The fact that the drafters chose a different verbal formula suggests that the "appropriate relationship" test is more stringent than the "reasonable relationship" test that governs choice-of-law agreements. Suppose, for example, that a case is litigated in State A, which has a sufficient relationship to the transaction to support *in personam* jurisdiction, but State B has the most significant contacts. Most courts have concluded that the courts in State A should apply the

---

[9] *See, e.g.,* Interfirst Bank Clifton v. Fernandez, 853 F.2d 292, 6 U.C.C. Rep. Serv. 2d 1275 (5th Cir. 1988) (court refused to apply Louisiana anti-deficiency statute to protect Louisiana resident); *see contra,* Lewis v. First Nat'l Bank of Miami, 216 S.E.2d 347, 17 U.C.C. Rep. Serv. 197 (Ga. Ct. App. 1975) (case decided under 1962 Official Text applying Georgia law to repossession, notwithstanding choice of Florida law).

[10] **This seems inevitable, although U.C.C. § R9-701, which contains a deferred effective date of July 1, 2001, represents an attempt to reduce the impact of the problem. See § 20.01 *infra.***

[11] 109 N.M. 161, 783 P.2d 471, 10 U.C.C. Rep. Serv. 2d 289 (N.M. 1989).

[12] U.C.C. § 1-105(1).

substantive law of State B,[13] although a minority have equated the "reasonable relationship" and "appropriate relationship" tests.[14]

While the Comments leave interpretation of the term "appropriate relationship" to the courts,[15] equating the two tests runs counter to the normal rules of statutory construction. It should be presumed that the drafters intended different tests since they used differing language. The courts that have taken the "most significant contacts" approach appear to have the better of the argument.

Even when the parties have selected a state that satisfies the reasonable relationship test, the courts should apply the appropriate relationship test when one of the disputants is a third party who did not participate in the agreement process.[16]

§ 9.02   Article 9 Choice-of-Law: Overview

Section 9-103 of the 1972 version of Article 9, which governs perfection and the effects of perfection or nonperfection, significantly limits the operation of the Code's basic choice-of-law provision.[17] The reason for the limitation should be clear. Perfection issues invariably involve the rights of third parties, and, as indicated in the preceding subsection, such parties ought not be bound by agreements to which they are not privy. Further, leaving the decision to the courts under the appropriate relationship test would not provide third parties with the clear guidance they require regarding the filing systems that need to be searched.

Section 9-103 is organized into six subsections, each of which deals with a different type of collateral. The general definitions of indispensable paper and purely intangible collateral used in intrastate transactions are applicable to section 9-103, but the categories of goods are different. Instead of the familiar categories — consumer goods, equipment, farm products and inventory — the most important subsections apply to "ordinary goods," "mobile goods," and "goods covered by a certificate of title." Each subsection contains one or more choice-of-law rules. The length of the section, its use of novel terms, and the general complexity of the subject matter create significant obstacles to understanding. The ensuing material tackles the issues that arise under each subsection.

Dissatisfaction with the choice-of-law rules of section 9-103 was one of the primary motivations impelling the revision of Article 9. Choice-of-law provisions are provided in the several sections that make up Subpart I of Part 3 of Revised Article

---

[13] *See, e.g.*, *In re* Nantahala Village. Inc., 976 F.2d 876, 18 U.C.C. Rep. Serv. 2d 1027 (4th Cir. 1992) (Florida law, rather than law of forum state, North Carolina, governed).

[14] *See, e.g.*, Bos Material Handling, Inc. v. Crown Controls Corp., 137 Cal. App. 3d 99, 186 Cal. Rptr. 740 (1982) (applying law of forum state even though it did not have most significant contacts with transaction).

[15] U.C.C. § 1-105 Cmt. 3.

[16] *See, e.g.*, Hong Kong & Shanghai Banking Corp. v. HFH USA Corp., 805 F. Supp. 133, 19 U.C.C. Rep. Serv. 2d 885 (W.D.N.Y. 1992). Many issues involving the rights of third parties will turn on perfection and the effects of perfection or nonperfection, and will be governed by section 9-103 rather than section 1-105(l).

[17] Section 1-105(2) expressly subjects section 1-105(1) to section 9-103.

9.[18] The revisions include several fundamental changes, including elimination of the distinction between ordinary goods and mobile goods.

The explanation of the changes in the revision will be provided in two ways in this chapter. The next subsection provides an overall explanation of the approach adopted in the revision. Explanations of the manner in which specific aspects of the revision deviate from the 1972 text will then be interspersed throughout the material describing that version.

§ 9.03   The Revision's Choice-of-Law Rules Generally — §§ R9-301-R9-307

The revision provides different choice-of-law rules for possessory and nonpossessory security interests. The general rule, which is the one that governs nonpossessory security interests, is that priority and perfection are governed by the local law of the jurisdiction in which the debtor is located.[19] Priority and perfection of possessory security interests are governed by the local law of the jurisdiction in which the collateral is located.[20]

This approach substantially simplifies the choice-of-law rules. One of the greatest advantages is the reduction in the circumstances under which the governing law will change once a financing statement has been properly filed.[21] The revision provides that perfection of nonpossessory security interests (other than interests in certain land-related collateral[22]) is determined by the law of the jurisdiction in which the *debtor* is located, whereas prior law looked to the law of the jurisdiction in which the *collateral* was located in cases involving instruments, documents, and certain types of goods. Because debtors are likely to change their domicile less frequently than they are the location of their assets, the move to determining choice of law based on debtor location will reduce the instances in which reperfection will be required in another jurisdiction.[23] Moreover, debtor location for a registered

---

[18] Part 3 is entitled "Perfection and Priority." Subpart I, entitled "Law Governing Perfection and Priority," contains seven sections.

[19] U.C.C. § R9-301(1). This approach eliminates the 1972 text's bifurcation in which nonpossessory security interests were sometimes governed by a rule based on the situs of the collateral and sometimes on a rule based on the debtor's domicile. *See* U.C.C. § 9-103(1),(3).

[20] U.C.C. § R9-301(2).

[21] U.C.C. § R9-301 Cmt. 3.

[22] A situs-of-collateral rule applies to certain types of collateral that are closely related to real property. It applies to perfection of a security interest in goods by fixture filing, U.C.C. § R9-301(3)(A), and perfection of a security interest in timber to be cut, U.C.C. § R9-301(3)(B). It also applies to perfection and priority of an agricultural lien on farm products, U.C.C. § R9-302, as well as to perfection and priority of a security interest in as-extracted collateral, U.C.C. § R9-301(4).

[23] Further efficiencies are created through the revision's elimination of two separate tests for nonpossessory security interests. One significant problem that was posed under the prior approach resulted when collateral consisting of ordinary goods was sold to produce intangible proceeds. After a short period of temporary perfection, a secured party who perfected by filing in the state in which the goods were located would become unperfected with respect to accounts generated by the sale of the goods unless the secured party had also filed in the

organization is deemed to be the jurisdiction under whose laws the debtor is organized, reducing further the chance that reperfection will become necessary. Secured parties should be able to detect changes in debtor location more easily than changes in collateral location.

Possessory security interests fall under a situs-of-collateral rule, and the efficiency of such an approach is obvious. Because the secured party, its representative, or a bailee obligated to follow the secured party's instructions is in possession of the collateral, movement of the collateral to another jurisdiction can be readily controlled. Moreover, possession will undoubtedly result in perfection under the law of the new jurisdiction at the moment the goods are moved there.

The determination of when the location-of-debtor rule and the situs rule apply is much easier under the revision. Section 9-103 drew a distinction between ordinary goods and mobile goods, applying the situs rule to the former and the location-of-debtor rule to the latter. The distinction at times, however, proved to be difficult to draw.[24] The revision eliminates this distinction. The situs rule applies only to perfection and priority of possessory security interests and nonpossessory security interests in certain land-related collateral; the location-of-debtor rule governs perfection and priority of all other nonpossessory security interests.

The elimination of the situs test to govern perfection of nonpossessory security interests in ordinary goods reduces the need for multiple filings. Under the prior approach, when a lender took a security interest in inventory or equipment located in several different states, the situs rule required a filing in each state to cover the goods in each location. Because perfection under the revision is accomplished by filing in the jurisdiction in which the debtor is located, a single filing will cover goods located in multiple jurisdictions.

Although most of the advantages to the revision enumerated above relate specifically to perfection, the drafters of the revision recognized a problem with respect to priority that could result from applying the location-of-debtor rule to nonpossessory security interests when the debtor and the collateral are located in different jurisdictions. The Comments explain the problem through the following example:

> For example, assume a security interest in equipment located in Pennsylvania is perfected by filing in Illinois, where the debtor is located. If the law of the jurisdiction in which the debtor is located were to govern priority, then the priority of an execution lien on goods located in Pennsylvania would be governed by rules enacted by the Illinois legislature.[25]

To address the problem, the revision includes another significant exception to the general rule that the law governing the perfection and priority of nonpossessory

state in which the debtor was located. By filing under the revision in the jurisdiction in which the debtor is located in order to perfect the security interest in the original collateral, the secured party can continue to use that filing with respect to the perfection rules on proceeds, despite the relationship of more than one jurisdiction to the transaction.

[24] See § 9.05[A] infra.

[25] U.C.C. § R9-301 Cmt. 7.

security interests is the law in which the debtor is located. With respect to the *effect of perfection or nonperfection and the priority* of a nonpossessory security interest, the law of the situs of the collateral governs for collateral consisting of goods, instruments, negotiable documents, money, or tangible chattel paper.[26] The affected collateral thus consists of goods and indispensable paper — the types of collateral that have a tangible form and thus can be located within a particular jurisdiction. The law governing *where to perfect* security interests in these types of collateral is determined under the general rule, which is the local law of the jurisdiction in which the debtor is located. In other words, the revision bifurcates the selection of the applicable law for these types of collateral according to issues of perfection and issues of priority. Although this bifurcated approach of the revision adds an element of complexity, it preserves the benefit associated with a location-of-debtor rule while avoiding the problems that would arise in allowing distant jurisdictions to control issues related to priorities.

The revision also includes new rules that establish the location of the debtor.[27] As explained above, the location of the debtor is the relevant standard to establish the law that governs both perfection and priority for security interests in pure intangibles,[28] and perfection for most nonpossessory security interests in goods and indispensable paper.[29]

Section R9-307(b) provides several baseline rules on debtor location. An individual is located at its residence.[30] Any other debtor is located at its place of business, and, if it has more than one place of business, at its chief executive office.[31] A registered organization[32] is located in the state under whose law it is organized.[33] Thus, a debtor corporation is located in the state in which it is incorporated.

The rule with respect to registered organizations represents a significant advantage over the rule in the 1972 text, which is based on the chief executive office of a debtor conducting business in multiple states. For example, a corporation is organized under the law of a single state, and the necessary information is readily

---

[26] U.C.C. § R9-301(3).

[27] U.C.C. § R9-307.

[28] U.C.C. § R9-301(1).

[29] U.C.C. § R9-301(1),(3).

[30] U.C.C. § R9-307(b)(1).

[31] U.C.C. § R9-307(b)(2),(3). "Place of business" is defined to mean "a place where a debtor conducts its affairs." U.C.C. § R9-307(a). This broad definition is included to encompass organizations that do not engage in "for profit" business activities. U.C.C. § R9-307 Cmt. 2.

[32] "Registered organization" means "an organization organized solely under the law of one State or the United States and as to which the State or the United States must maintain a public record showing the organization to have been organized." U.C.C. § R9-102(a)(70). The term includes, *inter alia*, corporations, limited partnerships and limited liability companies.

[33] U.C.C. § R9-307(e). Events like dissolution of a corporation or suspension or revocation of its charter that affect its corporate status do not affect its location for purposes of this rule. U.C.C. § R9-307(g).

available through public records, typically computer files. Comparable information is not available to determine a debtor's chief executive office, and doubts concerning the correct office often led to multiple filings as the only means to provide adequate protection. Reliance on the incorporation records should also lead to a substantial reduction in errors with respect to the debtor's name, as both filers and searchers will need to consult the incorporation records to determine the proper jurisdiction in which to file or search. The Comments point out that a jurisdiction could even program its filing system to reject any filing that designates an incorrect debtor name for a registered organization. [34]

The revision also provides new rules for determining the location of non-U.S. debtors. The general location-of-debtor rules of section R9-307(b) apply only if the debtor's applicable residence, place of business, or chief executive office is located in a jurisdiction whose law generally requires information concerning the existence of a nonpossessory security interest to be made generally available in a filing, recording, or registration system as a condition or result of the security interest's obtaining priority over the rights of a lien creditor with respect to the collateral." [35] The law of the foreign jurisdiction will apply, but only if it provides a means for public notice of security interests. Without a public notice system, the advantages of applying the location-of-debtor test would be lost. Accordingly, in such cases the revision establishes the debtor's location as Washington, D.C. [36]

The revision includes a method for continuing perfection even though the location of the debtor changes to another jurisdiction. [37] For the most part the rule is the same as that included in the 1972 text. [38] If the security interest is properly perfected under section R9-301(1) under the local law of the jurisdiction in which the debtor is located, the general rule is that the security interest remains perfected for four months after the change of the debtor's location to another jurisdiction. [39] Thus, the prior perfection continues for an additional four months.

The four-month grace period is altered under certain circumstances. If perfection uld cease sooner under the law of the jurisdiction of removal, the grace period extends only for the duration that the perfection would have been effective. [40] Thus, 'f proper perfection by filing would have lapsed in State A within one month of ;ic debtor changing its location to State B, the security interest remains perfected under the filing in State A only for the one-month period. If collateral is transferred to a person that becomes a debtor and is located in another jurisdiction, the grace

---

[34] U.C.C. § R9-307 Cmt. 4.

[35] U.C.C. § R9-307(c).

[36] U.C.C. § R9-307(c). The same location is designated for the United States as a debtor. U.C.C. § R9-307(h).

[37] U.C.C. § R9-316(a).

[38] *See* U.C.C. § 9-103(3)(e). The revision applies the same analysis developed in § 9.04[C] of this text, and the reader is referred to that discussion of the underlying rationales for the provisions.

[39] U.C.C. § R9-316(a)(2).

[40] U.C.C. § R9-316(a)(1).

period is extended for a period of one year.[41] The greater time is allowed because of the great difficulty of discerning such events even with due diligence.[42]

The grace period gives the secured party an opportunity to reperfect in the jurisdiction to which the debtor moves. If reperfection is accomplished before the applicable grace period ends, the secured party remains continuously perfected.[43] Failure to reperfect within the grace period leaves the security interest unperfected prospectively; further, as against a purchaser for value[44] who acquires rights in the collateral during the grace period, the security interest is deemed to be unperfected.[45] Thus, for example, a secured party perfected by filing in State A who does not take the necessary step of reperfecting in State B during the applicable grace period will be unperfected against a lien creditor only if the lien creditor's interest arises after the expiration of the grace period. As against a purchaser whose interest arises after the change in the debtor's location, however, the secured party will be deemed unperfected from the date of the move. With respect to purchasers, the failure to reperfect during the grace period results in retroactive invalidation of the perfection initially recognized under the grace period.

With its expansion to include deposit accounts within the scope of Article 9, the revision provides that the local law of the bank's jurisdiction governs perfection and priority of security interests in these accounts.[46] Rules that determine a bank's jurisdiction for purposes of this section are included. The parties can choose the law of a jurisdiction that they want to apply, even if the jurisdiction does not have any relationship to the parties or to the transaction.[47] If the parties do not make a selection, the jurisdiction will be the one in which the bank office that maintains the deposit account is located if the parties' agreement expressly identifies that location. Otherwise, the jurisdiction will be the location of the bank office identified in an account statement as the office serving the customer's account. If none of the preceding tests apply, the jurisdiction will be the location of the bank's chief executive office.[48]

---

[41] U.C.C. § R9-316(a)(3).

[42] U.C.C. § R9-316 Cmt. 2.

[43] U.C.C. § R9-316(b).

[44] "Purchaser" means any person with a voluntarily acquired interest in property and includes a secured party. U.C.C. § 1-201(33),(32). The 1998 text makes it clear that only a purchaser *for value* gains the protection of the retroactive invalidation rule. This is implicit in the 1972 text.

[45] U.C.C. § R9-316(b).

[46] U.C.C. § R9-304.

[47] U.C.C. § R9-304 Cmt. 2. The parties can choose to apply the law of one jurisdiction to perfection and priority and the law of another jurisdiction for other purposes. *Id.*

[48] The rules in section R9-304 are similar to the rules to determine a "security intermediary's jurisdiction" under former section 8-110(e). The latter section has been conformed to the somewhat greater flexibility included in section R9-304(b)(1). The revision's multistate rules for investment property are set forth in § R9-305 and are unchanged from current law as found in § 9-103(6).

§ 9.04 The Situs Rule — §§ 9-103(1), R9-301(2),(3)

Section 9-103(1) of the 1972 text adopts what is sometimes called a "situs rule" to deal with certain types of collateral that are generally expected to remain in one location. The basic rule is that the secured party should perfect under the laws of the jurisdiction in which the collateral is physically located. This approach is explored in the ensuing subsections.

The general rule under the revision is that the law governing the perfection of *nonpossessory* security interests (other than a few instances involving land-related collateral)[49] is the law of the jurisdiction where the debtor is located. For *possessory* security interests in goods and indispensable paper,[50] perfection is governed by the law of the jurisdiction where the collateral is located.[51]

With regard to the *effects* of perfection and nonperfection and the priority of both possessory and nonpossessory security interests in goods and indispensable paper, the revision consistently applies a situs rule.[52] In other words, if goods are located in State A and the debtor is located in State B, a nonpossessory security interest will be perfected by filing in State B, but priority contests will be resolved under the law of State A. The law of State A will govern every aspect of a possessory security interest.[53]

[A] The Last-Event Test

Section 9-103(1) of the 1972 text governs perfection and priority issues that arise when the collateral is documents, instruments, the right to proceeds of letters of credit, or ordinary goods. The basic rule for these categories is as follows:

> Except as otherwise provided in this subsection, perfection and the effect of perfection or non-perfection of a security interest in collateral are governed by the law of the jurisdiction where the collateral is when the last event occurs on which is based the assertion that the security interest is perfected or unperfected.[54]

The "events" upon which a secured party will ordinarily base its assertion that it is perfected are the conditions for attachment[55] plus whatever additional step may be

---

[49] The revision adopts a situs rule for nonpossessory security interests when a fixture filing is made, U.C.C. § R9-301(3)(A), when the collateral is timber to be cut, § R9-301(3)(B), and when the collateral is as-extracted collateral, § R9-301(4).

[50] Recall that these are the types of collateral *capable* of being perfected by possession.

[51] U.C.C. § R9-301(2).

[52] U.C.C. § R9-301(2)(possessory security interests), R9-301(3)(C)(nonpossessory security interests).

[53] The rationale for this distinction is explained in the preceding subsection. *See* § 9.03 *supra.*

[54] U.C.C. § 9-103(1)(b).

[55] *See generally* U.C.C. § 9-203. The conditions for attachment are that there be an agreement (in a proper type of signed writing for nonpossessory security interests), that the secured party give value, and that the debtor have rights in the collateral. These conditions are discussed in detail in Chapter 2 *supra.*

required for perfection.[56] Thus, the "last-event" test looks to the law of the state where the collateral is physically located (the situs) when the last of these events occurs to determine whether the secured party has perfected properly and to determine the consequences of perfection or nonperfection.

The revision abandons the last-event test. As indicated above,[57] except for possessory security interests, the situs test is largely abandoned in favor of a location-of-debtor test.[58] With a possessory interest, the secured party, its representative, or a bailee who is obligated to follow the secured party's instructions must acquire possession of the collateral. The dilemma created by the goods changing states while the steps for attachment and perfection are being undertaken simply does not confront a party with a possessory security interest. Accordingly, the last-event test is unnecessary.

With instruments and rights to proceeds of letters of credit, the basic rule in the 1972 text is that perfection requires possession and that the filing of a financing statement is neither necessary nor effective.[59] Because this rule is in effect in every state, the fact that there exists a choice-of-law rule governing the appropriate method of perfection is largely immaterial. No matter where the instrument is located, the secured party must take possession. In theory, an issue could arise involving an instrument, but it would be exceedingly rare. For example, states might differ as to the steps necessary to effectuate constructive possession,[60] with State A (where the instrument is located) requiring that the bailee be given notice by the debtor and State B permitting the notice to come from either the debtor or the secured party. A choice-of-law provision designating State B would not protect a secured party attempting to gain constructive possession by sending notice directly to the bailee rather than having the notice come from the debtor. Section 9-103 preempts the parties' choice and mandates the application of State A's law.

A security interest in negotiable documents can be perfected either by possession or filing.[61] If the secured party takes possession, the issues are the same as with instruments. If perfection is achieved by filing, the secured party must file in the state where the document is located when the last event occurs. The test is identical to the one used for ordinary goods and discussed *infra* this subsection.

The revision makes perfection by filing permissible for instruments as well as documents,[62] but perfection with respect to letter-of-credit rights must be by

---

[56] The various methods of perfection are discussed generally in Chapter 4 *supra.*

[57] *See* § 9.04 *supra.*

[58] **The last-event test has no relevance in this context because the applicable events are unrelated to debtor location.**

[59] U.C.C. § 9-304(1). There are exceptions for instruments, but each involves temporary perfection, and the rules governing this concept do not vary from state to state.

[60] Constructive possession is validated by section 9-305 of the 1972 text and discussed in Chapter 6 *supra.* **The steps necessary for constructive possession to occur are changed in the revision.** *Id.*

[61] U.C.C. §§ 9-305, 9-304. As with instruments, section 9-304 provides for periods of temporary automatic perfection.

[62] U.C.C. § R9-312(a).

control.[63] Perfection by filing of a security interest in instruments or negotiable documents is no longer governed by the law of the jurisdiction where the collateral is located. As indicated above, perfection by filing is based on the law of the jurisdiction where the debtor is located, although the effects of perfection or nonperfection and the priority of the security interest are governed by a situs rule.[64] Only in the case of a possessory security interest in an instrument or document does the law of the situs govern perfection.[65]

A separate provision of the revision addresses the law governing perfection and priority with respect to security interests in letter-of-credit rights.[66] The applicable law is the local law of the issuer's jurisdiction (or the local law of a nominated person's jurisdiction), provided that such jurisdiction is a state. If that jurisdiction is not a state, the general choice-of-law rule applies, meaning that perfection and priority are governed by the law of the debtor's location.[67] The objective is to prevent foreign law from controlling a transaction that, from the perspective of the debtor-beneficiary, its creditors, and a domestic nominated person, is essentially domestic.[68] The determination of an issuer's or nominated person's jurisdiction is to be made in accordance with provisions in Article 5 on letters of credit.[69]

All goods are by definition movable,[70] but ordinary goods in the 1972 text are goods that are expected to remain in one place.[71] A situs rule applies with ordinary goods. Ordinary goods must be contrasted with mobile goods, which are of a type normally used in more than one state and for which a location-of-debtor rule applies.[72] The assumption that underlies the situs rule for ordinary goods is that third parties will naturally search for financing statements in the state where such collateral is located, and therefore the secured party must perfect there. For example, if the debtor is a multinational corporation with offices and assets located all over the world, a security interest in shop machinery located at its plant in State A must be perfected according to State A's filing rules.[73]

---

[63] U.C.C. § R9-312(b)(2).

[64] *See* § 9.04 *supra.*

[65] *Id.*

[66] U.C.C. § R9-306.

[67] U.C.C. § R9-306 Cmt. 2. *See* U.C.C. § R9-301(1).

[68] U.C.C. § R9-306 Cmt. 2.

[69] U.C.C. § R9-306(b)(referencing U.C.C. § 5-116).

[70] U.C.C. § 9-105(l)(h).

[71] "Ordinary goods" is a residual category for purposes of section 9-103. They consist of goods that do not fit within the other categories — mobile goods, goods covered by a certificate of title, and minerals. U.C.C. § 9-103(1)(a).

[72] Mobile goods are discussed in detail in § 9.05[A] *infra.*

[73] U.C.C. § 9-109. Having identified the state whose law governs, the collateral must be recategorized using the ordinary classifications (the shop machinery would likely be equipment) and the intrastate filing rules for State A must be consulted to determine whether a local or centralized filing (or both) is required in State A. For discussion of the intrastate filing rules, *see* U.C.C. § 9-401 and § 5.04[B] *supra.*

The revision eliminates the distinction between ordinary goods and mobile goods. Because the general rule for nonpossessory security interests is that perfection is governed by a location-of-debtor test, the distinction is not meaningful.[74] The illustration of the multinational corporation serves to demonstrate the increased efficiency that accrues through the approach taken in the revision. Even though the debtor has goods that are subject to the security interest located in several states, the secured party needs to file and searchers need to search only in the state in which the debtor is located. The revision thus eliminates the need for multiple filings covering different types of collateral.

When the collateral remains in one state throughout the attachment and perfection process, the last-event test of the 1972 text presents few difficulties. If the collateral changes location during this process, however, the test creates a number of pitfalls for the careless lender. For example, suppose that the debtor and the secured party are both located in State A, and that all the debtor's assets are normally located in that state as well. Suppose further that the secured party agrees to make a loan against a particular piece of equipment which happens to be at a repair shop in State B when the secured party, assuming that the collateral is at the debtor's location, files in State A. If a judgment creditor of the debtor levies on the collateral before it returns to State A, the creditor will obtain priority over the secured party. The last-event test directed that the filing be made in State B, and the filing in State A was not sufficient. Under State B's priority rules (which for this purpose will be the same as State A's, since section 9-301(1)(b) will be in effect in both states), the judgment creditor will qualify as a lien creditor and take priority over the unperfected secured party. **This dilemma cannot exist under the revision. Perfection by filing will be governed by the law of the jurisdiction where the debtor is located, thus making the location of the collateral irrelevant. With a possessory security interest, the very fact of possession by the secured party eliminates the problem.**

Continuing with the prior example, suppose that the equipment is repaired in State B and returned to State A without incident. After its return, it is seized by a lien creditor. Will the secured party's interest be perfected by its filing in State A the moment the equipment crosses the state line, or will the secured party have to file first in State B before its filing in State A can become effective? Surely, the correct answer is that the initial filing becomes effective the moment the asset reenters State A; however, if the only "events" that count for purposes of the test are the steps leading to attachment and perfection, one might argue that section 9-103(1)(b) yields a different result. Because the collateral was in State B when the last of these events occurred, State B's version of the Code still controls, even though the collateral has been moved back to State A, rendering the filing in State A ineffective. To be perfected in State A, the secured party would first have to satisfy the last-event test by filing in State B. This filing would then be effective for four months after the equipment was returned to State A, and the secured party's filing in State A would ensure that there was never a gap in perfection.[75]

This result is absurd. Under a situs rule the mere fact that the collateral is physically located in State A should validate a filing within that state. One way to resolve the

---

[74] U.C.C. § R9-301 Cmt. 7.

[75] U.C.C. § 9-103(1)(d). For discussion of the four-month rule, *see* § 9.04[C] *infra*.

problem is to conclude that events other than those surrounding attachment and perfection can be used to satisfy the test. Under this approach the last event upon which the secured party would base its assertion that its interest is perfected would be the movement of the equipment from State B to State A.[76] Because the collateral was in State A at the time of the last event, State A's laws would control and the secured party's filing would be effective.

The example discussed above demonstrates some of the weakness inherent in the last-event test. The test creates uncertainty because it does not indicate which events are relevant. Elimination of the test is beneficial even for possessory security interests, which remain subject to a situs test under the revision. If a secured party takes possession of the collateral while it is located in State B, the secured party will control the movement of the collateral to State A. Assuming that the secured party does not surrender possession, its interest will become perfected under the law of State A as soon as it moves the collateral there.

The only way for a secured party to be certain that it has perfected properly under the last-event test is to make certain that it assesses the location of the collateral at the time the last event occurs, but this can be difficult. The last event is normally the filing of the financing statement, but suppose the secured party takes advantage of the pre-filing rule set forth in section 9-402(l).[77] Such a filing would not perfect a security interest since one does not yet exist, but if the events of attachment are subsequently satisfied, the security interest will be perfected at the moment of attachment (assuming the description in the financing statement covers the assets described in the security agreement). If the collateral changes states between the time of filing and the time of attachment, however, the secured party will be unperfected because the last-event test could not be satisfied without a filing in the new state. Lenders who pre-file must be aware of this possibility and make certain that their collateral is still within the state of filing when they subsequently take steps to have their security interest attach.

A secured party who pre-files under the revision does not incur this risk. With perfection by filing governed by a location-of-debtor rule rather than a situs rule, the secured party will become perfected upon attachment unless the debtor has changed its location in the interim. The secured party is much less likely to make a mistake under the revision's approach.

Another trap can spring into play under the 1972 text when a secured party takes a security interest in "lease paper"— chattel paper that represents a lease of goods — and also takes an interest in the debtor's reversionary interest in the leased goods. If the

---

[76] For conflicting views on whether the last event must be one of the normal events of attachment and perfection, see Kripke, *The "Last Event" Test for Perfection of Security Interests Under Article 9 of the Uniform Commercial Code,* 50 N.Y.U. L. Rev. 47 (1975) (arguing that the last event can be a "nonevent") and Coogan, *The New UCC Article 9, 86* Harv. L. Rev. 477 (1973) (arguing that last event must be one associated with attachment or perfection).

[77] By filing its financing statement before it commits to making a loan, the secured party can gain an important advantage. It can search the system for adverse filings and, if it finds none, be confident that no one can file between the time of the search and the time of the loan and thereby gain an advantage.

secured party chooses to file to perfect its interest in the chattel paper, the Code directs it to the state in which the debtor is located; with a multistate debtor, this means the place where the debtor maintains its chief executive office.[78] The right to the debtor's reversionary interest in the goods, however, will be subject to the last-event test because the goods will, upon return, be part of the debtor's inventory. If the place to which the goods will be returned is in a different state from the debtor's chief executive office, a filing will have to be made in that state as well.[79] **This problem is eliminated in the revision, which applies the general location-of-debtor test to both the chattel paper and the underlying goods.**

A similar problem can arise under the 1972 text when proceeds are involved. For example, suppose that the secured party takes a security interest in the inventory of a store that is located in State A but is part of a larger entity headquartered in State B. Under the situs rule, the secured party must file in State A, but that filing will not perfect its security interest in the accounts and chattel paper that are the likely proceeds of the inventory. After a ten-day period of temporary perfection, the secured party will become unperfected unless it has filed a financing statement in State B.[80] **This problem is also eliminated under the revision. With both the inventory and its proceeds subject to the location-of-debtor test, the party will have continuous automatic perfection beyond the grace period because the office in which filing was made for the inventory is the same office in which filing would be made for accounts or chattel paper.**[81]

[B]   The Thirty-Day Rule

Suppose a seller located in State B agrees to the credit sale of a piece of equipment that the buyer will use in its factory in State A. Assuming that the 1972 text's situs rule for ordinary goods is in effect, should the seller, who is retaining a purchase-money security interest, file in State A, where the goods will be kept, or in State B? Ultimately, of course, there will have to be a filing in State A because the equipment will be an ordinary good, but the seller should make certain that its interest is perfected while the equipment is en route.

If our seller files in State A only and the last-event test is used, the security interest will be at risk if a third party acquires an interest in the equipment before it reaches its destination. For example, suppose that a lien creditor seizes the equipment while it is passing through State C. On our facts, the last-event test will almost certainly dictate

---

[78] U.C.C. §§ 9-103(4),(3). If the secured party chooses to perfect by possession, the last-event test *is* used. *See* U.C.C. § 9-103(4),(1) and the discussion of perfection as to instruments in this subsection. The rules of section 9-103(3) are discussed in § 9.05 *infra.*

[79] *See, e.g., In re* Leasing Consultants, Inc., 486 F.2d 367, 13 U.C.C. Rep. Serv. 189 (2d Cir. 1973) (filing in New York effective as to chattel paper but ineffective as to leased goods returned to debtor's New Jersey location). This problem is discussed in more detail in the context of the domicile rule of section 9-103(3). *See* § 9.05[A] *infra.*

[80] U.C.C. § 9-306(3). The debtor need not sign the financing statement covering proceeds. *See* U.C.C. § 9-402(2)(b). This problem is discussed in more detail in the context of the domicile rule of section 9-103(3). *See* § 9.05[B] *infra.*

[81] **U.C.C. § R9-315(d)(1). Temporary perfection with regard to proceeds is 20 days in the revision. U.C.C. § R9-315(d). Temporary perfection for proceeds is discussed in § 8.02** *supra.*

that State B's laws control,[82] and the filing in State A will be ineffective. The seller would have to file in State B first and then make a subsequent filing in State A. The filing in State B would be effective in State C under the "four-month" rule.[83]

The drafters concluded that requiring the seller to make duplicate filings in such situations was too onerous, and they resolved the problem with section 9-103(1)(c), sometimes called the "thirty-day" rule. That subsection states:

> If the parties to a transaction creating a purchase money security interest in goods in one jurisdiction understand at the time that the security interest attaches that the goods will be kept in another jurisdiction, then the law of the other jurisdiction governs the perfection and the effect of perfection or non-perfection of the security interest from the time it attaches until thirty days after the debtor receives possession of the goods and thereafter if the goods are taken to the other jurisdiction before the end of the thirty-day period.

Applying this rule to the prior fact situation, our seller's filing in State A would be effective from the moment of attachment until thirty days after the debtor received possession of the equipment. If the equipment reached State A before the expiration of that period, there would never be a gap in perfection. The filing in State A would give the seller priority over the State C lien creditor, although a new filing in State C would be necessary if the thirty-day period had commenced and the goods were going to remain there after the period expired.

As with the last-event test, the logic behind the thirty-day rule is not difficult to understand, but the drafting creates traps for the unwary. For example, suppose that a purchase-money seller in State A enters into a contract to sell an identified piece of machinery to a buyer and the contract calls for the buyer to designate the place to which the machine is to be delivered. A few days later, the buyer advises the seller to ship the goods to State B. The seller, relying on the thirty-day rule, files in State B, but before the goods leave State A they are seized by a lien creditor. The lien creditor will have priority. The parties did not understand that the goods were to be kept in State B *at the time the security interest attached* and, therefore, the thirty-day rule did not apply. Under the last-event test, the law of State A governed, and perfection was contingent on a filing in that state.

The 1972 text provides that the thirty-day period begins to run when the debtor "receives possession" of the goods. Although the meaning of the term "possession" can be elusive, the use of the word "receives" in conjunction with it suggests that the drafters intended that the thirty-day period not begin to run until there is physical receipt of the goods by the debtor.[84] For example, suppose that the buyer and seller understand at the

---

[82] The filing in State A will probably be the last event upon which the seller bases its claim that its interest is perfected. Attachment will probably have occurred when the goods were identified to the contract of sale. *See* U.C.C. § 2-501 and the discussion in § 2.02[C] *supra.*

[83] The four-month rule is discussed in subsection [C] *infra.* If the goods remained in State C for more than four months, a filing in that state would be necessary to avoid a gap in perfection.

[84] *Cf.* U.C.C. § 2-103(1)(c), which defines "receipt" to mean taking physical possession of the goods.

time of attachment that the goods will be kept in State B and the seller files in that state. Suppose further that the contract calls for the seller to ship the goods from State A, and the seller turns them over to a common carrier for delivery. For certain Article 2 purposes, primarily risk of loss,[85] the goods will be deemed to have been tendered to the buyer when they were duly delivered to the carrier.[86] The buyer will not physically receive them, however, until the carrier in turn makes the delivery. On these facts, the seller should be protected by its State B filing even if the goods are held up for several months in another jurisdiction. Under the thirty-day rule, the seller is protected from the time of its filing until thirty days after the buyer receives delivery, and the time period cannot begin to run while the goods are still in the hands of the carrier.

Despite the logic of the foregoing analysis, a purchase-money secured party would be foolish to rely on it. The risk that a court might misapply the thirty-day rule is significant, and obtaining protection against such a possibility is inexpensive. With any doubt about whether the rule applies, or any risk that the goods will be delayed more than thirty days before they reach the destination state, the secured party should cover itself under both the last-event test and the thirty-day rule.[87] It should file first in the state of origin, thereby assuring protection for so long as the goods are in that state. This also assures the secured party a four-month grace period to refile if the goods are unexpectedly delayed in another state (other than the destination state). The secured party should also file in the destination state. This filing will satisfy the thirty-day rule if it is applicable and, if it is not applicable, a filing in the destination state would ultimately be required anyway. The dual-filing approach provides the secured party with the maximum protection possible.

The revisions eliminates the problem addressed by the thirty-day rule. Perfection with respect to nonpossessory security interests is governed by the law of the jurisdiction in which the debtor is located. Because that location is unaffected by the changing location of the goods, there is no need for a thirty-day rule.[88]

[C]   The Four-Month Rule

Suppose assets that are subject to the 1972 text's situs rule are taken from the state where initial perfection occurred and kept in another state. Because interested parties ill naturally search the records in the new state, a filing is needed there, but the secured arty may not become aware of the change for a significant time. The "four-month" rule described in this subsection was designed as a compromise between the interests of third parties and secured parties and, as such, it is not totally fair to either group. A secured party must check on the location of its collateral every four months to be safe and, if the collateral has changed states, make a filing in the new state.[89] A third party who has searched the records in the state where an asset is located and found nothing should make certain that the asset has been kept in that state for more than four months.

---

[85] *See* U.C.C. § 2-509(1)(a).

[86] *See* U.C.C. §§ 2-503(2), 2-504.

[87] *See* U.C.C. § 9-103 Cmt. 3.

[88] U.C.C. § R9-301 Cmt. 4.

[89] The filing is facilitated by the fact that the secured party need not obtain the debtor's signature. *See* U.C.C. § 9-402(2)(a).

(Matthew Bender & Co., Inc.)

The four-month rule is set forth as follows:

When collateral is brought into and kept in this state while subject to a security interest perfected under the law of the jurisdiction from which the collateral was removed, the security interest remains perfected, but if action is required by Part 3 of this Article to perfect the security interest,

  (i) if the action is not taken before the expiration of the period of perfection in the other jurisdiction or the end of four months after the collateral is brought into this state, whichever period first expires, the security interest becomes unperfected at the end of that period and is thereafter deemed to have been unperfected as against a person who became a purchaser after removal;

  (ii) if the action is taken before the expiration of the period specified in subparagraph (i), the security interest continues perfected thereafter;

  (iii) for the purpose of priority over a buyer of consumer goods (subsection (2) of Section 9-307), the period of the effectiveness of a filing in the jurisdiction from which the collateral is removed is governed by the rules with respect to perfection in subparagraphs (i) and (ii).[90]

In a simple example of this rule, suppose the collateral is ordinary goods that have been properly perfected in State A before they are permanently removed by the debtor to State B. Two months after removal, they are purchased by a nonordinary-course buyer who has searched the filing system in State B and found nothing. Before the four-month grace period expires, the secured party discovers what has happened and properly files in State B. In a priority contest between the secured party and the buyer, the secured party will prevail. The filing in State A was effective at the time of purchase, and the rights of a nonordinary-course buyer are subordinate to those of a perfected secured party.[91] Because the secured party filed in State B during the four-month grace period, it never had a gap in its perfection. The result is somewhat harsh because the buyer could only protect itself by inquiring (and getting a truthful answer) about the collateral's whereabouts during the four months preceding the purchase, but the buyer is not without a remedy. The debtor will be liable for breach of the Article 2 implied warranty of title.[92]

Now suppose the secured party fails to file during the grace period. The buyer will prevail because of the retroactive invalidation rule embedded in section 9-103(1)(d)(i). Although the security interest was technically perfected by the filing in State A at the time of purchase, the failure to file during the grace period undoes that perfection. A nonordinary-course buyer qualifies as a "purchaser,"[93] and the once-perfected secured party is deemed to have been unperfected as against any person who qualifies as a purchaser following removal.[94]

---

[90] U.C.C. § 9-103(1)(d).

[91] U.C.C. § 9-301(1)(c).

[92] U.C.C. § 2-312.

[93] U.C.C. § 1-201(33),(32). The term would also encompass a secured party, but not a lien creditor or any other party acquiring rights in the collateral by a nonvoluntary mechanism.

[94] The secured party could still prevail if it could prove that the buyer had knowledge of its security interest at the appropriate time. *See* U.C.C. § 9-301(1)(c) and § 14.03 *infra*.

Next, suppose the secured party allows the grace period to expire without filing in State B and the buyer purchases thereafter. The secured party's perfection based on its State A filing will have ended, and because it did not file in State B it will be unperfected.[95] In this context, however, the termination of State A perfection is not necessarily fatal. If the secured party had discovered the facts after its perfection ended but before purchase by the buyer and had filed in State B, it would have gained priority over the buyer based on its State B filing. The belated filing in State B would not have prevented a gap in perfection, but it would have given the secured party five years of perfection against subsequent parties in State B and would have provided a basis for a new four-month grace period if the goods were subsequently removed to another state.

What if the collateral is taken to a new state for a temporary purpose but remains there for more than four months? The four-month rule is triggered when collateral is "brought into and kept" in a new state, and the Comments indicate that this implies "a stopping place of a permanent nature in the state, not merely transit or storage intended to be transitory."[96] This approach was followed in *In re Potomac School of Law, Inc.*,[97] where a law school in the District of Columbia moved its library, which contained books subject to a publishing company's security interest, into storage in Virginia while it moved to a new location in the District. After the books had been in storage for more than four months, the law school filed for bankruptcy, and the court held that the publisher's filing in the District was still effective because the temporary movement of the collateral to Virginia did not trigger the four-month rule.

The retroactive invalidation rule of section 9-103(1)(d)(i) differs subtly from the intrastate lapse rule contained in section 9-403(2). The latter section includes lien creditors within the class of protected parties, but the choice-of-law rule protects only purchasers. Lien creditors (including bankruptcy trustees) do not generally rely on the filing system, so it seems that the approach of section 9-103 is superior.[98] Nevertheless, the adoption of different approaches for similar circumstances in the same Code is curious.

How does the four-month rule operate when a lien creditor is involved? For example, suppose that the secured party files properly in State A but fails to file within four months after removal to State B. If a lien creditor seizes the collateral after the grace period expires, the lien creditor will have priority,[99] but if it seizes the collateral during the grace period, it will lose, because the secured party will be perfected by its State A filing. The fact that the grace period has expired will not undo that perfection, because the lien creditor is not protected by the retroactive invalidation rule. Thus, the secured party could safely repossess the collateral from the lien creditor.[100] If it failed to do so and the

---

[95] In this context, the secured party will not be "deemed" unperfected under the retroactive invalidation rule; it will be actually unperfected.

[96] U.C.C. § 9-103 Cmt. 3.

[97] 16 B.R. 102, 32 U.C.C. Rep. Serv. 1598 (Bankr. D.D.C. 1981).

[98] **The revision's rule, applicable to changes in debtor location, operates in favor of purchasers for value but not lien creditors. U.C.C. § R9-515(c).**

[99] *See* U.C.C. § 9-103(1)(b).

[100] In most cases, the collateral will be in the possession of a levying sheriff and, to repossess, the secured party would have to obtain a writ of replevin directing that the sheriff turn the collateral over to it. If the lien creditor is a bankruptcy trustee, the secured party cannot gain possession unless the trustee abandons the collateral or the secured party obtains a turnover order.

collateral was sold at a sheriff's sale, the buyer would qualify as a purchaser and gain the protection of the retroactive invalidation rule.[101]

The grace period will be shorter than four months if the filing in the first state lapses in less than four months after removal.[102] The grace period is designed to provide interim recognition in the state of removal of a security interest that would continue perfected if the collateral were still located in the state in which the interest was perfected. If the original perfection would lapse less than four months from the date of removal, the justification to continue recognizing that perfection ceases at the same time. For example, if perfection by filing will lapse one month after the collateral is moved to another state, the grace period for reperfection in the other state will be reduced to one month. The grace period cannot exceed the period of continued validity of the original perfection.

Suppose, however, that the original filing would ordinarily lapse two months after removal but the secured party, after removal and before lapse, files a continuation statement. Technically, the filing in the original state would not lapse and, if section 9-103(1)(d)(i) is read narrowly, the secured party will get the full four months as its grace period. Arguably, however, the secured party should check on the status of its collateral at the time it files its continuation statement and, if it discovers that its collateral has left the state, it should file in the new state before its original lapse date. The following Comment provides some implicit support for this approach:

> If the removal occurs within a short period, like two weeks, before the lapse of the filing in the original state, the secured party has only that period, not the full four months, to reperfect in "this state." But ordinarily he would have filed a continuation statement in the original jurisdiction; and he may do so to avoid lapse and allow himself the full four months if he is searching for the collateral and needs more time.[103]

The Comment suggests that if the secured party knows where the collateral is located following removal, it ought to file in the new state before lapse in the first state. While the outcome in such a case is unclear, the smart creditor will refile in the new state as soon as possible in order to avoid litigation over the issue.[104]

Section 9-103(1)(d) does not address the rights of a party who has already acquired a junior interest before the goods are removed to State B. Suppose, for example, that SP-1 and SP-2 both have perfected security interests in the collateral, with SP-1 having priority by virtue of having filed first in State A, the original situs. After removal, SP-2 files in State B during the grace period, but SP-1 does not.[105] A straightforward application of section 9-312(5)(a) would give priority to SP-2,[106] and that is the correct

---

[101] This conclusion would hold even if the levying creditor bought at its own sheriff's sale.

[102] U.C.C. § 9-103(i)(d)(i).

[103] U.C.C. § 9-103 Cmt. 7.

[104] Indeed, the secured party should refile as soon as possible in the new state, even when it clearly has the full four months. If a third party acquires an interest in the collateral before there is a filing in the new state, the secured party may have to litigate to establish its priority.

[105] The same problem would arise if both creditors allowed the grace period to expire and then SP-2 filed in State B before SP-1.

[106] SP-1 cannot rely on its original filing in State A because there is a gap in its perfection. The relevant language is the last clause in section 9-312(5)(a) ("provided there is no period thereafter when there is neither filing nor perfection").

result. As between two secured parties, the Code adopts a pure race system, and the fact that SP-2 was on notice of SP-1's interest should not provide a basis for continuing its subordinated status.[107] In effect, SP-2 is rewarded for its diligence in filing in State B before expiration of the grace period.

If the security interest was perfected automatically in State A and the collateral is moved to State B, the interest ordinarily remains perfected automatically in State B. For example, suppose that the secured party acquires a purchase-money security interest in consumer goods located in State A and relies on automatic perfection. If the debtor moves the assets to State B, the security interest ordinarily will continue to be perfected under the laws of State B because no action would be required for automatic perfection in State B.

Some states, however, have placed monetary limits on the value of consumer goods that qualify for automatic perfection. In Kansas, for example, automatic perfection is not available if the value of the asset exceeds $2,500. Thus, if the secured party is a Missouri seller with a purchase-money security interest in a computer costing over $2,500 and the debtor moves the computer to Kansas, Missouri's automatic perfection rules will cease to govern at the end of the four-month period. Without a filing in Kansas during the grace period, the secured party will suffer the consequences of becoming unperfected.[108]

The four-month rule of section 9-103(1)(d) is not needed under the revision. The situs rule for perfection applies when the secured party takes a possessory security interest, and in such cases the secured party will control any change in the location of the collateral. Even if the collateral is moved to another jurisdiction, the secured party will continue perfected by possession in the new jurisdiction. The elimination of a situs rule to govern perfection for nonpossessory security interests also eliminates the need for the section 9-103(1)(d) rule to cover perfection by methods other than possession. With perfection based on the law of the jurisdiction in which the debtor is located, a change in the location of the collateral becomes irrelevant. Secured parties with nonpossessory interests need only worry about changes in the debtor's location.[109]

§ 9.05   The Location-of-Debtor Rule — §§ 9-103(3), R9-301(1),(3), R9-307

Although it has been heavily criticized, at least some logic underlies the situs rule when it is applied to tangible assets that are expected to stay in one place and to indispensable writings. When tangible collateral is so mobile, however, that it is likely to change location frequently, or when intangible rights have not been reified, the situs rule makes no sense at all. The mobile collateral can be taken anywhere and a situs rule would require that there be a financing statement on file everywhere. The "pure"

---

[107] *Cf. In re* Halmar Distribs., Inc., 968 F.2d 121, 18 U.C.C. Rep. Serv. 2d 337 (1st Cir. 1992) (first to file in original situs state continued priority because debtor's bankruptcy filing during four-month grace period froze its perfected status under U.C.C. § 9-403(2)).

[108] Section 9-103(1)(d)(iii) makes it clear that if the secured party filed in Missouri to protect itself from a consumer buyer who might otherwise claim priority under section 9-307(2), the filing will be effective against such a buyer in Kansas during the normal four-month grace period.

[109] *See* § 9.03 *supra* and § 9.05[C] *infra.*

intangibles (accounts and general intangibles[110]) have no situs and are ordinarily seen as following the debtor.[111] Thus, for these types of collateral, the Code adopts a rule that is predicated on the location of the debtor rather than the location of the collateral. This "location-of-debtor" rule is explored in the ensuing subsections.

The revision makes the location-of-debtor test the general test for determining the law governing perfection.[112] It is also used to determine the effects of perfection and nonperfection and the priority of security interests when the collateral is a pure intangible.[113] With nonpossessory security interests in goods and indispensable writings, the law of the jurisdiction where the collateral is located governs these latter issues.[114] The distinction between perfection and its effects are discussed earlier in this chapter, and the reader is referred to that discussion for more detail.[115]

[A] Mobile Goods

In addition to pure intangibles, section 9-103(3) of the 1972 text applies to "mobile goods," meaning goods which are:

> mobile and which are of a type normally used in more than one jurisdiction, such as motor vehicles, trailers, rolling stock, airplanes, shipping containers, road building and construction machinery and commercial harvesting machinery and the like, if the goods are equipment or are inventory leased or held for lease by the debtor to others, and are not covered by a certificate of title described in subsection (2).

Numerous problems lurk within this long and complex definition. Goods are, by definition, tangible assets that are "movable at the time the security interest attaches,"[116] so the word "mobile" must indicate something more than the normal movability of the collateral. Further, they must be of a "type" that is normally used in multiple states. The

---

[110] Investment property other than certificated securities consists of pure intangibles, but investment property is the subject of special multistate rules. *See* U.C.C. §§ 9-103(6), **R9-305**.

[111] Chattel paper has certain quasi-negotiable characteristics, meaning that, for some purposes, it is treated as a pure intangible and, for other purposes, it is treated as an indispensable writing. The Code reflects the dual nature of chattel paper by permitting perfection by both possession and by filing. When the secured party perfects by possession, the situs rule is applied and chattel paper receives the same treatment as instruments. When the secured party perfects by filing, the domicile rule is applied and chattel paper receives the same treatment as accounts. U.C.C. § 9-103(4).

Under the revision, when the secured party takes a possessory security interest in chattel paper, the local law of the jurisdiction in which the collateral is located governs perfection and priority. U.C.C. § R9-301(2). With a nonpossessory security interest in chattel paper, the local law of the jurisdiction in which the collateral is located governs only the effect of perfection or nonperfection and priority. U.C.C. § R9-301(3)(c). Perfection is governed under the local law of the jurisdiction in which the debtor is located. U.C.C. § R9-301(1).

[112] U.C.C. § R9-301(1).

[113] *Id.*

[114] U.C.C. § R9-301(3)(C).

[115] *See* § 9.03 *supra.*

[116] U.C.C. § 9-105(1)(h).

particular asset involved in the transaction is not required actually to be used in more than one jurisdiction.[117] **All of the problems associated with the definition of mobile goods are eliminated under the revision because the revision no longer draws the distinction between mobile goods and ordinary goods. As indicated above, the revision makes the location-of-debtor rule the basic choice-of-law rule for security interests perfected by filing.[118]**

What is the difference between goods being "mobile" on the one hand and "of a type normally used in more than one jurisdiction" on the other? A case that explores the difference between these requirements is *In re Varsity Sodding Serv., Inc.,*[119] in which the secured party took a security interest in landscaping equipment, including backhoes, mulch spreaders, loaders and trenchers. Many pieces of equipment were on wheels and self-propelled, thereby making them mobile in nature,[120] but the court concluded that they were ordinary rather than mobile goods because they were not of a type normally used in multiple states. The court's rationale was that the category of mobile goods includes only assets that ordinarily would be located in several states over the course of a given week (such as shipping containers), or that are so expensive that recouping the investment in them requires that they be used over a multi-state area (such as road building and construction machinery). The court concluded that a landscaping company could recoup its investment by using the collateral within a more limited geographic area.[121]

For another example of the confusion created by the definition, suppose a farmer lives on the Missouri side of the border with Iowa, but farms only on land located in Iowa. The farmer owns numerous pieces of equipment, and among them is a commercial harvester. While such harvesters typically are used by migratory workers who harvest crops in multiple jurisdictions, this farmer uses it exclusively to harvest her own crops. All the equipment is kept in a shed located in Iowa. Except for the harvester, the equipment is clearly within the category of ordinary goods, so that a secured party would apply the situs rule and file in Iowa. Because the typical use of the harvester places it within the definition of mobile goods,[122] the domicile rule applies to it and the secured

---

[117] U.C.C. § 9-103 Cmt. 5(b); *In re* Minnesota Utility Contracting, Inc., 101 B.R. 72, 10 U.C.C. Rep. Serv. 2d 519 (Bankr. D. Minn. 1989), *aff'd in part, rev'd in part,* 110 B.R. 414(D. Minn. 1990) (whether goods are of type normally used in more than one jurisdiction is to be determined by general business practices of all persons, based on type of goods involved, not debtor's particular use).

[118] *See* **§ 9.04[A]** *supra.*

[119] 191 B.R. 306, 28 U.C.C. Rep. Serv. 2d 761 (Bankr. M.D. Pa. 1996), *aff'd in part, rev'd in part,* 139 F.3d 154, 34 U.C.C. Rep. Serv. 2d 891 (3d Cir. 1998). .

[120] Assets need not be on wheels or be self-propelled to be mobile in nature. A classic example used by the drafters is shipping containers, that are made to be placed on trains and trucks and transported from state to state.

[121] The court reached this conclusion even though the particular debtor had, in fact, used the collateral in more than one state. This approach is consistent with the Code's emphasis on the "type" of goods involved, rather than the use to which the particular goods are put.

[122] It is quite possible to have goods that are typically used in multiple states in one part of the country but are typically kept in one location in another part of the country. Given the national

party would have to file in Missouri. Many secured lenders routinely file in multiple states in order to avoid the catastrophic consequences of misclassifying their collateral.

In addition to being mobile and of a type normally used in more than one jurisdiction, the collateral must be either equipment or inventory that is held for lease. Even though road building machinery fits within the other parts of the definition, such assets would not be mobile goods if they were inventory being held for sale. A bank financing the dealer's inventory would perfect its interest under the situs rule. If the dealer sold the machinery on secured credit to a buyer in the construction business, the collateral would be equipment and the dealer would have to perfect its purchase-money security interest under the location-of-debtor rule. [123] If as is often the case the inventory is held for either sale or lease depending upon the needs of the purchaser, [124] the secured party must file in the state where the collateral is located *and* in the state where the debtor is located. Note that if the inventory consists of ordinary rather than mobile goods, the distinction between sale and lease is irrelevant. The situs rule governs the secured party's filing.

The reason for the distinction between inventory held for sale and inventory held for lease should be obvious. If inventory is held for sale, it will typically be kept at the dealer's place of business until it is sold, at which point the secured party's interest will be severed if the buyer qualifies as a buyer in the ordinary course of business. [125] Inventory held for lease, however, can wind up anywhere. A lender financing inventory that will be leased and is of a type normally used in more than one jurisdiction cannot predict where its collateral will be located. If the Code did not place such assets within the mobile-goods category, the lender might have to file in every state.

The problem of leased assets is not resolved entirely by section 9-103(3). Most assets held for lease will qualify as ordinary goods because they will not fit within all aspects of the mobile-goods definition. For example, photocopiers being held for lease by a dealer are neither mobile nor of a type normally used in more than one jurisdiction. A lender with a security interest in such inventory must file first in the state where the dealer/lessor's showroom is located and then, within four months after its removal from the first state, file in the state where the collateral will be kept by the lessee. [126] Each filing, of course, should be under the name of the dealer/lessor. A lender financing a large leasing operation could wind up filing in every jurisdiction.

During the time that the asset is subject to the lease, the lender will be relying primarily on its rights in the chattel paper acquired by the dealer/lessor from the lessee, and the secured party will want to make certain that its security interest in this asset is also

---

financing available today, the better approach is to consider the typical use on a national scale. This approach will, however, cause confusion to small lenders who are familiar only with the customs in their particular area.

[123] The financing bank's security interest would have been severed by the sale to a buyer in the ordinary course. U.C.C. § 9-307(1). *See* § 11.03[A][1] *infra.*

[124] "Purchaser" includes a lessee. U.C.C. § 1-201(33), (32).

[125] Priority rights of buyers in the ordinary course of business are discussed in § 11.03[A][1] *infra.*

[126] *See, e.g., In re* Leasing Consultants, Inc., 486 F.2d 367, 13 U.C.C. Rep. Serv. 189 (2d Cir. 1973).

perfected.[127] The best method of perfection is possession but, if the secured party intends to rely on filing, it must make certain that it has filed under the location-of-debtor rule.[128]

[B] Where Debtor Is Located

The location-of-debtor rule requires the secured party to file in the state where the debtor is located, which can cause difficulties when the debtor has ties to more than one state. For example, suppose that the debtor is incorporated in Delaware, owns retail outlets in every state, and has major management facilities in Los Angeles and Chicago. Under the 1972 text, a secured party seeking to perfect a security interest in the debtor's mobile goods or pure intangibles must first consult section 9-103(3)(d), which states that "[a] debtor shall be deemed located at his place of business if he has one, at his chief executive office if he has more than one place of business, otherwise at his residence."[129] This provision narrows the search in our example to Los Angeles and Chicago. In *In re J.A. Thompson & Son, Inc.*,[130] the court identified the debtor's chief executive office by focusing on such factors as the location of the bulk of the debtor's business records, its top management offices, its directors' meetings, and its payroll operations. In addition to these factors, other courts have considered the place where creditors would reasonably be expected to conduct a search concerning the debtor.[131] With a decentralized company, an analysis of all these factors may leave room for doubt, and the safest course is to make multiple filings.

Under the revision the place in which to file in the hypothetical stated above will be the state of incorporation — Delaware.[132] A corporation is a registered organization,[133] and such an organization is deemed located in the state under whose laws it is organized.[134] The shift from the location of the chief executive office to the state of organization is one of the most beneficial aspects of the revision's treatment of this complex area. Of course, individuals and many types of organizations are not registered organizations, and the revision's rules in such cases are similar to those in current law. An individual is deemed located at his or her

---

[127] If the dealer/lessor filed for bankruptcy, a perfected security interest in the chattel paper would give the secured party priority over the trustee as to the lease payments (and any value associated with the remaining term of the lease), but the trustee would have priority as to any residual interest if the secured party failed properly to perfect its interest in the leased asset under the situs rule.

[128] U.C.C. § 9-103(4)(perfection by filing as to chattel paper governed by location-of-debtor rule; perfection by possession governed by situs rule).

[129] This rule is analogous to the rule in section 9-401(6), which deals with intrastate filing issues. Section 9-103(3) has special rules in subsection (d) for foreign air carriers and in subsection (c) for certain debtors located outside the United States.

[130] 665 F.2d 941, 33 U.C.C. Rep. Serv. 356 (9th Cir. 1982).

[131] *See, e.g.*, Mellon Bank v. Metro Communications, Inc., 945 F.2d 635, 15 U.C.C. Rep. Serv. 2d 1119 (3d Cir. 1991), *cert. denied*, 503 U.S. 937, 112 S.Ct. 1476, 117 L.Ed 2d 620 (1992).

[132] **The place of filing under the revision is also discussed in § 9.03 *supra*.**

[133] **U.C.C. § R9-102(a)(70).**

[134] **U.C.C. § R9-307(e).**

principal residence,[135] an organization that has only one place of business is deemed located at that place,[136] and an organization that has more than one place of business is deemed located at its chief executive office.[137] The revision defines "place of business" as the place where the debtor conducts its affairs,[138] but it does not provide a test for determining a multistate organization's chief executive office. The Comments, however, focus on the place from which the debtor conducts the main part of its business and indicate that this is the place where creditors would most likely conduct a search.[139]

Under the 1972 text, the location-of-debtor rule creates a subtle trap for a secured party claiming an interest in certain types of proceeds. For example, suppose a bank located in State A finances the inventory of what appears to be a local retailer but is in fact a branch of a larger operation headquartered in State B. Its security agreement describes the collateral as "inventory," but the bank expects the inventory to be sold on credit and is relying on both the inventory and the accounts it generates as security for the indebtedness. The bank's interest will attach to identifiable proceeds automatically.[140] Under the situs rule,[141] even if the bank had been aware of all the facts, it would have perfected its security interest in the inventory by filing in State A. If the debtor's headquarters had been in State A, as the bank believed, a single filing on inventory would have been sufficient to perfect its interest in accounts.[142]

Under the actual facts, however, an original security interest in the debtor's accounts would not have been perfected in the same office or offices as a security interest in the debtor's inventory — it would have been perfected by filing in the appropriate office or offices in State B. Thus, the bank will become unperfected as to each account ten days after the account is generated unless it has filed a financing statement covering accounts in State B.[143]

The problem with respect to proceeds is alleviated under the revision. The security interest in the inventory will be perfected in the state in which the debtor is located and that will be the same jurisdiction in which a security interest in accounts would have been filed if accounts had been the original collateral. This facilitates the

---

[135] U.C.C. § R9-307(b)(1).

[136] U.C.C. § R9-307(b)(2).

[137] U.C.C. § R9-307(b)(3).

[138] U.C.C. § R9-307(a).

[139] U.C.C. § R9-307 Cmt. 2.

[140] U.C.C. §§ 9-203(3), 9-306(2). For discussion of attachment of a security interest to proceeds, see § 2.04[B] supra.

[141] The situs rule would apply unless the inventory was held for lease and otherwise qualified as mobile goods.

[142] This analysis is based on section 9-306(3)(a). Because an original security interest in the debtor's accounts would have been perfected by filing in the same office or offices as a security interest in the debtor's inventory, no new filing describing the collateral as "accounts" would have been necessary. For discussion of perfection of a security interest in proceeds, see § 8.02 supra.

[143] U.C.C. § 9-306(3)(d).

secured party's ability to obtain the benefit of the automatic perfection rule for proceeds.[144]

[C] Change in Debtor's Location

If the secured party files properly under the location-of-debtor rule and the debtor then changes its state of domicile, the problem is similar to that faced by a secured party who files properly under the situs rule and then finds that its collateral has been moved to a different state. Indeed, the 1972 text applies precisely the same analysis to the two situations, and the reader is referred back to the discussion of the four-month rule set forth above.[145] In short, the secured party is given a four-month grace period to refile in the new state and, if it fails to do so, its interest becomes unperfected prospectively and is deemed to have been unperfected retroactively as against a party that purchased the collateral after the move.[146]

Comparable provision is made in the revision for grace periods, continuous perfection, and retroactive invalidation in the event of failure to reperfect within the applicable grace period. The reader is referred back to the earlier discussion of these provisions for greater details.[147]

§ 9.06   Certificate of Title Laws — §§ 9-103(2), R9-303, R9-316(d),(e), R9-337(1)

As was indicated in the material on perfection,[148] the Code does not govern perfection of certain assets that are subject to state certificate of title laws.[149] It does, however, govern the effects of perfection and nonperfection, and section 9-103(2) of the 1972 text deals with the interstate problems that arise concerning such assets.

The most important assets in this category are motor vehicles. Almost every state has a statute that requires security interests in motor vehicles to be perfected by noting the secured party's lien on a certificate issued by the state.[150] The idea is quite simple:

---

[144] U.C.C. § R9-315(d).

[145] *See* § 9.04[C] *supra.*

[146] *See, e.g., In re* Specialty Contracting & Supply, Inc., 140 B.R. 922, 18 U.C.C. Rep. Serv. 2d 917 (Bankr. N.D. Ga. 1992) (because secured party never filed in Georgia, its security interest became unperfected four months after debtor moved its corporate offices from Texas to Georgia).

[147] *See* § 9.03 *supra.*

[148] *See* § 4.02[F] *supra.*

[149] **The revision includes the following definition of "certificate of title": "[A] certificate of title with respect to which a statute provides for the security interest in question to be indicated on the certificate as a condition or result of the security interest's obtaining priority over the rights of a lien creditor with respect to the collateral." U.C.C. § R9-102(a)(10).**

[150] Article 9 defers to such statutes. *See* U.C.C. §§ 9-302(3),(4), **R9-310(b)(3), R9-311(a)(2),(3)**. A few states have enacted the Uniform Motor Vehicle Certificate of Title and Anti-Theft Act, whereas others have their own systems. Some states have adopted an alternative procedure that allows the secured party to file a notice of its interest with the state department of motor vehicles. The Federal Motor Vehicle Lien Act of 1958, which regulates motor vehicles owned by carriers with an Interstate Commerce Commission license, defers to state perfection laws (49 U.S.C. § 11304), and cases like *In re* Paige, 679 F.2d 601, 33 U.C.C. Rep. Serv. 1218 (6th Cir. 1982),

everyone should understand the imprudence of buying or lending against a motor vehicle without first seeing (and later taking an assignment of) the certificate of title. If the certificate shows the lien, notice has been given.

Motor vehicles are not the only assets subject to state certificate of title acts. Assets such as boats, farm tractors, and mobile homes are the subject of certificate legislation in some states, while interests in such assets are perfected by the normal Code methods (filing, possession, or automatic perfection) in other states. As is explained below, the lack of uniformity among state certificate of title laws is the source of considerable confusion.

Even in title states, not all security interests in such assets can be perfected using the certificate method. The 1972 text of Article 9 makes it clear that "during any period in which collateral is inventory held for sale by a person who is in the business of selling goods of that kind, the filing provisions of [Article 9] apply to a security interest created by him as debtor."[151] The reason should be obvious. The titling process is complicated, time-consuming and, when applied to a large volume of vehicles, expensive. If inventory held for sale were covered, the secured party would no sooner apply for a certificate than its interest would be severed by the dealer's sale of the vehicle in question to a buyer in the ordinary course. To avoid the paperwork and expense associated with such a procedure, the Code allows the secured party to perfect its interest in all assets held by its debtor by making a single Article 9 filing describing its collateral as inventory.

Under the 1972 text, the filing option will not work for inventory held for purposes of leasing. If, for example, the secured party is financing a car-rental agency's fleet of cars, it must have its lien noted on each car's certificate. Because the cars can be expected to remain with the agency for a significant period of time, such a system is not unduly burdensome.

The revision eliminates the distinction between inventory held for sale and for lease. Compliance with a state certificate of title law is neither necessary nor effective under the revision to perfect a security interest in inventory that is held by a person in the business of selling or leasing goods of that kind.[152] Perfection of such an interest in inventory is subject to the normal filing rules.[153]

---

permit titling of such vehicles in states that have little or no connection with the secured transaction. Under this approach, for example, a secured party would be protected by the notation of its lien upon an Oklahoma certificate of title, even if the debtor did not purchase the vehicle in Oklahoma and had no other connection to the state of Oklahoma. A few bankruptcy courts, however, have interpreted the certificate-of-title laws of particular states to have a "nexus" requirement. Under this interpretation, a secured party's lien would not be perfected by mere notation of the lien upon a certificate of title if the parties to the transaction had no meaningful connection to the titling state. *See, e.g., In re* Westfall, 227 B.R. 734 (Bankr. W.D. Mo. 1998). **The revision directly addresses the issue of connection between the titling state and the secured transaction: It applies the law of the titling state "even if there is no other relationship between the jurisdiction under whose certificate of title the goods are covered and the goods or the debtor." U.C.C. § R9-303(a). This result is consistent with modern trucking practices. U.C.C. § R9-303 Cmt. 2.**

[151] U.C.C. § 9-302(3)(b).

[152] **U.C.C. § R9-311(d).**

[153] **U.C.C. § R9-303 Cmt. 5.**

The most difficult problems again occur in the multistate context. One set of problems arises when an asset in which an interest has been perfected under a certificate law in one state is moved permanently to another state (which may or may not subject such assets to its certificate laws). Other problems follow when an asset in which an interest has been perfected under normal Code rules in one state is moved permanently to another state which subjects such assets to its certificate laws. The ensuing subsections deal with these problems.

[A] The 1972 Text

[1] Movement from Title State to Either Title State or Nontitle State

Suppose that the debtor lives in State A, which requires its domiciliaries to register their motor vehicles with the state and upon the happening of this event issues a certificate of title. If the debtor takes out a loan from the secured party using a car as collateral, the secured party will perfect by having its lien noted on the certificate pursuant to State A's certificate of title act. [154] Under that act the state will forward the certificate to the secured party for safekeeping. [155] If the debtor later wants to sell (or borrow against) the car, she will have to explain why she does not have a certificate. This inability of the debtor to produce a certificate puts the buyer (or lender) on notice to investigate with respect to the secured party's interest.

Suppose our debtor moves permanently to State B, which also requires its domiciliaries to register their cars and obtain a certificate. When the debtor registers the car, an official in State B will ask her to produce her title. At that point, she should advise the official of the secured party's security interest. State B will contact the secured party, which will surrender its State A certificate and receive in exchange a new certificate issued by State B. The secured party, which was originally perfected under the laws of State A, will now be perfected under the laws of State B.

Although fairly simple and straightforward, this scenario raises a host of issues. Does perfection in State A protect the secured party after the vehicle is removed to State B but before it is registered there, or is there a gap in protection? If the debtor violates the laws of State B by failing to register her car there, will the secured party continue to be protected by its perfection in State A? What if the debtor somehow acquires possession of a "clean" State B certificate — that is, a certificate that shows her as the

---

[154] This observation is true even if the secured party is taking a purchase-money security interest in a consumer good. U.C.C. § 9-302(1)(d) states confusingly that filing is required for a motor vehicle that must be registered. It clarifies that automatic perfection is not available, but it suggests that a normal Article 9 filing will work. The confusion is resolved by § 9-302(3), which states that an Article 9 filing is neither necessary nor effective with regard to vehicles that are not inventory held for sale, and by § 9-302(4), which gives compliance with a state's certificate of title act an effect that is equivalent to that ordinarily obtained by filing. The reference to filing in § 9-302(1)(d) should be read to mean an act that gives the same effect as filing. **The revision makes this correction by noting that a purchase-money security interest in consumer goods is perfected when it attaches, except "with respect to consumer goods that are subject to a statute or treaty described in § 9-311(a)." U.C.C. § R9-309(1).**

[155] If the car had been owned free and clear, the certificate would have been sent to the owner, who could have used it to facilitate a later sale or loan transaction.

owner and does not reflect the secured party's interest. If she then sells her car (or uses it as collateral for a new loan) using the clean certificate, will the secured party be protected against the buyer (or lender)? Section 9-103(2) of the 1972 text addresses these questions.

Section 9-103(2) does not come into play at all unless the goods are subject to certificate of title legislation in one of the states connected to the transaction.[156] If an asset moves from one certificate state to another certificate state, which often occurs with motor vehicles, the consequences of the move are governed by section 9-103(2)(b), which states that:

> Except as otherwise provided in this subsection, perfection and the effect of perfection or non-perfection of the security interest are governed by the law (including the conflict of laws rules) of the jurisdiction issuing the certificate until four months after the goods are removed from that jurisdiction and thereafter until the goods are registered in another jurisdiction, but in any event not beyond surrender of the certificate. After the expiration of that period, the goods are not covered by the certificate of title within the meaning of this section.

Section 9-103(2)(b) also governs movement of an asset from a title state to a nontitle state. Although rare today, it can occur with assets such as boats, farm tractors, and mobile homes. Most of the discussion in this section deals with movement from one title state to another title state.

As with ordinary goods and mobile goods, the 1972 version of the Code provides a grace period to allow a secured party to react after the events that caused it to perfect in one state have changed.[157] Unlike the other rules, however, the grace period may be shorter or longer than four months. For example, suppose a secured lender properly perfects by having its lien noted on a certificate issued by State A, which is where the debtor lives at the time of perfection. Later, the debtor moves to State B but fails to obey State B's laws, which require that she register her car in that state and obtain a State B certificate. Two years later, the car is still unregistered and the debtor files for bankruptcy relief. The secured party will have priority over the trustee because its perfection in State A will still be effective. The law of the issuing state continues to govern the transaction until the car is registered in another state. This rule does not prejudice third parties; because the debtor cannot produce a certificate, such parties are on notice of the secured party's interest.

Irrespective of when registration occurs, the grace period cannot be less than four months unless the secured party surrenders the old certificate. In the prior example, suppose the debtor registers her car in State B three weeks after she moves there, and State B contacts the secured party and asks it to surrender its State A certificate in exchange for a new State B certificate. If the secured party does so just six weeks after removal, it loses the protection of State A's laws. This loss is not prejudicial to the secured

---

[156] U.C.C. § 9-103(2)(a).

[157] The events are, in the case of ordinary goods, removal of the goods from the jurisdiction where perfection occurred or, in the case of mobile goods, movement of the debtor to a new jurisdiction.

party, however, because it will have become perfected under the laws of State B without ever experiencing a gap in its perfection. In other words, if the secured party surrenders the certificate in exchange for a certificate from a new state, it does not need the full four months.

The previous examples have assumed that "registration" by a state includes the issuance of a certificate from that state and that the issuing state will contact the secured party for surrender of the old certificate. That assumption is not always valid, however. For example, the debtors in *In re Males*[158] lived in New Hampshire and the secured party properly obtained a New Hampshire certificate listing its lien on their cars. The debtors then moved to New York, where they registered their cars and obtained license plates. The State of New York, however, never issued a new certificate and the secured party thus was never contacted and asked to surrender its old certificate. More than four months after the move, the debtors filed for bankruptcy relief and their trustee argued that the secured party had become unperfected under section 9-103(2)(b). The Second Circuit held that the car had not been "registered" in New York within the meaning of the Code, even though the debtors had advised that state of their presence and had obtained license plates. According to the court, "registration" requires that the new state issue a certificate of title upon being advised of a debtor's presence, not just issue license plates. Unless a new certificate is issued to the debtor, the rights of third parties will not be prejudiced.

The Second Circuit was correct as a matter of policy. The drafters were worried that another state might issue a clean certificate to the debtor, who could then use it to mislead third parties. For example, if the debtor registered the car in State B and signed a false affidavit claiming that she owned the car free and clear and that she had lost her certificate from State A, State B might issue a new certificate showing her to be the owner of an unencumbered vehicle.[159] Unless State B issues a new certificate, the effectiveness of the old certificate from State A should not lapse.

The drafters did not likely consider the meaning adopted by the Second Circuit.[160] Section 9-103(2)(b) was drafted before certificate laws for motor vehicles became universal, and it governs movement from title states to nontitle states as well as movement from one title state to another. Without registration in the second state, the effectiveness of a certificate obtained in the first state never lapses.

The following example is one that would have worried the drafters. Suppose the secured party perfects its interest in a car by obtaining a lien notation on a certificate issued by State A, and the debtor then moves to State B, a nontitle state (a distinct possibility at the time the current Code was drafted). State B requires motor vehicles to be listed with

---

[158] 999 F.2d 607, 21 U.C.C. Rep. Serv. 2d 108 (2d Cir. 1993). *Accord* General Motors Acceptance Corp. v. Rupp, 951 F.2d 283, 16 U.C.C. Rep. Serv. 2d 510 (10th Cir. 1991)

[159] With nationwide computer links, these events are much less likely to occur today than at the time the Code was drafted. When the debtor files the affidavit in State B, that state should contact State A and confirm that it issued a certificate. The confirmation will disclose whether the old certificate reflected a lien.

[160] For a case that reaches a result inconsistent with the Second Circuit's approach, *see* City of Boston v. Rockland Trust Co., 391 Mass. 48, 460 N.E.2d 1269, 37 U.C.C. Rep. Serv. 1338 (1984) (obtaining license plates without issuance of new certificate constitutes registration).

the state so that license plates can be issued, but State B does not have a certificate law and perfection is governed by the normal Code methods. Using the Second Circuit's limited definition of "registered," the debtor's listing of the car in State B would not trigger the statutory grace period and the secured party would be perfected indefinitely by its State A certificate.[161] Given the current universality of certification laws for motor vehicles, however, the Second Circuit's approach is eminently sensible.

Returning now to the scenario of moving from one title state to another, registration in the second state should lead to surrender of the old certificate and issuance of a new one reflecting the lien. Whether these events occur during the four months following removal or thereafter, the secured party's rights will not be prejudiced. It will at all times be protected by an effective certificate.

Suppose, however, that the debtor somehow gets a clean certificate from the new state — one that shows the debtor as the owner and that does not disclose the existence of the secured party's lien. A clean certificate can be obtained in a variety of ways, almost all involving fraud by the debtor.[162] For example, the debtor might move from State A to State B and, two weeks after removal, register her car in State B and fraudulently obtain a clean certificate. On these facts, the secured party's old certificate from State A will be effective until four months after the car was removed from that state, but if the secured party has not applied for a State B certificate within that time period, it will become unperfected. If the debtor files for bankruptcy three months after removal, the secured party is safe.[163] If she files for bankruptcy six months after removal, the trustee will have priority over the secured party's unperfected interest.[164]

Suppose now that the debtor uses the clean certificate to effect a fraudulent sale to a used-car dealer during the first four months following removal. Even though the dealer is misled by the clean certificate, the secured party will have priority. The secured party will still be protected by its certificate from State A, and because the used-car dealer will be a nonordinary-course buyer, it will take subject to the secured party's perfected interest.[165] The assumption is that the used-car dealer will know to ask the debtor questions that will lead the dealer to the secured party, but the truth is that this scenario

---

[161] If the Second Circuit's definition of "registered" in *In re Males* in correct, it is difficult to imagine a circumstance where the effectiveness of the original certificate would lapse. Thus, it might be best to limit the narrow definition of "registered" to the motor-vehicle context. Even if a broader definition is used, so that any listing with the state amounts to registration, however, there will be cases where an asset (like a farm tractor or a sailboat) moves from a title state to a nontitle state that does not have even a listing procedure. Under these circumstances, purchasers in the second state are likely to be misled. The problem stems from the fact that § 9-103(2)(b) was drafted with motor vehicles in mind, and it is ill-suited to other types of collateral.

[162] Although debtor fraud is a common theme, issuance of a clean certificate can occur innocently. The officials in the new state could simply misread the debtor's registration form and issue a clean certificate.

[163] U.C.C. § 9-201.

[164] U.C.C. § 9-301(1)(b).

[165] U.C.C. § 9-306(2).

rarely happens and the provision simply reflects a policy choice.[166] If the sale to the used-car dealer had occurred more than four months after removal, the dealer would take free of the unperfected security interest unless it had knowledge of that interest at the time of purchase.[167]

Suppose the sale to the used-car dealer occurs during the first four months following removal, but the secured party fails to take steps to perfect in State B before the grace period expires. If the transaction had been governed by section 9-103(1) (ordinary goods), this failure would cause the secured party's perfection to be retroactively invalidated as against all purchasers.[168] The Comments[169] suggest that the drafters intended the same result as for ordinary goods, but the text of section 9-103(2)(b) does not contain a retroactive invalidation rule.[170] The presence of such a rule in the text for the other subsections makes it difficult to avoid the conclusion that there is no retroactive invalidation here. If that is the case, a secured party that has priority at the time its adversary's interest becomes fixed will not be demoted because of a later failure to perfect in the new state. The result is curious, however, and the conclusion that retroactive invalidation permeates section 9-103 and should be applied in this context would not be unreasonable.

Suppose now that the debtor uses a clean certificate to sell the car to someone other than a used-car dealer (or that the dealer resells the car to a buyer who relies on the clean certificate).[171] Section 9-103(2)(d)[172] contains a special rule that protects all buyers except dealers. If the certificate relied upon by such a buyer does not show the secured party's interest or contain a general statement to the effect that the car may be subject to liens not shown on the certificate, the buyer who gives value and receives delivery of the car without knowledge of the security interest takes free of the security interest. This result follows even though that interest may still be perfected under the laws of the state of removal.

The rule is a fair compromise, although the exception for certificates containing general language regarding hidden liens is problematic. It assumes that buyers will take note of such language, realize its importance, and ask questions that will lead them to the

---

[166] Because § 9-103(2)(d) only protects buyers, not purchasers, a secured party who made a loan against the car relying on the clean certificate would be in the same position as the used-car dealer.

[167] U.C.C. § 9-301(1)(c).

[168] The retroactive invalidation rule is discussed in § 9.04[C] *supra.* Section 9-103(3) governing mobile goods also contains a retroactive invalidation rule. *See* § 9.05[C] *supra.*

[169] U.C.C. § 9-103 Cmt. 4(c).

[170] Indeed, there is retroactive invalidation when goods move from a non-title state to a title state because section 9-103(2)(c) incorporates the rule of § 9-103(1)(d).

[171] If the buyer purchases from a dealer in reliance on the clean certificate, the buyer would be a buyer in the ordinary course, but would not take free of the security interest under § 9-307(1) because the security interest was not created by the buyer's immediate seller (the dealer).

[172] This subsection, which deals generally with goods moving from one title state to another title state, is also applicable when goods move from a non-title state to a title state and buyers rely on a clean certificate issued by the second state.

secured party. If the assumption that used-car dealers will ask such questions as a matter of course is unrealistic, surely the assumption that nondealers will know to do so is insupportable.

[2] Movement from Nontitle State to Title State

With assets other than motor vehicles, there is a real chance of movement from a nontitle state to a title state. The effective period for perfection in the first state is governed under the 1972 text by section 9-103(2)(c), which states that:

> Except with respect to the rights of a buyer described in the next paragraph, a security interest, perfected in another jurisdiction otherwise than by notation on a certificate of title, in goods brought into this state and thereafter covered by a certificate of title issued by this state is subject to the rules stated in [section 9-103(1)(d).

In other words, suppose the debtor, who lives in State A, grants the secured party a purchase-money security interest in a pleasure boat. Boats are not governed by a title act in State A, and the secured party either relies on automatic perfection or files a financing statement. If the debtor then moves to State B, which has title legislation for boats, the secured party will have four months after removal to take whatever steps are necessary to have a certificate issued in State B showing its lien. If it fails to do so, it will become unperfected, and it will be deemed to have been unperfected as against parties who became purchasers during the four-month period following removal. The same analysis set forth with regard to ordinary goods applies.[173]

[B] The 1998 Text

The 1998 revision simplifies this area of the law considerably. The general rule eliminates references to registration of the goods in another jurisdiction and surrender of an issued certificate of title. Instead it provides as follows:

> **The local law of the jurisdiction under whose certificate of title the goods are covered governs perfection, the effect of perfection or nonperfection, and the priority of a security interest in goods covered by a certificate of title from the time the goods become covered by the certificate of title until the goods cease to be covered by the certificate of title.[174] Thus, the law of the state that issues a certificate of title governs for so long as the certificate covers the goods.**

The revision also indicates when goods become covered and cease to be covered by a certificate of title. Goods are covered "when a valid application for the certificate of title and the applicable fee are delivered to the appropriate authority."[175] Note that if the state does not actually issue a certificate following these actions by the applicant, the goods nevertheless are still covered by a certificate of title. The goods cease to be covered when the certificate of title ceases to be effective

---

173 *See* § 9.04[C] supra.

174 U.C.C. § R9-303(c).

175 U.C.C. § R9-303(b).

under the law of the issuing jurisdiction or when the goods subsequently become covered under a certificate of title issued by another jurisdiction, whichever occurs earlier.[176]

The provisions described above are choice-of-law provisions only. They determine the state whose law governs perfection and its effects, but they do not indicate how or when a security interest in goods subject to a state's certificate of title law *becomes* perfected. In other words, "coverage" is not the equivalent of "perfection." Perfection is governed by the procedural requirements of the certificate of title law. Coverage and perfection will coincide if the certificate of title law provides that perfection occurs when the application and fee are delivered to the proper state official. That is the case in many states, but in others perfection is conditioned upon surrender of any existing certificate of title and/or upon the actual issuance of a certificate of title with the security interest noted thereon. Analysis of the movement of goods from one title state to another title state, or from a nontitle state to a title state, requires an understanding of this distinction.

For example, assume that a secured party's interest in a State A resident's boat is perfected by a certificate of title issued by State A and the debtor moves to State B, another title state. State A law governs perfection, the effects of perfection and nonperfection, and priorities until the goods become covered by a certificate of title issued by State B. That will occur when an application and fee are delivered to the proper official in State B.[177] From that time forward, State B law will govern. Further analysis requires an understanding of section R9-316(d), which of course becomes State B law after it adopts the revisions.

Section R9-316(d) provides that, under State B law in the hypothetical, perfection by the State A certificate continues until the security interest would have become unperfected under State A law. In other words, the State A certificate continues to perfect the secured party's interest for *general purposes* without special time limitations.[178] This means that the secured party will have priority over lien creditors, including bankruptcy trustees, even if it never completes the steps for perfection under State B certificate of title law.[179] On the other hand, the State A certificate of title statute might provide that the notation on a State A certificate will no longer perfect the interest once the certificate is surrendered to authorities

---

[176] *Id.* Due to the differences in state certificate of title laws, the revision does not address when a certificate of title ceases to be effective. In most states, certificates remain effective until the indebtedness is satisfied.

[177] At the same time the boat will cease to be covered by the State A statute. U.C.C. § R9-303(b) (goods cease to be covered by a certificate of title when they subsequently become covered under a certificate of title issued by another jurisdiction).

[178] The exceptions with respect to purchasers are discussed below.

[179] Note in this situation that if the State A certificate was not surrendered as part of the application process in State B, the goods would be covered by a State B certificate (whether or not actually issued) and not covered by the issued State A certificate. Perfection of the security interest in the goods, however, would be pursuant to the notation of that interest on the State A certificate.

in another jurisdiction for purposes of re-titling the boat.[180] The secured party should then be able to tack its perfection from notation on the State A certificate of title through notation on the State B certificate without any intervening period of nonperfection.[181]

For another example, assume that State A does not have a certificate of title law governing boats but that State B does. Assume further that the security interest was perfected in State A by filing a financing statement[182] before the boat was covered by a certificate of title in State B. The law of State B would recognize the perfection of the security interest, even if the steps for perfection in State B are not completed, until the financing statement lapses or is terminated under the law of State A. Finally, consider the converse situation in which the security interest in the boat was perfected by notation on a State A certificate and moved to State B as a nontitle state. Obviously, the boat would not be covered by a State B certificate. State A law would continue to govern perfection, therefore, meaning that the State A certificate will continue to perfect the secured party's interest for as long as it remains effective under the State A certificate of title statute. These policy choices place an enormous burden on searchers in states that do not have certificate of title laws for assets like boats and mobile homes.

The general rule discussed above with respect to the continuation of perfection in the boat for as long as it remains perfected under State A law does not apply if the boat is acquired by a purchaser for value after its removal to State B. The security interest becomes unperfected as against a purchaser for value if the secured party does not reperfect within State B before the earlier of four months after the goods become covered by a certificate of title in State B or the time that the State A certificate ceases to be effective under State A law.[183] Thus, with respect to purchasers for value, the secured party must complete the steps necessary for an effective perfection in State B within a grace period that will never exceed four months. The failure to reperfect within the allowable grace period results not only in the security interest becoming unperfected *prospectively* as against a purchaser of the goods for value, but the interest also "is deemed never to have been perfected as against a purchaser of the goods for value."[184] Thus, the perfected status of the secured party during the allowable grace period is retroactively invalidated, thereby relegating the secured party to unperfected secured status from the time that the boat became covered by the certificate of title in State B.

The same rule applies if goods are moved from a nontitle state to a title state. Assume again that State A does not have a certificate of title law governing boats but that State B does, and that the secured party has properly perfected under State A law. State A law continues to govern until the boat becomes covered by a certificate

---

180 *See* U.C.C. § R9-316 Cmt. 5.

181 U.C.C. § R9-316(d).

182 Perfection might also occur automatically because the secured party has a purchase-money security interest in a boat that qualifies as consumer goods.

183 U.C.C. § R9-316(e)(2).

184 U.C.C. § R9-316(e).

issued by State B . Even after that time, State B law makes State A's perfection effective until it would have lapsed under State A law.[185] However, the secured party's interest will be unperfected as against a purchaser for value if the secured party fails to take the steps necessary to perfect its interest under State B's certificate of title law before the earlier of four months after the goods become covered in State B or the time perfection would have lapsed under State A law.

The revision continues the priority provided under the 1972 text for buyers who are likely to rely upon a "clean" certificate of title.[186] Priority applies only when a state actually issues a certificate of title with respect to goods that are perfected by any method in another jurisdiction. The certificate must be "clean" in the sense that it neither shows that the goods are subject to the security interest nor contains a statement that the goods may be subject to security interests that are not shown on the certificate. To qualify for priority, the buyer must give value and receive delivery of the goods after the certificate is issued and without knowledge of the security interest. The buyer cannot qualify if it is in the business of selling goods of that kind.

---

[185] U.C.C. § R9-316(d).

[186] U.C.C. § R9-337(1).

PART IV:

PRIORITIES

[A]   The Priority Concept

To the extent that it goes beyond the relationship between a debtor and a secured party, the discussion thus far has focused primarily on the means to perfect a security interest. The discussion has chiefly addressed the various mechanisms by which a secured party can attain and retain perfected status. Whether a secured party is perfected has significant consequences in the event of a competing claim to the collateral. The discussion now turns to the rules and policies that determine the outcome of these contests. The focus is on priorities.

A wide variety of different classes of third-party interests, including claims by other secured parties, general creditors, lien creditors, buyers, lessees, licensees, and trustees in bankruptcy, can compete for priority in the secured party's collateral. Perfection generally will enhance a secured party's position against these claimants. As the discussion in the next few chapters will demonstrate, however, a secured party's position, even with perfection, is rarely completely unassailable.

The importance of prevailing in a priority battle can be demonstrated through a simple illustration. Assume that Debtor defaults on its outstanding indebtedness to the following three creditors: Secured Party One (SP-1) for $10,000, Secured party Two (SP-2) for $20,000, and General Creditor (GC) for $5,000. The only asset of any value owned by Debtor is equipment that is the collateral for both of the secured loans. Sale of this equipment, however, will provide only $14,000.

If these three creditors were asserting unsecured claims in a bankruptcy distribution, a principle of *pro rata* distribution would be applied. All three of the interests would share in the proceeds from the sale of the equipment. The amount received by each claimant would be determined by each party's proportionate share of the total of the three claims. SP-1 would be entitled to two times more than GC, and SP-2 would be entitled to four times more than GC. Accordingly, GC would receive $2,000, SP-1 would receive $4,000, and SP-2 would receive $8,000.

Priority determinations under Article 9 are different. The competing claims are rank-ordered. The claimant with the top priority has the initial claim. If the collateral has enough value to satisfy all of the outstanding indebtedness on that claim, the remaining value is available to the second-ranked claimant. Lower-ranked claimants will realize nothing from the collateral unless it has enough value to satisfy all prior claims in full.

Priority allocations mean that some of the claimants in the illustration will not receive anything from the sale of the equipment. Under priority rules to be explained later, GC will be ranked third and thus will receive nothing. If SP-1 has top priority, the entire $10,000 debt will be satisfied, leaving only $4,000 for SP-2. If, on the other hand, SP-2 has top priority, the entire $14,000 sale proceeds will be applied to its $20,000 claim, leaving nothing for SP-1 or GC.

Priorities can be the ultimate factor that decides the benefit of a security interest. A secured party whose collateral is gobbled up by other claimants with superior priority rankings is effectively relegated to the position of a general creditor. The debt still exists, but the collateral that the secured party initially relied upon is gone. The secured party can only pursue the debt claim against the debtor, and may receive only a portion of its claim if the debtor files for bankruptcy protection.

Priority battles arise whenever two or more parties assert claims to the same specific assets. Many of these conflicts will not involve a secured party, such as competing claims between a buyer and a lessor of the same goods, or between a mortgagee and a trustee in bankruptcy competing for a parcel of real property. All of these conflicts are outside the scope of this book. In contrast, Article 9 governs priority conflicts between secured parties and other classes of claimants. Article 9 priorities thus are a part of a larger area of the law.

[B] Understanding Priorities

An understanding of Article 9 priorities can be furthered by seeing the relationship among the various priority rules, and how they operate together to cover an entire category of cases. Certain themes also run through the priority provisions. The fundamental principle of prioritization is "first-in-time, first-in-right." The party that has taken specified action first will win under this principle. Numerous exceptions to this general rule also follow certain patterns, particularly in cases of purchase-money security interests. Understanding Article 9 priorities requires an understanding of the overall picture, as well as each individual rule. Such understanding inevitably requires an appreciation of the policies that underlie the provisions. The discussion of priorities in this book is designed to advance insight from all of these perspectives.

The Code priority rules are quite precise, and with good reason. Although a security interest is created through a contract between a secured party and a debtor, the secured party's interest can have a competing or adverse effect on the interests of third parties. The broader contracts standards that apply to transactions like sales of goods thus are not workable in the secured transactions context. Other parties must know with certainty what their respective rights are with respect to collateral.

The starting point for priority issues is the Article 9 provision on the general validity of security agreements, which renders a security agreement effective according to its terms "between the parties, against purchasers of the collateral and against creditors."[1] This provision favors secured parties in priority conflicts with third parties: A security interest prevails even if it is unperfected.

The baseline established by the general validity provision is subject, however, to any exceptions that Article 9 otherwise provides. Those exceptions are numerous. The

---

[1] U.C.C. §§ 9-201, **R9-201(a)**. *See* § 14.01 *infra.*

discussion of priorities in the next few chapters of this book, is technically, a discussion of the exceptions to the general validity provision.

The determination of a priority dispute involves two basic steps. Initially, the status of each of the competing claimants in the conflict must be established; then, the appropriate rule can be applied to decide the outcome of a conflict between any pair of the claimants. Students often overlook the critical importance of the first step. One simply cannot select the correct priority rule without properly characterizing the status of each competing party. Making assumptions about a party's status will often lead to application of the wrong rule, and care must be exercised in ascertaining that status. In the case of some parties, that examination will encompass the issues covered thus far in this book -the determination of whether the claimant is a secured party, and, if so, whether the secured party is perfected.

CHAPTER 10

AMONG SECURED CREDITORS

SYNOPSIS

---

§ 10.01 First to File or Perfect — §§ 9-312(5)(a), R9-322(a)

If a debtor grants a security interest to two or more secured lenders and defaults on those obligations, competing claims might be made by those secured parties with respect to the same collateral. Priorities among conflicting security interests in the same collateral are governed by section 9-312 of the 1972 text. The general rules of that section are provided in subsection (5), which provides:

> In all cases not governed by other rules stated in this section (including cases of purchase money security interests which do not qualify for the special priorities set forth in subsections (3) and (4) of this section), priority between conflicting security interests in the same collateral shall be determined according to the following rules:
>
> (a) Conflicting security interests rank according to priority in time of filing or perfection. Priority dates from the time a filing is first made covering the collateral or the time the security interest is first perfected, whichever is earlier, provided that there is no period thereafter when there is neither filing nor perfection.
>
> (b) So long as conflicting security interests are unperfected, the first to attach has priority.

Because an unperfected secured party that realizes it faces a priority dispute with another unperfected secured party can simply perfect to attain priority under subsection (a),[1] recourse to subsection (b) is relatively rare.[2] Consequently, the basic general rule awards priority to the secured party that is the first to either file or perfect.[3]

The general rules of the revision are comparable, although the language is more precise and somewhat more expansive.[4] The same rules provided in the 1972 version govern priority of competing perfected security interests and agricultural liens,[5] and competing unperfected security interests and agricultural liens.[6] The revision states an additional general rule that a perfected security interest or agricultural lien has priority over a competing unperfected security interest or agricultural lien.[7]

The general rule on competing perfected security interests does not simply recognize filing as the predominant method of perfecting a security interest. It affords a special priority advantage to filing that is not available through any alternative method of

---

[1] *See* U.C.C. § 9-312 Cmt. 5. (Example 2); Engelsma v. Superior Prods. Mfg. Co., 298 Minn. 77, 212 N.W.2d 884, 13 U.C.C. Rep. Serv. 944 (1973).

[2] "The last mentioned rule [subsection (5)(b)] may be thought to be of merely theoretical interest, since it is hard to imagine a situation where the case would come into litigation without either [party] having perfected his interest." U.C.C. § 9-312 Cmt. 5. The provision has been relevant in an occasional case. Milwaukee Mack Sales, Inc. v. First Wis. Nat'l Bank of Milwaukee, 93 Wis. 2d 589, 287 N.W.2d 708, 28 U.C.C. Rep Serv. 540 (1980).

[3] Board of Cty. Comm'rs, Cty. of Adams v. Berkeley Village, 40 Colo. App. 431, 580 P.2d 1251, 24 U.C.C. Rep Serv. 975 (1978) (first secured party to perfect by filing had priority over both secured party who filed later and creditor who never filed); S. Lotman & Son, Inc. v. Southeastern Fin. Corp., 288 Ala. 547, 263 So. 2d 499, 11 U.C.C. Rep. Serv. 218 (1972) (B took security interest; A took competing security interest and filed; B filed later; A won as first to file and first to perfect).

[4] U.C.C. § R9-322(a).

[5] U.C.C. § R9-322(a)(1).

[6] U.C.C. § R9-322(a)(3).

[7] U.C.C. § R9-322(a)(2).

perfection.[8] A security interest cannot be perfected until all of the applicable steps required for perfection have been taken and the security interest has attached.[9] Nevertheless, a secured party may "pre-file" a financing statement before the security interest attaches. The secured party who files a financing statement but does not complete the process of attachment until later will achieve priority under the general rule against any secured lenders who perfect after that filing.[10]

The significance of the priority advantage associated with pre-filing can be illustrated by comparing the position of a secured party who files prior to attachment with what its position would have been had it taken possession of the collateral prior to attachment. Assume that SP-1 files a financing statement before it enters into a security agreement with a prospective debtor. SP-2 afterwards takes and perfects a security interest in the same property described in SP-1's financing statement. SP-1 and the debtor subsequently complete the steps necessary for SP-1's security interest to attach. If the debtor later defaults on both loans, SP-1 will have priority in the collateral. Even though SP-2 perfected first, the pre-filing by SP-1 provides it with priority.[11]

In contrast, if SP-1 had merely taken possession of the collateral, it would not have attained priority simply on the basis of possession. SP-1's perfection would have had to precede perfection by SP-2, which means that both attachment and any necessary steps for perfection would have had to predate filing by SP-2.[12]

The reason for affording a special priority protection for filing, even filing done prior to attachment, is stated in the Comments: "The justification for the rule lies in the necessity of protecting the filing system — that is, of allowing the secured party who has first filed to make subsequent advances without each time having, as a condition of protection, to check for filings later than his."[13] The existence of this special protection and the reasoning that supports it explain why creditors commonly insist upon having a prospective debtor execute a financing statement as a precondition to finalizing a secured financing transaction. The creditor can make a search and file its financing statement if the search does not show a competing claim. The creditor then can finalize

---

[8] Priority in favor of the first secured party to file requires the filing to be made properly. Mountain Credit v. Michiana Lumber & Supply, Inc., 31 Colo. App. 112, 498 P.2d 967, 10 U.C.C. Rep. Serv. 1347 (1972) (defendant's financing statement was filed first but in wrong office). *See also* **U.C.C. § R9-322 Cmt. 4.**

[9] U.C.C. §§ 9-303(1), **R9-308(a)**. *See* § 4.03 *supra.*

[10] *In re* McCorhill Pub., Inc., 86 B.R. 783, 8 U.C.C. Rep. Serv. 2d 203 (Bankr. S.D.N.Y. 1988). The priority also extends to after-acquired property. Wade Credit Corp. v. Borg-Warner Acceptance Corp., 83 Or. App. 479, 732 P.2d 76, 3 U.C.C. Rep. Serv. 2d 289 (1987).

[11] Enterprises Now, Inc. v. Citizens & S. Dev. Corp., 135 Ga. App. 603, 218 S.E.2d 309, 17 U.C.C. Rep. Serv. 1114 (1975) (having filed first, appellee had priority over appellant even though appellant perfected first).

[12] Bank of Okla., City Plaza v. Martin, 744 P.2d 218, 5 U.C.C. Rep Serv. 2d 222 (Okla. Ct. App. 1987) (first to record security interest in airplane with FAA); Barry v. Bank of N.H., N.A., 113 N.H. 158, 304 A.2d 879, 12 U.C.C. Rep. Serv. 732 (1973) (plaintiff perfected at the latest when it took possession of collateral).

[13] U.C.C. § 9-312 Cmt. 5. *See also* **U.C.C. § R9-322 Cmt. 4;** Enterprises Now, Inc. v. Citizens & S. Dev. Corp. 135 Ga. App. 603, 218 S.E. 2d 309, 17 U.C.C. Rep. Serv. 1114 (1975).

its transaction with the debtor free of concerns that the debtor might be dealing with another lender at the same time. The general rule is a pure race statute — the first party to take the required action prevails.[14] Being able to rely upon filing rather than perfection as the required action enables a creditor to establish its priority position before committing itself to any financing.[15]

If the party that pre-files a financing statement later makes a loan but never enters into a security agreement with the debtor, should that party nevertheless prevail against a secured party that files later? Although the general rule awards priority to the secured party that was the first to file, the general rule does not apply in this situation. The general rule governs priority battles between secured parties. If the first party to file never enters into a security agreement, that party never becomes a secured party and the filing is irrelevant for purposes of the general rule.[16] These facts vividly illustrate the importance of properly characterizing the competing claimants before selecting a rule to govern priority between them.

The characterization of the secured party's status may have to be determined over a period of time. The general rule confers priority on the secured party that was the first to file or perfect, provided that this secured party does not thereafter allow the intervention of a period during which it is neither filed nor perfected.[17] In other words, to retain the advantage from being the first to file or perfect, the secured party's filing or perfection must be continuous.[18]

§ 10.02 Future Advances — §§ 9-312(7), R9-323

Section 9-312 of the 1972 text also addresses priorities with respect to future advances that a secured party makes to a debtor. It provides that when a secured party makes a future advance while its security interest is perfected by any method other than automatic perfection or temporary perfection (*i.e.*, filing, possession, control or delivery), "the security interest has the same priority for the purposes of subsection (5) . . . with respect

---

[14] Knowledge that a prior party has taken a security interest that has not been perfected is irrelevant in the priority determination. *See also* **U.C.C. § R9-322 Cmt. 4;** State of Alaska, Div. Of Agr. v. Fowler, 611 P.2d 58, 29 U.C.C. Rep. Serv. 696 (Alaska 1980). Some priority provisions of Article 9 do refer to knowledge or notice, but not these general rules.

[15] A prospective secured party can also use this approach to protect itself against the delay in placing financing statements into the public record that plagues some states. Upon running a search and finding no competing financing statements, the lender can then wait for the period of time that covers the delay in obtaining any financing statements that have been previously presented into the public records. If another search conducted at the end of this time period reveals no competing financing statements, the lender has strong assurances that its financing statement will be the first to have been filed.

[16] Although it reached the correct result, the Tenth Circuit could have been more accurate by recognizing these principles. Transport Equip. Co. v. Guaranty State Bank, 518 F.2d 377, 17 U.C.C. Rep. Serv. 1 (10th Cir. 1975).

[17] Stearns Mfg. Co., Inc. v. National Bank & Trust Co. of Cent. Pa., 12 U.C.C. Rep.Serv. 189 (Pa. Ct. Com. Pl. 1972) (defendant obtained priority when plaintiff's previously filed financing statement lapsed).

[18] *See* U.C.C. §§ 9-312 Cmt. 5 (Example 3), **R9-322 Cmt. 4 (Example 3).**

to the future advances as it does with respect to the first advance."[19] Priority with respect to a future advance thus goes to the first secured party to either file or perfect (if continuous perfection has been maintained).

The priority achieved under the general rule will apply irrespective of whether the advances were made "pursuant to commitment."[20] An advance made pursuant to a commitment entered into before or while the security interest is perfected by one of the methods mentioned in the preceding paragraph also achieves priority under the general rule, even if the advance is made at a time when the security interest is temporarily perfected.[21] In other cases of temporary or automatic perfection, a secured party can have priority as to a particular advance only from the date of the advance.[22] For example, suppose Secured Party has a security interest in a negotiable promissory note executed by Obligor and payable to the order of Debtor. Secured Party has perfected its security interest in the instrument by possession, and the security agreement contains an optional future advances clause. Secured Party later delivers the instrument to Debtor so that Debtor can present it to Obligor for payment, thereby becoming temporarily perfected.[23] If Secured Party makes an advance during the period of temporary perfection, its priority for the advance will date only from the time the advance is made. If the security agreement had obligated the secured party to make the advance, however, priority as to the advance would date from the time Secured Party initially took possession.

Although they achieve the same result, the provisions in the revision differ. The revision does not include the above-quoted language from the 1972 text. Under a proper reading of section R9-322(a)(1)'s "first-to-file-or-perfect" standard,[24] however, a security interest with priority under the general rule also gives the secured party priority for all subsequent advances secured by its security interest.[25] The comments to section R9-323 make clear that the timing of an advance generally is not relevant to a priority conflict between secured parties.[26] Section R9-323 then

---

[19] U.C.C. § 9-312(7).

[20] "An advance is made 'pursuant to commitment' if the secured party has bound himself to make it, whether or not a subsequent event of default or other event not within his control has relieved or may relieve him from his obligation." U.C.C. § 9-105(1)(k). **The definition in the revision is comparable. U.C.C. § R9-102(a)(68).**

[21] U.C.C. § 9-312(7) & Cmt. 7.

[22] U.C.C. § 9-312(7). This last provision will govern very few cases, as secured parties rarely make future advances "without commitment while the security interest is perfected temporarily without either filing or possession." U.C.C. § 9-312 Cmt. 7.

[23] U.C.C. §§ 9-304(5)(twenty-one day period of temporary perfection), **R9-312(f) (twenty day period).** To maintain continuous perfection beyond the grace period under the 1972 text, Secured Party must reacquire possession. § 9-304(1). **Secured Party can either take possession or file under the revision. §§ R9-313(a) (possession), R9-312(a) (filing).** Temporary perfection is discussed generally in §§ 8.01, 8.02 *supra.*

[24] *See* § 10.01 *supra.*

[25] U.C.C. § R9-323 Cmt. 3.

[26] "[I]t is abundantly clear that the time when an advance is made plays no role in determining priorities among conflicting security interests except when a financing statement was not filed and the advance is the giving of value as the last step for attachment and perfection." *Id.*

identifies the one instance when the timing of an advance will affect priority — perfection of the security interest will date from the time an advance is made to the extent that the security interest secures an advance (1) that is made while the interest is perfected automatically or by temporary perfection, and (2) that is not made pursuant to a commitment entered into before or while the security interest was perfected by some other method.[27] Thus, under the revision, priority based on the time of advance continues to be confined to the same rare case identified under the 1972 text.[28]

Consider the following hypothetical. Creditor X loans Debtor $50,000, takes a security interest in Debtor's equipment, and files a financing statement, all on Day 1. On Day 20, Creditor Y takes a security interest in the same equipment, files a financing statement, and loans Debtor $75,000. On Day 30, Creditor X loans Debtor an additional $40,000. Under the provisions of section 9-312(5)(a), Creditor X clearly has priority with respect to its initial loan of $50,000. Does Creditor X have priority, however, with respect to the additional $40,000 loan?

The question cannot be answered without first characterizing Creditor X's status with respect to the second loan. That status cannot be established based on the facts presented because three relevant scenarios are still possible. Under two of them, Creditor X will prevail under the general rule. Under the third scenario, Creditor X will be an unsecured creditor with respect to the second loan, and thus will fall outside the scope of the provisions governing priority between secured parties.

One possibility is that Creditor X made the subsequent loan of $40,000 pursuant to a future advances clause in the security agreement between Creditor X and Debtor. The future advances clause would serve as the basis to establish that Creditor X was a secured party in the same collateral with respect to the subsequent loan. Because Creditor X had already filed a financing statement with respect to that collateral and it preceded the filing by Creditor Y, Creditor X would prevail even with respect to the future advance of $40,000.[29]

A second possibility is that the security agreement did not contain a future advances clause, but that Creditor X nevertheless claims secured status for the second loan pursuant to a new security agreement between Creditor X and Debtor that describes the same collateral covered in the original transaction between the two parties. The second security agreement clearly would give Creditor X secured status with respect to the second loan. The issue is whether the interest would be perfected and give priority to Creditor X over Creditor Y with respect to the $40,000 advance.

This issue proved to be controversial under the original enactments of Article 9. A minority position that attracted considerable attention was epitomized by the decision in *Coin-O-Matic Service Co. v. Rhode Island Hospital Trust Co.*[30] The original parties

---

[27] U.C.C. § R9-323(a).

[28] U.C.C. § R9-323 Cmt. 3 (Example 2).

[29] *In re* Leslie Brock & Sons, 147 B.R. 426, 21 U.C.C. Rep. Serv. 2d 154 (Bankr. S.D. Ohio (1992); Thorp Commercial Corp. v. Northgate Indus., Inc., 654 F.2d 1245, 31 U.C.C. Rep. Serv. 801 (8th Cir. 1981).

[30] 3 U.C.C. Rep. Serv. 1112 (R.I. Super. Ct. 1966).

in that case entered into a new security agreement at the time of the subsequent loan because, at the time of the first loan, they had not contemplated additional advances by the secured party. The court held that the "first-to-file" rule did not apply when the original security agreement did not provide for future advances, and concluded that the secured party did not have priority over a conflicting secured party whose interest was perfected prior to the subsequent loan.[31]

Fortunately, most courts refused to follow the *Coin-O-Matic* case.[32] The drafters of Article 9 rejected the decision and its progeny and, to emphasize this position, added subsection (7) to section 9-312 in the 1972 revision of Article 9.[33] The bankruptcy court in Rhode Island, where the *Coin-O-Matic* case was decided, later rejected the *Coin-O-Matic* approach based on the changes stressed by the drafters.[34]

Thus, if the second security agreement covers the same collateral described in the filed financing statement, Creditor X should have priority for its second loan, with or without subsection (7).[35] A new paragraph added to the Comments makes it clear that Creditor X should prevail.[36] Although the subsequent loan is not really a future advance at all, but rather an advance made contemporaneously with the new security agreement, Creditor X should still prevail on the strength of the language and policy of the general rule. The earlier discussion of the general rule[37] demonstrated that, if Creditor X had simply filed a financing statement and later entered into a security agreement with Debtor after Creditor Y entered into a security agreement and perfected, Creditor X would attain

---

[31] A few cases followed the same approach. ITT Indus. Credit Co. v. Union Bank & Trust Co., 615 S.W.2d 2, 30 U.C.C. Rep. Serv. 1701 (Ky. Ct. App. 1981) (future advances clause required in security agreement to cover future advances). Some more recent decisions have also suggested that a clause in the security agreement is needed. *In re* Comprehensive Review Technology, Inc., 138 B.R. 195, 17 U.C.C. Rep. Serv. 2d 954 (Bankr. S.D. Ohio 1992).

[32] Provident Fin. Co. v. Beneficial Fin. Co., 36 N.C. App. 401, 245 S.E.2d 510, 24 U.C.C. Rep. Serv. 1332 (1978); *In re* Rivet, 299 F. Supp. 374, 6 U.C.C. Rep. Serv. 460 (E.D. Mich. 1969).

[33] The Committee disapproves this line of cases, and believes that an appropriate financing statement may perfect security interests securing advances made under agreements not contemplated at the time of the filing of the financing statement, even if the advances then contemplated have been fully paid in the interim. Under the notice-filing procedures of the Code, the filing of a financing statement is effective to perfect security interests as to which the other required elements for perfection exist, whether the security agreement involved is one existing at the date of filing with an after-acquired property clause or a future advance clause, or whether the applicable security agreement is executed later.
Review Commitee for Article 9 of the Uniform Commercial Code, Final Report 226-27 (1971).

[34] *In re* Nason, 13 B.R. 984, 31 U.C.C. Rep. Serv. 1739 (Bankr. D.R.I. 1981). For consistent cases, see UNI Imports, Inc. v. Aparacor, Inc., 978 F.2d 984, 18 U.C.C. Rep. Serv. 2d 933 (7th Cir. 1992); State Bank of Sleepy Eye v. Krueger, 405 N.W.2d 491, 3 U.C.C. Rep. Serv. 2d 1145 (Minn. Ct. App. 1987).

[35] Allis-Chalmers Credit Corp. v. Cheney Inv., Inc., 227 Kan. 4, 605 P.2d 525, 28 U.C.C. Rep. Serv. 574 (1980).

[36] U.C.C. § 9-312 Cmt. 7 (last paragraph in Example 5). *See also* **U.C.C. § R9-323 Cmt. 3 (last sentence in Example 1).**

[37] *See* § 10.01 *supra.*

priority as the first to file.[38] Conceptually, the relationship between Creditor X's filed financing statement and its second security agreement with Debtor is no different just because Creditor X also entered into an initial security agreement with Debtor that was contemporaneous with the filing.

The third possible scenario with respect to the second loan advanced by Creditor X would be that the loan was made without any future advances clause in Creditor X's security agreement with Debtor and without any subsequent security agreement between the parties. In this case, Creditor X would be characterized as an unsecured creditor with respect to the second loan. Creditor X could not establish any way in which Debtor consented to attachment so that the collateral described in the original transaction would also be encumbered by the amount of the second loan. The general rule would not apply because, beyond Creditor X's initial loan, Creditor Y would be the only secured party. Creditor X would be only a general creditor on the second loan and would thus lack a property interest in any of Debtor's assets with respect to that claim. A lender in Creditor X's position, therefore, must either include a future advances clause in its initial security agreement or remember to enter into another agreement in order to secure any subsequent loans.

Creditor X's priority position would be evaluated in like fashion under all three scenarios if, rather than filing a financing statement, Creditor X had perfected its initial security interest by taking possession.[39] As the first to perfect, Creditor X would have priority with respect to its initial advance. If future advances were made pursuant to either a future advances clause in the security agreement or to new security agreements in the same collateral, Creditor X would also prevail with respect to later advances.

The first-to-file-or-perfect rule has enormous practical consequences on the way in which secured financing should be conducted. The practical reality is that there is no real safety in being a subordinate creditor.[40] If a debtor owes only $10,000 to a prior-perfected secured party and the collateral is worth in excess of $100,000, it might initially appear safe to lend several thousand dollars against the same collateral. The second lender's interest in the collateral could be wiped out in a practical sense, however, by subsequent advances from the first secured party. The second lender is not safe even if the original security agreement does not include a future advances clause or even if the outstanding debt to the first secured party has been paid in full. All that need happen to undercut the second lender's position is for the first lender to make a subsequent advance and enter into a new security agreement.

A prospective lender who wishes to proceed with a loan to the debtor but wants to avoid this risk should follow one of three courses. If the debt to the first lender has been fully paid, the second lender should insist upon a termination statement to end any basis for continuous perfection in the first lender.[41] If money is still owed to the first lender,

---

[38] U.C.C. §§ 9-312(5)(a), **U.C.C. § R9-322(a)(1)**. First Nat'l Bank & Trust Co. of Vinita, Okla. v. Atlas Credit Corp., 417 F.2d 1081, 6 U.C.C. Rep. Serv. 1223 (10th Cir. 1969).

[39] U.C.C. §§ 9-312 Cmt. 7 (last two paragraphs), **U.C.C. § R9-323 Cmt. 3 (Example 1)**.

[40] *In re* Martin Grinding & Machine Works, Inc., 793 F.2d 592, 1 U.C.C. Rep. Serv. 2d 1329 (7th Cir. 1986) (not safe to loan against property described in prior financing statement).

[41] Provident Fin. Co. v. Beneficial Fin. Co., 36 N.C. App. 401, 245 S.E.2d 510, 24 U.C.C. Rep. Serv. 1332 (1978) (defendant could have protected itself by insisting that a termination statement be filed, but failed to do so).

the second lender could increase the amount of its loan, pay off the first lender and require a termination statement, thereby attaining the status of the first secured party to file or perfect.[42] The third option would be to negotiate with the first lender[43] to obtain a subordination agreement[44] by which the first lender would agree to subordinate itself with respect to any further loans that it might advance to the debtor.[45] Although such an agreement is not generally in the interest of the first lender, it might be attainable if the first lender would like to see a new infusion of capital into the debtor's operation, or if the first lender is certain that it will not advance any more money to the debtor.[46]

§ 10.03 Exceptions for Non-filing Collateral

The Comments to the revision draw a distinction between "non-filing collateral" and "filing collateral." The distinction is described as follows:

These new provisions distinguish what these Comments refer to as "non-filing collateral" from what they call "filing collateral." As used in these Comments, non-filing collateral is collateral of a type for which perfection may be achieved by a method other than filing (possession or control, mainly) and for which secured parties who so perfect generally do not expect or need to conduct a filing search. More specifically, non-filing collateral is chattel paper, deposit accounts, negotiable documents, instruments, investment property, and letter-of-credit

---

[42] A bank received correspondence noting its payment of a prior-perfected finance company, but a termination statement was not filed. The court held that an enforceable subordination agreement was entered into with respect to the noted inventory, but that it did not extend to after-acquired units. *In re* Bishop, 52 B.R. 470, 41 U.C.C. Rep. Serv. 1491 (Bankr. N.D. Ala. 1985).

[43] Subordination agreements are generally entered into between two or more creditors. A secondary creditor who was not a party to a subordination agreement between the primary secured party and the debtor has been held to be a beneficiary of that agreement. *In re* Thorner Mfg. Co., Inc., 4 U.C.C. Rep Serv. 595 (Bankr. E.D. Pa. 1967).

[44] A secured party's priority can also be subordinated through estoppel. Hillman's Equip., Inc., v. Central Realty, Inc., 144 Ind. App. 18, 242 N.E.2d 522, 5 U.C.C. Rep. Serv. 1160 (Ind. Ct. App. 1968), *rev'd on other grounds,* 246 N.E.2d 383 (Ind. 1969) (junior secured party changed his position in reliance on senior secured party's statement, prior to sale of collateral, that he would get his equipment).

[45] "Nothing in this Article prevents subordination by agreement by any person entitled to priority." U.C.C. § 9-316. *See also In re* Smith, 77 B.R. 624, 5 U.C.C. Rep. Serv. 2d 496 (Bankr. N.D. Ohio 1987) (bank agreed to subordinate its lien on proceeds up to $8000 per year for seven years). *But see* H. & Val J. Rothschild, Inc. v. Northwestern Nat'l Bank of St. Paul, 309 Minn. 35, 242 N.W.2d 844, 19 U.C.C. Rep Serv. 673 (1976) (telephone conversation in which parties assumed mistakenly that plaintiff had prior claim did not subordinate defendant's claim).

[46] Western Auto Supply Co. v. Bank of Imboden, 17 Ark. App. 4, 701 S.W.2d 394, 42 U.C.C. Rep. Serv. 1506 (1985) (prior-perfected secured party consented because it recognized its own interest in debtor's obtaining bank loan). A secured creditor should be careful in agreeing to subordination. *In re* Bar C Cross Farms & Ranches, Inc., 48 B.R. 976, 1 U.C.C. Rep. Serv. 2d 256 (Bankr. D. Colo. 1985) (waiver by secured party did not merely subordinate its interest to another claimant but terminated the interest).

rights. Other collateral — accounts, commercial tort claims, general intangibles, goods, nonnegotiable documents, and payment intangibles — is filing collateral. [47]

The distinction is important because the revision provides special priority rules with respect to non-filing collateral that override the first-to-file-or-perfect rule of section R9-322(a). [48] Depending on the specific types of property, these rules on non-filing collateral extend priority based on the first to perfect through taking control or possession.

The 1972 text also includes several comparable rules that enable a secured party who takes possession of the collateral to obtain priority over even earlier-perfected secured parties in the same collateral. [49] It has fewer of these rules, because not all of the types of non-filing collateral recognized under the revision are within the scope of the 1972 text.

[A] Deposit Accounts — § R9-327

A secured party that has perfected a security interest in a deposit account by control will have priority over a secured party that has a competing interest perfected by any other method. [50] The only alternative method for perfection of a security interest in a deposit account would be the automatic continuous perfection available for identifiable cash proceeds within a deposit account. [51]

If the bank with which a deposit account is maintained holds a security interest in the deposit account, that interest takes priority over a conflicting security interest in the deposit account, whether the conflicting interest is as original collateral or as cash proceeds. [52] This rule leaves banks free to extend credit to their customers without having to consult records to determine whether another security interest has been created in the account. [53] A secured party that wishes to avoid such bank priority must either take control by having the account in its name and thereby becoming the bank's customer, [54] or obtain a subordination agreement from the bank. These rules governing priority of conflicting security interests in deposit accounts do not cover the proceeds of a deposit account. [55]

---

[47] U.C.C. § R9-322 Cmt. 7. The Comments to the 1972 text do not draw this distinction between non-filing collateral and filing collateral overtly. Nevertheless, as discussed in the text, the 1972 Code does provide special priority rules for conflicting security interests in certain collateral, such as chattel paper and instruments.

[48] U.C.C. §§ R9-327, R9-328, R9-329, R9-330.

[49] U.C.C. §§ 9-115(5), 9-308, 9-309.

[50] U.C.C. § R9-327(1). For a discussion of perfection by control in a deposit account, *see* U.C.C. §§ R9-312(b)(1), R9-314, R9-104 and § 6.04[B] *supra.* Under the 1972 text, a secured party cannot take a security interest in a deposit account (although a secured party can hold a security interest in identifiable cash proceeds within such an account).

[51] *See* U.C.C. §§ R9-312(b)(1), R9-315(c),(d)(2).

[52] U.C.C. § R9-327(3).

[53] U.C.C. § R9-327 Cmt. 4.

[54] U.C.C. §§ R9-327(4), R9-104(a)(3).

[55] U.C.C. § R9-327 Cmt. 5. For discussion on priorities in proceeds, *see* § 10.05 *infra.*

[B] Investment Property — §§ 9-115(5), R9-328

A secured party that has perfected a security interest in investment property by control will have priority over a competing interest perfected by any other means under both the 1972 text **and the revision.** [56] This rule reflects the unique aspects of the securities markets. It provides a clear mandate that a secured party that wants the greatest level of protection available must obtain control. The availability of filing as an alternative method of perfection for investment property is not intended to alter the established practice of not searching the U.C.C. files before entering into securities transactions. [57] Thus, a secured party can still obtain control and be unaffected by any prior filings. Filing provides protection against lien creditors (including bankruptcy trustees) and other secured parties that fail to obtain control.

A variety of rules under both the 1972 text **and the revision** determine priority of conflicting security interests in investment property when each of the interests is perfected by control. A primary advantage is afforded to a securities intermediary that holds a security interest in a security entitlement or a securities account that is maintained with the securities intermediary. Such an intermediary has priority over a conflicting security interest held by another secured party. [58]

In other cases involving conflicting security interests that are perfected by control, the 1972 text provides that such interests rank equally. [59] **The revision changes this result and resolves such conflicts under a temporal rule.** [60] **In other words, the first party to have obtained control or to have completed the steps required to achieve control will have priority.** The circumstances of such dual interests perfected by control are likely to be rare. [61]

A security interest in a certificated security in registered form which is perfected by delivery has priority over a conflicting security interest that is perfected by any method other than control. [62] Thus, a secured party that takes possession of a certificated security without obtaining a necessary indorsement will have priority over a prior secured party who perfected with respect to the security by filing. [63]

---

[56] U.C.C. §§ 9-115(5)(a), **R9-328(1).** For discussion of perfection by control in investment property, *see* U.C.C. §§ 9-115(4)(a), 9-115(1)(e), **R9-314, R9-106** and § 6.04[A] *supra.*

[57] The drafters added filing as an alternative method of perfection that provides more limited protection against general creditors and other secured creditors who rely upon filing. For discussion of practices in the securities markets, *see* § 6.04[A] *supra.*

[58] U.C.C. §§ 9-115(5)(c), **R9-328(3).** Comparable priority is available for a commodity intermediary. U.C.C. §§ 9-115(5)(d), **R9-328(4).**

[59] U.C.C. §§ 9-115(5)(b).

[60] **U.C.C. § R9-328(2).**

[61] U.C.C. §§ 9-115 Cmt. 5.

[62] U.C.C. §§ 9-115(6), **R9-328(5).**

[63] Priority between secured parties that both perfect by filing will be governed by the general rule of the first to file. U.C.C. §§ 9-115(5)(f), 9-312(5)(a), **R9-328(7), R9-322(a)(1).**

[C] Letter-of-Credit Rights — § R9-329

A secured party having control of a letter-of-credit right will have priority over a conflicting security interest held by a secured party that does not have control.[64] The only alternative methods of perfection in a letter-of-credit right would be automatic perfection as a supporting obligation[65] or temporary perfection as a proceed.[66] This allocation of priority is consistent with international practice and promotes finality of payment made to recognized assignees of letter-of-credit proceeds.[67] Multiple secured parties with control rank according to the time of obtaining control.[68]

[D] Chattel Paper, Instruments, Negotiable Documents, and Securities — §§ 9-308, 9-309, R9-330, R9-331

Article 9 includes provisions under which a purchaser can obtain priority against even a prior-perfected secured party in chattel paper, instruments, negotiable documents, and securities.[69] These provisions are covered in detail in a subsequent chapter covering other parties (such as buyers) whose interests conflict with a security interest in these types of property.[70] For present purposes, note that "purchaser" is defined broadly to include a secured party.[71] Consistent with the approach taken for other non-filing collateral, priority that is an exception to the first-to-file-or-perfect rule is available under these provisions for secured parties with interests in chattel paper, instruments, negotiable documents, or securities if they take possession of the collateral. **Under the revision, such priority is also available for secured parties who take control of electronic chattel paper.[72]**

§ 10.04 Purchase-Money Security Interests

The "first-to-file-or-perfect" rule and the rules on priorities with respect to future advances could place a debtor in a difficult position. The debtor's present secured lender might be unwilling to advance additional capital that the debtor needs to acquire more property of the type covered in a filed financing statement, while other financers could refuse to extend credit because they would be vulnerable to any advances that the present secured lender might later make. The "first-to-file-or-perfect" rule and the priority rules governing future advances could practically enable a secured lender to eliminate

---

64 U.C.C. § R9-329(1). For discussion of perfection by control for letter-of-credit rights, *see* U.C.C. §§ R9-312(b)(2), R9-314, R9-107 and § 6.04[B] *supra.*

65 U.C.C. § R9-308(d).

66 U.C.C. § R9-315(c).

67 U.C.C. § R9-329 Cmt. 2.

68 U.C.C. § R9-329(2).

69 U.C.C. §§ 9-308, 9-309, **R9-330, R9-331**.

70 *See* § 11.03[C],[D] *infra.*

71 U.C.C. § 1-201(33), (32).

72 U.C.C. § R9-330(a),(b). For discussion of perfection by control for electronic chattel paper, *see* U.C.C. §§ R9-314, R9-105 and § 6.04[B] *supra.*

competing sources of financing and to exert excessive control over the direction of the debtor's business.

This position of excessive control is tempered by other provisions that favor purchase-money secured parties. Under these provisions a purchase-money secured party can finance the debtor's acquisition of additional property that is subject to a prior-filed financing statement and obtain priority with respect to the additional property. Even if the initial secured party's perfected security interest extends to the new property under an after-acquired property clause, the interest of the initial secured creditor will be subordinate with respect to this new property.

The prior secured party should have no complaints, however, about this priority granted to later purchase-money secured parties. Because of the secondary source of financing, the collateral of the debtor is expanded, without the prior secured party having to finance its acquisition. Furthermore, the prior secured party never relied upon this additional collateral in making its decision to extend financing. The exceptions in favor of purchase-money secured parties are crucial to allow debtors to obtain alternative financing once they have permitted the filing of a financing statement.

[A]   Collateral Other Than Inventory — §§ 9-312(4), R9-324(a)

One of the priority rules included in the 1972 text favors purchase-money secured parties who have interests in collateral other than inventory:

> A purchase money security interest in collateral other than inventory has priority over a conflicting security interest in the same collateral . . . if the purchase money security interest is perfected at the time the debtor receives possession of the collateral or within ten days thereafter.[73]

As long as the transaction qualifies as a purchase-money security interest and the collateral is not inventory, this exception is available for a subsequent creditor to obtain priority against a prior party claiming through an after-acquired property clause.

Revised section R9-324(a) is based on section 9-312(4) and is designated in the revision as the general rule on purchase-money priority. Under the revision, a purchase-money security interest can only be created in goods and software.[74] The general rule thus applies to purchase-money priority in goods other than inventory, with an additional exclusion for livestock. Like the 1972 version, a perfected purchase-money security interest in such goods has priority over a conflicting security interest in the same goods if the purchase-money security interest is perfected when the debtor receives possession of the collateral or within a grace period that is expanded in the revision to 20 days.

---

[73] U.C.C. § 9-312(4).

[74] U.C.C. § R9-103. *See* § 1.05 *supra.* A purchase-money security interest in software can arise only if the debtor acquires its interest in the software for the purpose of using the software in goods subject to a purchase-money security interest. U.C.C. § R9-103(c). A perfected purchase-money security interest in software is given the same priority as the purchase-money security interest in the goods for which the software was acquired. U.C.C. § R9-324(f).

The only requirement imposed on the purchase-money secured party is to perfect in a timely manner.[75] The secured party may perfect by filing or by any other available method. This makes temporary perfection, or automatic perfection in the case of consumer goods, potentially relevant (perfection by possession is possible, but very unlikely given the nonpossessory nature of the typical purchase-money secured transaction). If the collateral is consumer goods, the purchase-money secured party's interest is automatically perfected upon attachment, and no filing is necessary to obtain priority over conflicting security interests.[76] If the collateral is not consumer goods, however, the purchase-money secured party effectively must file a financing statement before the expiration of the grace period.[77] The purchase-money secured party has a ten-day grace period during which to accomplish perfection.[78] Most states **and the revision** have increased the grace period to twenty days.

The grace period facilitates the completion of commercial transactions. A supplier thus can sell goods, retaining a security interest in them, and conveniently allow the debtor to take possession of them, without having to interrupt this sequence by first filing a financing statement. The supplier can proceed in its dealings with the debtor, confident that it can achieve priority if it completes the steps for perfection within the allotted grace period. The rationale that underlies prefiling of financing statements is not applicable here, where the secured party can obtain priority over any interest that is already of record.

The grace period for perfection begins from the time that the debtor receives possession of the collateral.[79] The provision has generated some controversy in cases in which the debtor acquires possession of goods by a lease containing an option to buy or by sale on approval. Assume that thirty days after receiving possession of the goods, the recipient decides to exercise the purchase option or agrees to buy the goods after satisfaction with the trial period under a sale on approval. If the parties then enter into a security agreement and the supplier files within ten days, the supplier might be challenged for priority by a prior-perfected secured party claiming an interest in the goods under an after-acquired property clause. The prior-perfected party might assert that the supplier does not qualify for the purchase-money priority rule because the supplier filed more than ten days after the debtor acquired possession.

The supplier's response should be that a debtor-in-possession[80] did not exist until the

---

[75] State Bank & Trust Co. of Beeville v. First Nat'l Bank of Beeville, 635 S.W.2d 807, 33 U.C.C. Rep. Serv. 1775 (Tex. Ct. App. 1982) (purchase-money secured party filed one day later to qualify under exception).

[76] Nevertheless, the purchase-money secured party may choose to file in order to ensure that it does not lose its priority as against a later consumer who buys the collateral without knowledge of the security interest. *See* § 11.03[A][2] *supra.*

[77] U.C.C. §§ 9-312(4), **R9-324(a).**

[78] The grace period is comparable to the ten days **(twenty-days under the revision)** allowed for a purchase-money secured party to file or take possession of the collateral to achieve priority over an intervening lien creditor. *See* U.C.C. §§ 9-301(2), **R9-317(e)** and § 14.02[B] *infra.*

[79] *In re* Ivy, 37 B.R. 285, 38 U.C.C. Rep. Serv. 651 (Bankr. E.D. Ky. 1983) (filing financing statement within ten days of debtor's receiving delivery of equipment was adequate even though security agreement was signed more than ten days before filing).

[80] Section 9-312(4) starts the grace period "at the time the *debtor* receives possession of the collateral." (Emphasis supplied.)

recipient of the goods became a "debtor" by entering into a security agreement.[81] Even if a financing statement had been filed earlier, it would not have resulted in perfection because no security interest existed until the recipient entered into the security agreement, and the exception in favor of a purchase-money secured party requires perfection within ten days of the debtor's receiving possession of the "collateral." Most courts have construed the language of Article 9 to support the supplier's position.[82] **The comments to the revision address the issue directly, indicating that "the 20-day period in subsection (a) does not commence until a [sic] the goods become 'collateral' (defined in Section 9-102), i.e., until they are subject to a security interest."[83]** This resolution of the issue obviously perpetuates problems of ostensible ownership, as third parties might deal with the recipient based on its possession of the goods, unaware of the supplier's superior interest.

The 1972 text does not address priority between two parties that both qualify as purchase-money secured parties. Such a conflict can arise when more than one lender finances acquisition of the same collateral. Clearly, any purchase-money secured party who does not act to qualify for the exception by filing within the allotted grace period is deprived of the exception and is relegated to the general "first-to-file-or-perfect" rule.[84] Despite the language in the 1972 text that applies the general "first-to-file-or-perfect" rule to purchase-money secured parties only when they do not qualify for purchase-money priority,[85] most courts have also applied the general rule when two or more purchase-money secured parties do qualify.[86] Thus, a purchase-money secured party who is not certain that it is the sole source of financing has a strong incentive not to delay in filing or perfecting its interest.

The revision includes a provision to govern priority among multiple purchase-money security interests. Priority is given to a security interest that secures the price of the collateral over a conflicting security interest acquired through an enabling loan.[87] The general "first-to-file-or-perfect" rule governs priority among multiple purchase-money security interests that secure enabling loans.[88]

---

[81] In the 1972 text, "Debtor" is defined as "the person who owes payment or other performance of the obligation secured . . . ." U.C.C. § 9-105(1)(d).

[82] *In re* Hooks, 40 B.R. 715, 39 U.C.C. Rep. Serv. 332 (Bankr. M.D. Ga. 1984) (shipment for inspection); Rainier Nat'l Bank v. Inland Mach. Co., 29 Wash. App. 725, 631 P.2d 389, 32 U.C.C. Rep. Serv. 287 (Wash. Ct. App. 1981) (lease with option to buy).

[83] **U.C.C. § R9-324 Cmt. 3.**

[84] "[A]ll cases not governed by other rules stated in this section (including cases of purchase money security interests which do not qualify for the special priorities set forth in subsections (3) and (4) of this section)" are governed by the general rule. U.C.C. § 9-312(5).

[85] U.C.C. § 9-312(5).

[86] John Deere Co. v. Prod. Credit Ass'n, 686 S.W.2d 904, 39 U.C.C. Rep. Serv. 684 (Tenn. Ct. App. 1984); Framingham U.A.W. Credit Union v. Dick Russell Pontiac, Inc., 41 Mass. App. Dec. 146, 7 U.C.C. Rep. Serv. 252 (1969). An alternative solution — although not adopted by any courts to date — would be to make a pro rata allocation between competing, qualifying purchase-money secured parties.

[87] **U.C.C. § R9-324(g)(1). This priority allocation reflects the rule adopted in the Restatement (Third) of Property (Mortgages) § 7.2(c) (1997). U.C.C. § R9-324 Cmt. 13.**

[88] **U.C.C. § R9-324(g)(2).**

[B] Inventory — §§ 9-312(3), R9-324(b),(c)

The exception favoring purchase-money secured parties is more involved when the collateral is inventory. The 1972 text provides:

A perfected purchase money security interest in inventory has priority over a conflicting security interest in the same inventory . . . if

(a) the purchase money security interest is perfected at the time the debtor receives possession of the inventory; and

(b) the purchase money secured party gives notification in writing to the holder of the conflicting security interest if the holder had filed a financing statement covering the same types of inventory (i) before the date of the filing made by the purchase money secured party, or (ii) before the beginning of the 21 day period where the purchase money security interest is temporarily perfected without filing or possession (subsection (5) of Section 9-304); and

(c) the holder of the conflicting security interest receives the notification within five years before the debtor receives possession of the inventory; and

(d) the notification states that the person giving the notice has or expects to acquire a purchase money security interest in inventory of the debtor, describing such inventory by item or type. [89]

Although these provisions may at first appear quite daunting, they essentially require the purchase-money secured party to do only two things: (a) to perfect its security interest at or before the time the debtor receives possession of the inventory, and (b) to provide proper notification, prior to the debtor receiving possession of the collateral, to a holder of a conflicting security interest who has filed a financing statement before the purchase-money secured party filed or attained temporary perfection. **The revision is comparable.** [90]

The specific requirements of this exception are best understood in the context of the underlying policy concerns. Consider a typical ongoing inventory-financing arrangement

---

[89] U.C.C. § 9-312(3). The purchase-money secured party's priority in inventory does not automatically extend to all proceeds of the inventory, but is limited only to "identifiable cash proceeds received on or before the delivery of the inventory to a buyer." *Id.* For discussion of the treatment of proceeds, *see* § 10.05[B] *infra.*

[90] **The same four requirements are stated in sections R9-324(b) and R9-324(c). The notification must be authenticated. U.C.C. § R9-324(b)(2). The reference to temporary perfection notes the 20-day period that is provided in the revision.** *See* **U.C.C. § R9-312(f). The revision also provides a priority rule for purchase-money security interests in livestock that is comparable to the purchase-money priority rule for inventory. U.C.C. § R9-324(d),(e).** The approach with respect to livestock differs from the 1972 text, under which a purchase-money security interest in livestock was governed by section 9-312(4). DeKalb Bank v. Klotz, 151 Ill. App. 3d 638, 502 N.E.2d 1256, 3 U.C.C. Rep. Serv. 2d 1214 (Ill. Ct. App. 1986) (notification under § 9-312(3) not required because livestock in possession of farmer is farm products rather than inventory and § 9-312(4) thus applies).

in which the secured party advances a specified percentage against invoices for new inventory acquired by the debtor. This type of arrangement is common in inventory financing, and inventory financers often rely upon such evidence as invoices in deciding whether to advance additional funds. If a purchase-money secured party has financed the debtor's acquisition of inventory covered by a particular invoice, the inventory financer could easily be deceived by a dishonest debtor who simply presents the same invoice as evidence for another advance. The purchase-money secured party, therefore, must protect the inventory financer by providing written notification [91] that it has acquired or intends to acquire [92] a purchase-money security interest in specific items or types of inventory. [93] The advance notice can protect the original secured party by alerting it to watch out for presentation by the debtor of an invoice that covers any of the inventory described in the notification. [94]

The notification process could become burdensome to a purchase-money secured party that contemplates a series of transactions with the debtor if it had to provide notification prior to each transaction. A manufacturer, for example, may decide to finance all of a retailer's subsequent acquisition of its products. The manufacturer can simply notify the prior inventory financer that it expects to acquire a purchase-money security interest in these items of inventory [95] and that notification will be valid for five years from the date that the inventory financer receives the notification. [96] It will then be incumbent upon the inventory financer to implement a business procedure by which, over the next five years, it can protect itself in light of the information received in the notification.

Because the notification may describe inventory in which the sender merely expects to acquire a purchase-money security interest, [97] a debtor might acquire some inventory that fits the description given in the notification but, in fact, is not financed by the sender of the notification. The inventory financer can then attain priority if it can reach those items of inventory as after-acquired property.

---

[91] Elhard v. Prairie Distrib., Inc., 366 N.W.2d 465, 40 U.C.C. Rep. Serv. 1968 (N.D. 1985) (oral notification invalid). **Authenticated notification is required under the revision. U.C.C. § R9-324(b)(2).**

[92] *In re* Daniels, 35 B.R. 247, 37 U.C.C. Rep. Serv. 967 (Bankr. W.D. Okla. 1983) (written notification upheld against attack that it should fail because it did not state explicitly that creditor planned to take purchase-money security interest).

[93] U.C.C. §§ 9-312(3)(b),(d), **R9-324(b)(2),(4).**

[94] The reason no comparable notification requirement applies to purchase-money security interests for collateral other than inventory is explained in the Comments: "Since an arrangement for periodic advances against incoming property is unusual outside the inventory field, no notification requirement is included in subsection (4)." U.C.C. § 9-312 Cmt. 3. *See also* **U.C.C. § R9-324 Cmt. 4.**

[95] U.C.C. §§ 9-312(3)(d), **R9-324(b)(4).**

[96] U.C.C. §§ 9-312(3)(c), **R9-324(b)(3).** The five-year duration of the notification corresponds to the period before a filed financing statement lapses. A purchase-money secured party engaged in ongoing financing of a debtor should provide new notification to all relevant parties when it files a continuation statement.

[97] Fedders Fin. Corp. v. Chiarelli Bros., 289 A.2d 169, 10 U.C.C. Rep. Serv. 880 (Pa. Super. Ct. 1972) (written notification that described variety of types of appliances was valid even though the purchase-money secured party took an interest only in the air conditioners).

The rules are available to enable any purchase-money secured party to take priority over a prior-perfected secured party. If a purchase-money secured party fails to comply with the procedures required to invoke them, however, it will be subordinate to a prior-perfected secured party who can use an after-acquired property clause to reach the collateral provided by the purchase-money secured party. [98]

§ 10.05 Proceeds

A secured party might take its interest in one form of collateral (such as inventory) and another lender might acquire a security interest from the same debtor in a different class of collateral (such as accounts). What happens when some of the inventory collateral is sold in transactions that create accounts? The accounts are proceeds of the inventory collateral, and a priority dispute might arise between the two creditors. Before turning to the priority rules, however, it is first necessary to characterize the interests of the two competing claimants in the accounts. Because the inventory-based secured party can claim the accounts only as proceeds, the provisions related to attachment and perfection in proceeds must be analyzed.

A security interest attaches automatically to identifiable proceeds received upon the disposition of collateral. [99] Thus, the inventory financer's interest would attach to the accounts created upon the sale of any of the inventory subject to its security interest. If the inventory financer perfected through a financing statement, perfection in the account proceeds would be continuous beyond the grace period of temporary perfection, because the office in which the financing statement was filed would be the same office in which to file with respect to such accounts. [100] After determining whether the accounts financer is perfected and whether the inventory financer has a perfected interest in the accounts as proceeds, the appropriate priority rule can be selected.

Article 9's priority provisions apply the rules governing purchase-money security interests as exceptions to the rules that establish priority among ordinary security interests. [101] This same approach is applied to priority with respect to proceeds: different rules govern transactions that involve nonpurchase-money security interests and those that involve purchase-money interests.

[A] Nonpurchase-Money Security Interests

[1] The 1972 Text — § 9-312(6)

The 1972 text provides that the priority that would be available with respect to the original collateral also extends to encompass proceeds: "For the purposes of subsection (5) a date of filing or perfection as to collateral is also a date of filing or perfection as to proceeds." [102]

---

[98] U.C.C. §§ 9-312(5), **R9-322(a)**.

[99] U.C.C. §§ 9-306(2), **R9-315(a)(2)**. For discussion of attachment of security interests in proceeds generally, *see* § 2.03[B] *supra*.

[100] U.C.C. §§ 9-306(3)(a), **R9-315(c),(d)(1)**. The example assumes that there are no multistate issues. For discussion of perfection of security interests in proceeds generally, *see* § 8.02 *supra*. For discussion of multistate issues in this context, *see* § 9.04 *supra*.

[101] *See* § 10.04 *supra*.

[102] U.C.C. § 9-312(6).

Thus, the general rule on proceeds provides that the priority of a secured party with a continuously perfected security interest in proceeds is governed by the first-to-file-or-perfect rule, and that the secured party's date of filing or perfection is established from the time that it took such action with respect to its original collateral.[103] Assume that an inventory financer files on the debtor's present and after-acquired inventory, whereas an accounts financer files on the same debtor's accounts. Some of the inventory is sold, producing accounts as proceeds, and a priority dispute develops between the two secured lenders. The inventory financer would claim a continuously perfected security interest in the accounts, as proceeds from the sale of its collateral.[104] Each party would have a perfected security interest in the accounts. Priority would depend upon which of the parties was the first to file its financing statement.

[2] Revised Article 9

The revision is more complex. It designates a general rule that is consistent with section 9-312(6) of the 1972 text, and also includes special rules that are new. Because the general rule for priority in proceeds applies the general rule of section R9-322(a)(1) governing priority of competing perfected security interests, it is a rule based on temporal priority ("first-to-file-or-perfect"). The special rules are provided for situations in which this temporal rule is no longer considered to be appropriate. The special rules apply only to what is designated as "non-filing collateral," and they encompass both a rule based on non-temporal priority and one based on special temporal priority. The explanation of these provisions and their application is provided below.

[a] General Rule — § R9-322(b)(1)

The general rule for priority in proceeds continues to make the time of filing or perfection as to proceeds the same as the time of filing or perfection as to a security interest in the original collateral, and it continues to apply the temporal first-to-file-or-perfect rule governing conflicting perfected security interests in the same collateral.[105] Thus, a priority dispute between an accounts financer and an inventory financer who claims a perfected security interest in accounts as proceeds from the disposition of its collateral will continue to be determined by which of the parties was the first to file its financing statement.

---

[103] *In re* Topsy's Shoppes, Inc. of Kansas, 118 B.R. 797, 12 U.C.C. Rep. Serv. 2d 1161 (Bankr. D. Kan. 1990) (secured party failed to establish priority in proceeds arising from sales of intangibles when it conceded that another secured party had prior perfection in the same intangibles); *In re* McBee, 20 B.R. 361, 34 U.C.C. Rep. Serv. 1011 (Bankr. W.D. Tex. 1982), *rev'd on other grounds,* 714 F.2d 1316, 36 U.C.C. Rep. Serv. 1473 (5th Cir. 1983) (inventory financers ranked according to time of filing with respect to cash proceeds).

[104] This position should be sustainable under sections 9-306(2) and 9-306(3)(a). One reason the filing as to inventory might not be effective for continuous perfection in the accounts proceeds would be if filing is required in a different state under § 9-103(3). *See* U.C.C. § 9-312 Cmt. 8.

[105] U.C.C. § R9-322(b)(1),(a)(1).

[b] Special Rules

The new special rules[106] are provided in the revision to cover situations in which the temporal priority of the general rule is considered to be inappropriate.[107] Both of these special rules apply only to what the Comments designate as "non-filing collateral."[108]

[i] Special Rule on Non-Temporal Priority — § R9-322(c)(2)

The revision includes a number of provisions whereby a secured party with a security interest in non-filing collateral can attain non-temporal priority, *i.e.*, priority over a prior-perfected conflicting security interest in the same collateral.[109] This priority is attained through perfection by possession or by control. Such priority is thus an exception to the temporal priority rule (first-to-file-or-perfect) that generally governs priority in conflicting perfected security interests in the same collateral.[110]

Whenever a secured party with a security interest in non-filing collateral has taken the steps necessary for such non-temporal priority,[111] section R9-322(c)(2) provides a baseline rule for proceeds of the non-filing collateral. It extends priority over a conflicting security interest in the proceeds of the collateral if the security interest in the proceeds is perfected and is either cash proceeds or is of the same type as the original collateral.

For example, assume that SP-1 perfects a security interest in instruments by filing. SP-2 later perfects in a promissory note of the debtor by taking possession. Debtor subsequently receives an installment payment on the note in the form of cash, and also receives a check for the balance of the note. The temporal rule of section R9-322(a)(1) would give priority in the proceeds of the note to SP-1. Section R9-322(c)(2) applies, however, and gives priority to SP-2. The cash and the check are both cash proceeds, and the check is also the same type of collateral as the promissory note, *i.e.*, an instrument.

When a secured party perfects in the original non-filing collateral by taking control, the additional step of filing can be beneficial in certain situations. For example, assume that SP-1 perfects a security interest in all of the investment property of Debtor by filing. Afterwards, SP-2 perfects in a certificated security of Debtor by taking control. Debtor subsequently receives a stock dividend on the certificated security controlled by SP-2, in the form of a new certificated security. Even though the proceed is the same type of property as the collateral, if SP-2 does

---

[106] U.C.C. § R9-322(c)-(e).

[107] U.C.C. § R9-322 Cmt. 7.

[108] The distinction between non-filing collateral and filing collateral is explained at § 10.03 *supra.*

[109] U.C.C. §§ R9-327 through R9-331. These provisions are discussed in § 10.03 *supra.*

[110] U.C.C. § R9-322(f)(1).

[111] An actual conflicting security interest in the original non-filing collateral is not necessary. U.C.C. § R9-322(c).

not take delivery or control, or file with respect to the proceeds before the expiration of its 20-day period of temporary perfection, SP-2 will be unperfected as to the proceeds[112] and SP-1 will have priority pursuant to section R9-322(a)(2). In contrast, if SP-2 had filed as to investment property in addition to perfecting in the original certificated security by taking control, SP-2 would be continuously perfected in the certificate constituting proceeds[113] and would attain priority in the proceeds under section R9-322(c)(2). The extent of benefit achievable through the additional step of filing with respect to original non-filing collateral, however, is limited. For example, if the proceeds received by Debtor took the form of a promissory note covering dividends, the filing by SP-2 in investment property would lead to continuous perfection in the note. SP-2 nevertheless could not prevail under section R9-322(c)(2), however, because the note is neither cash proceeds nor proceeds of the same type as the original collateral (*i.e.*, an instrument as opposed to investment property). SP-1 thus would have priority in the proceeds under sections R9-322(a) and (b).

The special rule of non-temporal priority in section R9-322(c)(2) also addresses proceeds of proceeds. Perfection under the special rule applies only if *all* of the intervening proceeds are cash proceeds, proceeds of the same type as the original collateral, or an account relating to the collateral.[114] If *any* of the intervening proceeds do not comply, priority in the proceeds is governed by the general first-to-file-or-perfect rule of sections R9-322(a) and (b).

[ii]   Special Rule on Temporal Priority — § R9-322(d),(e)

When a secured party perfects a security interest in non-filing collateral by possession or control, the secured party does not achieve any priority under section R9-322(c)(2) in proceeds that are designated as filing collateral.[115] Furthermore, the first-to-file-or-perfect rule of section R9-322(a) also will not apply. Subsections (d) and (e) provide a different temporal rule based on first-to-file to determine priority in such proceeds against a competing claimant.[116] This first-to-file priority rule is consistent with normal expectations concerning proceeds that are filing collateral.[117]

For example, assume that SP-1 perfects its security interest in Debtor's letter-of-credit rights by control. SP-2 thereafter files with respect to Debtor's inventory. Debtor subsequently uses funds acquired from the letter of credit to purchase additional inventory, and SP-1 promptly files with respect to the inventory. SP-1 claims the inventory as proceeds and SP-2 claims it as original collateral through an after-acquired property clause. SP-2 would have priority under section R9-322(d) as the first party to file with respect to the proceeds that are filing collateral. Note

---

[112] *See* U.C.C. § 9-315(e)(2) and § 8.02 *supra.*

[113] *See* U.C.C. § 9-315(d)(1) and § 8.02 *supra.*

[114] U.C.C. § R9-322(c)(2)(C).

[115] Filing collateral could not qualify under subsection (c) as either cash proceeds or proceeds of the same type that constitute the secured party's non-filing collateral.

[116] U.C.C. § R9-322(d),(e).

[117] U.C.C. § R9-322 Cmt. 9 (Example 12).

that this result is an exception to the priority rule based on temporal perfection under section R9-322(a). If that subsection applied, SP-1 would prevail as the first party to perfect without any subsequent period during which it was unperfected.

[B] Purchase-Money Security Interests — §§ 9-312(3),(4), R9-324(a),(b)

An earlier discussion in this chapter explains how Article 9 enables a purchase-money secured party to obtain priority over an earlier-perfected competing secured party in the same collateral.[118] As explained, this beneficial treatment varies depending upon whether the purchase-money security interest is taken in inventory or another type of collateral.[119] Those same Article 9 provisions include opportunities for the purchase-money secured party to obtain priority with respect to at least some types of proceeds.

When the purchase-money security interest is in collateral other than inventory,[120] the priority for that interest extends to proceeds to the same extent as it does to the original collateral under both the 1972 text **and the revision**.[121] Thus, if a perfected purchase-money secured party finances the acquisition of equipment for the debtor, priority extends in favor of this lender against a prior equipment lender that has an after-acquired property clause in its security agreement (assuming that the purchase-money secured party perfects in a timely fashion to obtain purchase-money priority). The priority extends to the equipment the purchase-money lender finances and to any proceeds in which a continuously perfected security interest is maintained.[122]

In contrast, when the original collateral consists of inventory, the extent of priority for proceeds under a purchase-money security interest is narrower. Priority in the 1972 text is limited to "identifiable cash proceeds received on or before the delivery of the inventory to a buyer."[123] Any priority under this exception is dependent upon the purchase-money inventory financer's timely compliance with the perfection and notification requirements regarding the collateral it finances.[124] A purchase-money secured party financing a line of inventory can achieve priority over a prior-perfected inventory financer in proceeds like cash or checks,[125] but not with respect to non-cash proceeds like

---

[118] *See* § 10.04 *supra*.

[119] U.C.C. §§ 9-312(3),(4), **R9-324(a),(b)**.

[120] Under the revision, a purchase-money security interest can only be created in goods and software. U.C.C. § R9-103. *See* § 1.05 *supra*.

[121] This result is accomplished in the 1972 text through insertion of the phrase "or its proceeds" in section 9-312(4). In § R9-324(a), this result follows from the words "a perfected security interest in its identifiable proceeds also has priority."

[122] Only disposition of equipment financed by the purchase-money lender could result in proceeds for that lender.

[123] U.C.C. § 9-312(3).

[124] Bank One, Lima, N.A. v. Duff Warehouses, Inc., 62 Ohio Misc. 2d 481, 601 N.E.2d 678, 19 U.C.C. Rep. Serv. 2d 634 (1992) (failure to comply with notification requirements relegated purchase-money secured party to general rule of priority in time of filing or perfection).

[125] Coachmen Indus., Inc. v. Security Trust & Sav. Bank of Shenandoah, 329 N.W.2d 648, 35 U.C.C. Rep. Serv. 1012 (Iowa 1983) (funds in deposit account).

promissory notes, chattel paper, or accounts.[126] **The revision is essentially comparable.**[127]

This limitation on the extent of proceeds priority might seem highly questionable. After all, inventory consists of goods that are held for sale and sales of inventory often produce accounts receivable or chattel paper. Pursuant to this limitation, a purchase-money secured party in inventory will lose priority in these proceeds to earlier secured parties with ongoing perfected financing arrangements in such property or inventory. The significance of the purchase-money priority in the inventory is thus substantially reduced.

Quite simply, this limitation is designed to favor accounts financing and chattel paper financing. These types of financing are a critical aspect of commercial finance. The danger associated with financing inventory as compared with the accounts or chattel paper that its sale generates are obvious and leave many lenders reluctant to lend against inventory.[128] For many lenders, inventory financing is only one facet of an ongoing financing arrangement that looks predominantly to the accounts or chattel paper proceeds generated by the sales of the inventory. Because accounts and chattel paper financing plays such a fundamental role in commercial finance, the drafters elected to protect the claims of these financers even against subsequent purchase-money secured parties who claim the accounts or chattel paper as proceeds.

Actually, the position of the purchase-money secured party in inventory is not as precarious as it might first appear. The independent financing made available through an accounts or chattel paper financer provides the debtor with funds that can be used to pay the inventory lender.[129] The purchase-money priority in the inventory will serve the inventory lender well in the event the debtor faces financial calamity. The lender then can repossess the unsold inventory free from the claims of other parties.

---

[126] The purchase-money secured party in inventory also loses on accounts as proceeds to a prior-perfected accounts financer. Mbank Alamo N.A. v. Raytheon Co., 886 F.2d 1449, 10 U.C.C. Rep. Serv. 2d 35 (5th Cir. 1989).

[127] **U.C.C. § R9-324(b),(c). This provision in the revision does allow purchase-money priority in inventory to carry over to chattel paper and instruments and their proceeds in certain limited circumstances provided in § R9-330.**

[128] *See* § 3.04[B] *supra.*

[129] U.C.C. § 9-312 Cmt. 8. ("In some situations, the party financing the inventory on a purchase money basis makes contractual arrangements that the proceeds of accounts financing by another be devoted to paying off the first inventory security interest."). *See also* **U.C.C. § R9-324 Cmt. 8.**

CHAPTER 11

PURCHASERS (OTHER THAN SECURED PARTIES) VERSUS PERFECTED SECURED PARTIES

SYNOPSIS

---

§ 11.01 General Rule on Disposition — §§ 9-306(2), R9-315(a)

The priority generally enjoyed by a perfected secured party may face a challenge from one who purchases[1] the collateral from the debtor. The purchaser will seek to establish that the collateral was transferred to it free of the secured party's interest. The secured party will contend that the transfer was subject to its security interest and that the collateral can be repossessed from the purchaser[2] in the event that the debtor defaults.[3] This chapter explains the provisions that govern disputes between purchasers (other than secured parties[4]) and secured parties who have perfected their interests.[5]

Article 9 contains a residual rule that grants priority to the secured party. The 1972 text provides, in part, that "a security interest continues in collateral notwithstanding sale, exchange or other disposition thereof."[6] **The 1998 revision amplifies on "other disposition" by expressly granting the secured party priority as against lessees and licensees from the debtor.**[7] The residual rule defeats any argument that mere disposition of the collateral in and of itself terminates a security interest in the collateral. To the contrary, the starting premise is that the security interest remains enforceable despite the disposition.[8] The rule, however, also indicates that continuation of the security interest is subject to two exceptions: 1) cases where the secured party has authorized the disposition free of the security interest; and 2) other rules that grant priority to the purchaser. To a large extent, the discussion in this chapter is directed to these exceptions.

The overall structure of section 9-306 of the 1972 text has created confusion. It deals so extensively with proceeds that some readers mistakenly assume that proceeds is the only topic. Section 9-306(2), however, also contains the residual rule continuing a secured party's rights notwithstanding a disposition of the collateral. Under the section's basic scheme, a secured party has dual interests following a disposition. The security interest remains enforceable against the collateral, which means that the purchaser's rights are subject to the security interest to the extent of the outstanding secured indebtedness. In addition, the security interest attaches to any identifiable proceeds received by the debtor.

---

[1] "Purchaser" is defined broadly to include a party who acquires an interest in property through a voluntary transaction. U.C.C. § 1-201(33), (32). The term includes, *inter alia*, secured parties, buyers, lessees and licensees.

[2] Alternatively, the purchaser may be liable in conversion for the collateral's fair market value. *See* U.C.C. § 9-306 Cmt. 3; **R9-315 Cmt. 2**; AAA Auto Sales & Rental, Inc. v. Security Fed. Sav. & Loan Ass'n, 114 N.M. 761, 845 P.2d 855, 19 U.C.C. Rep. Serv. 2d 923 (N.M. Ct. App. 1992). The mere fact of purchase does not make the purchaser personally liable for the secured obligation.

[3] Most security agreements make disposition by the debtor an event of default. *See* § 17.01 *infra.*

[4] Priority rights of secured parties as purchasers are discussed in Chapter 10 *supra.*

[5] Priorities between purchasers and unperfected secured parties are discussed in § 14.03 *infra.*

[6] U.C.C. § 9-306(2).

[7] **U.C.C. § R9-315(a)(1).**

[8] The continuation of the security interest had extensive reach in Marine Midland Bank, N.A. v. Smith Boys, Inc., 129 Misc. 2d 37, 492 N.Y.S.2d 355, 41 U.C.C. Rep. Serv. 1843 (1985). The debtor traded in two inboard motors that were subsequently sold three times. The ultimate purchaser took subject to the bank's security interest.

These dual interests give the secured creditor the option to pursue the proceeds, the collateral, or both.[9] Previous chapters have covered the secured party's right to proceeds.[10] This chapter covers the secured party's rights in the collateral following its voluntary transfer to a purchaser.

Another provision of Article 9 that sometimes causes confusion preserves the alienability of a debtor's rights in collateral. Notwithstanding an agreement between the debtor and the secured party which prohibits transfer or makes transfer an event of default (sometimes called a "negative-pledge" covenant), the debtor's legal and equitable rights in the collateral may be voluntarily or involuntarily transferred.[11] This provision appears at first glance to conflict with the residual rule preserving security interests in transferred collateral, but in fact the two provisions are complementary and must be read together. The provision preserving alienability focuses on the *debtor's* rights only. Those rights can be transferred notwithstanding a negative-pledge covenant, but the transferee takes those rights subject to any enforceable security interest unless it can take advantage of an exception to the residual rule.

For example, suppose Manufacturer grants a security interest in its equipment to Secured Party and agrees that it will not sell any item of equipment without Secured Party's written consent. In breach of this covenant, Manufacturer sells and delivers an item of equipment to Buyer. The sale is effective to transfer Manufacturer's rights to Buyer,[12] but those rights are encumbered by Secured Party's interest. Unless Buyer can take advantage of an exception to the residual rule, the security interest can be enforced notwithstanding the sale.[13] In addition, the sale is a breach of the security agreement, entitling Secured Party to exercise its remedies under the agreement.

§ 11.02   Authorized Disposition — §§ 9-306(2), R9-315(a)(1)

If the secured party authorizes the debtor to dispose of all or part of its rights in the collateral, those rights will no longer be encumbered by the security interest.[14] If, for example, a secured party authorizes the debtor to sell the collateral, it effectively releases the purchaser from the reach of the security interest[15] and must rely on its right to

---

[9] The secured party is, of course, entitled to only one satisfaction. *See* U.C.C. § 9-306 Cmt. 3; **R9-315 Cmt. 2.**

[10] *See* §§ 2.04, 8.02, and 10.04 *supra.*

[11] U.C.C. §§ 9-311, **R9-401(b).** An example of an involuntary transfer is a lien creditor's levy on collateral. *See* § 14.02[A] *infra.* Voluntary transfers are the focus of this chapter.

[12] Since the transaction is a sale, Buyer acquires Manufacturer's title to the equipment. U.C.C. § 2-106(1)(sale consists of passage of title for a price).

[13] Production Credit Ass'n v. Columbus Mills, 22 U.C.C. Rep. Serv. 228 (Wis. Cir. Ct. 1977). *See also* Decatur Prod. Credit Ass'n v. Murphy, 119 Ill. App. 3d 277, 456 N.E.2d 267, 37 U.C.C. Rep. Serv. 1736 (1983) (transferee acquired only rights of debtor and was not free of security interest).

[14] U.C.C. §§ 9-306(2), **R9-315(a)(1).**

[15] *See In re* Pearson Indus., Inc., 142 B.R. 831, 18 U.C.C. Rep. Serv. 2d 1267 (Bankr. C.D. Ill. 1992) (authorization is required only for disposition of collateral; it need not include an express release of secured party's interest).

proceeds. If it authorizes the debtor to lease or license the collateral, the purchaser's interest is unencumbered, but the debtor's residual rights remain subject to the security interest. The requisite authorization can be either express or implied.

Confusion has resulted from an apparent conflict between sections 9-306(2) and 9-402(7) of the 1972 text. Section 9-306(2) provides that a security interest does not continue in collateral following an authorized disposition. Section 9-402(7), by contrast, provides that "[a] filed financing statement remains effective with respect to collateral transferred by the debtor even though the secured party knows of or consents to the transfer." The apparent conflict arises because the former section refers to security interests that are severed by authorized dispositions while the latter section refers to security interests that continue notwithstanding such dispositions. In fact, the sections are easily harmonized. If the secured party authorizes a disposition *free and clear* of its security interest, section 9-306(2) properly protects purchasers from the interest's reach. If, on the other hand, the secured party authorizes a disposition *subject to* its security interest, that interest continues in the collateral in the hands of the transferee. Moreover, if the interest was perfected by filing, the secured party need not refile in the name of the transferee.[16]

Revised Article 9 avoids even the appearance of conflict. The residual rule continuing security interests and agricultural liens[17] is not operative if the secured party "authorized the disposition *free of* the security interest or agricultural lien,"[18] and the relevant filing rule states that "[a] filed financing statement remains effective with respect to collateral that is . . . disposed of *and in which a security interest or agricultural lien continues*, even if the secured party knows of or consents to the disposition."[19]

[A]   Express Authorization

Secured parties most commonly authorize disposition of collateral in the context of inventory financing. By definition, most inventory consists of goods held for sale or lease.[20] It would be nonsensical for a secured lender to take a security interest in retail inventory and then prohibit its sale. Without sales, the debtor would not generate the income necessary to pay the obligation owed to the secured party or to stay in business. Consequently, a secured party generally will authorize sales or leases of inventory and look to the proceeds generated by such transactions to protect its security interest.

Even in inventory financing, secured lenders are not likely to give a blanket authorization sufficient to support any disposition. For example, inventory financers typically authorize only sales that are made in the ordinary course of the debtor's

---

[16] *See* U.C.C. § 9-306 Cmt. 3 and § 9-402 Cmt. 8 (as amended by P.E.B. Commentary No. 3 (March 10, 1990)).

[17] *See* § 13.02 *infra.*

[18] U.C.C. § R9-315(a)(1)(emphasis supplied).

[19] U.C.C. § R9-507(a)(emphasis supplied).

[20] *See* § 1.04[A][3] *supra.*

business.[21] Another provision of Article 9 that will be explained later in this chapter automatically terminates even a perfected security interest in inventory if it is sold to a buyer in the ordinary course of business.[22] Because inventory sales that are not made in the ordinary course of business often include features that would be disadvantageous to a secured lender's interests,[23] lenders wisely avoid authorizing such sales.

Another commonly utilized limitation is to condition any authorization on the prior written consent of the secured party.[24] This participation of the secured party near the time of the proposed disposition enables the secured party to protect its interests.[25] It can deal directly with the prospective purchaser to devise a method of payment that will preserve its interest in proceeds.[26] If payments are to be made over a period of time, as when a retail buyer purchases a big-ticket item from a dealer, the secured party can withhold its consent to the sale if the prospective buyer's creditworthiness is less than desirable.[27]

With security agreements that require the prior written consent of the secured party, the requisite consent is often given on condition that the debtor remit the proceeds of the disposition to the secured party. In cases in which the debtor subsequently failed to account for the proceeds, the secured party sometimes has contended that its interest in the collateral continued, on the basis that the debtor's failure to satisfy the condition made the disposition unauthorized. A few courts have accepted this position.[28] The Ninth

---

[21] Universal C.I.T. Credit Corp. v. Middlesboro Motor Sales, Inc., 424 S.W.2d 409, 4 U.C.C. Rep. Serv. 1126 (Ky. 1968) (sales of automobiles by dealer to owner's wife and employee were in ordinary course of business).

[22] See § 11.03[A][1] infra.

[23] The court in Crocker Nat'l Bank v. Ideco Div. Of Dresser Indus., Inc., 889 F.2d 1452, 10 U.C.C. Rep. Serv. 2d 573 (5th Cir. 1989), held that a transfer of goods back to the seller who supplied them was not a sale in the ordinary course of business. The transfer was to cancel the debt owed for their purchase, which would not leave any proceeds to protect the security interest.

The bad faith of the debtor precluded finding a sale in the ordinary course of business in Central Fin. Loan Corp. v. Bank of Ill., 149 Ill. App. 3d 724, 500 N.E.2d 1066, 3 U.C.C. Rep. Serv. 2d 1178 (1986). A car dealer used false pretenses to obtain a duplicate certificate of title for a sale of an automobile in its inventory.

[24] United States v. E. W. Savage & Son, Inc., 343 F. Supp. 123, 10 U.C.C. Rep. Serv. 1093 (D.S.D. 1972) (cattle sold without written consent as required in security agreement).

[25] First Nat'l Bank & Trust Co. of Okla. City v. Atchison Cty. Auction Co., Inc., 10 Kan. App. 2d 382, 699 P.2d 1032, 41 U.C.C. Rep. Serv. 219 (1985) (where secured party waived written consent requirement, but still required prior oral consultation, sale of livestock without consultation was unauthorized).

[26] A secured lender required the debtor to have buyers of hogs issue checks jointly to the lender and debtor, and it informed buyers of this requirement. Sales made without compliance were unauthorized and the buyers were liable for conversion. Lafayette Prod. Credit Ass'n v. Wilson Foods Corp., 687 F. Supp. 1267, 6 U.C.C. Rep. Serv. 2d 1278 (N.D. Ind. 1987).

[27] This consideration is important because the value of the secured party's proceeds from the sale will be tied to the ability of the account debtor to make the required payments.

[28] See, e.g., Southwest Wash. Prod. Credit Ass'n v. Seattle-First Nat'l Bank, 92 Wash. 2d 30, 593 P.2d 167, 26 U.C.C. Rep. Serv. 1346 (1979).

Circuit has held, for example, that the secured party did not release its security interest in cattle until it actually received the cash proceeds from the debtor's sales.[29]

These decisions are incorrect. The authorized-disposition rule is essentially an estoppel rule. Having clothed the debtor with authority to dispose of the collateral, a disappointed secured party ought not be allowed to pursue a good-faith purchaser.[30] The purchaser pays the debtor but cannot control what the debtor does with the proceeds.[31] To impose a condition of debtor compliance would make the purchaser an insurer of acts that are beyond its control.[32] Most courts have correctly recognized that the failure to remit the proceeds constitutes a breach[33] by the debtor but does not retroactively negate the authority to dispose of the collateral.[34]

The result should be different, however, when the purchaser knows that authorization for the sale has been conditioned on debtor remittance of the proceeds.[35] The equities in that situation require that the purchaser take steps, such as issuance of a check naming the secured party as joint payee, that will protect the secured party's interest.[36]

Authorization can be provided by the secured party in the security agreement or otherwise.[37] When disposition is anticipated at the time of attachment, the security agreement itself can include an express authorization provision.[38] Express authorization

---

[29] In re Ellsworth, 722 F.2d 1448, 37 U.C.C. Rep. Serv. 1376 (9th Cir. 1984).

[30] Moffat Cty. State Bank v. Producers Livestock Mktg. Ass'n, 598 F. Supp. 1562, 40 U.C.C. Rep. Serv. 314 (D. Colo. 1984).

[31] In the Matter of Cullen, 71 B.R. 274, 3 U.C.C. Rep. Serv. 2d 815 (Bankr. W.D. Wis. 1987) (condition ineffective unless purchaser can control satisfaction of condition).

[32] Production Credit Ass'n of Baraboo v. Pillsbury Co., 132 Wis. 2d 243, 392 N.W.2d 445, 1 U.C.C. Rep. Serv. 2d 1352 (Wis. Ct. App. 1986) (conditions on authorization to sell are effective only if satisfaction of condition is within buyer's control).

[33] Moffat Cty. State Bank v. Producers Livestock Mktg. Ass'n, 598 F. Supp. 562, 40 U.C.C. Rep. Serv. 314 (D. Colo. 1984).

[34] Parkersburg State Bank v. Swift Indep. Packing Co., 764 F.2d 512, 41 U.C.C. Rep. Serv. 248 (8th Cir. 1985) (sale had been authorized, even though debtor subsequently failed to apply sale proceeds to secured debt).

[35] Lafayette Prod. Credit Ass'n v. Wilson Foods Corp., 687 F. Supp. 1267, 6 U.C.C. Rep. Serv. 2d 1278 (N.D. Ind. 1987) (secured party notified buyers that checks should be issued jointly to lender and farmer).

[36] The same principle applies when the buyer agrees to the condition on transfer imposed by the secured creditor that the buyer assume the debtor's obligations. In re Hanson Restaurants, Inc., 155 B.R. 758, 21 U.C.C. Rep. Serv. 2d 810 (Bankr. Minn. 1993); In the Matter of Dawley, 44 B.R. 738, 40 U.C.C. Rep. Serv. 1893 (Bankr. W.D. Pa. 1984).

[37] U.C.C. § 9-306(2). **The "or otherwise" proviso does not appear in the revision, but no change is intended. See § R9-315, Cmt. 2.**

[38] Attempts by litigants to stretch common clauses in security agreements to include an authorization to dispose of the collateral have been rebuffed by the courts. Northern Commercial Co. v. Cobb, 778 P.2d 205, 10 U.C.C. Rep. Serv. 2d 197 (Alaska 1989) (inclusion of right to proceeds). The Northern Commercial case also holds that the absence of any restrictions on sale in the security agreement cannot be construed as implying an authorization to sell.

can also be provided in another writing,[39] or can even be made orally.[40] The authorization need not even be express. A secured party can engage in conduct from which a court will infer authorization. These cases, often referred to as implied waivers of the security interest, have led to considerable differences among the courts and are discussed in the ensuing subsection.

[B] Implied Authorization

Even though a secured party says nothing that expressly authorizes a disposition of collateral, consent might be implied from its conduct. A secured party's knowing acquiescence in the debtor's disposition has sometimes been argued to establish implicit authorization. Some courts have held that a secured party who is aware of transfers by the debtor and does not object to them tacitly consents to the transfers,[41] while other courts have refused to recognize this as a sufficient basis for a finding of implicit authority.[42]

A purchaser will sometimes argue that authorization for the disposition stems from the secured party's acceptance of proceeds of the sale. If successful, the argument would preclude a secured party from pursuing the collateral in the hands of the transferee to cover any deficiency that remains in the debtor's obligation. Whether the argument should succeed depends upon the conceptual basis for advancing it.

An acceptance of proceeds should not be considered a ratification by the secured party of an unauthorized transfer.[43] Article 9 explicitly provides that a security interest continues in identifiable proceeds and, absent authorization or a contrary rule, in the collateral as well.[44] A secured party thus has a right to the proceeds. The Comments to the 1972 text state that "[t]he right to proceeds, either under the rules of section § 9-306(2) or under specific mention thereof in a security agreement or financing statement does not in itself constitute an authorization of sale."[45]

---

[39] In the Matter of Dawley, 44 B.R. 738, 40 U.C.C. Rep. Serv. 1893 (Bankr. W.D. Pa. 1984) (written consent of secured party for debtor to transfer its equity in collateral to another person); Ottumwa Prod. Credit Ass'n v. Keoco Auction Co., 347 N.W.2d 393, 38 U.C.C. Rep. Serv. 624 (Iowa 1984) (letter instructing debtor to liquidate its hog holdings).

[40] Wright v. Vickaryous, 611 P.2d 20, 28 U.C.C. Rep. Serv. 1177 (Alaska 1980) (secured creditors consented to auction sales of cattle in conversations with owner). *See also,* First Nat'l Bank of Bethany v. Waco-Pacific, Inc., 9 U.C.C. Rep. Serv. 1064 (Okla. Ct. App. 1971) (secured party's promise to release its interest in airplane to facilitate its sale was not subject to statute of frauds).

[41] Vacura v. Haar's Equip., Inc., 364 N.W.2d 387, 40 U.C.C. Rep. Serv. 1493 (Minn. 1985). *See also* Cessna Fin. Corp. v. Skyways Enters., Inc., 580 S.W.2d 491, 26 U.C.C. Rep. Serv. 212 (Ky. 1979) (prior consent requirement waived by secured party's acquiescence in sales of other airplanes subject to same requirement).

[42] *See, e.g.,* Oxford Prod. Credit Ass'n v. Dye, 368 So. 2d 241, 26 U.C.C. Rep. Serv. 217 (Miss. 1979).

[43] J.I. Case Credit Corp. v. Crites, 851 F.2d 309, 6 U.C.C. Rep. Serv. 2d 551 (10th Cir. 1988). *See also* Brown v. Arkoma Coal Corp., 276 Ark. 322, 634 S.W.2d 390 (1982) (no waiver of security interest in trying to prevent distribution of proceeds from judicial sale after collateral was taken by lien creditor).

[44] U.C.C. §§ 9-306(2), **R9-315(a)**. *See* § 11.01 *supra.*

[45] U.C.C. § 9-306 Cmt. 3.

A better case for the purchaser can be made if the secured party has engaged in a pattern of accepting proceeds from unauthorized sales that is sufficient to establish a course of dealing or a course of performance. A course of dealing is "a sequence of previous conduct between the parties to a particular transaction which is fairly to be regarded as establishing a common basis of understanding for interpreting their expressions and other conduct."[46] For example, a course of dealing might arise between a farmer and a bank that have entered annually into a secured transaction with respect to the farmer's livestock, with each year's security agreement including a prohibition against the farmer's sale of any of the collateral without the bank's prior written approval.[47] If, in a sequence of annual transactions, the bank had ignored the prior-approval requirement and acquiesced in the debtor's sales, a purchaser could argue that this pattern of conduct created a course of dealing that implicitly authorized the sale to it under the current security agreement.[48]

A course of performance arises when a contract "involves repeated occasions for performance by either party with knowledge of the nature of the performance and opportunity for objection to it by the other."[49] A course of performance is comparable to a course of dealing, except that, rather than a course of repeated conduct within the context of prior transactions between the same two parties, the course of conduct that comprises a course of performance transpires under the existing contract. For example, the bank's repeated acquiescence to livestock sales by the debtor with respect to the current security agreement could result in implicit authorization to make additional, similar sales under that agreement.[50]

Although similar in that each is based on a course of conduct, the Code makes a functional distinction between a course of dealing and a course of performance. Evidence of either is admissible to resolve an ambiguity.[51] The Code also explicitly provides that

---

[46] U.C.C. § 1-205(1).

[47] The U.C.C.'s "farm-products rule," discussed in § 12.01 *infra*, continued security interests in farm products notwithstanding their purchase by a buyer in the ordinary course of business. The bulk of the implied-authorization cases arose in the context of such purchases. The rights of most farm-products buyers have now been preempted by the federal Food Security Act of 1985, discussed in §§ 12.02 and 12.03 *infra*.

[48] *See, e.g.*, Producers Cotton Oil Co. v. Amstar Corp., 197 Cal. App. 3d 638, 242 Cal. Rptr. 914, 5 U.C.C. Rep. Serv. 2d 32 (Cal. Ct. App. 1988).

[49] U.C.C. § 2-208(1). Although course of performance is defined in Article 2, its use in the context of Article 9 is appropriate. A security agreement is a type of agreement (U.C.C. §§ 9-105(1)(l), **R9-102(a)(73)**), and "agreement" is defined in Article 1 as "the bargain of the parties as found in their language or by implication from other circumstances" including, *inter alia*, course of performance. § 1-201(3). The discussion in this subsection assumes that provisions of Article 2 are applicable by analogy.

[50] Farmers State Bank v. Farmland Foods, Inc., 225 Neb. 1, 402 N.W.2d 277, 3 U.C.C. Rep. Serv. 2d 902 (1987), *overruling* Garden City Prod. Credit Ass'n v. Lannan, 186 Neb. 668, 186 N.W.2d 99, 8 U.C.C. Rep. Serv. 1163 (1971).

[51] U.C.C. § 1-205(3)(course of dealing), 2-208(1)(course of performance). *Cf.* § 2-202 (evidence of course of dealing or course of performance admissible to resolve ambiguity in final writing representing contract for sale of goods).

evidence of a course of dealing can be used to supplement or qualify an express term.[52] The same result is implicit with a course of performance, which can be used as evidence that an express term has been waived or modified.[53] Suppose, however, that a security agreement contains an express term prohibiting disposition by the debtor without the written consent of the secured party. Evidence of a course of conduct permitting sales without consent clearly contradicts such a term. Under a hierarchical provision of Article 1, express terms and terms derived from a course of dealing are to be construed wherever reasonable as consistent with each other, but when such construction is unreasonable express terms control.[54] If this hierarchical provision is applied literally, a course of dealing could not displace an express term prohibiting disposition. Several courts have used this rationale to defeat course-of-dealing arguments advanced by purchasers,[55] and at least two states have amended their versions of Article 9 to overrule prior cases that permitted the use of course of dealing as the basis for consent to disposition free of a security interest.[56]

By contrast, "course of performance" is defined in Article 2, and Article 1's hierarchical provision is silent with regard to the effect of a course of performance. Article 2, however, contains its own hierarchy which, not surprisingly, assigns express terms a higher value than terms derived from a course of performance.[57] There is, however, a statutory mechanism for avoiding the impact of this rule. A course of performance can be used to demonstrate waiver or modification of an inconsistent express term.[58] Again reading the Code literally, a course-of-performance argument may succeed where a course-of-dealing argument would fail.

The distinction between course of dealing and course of performance is somewhat artificial in the context of most secured financing. At the time most of the early cases were decided, Article 9 permitted the use of after-acquired property clauses for every category of nonconsumer collateral[59] except crops.[60] Thus, nonfarm lenders would enter into a single security agreement that would continue to be performed over a period of years, while crop lenders had to obtain annual security agreements from their borrowers

---

[52] U.C.C. §§ 1-205(3). This provision applies without regard to the existence of a final writing. It is consistent with Article 2's parol evidence rule. *See* § 2-202.

[53] U.C.C. § 2-208(3).

[54] U.C.C. § 1-205(4).

[55] First Bank v. Eastern Livestock Co., 886 F. Supp. 1328, 27 U.C.C. Rep. Serv. 2d 1045 (S.D. Miss. 1995); *In re* Environmental Elec. Sys., Inc., 2 B.R. 583, 29 U.C.C. Rep. Serv. 271 (Bankr. N.D. Ga. 1980); Wabasso State Bank v. Caldwell Packing Co., 251 N.W.2d 321, 19 U.C.C. Rep. Serv. 315 (Minn. 1976).

[56] Ark. Stat. Ann. § 85-9-306(2)(Supp. 1975), *overruling* Planters Prod. Credit Ass'n v. Bowles, 256 Ark. 1063, 511 S.W.2d 645, 14 U.C.C. Rep. Serv. 1435 (1974); N.M. Stat. Ann. § 55-9-306(2)(1978), *overruling* Clovis Nat'l Bank v. Thomas, 77 N.M. 554, 425 P.2d 726, 4 U.C.C. Rep. Serv. 137 (1967).

[57] U.C.C. § 2-208(2).

[58] U.C.C. § 2-208(3).

[59] The Code has always limited the effectiveness of after-acquired property clauses covering consumer goods. *See* § 3.02[B] *supra.*

[60] U.C.C. § 9-204(1)(a)(1962 Official Text).

even though they intended a long-term relationship. This practice continued in the agricultural lending community long after the limitation on after-acquired interests in crops was eliminated by the 1972 text.[61] The course of conduct relied upon by a purchaser from a commercial borrower would be a course of performance, while the course of conduct relied upon by a purchaser from a farmer would be a course of dealing. Ascribing different legal effects to the two transactions is inconsistent with the Code's stated purposes, which include permitting the "continued expansion of commercial practices through custom, usage and agreement of the parties."[62] As long as the parties have entered into a continuing relationship, the courts ought not differentiate between those that do so through a single agreement with an after-acquired property clause and those that do so through a series of annual agreements.

§ 11.03 Priorities

When a secured party authorizes disposition by the debtor, the security interest no longer continues in the collateral. The disposition following authorization terminates the security interest that had previously attached to the collateral. The termination avoids any priority conflict between the formerly secured party and the purchaser or a transferee from the purchaser. The situation differs when the disposition is not authorized. Under Article 9's residual rule,[63] the secured party's interest continues in the collateral notwithstanding its disposition. The residual rule is, however, expressly subordinated to exceptions provided in other sections of Article 9.[64] The remainder of this Chapter explains the priority rules that protect purchasers (other than secured parties) of different types of collateral from a prior-perfected secured party. The rights of such purchasers against unperfected secured parties are discussed in Chapter 14.[65]

[A] Goods

[1] Buyers and Lessees in Ordinary Course of Business — §§ 9-307(1), R9-320(a), R9-321(c)

Article 9 provides that a buyer in the ordinary course of business (other that one who buys farm products from a farmer) takes free of a security interest created by the buyer's immediate seller even though the security interest is perfected and the buyer knows of

---

[61] There is some basis for the continued practice. Under the 1972 text, a security agreement covering crops must contain a description of the underlying land. U.C.C. § 9-203(1)(a). Since the land used by farmers often changes from year to year, many lenders require new security agreements annually to ensure that their land descriptions are accurate. **The 1998 text eliminates the land-description requirement for crops. See § R9-203(b)(3)(A)(land-description requirement limited to timber to be cut).**

[62] U.C.C. § 1-102(2)(b).

[63] See § 11.01 supra.

[64] U.C.C. §§ 9-306(2), **R9-315(a). The revision also resolves the "remote entrusting" prob-lem by subordinating the residual rule to § 2-403(2). See § 11.03[A][1][b]** infra.

[65] See § 14.03 infra.

its existence.[66] The rule is primarily designed to protect parties who buy goods in good faith from the inventory of a dealer.[67]

This exception to the general rule validating security interests against purchasers reflects the desire to remove obstacles that would unduly impede the free flow of commerce in goods. When buying in the ordinary course through established business channels, buyers rely on the integrity of the marketplace to pass them good title. The ordinary-course-buyer exception relieves customers who buy goods from inventory of the burdens of checking the filing system for public notices and of negotiating for releases from secured parties of whom they are aware. To require otherwise would unduly impede commerce in goods because of the sheer volume of buyers and because most secured parties financing inventory actually authorize sales of the collateral by their debtors.

As indicated above, the 1972 text provides priority for *buyers* of goods in the ordinary course of business. Should a *lessee* of goods in the ordinary course of business have the same protection? Article 2A governing leasing of goods did not exist in 1972, nor was there a sufficient volume of leasing transactions in the marketplace to justify a special rule. **The 1998 text explicitly provides that lessees of goods in ordinary course of business take their interests free of perfected security interests created by their immediate lessor, even those of which they have knowledge.[68]**

[a]   Defining the Buyer or Lessee — §§ 1-201(9), 2A-103(o)

A buyer must qualify as a "buyer in ordinary course of business" to take free of a perfected security interest. The definition of this term establishes criteria for the buyer, the seller, and the sales transaction.[69] A buyer in the ordinary course of business essentially is: 1) a bona-fide purchaser for value of goods, 2) from one who deals in such goods, 3) in the type of transaction by which such dealers normally conduct sales.

To qualify, a buyer must buy from a person, other than a pawnbroker, who is in the business of selling goods of the kind being purchased.[70] This requirement effectively limits the status to buyers from the inventory of a merchant.[71] The primary issue that

---

[66] U.C.C. §§ 9-307(1), **R9-320(a).**

[67] *See* U.C.C. § 1-201(9)(defining buyer in ordinary course of business) and the discussion in § 11.03[A][1][a] *infra.*

[68] U.C.C. § **R9-321(c). "Lessee in ordinary course of business"** is defined in § **2A-103(o).** **The priority rule is derived from § 2A-307(3).**

[69] U.C.C. § 1-201(9). **The 1998 Official Text amends the section to conform to revised Article 9. Changes in the definition are discussed in the text.**

[70] *Id.* Sindone v. Farber, 105 Misc. 2d 634, 432 N.Y.S.2d 778, 31 U.C.C. Rep. Serv. 329 (N.Y. Sup. Ct. 1980) (goods sold were equipment, not inventory, as debtor did not hold them for purposes of sale). The courts have clarified that sales between dealers can qualify because they frequently sell to one another. Taft v. Jake Kaplan, Ltd., 28 U.C.C. Rep. Serv. 253 (Bankr. D.R.I. 1980); Weidinger Chevrolet, Inc. v. Universal CIT Credit Corp., 501 F.2d 459, 15 U.C.C. Rep. Serv. 197 (8th Cir.), *cert. denied*, 419 U.S. 1003 (1974).

[71] A buyer of farm products from a farmer can qualify as a buyer in the ordinary course of business, but such buyers do not get the benefit of the Article 9 priority rule and, in any event, their rights are determined by preemptive federal law. *See* Chapter 12 *infra.*

has developed with respect to this part of the definition is whether a buyer can qualify when the transaction at issue falls outside the seller's most common business activity. In *Hempstead Bank v. Andy's Car Rental System, Inc.*,[72] for example, a car rental agency was generally in the business of leasing automobiles, but it periodically sold automobiles in its inventory in order to keep its fleet modern. The court characterized the sale of automobiles as merely incidental to the leasing business and therefore held that these sales were not made by a person engaged in the business of selling automobiles.[73]

By contrast, the court in *Tanbro Fabrics Corporation v. Deering Milliken, Inc.*[74] held in favor of a buyer even though the transaction differed from the seller's most common business practice. Deering sold unfinished fabric to Mill Fabrics, which then finished the fabric and resold it in the course of its business. Mill Fabrics lacked storage capacity, so Deering retained possession of the fabric, even after it had been paid for, until it was needed. Deering also retained a security interest in the fabric for obligations owed it by Mill Fabrics under an open account. On occasion, Mill Fabrics sold unfinished fabric to other fabric converters and ordered Deering to make delivery to the buyer. Tanbro was such a buyer. When Deering refused to make delivery, Tanbro sued it for conversion, arguing that it was a buyer in the ordinary course of business and therefore took free from Deering's security interest, which was perfected by possession. The court held in Tanbro's favor.

The finding that the sale to Tanbro was an ordinary-course transaction is not surprising. Although Mill Fabrics more commonly sold finished fabric, its sales of unfinished fabric were consistent with an industry-wide norm and thus reasonably to be expected.[75] **In the revision, a conforming amendment to section 1-201(9)'s definition of buyer in the ordinary course of business ratifies this aspect of *Tanbro*. It provides that "[a] person buys in the ordinary course if the sale to the person comports with the usual or customary practices in the kind of business in which the seller is engaged or with the seller's own usual or customary practices."[76]**

Tanbro's grant of priority to a buyer in the ordinary course of business over a security interest perfected by possession caused a stir in the marketplace. Nothing in section 9-307(1) of the 1972 text restricts the exception favoring such buyers to security interests perfected by filing, nor does pre-revision section 1-201(9) expressly require that a buyer have possession of goods to qualify for ordinary-course status. Nevertheless, possession is a common element in rules that protect bona-fide purchasers,[77] **and the 1998 text reverses this aspect of *Tanbro*. Section R9-320(e) modifies the exception by providing**

---

[72] 35 A.D.2d 35, 312 N.Y.S.2d 317, 7 U.C.C. Rep. Serv. 932 (N.Y. Sup. Ct. 1980).

[73] *Accord*, O'Neill v. Barnett Bank of Jacksonville, N.A., 360 So. 2d 150, 24 U.C.C. Rep. Serv. 779 (Fla. Dist. Ct. App. 1978) (occasional sale of used airplane by seller in business of airplane rental and service held insufficient to qualify).

[74] 39 N.Y.2d 632, 385 N.Y.S.2d 260, 350 N.E.2d 590, 19 U.C.C. Rep. Serv. 385 (1976).

[75] *Accord*, Sea Harvest, Inc. v. Rig & Crane Equip. Corp., 181 N.J. Super. 41, 436 A.2d 553, 32 U.C.C. Rep. Serv. 1005 (Ch. Div. 1981) (sales of equipment were substantial part of lessor's business).

[76] **U.C.C. § 1-201(9)(1998 Official Text).**

[77] *See* discussion in § 14.03 *infra.*

that it does "not affect a security interest in goods in the possession of the secured party," and another conforming amendment to section 1-201(9) states that "[o]nly a buyer that takes possession of the goods or has a right to recover the goods from the seller under Article 2 may be a buyer in the ordinary course of business."

A person must have the requisite bona fides in order to qualify as a buyer in the ordinary course of business. The buyer must be in good faith, must give present value,[78] and must be without knowledge that the sale violates the rights of another person, including a secured party.[79] The latter part of the definition might appear to conflict with that part of the Article 9 priority rule that allows an ordinary-course buyer to take free of a perfected security interest even though the buyer knows of its existence. In fact, the provisions do not conflict. A buyer who knows that a security interest exists qualifies for protection; a buyer who knows that the sale violates the terms of the security agreement does not qualify.[80] The Comments to the 1972 text reconcile the two provisions as follows:

> Reading the two provisions together, it results that the buyer takes free if he merely knows that there is a security interest which covers the goods but takes subject if he knows, in addition, that the sale is in violation of some term in the security agreement not waived by the words or conduct of the secured party.[81]

Suppose, for example, Bank has a perfected security interest in Dealer's inventory of consumer electronics. The security agreement requires Dealer to obtain a check made jointly payable to it and Bank on any cash sale in excess of $3,000. Suppose further that two buyers purchase big-screen TVs on the same day, each paying with a $3,500 check made payable to Dealer alone. Both buyers know of Bank's security interest, but only Buyer 1 knows of the joint-check requirement. If Dealer defaults, Bank can enforce its security interest against Buyer 1, who does not qualify as a buyer in the ordinary course of business. Buyer 2 does qualify and takes free of Bank's security interest.

The courts have disagreed on which definition of "good faith" to apply in determining whether a buyer qualifies for ordinary-course status.[82] Section 1-201(19) defines the term under a purely subjective standard as "honesty in fact in the conduct or transaction concerned." The transaction by which the buyer acquires the goods will be within the scope of Article 2, however, and section 2-103(1)(b) adds, in the case of merchants, an

---

[78] U.C.C. § 1-201(9)(transfer as security for or in total or partial satisfaction of antecedent debt excepted). *See* Fifth Third Bank of Southeastern Indiana v. Bentonville Farm Supply, Inc., 629 N.E.2d 1246, 25 U.C.C. Rep. Serv. 2d 279 (Ind. Ct. App. 1994)(sale not in ordinary course of business where debtor transferred collateral to buyer to reduce balance of open account).

[79] U.C.C. § 1-201(9). Under the definition bulk transferees do not qualify. *In re* Griswold, 18 B.R. 33, 32 U.C.C. Rep. Serv. 1643 (Bankr. M.D. Ga. 1982).

[80] Quinn v. Scheu, 675 P.2d 1078, 388 U.C.C. Rep. Serv. 367 (Or. Ct. App. 1984) (buyer who paid seller after notification that payment was to be made directly to secured party bought in knowing violation).

[81] U.C.C. § 9-307 Cmt. 2.

[82] To purchase in good faith, a dealer-buyer need not search the filing system for outstanding security interests. General Elec. Credit Corp. v. Humble, 532 F. Supp. 703, 33 U.C.C. Rep. Serv. 394 (M.D. Ala. 1982).

objective standard of "observance of reasonable commercial standards of fair dealing in the trade." Over a strong dissent, the appellate court in *Sherrock v. Commercial Credit Corp.* [83] reversed the lower court's application of the Article 2 definition in a sale of automobiles from one dealer to another. Other cases demonstrate the lack of a consistent judicial approach to the question. [84] **Although not dispositive of the meaning of "good faith" in the Article 1 definition of buyer in ordinary course of business, revised Article 9 adopts a definition of good faith that is consistent with the Article 2 merchant rule. [85] Indeed, with the exception of Article 5, [86] all recent Code revisions have moved to a standard that combines subjective and objective elements. [87] Accordingly, future cases are less likely to apply a purely subjective test of good faith.**

An additional requirement is that the buyer purchase the goods in ordinary course. The phrase "of business" is omitted in this context, and thus the requirement is satisfied by a consumer who buys for a personal, family or household purpose. A commercial buyer, however, must do so in the ordinary course of its business to qualify.

In a parallel provision, revised Article 9 provides that a lessee of goods in ordinary course of business takes its leasehold interest [88] free of a security interest even though it is perfected and the lessee knows of its existence. The Article 2A definition of "lessee in ordinary course of business" [89] is consistent with the Article 1 definition of similarly situated buyers. [90] Assume, for example, that Lessee leases a photocopier from a merchant lessor for a term of one year. Even though Lessee knows that Merchant's inventory [91] is subject to Bank's perfected security interest, a default by Merchant to Bank does not place Lessee's leasehold interest at risk. Bank's security interest can be enforced against Merchant's residual interest, [92] but Bank cannot deprive Lessee of its right to possess and use the photocopier during the lease term.

[b] Created by Its Seller or Lessor

A buyer in the ordinary course of business will take free of a perfected security interest only if the security interest was created by the buyer's immediate seller. [93] **Revised**

---

[83] 277 A.2d 708, 9 U.C.C. Rep. Serv. 294 (Del. Super. Ct. 1971).

[84] Frank Davis Buick AMC-Jeep, Inc. v. First Alabama Bank of Huntsville, N.A., 423 So. 2d 855, 35 U.C.C. Rep. Serv. 249 (Ala. Ct. App. 1982) (subjective standard); Hempstead Bank v. Andy's Car Rental Sys., Inc., 35 A.D.2d 35, 312 N.Y.S.2d 317, 7 U.C.C. Rep. Serv. 932 (1970) (objective standard).

[85] *See* § 18.02[E] *infra.*

[86] U.C.C. § 5-102(a)(7).

[87] See U.C.C. §§ 3-103(4), 4-104(c), 8-102(a)(10).

[88] A lessee's "leasehold interest" is its right to possession and use of the goods during the lease term. U.C.C. §§ 2A-103(m), (n).

[89] U.C.C. § 2A-103(o).

[90] U.C.C. § 1-201(9)(1998 Official Text).

[91] Assets that are leased or held for lease are inventory. U.C.C. §§ R9-102(a)(48)(B)(held for lease), R9-102(a)(48)(A)(leased).

[92] U.C.C. §§ 2A-103(q).

[93] U.C.C. §§ 9-307(1), R9-320(a).

Article 9 similarly limits the rights of a lessee in the ordinary course of business.[94] Put another way, only a person who acquires an interest in goods directly from the Article 9 debtor can take advantage of the special priority rules protecting ordinary-course buyers **and lessees.**

The effect of the limitation is easily illustrated. Assume, for example, that Bank has a perfected security interest in Retailer's inventory of main-frame computers. If Corporation buys a computer from Retailer for use in its business operations, Corporation will almost certainly take the computer free of Bank's security interest. The sale of the computer was probably authorized by Bank. Even if it was not, Corporation probably qualifies as a buyer in the ordinary course of business, and the security interest was created by Corporation's immediate seller, Retailer. For purposes of comparison, assume now that Bank provides an enabling loan for Partnership to acquire a computer for use in its business, and Bank perfects its interest. Partnership sells the computer to Dealer, who specializes in used computers. Dealer will not qualify as an ordinary-course buyer (assuming Partnership is not in the business of selling computers), and Dealer will thus take the computer subject to Bank's perfected security interest. If Dealer then resells the used computer to Buyer, Buyer will probably qualify as a buyer in the ordinary course. Buyer cannot, however, take free of Bank's security interest because that interest was not created by Dealer, Buyer's immediate seller. For priority purposes, Buyer is lumped together with buyers not in the ordinary course of business and takes the computer subject to security interests that are perfected or of which Buyer is aware.[95]

What explains the differing treatment afforded Corporation, an ordinary-course buyer who takes free of a perfected security interest, and Buyer, an ordinary-course buyer who is subordinated to a perfected security interest? It cannot be explained in terms of the perspectives of the two buyers. Both made good-faith purchases of similar goods from a merchant, and neither expected anything other than clear title.[96] As is explained below, the answer is based on the doctrine of apparent authority,[97] and thus focuses instead on the actions of the secured party and the business status of the debtor.

Inventory financers invariably give their debtors authority to sell collateral in ordinary-course transactions, although they often impose conditions that limit the debtor's authority. Buyers in such transactions do not need a special priority rule to take free of the financer's interest if all conditions imposed by the secured party are satisfied because the debtor has actual authority to conduct the sale.[98] Suppose, however, that a debtor sells inventory on credit in violation of a requirement that the secured party

---

[94] U.C.C. § R9-321(c)(ordinary-course lessee takes free of security interest created by the lessor). The discussion in this subsection thus applies equally to lessees in the ordinary course of business. The same limitation applies to a licensee of a general intangible in ordinary course. *See* § R9-331(b), discussed in § 11.03[B] *infra.*

[95] *See* § 14.03 *infra.*

[96] Indeed, both buyers are beneficiaries of the Article 2 implied warranty of title. U.C.C. § 2-312. A similarly situated lessee is entitled to a warranty against interference. § 2A-211(1).

[97] *See generally,* Lawrence, *The "Created by His Seller" Limitation of Section 9-307(1) of the UCC: A Provision in Need of an Articulated Policy,* 60 Ind. L.J. 73, 80-83 (1984).

[98] *See* § 11.02 *supra.*

must first determine the creditworthiness of the prospective buyer and approve the sale. Even though the sale is unauthorized, the secured party will lose to a buyer in the ordinary course of business. The rationale for this result is that the secured party has clothed the debtor with the indicia of apparent authority to make the sale.

The Article 9 approach for ordinary-course buyers is similar to the Article 2 entrustment rule. Under that rule a person who delivers goods to, or allows them to be retained by, a merchant who deals in goods of that kind gives the merchant the power to transfer the entruster's rights to a buyer in the ordinary course of business.[99] The entruster loses to a buyer in the ordinary course of business because the goods were entrusted to the only entity capable of selling to such a buyer — a merchant whose inventory is the same type of goods.[100] Similarly, an inventory financer who entrusts its collateral to a merchant empowers the merchant to convey the financer's rights in the collateral to an ordinary-course purchaser. By placing a debtor in possession of goods when the debtor is in the business of selling goods of the same kind, the secured party vests the debtor with indicia of apparent authority.

The basis for apparent authority is missing when the debtor is in possession of goods other than inventory. A secured party's acquiescence in its debtor's possession of noninventory collateral does not create appearances to third parties that the debtor's primary purpose for holding the goods is to sell them. The secured party has not entrusted the goods to a debtor who can make a sale in ordinary course.

Only in rare circumstances would a secured party be responsible for clothing anyone other than its debtor with apparent authority. Thus, the general rules protecting ordinary-course buyers are limited to security interests created by their immediate sellers. If, however, a secured party delivers or acquiesces in the delivery of its collateral to a remote party who deals in goods of that kind, its security interest should be subordinated to a subsequent buyer in the ordinary course of business under the Article 2 entrustment rule.[101] Suppose, for example, that a financially distressed debtor convinces a secured party to permit the collateral to be placed with a dealer for sale on commission. A buyer in the ordinary course of business from the dealer should take free of the security interest under the entrustment rule of Article 2. Under the 1972 text, however, it is difficult to reach this result. Section 9-306(2), the rule continuing security interests in collateral notwithstanding disposition by the debtor, states that it is subject to exceptions contained in Article 9, and this might be read to preclude a court from protecting a buyer under the entrustment rule, which is contained in section 2-403(2).[102] **Section R9-315(a), the**

---

[99] U.C.C. §§ 2-403(3), (2).

[100] Qualification for buyer-in-ordinary-course-of-business status requires that the buyer purchase from a person in the business of selling goods of that kind. U.C.C. § 1-201(9). *See* § 11.03[A][1][a] *supra.*

[101] Article 2A does not have a parallel rule for lessees in the ordinary course of business. Nevertheless, if goods are entrusted by a secured party to a merchant who deals in goods of that kind and then leased to an ordinary-course lessee, the lessee should take free of the security interest on estoppel grounds.

[102] *See* National Shawmut Bank of Boston v. Jones, 108 N.H. 386, 236 A.2d 484, 4 U.C.C. Rep. Serv. 1021 (1967). *But see* Executive Fin. Servs., Inc. v. Pagel, 238 Kan. 809, 715 P.2d 381, 59 A.L.R.4th 553, 42 U.C.C. Rep. Serv. 1185 (1986)(applying U.C.C. § 2-403(2) to protect ordinary-course buyer from security interest created by remote seller).

revision's counterpart to section 9-306(2), achieves the proper result by providing that a security interest or agricultural lien continues in collateral "[e]xcept as otherwise provided in this article and in Section 2-403(2)."

[2] Consumer Goods — §§ 9-307(2), R9-320(b)

Article 9 includes a provision that allows certain consumer buyers to take free of automatically-perfected security interests. Automatic perfection of purchase-money security interests in consumer goods [103] is a practical necessity given the enormous volume of such transactions, but it does create hidden liens. Enforcement of such liens against nonreliance creditors (*e.g.*, bankruptcy trustees) is fully justified. Enforcement against commercial buyers (*e.g.*, second-hand stores) is a closer case, but the policy decision has been made to subordinate such buyers. Commercial buyers of consumer goods should at least be aware of the possibility of hidden liens and ask appropriate questions of their seller. Enforcement against consumer buyers (*i.e.*, persons who buy for their own personal, family or household purposes) clearly goes too far. Accordingly, consumer buyers who give value take free of automatically-perfected security interests unless they know of the security interest's existence. [104]

The priority available through this provision has a narrow range of applicability. It applies only when a secured party relies upon automatic perfection in consumer goods, and the buyer must also intend to use the goods for consumer purposes. The section thus governs only consumer-to-consumer sales [105] and is, for that reason, sometimes referred to as the "backyard-sale" or "garage-sale" rule. The secured party can avoid the impact of the rule by filing a financing statement covering the goods prior to the purchase. Although it is far-fetched to believe that an average consumer will know to check the filings before buying used goods from another consumer, as a practical matter filing is all the secured party can do to avoid the problem of ostensible ownership.

[3] Future Advances — §§ 9-307(3), R9-323(d)-(g)

Article 9 also includes provisions that govern priority between a security interest covering future advances and a buyer **or lessee** not in the ordinary course of business. [106] The provisions provide that such a buyer **or lessee** takes free of a security interest to the extent that it covers future advances made after the earlier of (1) the time the secured party acquired knowledge of the sale **or lease**, or (2) 45 days after the sale **or lease**. [107] Notwithstanding these limitations, the secured party has priority if the advance was made pursuant to a commitment entered into without knowledge of the buyer's purchase **or the lessee's lease** and before the expiration of the 45-day period. [108] The

---

[103] *See* § 7.01 *supra.*

[104] U.C.C. §§ 9-307(2), **R9-320(b)**.

[105] Security Pac. Nat'l Bank v. Goodman, 24 Cal. App. 3d 131, 100 Cal. Rptr. 763, 10 U.C.C. Rep. Serv. 529 (1972).

[106] U.C.C. §§ 9-307(3), **R9-323(d)**, **(e)(buyer)**, **R9-323(f)**, **(g)(lessee)**.

[107] U.C.C. §§ 9-307(3), **R9-323(d)(buyer)**, **R9-323(f)(lessee)**.

[108] U.C.C. §§ 9-307(3), **R9-323(e)(buyer)**, **R9-323(g)(lessee)**.

"45-days-or-less" rule for gaining priority stands in contrast to the "45-days-or-more" rule adopted when a perfected secured party makes a future advance against a lien creditor.[109]

A buyer or lessee in the ordinary course of business will take free of any security interest created by the buyer's immediate seller or lessor and thus does not need protection against future advances.[110] Likewise, a buyer or lessee[111] who takes delivery of the goods for value and without knowledge of an unperfected security interest will take its interest free of that security interest[112] and, accordingly, free from future advances. Thus, the rules regarding future advances only apply when the purchaser is not entitled to priority over perfected security interests and the secured party has perfected prior to the buyer's or lessee's receipt of the goods.

Obviously, a secured party who knows that its debtor has entered into an unauthorized transaction should not expect to be able to further encumber the collateral in the hands of a buyer or lessee by continuing to advance money to the debtor. Even in the absence of such knowledge, the secured party's interest will be cut off with respect to any advances that are committed more than forty-five days after the purchase.[113] Secured lenders thus have a grace period during which to extend advances, but they should be concerned that their debtors have not wrongfully sold the collateral before they extend additional advances beyond the 45-day grace period.

Buyers and lessees will be on notice of the secured party's perfected interest and, as a practical matter, should contact the secured party and disclose the intended transaction before completing the sale or lease. This advice serves two functions: 1) it cuts off the secured party's right to make advances that will have priority against the buyer or lessee (absent a commitment, which can be inquired about); and 2) the buyer or lessee can determine whether the secured party intends to treat the sale or lease as a default under the security agreement. If the latter question is answered affirmatively, the buyer or lessee can take steps to avoid negative consequences. For example, the buyer or lessee might negotiate a waiver of the security interest by agreeing to pay all or part of the outstanding balance owed to the secured party by the debtor. If the secured party will not agree to a waiver, the buyer or lessee should cancel the transaction.[114]

The following hypothetical demonstrates the application of the future-advances provision. Assume that a secured party took a perfected security interest in the debtor's

---

[109] See § 13.03 infra.

[110] See § 11.03[A][1] supra.

[111] This includes a buyer or lessee in ordinary course of business whose seller or lessor did not create the security interest.

[112] See § 14.03 infra.

[113] The court in Spector United Employees Credit Union v. Smith, 45 N.C. App. 432, 263 S.E.2d 319, 28 U.C.C. Rep. Serv. 310 (N.C. Ct. App. 1980), held that a refinancing of the original secured debt, as distinct from a future advance, is not within the scope of § 9-307(3). It denied summary judgment and remanded to determine the extent to which a subsequent loan extended to the debtor well beyond 45 days after the sale of the collateral was a refinancing of the original debt.

[114] In a sales transaction, the buyer's right to cancel is predicated on a breach of the implied warranty of title. U.C.C. § 2-312. In a lease transaction, the lessee's right to cancel is predicated on a breach of the implied warranty against interference. § 2A-211(1).

business assets on June 1. On October 1, the secured party loaned additional funds. If the debtor had wrongfully sold the collateral on September 1, the buyer would take its interest free of the subsequent advance only if the secured party was not committed on that date to extend the advance and the secured party knew of the purchase. Similarly, the buyer would prevail with respect to the advance if the purchase had occurred more than 45 days prior to the advance (*e.g.*, on August 1), again provided that the secured party was not committed before lapse of the grace period (and at a time when it lacked knowledge of the purchase) to extend the advance.

[B] General Intangibles (Licensees in Ordinary Course of Business) — §§ R9-321(a), (b)

With regard to general intangibles, revised Article 9 provides that "[a] licensee in ordinary course of business takes its rights under a nonexclusive license free of a security interest in the general intangible created by the licensor, even if the security interest is perfected and the licensee knows of its existence."[115] The revision also provides a definition for "licensee in ordinary course of business" that parallels the definitions of ordinary-course buyers and lessees except that it eliminates any reference to possession.[116]

A license is a contract that authorizes the use of an asset without an accompanying transfer of ownership. Consider software[117] as an example. A security interest granted by the owner of software covers the owner's right to license authorized persons to use the software and the owner's right to prohibit unauthorized persons from doing so. If, however, a licensee acquires its rights from the owner in the ordinary course of business, the secured party cannot interfere with the licensee's right to continue using the software in a manner consistent with the license. The secured party can enforce its rights against the owner's interest in the software.

[C] Chattel Paper and Instruments — §§ 9-308, R9-330

Section 9-308 of the 1972 text includes two ways in which a purchaser of chattel paper or an instrument can achieve priority over a perfected security interest in the same property. To prevail under either approach, the purchaser must give new value and take possession of the chattel paper or instrument in the ordinary course of the purchaser's business.[118] A secured party, thus, could assure itself of priority against purchasers by perfecting its security interest through possession of the chattel paper or instrument.[119]

---

[115] U.C.C. § R9-321(b).

[116] U.C.C. § R9-321(a).

[117] "Software" is defined in U.C.C. § R9-102(a)(75) and is within the definition of general intangible in § R9-102(a)(42). Users of software generally acquire their rights by license rather than sale.

[118] The "ordinary course" requirement in this provision of Article 9 is individualized to the specific purchaser, as distinct from the "buyer in the ordinary course of business" requirement in § 9-307(1). Blazer Fin. Serv., Inc. v. Harbor Fed. Sav. & Loan Ass'n, 623 So. 2d 580, 23 U.C.C. Rep. Serv. 2d 1241 (Fla. Dist. Ct. App. 1993) (bulk purchase of installment sales contracts was transaction in ordinary course of purchaser's business).

[119] Except for periods of temporary automatic perfection (*see* § 8.01 *supra*), the 1972 text requires

Chattel paper typically arises from a secured sale or lease of inventory. A secured party may: 1) take a security interest in chattel paper without an accompanying security interest in inventory, 2) take a security interest in both inventory and chattel paper and consider each a primary part of its collateral, or 3) take its primary security interest in inventory and claim chattel paper merely as a proceed of that inventory. In the first two situations, a purchaser can take free of a security interest perfected by a method other than possession only if the purchaser is without knowledge of the security interest.[120] When the secured party claims chattel paper merely as a proceed of inventory,[121] however, a purchaser can prevail "even though [the purchaser] knows that the specific paper . . . is subject to the security interest."[122]

When inventory is sold on an unsecured basis, it is usually on open account. Although a merchant might require its buyers to execute instruments, this is not commonly done. Nevertheless, under the 1972 text the rules stated above for chattel paper also apply to instruments. Thus a security interest in any instrument can be severed by a purchaser who gives new value, takes possession in the ordinary course of business, and lacks knowledge of the security interest. If the instrument is claimed merely as a proceed of inventory, a purchaser who otherwise qualifies prevails even though the purchaser knows of the security interest. Note that a purchaser need not qualify as a holder in due course under Article 3 to take free of a security interest in a negotiable instrument.[123] The purchaser need only have the characteristics described above.

The policy objectives that underlie the broader protection granted purchasers when chattel paper or an instrument is claimed merely as a proceed of inventory are comparable to those advanced by the Article 9 rule favoring accounts financers over secured parties with purchase-money security interests in inventory. A secured party's purchase-money priority in a merchant's inventory extends only to identifiable cash proceeds received on or before delivery of that inventory to a person who purchases it from the merchant. Purchase-money priority does not extend to the merchant's accounts, chattel paper, or time instruments,[124] nor does it extend to any cash proceeds generated when the merchant later collects from the account debtor (or obligor).[125] This approach was adopted to

---

possession for perfection of a security interest in instruments. U.C.C. § 9-304(1). With chattel paper, the secured party can choose between possession and filing a financing statement. U.C.C. §§ 9-305, 9-304(1). **Revised Article 9 permits filing as an alternative method of perfection for instruments. U.C.C. § R9-312(a).**

[120] U.C.C. § 9-308(a).

[121] Attachment of a security interest to proceeds is discussed in § 2.04[B] *supra.*

[122] U.C.C. § 9-308(b). International Harvester Credit Corp. v. Assocs. Fin. Serv. Co., Inc., 133 Ga. App. 488, 211 S.E.2d 430, 16 U.C.C. Rep. Serv. 396 (1974).

[123] A negotiable instrument payable to the order of a named person must be indorsed by that person for a subsequent transferee to acquire holder-in-due-course status. U.C.C. § 3-201(b).

[124] A check is an instrument, but it qualifies as a cash proceed. U.C.C. §§ 9-306(1), **R9-102(a)(9).**

[125] In the 1972 text, the purchaser from the merchant is an account debtor if the proceeds are an account or chattel paper. U.C.C. § 9-105(1)(a). The term "obligor" is used to describe the issuer of an instrument. *See* § 9-502. **In the revision, "account debtor" includes a person obligated on an account or on chattel paper that does not include a negotiable instrument. § R9-102(a)(3). The issuer of an instrument, including a negotiable instrument that is part**

protect financers who acquire security interests in accounts because of their important role in the financing of many debtors.[126] No person would buy or lend against a merchant's accounts if another person could obtain priority in those accounts simply by financing the merchant's acquisition of inventory.

Similarly, section 9-308(b) of the 1972 text favors independent chattel paper and instrument financers by eliminating the lack-of-knowledge requirement. The drafters considered them to be too important a source of commercial financing to be hampered by proceeds claims asserted by inventory financers. The interests of the inventory financers were also considered not to be unduly burdened because the proceeds received by the debtor from the purchaser of the chattel paper can be used to pay off the debt owed to the inventory financer.

When a security agreement covers inventory alone, the secured party obviously is interested in any resulting chattel paper or instruments "merely as proceeds" of its collateral. This conclusion does not change merely because the security agreement also explicitly covers chattel paper or instruments. A court can still conclude that the secured party's primary interest is in the inventory and that any additional category was included to avoid the impact of section 9-308(b).[127] This conclusion is appropriate when the inventory consists of big-ticket items that are being financed under a floor-plan arrangement.[128] In a typical floor plan, the secured party advances money to enable the debtor to purchase specific items of inventory and expects to be repaid as each item is sold. When the security interest at issue is a general floating lien, however, the typical secured party relies upon a shifting pool of collateral that consists of the inventory and receivables (i.e., accounts, chattel paper, instruments). Indeed, debtors are commonly permitted to borrow up to a pre-set percentage of the cost of the inventory and a different percentage of the face amount of the receivables. With a general floating lien, the secured party's interest in chattel paper or instruments can hardly be described as a "mere proceeds" interest.[129]

When a secured party has more than a "mere proceeds" interest, a purchaser of chattel paper or an instrument must lack knowledge of the security interest to achieve priority.[130] The lack-of-knowledge requirement does not create a duty for purchasers to check the filing system prior to making their purchase.[131] The rights of a chattel paper financer who gives new value and takes possession of the paper in the ordinary course of its business are not limited by the awareness that a prior filing might exist; and filing is not even a permissible method of perfection for instruments under the 1972 text.[132] When

---

of chattel paper, is referred to as a "person obligated." See § R9-607. This term was chosen because the revision uses "obligor" differently. See § R9-102(a)(59) and discussion in § 1.02 supra.

[126] For discussion of the favored position of accounts financers, see § 10.04[B] supra.

[127] International Harvester Credit Corp. v. Assocs. Fin. Serv. Co., Inc., 133 Ga. App. 488, 211 S.E.2d 430, 16 U.C.C. Rep. Serv. 396 (1974).

[128] Floor planning is discussed in § 3.04[C] supra.

[129] See P.E.B. Commentary No. 8 (December 10, 1991).

[130] U.C.C. § 9-308(a).

[131] U.C.C. § 9-308, Comment 3 (as amended by P.E.B. Commentary No. 8 (December 10, 1991)).

[132] See U.C.C. § 9-304(1) and § 6.01[C] supra. Filing is a permissible method of perfection for instruments under the revision. § R9-312(a).

it is desirable for the secured party to leave the paper in the hands of the debtor, as is common in the furniture field where the debtor continues to collect the installment payments of the account debtors, the secured party can protect itself by stamping the paper or making a notation on it to indicate that the paper has been assigned to the secured party.[133] The stamp or notation serves to notify any potential purchaser of the secured party's prior interest.

To qualify for protection, the purchaser must give new value. The 1972 text does not define what constitutes "new value,"[134] but the courts have refused to recognize a setoff against a pre-existing debt owed to the purchaser by the Article 9 debtor.[135] The refusal is justified on policy grounds. Although the secured party's interest in the chattel paper can be severed, the new value provided by the purchaser is a proceed of the chattel paper that provides some protection for the secured party. If the purchaser simply sets off a prior debt, the purchase transaction does not generate any proceeds that might benefit the secured party. The courts, therefore, appropriately preclude priority for the purchaser under these circumstances on the ground that the purchaser did not give new value. **Revised Article 9 provides a definition of "new value" that is consistent with the foregoing analysis.[136]**

Revised Article 9 retains the distinction between primary and proceeds interests in chattel paper with one important exception. While a security interest that is claimed merely as a proceed of inventory is generally subordinated to a purchaser for new value who takes possession in the ordinary course of business even though the purchaser knows of the security interest,[137] the secured party can protect itself from such a purchaser by having its interest as assignee noted on the chattel paper.[138] Under the 1972 text, this technique was available only for paper in which the secured party claimed a primary interest.

With regard to instruments, the revision eliminates the "mere proceeds" category. It also eliminates the requirements that the purchaser give "new" value and be acting in the ordinary course of business. To take priority over a security interest perfected

---

[133] U.C.C. § 9-308, Comment 3.

[134] While not defining new value, U.C.C. § 9-108 provides that certain persons who take after-acquired collateral for pre-existing claims give new value. **The revision omits this provision as "unnecessary, counterintuitive, and ineffective for its original purpose of sheltering after-acquired collateral from attack as a voidable preference in bankruptcy." § R9-102, Cmt 21.** *See* **discussion of new value in § 8.01[A]** *supra.*

[135] General Elec. Capitol Corp. v. Deere Credit Serv., Inc., 799 F. Supp. 832, 19 U.C.C. Rep. Serv. 2d 933 (S.D. Ohio 1992); *In re* Dr. C. Huff Co., Inc., 44 B.R. 129, 40 U.C.C. Rep. Serv. 284 (Bankr. W.D. Ky. 1984).

[136] U.C.C. § R9-102(a)(57).

[137] U.C.C. § R9-330(a)(1). The revision also gives priority to a qualifying purchaser who obtains control of electronic chattel paper. *See* § 6.04[B] *supra.*

[138] U.C.C. § R9-330(a)(2)(chattel paper must indicate that it has been assigned to an identified assignee other than the purchaser). *See also* § R9-330(f)(indication of security interest on chattel paper or instrument gives purchaser knowledge that the purchase violates secured party's rights).

by a method other than possession, a purchaser must be in good faith,[139] lack knowledge of the security interest, give value[140] and take possession. The purchaser need not qualify as a holder in due course.[141]

[D] Negotiable Instruments, Negotiable Documents, and Securities — §§ 9-309, R9-331

While the provisions of Article 9 discussed in the preceding subsection provide protection for purchasers of nonnegotiable instruments and for purchasers of negotiable instruments who do not qualify for holder-in-due-course status, another provision[142] covers only purchasers who qualify for the highest status with respect to fully negotiable personal property. That provision states that nothing in Article 9 limits the rights of a holder in due course of a negotiable instrument under Article 3,[143] a holder to whom a negotiable document of title has been duly negotiated under Article 7,[144] or a protected purchaser of a security.[145] Moreover, filing under Article 9 does not constitute notice of the security interest to such holders or purchasers.[146]

The holders and purchasers referred to are types of bona fide purchasers for value who are given priority over adverse claims of ownership under Articles 3 (negotiable instruments), 7 (negotiable documents) and 8 (securities). The provision of Article 9 under discussion provides an interface with those other Articles and defers to the results that would follow under those Articles.[147] The 1972 text provides that such holders and purchasers take priority over even a perfected security interest,[148] but that statement is overly broad. **The revision appropriately clarifies that such holders and purchasers take priority only to the extent provided in the other Articles.[149] For example, a holder to whom a negotiable document has been duly negotiated takes it subject to any security interest in the covered goods that attached and was perfected before the document was issued.[150]** Nothing in Article 9 changes this result.

---

[139] The revision makes the good-faith requirement explicit for all purchasers of chattel paper and instruments. U.C.C. §§ R9-330(a)(chattel paper claimed merely as proceeds), R9-330(b)(chattel paper claimed other than merely as proceeds), R9-330(instruments).

[140] U.C.C. § 1-201(44).

[141] U.C.C. § R9-330(d) controls over § 3-306, which subordinates transferees who are not holders in due course to existing claimants. *See* § 3-102(b)(Article 9 controls in case of conflict with Article 3).

[142] U.C.C. § 9-309, R9-331.

[143] U.C.C. §§ 3-302, 3-305, 3-306.

[144] U.C.C. § § 7-501, 7-502.

[145] U.C.C. § 8-303. Even though uncertificated securities are not represented by indispensable paper, they are fully negotiable in that Article 8 provides protection for good-faith purchasers who give value, lack notice of adverse claims, and take control. Control is discussed in § 6.04 *supra.*

[146] U.C.C. §§ 9-309, R9-331(c).

[147] U.C.C. §§ 9-309, R9-331(a).

[148] U.C.C. § 9-309.

[149] U.C.C. § R9-331(a).

[150] U.C.C. § 7-503(1). *See* § 6.02[B][1] *supra.*

This provision shows the risk in leaving fully negotiable collateral in the possession or under the control of the debtor. The security agreement may flatly prohibit any transfers of the property by the debtor absent the secured party's authorization. By retaining possession or control, however, the debtor is nevertheless empowered to transfer the collateral to a qualifying purchaser free from the security interest.[151] Filing[152] and temporary methods of perfection are extremely convenient ways to transact business, but they carry the risk associated with wrongful transfers.

[151] Louisiana State School Lunch Employees Retirement Sys. v. Legel Braswell Gov't Securities Corp., 699 F.2d 512, 35 U.C.C. Rep. Serv. 737 (11th Cir. 1983) (priority to bona-fide purchaser of securities); Bowles v. City Nat'l Bank & Trust Co. of Oklahoma City, 537 P.2d 1219, 16 U.C.C. Rep. Serv. 1396 (Okla. Ct. App. 1975) (priority to pledgee of negotiable instrument that qualified as holder-in-due-course).

[152] Filing is available as an alternative method of perfection for instruments under the revision. U.C.C. § R9-312(a).

CHAPTER 12

THE FARM PRODUCTS RULE

SYNOPSIS

---

§ 12.01   The Rule

Article 9 contains an exception to the priority that favors a buyer in the ordinary course of business over a prior-perfected security interest created by the buyer's seller.[1] The relevant priority provision states an exclusion for "a person buying farm products from a person engaged in farming operations."[2] Even though a farmer's farm products are analogous to a merchant's inventory and a buyer of farm products can qualify as a buyer in the ordinary course of business, the Code does not permit such a buyer to prevail over a prior-perfected agricultural lender.

Several arguments have been advanced in favor of the rule. Buyers of farm products generally are merchants who, unlike ordinary consumers who buy from the inventory of a seller, ought to be aware of the need to check the filed financing statements before proceeding with a purchase. These buyers are, accordingly, in a better position to protect their interests. Agricultural lenders are also somewhat more vulnerable than other lenders who finance the inventory of their debtors. Farmers are much more likely to sell all of their farm products at one time.[3] The policing measures that can detect a retailer

---

[1] For discussion of this priority rule, see § 11.03[A][1] *supra.*

[2] U.C.C. §§ 9-307(1), **R9-320(a)**.

[3] In any event, such a bulk sale by a nonfarmer would be unlikely to qualify as an ordinary-course transaction. *See* U.C.C. § 1-201(9).

beginning to sell merchandise "out of trust"[4] cannot aid a lender once a farmer has wrongfully sold all the crops or livestock. Although the lender's interest does extend automatically to the cash proceeds of the sale,[5] that protection can be meaningless when the debtor is dishonest and the lender is not included as a joint payee on the buyer's check.

The farm-products rule has also had its detractors. The general rule favoring buyers in the ordinary course of business protects the free flow of commerce and that principle, arguably, should apply to agricultural commodities as well as to other kinds of goods. A search of the filing system also was often particularly impractical and costly because of federal laws that require prompt payment for certain commodities.[6] The impact of the farm-products rule was also depicted as falling with undue harshness on small buyers of farm products, who derisively called it the "double-jeopardy" rule. The term referred to the fact that they paid the farmer for the products and then had to pay the secured party a second time to avoid foreclosure.

§ 12.02 The Food Security Act of 1985

In a move that caught farm lenders by surprise, Congress included a section in the Food Security Act of 1985[7] that is captioned "Protection for Purchasers of Farm Products."[8] The Congressional findings for the provision determined that the possibility of double payment by a purchaser who did not discover the existence of a perfected security interest in farm products constitutes a burden on and an obstruction to interstate commerce. Congress, therefore, provided that, unless one of two exceptions applies, buyers of farm products in the ordinary course of business[9] are treated like other buyers in the ordinary course of business;[10] *i.e.*, they take free of perfected security interests, even if they have knowledge of such interests.[11] The federal legislation, which became effective in December 1986, preempts the farm-products rule.[12]

Federal law provides two alternative mechanisms by which a perfected secured party's interest can continue in farm-products collateral following its unauthorized disposition

---

[4] This term is used primarily in floor planning, a type of inventory financing discussed in § 3.04[C] *supra*. It refers to a failure to remit to the lender an agreed percentage of the purchase price of big-ticket inventory items.

[5] *See* § 2.04 *supra*.

[6] *See* Packers & Stockyard Act, 7 U.S.C. § 2286(1994) (full payment before close of next business day following purchase and transfer of livestock).

[7] Pub. L. No. 99-198, § 1324, 99Stat. 1535 (1985).

[8] 7 U.S.C. § 1631.

[9] Although defined by federal law, the terms "farm products" and "buyer in the ordinary course of business" have essentially the same meanings as those set forth in the U.C.C. 7U.S.C. §§ 1631(c)(1)(buyer in the ordinary course of business), 1631(c)(5)(farm products).

[10] The protection of the federal legislation also extends to "commission merchants" and "sales agents" who sell farm products in the ordinary course of business so that they will not be liable in conversion.

[11] 7 U.S.C. § 1631(d).

[12] Lisco State Bank v. McCombs Ranches, Inc., 752 F. Supp. 329, 13 U.C.C. Rep. Serv. 2d 927 (D. Neb. 1990) (federal statute applies retroactively to previously perfected security interests).

by the debtor. One approach is for the secured party or the debtor-seller to provide advance notice of the security interest to the buyer of the farm products. The other approach is to utilize a new central registry that a state may create for purposes of providing notification to buyers who request information concerning farm products. The two mechanisms are discussed below.

[A] Advance-Notice Approach

A buyer of farm products who receives, within one year prior to the sale, a written notice in proper form from either the lender or the seller advising of the security interest will take subject to the security interest, unless the buyer complies with payment instructions that are included in the notice. The expectation is that the secured party will require payment to be made by way of a jointly payable check so that the secured party can be assured of having access to and control over the proceeds of the sale.[13] This approach essentially shifts the burden that Article 9 generally imposes on a third-party buyer to check the filing system for perfected interests onto the secured party, who must locate and provide direct notice to potential buyers.

The advance notice to buyers must satisfy several requirements.[14] It must be organized by the type of farm product affected. It must contain the names and addresses of the secured party and the debtor, the Social Security number or the taxpayer identification number of the debtor, a description of the farm products subject to the security interest, the amount of the farm products where applicable (*e.g.*, where less than all of a particular category is claimed), the crop year, the county or parish, a reasonable description of the real property where the crops will be grown, and any payment obligations imposed on the buyer as a condition for release of the security interest.[15] In addition, written notices must be amended in writing within three months following any material change.[16]

To facilitate provision of effective notice, the secured lender can require the debtor to provide a list of the prospective buyers to which the debtor might sell its farm products.[17] The secured party should require covenants in the security agreement under which the debtor promises to provide such a list and to sell only to buyers on the list. A debtor is subject to a fine of $5,000, or 15% of the value of the farm products, whichever is greater, as a penalty for either selling to an unlisted buyer without notifying the secured lender at least seven days prior to the sale or for failing to remit proceeds of the sale within ten days following an unauthorized sale.[18] The off-list buyer takes

---

[13] Farm Credit Bank of St. Paul v. F&A Dairy, 165 Wis. 2d 360, 477 N.W.2d 357, 16 U.C.C. Rep. Serv. 2d 885 (Ct. App. 1991) (buyer liable in conversion for failure to comply with advance direct notice for monthly milk payments to be made directly to secured party). *But see* Mercantile Bank of Springfield v. Joplin Regional Stockyards, Inc., 870 F. Supp. 278, 27 U.C.C. Rep. Serv. 2d 269 (W.D. Mo. 1994) (buyer who did not comply with payment instructions still prevailed, based on course of conduct created by secured party's acquiescence).

[14] Lisco State Bank v. McCombs Ranches, Inc., 752 F. Supp. 329, 13 U.C.C. Rep. Serv. 2d 927 (D. Neb. 1990) (oral direct notification is ineffective).

[15] 7 U.S.C. § 1631(e)(1)(A)(ii).

[16] 7 U.S.C. § 1631(e)(1)(A)(iii).

[17] 7 U.S.C. § 1631(h)(1).

[18] 7 U.S.C. § 1631(h)(2).

the farm products free of the security interest, even if the buyer knows of the security interest's existence.

[B] State Central-Registry Approach

The alternative approach for a perfected farm-products lender to obtain priority as against a buyer in ordinary course requires first that the state select the option of creating a central-filing registry that complies with the federal law. Such a system must require the secured lender to file with the registry (maintained by the Secretary of State) a notice that is referred to in the federal statute as an "effective financing statement" and that is known to lenders as an "EFS." An EFS must include all of the same information mandated under the direct-notice alternative,[19] and it must be amended within three months following any material change.[20] Once filed it provides constructive notice of the security interest to all potential farm-product buyers.[21] Like an Article 9 financing statement, an EFS is effective for a period of five years.[22]

The registry contains several master lists. One of them is organized around each type of farm product. Each farm-product list is arranged alphabetically by the debtor's name, numerically by Social Security and taxpayer identification numbers, geographically by county, and by crop year. Another master list is maintained of all of the buyers of farm products that register with the Secretary of State's office. That list shows the name and address of each buyer and the types of farm products in which the buyer is interested. The Secretary of State is required on a regular basis to send buyers a written notification of the registered information about the types of farm products indicated on the buyers' forms. The Secretary of State must also provide oral confirmation within 24 hours when a buyer makes a request.

A buyer that does not register with or make a direct request of the Secretary of State prior to purchasing farm products that are subject to a perfected security interest takes subject to that interest if the secured party has filed an EFS.[23] If the secured party has not filed an EFS, even an unregistered buyer prevails.[24] If a registered buyer receives notification from the Secretary of State that an EFS has been filed by a secured party, the buyer will take subject to the security interest unless it complies with the payment conditions specified by the secured party in the EFS.[25]

§ 12.03 A Critique

The federal statute contains some significant deficiencies. It was adopted based on a finding that the farm-products rule burdens interstate commerce. The mechanisms

---

[19] 7 U.S.C. § 1631(c)(4)(D).

[20] 7 U.S.C. § 1631(c)(4)(E).

[21] Lisco State Bank v. McCombs Ranches, Inc., 752 F. Supp. 329, 13 U.C.C. Rep. Serv. 2d 927 (D. Neb. 1990) (perfected secured party failed to file effective financing statement to take advantage of Nebraska's implementation of central-filing system).

[22] 7 U.S.C. § 1631(c)(4)(F).

[23] 7 U.S.C. § 1631(e)(2).

[24] Id.

[25] 7 U.S.C. § 1631(e)(3).

introduced in the statute seem poorly designed, however, to overcome such burdens. They are cumbersome and unlikely to promote efficiency in agricultural transactions. They also impede the national goal of promoting uniformity in commercial law. The alternative mechanisms made available to the states undercut uniformity and suggest that Congress lacked adequate information to assess the desirability of the alternatives.

Uniformity is undermined under either of the two mechanisms used. The legislation leaves to individual states the determination of what constitutes "receipt" of an advance notification.[26] Under the state central-registry approach, each state is allowed to prescribe what constitutes "regular" distribution by the state of written notices to buyers who have requested that notices be sent regarding specific types of farm products.[27]

The central-filing registry, in particular, is a potential source for considerable confusion. It does not in any way replace or operate as a substitute for the Article 9 filing systems for perfection of a security interest. Interests in farm products must still comply with the Article 9 requirements in order to be perfected by filing.[28] The central-filing registry is a creation of federal law that the states may elect to implement.[29] It has relevance only in determining priority between a perfected secured party in farm products and a buyer of farm products in the ordinary course of business.

The federal legislation can serve as a trap for the unwary. By describing the applicable mechanism as a "central filing system" and referring to the secured party's filing as an "effective financing statement," the federal legislation can easily create the impression that it supplants the Article 9 filing requirements for purposes of perfection. Needless confusion is generated by duplicating terms used in Article 9 but assigning to them different meanings.

The mechanisms established in the federal legislation also pose some workability concerns. The provisions imposing fines on farmers who sell collateral to buyers that do not appear on the list of potential buyers submitted to the secured party does not appear to provide sufficient deterrent effect for farmers who are facing financial ruin. In addition, these fines are collected by the government, rather than being applied to compensate the secured party.

The advance-notice approach also creates an incentive for secured lenders to send their notifications to all potential buyers of the debtor's farm products. Rather than limiting notification to the buyers listed by the debtor, the secured party might be inclined to notify other buyers in a relevant geographic area as a hedge against the debtor's

---

[26] 7 U.S.C. § 1631(c)(2)(e).

[27] 7 U.S.C. § 1631(f).

[28] The commission agent in Food Services of Am. v. Royal Heights, Inc., 123 Wash. 2d 779, 871 P.2d 590, 23 U.C.C. Rep. Serv. 2d 949 (1994), claimed priority in the proceeds of its sale of the debtor's apple crop made free of the competing bank's prior-perfected security interest. The court denied priority to the commission agent because of its failure to comply with Article 9 perfection requirements. The federal statute's protection extended to protect the commission agent as a seller but not as a competing secured creditor.

[29] States that have implemented central registry systems include Alabama, Arkansas, Colorado, Idaho, Louisiana, Maine, Mississippi, Montana, Nebraska, New Hampshire, New Mexico, North Dakota, Oklahoma, Oregon, South Dakota, Utah, Vermont, West Virginia, and Wyoming.

wrongfully selling the collateral to a non-listed buyer. This creates additional, unnecessary transactional costs for the secured lender. This incentive to over-notify can also present paperwork problems for buyers blitzed with an extensive array of notices. Because the federal legislation requires only that specified information must be included in notices from the secured party without stipulating a uniform format, buyers must be prepared to assimilate information that will be sent in a variety of different formats.

CHAPTER 13

CREDITORS WITH LIENS ARISING BY OPERATION OF LAW

SYNOPSIS

§ 13.01   Possessory Liens that Arise by Operation of Law — §§ 9-310, R9-333

Article 9 provides priority over even perfected secured parties for liens that arise by operation of law in favor of certain persons who provide services or materials with respect to goods.[1] **The 1998 text refers to such liens as "possessory liens," which is an apt description in that only those liens whose effectiveness depends upon possession of the goods by the provider qualify for priority.[2]**

The classic example is a lien that arises when repair work is conducted on goods like a car.[3] The common law of most states gives the garage that does the repair work an artisan's lien[4] on the car so long as it retains possession. In other words, the garage can sell the car at foreclosure if the owner fails to pay the repair bill. The lien will have

---

[1] U.C.C. §§ 9-310, **R9-333**.

[2] A nonpossessory lien may qualify as an agricultural lien, discussed in § 13.02 *infra*.

[3] Schleimer v. Arrowhead Garage, Inc., 46 Misc. 2d 607, 260 N.Y.S.2d 271, 2 U.C.C. Rep. Serv. 753 (N.Y. Civ. Ct. 1965).

[4] The term "mechanic's lien" generally refers to liens arising by operation of law in favor of persons who provide services or materials to improve land. An architect, who is an artisan, might have the benefit of a mechanic's lien, while a mechanic who repairs a car might have the benefit of an artisan's lien. Go figure!

priority over even a perfected Article 9 security interest because the following elements are present: 1) the services or materials are furnished in the ordinary course of the provider's business; 2) the effectiveness of the lien depends upon retention of possession by the provider; and 3) the lien arises by operation of a statutory or common-law rule.[5] The key point with regard to the last element is that the lien must not be consensual and it must not result from a judicial or quasi-judicial proceeding. Thus, the provider must be neither an Article 9 secured party nor a lien creditor.

The rationale for the priority granted for possessory liens is akin to the rationale that undergirds the special priority granted purchase-money security interests.[6] If a car is in need of repair, for example, its value as collateral will have been reduced. Because the services and materials supplied by the garage restore the car's value, it is only fair that the garage obtain priority in the car for the purpose of recovering its repair bill. The remaining value of the car — the value that was present before the repairs were done — is still available to the secured party.[7]

States provide liens for a wide array of interests. Some liens are rooted in the common law; others arise by statute. In addition to artisans' liens, there are carriers' liens, loggers' liens, innkeepers' liens, and even plastic fabricators' liens. The Code's priority rule is designed to favor "liens securing claims arising from work intended to enhance or preserve the value of the collateral,"[8] and even storage liens have been held to be within the scope of the rule when storage has preserved the value of the goods.[9]

As indicated above, the lien must be possessory in nature to fall within the priority rule of Article 9. It does not benefit a person who never acquires possession of the goods[10] or one who voluntarily surrenders possession.[11] Reacquiring possession of the goods after they have been surrendered will also leave the lienholder unprotected.[12] On the other hand, involuntary relinquishment of possession, such as by a secured party's replevy[13] of the property, will not defeat a lienholder's priority.[14] One court has properly

---

[5] U.C.C. §§ 9-310, **R9-333**.

[6] For discussion of the policy underlying purchase-money secured party priority, *see* §§ 10.03, 10.04[B] *supra*.

[7] The secured party must be careful or this value could be lost. If the car is sold at the garage's foreclosure sale, the purchaser will take free of the secured party's interest. See § 18.02[E] *infra* (junior liens destroyed through foreclosure). Whether the secured party is entitled to share in any surplus (*i.e.*, amount in excess of the repair bill) received at the sale turns on the state law governing the foreclosure. Because of these risks, the secured party may simply choose to pay the repair bill prior to foreclosure and add the amount to the obligation owed by the debtor.

[8] U.C.C. § 9-310, Cmt 1.

[9] Central Trust Co., N.A. v. Dan's Marina, 858 S.W.2d 211, 23 U.C.C. Rep. Serv. 2d 308 (Ky. Ct. App. 1993).

[10] Circle 76 Fertilizer, Inc. v. Nelson, 219 Neb. 661, 365 N.W.2d 460, 41 U.C.C. Rep. Serv. 1079 (1985) (supplier of fertilizer with statutory lien never had possession of debtor's crops).

[11] Forrest Cate Ford, Inc. v. Fryar, 62 Tenn. App. 572, 465 S.W.2d 882, 8 U.C.C. Rep. Serv. 239 (1970).

[12] Balzer Mach. Co. v. Klineline Sand & Gravel Co., 271 Or. 596, 533 P.2d 321, 16 U.C.C. Rep. Serv. 1160 (1975).

[13] Replevin is discussed in § 18.01[B] *infra*.

[14] Finch v. Miller, 271 Or. 271, 531 P.2d 892 (1975).

held that a statutory lienholder that temporarily surrenders possession to a subcontractor for purposes of doing a portion of the repair work does not jeopardize its priority.[15] This is consistent with the constructive possession doctrine available to secured parties with possessory security interests.[16]

In some instances a state statute may entitle a lienholder to file a notice of its lien and return the property to the debtor rather than retain possession.[17] When this option is pursued, the lienholder does not enjoy the benefit of Article 9's priority rule. The secured party does not necessarily prevail, however. The statutory lien is then outside the scope of Article 9[18] and most courts have determined priority under some other law, without application of Article 9.[19]

If the possessory lien arises from the common law, it has priority over even a perfected security interest. The same is true of statutory liens with one exception: A possessory lien created by a statute which expressly subordinates the lien to an Article 9 security interest loses the priority that would otherwise be available.[20] In the absence of express subordination, a statute creating a possessory lien might still have been construed under pre-Code case law as subordinating the lien to a security interests. When the subordination of the lien is based on case law rather than the express provisions of the statute, however, the drafters' position is that Article 9 "provides a rule of interpretation that the lien should take priority over the security interest."[21]

Most jurisdictions have enacted forfeiture statutes under which a government entity can seize property. Sometimes the seized property is subject to a perfected security interest. Although the government's interest appears to be analogous to a possessory lien, the claim of the governmental entity that seizes the goods does not fit within the parameters of the Code's priority rule because the seizure does not preserve or enhance the value of the goods. Resolution of the dispute in these cases falls outside the scope of Article 9.[22]

---

[15] Beverly Bank of Chicago v. Little, 527 So. 2d 706, 7 U.C.C. Rep. Serv. 2d 1272 (Ala. 1988).

[16] *See* § 6.03[B] *supra.*

[17] *See, e.g.*, Kan. Stat. Ann. § 58-201.

[18] U.C.C. §§ 9-104(c), **R9-109(d)(2)**. *See* § 1.07[B] *supra.*

[19] Church Bros. Body Serv., Inc. v. Merchants Nat'l Bank & Trust Co. of Indianapolis, 559 N.E.2d 328, 13 U.C.C. Rep. Serv. 2d 537 (Ind. Ct. App. 1990) (pre-Code law applied to priority dispute between security interest and nonpossessory artisan's lien). A court might grant priority to the secured party under the Code's residual rule. U.C.C. §§ 9-201, **R9-201**. *See* discussion in § 14.04 *infra.*

[20] Affiliated Bank v. Evans Tool & Mfg. Co., Inc., 229 Ill. App. 3d 464, 593 N.E.2d 145, 19 U.C.C. Rep. Serv. 2d 928 (1992).

[21] U.C.C. § 9-310 Cmt. 2.

[22] *Compare* State v. One 1976 Pontiac Firebird, 168 N.J. Super. 168, 402 A.2d 254, 26 U.C.C. Rep. Serv. 1306 (N.J. Super. Ct. 1979) (state statute made seizure subject to prior security interest), *with* United States v. One 1969 Plymouth Fury Auto., 476 F.2d 960, 12 U.C.C. Rep. Serv. 1228 (5th Cir. 1973) (forfeiture to government held superior to security interest because statute did not provide for subordination). *See also* discussion in § 14.04 *infra.*

§ 13.02 Agricultural Liens — §§ R9-317, R9-322(a)(1)

Revised Article 9's scope has been expanded to govern certain aspects of "agricultural liens."[23] An agricultural lien is a nonpossessory statutory lien on farm products[24] that is not a security interest (*i.e.*, is not consensual) and that secures payment to a person who in the ordinary course of business furnishes goods or services, or leases real property, to assist with a debtor's farming operation.[25] Examples include a landlord's lien for unpaid rent on crops raised on the demised premises, a commercial harvester's lien for services rendered on crops left in the farmer's possession, and a feeder's lien for services rendered on livestock that remain on a rancher's land. Such liens arise by operation of law other than Article 9, but once created they are swept into Article 9 for perfection and priority purposes. In other words, once the agricultural lien becomes effective, it is afforded the same treatment as an Article 9 security interest. "Effectiveness" of an agricultural lien is the equivalent of "attachment" of a security interest.[26]

Since agricultural liens are by definition nonpossessory, perfection is accomplished by filing a financing statement.[27] Many of the priority rules contain specific provisions dealing with agricultural liens, inevitably affording them the same treatment as ordinary security interests. For example, section R9-317(a) provides that an unperfected security interest or agricultural lien is subordinate to the rights of a lien creditor, and section R9-317(b) allows a buyer who gives value and takes delivery of goods without knowledge of a security interest or agricultural lien to take free of the interest or lien if it is unperfected. Similarly, section R9-322(a)(1) provides that "conflicting security interests and agricultural liens rank according to priority in time of filing or perfection." If, for example, a bank takes a security interest in a farmer's crops and files its financing statement on November 5, it will be subordinate to a commercial harvester with a statutorily created agricultural lien on the same crops who filed on November 1.

§ 13.03 Federal Tax Liens

The Tax Lien Act of 1966 grants to the federal government a lien on all property belonging to a taxpayer who neglects or refuses to pay taxes following a demand for payment.[28] The lien arises when the following events have occurred: 1) the government has made a valid tax assessment; 2) notice has been given to the taxpayer stating the amount owed and demanding that it be paid; and 3) the taxpayer has failed to make

---

[23] U.C.C. § R9-109(a)(2). *See* § 1.07[B] *supra.*

[24] U.C.C. § R9-102(a)(34), discussed in § 1.04[A][2] *supra.*

[25] U.C.C. § R9-102(a)(5).

[26] *Compare* U.C.C. § R9-308(a)(security interest is perfected when it *attaches* and all applicable requirements of § R9-310 are satisfied) *with* § R9-308(b)(agricultural lien is perfected when it becomes *effective* and all applicable requirements of § R9-310 are satisfied).

[27] U.C.C. § R9-310(a).

[28] I.R.C. § 6321. The best analysis of these issues is M. Cecil, "Bankruptcy: Tax Issues Affecting Insolvent and Bankrupt Debtors," which comprises Ch. 158 of *Business Organizations with Tax Planning* (Matthew Bender, 1996).

payment within ten days following the demand.[29] Once created, the lien relates back to the date on which the assessment was made,[30] and its scope is exceptionally broad, attaching to all existing and after-acquired real and personal property in which the taxpayer has an interest.[31] The lien is a "secret lien," meaning that the Internal Revenue Service need not give any public notice in order for it to arise and be enforced. It continues in effect until the tax is paid or a ten-year limitation period has expired.[32]

Because the lien is secret, third parties, including Article 9 secured parties, who are unaware of it and acquire an interest in the taxpayer's property are potentially at risk. To reduce the level of risk, the tax laws encourage the government to file a public notice of its lien[33] by providing that the lien is invalid as against certain interests that arise before the filing is made. The protected parties are purchasers, judgment lien creditors, mechanic's lienors and, most importantly for our purposes, holders of security interests.[34]

Federal law defines "security interest" to include only interests that have been properly perfected under state law.[35] Thus, under Article 9, it is appropriate to speak in terms of perfected and unperfected security interests, but for tax-law purposes the holder of an unperfected Article 9 security interest does not have a "security interest" at all and has no protection against even an unfiled tax lien. Only secured parties who have perfected prior to the government's filing have any hope of prevailing in a priority contest.

Even if the secured party has properly perfected before notice of the federal tax lien is filed, it will not prevail over the government unless its security interest is *choate*.[36] A security interest is choate if the identity of the secured party, the property to which the interest attaches, and the amount of the debt can all be accurately established. For the secured party with a single loan and a security interest in a readily identifiable asset, choateness is not a problem. If, for example, the secured party has a security interest in the debtor's car and has properly perfected by having its lien noted on the certificate of title, the fact that the car was subject to a hidden federal tax lien at the time of perfection is irrelevant. All that matters is that the secured party perfected its interest before the government filed its tax-lien notice. The secured party will have no difficulty proving the elements necessary to show choateness.

The choateness doctrine is most troublesome when the secured party is attempting to enforce a lien on after-acquired property or on an indebtedness that is secured by way of a future-advances clause. In *Rice Investment Co. v. United States*,[37] for example, a

---

[29] I.R.C. §§ 6303(a), 6321, 6331(a).

[30] I.R.C. § 6322.

[31] Treas. Reg. § 301.6321-1.

[32] I.R.C. § 6322.

[33] In the case of personal property, the filing must be made in a single office located in the taxpayer's state of residence. I.R.C. § 6323(f)(1)(A)(ii), (2)(B).

[34] I.R.C. § 6323(a).

[35] I.R.C. § 6323(h)(1).

[36] Choateness is a judicially created doctrine. The seminal case under the Tax Lien Act of 1966 is United States v. McDermott, 507 U.S. 447 (1993).

[37] 625 F.2d 565 (5th Cir. 1980).

secured party with a properly perfected security interest in the debtor's inventory, including after-acquired inventory, lost a priority battle with the government because it was unable to establish that the inventory it was claiming was in existence and owned by the debtor at the time the government filed its notice of tax lien. Similarly, in *Texas Oil & Gas Corp. v. United States,* [38] the court held that a secured party's perfected security interest was inchoate because its future-advances clause rendered the amount of the indebtedness uncertain as of the time the government's notice was filed.

The Tax Lien Act contains two important exceptions to the choateness doctrine. The first exception, [39] which applies only to security agreements that contain future-advances clauses, allows a secured party to obtain priority for its advances over a filed tax lien if certain conditions are met. To obtain priority for amounts advanced before the tax-lien notice is filed, the secured party need only be perfected. To obtain priority for a subsequent advance: 1) the advance must be made before the 46th day following the tax-lien filing; 2) the collateral must have been covered by the terms of a written security agreement entered into before the tax-lien filing; and 3) the advance must be protected under state law against a creditor with a judgment lien arising out of an unsecured obligation. The period during which the secured party can obtain priority for future advances terminates early if the secured party acquires knowledge or actual notice of the tax-lien filing.

This provision can best be understood by contrasting it with the Article 9 provision dealing with priority for future advances as against a lien creditor. [40] That provision was drafted with the Tax Lien Act in mind and, because of its provisions, the third requirement for priority over the government (that future advances made before the 46th day after tax-lien filing be protected under state law from a judgment lien creditor) is always satisfied. Specifically, Article 9 provides that a secured party has priority over a person who becomes a lien creditor while the security interest is perfected for: 1) all advances made before the person becomes a lien creditor; 2) all advances made within 45 days following the date on which the person becomes a lien creditor, irrespective of the secured party's knowledge of the person's interest; 3) all advances made more than 45 days following the date on which the person becomes a lien creditor if the secured party lacks knowledge of the person's interest at the time of the advance; and 4) all advances made pursuant to a commitment entered into without knowledge of the person's lien.

A few examples will help to illustrate the differences between the treatment of future advances under the U.C.C. and under the Tax Lien Act. Suppose SP has a perfected security interest in D's equipment, which is collateral for a $10,000 loan. The security agreement contains a future-advances clause. On May 1, the government files its tax-lien notice. On May 31, SP, who has neither actual notice [41] nor knowledge of the

---

[38] 466 F.2d 1040 (5th Cir. 1972), *cert. denied,* 410 U.S. 929 (1973).

[39] I.R.C. § 6323(d).

[40] U.C.C. §§ 9-301(4), **R9-323(b)**.

[41] The Internal Revenue Code does not define the term, but actual notice obviously means less than actual knowledge and more than either constructive or inquiry notice. Suppose, for example, the secured party does not know that the government has a tax lien but learns from a reliable source that the government has padlocked the debtor's plant. This information ought to constitute actual notice, and a future advance made after acquiring such information would be subordinate to the tax lien. *Cf.* U.C.C. § 1-201(25)(defining notice).

government's filing, lends D an additional $10,000. SP will have priority over the government for both the original loan and the advance. If SP had made the advance on June 30, more than 45 days after the tax-lien filing, the government would have had priority as to the advance (but not the original loan). The fact that SP was still without actual notice or knowledge when it made the advance on June 30 would be irrelevant. The period of protection for future advances never exceeds 45 days, and actual notice or knowledge shortens it. The only way for a secured party making a series of future advances to be perfectly safe is to check for tax-lien filings every 45 days.

Article 9 operates somewhat differently. Again, assume SP has a perfected security interest in D's equipment as security for a $10,000 loan, and the security agreement has a future-advances clause. On May 1, L, an erstwhile unsecured creditor who has obtained a judgment against D, has the sheriff levy on the equipment. On May 31, SP, who does not have knowledge [42] of the levy, makes an advance. SP will have priority over L for both the original loan and the advance. The result would be the same if SP had knowledge of the levy, because Article 9 protects all advances made during the 45-day period without regard to knowledge. Even if the advance was made on June 30, SP would have priority if it still lacked knowledge of the levy. In short, the tax laws protect future advances for 45 days at most and perhaps for a shorter period; the U.C.C. protects such advances for at least 45 days and perhaps longer. [43]

The second exception to the choateness doctrine applies to after-acquired property clauses. [44] The exception applies to "commercial transactions financing agreements," [45] meaning agreements entered into by lenders to make loans to taxpayers secured by "commercial financing security." [46] Commercial financing security in turn means collateral of a kind ordinarily arising in commercial transactions: accounts receivable and inventory. If the secured party has a written security agreement with the taxpayer that covers commercial-financing security, including after-acquired assets, and its security interest is protected under state law from a judgment lien arising out of an unsecured obligation (meaning that it is properly perfected before the government files its notice),

---

[42] Article 9 does not use the term "actual notice."

[43] The discussion of this area would not be complete without a reference to U.C.C. §§ 9-307(3), R9-323(d), (e) which provide a "forty-five day or less" rule for future advances made after a buyer not in the ordinary course purchases the collateral. **The revision contains a similar rule in the context of lessees. § R9-323(f), (g).** *See* § 11.03[A][3] *supra. See also* §§ 9-312(7), **R9-323(a)** which provide for unlimited priority for future advances against another secured party, discussed in § 10.02.

[44] I.R.C. § 6323(c). This provision also applies to a limited class of obligatory future-advances clauses.

[45] I.R.C. § 6323(c)(1)(A)(i). The provision also applies to real property construction or improvement financing agreements and to obligatory disbursement agreements. § 6323(c)(1)(A)(ii), (iii). Discussion of these agreements is beyond the scope of this work.

[46] I.R.C. § 6323(c)(2)(A). The lender must make the loan in the ordinary course of business and the taxpayer must acquire the commercial financing security in the ordinary course of business. This section of the Tax Lien Act also applies to certain agreements to purchase commercial financing security (other than inventory) from the taxpayer. This is roughly analogous to, although somewhat broader than, Article 9's coverage of sales of certain intangibles.

it will have priority over the government as to commercial-financing security acquired by the taxpayer before the 46th day following tax-lien filing. As with the future-advances exception discussed above, the period during which the secured party can obtain priority for after-acquired property terminates early if the secured party acquires knowledge or actual notice of the tax-lien filing.

As with the exception for future advances, the only sure way for a secured party to protect itself is by checking for tax-lien filings every 45 days. If such a filing is discovered during a search (or otherwise comes to the attention of the secured party), the secured party should move immediately to repossess its collateral. If it allows the debtor to retain the collateral beyond the protected period (45 days or less), it will later have to prove what collateral was in the debtor's hands when the period ended or it will face the inchoateness problem described in connection with the *Rice Investment Co.* case.

CHAPTER 14

PURCHASERS (OTHER THAN SECURED PARTIES), LIEN CREDITORS, AND OTHER CLAIMANTS VERSUS UNPERFECTED SECURED PARTIES

SYNOPSIS

---

§ 14.01 Article 9's Residual Priority Rule — §§ 9-201, R9-201(a)

Article 9 contains a residual rule that renders a security interest, even one that is unperfected, effective against the debtor, purchasers from the debtor, and creditors.[1] This rule is subject to numerous exceptions that subordinate unperfected security interests to the rights of competing claimants, and the ensuing sections of this chapter examine those exceptions. If there is no exception, however, the residual rule becomes the rule of decision.

---

[1] U.C.C. § 9-201, **R9-201(a)**.

§ 14.02 Lien Creditors

[A] General Rule — §§ 9-301(1)(b), R9-317(a)(2)

Article 9 also includes rules that establish priority between a secured party and a lien creditor.[2] The term "lien creditor" means: 1) a creditor who has acquired a lien on the collateral through a legal process such as attachment, levy or the like; 2) an assignee for the benefit of creditors from the time of the assignment; 3) a trustee in bankruptcy from the date of filing of the petition in bankruptcy; or 4) a receiver in equity from the time of that person's appointment.[3] "Lien creditor" is misleading[4] since Article 9 refers to parties with liens who do not fall within the term's definition. A secured party's security interest is a lien, for example, but it is consensual in nature and secured parties are not lien creditors. A creditor may also have a lien arising by operation of a common-law or statutory rule,[5] but again such creditors are not lien creditors. The common element among parties who qualify as lien creditors is that their property rights arise as the result of a judicial or quasi-judicial proceeding. The most important lien creditor, the trustee in bankruptcy, is covered extensively in Chapter 16.[6]

Next in order of importance is an unsecured creditor who acquires lien-creditor status through levy or a similar process. For example, suppose Seller sells hard drives to Debtor, a computer manufacturer, on unsecured credit. This transaction is governed by Article 2 of the U.C.C. Because it is a sale, Debtor acquires title to the drives.[7] Calling it an unsecured sale on credit tells us that Seller chose to convey title without retaining any property interest in the drives whatsoever. In effect, Seller traded the drives for a legally enforceable promise to pay the contract price. If Debtor fails to pay the price as it comes due, Seller cannot repossess the drives.[8] Instead, Seller must file suit against Debtor claiming breach of contract. After recovering a judgment, Seller is entitled to use the state's debt-collection machinery. That machinery is called the "execution" process.

Missouri's execution process is typical and is used here for illustrative purposes. Seller's judgment entitles it to apply to the court clerk for a writ of execution,[9] which is an order directing the sheriff to levy on Debtor's assets. In effect, the sheriff acts as Seller's agent for purposes of satisfying the judgment. "Levy" means to take into legal custody and, in the case of tangible goods capable of being moved, requires physical

---

[2] U.C.C. §§ 9-301(1)(b), **R9-317(a)(2)**.

[3] U.C.C. §§ 9-301(3), **R9-102(a)(52)**.

[4] The term was labeled "gibberish" by one scholar. Mellinkoff, *The Language of the Uniform Commercial Code*, 77 Yale L.R. 185 (1967).

[5] *See* Chapter 13 *supra.*

[6] *See* § 16.01[C] *infra.*

[7] *See* U.C.C. §§ 2-106(1)("sale" means passing title from seller to buyer for a price); 2-401(2)(unless otherwise agreed, title passes to buyer on physical delivery of goods).

[8] U.C.C. § 2-702 creates a limited exception to this rule. Seller can reclaim the drives *in specie* if Debtor was insolvent on the delivery date and Seller demands their return within ten days thereafter (or a longer reasonable time if Debtor misrepresented its solvency in writing during the three months preceding delivery).

[9] Rule 76.01, Mo. R. Civ. P.

seizure by the sheriff.[10] Note that a writ of execution allows levy on *any* asset.[11] The drives may be subjected to levy, but Seller has no more (or less) right to have the sheriff levy on them than it has to have the sheriff levy on any other particular asset, including real estate. The act of levy confers on the sheriff a power of sale,[12] and any proceeds derived from the execution sale will (after paying the sheriff's expenses) go to Seller in full or partial satisfaction of the judgment. The act of levy also creates a lien in favor of Seller and converts Seller into an Article 9 lien creditor.[13]

Under the "first-in-time, first-in-right" rule, a lien on assets acquired by levy gives the judgment creditor priority over persons who acquire property interests in them subsequent to their seizure by the sheriff, but it does not give priority over existing property interests. The U.C.C. contains an exception to this rule, providing that an unperfected security interest is subordinate to the rights of a lien creditor.[14] The practical effect of granting priority to the lien creditor is that the security interest in the collateral will be eliminated by the sheriff's execution sale.[15] Had the security interest been perfected prior to the sheriff's levy, the secured party would have had priority, and the security interest would remain enforceable against the collateral in the hands of the execution-sale purchaser.

[B] Purchase-Money Security Interest — §§ 9-301(2), R9-317(e)

Article 9 includes an exception to the general rule by allowing a secured party to prevail even though it perfects after a lien creditor's interest attaches to the property that serves as the secured party's collateral. Section 9-301(2) of the 1972 text provides:

> If the secured party files with respect to a purchase money security interest before or within ten days after the debtor receives possession of the collateral, he takes priority over the rights of a transferee in bulk or of a lien creditor which arise between the time the security interest attaches and the time of filing.

---

[10] Rule 76.06, Mo. R. Civ. P. Different procedures are prescribed for levy on other types of assets. If an asset is in the custody or under the control of a third person, levy requires that the person be served with a writ of garnishment. Rule 90.01 *et seq.*, Mo. R. Civ. P.

[11] Certain assets can be claimed by a judgment debtor as exempt, meaning that they can be placed beyond the reach of an executing creditor. *See generally* § 513.430, R.S.Mo. (list of exemptions), Rule 76.075 (procedure for claiming exemptions). Each state has its own list of exempt property.

[12] The procedures to be employed at an execution sale are set forth in Rule 76.18, Mo. R. Civ. P.

[13] Rule 76.07, Mo. R. Civ. P. In limited circumstances, levy may proceed from an attachment rather than an execution. Rule 85.0 *et seq.*, Mo. R. Civ. P. Attachment, an ancillary process used in conjunction with a creditor's suit for a money judgment, permits levy prior to judgment. Assets subjected to an attachment levy are held *in custodia legis* pending the outcome of the litigation. If the creditor recovers a money judgment, the assets are sold at an execution sale. For purposes of Article 9, the creditor becomes a lien creditor at the moment of levy.

[14] U.C.C. §§ 9-301(1)(b), R9-317(a)(2).

[15] It is axiomatic that junior interests are eliminated by foreclosure sales, including execution sales and Article 9 foreclosure sales. *See* § 18.02[E] *infra.* Any excess from the execution sale is a proceed to which the security interest attaches automatically. *See* § 2.04[B] *supra.*

This provision operates only in favor of a purchase-money secured party.[16] Its primary rationale is the facilitation of secured sales[17] by allowing the buyer to take delivery[18] without the seller first having to file a financing statement.[19] If a lien creditor's interest arises shortly after delivery, a diligent secured party should not suffer a loss of priority. Although the 1972 Official Text permitted only a ten-day grace period commencing with the debtor's receipt of possession,[20] most states increased the grace period to twenty days. **The 1998 Official Text permits a twenty-day grace period.** [21] The lien creditor is not prejudiced unduly because this type of creditor does not rely upon the absence of a filed financing statement in attaching its lien to property in the debtor's possession.

This purchase-money exception is comparable to the noninventory purchase-money exception to the "first-to-file-or-perfect" priority rule that governs conflicting security interests in the same collateral.[22] The latter section protects a purchase-money secured party who perfects during the grace period from a prior-perfected secured party with an after-acquired security interest in the same collateral, as well as a secured party whose interest attaches during the grace period and who perfects before the purchase-money secured party perfects.

The purchase-money exception also protects secured parties from bulk transferees whose rights arise between the time the security interest attaches and the time the secured party files.[23] A bulk transferee is a buyer whose purchase is subject to the provisions of Article 6 of the Code.[24] Under the 1972 text, the relation-back rule does not operate against any other kind of buyer. For example, suppose Seller sells a computer to Buyer on secured credit, taking back a purchase-money security interest in the computer as collateral for the unpaid price. If Buyer resells the computer to Purchaser, who gives value and takes delivery before Seller files a financing statement, Purchaser takes free of Seller's interest even though Seller's filing occurred within the grace period. **In contrast, the revision permits relation-back to operate against buyers generally.**[25]

---

[16] *See* § 1.05 *supra.*

[17] Although the rule was adopted to protect sellers, it applies to all purchase-money secured parties.

[18] U.C.C. § 1-201(14)("delivery" means voluntary transfer of possession).

[19] In re Moore, 7 U.C.C. Rep. Serv. 578 (Bankr. C.D. Me. 1969) (provisions concerned only with allowing retroactive priority during the applicable grace period).

[20] Secured sellers do not ordinarily file financing statements before goods have been delivered. Thus, the Code selects the buyer's receipt of possession as the triggering date for the grace period even though attachment of the security interest may have occurred earlier. *See, e.g.,* U.C.C. §§ 2-501(1)(buyer obtains rights in goods — a "special property interest" — upon their identification to a contract for sale); 1-201(44)(d)(value includes any consideration sufficient to support a simple contract). A filing before the end of the grace period defeats any lien creditor whose rights arise between the time of attachment and the time of filing.

[21] **U.C.C. § R9-317(e).**

[22] *See* § 10.03[A] *supra.*

[23] U.C.C. §§ 9-301(2), **R9-317(e).**

[24] The Code's sponsoring bodies have recommended that Article 6 be repealed, and a majority of states have done so. *See* Article 6, Alternative A.

[25] **U.C.C. § R9-317(e). Revised Article 9 also permits relation back to defeat the rights**

Thus, Purchaser would be subordinate to Seller's security interest in the preceding example.

[C]   Future Advances — §§ 9-301(4), R9-323(b)

Article 9 also contains a provision that governs priority between a perfected security interest covering future advances[26] and the interest of a lien creditor. Under this provision, the lien creditor takes subject to the security interest only to the extent that it secures advances made: 1) before the lien creditor's interest arises; 2) within 45 days after the lien creditor's interest arises, even if the secured party knows of that interest at the time it makes the advance; 3) more than 45 days after the lien creditor's interest arises if made without knowledge of that interest; or 4) pursuant to a commitment entered into without knowledge of the lien creditor's interest.[27] The absolute protection afforded the secured party for the initial 45-day period was included to protect security interests against liens arising under the Federal Tax Lien Act of 1966, and the future-advances rule is discussed more fully in that context.[28]

§ 14.03   Other Purchasers — §§ 9-301(1)(c),(d), R9-317(b)-(d)

Section 9-301(1)(c) of the 1972 text provides that an unperfected security interest is subordinate to the following rights:

[I]n the case of goods, instruments, documents, and chattel paper, a person who is not a secured party and who is a transferee in bulk or other buyer not in ordinary course of business, or is a buyer of farm products in ordinary course of business, to the extent that he gives value and receives delivery of the collateral without knowledge of the security interest and before it is perfected.

Although the provision seems somewhat unwieldy, it is crafted to correlate with other Article 9 priority provisions. Careful dissection of the language readily reveals the focus of the priorities it covers.

Section 9-301(1)(c) covers conflicts over goods, instruments, documents, and chattel paper. Because a buyer under this provision can prevail only by taking delivery[29] of the property, the section can apply only in cases in which delivery is possible. Accordingly, the section was limited to goods and the forms of indispensable paper recognized at the time the 1972 text was promulgated, and section 9-301(1)(d) was drafted to deal with buyers of intangibles (i.e., collateral incapable of being delivered). In 1972 all securities were represented by certificates[30] and qualified as instruments for purposes of Article 9.[31] Securities were removed to the category "investment property"[32] in 1994,

---

of a lessee of goods, a type of purchaser not covered by the 1972 text. The revision's basic priority rule governing disputes between lessees of goods and unperfected secured parties is discussed in § 14.03 infra.

[26] See § 3.03 supra.

[27] U.C.C. §§ 9-301(4), **R9-323(b)**.

[28] See § 13.03 supra.

[29] See U.C.C. § 1-201(14).

[30] U.C.C. § 8-102(1)(1962 Official Text).

[31] U.C.C. § 9-105(1)(i)(1972 Official Text). Uncertified securities were first introduced in the Code with the 1978 revision of Article 8.

and "certificated securities" became a subcategory. Certificated securities are indispensable paper; other types of investment property are intangibles. For purposes of section 9-301(1), certificated securities should have been included in subsection (c) in 1944 and investment property other than certificated securities should have been included in subsection (d). [33] Instead, all investment property was included in subsection (d), **an oversight that has been corrected in the 1998 text.** [34]

A claimant who buys goods in the ordinary course of business from an Article 9 debtor takes free of a security interest in the goods created by the debtor without regard to either perfection or the claimant's knowledge of the security interest. [35] In addition, certain buyers of instruments, documents and chattel paper are entitled to priority over either a perfected or unperfected secured party. [36] Section 9-301(1)(c) addresses the rights of a buyer not protected under other provisions: 1) a buyer of goods who does not buy in the ordinary course of business; 2) a buyer in the ordinary course of business whose seller did not create the security interest; 3) a bulk transferee; [37] and 4) a buyer of an instrument, document or chattel paper not entitled to priority over a perfected secured party. Although buyers of farm products in the ordinary course of business are listed in the statute, the rights of such buyers are governed by preemptive federal law. [38]

To prevail, a buyer within the scope of section 9-301(1)(c) must meet certain requirements. The buyer must both give value and receive delivery without knowledge of the security interest and before it is perfected. [39] A buyer who qualifies is a type of bona-fide purchaser for value — one who does not meet all the requirements set forth in other sections for priority over perfected security interests. Such buyers are presumed to rely on the Code's filing system and are protected from secured parties who fail to give notice in that system. [40] This rationale also explains the 1972 text's rule limiting

---

[32] *See generally* § 1.04[E] *supra.*

[33] Discussed *infra* this subsection.

[34] **U.C.C. §§ R9-317(b)(section dealing with buyers that receive delivery includes certificated securities); R9-317(d)(section dealing with buyers that do not receive delivery includes investment property other than certificated securities).**

[35] U.C.C. §§ 9-307(1), **R9-320(a).**

[36] *See* § 11.03[C], [D] *supra.*

[37] *See* § 14.02[B] *supra.*

[38] *See* Chapter 12 *supra.* The reference in U.C.C. § 9-301(1)(c)dovetails with the farm-products rule in § 9-307(1), also preempted by the federal law.

[39] Chase Manhattan Bank, N.A. v. J & L General Contractors, Inc., 832 S.W.2d 204, 18 U.C.C. Rep. Serv. 2d 1286 (Tex. Ct. App. 1992) (purchaser was buyer not in ordinary course that gave value and received delivery of goods with no knowledge of creditor's security interest).

[40] The primary method of perfection contemplated by this section is filing a financing statement. If the secured party perfected by possession or control, the buyer could not take delivery and therefore could not prevail. Further, the Code has separate rules protecting consumer buyers of consumer goods from purchase-money secured parties who rely on automatic perfection (U.C.C. §§ 9-307(2), **R9-320(b))** and protecting buyers who rely on clean certificates of title from secured parties who perfect as to goods covered by certificates of title. (§§ 9-103(2)(d), **R9-337(1)).**

relation back to bulk transferees and lien creditors, parties who are unlikely to rely on the filing system.[41]

Section 9-301(1)(d) of the 1972 text is a comparable provision that applies to buyers of accounts, general intangibles, and investment property. Because these types of property are largely intangible,[42] the requirement that the buyer take delivery in order to prevail is deleted. In addition, the section omits any reference to buyers not purchasing in the ordinary course of business because that term is limited to buyers of goods.[43]

Revised Article 9 follows the same basic structure,[44] although it moves certificated securities to the category of collateral that can be delivered. The revision also divides the treatment of chattel paper, logically categorizing tangible chattel paper as indispensable paper and electronic chattel paper as an intangible. It furthermore provides that buyers of farm products entitled to priority take free from both security interests and agricultural liens.

The revision also deals with the rights of two types of purchasers not explicitly covered by the 1972 text — lessees of goods and licensees of general intangibles (other than lessees and licensees in the ordinary course of business[45]). The rights of lessees and licensees are similar to the rights of buyers. A lessee of goods takes free of a security interest or agricultural lien[46] if the lessee gives value and takes delivery before perfection and without knowledge of the interest or lien. A licensee of a general intangible need only lack knowledge at the time value is given. This provision is of particular importance in that most software, a general intangible under the revision,[47] is licensed rather than sold.

---

[41] *See* § 14.02[B] *supra.* The 1998 text's extension of the rule to purchasers is somewhat troubling. *See* U.C.C. § R9-317(e). It makes this relation-back rule congruent with similar rules applicable in priority contests between secured parties (*see* § 10.03 *supra*), but it is reasonable to expect a secured party to be aware of grace-period risks and to take protective measures. A buyer's (or lessee's) reliance on the filing system may deserve greater protection. On the other hand, the revision's approach is consistent with multistate perfection rules first promulgated with the 1972 text that permit filings in new states made during four-month grace periods to be effective against reliance purchasers that acquire interests after the grace period commences and prior to the filing. *See* §§ 9.03[C], 9.04[C] *supra.*

[42] Certificated securities, a subcategory of investment property, are indispensable paper. *See* discussion *supra* this subsection. The revision removes certificated securities to the subsection dealing with buyers who take delivery. U.C.C. §§ R9-317(b).

[43] U.C.C. § 1-201(9).

[44] U.C.C. § § R9-317(b) (goods and indispensable paper), 9-317(c) (intangibles).

[45] As might be expected, a lessee or licensee in the ordinary course of business takes free of a perfected security interest created by the lessor or licensor even if the lessee or licensee knows of its existence. U.C.C. §§ R9-321(c)(lessee), R9-321(b)(licensee). See also § R9-321(a)(defining licensee in ordinary course of business), 2A-103(1)(o)(defining lessee in ordinary course of business). *See also* § 11.03 *supra.*

[46] Agricultural liens are effective only as to farm products (U.C.C. § R9-102(a)(5)), and thus lessees are unlikely.

[47] U.C.C. § R9-102(a)(42). *See also* § R9-102(a)(75)(defining software).

§ 14.04 Claimants Not Expressly Governed by Article 9

Article 9 contains rules that explicitly govern priority contests between a secured party and a purchaser, a lien creditor, another secured party, and certain persons with liens that arise by operation of law. This list by no means exhausts the types of persons that may claim a competing interest. When the adverse claimant does not fall within one of the articulated categories, the court must decide between resolving the contest under the Code's residual priority rule[48] or resolving it by application of rules derived from the common law or equity.[49] If the residual priority rule is applied, the secured party prevails regardless of perfection. The outcome is less certain when non-Code rules are applied.

For example, suppose Finance Company, which has a security interest in Debtor's inventory, permits Debtor to retain cash proceeds from the sale of inventory and to commingle those proceeds with other funds in its general operating account, which is maintained at Bank. Suppose further that Debtor owes money to Bank and is in default on its obligation. Under the common law, Bank has a right of "setoff" — a right to seize the funds in the account and apply them to reduce the outstanding indebtedness to Bank. Who will have priority if Bank seizes proceeds that can be identified[50] by Finance Company?[51]

Bank will, of course, assert the residual priority rule. In deciding whether to apply that rule as the rule of decision, the court must first determine whether the express provisions of Article 9 *preclude* its application. The 1972 text of Article 9 excludes from its scope "any right of setoff."[52] If this excludes from coverage every aspect of a contest involving the exercise of setoff, then the residual rule is inapplicable. Most courts have interpreted the exclusion narrowly, however, to mean simply that a bank need not enter into a security agreement with its depositor to have a right of setoff.[53] In other words, the exclusion merely affirms that Bank's right of setoff arises under the common law and is not a security interest under Article 9. Courts that interpret the exclusion narrowly

---

[48] U.C.C. §§ 9-201, **R9-201(a)**, discussed in § 14.01 *supra*.

[49] *See* U.C.C. § 1-103(unless preempted, common-law and equitable rules applicable).

[50] Mechanisms used to identify commingled cash proceeds are discussed in § 2.04[B] *supra*.

[51] *See generally* Henning, *Article 9's Treatment of Commingled Cash Proceeds in Noninsolvency Cases,*35 Ark. L. Rev. 191 (Winter 1982).

Setoff is only one method by which a depositary bank can gain control of deposited funds. An advantage of setoff is that it is a self-help remedy that can be implemented without the cooperation of the debtor (depositor). If the debtor will cooperate, the bank will be better off having the funds in the account paid to it voluntarily. Comment 2(c) to U.C.C. § 9-306indicates that when cash proceeds in a deposit account are paid to a transferee in the course of the debtor's business, the transferee takes free of any security interest in the proceeds unless the transfer is a fraudulent conveyance or is in some other respect a collusive attempt to defraud the secured party. **§ R9-332 elevates this principle to the text of the act.** Further, if the funds are paid by check the transferee may qualify as a holder in due course and thereby defeat the security interest. §§ 9-309, **R9-331**. The rights of holders in due course are discussed in § 11.03[D] *supra*.

[52] U.C.C. § 9-104(i).

[53] *See, e.g.,* Citizens Nat'l Bank of Whitley County v. Mid-States Dev. Co., 177 Ind. App. 548, 380 N.E.2d 1243, 3 A.L.R.4th 987, 24 U.C.C. Rep. Ser. 1321 (1978); Insley Mfg. Corp. v. Draper Bank & Trust, 717 P.2d 1341, 1 U.C.C. Rep. Serv. 2d 961 (Utah 1986).

then proceed to grant priority to the secured party under the residual rule. A few courts have interpreted the exclusion broadly to remove all issues involving setoff, including priority issues, from the scope of Article 9.[54]

Perhaps the best discussion of the issues can be found in *National Acceptance Co. of America v. Virginia Capital Bank*,[55] where a federal district court was called upon to resolve a dispute under Virginia law. Since Virginia's courts had not ruled on the proper interpretation of the exclusion for rights of setoff, the district court gave alternative analyses. Under a narrow interpretation, of course, the party claiming a security interest in the deposited funds would prevail under Article 9's residual rule. Under a broad interpretation, resolution would turn on non-Code law. The court found that the non-Code law of Virginia follows the majority rule that a bank exercising setoff is subordinate to an adverse claimant if it knows or has reason to know of the claimant's interest.[56] Because the evidence indicated that the bank had (at a minimum) notice of the secured party's interest, the court concluded that the secured party would prevail under either a narrow or broad interpretation.

Under revised Article 9, a secured party can assert a security interest in funds on deposit if they represent identifiable proceeds of its collateral,[57] or, except in a consumer transaction, it can acquire a security interest in an entire deposit account as original collateral.[58] If the security interest is a proceeds interest, the analysis set forth above in connection with the 1972 text remains applicable.[59] If, however, the interest is a nonproceeds interest in a deposit account, the revision provides that an exercise of setoff is ineffective if the secured party has perfected its interest by control under section R9-104(a)(3)[60] This section permits a secured party to obtain control by becoming the named customer on the deposit account. If the secured party instead utilizes a control agreement under the alternative procedure of section R9-104(a)(2),[61] it should make certain that the agreement provides for the subordination of any setoff rights held by the bank that maintains the account.[62]

A bank exercising setoff is but one example of a third party whose rights are not expressly governed by the provisions of Article 9. In each such instance, the court must

---

[54] *See, e.g.,* State Bank of Rose Creek v. First Bank of Austin, 320 N.W.2d 723, 33 U.C.C. Rep. Serv. 1755 (Minn. 1982).

[55] 498 F. Supp. 1078, 30 U.C.C. Rep. Serv. 1145 (E.D. Va. 1980).

[56] The majority rule is sometimes referred to as the "legal" rule. Under the minority, or "equitable," rule a third-party claimant has priority even if the bank exercising setoff lacks knowledge or notice.

[57] U.C.C. § R9-315(a)(2).

[58] U.C.C. § R9-109(d)(13)(narrowing exclusion from Article 9 to assignments of deposit accounts in consumer transactions). Even in a consumer transaction, a secured party can attempt to trace proceeds into a deposit account. *Id.*

[59] *See* U.C.C. § R9-109(d)(10)(excluding right of setoff).

[60] Control of deposit accounts is discussed generally in § 6.04[b] *supra.*

[61] A bank is not under a duty to enter into a control agreement. § R9-342.

[62] Parties can alter the Code's normal priority rules through a subordination agreement. U.C.C. §§ 9-316, **R9-339.**

(Matthew Bender & Co., Inc.)

decide whether to confer priority on the secured party through application of the residual rule or to decide the case based on the non-Code law of the state.

CHAPTER 15

FIXTURES, ACCESSIONS AND PRODUCTS

SYNOPSIS

---

§ 15.01 Fixtures Defined — §§ 9-313(1)(a),(2), R9-102(a)(41)

The U.C.C. defines "fixtures" as goods that have become so related to a particular parcel of land that an interest in those goods arises under applicable real estate law.[1] Thus, although Article 9 establishes a complex system of perfection and priority for security interests in fixtures, it leaves the basic definition of "fixtures" to the non-Code law of the jurisdiction. Under real estate law, a fixture is an item of personalty so affixed to land or to a structure on land that a purchaser[2] would believe that it would pass with a deed to the land. A fixture does not lose its separate identity and become merged into the realty for all purposes, however; as a result, it can be removed from the realty and sold at an Article 9 foreclosure sale. In other words, a fixture has attributes associated with both realty and personalty. An Article 9 secured party can have a security interest in a fixture,[3] but a buyer of the land would expect to become the owner of the fixture and a mortgagee would expect the fixture to serve as collateral for a mortgage loan. Because of the potential conflict between a secured party (with an interest in the fixture as personalty) and parties with an interest in the fixture as realty, the U.C.C. contains provisions that encourage secured parties to place notices of their interests in the real estate records.

Whether a particular asset qualifies as a fixture under real estate law is determined by a facts-and-circumstances test, which leads the courts to focus on three elements: 1) the intent of the annexor;[4] 2) the degree of physical affixation to the realty; and 3) the degree to which the asset is adapted to the particular characteristics of the real estate. Although the intent of the annexor is important when the dispute is between the secured party and the party who owned the land at the time of affixation,[5] it is largely ignored by the courts when the dispute is between the secured party and subsequent purchasers. Such purchasers will have relied on appearances in deciding whether to buy the land or to make a loan, and their reasonable expectations outweigh the hidden intentions of the annexor.

Accordingly, in most disputes involving whether a good constitutes a fixture, the issue turns on the degree of affixation and adaptation. A good that is plugged into the wall

---

[1] U.C.C. §§ 9-313(1)(a); R9-102(a)(41).

[2] Under both the Code and real estate law, the term "purchaser" includes, at a minimum, both buyers and mortgagees. *See* U.C.C. §§ 1-201(32), (33).

[3] The Code does provide, however, that an Article 9 security interest cannot exist in "ordinary building materials incorporated into an improvement on land." U.C.C. § 9-313(2); **R9-334(a).** For classification purposes, then, there are three categories of goods: 1) goods that are pure personalty; 2) goods that are so affixed to land that they qualify as fixtures under local real estate law but are not "ordinary building materials incorporated into an improvement on land"; 3) goods that are so integrally incorporated into a structure that they lose their separate identity and become merged into the land for all purposes. Included within category 3) are virtually all "ordinary building materials incorporated into an improvement on land" (*e.g.*, nails and lumber after being used to construct a home). Sections 9-313 and **R9-334** deal only with goods in the second category.

[4] The "annexor" is the person affixing the asset to the realty.

[5] If the asset would not be considered a fixture in a contest between the annexor and the owner of the land, it should not be considered a fixture when the secured party is asserting its rights against that owner.

is "affixed" to the land, but a court would not likely characterize it as a fixture. If a couple of screws connect a good to the land to keep it from vibrating, it may or may not be a fixture. If the good is so deeply attached to or embedded in the real estate that one could not remove it without hours of intensive labor, the good is almost certainly a fixture. Adaptation comes into play when the physical connection between the good and the land is slight but the good has been specially designed to fit into a particular area. For example, drapes that are loosely attached but that are specially designed for a particular room may qualify as fixtures. [6]

Certain goods become so embedded in the land that they lose their individual identity and become purely part of the land. Many houses, for example, are technically movable [7] in that they can be lifted from their foundations; as a whole, however, a court will characterize a house as pure real estate. [8] Likewise, real estate law considers most ordinary building materials that have been incorporated into a structure — such as bricks and mortar — to be pure realty. Real estate law does not treat such materials as fixtures, because they are unlikely to retain their integrity and/or their value once removed from the land.

Conceptually, some ordinary building materials may qualify as fixtures under non-Code law (not as pure realty) and yet should not be subject to an Article 9 security interest as a matter of policy. For example, the bricks used to erect a house might still have separate value if removed from the house, but no Article 9 secured party should be able to remove the bricks because doing so will destroy the economic value of the structure. Although removing a fixture often requires the secured party to inflict some physical damage to the land and often decreases the land's fair market value, it would be wasteful to allow a secured party to disassemble a structure piecemeal and thereby destroy its capacity to carry out the basic functions for which it was designed. Accordingly, the Code precludes parties from maintaining a security interest in ordinary building materials once they have been incorporated into an improvement, *regardless* of their classification under real estate law. [9] The distinction is more theoretical than practical. Any ordinary building materials that are so incorporated would almost certainly be classified as pure realty under non-Code state law. [10]

§ 15.02 Fixture Filings — §§ 9-313(1)(b), R9-102(a)(40)

As indicated in the preceding section, disputes involving fixtures often pit an Article 9 secured party against a buyer or mortgagee of the land. One who buys land after a good has been affixed likely will have relied on acquiring an interest in that good in

---

[6] *See, e.g.,* Sears, Roebuck & Co. v. Seven Palms Motor Inn, 530 S.W.2d 695 (Mo. 1975). The concept of adaptation is sometimes called "constructive annexation."

[7] "Goods" are "all things which are movable at the time the security interest attaches or which are fixtures." U.C.C. §§ 9-105(1)(h); **R9-102(a)(44)**. *Cf.* § 2-107.

[8] Smaller structures such as sheds may qualify as goods.

[9] U.C.C. § 9-313(2); **R9-334(a)**.

[10] An unpaid supplier of building materials typically acquires a mechanic's lien, giving it a right to foreclose on the land (as opposed to any specific materials). The creation and enforcement of mechanics' liens is beyond the scope of this book.

(Matthew Bender & Co., Inc.)

deciding on a purchase price; likewise, one who takes a mortgage upon land after affixation likely will have relied upon acquiring an interest in that good in determining the mortgage loan amount. Thus, any system that permits a security interest in such goods should provide for notice of that security interest in the chain of title to the land.

Article 9 facilitates this notice through the "fixture filing." Under the 1972 text, a fixture filing is a financing statement that describes goods that are or are to become fixtures and conforms to the requirements of Section 9-402(5).[11] Section 9-402(5) provides in relevant part:

> a financing statement filed as a fixture filing (Section 9-313) where the debtor is not a transmitting utility,[12] must show that it covers this type of collateral, must recite that it is to be filed [for record] in the real estate records, and the financing statement must contain a description of the real estate [sufficient if it were contained in a mortgage of the real estate to give constructive notice of the mortgage under the law of this state]. If the debtor does not have an interest of record in the real estate, the financing statement must show the name of the record owner.

A substantially similar definition appears in revised Article 9.[13] As one might expect, the Code dictates that fixture filings be made in the office where a mortgage on the underlying real estate would be filed or recorded.[14]

In other words, to serve as a fixture filing, an ordinary financing statement must be adapted so that it can serve the functions of the real estate recording system[15] and the filing officer who normally files financing statements in the chattel records must be instructed to index the fixture filing into the land records.[16] To do so, the filing officer must have the name of the record owner of the land, if that owner is someone other than the debtor. As we shall see, many (but not all) priority contests turn on whether the secured party has made a timely fixture filing.

---

[11] U.C.C. § 9-313(1)(b).

[12] The Code contains special provisions allowing a security interest in the land-related assets of a transmitting utility to be perfected by a single, central filing that has the effect of a fixture filing and that remains effective until a termination statement is filed. The rationale is that many utilities span large parts of a state, such that the normal fixture filing rules would require filings in multiple counties. See U.C.C. §§ 9-105(n), **R9-102(a)(80)** (defining "transmitting utility"); §§ 9-401(5), **R9-501(b)** (central filing operates as a fixture filing); §§ 9-403(6), **R9-515(f)** (duration of filing).

[13] U.C.C. §§ **R9-102(a)(40), R9-502(b)**.

[14] U.C.C. §§ 9-401(1)(b)(all three alternatives); **R9-501(a)(1)(B)**.

[15] A recorded mortgage can serve as a fixture filing if the mortgage sufficiently describes the goods, if the goods are or will become fixtures to the land described in the mortgage, and if the mortgage contains all the information necessary for a valid financing statement (other than an instruction directing that it be filed in the land records). U.C.C. §§ 9-402(6); **R9-502(c)**. When a mortgage serves as a valid fixture filing, it remains effective until the secured debt is released or satisfied of record. U.C.C. §§ 9-403(6); **R9-515(g)**.

[16] If the fixture filing is in proper form and is presented for filing with the proper fees, the secured party is perfected even if the filing officer mistakenly files it in the chattel records. U.C.C. §§ 9-403(1); **R9-516(a), R9-517**.

§ 15.03 Priorities in Fixtures

[A] The Code's Residual Rule — §§ 9-313(7), R9-334(c)

The Code's residual priority rule is set forth in section 9-313(7) of the 1972 text, which provides that "a security interest in fixtures is subordinate to the conflicting interest of an encumbrancer [17] or owner of the related real estate who is not the debtor." **Revised Article 9 provides the same residual priority rule.** [18] Thus, in contrast to the Code's residual rule for priorities generally, [19] the residual rule for priority in fixtures is that the secured party loses. The potential reach of this residual rule, however, is limited by a number of exceptions that, if satisfied, enable an Article 9 secured party with a security interest in fixtures to take priority over certain conflicting real estate interests. The most significant exception to the residual rule is the purchase-money priority rule. [20] In practice, most Article 9 secured parties who take a security interest in goods that become fixtures have purchase-money security interests; accordingly, we begin our discussion of the exceptions with the purchase-money priority rule.

[B] The Purchase-Money Priority Exception — §§ 9-313(4)(a), R9-334(d)

The 1972 text's purchase-money priority exception to the residual rule provides that a party holding a perfected security interest in fixtures has priority over the conflicting claim of an encumbrancer or owner of the related land where:

> the security interest is a purchase money security interest, the interest of the encumbrancer or owner arises before the goods become fixtures, the security interest is perfected by a fixture filing before the goods become fixtures or within ten days thereafter, and the debtor has an interest of record in the real estate or is in possession of the real estate . . . . [21]

The revision contains a similar purchase-money exception, although the grace period for making a fixture filing is extended to twenty days following affixation. [22]

One should note that the purchase-money priority exception does not provide protection against real estate interests that arise *after an asset becomes a fixture.* As explained earlier, buyers and mortgagees of land and fixtures may rely upon the presence of the fixture and the absence of conflicting claims in the land records; [23] for a secured party's conflicting interest in existing fixtures that have been relied upon to take priority, there

---

[17] "Encumbrance" is defined in U.C.C. § 9-105(1)(g) to include "real estate mortgages and other liens on real estate and all other rights in real estate that are not ownership interests." **A similar definition appears in § R9-102(a)(32).**

[18] U.C.C. § R9-334(c).

[19] Under the Code's normal residual rule, U.C.C. §§ 9-201; **R9-201(a)**, the secured party *wins* unless other provisions dictate a contrary result.

[20] U.C.C. §§ 9-313(4)(a), **R9-334(d)**.

[21] U.C.C. §§ 9-313(4)(a).

[22] U.C.C. § R9-334(d).

[23] A buyer or mortgagee may not actually rely on fixtures in a particular case, but the priority rules are predicated on the assumption of reliance.

should be notice in the chain of title to the land. Thus, the grace period for making a fixture filing is not a "relation back" rule.[24]

For example, suppose that Secured Party sells Grocer a walk-in freezer on credit and takes back a purchase-money security interest. On August 1, Grocer installs the freezer in its store and it qualifies as a fixture under local real estate law. On August 5, Grocer and Bank hold a mortgage loan closing and Grocer grants Bank a mortgage on the store. On August 9, within ten days after the freezer became a fixture, Secured Party makes a proper fixture filing. Secured Party cannot claim purchase-money priority over Bank, and thus Bank's mortgage will take priority over Secured Party's interest under the residual priority rule. This result makes sense; as Bank's title search would not have revealed Secured Party's interest, a reasonable person in Bank's position would have concluded that the freezer was unencumbered.

The purchase-money priority exception operates against parties whose interests arose before the good became a fixture and who thus could not reasonably have relied on acquiring an interest in the good. For example, suppose that Bank had acquired its mortgage on Grocer's land before Secured Party sold the freezer to Grocer. In this example, granting purchase-money priority to Secured Party facilitates commerce by encouraging credit sales and has no deleterious effect on Bank, because Bank did not rely on the freezer in making its loan.[25] One might ask why any form of perfection — much less a fixture filing — is necessary to enable a purchase-money creditor like Secured Party to prevail over Bank in this example (assuming Bank has made no future advances after the good became a fixture).[26] Nevertheless, for purchase-money priority, the Code requires a fixture filing within the grace period after the goods become fixtures.

Finally, suppose that Secured Party sells an asset to Contractor, who is doing remodeling work on Owner's building, and takes back a purchase-money security interest. Suppose further that Bank holds a previously recorded mortgage on Owner's land. Even Secured Party makes a fixture filing within ten days after the asset becomes a fixture, will not obtain priority over Bank. Because Contractor, the Article 9 debtor, had neither n interest of record in the land nor possession of the land, the purchase-money priority ception does not apply. Therefore, Bank takes priority under the residual priority rule.[27]

---

[24] U.C.C. § 9-313 Cmt. 4.

[25] Indeed, the drafters assumed that in most instances involving mortgagees, who are usually institutional lenders and can afford to take a long-term view, the purchase-money priority rule would have a beneficial effect by encouraging mortgagors to modernize their facilities. *See* U.C.C. § 9-313 Cmt. 8.

Any adverse effect of the purchase-money priority exception is mitigated by § 9-313(8) and **§ R9-604(d)**, which require that secured parties must reimburse third parties for physical damage to land resulting from removal of fixtures.

[26] The original version of Article 9 did not require perfection to defeat such a party (*see* U.C.C. § 9-313[1962 Official Text]).

[27] U.C.C. §§ 9-313(7); **R9-334(c)**. If Secured Party wants priority over either Bank or Owner, it should obtain their respective consent to its security interest. §§ 9-313(5)(a); **R9-334(f)(1)**.

[C] The "First-to-File" Exception — §§ 9-313(4)(b), R9-334(e)(1)

A secured party with a security interest in fixtures can also claim priority over persons who *subsequently* obtain a conflicting interest in the real estate by using the "first-to-file" exception to the residual priority rule. Under this exception, a party who takes a security interest in fixtures and perfects that interest with a fixture filing will take priority over the interest of an owner or encumbrancer whose interest is recorded after the secured party's fixture filing.[28]

For example, suppose that Secured Party sells Grocer a walk-in freezer on August 1, taking a security interest to secure the purchase price. The freezer is installed in the Grocer's store later that same day and becomes a fixture. Grocer's store is subject to a previously existing, properly recorded mortgage in favor of Bank. If Secured Party makes a fixture filing within the grace period for purchase-money priority,[29] it will have priority over Bank's mortgage. If Secured Party delays beyond that date, it will be relegated to the general priority rule and, because Bank has already recorded its mortgage, Secured Party's interest would be subordinate to Bank's mortgage. Secured Party's interest will take priority, however, over any mortgage that Grocer should grant in the future. Furthermore, if Bank had failed to record its mortgage prior to Secured Party's fixture filing, Secured Party's interest would have taken priority over Bank's mortgage — even if Bank had subsequently recorded that mortgage, and even if Secured Party had possessed actual knowledge of Bank's unrecorded mortgage at the time it extended credit.

The first-to-file exception also applies to nonpurchase-money security interests. For example, suppose that Merchant borrows money from Bank and, as collateral, grants Bank a security interest in all of its existing fixtures. Merchant then sells the underlying land to Buyer. If Bank has made a fixture filing before Buyer records its deed to the land, then Buyer will take the land subject to Bank's perfected security interest in the fixtures. If Bank fails to make a fixture filing before Buyer records its deed, then Buyer will take the land free of Bank's security interest in the fixtures, regardless of whether Buyer has knowledge of Bank's interest.

A secured party that makes its fixture filing before the conflicting real estate interest is recorded will not prevail if the holder of the conflicting interest is a successor in interest to a party that would have had priority over the secured party. For example, suppose that on August 1, Secured Party sells a walk-in freezer to Grocer and takes a security interest to secure the purchase price. Later that same day, the freezer is installed and becomes a fixture. Grocer's store is subject to a previously recorded mortgage in favor of Bank. Secured Party fails to make its fixture filing until October 1. On November 1, Bank forecloses on Grocer's mortgage and Buyer purchases the land at the foreclosure sale. Buyer records its deed on November 2. It is irrelevant that Secured Party made its fixture filing before Buyer recorded its deed; the first-to-file exception embraces the derivative title principle, and Buyer succeeds to Bank's priority over Secured Party.

---

[28] U.C.C. §§ 9-313(4); **R9-334(e)(1).**

[29] *See* U.C.C. § 9-313(4)(a) and the discussion in the preceding subsection. **Recall that under § R9-334(d), Secured Party would have a grace period of 20 days for filing.**

[D]   The Nonreliance-Creditor Exception — §§ 9-313(4)(d), R9-334(e)(3)

Article 9 requires a secured party to make a fixture filing to obtain priority against what might be called "reliance creditors" — parties who typically rely on the real estate recording system in deciding whether to buy land or lend against it. Other creditors, such as creditors who acquire encumbrances on land and any attached fixtures by virtue of a judgment or the execution process,[30] were deemed by the drafters to be nonreliance creditors of the sort not typically protected by recording statutes.[31] Thus, perfection using the standard Article 9 rules (as opposed to the fixture filing rules) is sufficient to defeat these nonreliance creditors. This principle finds expression in section 9-313(4)(d) of the 1972 text, which states that a perfected secured party has priority where "the conflicting interest is a lien on the real estate obtained by legal or equitable proceedings after the security interest was perfected *by any method permitted by this Article.*"[32] **Revised Article 9 contains an essentially identical provision.[33]**

Invariably, goods that become fixtures would otherwise have been classified for Article 9 purposes as either equipment or as consumer goods (depending upon the nature of the debtor's use). If an affixed good would constitute equipment in its unattached form, and the secured party has filed an ordinary financing statement in the office(s) necessary to perfect a security interest in that good as equipment, the secured party will defeat a nonreliance creditor. For example, suppose that Secured Party sells a walk-in freezer to Grocer on credit, retaining a security interest to secure the purchase price. Secured Party does not make a fixture filing, but does file an Article 9 financing statement describing "equipment" in all offices necessary to perfect a security interest in Grocer's equipment. The freezer is installed and becomes a fixture. Thereafter, Customer obtains a judgment against Grocer arising out of a slip-and-fall accident, and the judgment constitutes a lien against all of Grocer's real estate. Although Customer obtains a judgment lien against the freezer, this lien is subordinate to Secured Party's perfected security interest under the nonreliance-creditor exception. Likewise, if an affixed good is a consumer good and the secured party has taken the steps necessary to perfect an ordinary security interest in the debtor's consumer goods, the secured party's interest will have priority over a nonreliance creditor. For example, suppose that Secured Party sells Tycoon a walk-in freezer on credit for use in his home, retaining a security interest to secure the purchase price. The freezer is installed and becomes a fixture. Thereafter, Creditor obtains a

---

[30] Creditors that acquire an interest in personalty by virtue of the execution process are called lien creditors in Article 9. *See* discussion in Chapter 14 *supra.* The concept is the same here, except that a creditor who levies upon the land (and, therefore, is deemed to have levied upon the fixtures as part of the land) is not strictly an Article 9 lien creditor (as the lien is attaching to realty, not personalty). It is possible, however, for such a creditor to have the sheriff levy on just the fixture and remove it from the land, at which point the creditor would be an Article 9 lien creditor.

[31] *See* U.C.C. § 9-313 Cmt. 4(c). State real estate law is not unanimous on this point; although many state recording acts do not protect judgment creditors, some states do permit judgment lien creditors to assert the benefit of their recording statutes. *See, e.g.,* Colo. Rev. Stat. Ann. § 38-35-109 (1)(unrecorded instrument is invalid as "against *any person with any kind of rights* in or to such real property who first records") (emphasis added).

[32] U.C.C. § 9-313(4)(d)(emphasis added).

[33] U.C.C. § R9-334(e)(3).

judgment against Tycoon, and the judgment constitutes a lien against Tycoon's home. Although Creditor obtains a judgment lien against the freezer, this lien is subordinate to Secured Party's security interest — which is automatically perfected upon attachment as a purchase-money security interest in consumer goods — under the nonreliance-creditor exception.

The most feared nonreliance creditor is, of course, the trustee in bankruptcy. If a secured party has failed to make a fixture filing and finds itself in a priority contest with the trustee, can it prevail if it has perfected using one of the Code's nonfixture methods? The drafters of the U.C.C. assumed that the answer was "yes," but the issue was open until 1984, when the Bankruptcy Code was amended to make clear that when the trustee is pursuing fixtures, it is exercising the rights of a lien creditor levying on personalty under state law and not the rights of a bona fide purchaser of real property. [34] Thus, suppose that Secured Party sells a walk-in freezer to Grocer on credit, retaining a security interest to secure the purchase price. Secured Party does not make a fixture filing, but does file an Article 9 financing statement describing "equipment" in all offices necessary to perfect a security interest in Grocer's equipment. The freezer is installed and becomes a fixture. Thereafter, Grocer files for bankruptcy protection. Thanks to the nonreliance-creditor exception, the bankruptcy trustee cannot take priority over Secured Party's perfected security interest in the freezer.

One can appreciate that when a prudent secured party takes a security interest in a good that it expects to become a fixture, that secured party not only should make a fixture filing, but also should file any financing statement necessary to perfect a security interest in the good in its nonaffixed form. This precaution protects the secured party against the risk that the debtor never affixes the good, or the risk that a court might later hold that the good did not qualify as a fixture under local real estate law.

[E] The "Readily Removable Equipment" Exception — §§ 9-313(4)(c), R9-334(e)(2)

The 1972 text contains an exception that is limited to security interests in "readily removable factory or office machines or readily removable replacements of domestic appliances which are consumer goods." [35] **The revision expands the scope of this exception to include fixtures that are "equipment that is not primarily used or leased for use in the operation of the real property."** [36] A secured party may perfect a security interest in such goods by any method permitted by Article 9, including filing and automatic perfection. Under this exception, no fixture filing is necessary, and ordinary perfection is sufficient against even reliance creditors. To qualify for protection under this section, the secured party must perfect the security interest before the good is affixed to the land. For all practical purposes, this requirement limits the exception to purchase-money security interests.

The rationale for this exception is the underlying reliance basis for the priority rules. For example, assume that Secured Party has a security interest in Debtor's photocopier,

---

[34] *See* 11 U.S.C. § 544(a)(3)(as amended). *See also id.* § 547(e)(1) (trustee treated as lien creditor of personalty rather than bona-fide purchaser for preferential transfer purposes).

[35] U.C.C. § 9-313(4)(c).

[36] U.C.C. § R9-334(e)(2).

which fits into a recess in the Debtor's office building. If Debtor obtains a mortgage on its office building from Bank, it is unlikely that Bank would be expecting that its mortgage would cover the photocopier; given its readily removable character, the Bank likely would not expect it to be a fixture that constitutes part of the building. Nevertheless, a court might conclude that the combination of affixation by a wall plug and adaptation [37] to a particular feature of the building renders the copier a fixture. The "readily removable" exception suggests, however, that even if such a good is technically a fixture under state law, it is not a type upon which a potential real estate buyer or mortgagee would likely rely; thus, ordinary perfection should suffice.

For domestic appliances that are consumer goods, note that the exception requires that the collateral be a *replacement*, not an original. This limitation serves to protect the lender (typically a construction lender) who may have relied on having a lien upon the original appliances when it provided financing to the debtor. Such a lender should realize that appliances depreciate and eventually break down, and that requiring a purchase-money secured party to make a fixture filing in order to obtain priority for an interest in a replacement appliance would drive up the transaction costs for what are routine sales (usually perfected automatically) and thus would serve no useful notice function.

[F] Special Rules for Construction Mortgages — §§ 9-313(6), R9-334(h)

The 1972 text states the following special priority rule designed to protect a construction lender's interest in fixtures under a construction mortgage: [38]

Notwithstanding paragraph (a) of subsection (4) but otherwise subject to subsections (4) and (5), a security interest in fixtures is subordinate to a construction mortgage recorded before the goods become fixtures if the goods become fixtures before the completion of the construction. To the extent that it is given to refinance a construction mortgage, a mortgage has this priority to the same extent as the construction mortgage.

The revision makes no substantive changes to this rule. [39]

This rule precludes the operation of the purchase-money priority exception against construction lenders. For example, suppose that Debtor is building an office building financed by a recorded construction mortgage from First Bank. Suppose further that Secured Party sells Debtor 50 units of cabinets for wall-mounted installation in the offices, taking a security interest in the cabinets to secure the unpaid purchase price. The cabinets are installed and become fixtures. The following day, Secured Party makes a fixture filing describing the cabinets. But for the special rule on construction mortgages, Secured Party would take priority over Bank under the purchase-money priority exception. [40] Under the construction mortgage rule, however, Secured Party's interest is subordinate to the lien of First Bank's mortgage. Why this solicitude for the construction lender? Recall

---

[37] Adaptation is discussed in § 15.01 *supra.*

[38] U.C.C. § 9-313(6). § 9-313(1)(c) states that "a mortgage is a 'construction mortgage' to the extent that it secures an obligation incurred for the construction of an improvement on land including the acquisition cost of the land, if the recorded writing so indicates." **§ R9-334(h) provides a substantially identical definition.**

[39] U.C.C. § R9-334(h).

[40] *See* § 15.03[B] *supra.*

that the purchase-money priority exception is predicated on the assumption that a mortgagee whose interest arose before a good became a fixture did not rely upon that good in deciding how much money to lend. This assumption is not valid for the construction mortgagee, however, who typically knows of the construction plans from the outset and makes its decision to lend assuming that the fixtures will become part of the structure.[41] Consequently, the construction mortgagee is a reliance creditor from the start of construction. A supplier of goods that become fixtures is, in essence, relegated to whatever rights accrue to it under the state's mechanic's lien laws. Furthermore, any priority accruing to a construction mortgagee can be passed along to the permanent or "take-out" lender to whom the mortgage is assigned when construction is complete.

When the construction lender or permanent lender acquires an interest in fixtures placed on the land after construction is complete (typically through an after-acquired fixtures provision in the mortgage), the rationale for this provision no longer applies. The priority for construction mortgages thus applies only to goods that become fixtures before construction is completed. For example, if Secured Party sells Debtor 50 units of cabinets that Debtor installs six months after construction is complete, and the cabinets become fixtures upon installation, Secured Party can acquire priority over a properly recorded construction mortgage or permanent take-out mortgage by making a proper fixture filing during the applicable grace period.[42]

Two other exceptions that are relatively less significant nevertheless deserve brief mention. First, if the construction lender or permanent take-out lender consents in writing to the security interest or disclaims an interest in the fixtures, or if it gives the debtor consent to remove the fixtures, the secured party acquires priority over the mortgage with respect to those fixtures.[43] Second, if the construction mortgagee fails to record its mortgage before the goods become fixtures (not likely, but possible if the construction lender is careless), it subjects itself to the risk of losing priority under the "first-to-file" exception to the residual priority rule.[44]

[G] Exception for Manufactured Homes — § R9-335(e)(4)

Revised Article 9 contains a special priority rule addressing the potential conflict between a party who financed the debtor's purchase of a "manufactured home"[45] and a party holding a lien upon the land to which the home is attached. In most states, mobile homes are covered by title-certification statutes. In those states, as would be the case with vehicles, a secured party would have to perfect its security interest in a mobile home by having it noted upon the home's title certificate. Under

---

[41] In fact, in many circumstances the construction lender will have factored the cost of the building fixtures into its construction loan amount and thus expects to be financing those fixtures. Thus, enabling the debtor to grant purchase-money priority in the fixtures to a competing secured party would allow the debtor to "double finance" the building's fixtures.

[42] See § 15.03[B] supra.

[43] U.C.C. §§ 9-313(5); **R9-334(f)**.

[44] See § 15.03[C] supra.

[45] **The definition of "manufactured home" in U.C.C. § R9-102(a)(53) would include the typical mobile home or prefabricated home that is movable in one or more sections.**

revised section R9-334(e)(4), a security interest in a manufactured home that is created in a "manufactured home transaction"[46] takes priority over the interest of an owner or encumbrancer of the land to which the home is attached, provided that the secured party's interest is perfected by notation on the home's certificate of title. Thus, suppose that Debtor purchases a mobile home on credit from Seller and grants Seller a purchase-money security interest in the home. Seller has its interest properly noted on the certificate of title covering the home. The home is then affixed to land that the Debtor is purchasing from Vendor on a contract for deed. Seller's security interest will have priority over the claim of Vendor under the contract for deed.

[H] Exception Based on Consent or Right of Removal — §§ 9-313(5), R9-334(f)

There are two additional exceptions to the residual priority rule that merit brief mention. The first exception is based upon consent: If an encumbrancer or owner who would otherwise have priority over the secured party consents in writing to the security interest or disclaims an interest in the fixtures, the secured party acquires priority.[47] This is merely a particular application of the general rule that parties may enter into subordination agreements reversing any of the U.C.C.'s normal priority rules.[48]

The final exception arises primarily in lease situations. A majority of jurisdictions have adopted what is sometimes called the "trade fixture" doctrine. Under this doctrine, goods affixed to leased business premises generally are treated as personalty as between the lessor and the lessee, and thus may be removed by the lessee at the conclusion of the lease term (unless the lease provides expressly to the contrary). Further, most jurisdictions have expanded this doctrine to include goods affixed by lessees of residential property. Article 9 incorporates this concept, giving a secured party with an interest in fixtures priority over the conflicting claim of an encumbrancer or owner of the land if "the debtor has a right to remove the goods as against the encumbrancer or owner," regardless of whether the secured party's interest in the fixtures is perfected.[49] The Code provides that "[i]f the debtor's right [to remove the goods] terminates, the priority of the security interest continues for a reasonable time."[50] This provision is important in those jurisdictions where the lessee's right to remove fixtures terminates upon expiration of the lease (or expiration of the period during which the lessee is a holdover tenant), as it affords the secured party priority for a reasonable time so that it can repossess the fixtures.[51]

---

[46] A "manufactured home transaction" is a transaction that creates a purchase-money security interest in a manufactured home, so long as the manufactured home is the primary collateral in the transaction. U.C.C. § R9-102(a)(54).

[47] U.C.C. §§ 9-313(5)(a); R9-334(f)(1).

[48] *See* U.C.C. §§ 9-316; R9-339.

[49] U.C.C. §§ 9-313(5)(b); R9-334(f)(2). The rationale does not apply to parties who buy the land from, or become mortgagees of, the lessor.

[50] *Id.*

[51] If the debtor no longer has access to the premises, the secured party would be well-advised to use judicial repossession rather than attempting to repossess by self-help. *See* discussion in Chapter 17 *infra.*

§ 15.04 Secured Party's Right to Remove Fixtures After Default —
§§ 9-313(8), R9-604(c),(d)

The secured party's rights to enforce its security interest in fixtures after default are set forth in section 9-313(8) of the 1972 text. A secured party may not repossess fixtures if there is an owner or encumbrancer against whom it lacks priority.[52] In other words, if the secured party is not first in line, it cannot repossess at all. Unless the secured party obtains the consent of all parties having priority, its security interest is worthless and it must rely for protection on any rights it may have under the state's laws governing mechanics' liens, if any.

Even if the secured party has first priority as to fixtures, however, its repossession and enforcement rights are limited. The 1972 text provides that the secured party repossessing fixtures must "reimburse any encumbrancer or owner of the real estate who is not the debtor and who has not otherwise agreed for the cost of repair of any physical injury, but not for any diminution in value of the real estate caused by the absence of the goods removed or by any necessity of replacing them."[53] For example, suppose that Secured Party has a perfected security interest in Grocer's walk-in freezer (which constitutes a fixture), and has priority over Bank, which holds a mortgage upon Grocer's store. Secured Party removes the fixture and sells it; in the process of removing the freezer, Secured Party does $400 in physical damage to the store (tearing down a wall to gain access to the freezer) and reduces the fair market value of the store by $4,000 (the cost to obtain and install a replacement freezer). Secured Party must reimburse Bank for the $400 in physical damage to the store premises, but need not pay any sum to reimburse the Bank for the reduction in the fair market value of the premises because the freezer is now missing. The rationale for this result should be apparent. Article 9 typically grants fixture priority to secured parties when the encumbrancer or owner has not relied on the presence of the fixture; thus, the fact that removal reduced the fair market value of the store premises by $4,000 should not seriously interfere with Bank's reasonable expectations (as Bank likely did not rely upon having priority over the freezer). When Secured Party causes physical injury to the land in removing the fixture, however, there is a direct and substantial interference with the Bank's expectations in the physical integrity of the mortgaged premises, and Secured Party should have to compensate Bank for this interference. In addition to granting the owner or encumbrancer a right of reimbursement, the Code also provides that the owner or encumbrancer may refuse permission to remove until the secured party gives adequate security for the performance of this obligation.[54] This represents a departure from the pre-Code rule in many jurisdictions barring removals that would cause material injury to the land.[55]

---

[52] Priorities are discussed in detail in § 15.03 *supra*.

[53] U.C.C. § 9-313(8). **The revision provides a similar limitation, although it omits the phrase "and who has not otherwise agreed." § R 9-604(d).**

[54] U.C.C. §§ 9-313(8), **R9-604(d).**

[55] U.C.C. § 9-313 Cmt. 9. If removal of a fixture would cause such massive harm as to be wasteful, the court might find that the good (whether or not it qualifies as a fixture under real estate law) is an ordinary building material and that, therefore, no security interest continues to attach to it. *See* § 15.01 *supra*.

Suppose that Secured Party had a perfected security interest in Debtor's fixtures and that Secured Party was entitled to priority over Bank, which held a mortgage on Debtor's land. Suppose further that Debtor was in default to Bank, which foreclosed on Debtor's land and sold the land to Buyer. Can Secured Party claim first priority in the sale proceeds? A leading case interpreting the 1972 text, *Maplewood Bank & Trust v. Sears, Roebuck & Co.*,[56] held that the answer was no. The court held that under section 9-313(8) of the 1972 text, Secured Party's right to priority against fixtures is limited to removal of the fixture; Secured Party has no priority claim against the land itself and thus no claim to priority against the proceeds of the foreclosure sale. Secured Party's priority against the fixture, however, continued as the fixture passed into the hands of the Buyer.

Revised section 9-604(b) provides that a party with a security interest in fixtures may enforce its interest under Article 9's enforcement provisions or under applicable state real estate law. If the secured party enforces its interest under state real estate law, none of Article 9's enforcement provisions apply to the secured party's actions. Thus, in the above hypothetical, if state law permitted Secured Party to claim an interest in the sale proceeds under the law governing real estate foreclosures, Secured Party would have first priority against the foreclosure sale proceeds.[57]

§ 15.05 Accessions — §§ 9-314, R9-335

[A] Nature of the Interest

Accessions are analogous to fixtures, except that an accession is an item of personalty that is attached to *another item of personalty* rather than to real estate. Accessions retain their identity and can be removed and sold separately. This distinguishes them from one of the two classes of products — the "commingled mass," or the product that arises when an item of personalty becomes so commingled into a larger whole (also personalty) that it loses its separate identity.[58] Section 9-314 of the 1972 text sets forth the U.C.C.'s

---

[56] 625 A.2d 537 (N.J. App. 1993).

[57] U.C.C. § R9-604 Cmt. 3 ("[R9-604(b)] makes clear that a security interest in fixtures may be enforced either under real-property law or under any of the applicable provisions of Part 6. . . . Subsection (b) also serves to overrule cases holding that a secured party's only remedy after default is the removal of the fixtures from the real property.").

[58] The other class of products that arises under existing Article 9 involves the situation where a secured party acquires an interest in an asset (e.g., a component part) that later will be manufactured, processed or assembled into a larger whole *without* losing its identity. For example, suppose that Secured Party has a security interest in a batch of computer hard disk drives that Debtor will later be assembling into completed desktop computer units. In other words, the whole (the desktop computer unit) is a type of product and the particular asset (the hard drive) is an accession. In this product/accession situation, Secured Party must make a choice regarding the collateral — the hard drives or the assembled computer units — at the time it files a financing statement perfecting its interest. If Secured Party checks the box on the financing statement marked "products," Secured Party thereby signifies that it has elected to give up its right later to claim the hard drives as accessions, and has decided instead to claim an interest in the assembled computer units (the products). U.C.C. § 9-315(1)(b). Secured Party's failure to check the box will limit its interest to the accessions (the hard drives) alone. **Revised Article 9 eliminates this class of products; under Revised Article 9, Secured Party could only claim an interest in the hard drives, unless Debtor granted it a separate and direct security interest in the assembled computer units.** Products are discussed generally in the ensuing section.

rules governing priorities in accessions, and section 9-315 of the 1972 text provides the rules governing priorities in products.

Section 9-314's definition of "accessions" differs somewhat from the common-law definition. At common law, an asset did not become an accession until it was so intertwined with the whole that, although retaining its separate identity, its removal would cause substantial harm to the whole.[59] For purposes of section 9-314, however, an item is an accession if it is "installed in or affixed to" other goods.[60] One should note carefully that this definition only applies to disputes governed by section 9-314,[61] and that section is relevant only if there is a priority contest between a secured party claiming an interest in an accession and a third party claiming an interest in the whole.

If the issue is simply whether a security agreement is sufficiently broad to grant the secured party an interest in a particular item that is somehow connected with a larger whole, the common-law definition of accessions governs. For example, if Secured Party has a security interest in Debtor's car, its interest extends to the motor because the motor, being integral to the functioning of the car, qualifies as a common-law accession. The security interest might not extend to Debtor's cellular phone installed in the car; the cellular phone likely would not constitute an accession, as its removal would not cause substantial harm to the car as a whole or compromise its operability. Thus, if Secured Party repossessed the car following Debtor's default and failed to remove the cellular phone and return it to Debtor, Secured Party likely would be liable for conversion. As a result, a well-drafted security agreement will contain language that extends the security interest to all attachments and accessories, whenever acquired.

[B] Priorities

Section 9-314 resolves the priority dispute that arises when the secured party has a security interest in an accession (as defined by the Code) and a third party claims a competing interest in the whole. For priority purposes, the 1972 text differentiates between security interests that attach to the accession before affixation and those that attach afterwards. As one might expect, a secured party would be unlikely to agree to finance an already-installed accession; under section 9-314, the secured party's interest will be "invalid against any person with an interest in the whole at the time the security interest attaches to the goods [meaning the accession] who has not in writing consented to the security interest or disclaimed an interest in the goods as part of the whole."[62]

For example, suppose Dealer has a security interest in Debtor's car, and further that Debtor takes the car to Bank and asks Bank for a loan secured only by the car's engine. Unless Dealer consents to the Bank's security interest or disclaims any interest in the

---

[59] *See generally* R. Brown, *The Law of Personal Property* §§ 6.1-6.7 (W. Raushenbush 3d ed. 1975).

[60] U.C.C. § 9-314(1). **Under Revised Article 9, accessions are "goods that are physically united with other goods in such a manner that the identity of the original goods is not lost." § R9-102(a)(1).**

[61] U.C.C. § 9-314(1)explicitly states that its definition is limited to "this section." **Revised Article 9 implicitly qualifies the definition of accessions in a similar manner. § R9-335.**

[62] U.C.C. § 9-314(2).

engine — which is extremely unlikely — Bank's security interest would not be valid as against Dealer, even if Bank properly perfected its security interest immediately (and even if Dealer's security interest was unperfected). Further, as is the case with fixtures,[63] because Bank's security interest would be subordinate to the Dealer's competing interest in the entire car, Bank would be unable to remove the engine from the car for foreclosure purposes in the event that Debtor defaulted.[64] Thus, Bank would be better advised to take and perfect a security interest in the entire car rather than the already-installed engine.[65]

Section 9-314 of the 1972 text provides better treatment for the secured party who finances a good that will be installed or affixed after the security interest has attached. Under the general priority rule set forth in section 9-314(1),[66] the secured party (who is typically, but not necessarily, a purchase-money secured party) who takes a security interest in an accession before installation or affixation takes priority over conflicting interests in the whole. For example, if Debtor asks Bank to finance a new motor to be installed in a car, Bank need not worry that Dealer has a perfected security interest in the car, as Bank would still have priority over the new engine — *even if Bank never perfects its interest.* Whether Bank perfects its security interest is relevant only as to certain parties (such as purchasers or lien creditors) whose interests in the whole arise after installation or affixation,[67] since such parties might be misled by the lack of notice of the secured party's interest in the accession. For example, suppose Bank finances a new motor for Debtor's tractor, which is subject to Finance Company's perfected security interest. As we have seen, Bank will have priority over Finance Company with respect to the motor, regardless of whether Bank perfects its interest, so long as Bank's interest attaches before the motor is installed. If Finance Company makes a future advance to Debtor after installation, however, and does so without knowledge of Bank's interest in the motor and before Bank perfects that interest, Finance Company would have priority as to the motor to the extent of the future advance.[68] Likewise, if Debtor sells the tractor to Buyer after affixation of the motor and before Bank perfects its security interest in the motor, Buyer will take the tractor free of Bank's interest in the motor so long as Buyer has no knowledge of Bank's unperfected security interest.

---

[63] *See* § 15.04 *supra.*

[64] U.C.C. §§ 9-314(4); **R9-335(f).**

[65] A secured party should almost never take an interest in an already-installed accession. If there is a prior conflicting interest in the whole, the secured party will be subordinate and unable to repossess the accession. Thus, such a secured party would be better off with a junior security interest in the whole, which it could foreclose. *See* discussion of the rights of junior secured parties in Chapter 17 *infra.* Further, even if the whole is unencumbered, a secured party is still better off with a security interest in the whole than with an interest in any particular accession.

[66] Under U.C.C. § 9-314(1), a security interest that attaches before installation or affixation "takes priority as to the goods installed or affixed . . . over the claims of all persons to the whole except as stated in subsection (3) and subject to Section 9-315(1)."

[67] U.C.C. § 9-314(3) identifies the parties whose interests will defeat an unperfected security interest in an accession.

[68] U.C.C. § 9-314(3).

Revised Article 9 has dramatically simplified the priority rules governing accessions. The revisions eliminate the distinction between security interests arising before affixation and those arising after affixation. Under the revisions, the general rule for priority disputes involving accessions is that disputes between a secured party claiming an interest in an accession and a party claiming a conflicting interest in the whole are resolved by the Code's ordinary priority rules.[69] For example, suppose that Debtor grants Bank a security interest in a new computer hard drive to be installed in Debtor's business computer, which is subject to an already perfected security interest in favor of Finance Company. If Bank's interest is a purchase-money security interest (*i.e.*, if Debtor acquired the hard drive with money advanced by the Bank), Bank would take priority as to the hard drive over Finance Company's interest in the entire computer so long as Bank perfected its interest within the 20-day grace period after Debtor receives possession of the hard drive.[70] If Bank fails to perfect its interest within this grace period, or if Bank's interest is not a purchase-money interest, Finance Company would take priority as to the installed hard drive based upon its prior perfected interest in the whole computer.[71]

Likewise, suppose that after installing the hard drive, Debtor sells the computer to Buyer. If Bank perfected its security interest in the hard drive before the sale to Buyer, Bank's security interest in the hard drive will remain effective even after the computer is in the hands of Buyer. If, however, Buyer gives value and takes possession of the computer without knowledge of Bank's security interest and before it is perfected, Buyer will take the computer free of Bank's interest in the hard drive.[72]

Revised section 9-335 does provide a special priority rule with regard to accessions to vehicles covered by certificate-of-title statutes. Under section R9-335(d), a security interest in an accession is subordinate to a security interest in the whole that is perfected under a certificate-of-title statute.[73] Thus, suppose that Debtor asks Bank to finance a new engine for its car, upon which GMAC has a perfected security interest by notation upon the car's title certificate. Under section R9-335, Bank cannot obtain priority as to the engine over GMAC, notwithstanding Article 9's traditional priority for a purchase-money secured party.

---

[69] U.C.C. § R9-335(c).

[70] U.C.C. § R9-324(e). If Debtor's computer was for household purposes and constituted consumer goods, Bank's purchase-money security interest would be automatically perfected upon attachment. § R9-309(1).

[71] U.C.C. § R9-322(a)(1).

[72] U.C.C. § R9-317(b).

[73] U.C.C. § R9-335(d) ("A security interest in an accession is subordinate to a security interest in the whole which is perfected by compliance with the requirements of a certificate-of-title statute under Section 9-311(d).").

§ 15.06 Products — §§ 9-315, R9-336

[A] Rights

Section 9-315 of the 1972 text sets out rules that govern the effectiveness of a secured party's interest in a particular good that has been commingled with other goods into a product or mass. Can the secured party assert a claim against the product or mass and, if so, will that claim have priority over third parties with competing interests in the product or mass? The right to assert a claim against the product or mass is governed by section 9-315(1), which states:

> If a security interest in goods was perfected and subsequently the goods or a part thereof have become part of a product or mass, the security interest continues in the product or mass if
>
> (a) the goods are so manufactured, processed, assembled or commingled that their identity is lost in the product or mass; or
>
> (b) a financing statement covering the original goods also covers the product into which the goods have been manufactured, processed or assembled.
>
> In a case to which paragraph (b) applies, no separate security interest in that part of the original goods which has been manufactured, processed or assembled into the product may be claimed under Section 9-314.

Note that if the secured party fails to perfect its security interest in the original good, it cannot later claim an interest in the product or mass. If the secured party perfects its interest in the original good and can meet the burden of tracing that good into the product or mass, the secured party can assert a claim to the product or mass.

As the language of section 9-315(1) suggests, the current Article 9 identifies two classes of products. The first class involves a product or mass that results when its component goods lose their identity as a result of commingling or processing. For example, suppose that Bank has a security interest in Debtor's flour, and Debtor later combines that flour with eggs, water and sugar to make a cake. The flour loses its identity in the process of baking the cake, but this does not completely eliminate Bank's security interest. If Bank had perfected its security interest in the flour and can prove that the flour went into the cake, it can claim an interest in the cake.

The second class of products involves a product or mass that results from the manufacturing or assembly of component goods that does not destroy the identity of the component goods. In this situation, the component goods would be accessions to the product or mass. Under section 9-315(1)(b), the secured party with an interest in a component good can elect between retaining a security interest in the good as an accession (governed by section 9-314) or instead claiming an interest in the whole product or mass into which the good is assembled. The secured party must make this election at the time it files its financing statement. If its financing statement shows that products are covered, the secured party has elected not to pursue its collateral under the accession rules, and its claim instead attaches to the assembled whole.[74]

---

[74] U.C.C. § 9-315(1)(b).

Revised Article 9 retains the first class of products, which it defines as "commingled goods," meaning "goods that are physically united with other goods in such a manner that their identity is lost in a product or mass."[75] If a secured party has an interest in goods that become commingled goods, the secured party receives an interest in the resulting product or mass.[76] Further, if the secured party perfected its interest in the goods before commingling, the secured party's interest in the product or mass is also perfected.[77]

Revised Article 9 eliminates the second class of products. When a secured party has an interest in component goods that do not lose their identity as part of the process of manufacturing and assembly, the secured party's interest is limited to the component goods as accessions.[78] Under the revision, the secured party cannot claim an interest in the whole product or mass unless it takes a direct security interest in the whole product or mass under the security agreement.

[B] Priorities

Most priority problems involving products are resolved fairly easily. A perfected security interest in a product or mass will have priority over a lien creditor or a buyer not in the ordinary course, but a buyer in the ordinary course will take free of the security interest.[79] Against competing security interests in the product or mass, the 1972 text applies the following formula to resolve the dispute:

> When under subsection (1) more than one security interest attaches to the product or mass, they rank equally according to the ratio that the cost of the goods to which each interest originally attached bears to the cost of the total product or mass.[80]

Determining whether there are competing security interests in the product or mass is not always easy. For example, suppose Supplier sells Debtor cattle feed on secured credit and Bank has a security interest in Debtor's cattle. If all the feed has been consumed when Debtor defaults, can Supplier argue that it has an interest in the cattle as a "product or mass" and that it therefore can share ratably with Bank under the formula set forth in section 9-315(2)? The cases to date have concluded that this situation was not within the contemplation of the drafters and have refused to allow feed suppliers to assert claims against cattle that have eaten the feed.[81] The theory behind these cases, however — that

---

[75] U.C.C. § R9-336(a).

[76] U.C.C. § R9-336(c).

[77] U.C.C. § R9-336(d).

[78] U.C.C. §§ R9-335, R9-336. Accessions are discussed in § 15.05 *supra.*

[79] This conclusion is implicit in U.C.C. § 9-315(2); that section does not address these priority disputes, thus leaving them to Article 9's general priority rules. **Section R9-336(e) makes this explicit.**

[80] U.C.C. § 9-315(2). This formula codifies the doctrine of "confusion of goods." *See* R. Brown, *The Law of Personal Property* §§ 6.8-6.14 (W. Raushenbush 3d ed. 1975).

[81] *See, e.g.,* First Nat'l Bank of Brush v. Bostron, 39 Colo. Ct. App. 107, 564 P.2d 964, 21 U.C.C. Rep. Serv. 1475 (Colo. Ct. App. 1977); Farmers Coop. Elevator Co. v. Union State Bank, 409 N.W.2d 178, 4 U.C.C. Rep. Serv. 2d 1 (Iowa 1987). The cases have also considered and rejected the argument that the cattle are proceeds of the feed.

there is nothing left of the feed after the cattle have eaten it — seems a bit strained. The feed has clearly been converted into meat, and there is no logical reason why section 9-315 should not apply. Nevertheless, based on the decisions under the current Article 9, a prudent feed supplier that wants an interest in the cattle as well as the feed should so specify in its security agreement.

Under revised Article 9, a perfected security interest in commingled goods takes priority over a conflicting unperfected security interest in the same goods.[82] Further, under the revision, conflicting perfected security interests in a commingled product or mass rank equally in proportion to the value of the original collateral at the time it became commingled goods.[83] For example, suppose that Bank has a perfected security interest in Debtor's flour (worth $100), Finance Company has a perfected security interest in Debtor's eggs (worth $200), and Debtor commingles the flour and eggs to make cakes. Suppose further that after the Debtor's default, the cakes sold for only $150. From this $150, Bank would receive $50 and Finance Company $100.

---

[82] U.C.C. § R9-336(f)(1).

[83] U.C.C. § R9-336(f)(2).

CHAPTER 16

BANKRUPTCY

SYNOPSIS

---

§ 16.01 Background

[A] Introduction

When a debtor files for bankruptcy protection, the secured party's ability to enforce its security interest becomes subject to the substantive and procedural limitations imposed by federal bankruptcy law. Thus, although Article 9 is "state" law, most current decisions interpreting and applying Article 9 arise in the federal bankruptcy courts. Accordingly, a thorough understanding of the law of secured transactions requires a basic understanding of bankruptcy law.

A variety of policies and concerns motivate our system of federal bankruptcy law. One concern is that, outside of bankruptcy, a debtor's financial distress can trigger a "race to the courthouse" by its creditors, with each creditor attempting to maximize its recovery before the debtor's assets are exhausted. Such a "race" has the potential to force the distressed but solvent debtor into insolvency, when time, planning, and some "breathing space" might have enabled the debtor to recover a sound financial position. Thus, one of the primary objectives of bankruptcy law is to provide a comprehensive system of debt collection that can help either avoid or mitigate the adverse consequences of the "race to the courthouse."

In bankruptcy an insolvent debtor's financial affairs are administered in a collective proceeding rather than through the ad hoc collection efforts of individual creditors.[1] Within this collective proceeding, there is a strong emphasis upon the equitable (as distinct from equal) treatment of all creditors; bankruptcy law generally treats similarly situated creditors in a similar fashion, and discourages attempts by creditors to "opt out" of the collective process.[2] Current bankruptcy law provides more, however, than just a collective debt collection system. Bankruptcy also provides insolvent debtors with the opportunity to obtain a "fresh start" or to "reorganize" their financial affairs. Individual debtors may choose to liquidate their prebankruptcy assets and thereby obtain an order discharging their prebankruptcy debts. In contrast, individual and business debtors may retain their assets and attempt to restructure and repay some or all of their prebankruptcy debts in a reorganization proceeding.

This variety of objectives is manifested in Title 11 of the United States Code, commonly known as the Bankruptcy Code. Enacted by Congress in 1978 and revised on several subsequent occasions, the Code divides bankruptcy law into separate "Chapters." Three of these Chapters (1, 3, and 5) contain general provisions that apply in all types of bankruptcy cases. The remaining Chapters govern the specific types of bankruptcy cases. Chapter 7 establishes the rules governing the liquidation of individual or business debtors.[3] Chapter 11 governs the attempt by a business debtor to implement a plan for restructuring its prebankruptcy debts and rehabilitating its business.[4] Chapter 12 establishes a procedure whereby farmers may restructure and repay prebankruptcy debts using postbankruptcy earnings.[5] Chapter 13 sets forth the rules that govern how an individual wage-earner's prebankruptcy debts may be restructured and repaid using postbankruptcy disposable income.[6] This book does not discuss the procedure that governs proceedings under each Chapter of the Code; instead, this book generally will

---

[1] Elizabeth Warren, *Bankruptcy Policy*, 54 U. Chi. L. Rev. 775 (1987).

[2] This objective explains, for example, the Bankruptcy Code provision allowing the bankruptcy trustee to avoid (*i.e.*, set aside or recover) certain transfers by the debtor prior to bankruptcy that had the effect of preferring certain creditors over other, similarly situated creditors (these transfers are called "preferences"). 11 U.S.C. § 547; *see* § 16.04[E] *infra*.

[3] 11 U.S.C. §§ 701-728.

[4] *Id.* §§ 1101-1146. Although the majority of Chapter 11 cases involve debtors that are corporations, partnerships, or other business entities, the Supreme Court has held that individual debtors can use the provisions of Chapter 11. Toibb v. Radloff, 501 U.S. 157 (1991).

[5] 11 U.S.C. §§ 1201-1231.

[6] *Id.* §§ 1301-1330.

focus only upon those aspects of bankruptcy law that have significant consequences for Article 9 secured transactions and the behavior of debtors and secured parties.[7]

[B] The Bankruptcy Estate

The filing of a bankruptcy petition creates a bankruptcy estate.[8] Subject to limited statutory exceptions, all of the interests in property (whether legal or equitable) owned by the debtor at the moment of the bankruptcy petition become part of the bankruptcy estate.[9] In a Chapter 7 case, the debtor essentially gives up all of its nonexempt property — which is used to repay the claims of creditors — in exchange for a fresh start and a discharge of its debts. Thus, the Chapter 7 debtor generally does not retain possession and control of property of the estate. Instead, the bankruptcy trustee distributes the estate's property in one of three ways: first, the trustee abandons any overencumbered property (*i.e.*, property that secures a debt in excess of its value) or otherwise worthless property;[10] second, the trustee abandons any exempt property (*i.e.*, property that the debtor is allowed to retain free of creditor claims under applicable state or federal exemptions);[11] third, the trustee liquidates the remaining property and distributes the proceeds to pay persons holding valid claims against the debtor and administrative expenses.[12]

In contrast, in reorganization cases under Chapters 11, 12, and 13, property of the estate generally remains in control of the bankrupt debtor. In these Chapters, the bankrupt debtor generally retains its prebankruptcy assets and attempts to repay the claims of creditors using assets obtained and income generated after the bankruptcy petition. Thus, the reorganizing debtor remains in possession of property of the estate, and may continue to use that property in its reorganization efforts (subject to the supervision of the bankruptcy court).[13]

[C] The Bankruptcy Trustee

The central figure in bankruptcy cases is the trustee. The trustee is the official representative of the bankruptcy estate.[14] In a Chapter 7 case, a trustee is always appointed. The Chapter 7 trustee collects and manages the property in the bankruptcy estate, investigates the bankrupt's financial affairs, sets aside improper prebankruptcy transfers by the debtor, liquidates the property of the estate and distributes the proceeds to those creditors entitled to payment under the Code's distributive scheme.[15]

---

[7] For further discussions of the general procedures of bankruptcy, *see generally* Michael J. Herbert, *Understanding Bankruptcy* (1995).

[8] 11 U.S.C. § 541(a).

[9] *Id.* § 541(a)(1).

[10] *Id.* § 554(a). When the trustee abandons property of the estate, title to that property is vested back into the debtor. Any creditor with a security interest in that property may then enforce that security interest, subject to obtaining relief from the automatic stay as discussed in § 16.03[B] *infra*.

[11] 11 U.S.C. § 554(a).

[12] *Id.* § 726.

[13] *Id.* §§ 1107(a), 1203(a), 1303.

[14] *Id.* § 323(a).

[15] *Id.* § 704.

In reorganization cases, however, the role of the trustee differs. A trustee is always appointed in Chapter 12 and 13 cases also, but that trustee does not collect and manage the property of the estate. Instead, the Chapter 12 or Chapter 13 trustee investigates the bankrupt debtor's financial affairs, sets aside improper prebankruptcy transfers by the debtor, and collects all of the debtor's postbankruptcy disposable net income, which is used to pay the claims of creditors in accordance with a plan of reorganization approved by the court.[16] Trustees are not appointed as a matter of course in Chapter 11 cases.[17] In the typical Chapter 11 case, the Code authorizes the bankrupt debtor (called the "debtor-in-possession" or "DIP") to carry out the powers of a Chapter 11 trustee.[18]

In any bankruptcy case, the trustee (or the DIP) presents the primary potential threat to the Article 9 secured party and its ability to enforce its security interest. In all cases, the trustee/DIP examines the claims of creditors and is entitled to enforce any legal claims that the estate might have against creditors or other third parties. Pursuant to its avoiding powers, the trustee/DIP may attack and set aside certain prebankruptcy transfers, including (among others) unperfected security interests,[19] fraudulent transfers,[20] and security interests or other transfers that had the effect of preferring the Article 9 secured party over other prebankruptcy creditors.[21]

§ 16.02 Contrasting Secured and Unsecured Claims

[A] What is a Claim?

Bankruptcy is a collective process in which the court resolves "claims" arising under nonbankruptcy law against financially distressed debtors. The Bankruptcy Code defines the term "claim" very broadly to incorporate any "right to payment, whether or not . . . reduced to judgment, liquidated, unliquidated, fixed, contingent, matured, unmatured, disputed, undisputed, legal, equitable, secured, or unsecured."[22] Likewise, the Code broadly defines "creditor" to include anyone or any entity that holds "a claim against the debtor" that arose prior to filing of the bankruptcy petition.[23] By defining the terms "claim" and "creditor" so broadly, the Code makes it possible for the bankruptcy process to address and resolve all of the debtor's legal obligations arising out of its prebankruptcy activities.[24]

---

[16] *Id.* §§ 1202(b); 1302(b).

[17] A trustee may be appointed upon request of any party in interest for cause (including the debtor's dishonesty, fraud, or incompetence), or if the court concludes that appointment of a trustee is otherwise necessary to protect the estate or the interests of creditors or other interest holders (such as stockholders of a bankrupt corporation). 11 U.S.C. § 1104(a).

[18] 11 U.S.C. § 1107(a). The powers of the Chapter 11 trustee are listed in § 1106(a) and are similar to the powers provided to trustees in the other bankruptcy chapters.

[19] *Id.* § 544(a).

[20] *Id.* §§ 544(b), 548.

[21] *Id.* § 547.

[22] *Id.* § 101(5)(A).

[23] *Id.* § 101(10).

[24] S. Rep. No. 989, 95th Cong., 2d Sess. 22.

[B] The Allowance of Claims

To make distributions to creditors, bankruptcy must identify those creditors holding valid claims against the debtor. Not surprisingly, bankruptcy law does not honor all prebankruptcy claims; instead, policy concerns justify the disallowance of some claims. Sometimes the rationale for disallowing a claim rests upon nonbankruptcy law. For example, claims that are not enforceable under nonbankruptcy law — such as a debt evidenced by a forged promissory note — are not enforced in bankruptcy, lest such claimants receive better treatment in bankruptcy courts than they would outside of bankruptcy.[25] In other cases, the rationale for disallowance is based on concerns of sound bankruptcy policy, such as the disallowance of claims for unmatured interest.[26]

Thus, Bankruptcy Code section 502 distinguishes between *allowed claims* and *disallowed claims*. Under section 502(a), claims are deemed "allowed" unless the trustee, the debtor, or some other party in interest raises a valid objection to the claim.[27] Once an objection is properly raised, the court must conduct a hearing and determine the amount of the creditor's allowed claim.[28]

[C] Secured Claims, Unsecured Claims, and Valuation

The Bankruptcy Code further separates claims into two primary categories — *secured claims* and *unsecured claims*. As a starting point, bankruptcy takes secured creditors as it finds them on the petition date — a security interest that is enforceable under nonbankruptcy law will also be respected in bankruptcy.[29] A creditor with a valid lien

---

25 11 U.S.C. § 502(b)(1).

26 *Id.* § 502(b)(2). For example, suppose that Creditor asserted an otherwise valid claim for $1,000 for goods shipped to Debtor on open account, and Creditor's terms included an 18% interest charge on past due accounts. Section 502 would allow the claim in the amount of $1,000, plus any interest that had accrued up to the date of the bankruptcy petition, but § 502(b)(2) would disallow the claim to the extent of any interest that otherwise would have accrued after the petition date outside of bankruptcy. Denial of unmatured interest on unsecured claims is a matter of administrative convenience. Debtors typically do not have the assets to pay 100% of the principal balance of unsecured claims — much less interest on those claims — and disallowing claims for unmatured interest thus avoids the accrual of interest (and the inconvenience of recomputing claim balances) as the case proceeds. Vanston Bondholders' Protective Comm. v. Green, 329 U.S. 156 (1946); *In re* Hanna, 872 F.2d 829 (8th Cir. 1989).

Notwithstanding § 502(b)(2), creditors holding oversecured claims (claims secured by property whose value exceeds the balance of the debt) are entitled to collect postpetition interest as part of their allowed claim, up to but not beyond the value of the collateral. 11 U.S.C. § 506(a)-(b). Interest on secured claims is discussed in further detail in § 16.03[B][1][a][ii] *infra*.

27 11 U.S.C. § 502(a)(claims deemed allowed unless party in interest objects).

28 *Id.* § 502(b) (if objection is filed, court must determine amount of allowed claim after notice and hearing). Section 502(b) elaborates the circumstances upon which the court must disallow a creditor's claim; its full reach is beyond the scope of this book.

29 This general statement is subject to two caveats regarding its scope. First, while the secured party's lien itself is respected, the secured party's nonbankruptcy remedies to enforce that lien (such as foreclosure) are stayed during the pendency of bankruptcy, as discussed in § 16.03[A] *infra*. Second, there are certain circumstances in which the Code gives the trustee or the debtor

upon certain of the debtor's assets (such as a mortgage or Article 9 security interest) is treated as the holder of a *secured claim* against those assets and retains its prebankruptcy priority for any distribution from those assets.[30] If Bank holds a valid Article 9 security interest in Chapter 7 Debtor's inventory (worth $100,000) to secure a debt of $40,000, Bank will be repaid its $40,000 from the proceeds of the inventory before any administrative expenses or general creditors will be paid.[31] In contrast, the holders of *unsecured claims* — general creditors without any prepetition lien against specific assets of the debtor — are repaid only on a pro rata basis to the extent that assets remain after payment of secured claims and the expenses of bankruptcy administration.[32]

In some cases, however, a creditor will hold an *undersecured* claim — a claim that is secured by a lien upon assets of the debtor, the value of which is less than the total balance of the creditor's allowed claim. For example, suppose Bank holds a valid Article 9 security interest in Chapter 7 Debtor's inventory (worth $40,000) to secure a debt of $100,000. Outside of bankruptcy, the creditor would be deemed to hold one legal claim against the debtor in the amount of $100,000. The Bankruptcy Code, however, "bifurcates" the claim of an undersecured creditor such as Bank. Section 506(a) treats Bank's claim as if it were *two separate claims* — a secured claim equal to the value of the collateral, and an unsecured claim to the extent of the deficiency balance of Bank's claim.[33] In this example, Bank would thus have a secured claim of $40,000 and an unsecured claim of $60,000.[34]

---

the power to avoid a creditor's security interest, either in whole or in part, in order to advance one or more of the Code's underlying policy objectives. These "avoiding powers" are discussed in § 16.04 *infra*.

[30] 11 U.S.C. § 506(a).

[31] The trustee could, however, first deduct the "reasonable, necessary costs and expenses" of preserving and disposing of the inventory to the extent those costs and expenses provided a benefit to Bank. *Id.* § 506(c).

[32] *Id.* §§ 726(a), 507(b).

[33] Section 506(a) literally states that an allowed claim secured by a valid lien on certain property is secured to the extent of "the value of such creditor's interest in the estate's interest in such property." 11 U.S.C. § 506(a). In interpreting § 506(a), the Supreme Court has equated the quoted language with "the value of the collateral." United Savings Ass'n of Tex. v. Timbers of Inwood Forest Assocs., Ltd., 484 U.S. 365 (1988).

[34] In this hypothetical, the most likely scenario is that the Chapter 7 trustee will abandon the property to Bank, which will conduct an Article 9 sale of the inventory and apply the proceeds to Bank's debt. The unsecured portion of the Bank's claim (the portion remaining after Bank sells the inventory) will be discharged in bankruptcy following any pro rata distribution to unsecured creditors.

In limited circumstances, Chapter 7 debtors may attempt to retain an overencumbered asset (such as a house or a valuable piece of art or jewelry). For example, suppose that a Chapter 7 debtor owns a home worth $60,000 that is subject to a mortgage held by Bank securing a debt of $70,000. Debtor wishes to retain possession of her home because she is worried that after bankruptcy, she will be unable to obtain credit to purchase another home. Thus, Debtor continues making her monthly mortgage payments in order to avoid losing her home (although she is not paying any of her other debts). Under § 506(a), Bank would have a secured claim for $60,000 and an unsecured claim of $10,000; further, Debtor's liability for the unsecured claim will be discharged. Bank's

Few issues have generated more controversy in bankruptcy than the proper method for determining the value of a secured party's collateral. Rather than specify one particular measure of value for all collateral valuations, section 506(a) instead provides a flexible, case-by-case standard, under which the court should determine the value of collateral "in light of the purpose of the valuation and of the proposed disposition or use of such property. . . ."[35] While bankruptcy courts have struggled to apply section 506(a) in a consistent fashion, section 506(a)'s fact-driven inquiry suggests that the court's determination of the collateral's "market value" should be influenced by both the debtor's proposed use of the collateral and the procedural context of the bankruptcy case.[36] In some contexts, the surrounding circumstances will justify a court's decision to value the collateral at its "wholesale" or "liquidation" value; in other contexts, the court may choose to value the collateral at its "retail" or "going concern" value.[37]

§ 16.03 The Automatic Stay

[A] Nature and Scope

Outside of bankruptcy, creditors can resort to their ordinary collection remedies upon the debtor's default. The filing of a bankruptcy petition, however, automatically triggers the stay authorized by section 362, which enjoins creditors from exercising their ordinary remedies to enforce or collect debts that arose prior to the bankruptcy petition.[38] Under section 362(a), the filing of a bankruptcy petition means that a creditor legally may not engage in any of the following customary collection activities: filing suit to collect a prepetition debt;[39] prosecuting a previously filed suit to collect a prepetition debt;[40] enforcing a judgment obtained prior to bankruptcy;[41] attaching, levying upon, or repossessing property of the bankruptcy estate;[42] obtaining, perfecting, or enforcing a lien

---

mortgage lien, however, will survive bankruptcy unaffected, and thus if Debtor wants to avoid foreclosure of the lien following bankruptcy, Debtor will have to repay the entire mortgage balance, not just the $60,000 secured portion of Bank's claim. Dewsnup v. Timm, 502 U.S. 410 (1992).

In Chapter 11 cases only, the Code gives the undersecured creditor an option: it can (i) allow its claim to be bifurcated under § 506(b); or (ii) elect to have its entire claim treated as secured under § 1111(b), notwithstanding § 506(a). 11 U.S.C. § 1111(b). In the example given in the text, if Bank exercises its § 1111(b) election, Bank would have a secured claim for $100,000 and no unsecured claim at all. As a result of this election, Bank would have no right to receive any distributions that are made to unsecured creditors.

35 11 U.S.C. § 506(a).

36 For a thoughtful treatment of valuation issues in bankruptcy, *see* Robert M. Lawless & Stephen P. Ferris, *Economics and the Rhetoric of Valuation*, 5 J. Bankr. L. & Prac. 3 (1995).

37 *See infra* § 16.03[B] (valuation in context of motions for relief from automatic stay); § 16.04[F] (valuation in context of fraudulent transfer actions); § 16.08 (valuation in context of redemption).

38 11 U.S.C. § 362(a). The stay is self-executing; it arises automatically upon the filing of the bankruptcy petition, without any action by the debtor or by the bankruptcy court.

39 *Id.* § 362(a)(1).

40 *Id.*

41 *Id.* § 362(a)(2).

42 *Id.* § 362(a)(3).

or security interest in property of the bankruptcy estate;[43] or taking any other action "to collect, assess, or recover" a prepetition debt (including setting off a mutual debt owed to the debtor).[44] Section 362(a) defines the scope of the stay in such broad and sweeping terms that dunning letters, phone calls to the debtor, and even polite requests for payment must stop once the debtor files its bankruptcy petition. Once a bankruptcy petition is filed, creditors "may continue to breathe, eat and sleep and are free to dream about the debtor,"[45] but cannot do anything else with regard to the debtor unless that action falls within the limited and exclusive set of exceptions specified in section 362(b).[46]

What happens when a creditor violates the automatic stay? Generally speaking, the debtor is unaffected; creditor actions taken in violation of the automatic stay are void.[47] A creditor cannot argue that its actions should be given effect because it lacked notice or knowledge of the debtor's bankruptcy filing; actions that violate the stay are void even if the creditor honestly was unaware of the bankruptcy filing. Furthermore, there are potentially serious financial consequences for the creditor who knowingly violates the stay. Under section 362(h), anyone who suffers injury as a result of a willful violation of the stay can recover actual damages (including costs and attorneys' fees).[48] In addition,

---

[43] *Id.* § 362(a)(4), (5).

[44] *Id.* § 362(a)(6), (7). The Supreme Court has held, however, that while a bank may not effect a setoff of the debtor's bank account without obtaining relief from the stay, a bank can place an "administrative freeze" on a debtor's bank account — thereby preventing any disbursements from the account — without violating the stay. Citizens Bank of Md. v. Strumpf, 516 U.S. 16 (1995).

[45] David G. Epstein, Steve H. Nickles & James J. White, *Bankruptcy*; § 3-1, at 61 (West 1992).

[46] Section 362(b) allows the commencement or continuation of certain actions to establish or enforce the debtor's noncommercial obligations. *See* 11 U.S.C. §§ 362(b)(1)(criminal proceedings against debtor); 362(b)(2) (actions to establish paternity or orders for alimony, maintenance or support); 362(b)(4)-(5) (actions by governmental units to enforce police or regulatory power); 362(b)(9) (governmental tax audits and issuance of tax deficiency notices). Section 362(b)(10) permits a landlord of nonresidential land to repossess land from the debtor if the lease has expired. Finally, section 362(b)(3) permits a secured party to perfect a lien against property of the estate (such as by filing an Article 9 financing statement) after the petition date, notwithstanding the stay prohibitions in section 362(a)(4)-(5), in two limited circumstances that will be discussed in conjunction with the trustee's avoiding powers in § 16.04[B] and § 16.04[E] *infra*.

[47] *In re* Schwartz, 954 F.2d 569 (9th Cir. 1992) (postpetition IRS tax assessment was void); *In re* Smith, 876 F.2d 524 (6th Cir. 1989) (postpetition disposition of collateral by secured party was void); *In re* Ward, 837 F.2d 124 (3d Cir. 1988) (postpetition sheriff's foreclosure sale was void).

[48] 11 U.S.C. § 362(h). On its face, section 362(h) limits the availability of damages to individual debtors. A number of courts have interpreted this provision literally and have refused to award damages or fees to corporate debtors harmed by willful stay violations. *In re* Chateaugay Corp., 920 F.2d 183 (2d Cir. 1990). Other courts have held that section 362(h)'s reference to "individual" debtors was likely a drafting error by Congress and have awarded damages or fees to corporate debtors. Budget Serv. Co. v. Better Homes of Va., Inc., 804 F.2d 289 (4th Cir. 1986). Courts have also disagreed as to whether the trustee can recover damages and fees under § 362(h). *Compare In re* Pace, 67 F.3d 187 (9th Cir. 1995) (no, trustee not an "individual") *with In re* Garofalo's Finer Foods, Inc., 186 B.R. 414 (N.D. Ill. 1995) (yes, trustee is an "individual").

section 362(h) authorizes the award of punitive damages for willful stay violations that involve egregious or outrageous conduct. [49]

Unless the bankruptcy court terminates or modifies the effectiveness of the stay, it remains in effect until the bankruptcy case is closed or dismissed, or until the debtor receives its discharge, whichever first occurs. [50] Further, the stay remains in effect to enjoin actions against any object that is property of the bankruptcy estate for as long as that object remains a part of the bankruptcy estate. [51]

By halting all external collection efforts, the stay essentially forces creditors to resolve their claims against the debtor through the collective bankruptcy process, under the supervision of the bankruptcy court. The injunctive nature of the stay thus helps to promote the key objectives of the bankruptcy process: to provide the debtor with a "breathing spell" during which the debtor can arrange a plan for its reorganization or its orderly liquidation without undue pressure or harassment from creditors, [52] and to preserve the assets of the bankruptcy estate for equitable distribution to similarly situated creditors. [53]

[B] Relief from Stay

In adopting a broad, self-executing stay, Congress recognized that there would be situations in which a creditor's interest in carrying out an otherwise stayed action (*e.g.,* repossession and foreclosure of collateral) would outweigh the interests of the estate or the debtor in having the stay remain in effect. Congress thus provided a mechanism whereby the court, at the request of an affected creditor, could grant relief from the automatic stay to permit that creditor to act in a manner otherwise forbidden by section 362(a). [54] The Bankruptcy Code sets forth two standards for relief from the stay that

---

49 *See, e.g., In re* Wagner, 74 B.R. 898 (Bankr. E.D. Pa. 1987) (secured party burst into debtor's home, extinguished lights, held finger to debtor's head and threatened to "blow [debtor's] brains out" unless debtor repaid debt). Such egregious examples are easy, but some bankruptcy courts have also awarded punitive damages for creditor activity that posed no such physical threats. For example, a Florida bankruptcy court awarded punitive damages totaling $10,000 to a married couple against a creditor who, after learning the couple had filed a Chapter 7 petition, continued to send dunning letters and phone the debtors in an attempt to collect a $770 debt. *In re* Miller, 200 B.R. 415, 417 (Bankr. M.D. Fla. 1996).

50 11 U.S.C. § 362(c)(2).

51 *Id.* § 362(c)(1). During the case, property of the estate remains in the estate unless it is liquidated, abandoned under section 554, or the debtor can and does claim the property as exempt under section 522. In reorganization cases, title to property of the estate is vested back into the reorganized debtor upon confirmation of a plan of reorganization. *Id.* §§ 1141(b) (Chapter 11); 1227(b) (Chapter 12); 1327(b) (Chapter 13).

52 H.R. Rep. No. 595, 95th Cong., 1st Sess. 340.

53 *In re* Richardson Builders, Inc., 123 B.R. 736, 738 (Bankr. W.D. Va. 1990).

54 Section 362(d) specifies four types of relief that the bankruptcy court might order. First, the court could *terminate* the stay, permitting a creditor to begin or resume its collection efforts, but without validating any prior actions taken in violation of the stay. Second, the court could *annul* the stay, thereby validating any prior actions taken in violation of the stay. Third, the court could *modify* the stay, permitting a creditor to take a particular action but otherwise leaving the stay

are relevant to Article 9 secured parties: section 361(d)(1), which entitles a creditor to relief for "cause," and section 362(d)(2), which entitles a creditor to relief if the debtor has no equity in the collateral and the collateral is not necessary for the debtor's effective reorganization.[55]

[1] Relief for "Cause" — 11 U.S.C. § 362 (d)(1)

Section 362(d)(1) provides that the court shall grant a creditor relief from the stay if that creditor demonstrates "cause, including the lack of adequate protection of an interest in property" held by that creditor.[56]

[a] Lack of adequate protection

The most frequently litigated ground in lifting the automatic stay for "cause" involves an allegation by a creditor that its interest in the debtor's property is not being "adequately protected." Because an unsecured creditor has no interest in any specific assets of the debtor, relief for lack of adequate protection is limited to creditors (such as Article 9 secured parties) with valid and enforceable interests in specific assets of the debtor under nonbankruptcy law.

[i] Preserving the value of the secured party's encumbrance

Outside of bankruptcy, following default, a secured party could repossess its collateral from the debtor, liquidate the collateral in compliance with applicable law, recover the collateral's value as of the date of the sale, and apply that amount to the underlying debt. By preventing the creditor from repossessing and selling the collateral, and by allowing the trustee or DIP to retain and use the collateral,[57] the stay imposes upon the secured party a risk that its collateral may depreciate during the pendency of the bankruptcy case. This depreciation could result from ordinary fluctuations in the value of the collateral,[58] from use of the collateral that physically exhausts the collateral's economic value,[59] or from damage to or destruction of the collateral in an uninsured casualty.

This risk of depreciation during bankruptcy poses an unacceptable threat to the secured party. Consider, for example, the plight of Bank, which possesses a valid lien upon

---

in place with respect to other actions (*e.g.*, allowing the creditor to reduce an unliquidated claim to judgment in state court, but not allowing any execution upon that judgment). Fourth, the court could *condition* the continued effectiveness of the stay upon some action by the trustee or the debtor (*e.g.*, allowing the stay to remain in effect upon the condition that the debtor file its reorganization plan within 30 days).

[55] 11 U.S.C. § 362(d). Section 362(d)(3) also permits relief from the stay to certain real estate mortgagees in cases involving "single asset real estate."

[56] *Id.* § 362(d)(1).

[57] Under section 363(d), the trustee generally may use property of the estate in the ordinary course of business, without notice or hearing. The debtor in possession in a Chapter 11 case, or the debtor in a Chapter 12 or 13 case, also has the powers of a trustee under section 363(d). 11 U.S.C. §§ 1107(a), 1203, 1303.

[58] For example, inventory might decrease in value due to functional or stylistic obsolescence.

[59] For example, by driving a car 2,000 miles per month during the pendency of the bankruptcy, Debtor would exhaust some portion of the car's useful life.

Debtor's car to secure a $5,000 debt. Debtor files a Chapter 11 petition, and on the petition date, the car's value is $5,000. During the Debtor's bankruptcy, however, the debtor's continued operation of the car will cause it to depreciate (for the sake of this example, assume that this depreciation can be measured at $150 per month). This depreciation would be of no consequence if Debtor could repay Bank the full $5,000 balance of the debt, but given Debtor's insolvency, full repayment is unlikely. Indeed, Debtor theoretically could remain in Chapter 11 for twelve months, fail to reorganize successfully, and then convert to a Chapter 7 liquidation. During that twelve months, the car would depreciate in value by $1,800, with the result that the car would bring only $3,200 at sale. Debtor's postpetition use of the car thus creates a threat that Bank — which could have recovered its claim in full but for the stay — will instead recover only a portion of its original secured claim. In this circumstance, Debtor's use of the car means that Bank's security interest in the car is not adequately protected.

In drafting section 362, Congress provided a mechanism for a secured party such as Bank to protect itself from the risk of depreciation during the pendency of bankruptcy. Because "cause" for relief from stay includes "lack of adequate protection," Bank can request that the bankruptcy court terminate the stay (to permit Bank to foreclose on its security interest immediately) or condition the continued effectiveness of the stay upon Debtor's providing "adequate protection" of Bank's security interest.[60] Once Bank makes this request,[61] Debtor must either provide Bank with adequate protection of its security interest or surrender the collateral to the secured party; if Debtor does neither, the bankruptcy court must lift the stay and permit Bank to pursue its nonbankruptcy remedies.

The trustee/DIP enjoys some flexibility under the Bankruptcy Code in how to provide adequate protection of a secured party's interest. Action by the trustee/DIP will be sufficient to provide adequate protection if it eliminates the risk that continuation of the stay will impose a depreciation loss upon the secured party.[62] As a result, it is perhaps easiest to think of adequate protection as being like "insurance" against depreciation in the collateral. To provide adequate protection of a secured party's interest in collateral, the trustee/DIP must ensure that the value of the secured party's collateral (either the original collateral or some substitute collateral) is preserved or that the secured party is compensated for any depreciation. Section 361 provides an illustrative list of the ways in which the trustee/DIP might provide adequate protection:

- *Cash payments.* If the estate has sufficient unencumbered funds, the trustee/DIP can make cash payments to the secured party in an amount necessary to offset the expected depreciation in the collateral's value. The

---

60 Although section 363(d) authorizes the trustee to use a secured party's collateral in the ordinary course of business, section 363(e) provides that, upon the secured party's request, the court may prohibit or condition the trustee's use of the collateral "as is necessary to provide adequate protection" of the secured party's interest in the collateral.

61 This request is typically made by way of a pleading filed with the court and entitled either "Motion to Lift Stay" or "Motion for Adequate Protection."

62 Thus, for example, if the debtor has allowed casualty insurance upon the collateral to lapse, adequate protection requires that the trustee/DIP insure the collateral up to its then-current value. *In re* Hancock, 126 B.R. 270 (Bankr. E.D. Tex. 1991) (lapse of insurance coverage resulted in lack of adequate protection).

secured party would apply these payments to reduce the debt, thereby maintaining the value of the collateral relative to the underlying debt. [63]

- *Replacement lien.* If the estate has equity in another asset and the equity in that asset exceeds the anticipated depreciation of the collateral, the trustee can grant the secured party an additional lien upon that other asset. [64]

- *The "Indubitable Equivalent."* The trustee can provide any other form of relief that will provide the secured party with the "indubitable equivalent" of its interest in the collateral. [65]

Although the term "indubitable equivalent" is maddeningly vague, [66] it includes the existence of an "equity cushion," meaning any surplus value (*i.e.*, equity) in the collateral over and above the balance of the debt. For example, in the immediately preceding hypothetical, if Debtor's car had a value of $9,000 on the petition date, Bank would have a $4,000 equity cushion (the car's excess value relative to the $5,000 debt). Even if Debtor remained in bankruptcy for two years and the car depreciated throughout the duration of the bankruptcy, Bank would still remain fully secured; thus, Bank's security interest is not seriously threatened as of the petition date. Under those circumstances, then, the court properly should refuse to grant Bank relief from the stay, because the equity cushion provides adequate protection for Bank's security interest. [67]

[ii]   The problem of lost opportunity costs

When the debtor files for bankruptcy, it typically ceases making payments on its debts. The consequence is that any creditor holding a claim against the debtor is not collecting the interest that the debtor is obligated to pay under their agreement and applicable

---

[63] 11 U.S.C. § 361(1).

[64] *Id.* § 361(2).

[65] *Id.* § 361(3).

[66] The phrase "indubitable equivalent" comes from an opinion by Judge Learned Hand in *In re* Murel Holding Corp., 75 F.2d 941 (2d Cir. 1935), where Judge Hand used the term "most indubitable equivalence" in attempting to explain the parameters of the term "adequate protection" as it was used under the Bankruptcy Act of 1898.

[67] *In re* Mellor, 734 F.2d 1396 (9th Cir. 1984); *In re* Colonial Ctr., Inc., 156 B.R. 452 (Bankr. E.D. Pa. 1993). Over time, of course, depreciation of the collateral would eventually consume the equity cushion. Once the equity cushion is consumed and the secured party is no longer oversecured, the secured party could again request adequate protection of its interest and thereafter, the trustee would be obligated to provide adequate protection sufficient to satisfy sections 361-363.

Occasionally, creditors have tried to argue that the equity cushion itself must be adequately protected. One could argue that, as an economic matter, the creditor who bargained for the security of an equity cushion may have agreed to accept a lower interest rate or may have made other concessions in return, such that protection of the equity cushion is necessary in order to provide the creditor with the assurance of its bargain. Courts, however, have generally rejected arguments that the trustee/DIP must provide adequate protection of the equity cushion itself. *In re* Senior Care Properties, Inc., 137 B.R. 527 (Bankr. N.D. Fla. 1992) (insufficient equity cushion does not justify relief from stay based upon lack of adequate protection); *In re* Lane, 108 B.R. 6 (Bankr. D. Mass. 1989) (same).

nonbankruptcy law. Outside of bankruptcy, of course, a secured party could repossess its collateral following default, liquidate the collateral, apply the proceeds to the debt, and then reinvest those proceeds in some alternative investment opportunity that would produce a return — *e.g.*, it could reloan the proceeds to a solvent borrower capable of paying interest. By preventing the secured party from pursuing this course of action, the stay imposes a lost opportunity cost upon the secured party. Further, as discussed earlier, bankruptcy law generally compounds this burden by disallowing claims for unmatured interest.[68]

For some secured creditors, Bankruptcy Code section 506(b)partially mitigates this effect of the automatic stay. Section 506(b) provides that *oversecured* creditors — creditors with collateral of a value that exceeds the balance of their allowed claims -are entitled to collect interest upon their secured claims, up to but not beyond the total value of the collateral.[69]

But what about undersecured creditors? On the one hand, section 506(b) by its terms includes only oversecured creditors; thus, one can argue, by negative implication, that Congress did not intend for undersecured creditors to receive interest upon their secured claims.[70] On the other hand, outside of bankruptcy, an undersecured creditor could have used its state law security interest to liquidate the collateral following default and reinvest the proceeds in some alternative interest-bearing investment. Thus, one could also argue that the creditor's right to immediate foreclosure upon default is an "interest in property" which is not adequately protected unless the creditor receives interest upon the secured portion of its claim during the pendency of the stay.

This debate generated a significant body of case law on the question of whether "adequate protection" required the trustee to pay postpetition interest on undersecured claims. A significant number of bankruptcy court decisions held that adequate protection did require the payment of postpetition interest.[71] When the issue finally reached the Supreme Court in *United Savings Ass'n of Texas v. Timbers of Inwood Forest Associates, Ltd.*,[72] the Court concluded that undersecured creditors were *not* entitled to interest during the pendency of the stay under the guise of "adequate protection." Writing for a unanimous Court, Justice Scalia found section 506(b) determinative:

> Since [section 506(b)] permits postpetition interest to be paid only out of the "security cushion," the undersecured creditor, who has no such cushion, falls within the general rule disallowing postpetition interest. If the Code had meant to give the undersecured creditor, who is thus denied interest on his claim, interest on the value of his collateral, surely [section 506(b)] is where that disposition would have been set forth, and not

---

[68] *See* § 16.02[B] *supra*.

[69] 11 U.S.C. § 506(b). If the trustee/debtor does not pay this interest to the oversecured creditor during the pendency of the bankruptcy stay, the unpaid interest accrues and is added to the creditor's secured claim.

[70] Justice Scalia relied upon this argument in rejecting the undersecured creditor's right to collect interest under the guise of "adequate protection" in United Savings Ass'n of Tex. v. Timbers of Inwood Forest Assocs., Ltd., 484 U.S. 365 (1988), discussed below.

[71] *E.g.*, *In re* American Mariner Indus., Inc., 734 F.2d 426 (9th Cir. 1984).

[72] 484 U.S. 365 (1988).

obscured within the "adequate protection" provision of § 362(d)(1).[73] The *Timbers* decision has been criticized for both its economic premises[74] and its method of statutory interpretation,[75] but the Court's subsequent bankruptcy decisions have never directly questioned *Timbers*. Accordingly, *Timbers* stands for the proposition that the trustee/DIP must provide "adequate protection" only in cases where the risk of depreciation in the value of the collateral poses a threat to the secured party's overall secured position.

[b]   Other cause for relief

Section 362(d)(1) does not limit "cause" for relief from stay only to those circumstances presenting lack of adequate protection. Instead, the bankruptcy court has the discretion to grant relief from the stay in other circumstances where the harm caused by the stay outweighs the benefit to the estate and the debtor from continuing the stay's effectiveness. Thus, courts have terminated the stay upon concluding that a debtor had filed its bankruptcy petition in bad faith or in a clear attempt to abuse the bankruptcy process.

An illustrative example is *In re Dixie Broadcasting, Inc.*,[76] where the debtor had entered into a contract to sell a radio station but later reneged when it received a better offer from another prospective purchaser. When the contract vendee sued for specific performance, the debtor filed a Chapter 11 petition in order to stay the state court from ordering specific performance. The court granted the vendee's motion to lift the stay, and the Eleventh Circuit affirmed, stating that "[t]he Bankruptcy Code is not intended to insulate financially secure sellers or buyers from the bargains they strike."[77] Likewise, courts have lifted the stay against pending litigation based upon the conclusion that the litigation would be more appropriately resolved in a forum other than the bankruptcy court.[78]

---

[73] *Timbers*, 484 U.S. at 372-373 (citations omitted).

[74] Douglas G. Baird, *The Elements of Bankruptcy* 204 (rev. ed. 1993) ("[o]ne can look at *Timbers* as essentially requiring Bank to make a forced, interest-free loan for the duration of the bankruptcy"); David Gray Carlson, *Adequate Protection Payments and the Surrender of Cash Collateral in Chapter 11 Reorganizations*, 15 Cardozo L. Rev. 1357, 1359 (1994) (*Timbers* "denies that time exists").

[75] Justice Scalia's statement that there is no express statutory authority for the payment of interest to undersecured creditors seems disingenuous in light of the "indubitable equivalent" language of section 361(3). In economic terms, part of the "indubitable equivalent" of a secured party's interest in collateral is the interest that the secured party could earn upon liquidation of the collateral and reinvestment of the proceeds.

[76] 871 F.2d 1023 (11th Cir.), *cert. denied*, 493 U.S. 853 (1989).

[77] *Id.* at 1028.

[78] For example, the Fourth Circuit has suggested that the court can consider lifting the stay where the issues involved in pending litigation involve only state law such that the expertise of the bankruptcy court is unnecessary, and where modifying the stay to permit litigation to proceed in state court would promote judicial economy. *In re* Robbins, 964 F.2d 342 (4th Cir. 1992). *See also In re* MacDonald, 755 F.2d 715 (9th Cir. 1985) (bankruptcy court lifted stay to permit pursuit of state court spousal support modification, in deference to state court expertise regarding family law matters); Garland Coal & Mining Co. v. United Mine Workers of Am., 778 F.2d 1297 (8th Cir. 1985) (bankruptcy courts ordinarily should lift stay to allow resolution of labor disputes through arbitration).

[2] Relief Under 11 U.S.C. § 362(d)(2)

Under section 362(d)(2), a secured party can obtain relief from the stay in order to repossess and foreclose upon its collateral, if "the debtor does not have an equity" in the collateral and the collateral "is not necessary to an effective reorganization."[79] If these grounds for relief are present, then relief from the stay is both necessary and appropriate; under such circumstances, neither the debtor nor general creditors will benefit if the collateral remains property of the estate.

[a] Does Debtor have equity in the collateral?

For purposes of section 362(d)(2), the debtor has no "equity" in an asset if the sum of all encumbrances on that asset exceeds the value of the asset.[80] To make this determination, of course, the bankruptcy court must determine the value of the collateral. The Bankruptcy Code does not specify a particular method of appraisal. Typically, the interested parties (usually the party seeking relief from stay and the trustee/DIP) present evidence regarding the value of the collateral, sometimes in the form of expert testimony. The bankruptcy court considers this evidence and makes a determination of the collateral's value "in light of the purpose of the valuation and of the collateral's proposed disposition or use,"[81] with the burden of persuasion placed upon the party seeking relief from the stay.[82] If the court's valuation reflects that the debtor does have equity in the collateral, the secured party's motion for relief from the stay under section 362(d)(2) must be denied — as it should be, because the purpose of the stay is to protect that equity for the benefit of general creditors and the debtor's potential reorganization.

As stated above, section 506(a) requires the court to value the collateral "in light of the purpose of the valuation and of the collateral's proposed disposition or use," but what does this statement really mean? The proper interpretation of this language has generated significant litigation in the bankruptcy courts, with significant disagreement among different courts. Perhaps the best example of the divergent judicial views has involved the valuation of vehicles. For example, suppose Debtor owns an automobile subject to a valid and properly perfected security interest in favor of Bank, securing Debtor's obligation to Bank in the amount of $10,000. Debtor files a Chapter 13 petition and wants to retain the automobile. This particular make and model of automobile has a "bluebook" retail value of $12,000 and a "bluebook" wholesale value of $9,900. In the context of a motion to lift the stay, should the court value Debtor's automobile at its retail value (leaving Debtor with equity in the automobile) or at its wholesale value (leaving Debtor with no equity)?[83] Prior to 1997, courts generally followed one of three approaches to

---

[79] 11 U.S.C. § 362(d)(2). In a liquidation proceeding under Chapter 7, the debtor is not contemplating any reorganization; thus, only the first ground (lack of equity) is relevant.

[80] *In re* Sun Valley Newspapers, Inc., 171 B.R. 71 (Bankr. 9th Cir. 1994); *In re* Hurst, 212 B.R. 890 (Bankr. W.D. Tenn. 1997).

[81] 11 U.S.C. § 506(a).

[82] 11 U.S.C. § 362(g)(1); *In re* Dandridge, 221 B.R. 741 (Bankr. W.D. Tenn. 1998); *In re* Food Barn Stores, Inc., 159 B.R. 264 (Bankr. W.D. Mo. 1993).

[83] It is more accurate to ask "which measure should be the *starting point*" for the court's valuation. Obviously, if the auto is in below-average condition and in need of repair, the court should

this question. A significant number of courts argued that where a debtor proposes to retain an automobile as a part of its reorganization, the court should value the auto at its "going concern" or "retail" value.[84] Many other courts argued that the court should value the automobile at its "wholesale" or "liquidation" value, on the theory that such a valuation more readily reflects the amount that a secured party like Bank would obtain if it could foreclose upon the automobile.[85] Yet other courts took a third, intermediate approach, holding that courts should value the automobile at the average of its retail and wholesale values.[86]

In 1997, the U.S. Supreme Court addressed this issue in *Associates Commercial Corp. v. Rash*.[87] In the *Rash* case, the debtor proposed to retain a tractor-trailer truck to use in his Chapter 13 reorganization efforts. The Fifth Circuit affirmed the bankruptcy court's valuation of the truck at its "net foreclosure value" (*i.e.*, its liquidation value) rather than its "going concern" value.[88] By an 8-1 margin, the Supreme Court reversed and remanded, holding that where the debtor proposed to retain the collateral in a Chapter 13 case, section 506(a) required the court to value the collateral at its "replacement value" — that is, "the price a willing buyer in the debtor's trade, business, or situation would pay to obtain like property from a willing seller."[89] Justice Ginsburg's opinion suggests that this replacement-value measure is appropriate based upon the risks presented to the secured party when the debtor proposes to retain the collateral:

> When a debtor surrenders the property, a creditor obtains it immediately, and is free to sell it and reinvest the proceeds. . . . If a debtor keeps the property and continues to use it, the creditor obtains at once neither the property nor its value and is exposed to double risks: The debtor may again default and the property may deteriorate from extended use. Adjustments in the interest rate and secured creditor demands for more "adequate protection" do not fully offset these risks.

> Of prime significance, the replacement-value standard accurately gauges the debtor's "use" of the property. . . . The debtor in this case elected to use the collateral to generate an income stream. That actual use, rather than a foreclosure sale that will not take place, is the proper guide under a prescription hinged to the property's "disposition or use."[90]

---

reduce the value of the auto below its "bluebook" value accordingly. In contrast, if the auto has low mileage and is generally in excellent condition, the court should increase the value of the auto above its "bluebook" value.

[84] *E.g., In re* Trimble, 50 F.3d 530 (8th Cir. 1995) (value of automobile properly based upon retail value, without deduction for costs of sale).

[85] *E.g., In re* Mitchell, 954 F.2d 557 (9th Cir.), *cert. denied*, 506 U.S. 908 (1992).

[86] *E.g., In re* Hoskins, 102 F.3d 311 (7th Cir. 1996).

[87] 90 F.3d 1036 (5th Cir. 1996), *rev'd*, 117 S. Ct. 1879 (1997).

[88] *Rash*, 90 F.3d at 1044 ("[T]he creditor's interest is in the nature of a security interest, giving the creditor the right to repossess and sell the collateral and nothing more. . . . [T]he valuation should start with what the creditor could realize by exercising that right.").

[89] *Rash*, 117 S. Ct. at 1884.

[90] *Id.* at 1885-86 (citations and footnotes omitted).

(Matthew Bender & Co., Inc.)

Just as soon as the Supreme Court "clarified" this issue by adopting the replacement-value standard, however, the Court immediately confused it again in a footnote, stating "[w]hether replacement value is the equivalent of retail value, wholesale value, or some other value will depend on the type of debtor and the nature of the property."[91] The Court's point is a legitimate one — although some debtors could only obtain a replacement vehicle through a retail dealer, other debtors could acquire a replacement vehicle at a wholesale price (such as through a private auto auction). For this latter type of debtor, "replacement value" should mean wholesale value.[92] Furthermore, the Court also noted that even where retail value is the appropriate starting point for valuation, the court could make an appropriate downward adjustment to the value to account for the fact that the typical retail price would include some items — like warranties and reconditioning expenses — that "the debtor does not receive when he retains his vehicle."[93]

In the wake of *Rash*, courts have struggled to interpret the Supreme Court's footnote and have (perhaps unsurprisingly) continued to reach different results. Some courts have held that the "replacement value" generally means the retail value with no reduction for items such as warranty or reconditioning costs.[94] Another court has concluded that the appropriate starting point for valuation is the retail bluebook value less five percent.[95] The majority of post-*Rash* decisions have concluded that the starting point for valuing vehicles is the midpoint between the retail and wholesale bluebook values.[96]

[b] Is the collateral necessary for Debtor's reorganization?

If the valuation reflects that the debtor has no equity in the collateral, the court must grant relief from the stay, unless the debtor can prove that the collateral is "necessary for an effective reorganization" of the debtor.[97] To carry the burden of persuasion on this point,[98] the debtor must prove two things. First, the debtor must prove that the particular item of collateral is "necessary" to the debtor's reorganization effort. Courts have not read the term "necessary" too literally, however, as is reflected in *In re Fields*.[99]

---

[91] *Id.* at 1886 n.6.

[92] *In re* Oglesby, 221 B.R. 515, 517-19 (Bankr. D. Colo. 1998).

[93] *Rash*, 117 S. Ct. at 1186 n.6.

[94] *In re* Russell, 211 B.R. 12 (Bankr. E.D.N.C. 1997) (starting point for valuation is bluebook retail value).

[95] *In re* Renzelman, 227 B.R. 740 (Bankr. W.D. Mo. 1998) (five percent reduction appropriate to account for warranties, reconditioning, cleaning, detailing, dealer preparation, and other services not provided when debtor simply retains its vehicle).

[96] *In re* Oglesby, 221 B.R. 515 (Bankr. D. Colo. 1998); *In re* Younger, 216 B.R. 649 (Bankr. W.D. Okla. 1998); *In re* Franklin, 213 B.R. 781 (Bankr. N.D. Fla. 1997).

[97] 11 U.S.C. § 362(d)(2). Obviously, Chapter 7 cases contemplate liquidation of the debtor's property rather than reorganization of the debtor's financial affairs. Accordingly, in a Chapter 7 case, relief from stay should be granted if the debtor has no equity in the property.

[98] 11 U.S.C. § 362(g)(2)(party opposing relief from stay has burden of proof on all issues other than issue of debtor's equity in property); *In re* Food Barn Stores, Inc., 159 B.R. 264 (Bankr. W.D. Mo. 1993).

[99] 127 B.R. 150(Bankr. W.D. Tex. 1991).

In the *Fields* case, the secured party sought relief from the stay against certain of the debtor's assets, arguing that because the debtor had other assets it could use to reorganize, the secured party's collateral was not "necessary" to the debtor's reorganization. The court properly rejected this argument. Consider for example an air line estate which owns airplanes, each financed with a different lender. No one plane is really *necessary*, under a literal reading of that term, but how many planes would have to be lost to stay litigation before the court finally had to draw the line and deny such motions on grounds that the remaining planes were necessary? Applying such a reading to "necessary" would reward impatient creditors, while punishing creditors who, by working with the estate, exercise self-restraint and do not immediately seek relief from the stay. This approach would only encourage a post-petition race to the courthouse, in direct conflict with clear bankruptcy policy which discourages such *pre*-petition races.[100]

Instead, the court must consider the particular asset's necessity in light of the kind of debtor involved and the kind of reorganization that the debtor contemplates.[101] For example, assume that Waters' Edge, Inc., which sells clothing in its own stores and by mail order, is attempting to reorganize in Chapter 11. If Waters' Edge contemplates a reorganization plan whereby it will continue to sell its merchandise in its own retail stores, then a court would consider the debtor's trade fixtures (clothing racks, shelves, counters, cash registers, etc.) to be "necessary" to the debtor's contemplated reorganization. If Waters' Edge plans to close its retail stores, however, and sell only by mail order in the future, the court would be more likely to consider the trade fixtures to be unnecessary to the debtor's reorganization.

Second, the debtor must prove that an "effective reorganization" is possible. As the Supreme Court noted in the *Timbers* decision, this means that "there must be a 'reasonable possibility of a successful reorganization within a reasonable time'."[102] If the debtor cannot prove that it is likely to reorganize successfully or within a reasonable period of time, then the stay should be lifted -further reorganization efforts by the debtor under those circumstances will waste estate resources that could otherwise go to satisfy the claims of creditors. As a practical matter, the debtor's burden of proof on this point becomes progressively harder for the debtor to meet the longer it remains in bankruptcy. As one court has explained:

> [I]n the initial stages of a Chapter 11 proceeding, the debtor should be granted significant leeway in attempting to establish that successful reorganization is a reasonable possibility. However, as the case progresses, so too does the debtor's burden of proving that successful reorganization may be reasonably expected. . . . [T]he test should be viewed as a continuum with the scales tipping in favor of the debtor in the early stages and the burden of proof becoming greater in the later stages.[103]

---

[100] *Id.* at 152.

[101] *Id.* at 154.

[102] *Timbers*, 484 U.S. at 376 (quoting the Fifth Circuit's *en banc* opinion in the *Timbers* case). Although the quoted statement was dicta in the *Timbers* case, bankruptcy courts, in subsequent cases, have followed this standard uniformly.

[103] *In re* Ashgrove Apts. of DeKalb County, Ltd., 121 B.R. 752, 756 (Bankr. S.D. Ohio 1990).

[3] Procedural Issues and Burden of Proof

The bankruptcy court does not order relief from the stay *sua sponte*; a secured party seeking relief from the stay must file a motion with the bankruptcy court requesting that the stay be lifted. Under section 362(e), the court must act upon the motion within 30 days; if not, the moving party automatically receives the requested relief. Typically, during this 30-day period, the court conducts a hearing, after which it either (a) enters an order granting or denying the requested relief, or (b) continues the stay temporarily, pending a later final hearing and determination of the motion.[104] If the court continues the stay pending a final hearing, such final hearing must be concluded within 30 days of the preliminary hearing, unless the court extends that 30-day period with the consent of the parties or based upon "compelling circumstances."[105] In exceptional circumstances, the court can order relief from the stay without notice if the party seeking relief would be "irreparably damaged" by the delay occasioned by notice and a hearing.[106]

The moving party bears the burden of persuasion on the issue of the debtor's equity in the property.[107] Accordingly, a secured party seeking relief from the stay under section 362(d)(2) bears the burden of persuasion as to the value of the collateral. The party opposing relief from the stay (typically the trustee/DIP) bears the burden of persuasion on all other issues, including the existence of adequate protection (or other "cause") and the debtor's prospects for reorganization within a reasonable time.[108]

§ 16.04 The Trustee's Avoidance Powers

[A] Background

As discussed previously, the bankruptcy process seeks to facilitate the debtor's fresh financial start while simultaneously preserving the value of estate property and providing for the equitable treatment of similarly situated creditors. Debtors typically file for bankruptcy protection following a period of financial difficulty. During this period, some creditors may have patiently "worked with" the debtor, extending payment deadlines in an attempt to alleviate the debtor's adverse financial circumstances. Other creditors, however, may have begun exercising their state law collection remedies — reducing their claims to judgment or levying upon the debtor's assets -or may have attempted to negotiate security arrangements with the debtor in exchange for their continued forbearance. The result of these prebankruptcy machinations is that creditors who were once similarly situated may no longer be in similar positions on the petition date. In addition, such prebankruptcy actions have the potential to cause a significant depletion of the debtor's property, thereby compromising the Bankruptcy Code's objective of preserving the estate for the benefit of the debtor's reorganization and equitable distribution to creditors.

---

[104] 11 U.S.C. § 362(e).

[105] *Id.*

[106] *Id.* § 362(f).

[107] *Id.* § 362(g)(1); *In re* Dandridge, 221 B.R. 741 (Bankr. W.D. Tenn. 1998); *In re* Food Barn Stores, Inc., 159 B.R. 264 (Bankr. W.D. Mo. 1993).

[108] *Id.* § 362(g)(2); *In re* Food Barn Stores, Inc., 159 B.R. 264 (Bankr. W.D. Mo. 1993).

To combat this problem, the Bankruptcy Code authorizes a series of *avoiding powers* — causes of action that allow the bankruptcy trustee (and the debtor in reorganization proceedings [109]) to avoid, or nullify, certain inequitable or illegitimate dispositions of property by the debtor or obligations incurred by the debtor during some period of time prior to bankruptcy. The avoiding powers include:

- the "strong-arm" power to avoid unperfected security interests and other transfers made or obligations incurred by the debtor that could have been avoided by judgment lien creditors (or bona fide purchasers in the case of land) under state law; [110]

- the power to avoid transfers made or obligations incurred by the debtor that could have been avoided by an actual unsecured creditor under applicable nonbankruptcy law; [111]

- the power to avoid preferential transfers that occurred within 90 days prior to bankruptcy; [112]

- the power to avoid fraudulent transfers made or obligations incurred within one year prior to bankruptcy; [113]

- the power to avoid certain statutory liens against the debtor's property; [114]

- the power to avoid unauthorized postpetition transfers of property of the estate; [115] and

- the power to avoid certain rights of setoff against the debtor. [116]

---

[109] In a Chapter 11 or Chapter 12 case, the debtor in possession receives the powers of a trustee, including the avoiding powers. 11 U.S.C. §§ 1107(a), 1203. The Code does not expressly delegate the avoiding powers to a Chapter 13 debtor. *Id.* § 1303. The legislative history, however, suggests that "[§ 1303] does not imply that the debtor does not also possess other powers concurrently with the trustee," 124 Cong. Rec. 32,409 (floor statement of Rep. Edwards), and a majority of courts have concluded that a Chapter 13 debtor can exercise the avoiding powers. *In re* Hernandez, 150 B.R. 29 (Bankr. S.D. Tex. 1993); *In re* Pinkstaff, 121 B.R. 596 (Bankr. D. Or. 1990); *In re* Robinson, 80 B.R. 455 (Bankr. N.D. Ill. 1987).

[110] 11 U.S.C. § 544(a).

[111] *Id.* § 544(b).

[112] *Id.* § 547.

[113] *Id.* § 548.

[114] *Id.* § 545.

[115] *Id.* § 549(a). The purpose of section 549 is the preservation of the estate; once the debtor is in bankruptcy, estate property can be transferred only as authorized by the express terms of the Bankruptcy Code or by the order of the bankruptcy court. The trustee's power to avoid unauthorized postpetition transfers of estate property is subject to certain exceptions (listed in §§ 549(b) and 549(c)) that are beyond the scope of this book.

[116] Generally speaking, a creditor can offset a mutual debt it owes to the debtor if each party's debt arose prior to the petition date and the creditor would have a right of setoff under nonbankruptcy law (such as a bank's right to exercise a setoff against the debtor's funds on deposit with the bank). The trustee can prevent a creditor from exercising its setoff right, however, to the extent any of the following is true: (1) the creditor holds a disallowed claim; (2) the creditor acquired its claim from a third party after the petition date; (3) the creditor acquired its claim from

The trustee's avoiding powers enable the trustee to preserve the estate by ameliorating the harm caused by actions of creditors or the debtor just prior to or in anticipation of bankruptcy. Further, the avoiding powers allow the trustee to negate some advantages obtained by creditors prior to or in anticipation of bankruptcy, thereby ensuring comparable and equitable treatment of otherwise similarly situated creditors.

Despite the seeming breadth of the trustee's avoidance powers, however, they do not enable the trustee to set aside all prebankruptcy transfers made or obligations incurred by the debtor. Not all transfers prior to bankruptcy result in an unjustified depletion of the estate or inequitable recovery by one or more creditors. Unlimited avoidance powers would threaten the security of credit transactions generally; the risk that all prebankruptcy transactions with a bankrupt debtor might be set aside could cause creditors to overreact by refusing to extend future credit to debtors in financial distress or by extending credit upon terms that are far more unfavorable to debtors. To prevent these potential adverse effects upon credit transactions generally, Congress focused the avoiding powers only upon those transactions it considered to be nefarious — transactions that would inappropriately diminish the bankruptcy estate and/or result in unequal or inequitable distribution to creditors.

[B] Strong-Arm Power — 11 U.S.C. § 544(a)

[1] The Trustee as Hypothetical Lien Creditor vs. the Unperfected Secured Party

Section 544(a)(1) provides that the trustee can avoid any transfer made or obligation incurred by the debtor that could have been avoided by a judgment lien creditor as of the date of the bankruptcy petition.[117] This "strong-arm" power primarily allows the

---

a third party during the 90 days prior to bankruptcy and while the debtor was insolvent; or (4) the creditor incurred its debt during the 90 days prior to bankruptcy, while the debtor was insolvent, for the purpose of acquiring a right to setoff. 11 U.S.C. § 553(a). For example, if Bank had accepted $15,000 of deposits by Debtor during the week prior to Debtor's bankruptcy, while Debtor was insolvent, Bank could not use those deposits to offset Debtor's $15,000 unsecured debt to Bank. *In re* United Sciences of America, Inc., 893 F.2d 720 (5th Cir. 1990). In addition, the trustee can set aside any setoff that a creditor exercised during the 90 days prior to bankruptcy to the extent that the setoff had the effect of improving the creditor's position. 11 U.S.C. § 553(b).

117 11 U.S.C. § 544(a)(1). In addition to granting the trustee the status of hypothetical judgment lien creditor, section 544(a) grants the trustee the status of two other hypothetical persons. Section 544(a)(2) endows the trustee with the powers of a hypothetical creditor who obtained an execution upon the debtor that was returned unsatisfied. Section 544(a)(2) only has significance in those states where an unsatisfied execution confers special rights of avoidance upon the execution creditor, and thus this section is rarely used. Section 544(a)(3) bestows upon the trustee the status of a hypothetical bona fide purchaser of the debtor's land (other than fixtures). Section 544(a)(3) would thus permit the trustee to avoid an unrecorded mortgage against the debtor's land. Giving the trustee the status of a bona fide purchaser would be necessary to achieve this result because, under most state recording statutes, unrecorded mortgages are effective against judgment lien creditors; thus, the trustee could not avoid an unrecorded mortgage under section 544(a)(1).

Because section 544(a)(2) is rarely used and section 544(a)(3) deals with land, the text focuses exclusively upon section 544(a)(1) and the trustee as hypothetical judgment lien creditor.

trustee to avoid security interests that are unperfected as of the petition date, by means of a two-step process involving the combined effect of the Bankruptcy Code and Article 9.

For example, suppose that Bank possesses a security interest in Debtor's inventory (worth $100,000) to secure a debt of $100,000, but that Bank filed its financing statement only in the local county filing office, not in the central filing office. If Debtor files for bankruptcy, section 544(a)(1) arms the trustee with all of the rights and powers of a judgment lien creditor as of the petition date (Step 1), — thereby allowing the trustee to assert any rights that such a creditor could have asserted under nonbankruptcy law. U.C.C. section 9-301(1)(b), of course, provides that a lien creditor takes priority over unperfected security interests, and thus the trustee/DIP can assert its status as a lien creditor under state law to avoid Bank's unperfected security interest (Step 2). The consequences of this avoidance are twofold. First, the trustee can liquidate the inventory and use the proceeds to pay administrative expenses and unsecured creditors, rather than having to distribute them to Bank in reduction of Bank's claim against Debtor. Second, while Debtor's underlying obligation to Bank remains enforceable, the Bank's claim is treated as unsecured, significantly reducing Bank's recovery on its claim.

Note that section 544(a)(1) clothes the trustee with the status of a judgment lien creditor *even if no such creditor actually existed on the petition date*. The trustee has the status of the "hypothetical lien creditor," regardless of whether any of the debtor's actual creditors had acquired judgment liens prior to bankruptcy. To illustrate, suppose that in the above hypothetical, none of Debtor's general creditors had reduced their claims to judgment and levied upon Debtor's assets prior to bankruptcy. Outside of bankruptcy, Bank's unperfected security interest would still have had priority over the claims of Debtor's other creditors, and Bank would have recovered its claim in full.[118] The Debtor's bankruptcy filing, however, permits the trustee to assert the status of a lien creditor anyway, thereby enabling the trustee to avoid Bank's unperfected security interest.[119]

Why should the trustee/DIP be able to assert rights in bankruptcy that no general creditor could have asserted outside of bankruptcy? There are two plausible justifications for this result. The first is that unperfected security interests are really "secret liens" that create the potential for abuse by the debtor and reliance by third parties. This explanation is not terribly satisfying. Unperfected security interests constitute "secret liens" outside of bankruptcy, but they are still enforceable against general creditors under nonbankruptcy law.[120]

The second justification is that the strong-arm power serves a preventative function that helps to facilitate bankruptcy law's underlying objectives. Outside of bankruptcy, a debtor's general unsecured creditors could race to reduce their claims to judgment and

---

[118] Recall that unperfected security interests are effective even against general creditors of the Debtor. U.C.C. §§ 9-201, **R9-201(a)**.

[119] *In re* Merritt Dredging Co., Inc., 839 F.2d 203, 5 U.C.C. Rep. Serv. 2d 900 (4th Cir.), *cert. denied*, 487 U.S. 1236 (1988); *In re* Kors, Inc., 819 F.2d 19 (2d Cir. 1987); *In re* Advance Insulation & Supply, Inc., 176 B.R. 390, 3 U.C.C. Rep. Serv. 2d 1957 (Bankr. D. Md. 1994), *aff'd*, 176 B.R. 401 (D. Md. 1995).

[120] U.C.C. §§ 9-201, **R9-201(a)**.

levy upon property subject to an unperfected security interest — thereby taking priority over unperfected secured parties and other general creditors. Practically speaking, each individual creditor must participate in this race; those who delay or do not participate at all may be left with a worthless judgment against the debtor. This sort of "race" by unsecured creditors, however, may produce consequences that bankruptcy law was intended to avoid. The pressure of creditor collection activity may make it difficult or impossible for the marginal debtor to carry out its business or financial affairs. Indeed, collection activity by unsecured creditors might force the debtor into bankruptcy prematurely, when informal negotiations with creditors instead might have enabled the debtor to restructure its debts and avoid bankruptcy altogether. By enabling the trustee (as representative of the debtor's general creditors) to assert the status of a judgment lien creditor if the debtor does go bankrupt, section 544(a)(1) ostensibly encourages the debtor's general creditors not to engage in this counterproductive collection race — thereby (hopefully) maximizing the debtor's ability to sort out its financial affairs and avoid a needless bankruptcy.[121]

Note that section 544(a) allows the trustee/DIP to exercise the strong-arm power to avoid an unperfected security interest without regard to any knowledge that the trustee, the debtor, or any creditor might have.[122] In this regard, section 544(a) treats the trustee/ DIP as having a pure heart and an empty head. For example, suppose that Bank holds a security interest in all of Debtor's equipment, but that Bank filed the financing statement in the wrong office. Under U.C.C. section 9-401(2)(1972 text), a financing statement that is filed in the wrong office is still effective to perfect a security interest as against any party with knowledge of the contents of that financing statement.[123] If the trustee has actual knowledge of the Bank's security interest and the contents of its financing statement, can Bank argue that its security interest is effective against the trustee/DIP under section 9-401(2)? *No.* Section 544(a) makes the knowledge of the trustee/DIP irrelevant; the strong-arm power bestows the status of a lien creditor without knowledge of Bank's security interest, *even if no such creditor actually existed as of the petition date.* Because such a creditor would have prevailed over Bank's unperfected security

---

[121] One might describe this as the optimistic or "the glass is half-full" theory of creditor behavior. Many critics of the strong-arm power instead adopt the pessimistic "the glass is half-empty" theory of creditor behavior, arguing that it is simply naive to think that section 544(a)(1) will discourage unsecured creditors from undertaking collection activity in anticipation of bankruptcy. The pessimists may have the better of the argument here — after all, if the debtor has not yet filed for bankruptcy, what's to say the debtor *actually will* file for bankruptcy? An unsecured creditor that can win the race to the courthouse improves its likelihood of a full recovery, and if no bankruptcy ever ensues, that creditor improves its position vis-a-vis general creditors and unperfected secured creditors. As a result, unsecured creditors without crystal balls or psychic abilities will often choose to engage in this race anyway, notwithstanding the rationale of section 544(a)(1).

[122] *In re* Kitchin Equip. Co., 960 F.2d 1242, 17 U.C.C. Rep. Serv. 2d 322 (4th Cir. 1992) (debtor's knowledge not imputed to trustee to defeat strong-arm power); McEvoy v. Ron Watkins, Inc., 105 B.R. 362 (N.D. Tex. 1987) (trustee's actual knowledge irrelevant under § 544(a)); *In re* Williams, 124 B.R. 311 (Bankr. C.D. Cal. 1991) (debtor's knowledge cannot be imputed to trustee to defeat strong-arm power).

[123] U.C.C. § 9-401(2).

interest, the trustee/DIP can avoid Bank's security interest notwithstanding its actual knowledge.

Finally, note that section 544(a) empowers the trustee/DIP to avoid security interests that are unperfected as of the moment of the debtor's bankruptcy petition. Section 544(a) essentially "freezes" the positions of the debtor's respective creditors as of that moment. Consequently, section 544(a) does not allow the trustee to avoid a security interest that was properly perfected as of the petition date but becomes unperfected thereafter (such as by lapse of the five-year effectiveness of the secured party's financing statement[124] or the movement of the collateral to another state).

[2]   Relation-Back Priority — 11 U.S.C. § 546(b)

The strong-arm power creates a potential statutory trap for certain creditors who might otherwise rely upon the existence of relation-back priority rules under nonbankruptcy law. For example, suppose that Debtor purchases a drill press from Seller, who takes a purchase-money security interest (PMSI) in the press. Knowing that it has the benefit of a grace period in which to perfect its PMSI against lien creditors,[125] Seller does not file its financing statement immediately. The day after the sale, Debtor files a bankruptcy petition. Two days later, and still within the applicable state law grace period, Seller files its financing statement in the appropriate filing office. As between Trustee and Seller, what is the status of Seller's security interest?

If one looked solely at the language of section 544(a)(1), Trustee would be able to avoid Seller's security interest on the ground that Seller had not perfected that interest prior to Debtor's bankruptcy filing. Outside of bankruptcy, however, Seller's PMSI would have taken priority over the claim of an intervening lien creditor because Seller perfected its PMSI by filing within the grace period specified in U.C.C. Article 9.[126] Given the rationale of the strong-arm clause, Trustee logically should do no better than a lien creditor could have done under nonbankruptcy law. To accomplish this result, Congress limited the Trustee's strong-arm power in section 546(b) by making the power subject to those provisions of nonbankruptcy law (such as U.C.C. Article 9's grace period for perfecting PMSIs) that permit relation-back priority over lien creditors.[127] Because Seller perfected

---

[124] General Elec. Credit Corp. v. Nardulli & Sons, Inc., 836 F.2d 184, 5 U.C.C. Rep. Serv. 2d 501 (3d Cir. 1988); *see also* U.C.C. § 9-403(2)(perfection of security interest does not lapse if 5-year effectiveness of financing statement expires during insolvency proceedings; perfection continues for 60 days following termination of insolvency proceedings). **This provision has been deleted from revised Article 9, because Bankruptcy Code section 362(b)(3)permits a secured party to continue its perfected status without first obtaining relief from the stay.**

[125] U.C.C. §§ 9-301(2), **R9-317(e).**

[126] Recall that under the 1972 text, a secured party holding a purchase-money security interest may perfect that interest within ten days after the debtor receives possession of the collateral and take priority over the rights of a lien creditor whose interest arose during the gap between attachment and perfection of the security interest. U.C.C. § 9-301(2). **Revised Article 9 extends this grace period to twenty days. U.C.C. § R9-317(e).**

[127] 11 U.S.C. § 546(b)(the avoiding powers are subject to "any generally applicable law that permits perfection of an interest in property to be effective against an entity that acquires rights in such property before the date of perfection"). Note that section 546(b) does not itself authorize relation-back priority for any secured party, but only recognizes and incorporates provisions of nonbankruptcy law that provide for relation-back priority over intervening lien creditors.

its PMSI within the grace period specified in Article 9, Trustee cannot avoid Seller's PMSI under the strong-arm clause.

This example requires a brief return to consider section 362 and the effect of the automatic stay. As discussed previously,[128] the filing of the bankruptcy petition operates to stay "any act to . . . perfect . . . any lien against property of the estate."[129] On its face, this would seem to prevent Seller's postpetition financing statement from having any legal effect to perfect Seller's PMSI. Section 362(b)(3) provides an exception, however, in this particular circumstance, allowing a creditor to undertake "any act to perfect an interest in property to the extent that the trustee's rights and powers are subject to perfection under section 546(b)."[130] This exception permits a secured party in Seller's position to file its financing statement without violating the automatic stay. Note, however, that this exception only protects the secured party if it acts to perfect its interest within the applicable state law grace period.[131] Further, the exception applies only to permit the secured party's *perfection* of the interest; the stay remains effective to prevent any action to *enforce* the lien, unless the court orders relief from the stay.

[C] Subrogation to State Law Avoidance Powers of an Unsecured Creditor — 11 U.S.C. § 544(b)

Section 544(b) authorizes the trustee to avoid "any transfer of an interest of the debtor in property or any obligation incurred by the debtor that is voidable under applicable nonbankruptcy law by a creditor holding an unsecured claim.. . ."[132] Section 544(b) thus allows the trustee to assert any state law avoidance claim that could have been asserted by one of the debtor's *actual* unsecured creditors. Unlike the strong-arm clause, section 544(b) does not endow the trustee with the status of a "hypothetical" creditor. To assert an avoidance claim under section 544(b), the trustee must establish that a particular unsecured creditor of the debtor could have asserted the power to avoid the particular transfer under state law; if so, the trustee is subrogated to the rights of that creditor and can assert this claim on behalf of the estate.[133]

As a practical matter, nonbankruptcy law rarely grants unsecured creditors the power to set aside transfers by the debtor, and thus section 544(b) is of limited use to the trustee/DIP. There are two primary circumstances under which trustees/DIPs have asserted section 544(b) avoidance claims. The first involves transfers that are fraudulent under

---

[128] *See* § 16.03[A] *supra.*

[129] 11 U.S.C. § 362(a)(4).

[130] *Id.* § 362(b)(3).

[131] *In re* Continental Country Club, Inc., 64 B.R. 177 (Bankr. M.D. Fla. 1986). In the example in the text, Debtor filed its petition the day after taking possession of the drill press. Thus, to qualify for the protection of section 546(b) and not violate the automatic stay, Seller must file its financing statement within nine days of the bankruptcy petition (under the 1972 text, U.C.C. § 9-301(2)) **or within nineteen days of the petition (under the revision, § R9-317(e))**. Any filing by Seller after that period elapses would violate the automatic stay and would not perfect Seller's security interest, which could then be avoided by Trustee under section 544(a)(1).

[132] 11 U.S.C. § 544(b).

[133] *In re* Acequia, Inc., 34 F.3d 800 (9th Cir. 1994); *In re* Agricultural Research and Technology Group, Inc., 916 F.2d 528 (9th Cir. 1990).

applicable state fraudulent transfer law; these transfers are treated in greater detail in conjunction with the discussion of Code section 548.[134] The second involves bulk sale transfers that did not comply with applicable state law governing bulk sales. In a jurisdiction in which U.C.C. Article 6still governs bulk sales,[135] section 544(b) allows the trustee to set aside a bulk sale under Article 6 if it can identify a particular creditor that did not receive notice of the bulk sale.[136]

[D]   Power to Avoid Statutory Liens

"Statutory liens" are liens that arise as a matter of nonbankruptcy law "solely by force of a statute on specified circumstances or conditions."[137] Often, statutory liens reflect a legislative judgment that particular types of creditors (such as mechanics who service automobiles) deserve special protection from the risk of nonpayment. Generally speaking, statutory liens arising under nonbankruptcy law are respected in bankruptcy and the trustee/DIP cannot avoid those that were validly obtained prior to the petition date.

Section 545, however, allows the trustee/DIP to avoid a statutory lien against an asset of the debtor in three limited circumstances. First, section 545(1) permits the trustee/DIP to avoid a statutory lien against any asset where that lien took effect only because the debtor became insolvent or filed for bankruptcy.[138] This provision is necessary to preserve the efficacy of federal bankruptcy law; otherwise, states could establish statutory "insolvency" liens that would circumvent the Bankruptcy Code's priority scheme for distribution to creditors. Second, section 545(2) permits the trustee/DIP to avoid a statutory lien against any asset if that statutory lien could not have been enforced against a bona fide purchaser of the asset outside of bankruptcy.[139] Section 545(2) would allow the trustee to avoid, for example, a federal tax lien against a debtor's assets if the IRS had not filed a notice of tax lien filing as of the petition date.[140] This allows the trustee/DIP to avoid secret statutory liens to the same extent as they would be avoidable by an innocent purchaser under nonbankruptcy law. Finally, sections 545(3) and 545(4) permit the trustee/DIP to avoid any common law or statutory landlord's lien for unpaid rent.[141] Note carefully that section 545 does not authorize the trustee to avoid a lien for rent for which the lienor contractually bargained — such a lien is a security interest, not a statutory lien.[142]

---

[134] See § 16.04[F][4] infra.

[135] The National Conference of Commissioners on Uniform State Laws has repealed Article 6 from the official version of the U.C.C. Article 6has not yet been repealed, however, by all of the states that originally enacted it.

[136] In re Villa Roel, Inc., 57 B.R. 835, 42 U.C.C. Rep. Serv. 1396 (Bankr. D.D.C. 1985).

[137] 11 U.S.C. § 101(53). See Chapter 13 supra.

[138] Id. § 545(1).

[139] Id. § 545(2).

[140] In re J.B. Winchells, Inc., 106 B.R. 384 (Bankr. E.D. Pa. 1989).

[141] 11 U.S.C. § 545(3), (4). Section 545(3) has been interpreted to permit the trustee to avoid a landlord's statutory lien against the proceeds of the tenant's crop. In re Harrell, 55 B.R. 203 (Bankr. E.D.N.C. 1985).

[142] Dallas v. S.A.G., Inc., 836 F.2d 1307 (11th Cir. 1988).

[E] Power to Avoid Preferential Transfers — 11 U.S.C. § 547

[1] Background

Suppose that Debtor has two creditors, A and B, to whom Debtor owes $100 each. Suppose further that Debtor has only $100 in assets, and uses those assets to make full payment to A before declaring bankruptcy. A receives payment in full, B receives nothing. One might say that the Debtor has chosen to "prefer" A to B, or that A has received a "preferential" payment. Outside of bankruptcy, generally speaking, commercial law does not concern itself with preferential transfers. For the most part, commercial law leaves creditors like A and B to their own wiles and efforts. If Debtor pays A in full (whether voluntarily or because of A's more insistent collection efforts) and pays B nothing, that is B's problem; B could have prevented this result by pursuing its remedies more promptly or by being more insistent in its collection efforts.

Bankruptcy law, however, does care about such transfers, because one of the goals of bankruptcy is to provide a collective debt resolution process that distributes Debtor's assets in a way that treats similarly situated creditors in similar fashion. In the above example, before the payment, A and B were similarly situated general creditors; in a Chapter 7 liquidation, each creditor would have received $50 on its claim. By choosing to pay A in full and B nothing, Debtor circumvents bankruptcy's distributive scheme to the detriment of B.

While the foregoing example involves a purposeful attempt to prefer one creditor over another, transfers can have preferential effect regardless of the debtor's motive or the impetus for the transfer. For example, suppose that the payment of $100 to A had occurred not voluntarily, but instead as the result of A's execution upon a judgment obtained against Debtor. The transfer still has precisely the same effect as the voluntary payment by Debtor; without the execution, each creditor would have received $50 in a Chapter 7 liquidation.

Unless bankruptcy law provided a mechanism to deal with such transfers, creditors would have a significant incentive to engage in "last-minute" or "eve-of-insolvency" collection activities — to reduce their unsecured claims to judgment and execute upon those claims before other creditors could act, or before a financially troubled debtor was pushed to the brink of bankruptcy. Such collection activity, of course, has the potential for triggering the "race to the courthouse" that bankruptcy law seeks to avoid (or at least mitigate) in the first place. Thus, to discourage the piecemeal dismemberment of the debtor and to facilitate equitable distribution to each class of similarly situated creditors, Congress provided the trustee with the power to avoid certain preferential transfers that occur just prior to the filing of a bankruptcy petition.

[2] Proving the Elements of a Preference

The trustee can avoid any transfer (whether or not voluntary) of an interest in the debtor's property if the transfer meets all of the following characteristics specified in section 547(b):

- *The transfer must have been made to a creditor or must have benefitted a creditor.*[143] Preference law is concerned only with pre-bankruptcy

---

[143] 11 U.S.C. § 547(b)(1).

actions that enable creditors to collect their pre-bankruptcy claims (*e.g.*, the debtor repays a loan to a creditor) or render those claims more secure (*e.g.*, the debtor grants a creditor a security interest in certain assets to secure a previously unsecured obligation). If the transfer does not benefit a creditor (*e.g.*, the debtor makes a gift of valuable property to a friend), preference law does not concern itself with avoiding that transfer.[144]

● *The transfer must have been made on account of an antecedent debt, i.e., a liability that the debtor incurred before the transfer was made.*[145] Again, preference law is concerned only with those transfers that enable a creditor to collect a pre-existing debt or render a pre-existing debt more secure. Thus, if Debtor grants Bank a security interest in a car to secure a simultaneous[146] $2,000 loan to Debtor by Bank, there is no preference; Bank is not engaging in activity intended to collect or secure an obligation previously incurred by Debtor. In contrast, if Debtor grants Bank a security interest in a car to secure a previously unsecured $2,000 loan made by Bank to Debtor two months earlier, Debtor has transferred an interest in its property on account of an antecedent debt.

● *The debtor must have been insolvent when the transfer took place.*[147] Preference law is not concerned with avoiding transfers that occurred when the debtor was solvent; if the debtor is solvent, it can repay all of its pre-existing obligations, and thus any transfer by the debtor could not have the effect of preferring the recipient over any other creditor. Note that section 547 provides that in any action to avoid a preferential transfer the debtor is presumed to have been insolvent during the 90 days prior to the filing of the bankruptcy petition.[148]

---

[144] In some cases, gift transfers by the debtor prior to bankruptcy may be avoidable as fraudulent transfers under section 548. *See* § 16.04[F][2] *infra*.

[145] 11 U.S.C. § 547(b)(2).

[146] As a practical matter, a truly simultaneous transfer is unlikely. Even when Buyer pays cash to Seller to purchase goods over the counter, Buyer's payment typically occurs at least a few seconds after Buyer's obligation to pay for the goods arises. Technically speaking, even a delay of one second between the arising of Buyer's obligation and Buyer's transfer would mean that the transfer occurred on account of an antecedent debt — a result that would stretch the trustee's preference avoiding power well past the bounds of reason. As a practical matter, courts have not been inclined to interpret the term "antecedent" so restrictively as to set aside payments made in cash sales. Furthermore, as discussed *infra* § 16.04[E][4][a], section 547(c)(1) provides an exception that prevents the trustee from recovering transfers such as cash sales that involve "substantially contemporaneous" exchanges for new value. Thus, in many cases, section 547(c)(1) would mitigate the effect of a court's decision to adopt an overtly technical interpretation of section 547(b)(2).

[147] 11 U.S.C. § 547(b)(3). The Bankruptcy Code applies a "balance sheet" test for insolvency — the debtor is "insolvent" if the sum of its debts exceed the value of its assets. *Id.* § 101(32).

[148] *Id.* § 547(f). This presumption is motivated primarily by efficiency. In most bankruptcy cases, the debtor will have been insolvent for some time prior to filing its bankruptcy petition, and thus it would serve no real purpose to force the trustee to spend the time and resources necessary to reconstruct the debtor's records to prove that the debtor was insolvent at the time of the allegedly preferential transfer. As a consequence of this presumption, the recipient of the allegedly preferential

- *The transfer must have taken place within 90 days prior to the filing of the bankruptcy petition (or within one year prior to the petition, in the case of a transfer to an "insider").* [149] Preference law is concerned about transfers of the debtor's property in anticipation of the debtor's bankruptcy. The aim of preference law is to prevent creditors from "opting out" of the collective bankruptcy process by trying to collect or secure their pre-bankruptcy claims during the debtor's "slide into bankruptcy." [150] Congress could have adopted a subjective standard that focused upon the creditor's state of mind (*i.e.*, was the creditor trying to "opt out"), but this would have been very difficult to apply. Instead, the Code opted for a bright-line preference period — the 90 days immediately prior to the bankruptcy petition. Transfers that occur within this period are conclusively suspect as potential preferences, even if the creditor had no idea of the debtor's financial difficulties. In contrast, the trustee cannot reach transfers that occurred more than 90 days prior to bankruptcy, even if the benefitted creditor fully expected the debtor to seek bankruptcy protection in the near future. Note carefully that the Code expands the preference period to one year if the transferee is an "insider." [151]

Because "insiders" have a close relationship with the debtor, they could possess inside information about the debtor's financial circumstances, or could exercise control over the debtor's financial decisions (such as when to seek bankruptcy protection). To prevent insiders from using this information or control to manipulate the timing of transfers in order to avoid the trustee's preference powers, [152] the Bankruptcy Code expands the preference period to one year for transfers to insiders.

- *Finally, the transfer must have actually improved the creditor's position.* [153] Preference law works on the "no harm, no foul" principle; it is not concerned with transfers that result in the creditor being paid no more

---

transfer thus bears the burden of coming forward with evidence to demonstrate that the debtor was solvent at the time of the transfer.

[149] *Id.* § 547(b)(4).

[150] H.R. Rep. No. 595, 95th Cong., 1st Sess. 177-78.

[151] 11 U.S.C. § 101(31)provides a list of characteristics that make a transferee an "insider." Generally speaking, an "insider" can be a relative, an officer or director of a corporation, a partner of a partnership — in other words, someone who possesses a sufficiently close relationship with the debtor that they can be presumed to be in a position to possess information about the debtor's financial condition, or to possess control over the debtor's financial decisionmaking.

Note, however, that if the trustee attempts to recover an allegedly preferential transfer from an insider, and that transfer occurred more than 90 days prior to the petition date, the trustee is *not* entitled to the presumption of insolvency at the time of the transfer. The presumption of insolvency in section 547(f) is strictly limited to the 90 days immediately prior to the petition date.

[152] For example, suppose that X is president and sole shareholder of Debtor, and that X had loaned $10,000 to Debtor. As an insider, X is in a position to cause Debtor to repay its debt to X, and is also in a position to cause Debtor not to file bankruptcy until 91 days later — after the general preference period would have passed.

[153] 11 U.S.C. § 547(b)(5).

than the creditor would have received if it had been paid only through a liquidation of the debtor's assets. Section 547(b) only reaches those transfers that enabled the recipient to recover more than the recipient would have recovered through liquidation alone. To apply section 547(b), the court must determine what amount the creditor would have received in a Chapter 7 liquidation case *if the alleged preferential transfer had not been made*. If the creditor actually received more than that "hypothetical liquidation" amount, then the transfer had the effect of improving the creditor's position. Thus, suppose Debtor repays a $10,000 unsecured loan to Bank 20 days prior to filing a bankruptcy petition. If the transfer had not been made, Bank would have received only a partial distribution on its claim in a Chapter 7 liquidation.[154] By receiving payment in full prior to bankruptcy, Bank has improved its position to the detriment of other general creditors. In contrast, if Bank's loan to Debtor had been secured by inventory worth $30,000, the loan would have been fully secured; under those circumstances, Bank would have received full payment on its claim in a Chapter 7 liquidation case and the payment thus would not have improved Bank's position. For this reason, courts have held that payment to a fully secured creditor cannot be set aside as a preference.[155] Finally, what if Bank's loan to Debtor had been secured by inventory worth $5,000? In that case, Bank would have been an undersecured creditor at the time it received payment. Had Bank not received the payment and had Debtor filed a Chapter 7 petition, section 506(b) would have bifurcated Bank's claim into a secured claim of $5,000 and an unsecured claim of $5,000. In that hypothetical Chapter 7 liquidation, Bank would have received full payment of its secured claim, but less than full payment on its unsecured claim; therefore, Debtor's payment to Bank improved its position and can be avoided as a preference.[156]

---

[154] This statement assumes that Debtor is insolvent at the time of the bankruptcy petition. [Note, however, that insolvency is *not* a condition precedent to the filing of a voluntary petition in bankruptcy.] If Debtor is insolvent, by definition it has insufficient assets to pay its creditors and thus general unsecured creditors will receive less than full payment in a Chapter 7 liquidation under the Bankruptcy Code's distributive scheme. *In re* Milwaukee Cheese Wisconsin, Inc., 164 B.R. 297 (Bankr. E.D. Wis. 1993); *In re* Lease-A-Fleet, Inc., 141 B.R. 853 (Bankr. E.D. Pa. 1992).

[155] *In re* EDC, Inc., 930 F.2d 1275 (7th Cir. 1991); Braniff Airways, Inc. v. Exxon Co., U.S.A., 814 F.2d 1030 (5th Cir. 1987); *In re* Pineview Care Center, Inc., 142 B.R. 677 (Bankr. D.N.J. 1992), *aff'd*, 152 B.R. 703 (D.N.J. 1993). The statement in the text assumes that the trustee has no legitimate basis upon which to avoid Bank's security interest. If the trustee can avoid Bank's security interest under any of the avoiding powers, then Bank will be treated as an unsecured creditor and the $10,000 payment in full will have improved Bank's position. *In re* Adams, 102 B.R. 271, 10 U.C.C. Rep. Serv. 2d 1014 (Bankr. M.D. Ga. 1989).

[156] *In re* Air Conditioning, Inc. of Stuart, 845 F.2d 293 (11th Cir.), *cert. denied*, 488 U.S. 993 (1988); *see also* 4 *Collier on Bankruptcy* ¶ 547.08, at 547-47 to 547-48 ("[p]ayments to a partially secured creditor from property not covered by its lien . . . have a preferential effect, because in a chapter 7 liquidation, that creditor would receive a distribution for its lien in addition to the payments already received"). In this example, the only way that Bank could prove that it had not

[3] Determining When the Transfer Occurred

A transfer cannot be preferential unless it occurred on account of an antecedent debt and within the applicable preference period. Given these standards, the trustee must establish the date on which a transfer took place in order to establish that the transfer satisfies section 547(b). To determine the effective date of prepetition transfers, section 547(e) provides rules that establish the date a transfer is deemed to occur for purposes of preference law. For example, an allegedly preferential payment generally will be deemed to have been made whenever it legally took effect between the parties under nonbankruptcy law.[157] Thus, a $10,000 payment to Bank by Debtor on December 4 would be deemed to have occurred on December 4 for purposes of section 547(b).[158]

The granting of a security interest by the debtor can also constitute a preferential transfer. Suppose Debtor grants a security interest in its equipment to Bank one month prior to bankruptcy in order to secure a previously unsecured debt owed to Bank. As a result, Debtor has improved Bank's position as compared to other general creditors — Bank would now receive full payment to the extent of the equipment's value, whereas general creditors would receive only pro rata distributions from unencumbered assets. When the allegedly preferential transfer is the debtor's granting of a security interest, section 547(e) provides an intricate timing rule that "dates" the security interest for purposes of section 547 based upon when that security interest was "perfected." A security interest will be deemed to have been granted when it legally took effect between the parties under nonbankruptcy law (*i.e.*, upon attachment under the U.C.C.), but only if the security interest was perfected[159] at that time or within ten days thereafter (or, in

---

been made better off would be for Bank to demonstrate that it applied the payments to reduce the secured, rather than the unsecured, portion of its claim. Vern Countryman, *The Concept of a Voidable Preference in Bankruptcy*, 38 Vand. L. Rev. 713, 744 (1985).

There is some disagreement in the cases as to the proper amount of the judgment that the trustee should receive from Bank in this example. Some courts have suggested that the trustee should be able to avoid the transfer only to the extent that it was preferential. Levit v. Ingersoll Rand Fin. Corp., 874 F.2d 1186 (7th Cir. 1989) (dicta). Under this view, the trustee could not recover the $5,000 portion of the payment allocable to Bank's secured claim, as Bank would have received that $5,000 anyway in a Chapter 7 liquidation.

The actual language of section 547, however, does not seem to support this view. Section 547 does not authorize the trustee to avoid transfers to the extent that they are preferential; instead, it authorizes the trustee to "avoid any transfer" that is preferential in effect. Taken literally, section 547 thus authorizes the trustee to avoid the entire $10,000 payment from Bank. In that case, however, Bank's secured and unsecured claims are revived; Bank would then hold a $5,000 secured claim and a $5,000 unsecured claim.

157 11 U.S.C. § 547(e)(2)(A).

158 One caveat is appropriate here. If a debtor makes a payment to a creditor using a check, the Supreme Court has held that transfer (for purposes of section 547(b)) does not occur when the debtor delivers the check to the creditor, but only when the check is *actually paid* by the drawee bank. Barnhill v. Johnson, 503 U.S. 393 (1992).

159 A transfer of an interest in personal property or fixtures is "perfected" for purposes of preference law "when a creditor on a simple contract cannot acquire a judicial lien that is superior to the interest of the transferee." 11 U.S.C. § 547(e)(1)(B). Under Article 9, of course, a lien creditor cannot acquire rights superior to the holder of a validly perfected Article 9 security interest. U.C.C.

the case of a purchase-money security interest, within twenty days thereafter).[160] If the creditor delays in perfecting the security interest for more than this "grace period" following attachment, the security interest will be deemed to have been granted on the date that the creditor actually perfected that interest.[161] If the creditor has not perfected its security interest at all by the later of the petition date or the end of the applicable grace period following attachment, the security interest will be deemed to have been granted on the date of the bankruptcy petition.[162]

Section 547(e)'s timing rule can be demonstrated by the following example. Suppose Debtor borrowed $20,000 from Bank on June 1, simultaneously granted Bank a security interest in certain equipment to secure repayment of this debt, and then filed for bankruptcy on June 20. If the Bank filed a proper financing statement in the correct office(s) on or before June 11, the security interest will be deemed to have been granted on June 1 — meaning that it is not a transfer on account of an antecedent debt, and thus cannot be avoided as a preference. In contrast, if Bank did not file its financing statement until June 15, the security interest will be deemed to have been granted on that date. Because the debt arose on June 1, the security interest would then be considered a transfer on account of an antecedent debt for purposes of section 547(b). Finally, if the Bank never filed its financing statement or took possession of the collateral, the security interest will be deemed to have been granted on June 20 (the petition date), and thus would be a transfer on account of an antecedent debt.

The rationale for this timing provision lies in the fact that delayed perfection of a security interest creates an ostensible-ownership or "secret-lien" problem. As explained previously, this secret-lien problem can operate to mislead the debtor's creditors or other

---

§§ 9-301(1)(b), **R9-317(a)(2).** Thus, if a security interest was validly perfected under Article 9, it is "perfected" for purposes of 11 U.S.C. § 547.

[160] 11 U.S.C. § 547(e)(2)(A); *In re* Loken, 175 B.R. 56, 25 U.C.C. Rep. Serv. 2d 1253 (9th Cir. Bankr. 1994). Prior to 1994, section 547(e)'s timing rule provided a fixed ten-day period that applied regardless of whether a security interest was a PMSI or a nonPMSI. This created a potential trap for secured parties in states that adopted nonuniform amendments to U.C.C. § 9-301(2) and § 9-312(4)(1972 text) to permit purchase-money secured parties to have a twenty-day grace period for filing. In 1994, to avoid this trap, Congress expanded the ten-day timing rule of section 547(e) to twenty days for PMSIs.

If the debtor files for bankruptcy before this ten-day period (or twenty-day period, for PMSIs) elapses, the secured party can still act to perfect its security interest for purposes of section 547 without violating the automatic stay as long as the secured party acts before the end of the applicable period. 11 U.S.C. §§ 362(b)(3), 547(e)(2)(C). Thus, if Debtor granted Bank a nonpurchase-money security interest on June 1 and filed a bankruptcy petition on June 3, Bank could file its financing statement (and thereby perfect its security interest for purposes of section 547) up to and including June 11 without violating the automatic stay. Caution: This timing rule is relevant only for purposes of section 547. In the above example, Bank's security interest would still have been unperfected under Article 9 as of the petition date, and thus the trustee could avoid that security interest under the strong-arm power. *See* § 16.04[B][1] *infra; In re* Planned Protective Servs., Inc., 130 B.R. 94 (Bankr. C.D. Cal. 1991).

[161] 11 U.S.C. § 547(e)(2)(B); *In re* Loken, 175 B.R. 56 (Bankr. 9th Cir. 1994).

[162] 11 U.S.C. § 547(e)(2)(C).

third parties into believing that encumbered assets are not encumbered.[163] Further, because an unperfected security interest is not effective against lien creditors such as the trustee, one might characterize delayed perfection of a security interest prior to bankruptcy as a last-minute attempt by a creditor to improve its position in anticipation of bankruptcy.[164]

Section 547(e) provides another timing rule that is implicated primarily in cases of security interests covering after-acquired property. Suppose that, on June 1, Debtor borrows $100,000 from Bank, which takes and properly perfects a security interest in all ten of Debtor's machines under a security agreement that also covers after-acquired equipment. Suppose further that Debtor files for bankruptcy on December 1, that Debtor had acquired two additional machines on November 1, that the value of all 12 machines is $80,000, and that Debtor still owes Bank $100,000. The trustee cannot avoid Bank's security interest in the original ten machines as a preference. Because the security interest in those ten machines is deemed to have been granted on June 1 (when the interest was perfected), it lacks two of the necessary elements of section 547(b) — it was not granted on account of an antecedent debt, nor was it granted within the 90-day avoidance period.

Preference law treats the security interest in the two after-acquired machines differently, however; under section 547(e)(3), the security interest in those two machines is deemed to have been granted on November 1, when Debtor acquired the machines.[165] Accordingly, the security interest in the two machines acquired on November 1 is an avoidable preference: there was a transfer of a security interest in Debtor's property (the two machines), to a creditor (Bank), on account of an antecedent debt (a transfer on November 1 on account of a debt that arose on June 1), within the 90 days prior to bankruptcy (30 days prior to the bankruptcy filing on December 1), while Debtor was insolvent (recall that Debtor is presumed to have been insolvent during the 90 days prior to bankruptcy). Finally, the transfer made Bank better off by reducing Bank's unsecured claim. With the transfer, the Bank has a security interest in twelve machines (worth $80,000) to secure a $100,000 claim; without the transfer, the Bank would have had a security interest in only ten machines (worth less than $80,000, assuming the two additional machines have some economic value) to secure a $100,000 claim.

It should be apparent that section 547(e)(3) places the trustee in a better position than a lien creditor would occupy outside of bankruptcy under Article 9. Outside of bankruptcy, a lien creditor could not avoid a properly perfected security interest against after-acquired collateral.[166] Upon reflection, this provision makes sense in light of the objectives of preference law. In this example, Debtor took funds that would have been unencumbered property of the estate and used them to improve the position of a partially unsecured creditor (*i.e.*, to render the creditor less undersecured) just prior to bankruptcy. In substance, this action had the same effect as if Debtor had taken the same dollars

---

[163] David G. Epstein, Steve H. Nickles, & James J. White, *Bankruptcy* § 6-11, at 542 (West Pract. ed. 1992).

[164] *Id.*

[165] 11 U.S.C. § 547(e)(3)("For purposes of this section, a transfer is not made until the debtor has acquired rights in the property transferred.").

[166] U.C.C. §§ 9-301(1)(b), **R9-317(a)(2)**.

and instead used them to pay an unsecured creditor — which would have been an obvious preference.

[4] Exceptions to the Trustee's Preference Avoidance Power

Section 547(b) casts a broad net designed to catch all transfers that have a preferential effect. Because it is drafted so broadly, however, section 547(b) also catches a variety of legitimate transfers that, while technically preferences, do not really bestow an improper advantage upon creditors who receive them. As discussed earlier, Congress did not want to authorize the avoidance of such benign transfers, out of concern for the impact that such a broad preference rule could have upon commercial transactions generally. To protect these benign transfers from the trustee's preference avoiding powers, Congress provided a series of exceptions in section 547(c).

[a] Substantially contemporaneous exchanges for new value

Suppose that, on June 1, Debtor purchases a machine from Seller, paying with a check. The following day, Seller presents the check for payment to the drawee bank and the bank pays the check. If Debtor goes bankrupt two weeks later, can Trustee recover the funds paid to Seller? Because payment by check is technically a credit transaction, the transfer of Debtor's funds to Seller does not occur until the drawee bank pays the check, and the transfer thus constitutes a preference under section 547(b).[167] This transfer, however, does not bestow any illegitimate advantage upon Seller, and there is no good reason to permit the trustee to avoid the transfer. Seller's acceptance of payment by check was a reasonable alternative to cash payment, given the significant amount of day-to-day commerce transacted by check. Further, Debtor received new value (the machine) in exchange for the transfer, and thus Debtor's estate was not diminished to the detriment of other creditors.[168] Allowing the trustee to recover the funds paid to Seller would give Debtor's other creditors a windfall at Seller's expense. To prevent this result, Congress provided that the trustee cannot avoid a transfer that was "intended by the debtor and the creditor . . . to be a contemporaneous exchange for new value given to the debtor," as long as the transfer was "in fact a substantially contemporaneous exchange."[169]

---

[167] Until the drawee bank pays the check, Seller has essentially extended credit to Debtor. Accordingly, there is a transfer of Debtor's property (payment of the check), to a creditor (Seller), on account of an antecedent debt (the check was paid on June 2 on account of a debt incurred on June 1), during the 90-day avoidance period (during which Debtor is presumed to have been insolvent), and the transfer enabled Seller to receive payment in full (better treatment than it would have received as an unsecured creditor in a Chapter 7 liquidation).

[168] "New value" is defined to include money, money's worth in goods, services, or new credit, and the release of an otherwise unavoidable lien against the debtor's property. 11 U.S.C. § 547(a)(2); *In re* Robinson Bros. Drilling, Inc., 877 F.2d 32 (10th Cir. 1989) (even though satisfaction of debt was not new value, release of lien against debtor's assets was new value). "New value" does not include satisfaction of an antecedent unsecured debt. *In re* Chase & Sanborn Corp., 904 F.2d 588 (11th Cir. 1990) (such an argument would render § 547 a "tautological nullity"). Further, "new value" does not include the mere substitution of a new unsecured obligation in place of the original obligation, *In re* Wellington Constr. Corp., 82 B.R. 424 (Bankr. N.D. Miss. 1987), or mere forbearance in the collection of a debt. *In re* Air Conditioning, Inc. of Stuart, 845 F.2d 293 (11th Cir.), *cert. denied*, 488 U.S. 993 (1988).

[169] 11 U.S.C. § 547(c)(1).

Although the legislative history of section 547(c)(1) suggests that Congress was primarily concerned with the "payment by check" scenario described above, the language of section 547(c)(1) is not so limited. For example, suppose that while shopping in a rural area 45 miles from home, Debtor locates and decides to purchase a rare antique vase for $5,000. Seller is only willing to accept cash or check, so Debtor calls Bank (where Debtor is a favored customer) and asks Bank for a $5,000 loan to be immediately deposited into Debtor's account to cover Debtor's check to Seller. Bank agrees to make the loan so long as Debtor will grant Bank a security interest in Debtor's equipment; Bank and Debtor agree that Debtor will come to the Bank when Debtor returns later that day to sign the necessary documents to reflect Bank's security interest. Later that day, Debtor indeed signs a security agreement to Bank and Bank properly perfects its security interest by filing. If Debtor files for bankruptcy one week later, Trustee cannot avoid Bank's security interest. Although Debtor's obligation to Bank arose before Bank's security interest attached (and therefore was an antecedent debt), the parties intended the security interest to be a contemporaneous exchange for new value (the $5,000 loan) given to Debtor by Bank, and the transfer was in fact *substantially* contemporaneous. Under the circumstances surrounding this transaction,[170] the delay of a few hours does not justify allowing the trustee to recover a windfall at Bank's expense.

Note carefully that section 547(c)(1) requires that the parties must have intended that the transfer constitute a contemporaneous exchange for new value. If this intent is not present at the time the debtor's obligation arises, the subsequent transfer does not qualify for the protection of section 547(c)(1), no matter how small the delay.[171]

Secured parties have often tried to use section 547(c)(1) in cases involving delayed perfection of security interests, but the section provides little practical assistance. For example, suppose that on June 1, Debtor borrows $10,000 from Bank, which takes a security interest in Debtor's equipment. Suppose further that Debtor files a bankruptcy petition on July 1. If Bank perfected its security interest on or before June 11, section 547(e) will deem the security interest to have been granted to Bank on June 1. Accordingly, a court likely would conclude that the security interest was not granted on account of an antecedent debt, and the trustee thus could not avoid the transfer anyway.[172] In contrast, if Bank did not perfect its security interest until after June 12,

---

[170] Case law clearly establishes that contemporaneity is a question of fact that must be determined on the merits of each case. Thus, drawing clear lines is hazardous; nevertheless, courts generally have concluded that delays of one week or less have satisfied section 547(c)(1)'s "substantially contemporaneous" requirement. Dean v. Davis, 242 U.S. 438 (1917) (mortgage executed to secure loan made one week earlier considered substantially contemporaneous); *In re* Quade, 108 B.R. 681 (Bankr. N.D. Iowa 1989) (substitution of collateral substantially contemporaneous even though substitution delayed by six days).

[171] *In re* Jolly N, Inc., 122 B.R. 897 (Bankr. D. N.J. 1991). This "intent" requirement derives from the Supreme Court's decision in National City Bank of N.Y. v. Hotchkiss, 231 U.S. 50 (1913). *Hotchkiss* involved a Bank which made an unsecured loan to Debtor but later that day demanded collateral. Debtor complied with Bank's request by pledging valuable securities. In Debtor's subsequent bankruptcy, the Court affirmed the trial court's conclusion that the pledge was a preferential transfer.

[172] Theoretically, the court might take a strict or literal interpretation of "antecedent" and con-

section 547(c)(1) will not save the Bank's lien, because most courts have concluded that any delay in perfection beyond the ten-day grace period in section 547(e)(2) prevents the transfer from being considered substantially contemporaneous in fact.[173] Furthermore, some courts have concluded that section 547(c)(1) cannot be applied at all in favor of a secured party holding a PMSI.[174]

[b] "Ordinary-course" transfers

A wide variety of prepetition transfers (such as utility payments, home mortgage payments, and timely payments for inventory or equipment purchased on open account) constitute preferences, even though these transfers are so routine that they occur millions of times daily in ordinary commerce. Congress felt that widespread avoidance of such routine transfers would be too disruptive of daily commercial activity, despite the fact that many of them clearly benefit the recipients as compared to other unpaid creditors. Further, Congress was concerned that widespread avoidance of such routine transfers could discourage a financially distressed debtor's primary creditors from extending further credit, thereby exacerbating the debtor's financial difficulties and perhaps even increasing the likelihood of the debtor's bankruptcy.[175] To avoid such effects, Congress enacted section 547(c)(2), which provides that the trustee cannot recover any transfer that was

(A) in payment of a debt incurred by the debtor in the ordinary course of business or financial affairs of the debtor and the transferee; (B) made in the ordinary course of business or financial affairs of the debtor and the transferee; and (C) made according to ordinary business terms.[176]

All three of the elements set forth above must be satisfied in order to protect a payment from avoidance under section 547(c)(2). Thus, if the debtor incurred the debt under atypical circumstances or the creditor extended the credit under atypical circumstances, section 547(c)(2) cannot protect payments on that debt.[177] Likewise, section 547(c)(2)

---

clude that the momentary delay between the loan and the signing of the security agreement rendered the debt "antecedent." In that case, the Bank would have to rely upon section 547(c)(1) to save its security interest from avoidance.

[173] *In re* Holder, 892 F.2d 29 (4th Cir. 1989); *In re* Petrewsky, 147 B.R. 27 (Bankr. S.D. Ohio 1992). *But see In re* Telecash Indus., Inc., 104 B.R. 401, 403-04 (Bankr. D. Utah 1989) ("a ten-day limitation in the contemporaneous exchange exception . . . is simply not there").

[174] *In re* Locklin, 101 F.3d 435 (5th Cir. 1996) (lender holding PMSI cannot assert protection of § 547(c)(1), but is instead limited to benefit of § 547(c)(3) exception for enabling loans); *In re* Holder, 892 F.2d 29 (4th Cir. 1989); *In re* Tressler, 771 F.2d 791 (3d Cir. 1985).

[175] Vern Countryman, *The Concept of a Voidable Preference in Bankruptcy*, 38 Vand. L. Rev. 713 (1985).

[176] 11 U.S.C. § 547(c)(2).

[177] *In re* Energy Co-op, Inc., 832 F.2d 997, 5 U.C.C. Rep. Serv. 2d 99 (7th Cir. 1987) (payment made to settle breach of contract claim not made in ordinary course); Industrial & Municipal Eng'g, Inc., 127 B.R. 848(Bankr. C.D. Ill. 1990) (payment made to settle lawsuit not made in ordinary course).

Prior to 1984, section 547(c)(2) provided that payments could not qualify for protection unless they were made within 45 days of the date that the debt arose. Under that provision, payments on long-term debt could not qualify for ordinary course protection. In 1984, Congress removed

will not protect payments that are made outside of the ordinary course of business (*e.g.*, the debtor pays in an inconsistent rather than timely fashion,[178] or pays involuntarily via levy or garnishment[179]), nor will it protect payments that are unusually large relative to the regular periodic payment amount.[180]

By its terms, the "ordinary-course" exception is limited to payments; the granting of a security interest could not qualify for protection from avoidance under section 547(c)(2), even if the debtor and creditor routinely enter into security agreements in the ordinary course of their financial dealings.[181]

[c] Security interests granted in conjunction with enabling loans

The typical PMSI transaction does not result in an illegitimate preferential transfer to a creditor; after all, the granting of a PMSI enables the debtor to acquire additional property, thereby expanding the size of the debtor's estate. The timing of certain enabling loan transactions, however, can result in security interests that technically satisfy each element for a preferential transfer under section 547(b).

For example, suppose that on June 1, Debtor borrows $40,000 from Bank to purchase a new punch press which Debtor plans to acquire later in June when Debtor expands its operations. Contemporaneously with the loan, Debtor signs a security agreement and financing statement describing the punch press, and Bank files the financing statement. Debtor purchases the punch press on June 19, and then files for bankruptcy protection on August 1. Under these circumstances, Bank's purchase money security interest (PMSI) is a transfer that satisfies each element of section 547(b): it is a transfer to a creditor (Bank), on account of an antecedent debt (the PMSI does not attach until June 19 when Debtor acquires rights in the punch press, whereas Debtor incurred the debt on June 1), during the 90 days prior to bankruptcy, while Debtor is presumed to have been insolvent, and the PMSI makes Bank better off than it would have been as an unsecured creditor in a Chapter 7 liquidation. But there is no defensible reason for preference law to allow Trustee to avoid Bank's PMSI; Bank did not take the PMSI to secure an existing obligation, but instead took the PMSI in exchange for credit that enabled Debtor to acquire a valuable asset. Allowing Trustee to avoid Bank's PMSI would bestow a windfall upon the Debtor's other creditors to the detriment of Bank.

To prevent this result, section 547(c)(3) provides that the trustee/DIP cannot avoid a security interest to the extent that it:

---

the 45-day limitation, and this triggered a debate in the courts regarding whether payments on long-term debt could qualify for protection as ordinary course transfers. In Union Bank v. Wolas, 502 U.S. 151 (1991), however, the Supreme Court held that payments on long-term debt can qualify for protection under section 547(c)(2).

[178] *In re* Xonics Imaging, Inc., 837 F.2d 763 (7th Cir. 1988); *In re* Cook United, Inc., 117 B.R. 884 (Bankr. N.D. Ohio 1990).

[179] WJM, Inc. v. Massachusetts Dept. of Public Welfare, 840 F.2d 996 (1st Cir. 1988).

[180] *In re* McElroy, 228 B.R. 791 (Bankr. M.D. Fla. 1999); *In re* Roemig, 123 B.R. 405 (Bankr. D.N.M. 1991).

[181] *In re* Blackburn, 90 B.R. 569 (Bankr. M.D. Ga. 1987).

- secures new value given at or after the signing of a written security agreement describing the collateral;

- secures new value given by/on behalf of the secured party;

- secures new value given to enable the debtor to acquire the collateral, as long as it was in fact used by the debtor to acquire the collateral; and

- was perfected on or before 20 days after the debtor took possession of the collateral.[182]

Note carefully that section 547(c)(3) does not protect PMSIs from avoidance in all cases. Delayed perfection of a PMSI results in a transfer that will not be excepted from avoidance under section 547(c)(3). Suppose that, in the previous hypothetical, Bank had not filed a financing statement to perfect its PMSI until July 20 (more than 20 days after Debtor took possession of the punch press). Because of this excessive delay, Bank's PMSI would not qualify for protection under section 547(c)(3) and trustee could avoid the PMSI as a preference.[183]

[d] Transfers ameliorating an earlier preference

Suppose that Debtor is a financially distressed baker seeking additional flour from Supplier. Supplier refuses to consider supplying any more flour to Debtor unless Debtor pays 50% of its existing account balance. Four days after Debtor pays $6,000 to Supplier in satisfaction of 50% of its account balance, Supplier agrees to and does ship to Debtor an additional $2,500 worth of flour. Debtor cannot extract itself from financial difficulty, however, and files for bankruptcy three weeks later. Debtor's payment to Supplier constitutes a preference under section 547(b), and cannot be protected as a contemporaneous exchange for new value or an ordinary course transfer. Nevertheless, Supplier subsequently ameliorated the effect of this payment by extending new credit that enabled Debtor to acquire additional assets. Thus, if Trustee were allowed to recover the full $6,000 payment to Supplier, Trustee and other general creditors would receive a windfall at Supplier's expense. Furthermore, creditors such as Supplier would be discouraged from extending additional credit to distressed debtors, which in turn could compromise the ability of debtors to resolve their financial affairs and avoid bankruptcy.[184]

To account for such "post-preference" extensions of new value, section 547(c)(4) provides that the trustee cannot recover an otherwise preferential transfer to the extent that after the transfer, the preferred creditor

---

[182] 11 U.S.C. § 547(c)(3).

[183] In this example, Bank might then attempt to argue that the PMSI should be treated as a contemporaneous exchange for new value under section 547(c)(1). Such an argument, however, will almost certainly fail. Most courts have concluded that section 547(c)(1) does not apply to enabling loan transactions. *In re* Locklin, 101 F.3d 435 (5th Cir. 1996); *In re* Tressler, 771 F.2d 791 (3d Cir. 1985). Courts have also held that any delay in perfection beyond the statutory grace period prevents the secured party from arguing that the PMSI is a substantially contemporaneous transfer for new value. *In re* Holder, 892 F.2d 29 (4th Cir. 1989).

[184] *In re* New York City Shoes, Inc., 880 F.2d 679 (3d Cir. 1989); *In re* IRFM, Inc., 144 B.R. 886 (Bankr. C.D. Cal. 1992), *aff'd*, 52 F.3d 228 (9th Cir. 1995).

(Matthew Bender & Co., Inc.)

gave new value to or for the benefit of the debtor (A) not secured by an otherwise unavoidable security interest; and (B) on account of which new value the debtor did not make an otherwise unavoidable transfer to or for the benefit of such creditor.[185]

The language of section 547(c)(4) is not a model of clarity, but the idea behind it is simple: the trustee should not be able to avoid a preferential transfer to the extent that the benefitted creditor subsequently extends new value or credit that ameliorates the effect of the earlier preference. In the above example, Supplier's extension of $2,500 of unsecured credit ameliorated the effect of the earlier $6,000 preferential payment; thus, trustee can only recover $3,500 from Supplier.[186] Likewise, if Debtor pays $10,000 owed to its lawyer on the 80th day prior to Debtor's bankruptcy petition, Trustee cannot recover this payment if Debtor's lawyer provided an additional $10,000 worth of services between the time of the payment and the time of the bankruptcy petition.[187]

In contrast, if Supplier in the earlier hypothetical had taken a purchase-money security interest when it sold Debtor the $2,500 of additional flour, Supplier's extension of new credit would have been fully secured and, thus, would not have ameliorated the preferential effect of the earlier $6,000 payment. In those circumstances, section 547(c)(4) would not protect Supplier, and the trustee could avoid the $6,000 payment in full.[188]

[e] Floating liens in inventory and accounts receivable

In a floating lien transaction covering inventory or accounts, the parties understand that the secured party will advance credit to the debtor as the debtor acquires inventory or generates accounts and that, in turn, debtor will repay some or all of that credit as the debtor sells inventory or collects accounts. This process of borrowing and repaying continues on a revolving basis, with the secured party possessing a lien upon whatever collateral the debtor owns at any point in time. As the debtor acquires new inventory or generates new accounts, they are added to the "pool" of collateral over which the secured party's lien "floats."

Section 547(e)(3)'s timing rule, however, presents a problem to secured parties with floating liens upon inventory and/or accounts. Under section 547(e)(3), the "transfer" of a security interest in any particular item of collateral does not occur until the debtor acquires rights in that item of collateral. For purposes of preference law, therefore, each time the debtor acquires a new item of inventory, the debtor's inventory lender receives a "transfer" of a security interest in that item of inventory. Because that security interest secures the balance of the debtor's previously incurred loan, the transfer of the security interest occurs on account of an antecedent debt. As a result, the security interest in any item of inventory acquired during the 90 days prior to bankruptcy qualifies as a

---

185 11 U.S.C. § 547(c)(4).

186 What if Supplier had shipped the flour before Debtor had repaid half of its account balance? The net effect of this transaction on Debtor's balance sheet would have been the same; in this situation, however, the advance of new credit would not ameliorate a prior preference, and thus, section 547(c)(4) would not protect Supplier. *In re* McLaughlin, 183 B.R. 171, 26 U.C.C. Rep. Serv. 2d 1110 (Bankr. W.D. Wis. 1995).

187 *In re* Sounds Distributing, Inc., 80 B.R. 749 (Bankr. W.D. Pa. 1987).

188 11 U.S.C. § 547(c)(4)(A); *In re* Toyota of Jefferson, Inc., 14 F.3d 1088 (5th Cir. 1994).

preferential transfer under section 547(b), unless the secured party was already fully secured at the time the debtor acquired that item of inventory.

This timing problem is exacerbated by the fact that, for many debtors, their inventory or accounts "turn over" (*i.e.*, their inventory is sold or their accounts collected, and replaced with new inventory or new accounts) every 90 days, if not more frequently. For example, suppose that Debtor files for bankruptcy protection on June 1, owing Bank $100,000 secured by a floating lien upon Debtor's inventory (worth $80,000). Further, suppose that each item of Debtor's inventory as of the petition date has been acquired during the previous 30 days. Under these circumstances, Bank's security interest in Debtor's entire inventory technically constitutes a preference under section 547(b). Unless bankruptcy law provides some measure of protection for floating liens, the trustee could avoid Bank's entire floating lien.

Allowing the trustee to avoid Bank's entire floating lien, however, would be counterproductive. Floating liens generally provide a convenient and efficient means for businesses such as Debtor to finance their business inventory or receivables, and do not inherently offend any policies underlying preference law. Thus, to protect floating liens [189] in inventory or accounts from blanket avoidance because of section 547(e)(3)'s timing rule, section 547(c)(5) provides an exception for certain perfected security interests in inventory and accounts. [190]

This exception for floating liens is not absolute, however, because purchases of new inventory can in fact create an illegitimate preferential benefit. For example, an undersecured creditor with a floating lien may bring pressure on the debtor to acquire additional collateral in order to bolster the creditor's overall secured position. To the extent that the debtor acquires this additional collateral with assets that would otherwise have remained available for payment to general creditors, the acquisition of the additional collateral bestows an illegitimate preferential effect upon the creditor. Thus, section 547(c)(5) permits the trustee to avoid a floating lien in inventory or accounts to the extent that the "transfers" (*i.e.*, the attachment of the secured party's lien when the debtor

---

[189] Because section 547(c)(5) uses the term "perfected security interest" rather than "floating lien," a question arises whether section 547(c)(5) protects a late perfected security interest in inventory or receivables that is *not* a floating lien. Suppose that Debtor grants Bank a security interest in its existing inventory (*not* including after-acquired inventory) to secure a previously unsecured debt, but Bank fails to perfect that security interest until 30 days later. If Debtor then files for bankruptcy one week later, Bank will argue that trustee cannot avoid its security interest because (a) that interest was perfected and (b) the Bank's secured position was not improved during the preference period because Bank did not receive a security interest in newly acquired inventory. In contrast, trustee will argue that section 547(c)(5) was intended to protect floating liens and should be limited to such liens. Courts have split on this issue. *Compare In re* Val Decker Packing Co., 61 B.R. 831 (Bankr. S.D. Ohio 1986) (§ 547(c)(5) inapplicable if creditor does not have floating lien) *with* In re American Ambulance Service, Inc., 46 B.R. 658 (Bankr. S.D. Cal. 1985) (§ 547(c)(5) applies to all perfected security interests in inventory or receivables, even nonfloating liens).

[190] Section 547(a)(1) defines the terms "inventory" and "receivable" more broadly than the corresponding Article 9 categories "inventory" and "account." For purposes of section 547, "inventory" includes farm products held for sale or lease, and "receivable" includes any right to payment (thus including Article 9 chattel paper, general intangibles and rights to payment under instruments).

(Matthew Bender & Co., Inc.)

acquires additional inventory or receivables) resulted in an improvement of the creditor's overall secured position to the detriment of unsecured creditors during the last 90 days prior to bankruptcy (or one year, in the case of an insider creditor).

To determine the amount that the trustee can avoid, section 547(c)(5) applies a "net improvement" test that requires the following calculations:

- Step One: Determine the debtor's outstanding loan balance on the 90th day prior to the debtor's bankruptcy filing[191] and the value of the collateral on that same day.

- Step Two: Determine the debtor's outstanding loan balance on the petition date and the value of the collateral on that same date.

- Step Three: Compare the creditor's overall secured position (*i.e.*, the value of its collateral less the outstanding loan balance) on the 90th day prior to bankruptcy with the creditor's overall position on the petition date.

Thus, if the creditor was fully secured on the 90th day prior to bankruptcy, the creditor's overall secured position cannot be improved to the detriment of unsecured creditors, and the trustee cannot avoid the creditor's floating lien to any extent. But if the creditor was undersecured on the 90th day prior to bankruptcy and that shortfall has been reduced by the petition date, the debtor's acquisition of additional inventory or receivables improves the creditor's position and trustee can avoid the creditor's floating lien to the extent of the improvement.[192]

The improvement in position must arise "to the prejudice of other creditors holding unsecured claims."[193] This means that the debtor must have used otherwise unencumbered assets to acquire additional collateral that improved the creditor's position. If the creditor's position is improved because the debtor's inventory appreciated in value, this improvement did not reduce the value of the debtor's estate to the prejudice of unsecured creditors, and, accordingly, trustee cannot avoid the creditor's lien on account of that improvement.[194]

To make the necessary calculations under section 547(c)(5), the court must determine the appropriate value of the collateral as of the relevant measuring dates. The trustee and the creditor will often disagree, however, on the proper valuation of the collateral. Because there is no avoidable improvement in position if the creditor was fully secured on the 90th day prior to bankruptcy, the trustee will argue that the collateral should be valued at its lowest possible value (*e.g.*, its liquidation or foreclosure sale value). In contrast, the creditor will argue that the collateral should be valued at its highest possible value (*e.g.*, the retail value of inventory or the face amount of receivables).

---

191 11 U.S.C. § 547(c)(5)(A)(i). If the creditor is an insider, the relevant date would be the date one year prior to debtor's bankruptcy. *Id.* § 547(c)(5)(A)(ii). If the creditor's first extension of credit to the debtor occurred within 90 days prior to bankruptcy, the relevant date would be the date of the creditor's first extension of credit to the debtor. *Id.* § 547(c)(5)(B).

192 *In re* Wesley Indus., Inc., 30 F.3d 1438 (11th Cir. 1994); *In re* Ebbler Furniture and Appliances, Inc., 804 F.2d 87 (7th Cir. 1986).

193 11 U.S.C. § 547(c)(5).

194 *In re* Castletons, Inc., 990 F.2d 551, 21 U.C.C. Rep. Serv. 2d 1062 (10th Cir. 1993).

As with valuation in other contexts, courts have developed no hard and fast rules for the appropriate valuation of inventory for purposes of section 547(c)(5); instead, courts conduct this valuation on a case-by-case basis, taking into account the likely manner of the use or disposition of the collateral. For example, in *In re Clark Pipe and Supply Co., Inc.,*[195] the evidence reflected that the debtor was in the process of liquidating its assets throughout the 90-day period prior to bankruptcy. Based upon this evidence, the Fifth Circuit concluded that the inventory properly was valued at its liquidation value.[196] In contrast, if a Chapter 11 debtor is seeking to operate and reorganize its retail department store operations, the court might more properly value the debtor's inventory using a "going concern" or "replacement value" measure.[197]

[f] Statutory liens

If a creditor obtains a valid statutory lien under nonbankruptcy law during the 90 days immediately prior to bankruptcy, the attachment of that lien satisfies the standards for a preferential transfer in section 547(b). The trustee/DIP cannot use section 547 to avoid a statutory lien, however; section 547(c)(6) provides that section 545 is the exclusive statutory authority by which the trustee/DIP can avoid a statutory lien.[198]

[g] Consumer transfers

If the debtor is an individual with primarily consumer debts, section 547(c)(8) provides that the trustee cannot recover any transfer in which the total value of the property transferred was less than $600.[199] If the value of the property transferred is $600 or more, however, section 547(c)(8) does not protect the creditor to any extent.[200]

[F] Power to Avoid Fraudulent Transfers

[1] Intentionally Fraudulent Transfers — 11 U.S.C. § 548(a)(1)

Sometimes debtors deliberately seek to frustrate the legitimate collection efforts of their creditors by transferring property to friends or relatives by gift or for nominal consideration. Since the Statute of 13 Elizabeth in 1570, the common law has allowed

---

[195] 893 F.2d 693 (5th Cir. 1990).

[196] *In re* Clark Pipe and Supply Co., 893 F.2d 693 (5th Cir. 1990) (appropriate measure of collateral value is net amount creditor could have received if/when it could have repossessed and sold inventory).

[197] Although the Supreme Court's decision in Associates Commercial Corp. v. Rash, discussed in § 16.03[B][2][a] *supra*, focused on the valuation of vehicles in Chapter 13, the Court's interpretation of section 506(a) suggests that a replacement-value approach would be required when a debtor was seeking to use the collateral in its reorganization efforts.

[198] 11 U.S.C. § 547(c)(6).

[199] 11 U.S.C. § 547(c)(8). A number of courts have concluded that multiple transfers to the same creditor can be aggregated and avoided if the total of those transfers exceeds $600. *See, e.g., In re* Djerf, 188 B.R. 586 (Bankr. D. Minn. 1995); *In re* Alarcon, 186 B.R. 135 (Bankr. D.N.M. 1995).

[200] Creditors have attempted to argue that § 547(c)(8) should protect the transfer to the extent of $600, but courts have rejected these arguments. *In re* Via, 107 B.R. 91 (Bankr. W.D. Va. 1989); *In re* Vickery, 63 B.R. 222 (Bankr. E.D. Tenn. 1986).

creditors harmed by intentionally fraudulent transfers to set such transfers aside. Today, both the Uniform Fraudulent Conveyance Act (UFCA) and the Uniform Fraudulent Transfer Act (UFTA) contain provisions that permit creditors to avoid transfers made by the debtor with the intent to hinder, delay, or defraud creditors.[201] Because these transfers also operate to disadvantage an insolvent debtor's unsecured creditors, section 548(a)(1) of the Bankruptcy Codepermits the trustee/DIP to bring an action to avoid intentionally fraudulent transfers made by the debtor within the one-year period prior to bankruptcy.[202]

[2]   Constructively Fraudulent Transfers — 11 U.S.C. § 548(a)(2)

More frequently, a financially distressed debtor makes a transfer by gift or for insufficient consideration without any specific intent to hinder, delay, or defraud creditors. The debtor's pure motives, however, provide cold comfort to the debtor's creditors, for whom the transfer has the same effect — assets that could have been used to satisfy creditor claims are instead diverted to other parties for less than their actual value, thereby depleting the assets available for unpaid creditors. In recognition of the fact that such transfers tend to have the same effect as intentionally fraudulent transfers, common law has long deemed such transfers by insolvent debtors to be avoidable as *constructively* fraudulent. Both the UFCA and the UFTA allow creditors to avoid constructively fraudulent transfers,[203] and the Bankruptcy Code provides a similar rule in section 548(a)(2), which permits the trustee/DIP to avoid any transfer of the debtor's property or any obligation incurred by the debtor, if

- the transfer was made or the obligation was incurred within one year prior to the debtor's bankruptcy;
- the debtor received less than a "reasonably equivalent value" in exchange; and
- the debtor
    - was insolvent at the time the transfer was made or obligation was incurred, or was rendered insolvent as a result; or
    - was engaging in business or a transaction with "unreasonably small capital"; or
    - intended to incur or expected to incur debts beyond its ability to repay.[204]

Thus, if Debtor sells its equipment (worth $100,000) to Buyer for a price of $50,000, thereby rendering Debtor insolvent, and Debtor files for bankruptcy within one year of the sale, Trustee can establish that the transfer was constructively fraudulent under section 548(a)(2). Trustee could, consequently, recover the equipment from Buyer, even if Buyer

---

[201] UFCA § 7, UFTA § 4(a)(1). The UFTA is the more recent of the two model fraudulent transfer statutes, and was designed to modernize and replace the UFCA.

[202] 11 U.S.C. § 548(a)(1).

[203] UFCA § 4, UFTA § 4(a)(2).

[204] 11 U.S.C. § 548(a)(2).

had acted in good faith and without knowledge that the transfer was fraudulent.[205] Because of the harshness of this result for Buyer, the Bankruptcy Code does provide some protection for good faith purchasers and their subsequent transferees. If Buyer did purchase the equipment in good faith, Buyer would receive a lien upon the equipment to secure repayment of the $50,000 that Buyer paid to Debtor.[206] Further, if Buyer has already conveyed the equipment to Third Party by the time that Trustee discovers the fraudulent sale to Buyer, Trustee cannot recover the equipment from Third Party if Third Party took the property for value, in good faith, and without knowledge of the fact that Buyer's purchase from Debtor violated section 548(a).[207]

Generally, section 548(a)(2) presents few significant threats to the typical secured party (except in the context of a prebankruptcy foreclosure sale, which will be discussed shortly). Prepetition payments by the debtor on the debt cannot be avoided as constructively fraudulent transfers, because the debtor receives equivalent value (*i.e.*, the pro tanto satisfaction of the debt) in exchange.[208] Likewise, because section 548 defines "value" to include "securing . . . [an] antecedent debt,"[209] the trustee/DIP cannot use section 548 to avoid a security interest just because the interest was granted to secure a previously unsecured obligation of the debtor.[210] If the debtor granted a security interest in its property to secure the debt of an unrelated person, however, the debtor would not have received any value in exchange. Under those circumstances, the trustee could avoid the security interest as a fraudulent transfer if the debtor was insolvent at the time or was rendered insolvent as a result of granting the security interest.[211]

[3] Prebankruptcy Foreclosure Sales as Fraudulent Transfers

Trustees have invoked section 548 most often in attempts to set aside prebankruptcy foreclosure sales as constructively fraudulent transfers. Foreclosure sales tend to bring notoriously low prices. Because they are typically conducted more quickly and with less

---

[205] *Id.* § 550(a)(1).

[206] *Id.* § 548(c) ("a transferee . . . that takes for value and in good faith has a lien . . . to the extent that such transferee . . . gave value to the debtor in exchange for such transfer. . . ."); Stratton v. Equitable Bank, N.A., 104 B.R. 713, 11 U.C.C. Rep. Serv. 2d 149 (D. Md. 1989), *aff'd*, 912 F.2d 464 (4th Cir. 1990).

[207] 11 U.S.C. § 550(b).

[208] *In re* United Energy Corp., 102 B.R. 757 (Bankr. 9th Cir. 1989), *aff'd*, 944 F.2d 589 (9th Cir. 1991). 11 U.S.C. 548(d)(2)(A)expressly defines "value" to include "satisfaction . . . of a present or antecedent debt."

[209] 11 U.S.C. § 548(d)(2)(A).

[210] *In re* Countdown of Conn., Inc., 115 B.R. 18 (Bankr. D. Conn. 1990).

[211] For purposes of determining whether the debtor is insolvent under section 548(a)(2), the court must take into account both the debtor's fixed liabilities and its contingent liabilities. In valuing the debtor's contingent liabilities (*e.g.*, the debtor's liability upon a guaranty of another's obligation), the court must take into account the probability that the contingency will occur. Covey v. Commercial Nat'l Bank of Peoria, 960 F.2d 657 (7th Cir. 1992). Thus, if Debtor grants a security interest in its equipment to Bank to secure the obligation of Third Party, the court, in valuing the contingent liability created by Debtor's granting of the security interest, must take into account the likelihood of default by Third Party.

advertising than arms-length sales, foreclosure sales often yield few bidders and bargain prices. For example, suppose that after default by Debtor, Bank repossesses Debtor's inventory pursuant to its security agreement and conducts a public sale at which Buyer purchases all of the inventory for a total price of $50,000. Suppose further that the inventory had a wholesale value of $90,000 if bought and sold in the ordinary course of business. If Debtor then files for bankruptcy three months later, Trustee might attempt to argue that the foreclosure sale should be set aside as a constructively fraudulent transfer. Nevertheless, there are countervailing policy concerns that could justify a contrary result. To the extent trustees can collaterally attack foreclosure sales based upon low sale prices, this could have the undesirable effect of discouraging or "chilling" bidding at foreclosure sales, which in turn could generally depress foreclosure sale prices.[212]

Assuming that Debtor was insolvent at the time of the foreclosure sale,[213] the foreclosure sale seems to fit the standard established in section 548(a)(2). There is a transfer of Debtor's property (the sale of the inventory), while Debtor was insolvent, and Debtor appears to have received less than "reasonably equivalent value" in exchange — Debtor received $50,000 (satisfaction of debt) in exchange for inventory that had a significantly higher market value. Further, there are good reasons that bankruptcy law *should* want to set aside such a sale; if Trustee can recover the sale and liquidate the inventory at its fair wholesale value, Trustee could capture $40,000 of additional value for the benefit of general creditors.

The question of whether Trustee can avoid a prebankruptcy foreclosure sale that generated a price below fair market value has raged through bankruptcy courts since Congress enacted section 548 in 1978, but the Supreme Court appears to have resolved the debate with its decision in *BFP v. Resolution Trust Corporation*.[214] The foreclosure sale at issue in *BFP* involved the debtor's house, which had an alleged fair market value of $725,000 but which sold at a prebankruptcy foreclosure for only $433,000. The trustee attempted to set aside the sale as constructively fraudulent because the sale yielded only 57% of the property's fair market value.[215] The purchaser argued, however, that the purchase price received at a regularly conducted, noncollusive foreclosure sale should

---

[212] This same "chilling effect" explains the rationale behind Article 9's rather strong finality rules that permit collateral attack against Article 9 foreclosure sales in only very limited circumstances. *See* § 18.02[E] *infra.*

[213] The trustee bears the burden of proving that the transfer was fraudulent, *In re* Colonial Realty Co., 226 B.R. 513 (Bankr. D. Conn. 1998), and thus must prove that the debtor was insolvent at the time of the transfer or was rendered insolvent as a result. *In re* North Am. Dealer Group, Inc., 62 B.R. 423 (Bankr. E.D.N.Y. 1986). Section 548 does not provide a presumption of insolvency similar to the one that exists in preference actions under section 547.

[214] 511 U.S. 531 (1994).

[215] The trustee's argument relied upon a rule that derived from the opinion in Durrett v. Washington Nat'l Insurance Co., 621 F.2d 201 (5th Cir. 1980), in which the court suggested that any sale for less than 70% of the property's fair market value was presumptively constructively fraudulent. Prior to *BFP*, a significant number of bankruptcy courts had adopted this rule of thumb, which became known as the "*Durrett*" rule. *See, e.g., In re* Littleton, 888 F.2d 90 (11th Cir. 1989). *See also* Henning, *An Analysis of* Durrett *and Its Impact on Real and Personal Property Foreclosures: Some Proposed Modifications,* 63 N.C. L. Rev. 257 (1985).

be deemed "reasonably equivalent value" under section 548(a)(2).[216] Unlike the UFTA, which contains express language adopting such a conclusive presumption,[217] section 548(a)(2) contains no language purporting to define the term "reasonably equivalent value" or to establish any presumption regarding its meaning. Nevertheless, the purchaser urged the Court to conclude that this conclusive presumption was implicit in section 548(a)(2).

In a 5-4 decision, the Court concluded that the trustee cannot use section 548 to set aside a regularly conducted, noncollusive foreclosure sale of land — regardless of the fact that the sale generated a price far below an ordinary market sale price.[218] Justice Scalia concluded that the term "reasonably equivalent value" as used in section 548(a)(2) did not mean "fair market value" in the context of a foreclosure sale:

> The language of § 548(a)(2)(A) . . . requires judicial inquiry into whether the foreclosed property was sold for a price that approximated its worth at the time of sale. An appraiser's reconstruction of "fair market value" could show what similar property would be worth if it did not have to be sold within the time and manner strictures of state-prescribed foreclosure. But property that must be sold within those strictures is simply worth less. No one would pay as much to own such property as he would pay to own real estate that could be sold at leisure and pursuant to normal marketing techniques.[219]

In an opinion ringing with strong federalist undercurrents, Justice Scalia concluded that state foreclosure and fraudulent transfer laws have never authorized the setting aside of a foreclosure sale solely because the sale generated an inadequate price. Given this long history of state laws designed to promote finality in foreclosure sales, Justice Scalia concluded that the words "reasonably equivalent value" in section 548(a)(2) do not reflect a clear legislative intent to displace state foreclosure law and permit bankruptcy trustees to set aside foreclosure sales based solely upon low sale prices.[220] Accordingly, the majority concluded that "a fair and proper price, or a 'reasonably equivalent value,' for foreclosed property, is the price in fact received at the foreclosure sale, so long as all

---

[216] Prior to *BFP*, two Circuits adopted the rule advocated by the purchaser. *In re* Winshall Settlor's Trust, 758 F.2d 1136 (6th Cir. 1985); *In re* Madrid, 21 B.R. 424 (9th Cir. Bankr. 1982), *aff'd on other grounds*, 725 F.2d 1197 (9th Cir.), *cert. denied*, 469 U.S. 833 (1984).

[217] UFTA § 3(b)("[A] person gives reasonably equivalent value if the person acquires an interest of the debtor in an asset pursuant to a regularly conducted, noncollusive foreclosure sale or execution of a power of sale for the acquisition or disposition of the interest of the debtor upon default under a mortgage, deed of trust, or security agreement."). The UFCA uses the term "fair consideration" instead of "reasonably equivalent value," UFCA § 3, and its definition of "fair consideration" contains no presumption comparable to the one found in UFTA § 3(b).

[218] *BFP*, 511 U.S. at 545.

[219] *Id.* at 538-39. Commentators have been extremely critical of Scalia's statement that property being sold at foreclosure is "worth less" than it would be if sold at arms-length, on the ground that Scalia is confusing the terms "value" and "price." The fact that a foreclosure sale brings a lower price does not mean that the property is actually worth less. Robert M. Lawless & Stephen P. Ferris, *Economics and the Rhetoric of Valuation*, 5 J. Bankr. L. & Prac. 3 (1995).

[220] *BFP*, 511 U.S. at 538-45.

the requirements of the State's foreclosure law have been complied with."[221] Thus, the trustee/DIP cannot use section 548(a)(2) to attack a prebankruptcy foreclosure sale of land unless there is some irregularity in the conduct of the sale.[222]

The Court explicitly limited the *BFP* decision to private foreclosures of land, purporting to leave open the question of whether section 548(a)(2) applies to other forced sales (such as tax sales or Article 9 sales).[223] Despite this limitation, however, it is almost certain that the Court would reach the same result if faced with a trustee's attempt to use section 548(a)(2) to avoid a prebankruptcy foreclosure of personal property. If the secured party complied with all of the requirements of U.C.C. Article 9 and conducted a commercially reasonable sale at which the buyer purchased in good faith, the debtor could not set aside the sale, regardless of the sale price.[224] Accordingly, the rationale of *BFP* would suggest that the trustee could not set aside the foreclosure sale under section 548(a)(2). In contrast, if the secured party failed to comply with the requirements of Article 9 and conducted a commercially unreasonable sale, a bankruptcy court might permit the trustee to assert section 548(a)(2) if the sale resulted in a manifestly low price relative to the collateral's fair market value.

[4] Avoiding Fraudulent Transfers Under State Law — 11 U.S.C. § 544(b)

As discussed earlier, section 544(b) allows the trustee to set aside any transfers of the debtor's property that could have been avoided under state law by one of the debtor's actual unsecured creditors.[225] State fraudulent transfer laws (either the UFTA, the UFCA, or some statutory descendant of the Statute of 13 Elizabeth) uniformly permit unsecured creditors to set aside both intentionally and constructively fraudulent transfers.[226] Thus, assuming that the trustee can identify an actual unsecured creditor of the debtor who is capable of asserting a state law fraudulent transfer claim, the trustee could also use section 544(b) to avoid the transfer based upon the applicable state fraudulent transfer law.

Because the applicable standards for establishing a fraudulent transfer are essentially the same under both section 548(a) and most applicable state fraudulent transfer laws, the trustee will choose to proceed under section 544(b) only if the transfer occurred more than one year prior to bankruptcy (and thus outside the one-year reach-back period of section 548). State law typically provides aggrieved creditors with a longer period of time in which to avoid fraudulent transfers. For example, the UFTA generally allows creditors a period of 4 years in which to seek avoidance of a fraudulent transfer.[227]

---

[221] *Id.* at 545.

[222] *Id.* at 545-46 ("Any irregularity in the conduct of the sale that would permit judicial invalidation of the sale under applicable state law deprives the sale price of its conclusive force under § 548(a)(2)(A), and the transfer may be avoided if the price received was not reasonably equivalent to the property's actual value at the time of the sale.").

[223] *Id.* at 537 n.3.

[224] U.C.C. §§ 9-504(4), **R9-617(b).** *See* § 18.02[E] *infra.*

[225] *See* § 16.04[C] *supra.*

[226] *See* notes 201 and 203 *supra.*

[227] UFTA § 9(a),(b).

§ 16.05 The Trustee's Right to Assert the Debtor's Defenses — 11 U.S.C. § 558

Under section 558, the trustee can assert on behalf of the estate "any defense available to the debtor as against any entity other than the estate."[228] Although section 558 technically is not an avoiding power, the trustee can use it to similar effect. First, the trustee can use section 558 to reduce or eliminate a creditor's security for its claim to the extent that the debtor had a valid defense to the claim. For example, suppose that Bank claimed a prepetition security interest against all of Debtor's inventory, but the security agreement did not contain the authorized signature of Debtor (or, under revised Article 9, was not properly authenticated). Under section 558, the trustee could assert that the requirements for attachment were not satisfied and thus that no valid security interest attached to Debtor's inventory. Alternatively, the trustee may use section 558 to attack the enforceability of the creditor's underlying claim. For example, suppose that Shark claims a security interest in Debtor's jewelry to secure a debt incurred when Shark made Debtor a loan at usurious interest rates. If the jurisdiction's usury law would have permitted Debtor to avoid the obligation to repay some or all of the principal or interest of this loan, the trustee may assert that usury law as a defense to Shark's claim, thereby reducing the debt and the lien which secures it.[229]

In asserting the debtor's defenses under section 558, the trustee stands no better or no worse than the debtor stood as of the bankruptcy petition date. Any attempted waiver of defenses by the debtor after the bankruptcy petition is filed has no legal effect; section 558 makes clear that the debtor's attempted postpetition waiver of defenses "does not bind the estate."[230] In contrast, if the debtor had waived the defense in question prior to the petition date and the waiver was enforceable under nonbankruptcy law, the trustee would be bound by the waiver and could not assert that defense under section 558.[231]

§ 16.06 Security Interests in After-Acquired Property — 11 U.S.C. § 552

[A] The General Rule Cutting Off Liens Against After-Acquired Property — 11 U.S.C. § 552(a)

Businesses commonly finance their activities through the use of floating liens covering presently-owned and after-acquired collateral of a particular type or types, such as inventory or accounts receivable. Outside of bankruptcy, the debtor cannot avoid an enforceable and properly perfected floating lien; each time the debtor acquires new assets of the type covered by the floating lien, the floating lien automatically attaches to those assets, and will continue to cover all new assets of that type until the debtor satisfies the underlying obligation.

While the operation of a floating lien outside of bankruptcy is a straightforward matter, its operation after bankruptcy ensues is more complicated. If a floating lien continued

---

[228] 11 U.S.C. § 558.

[229] *In re* McCorhill Publishing, Inc., 86 B.R. 783, 8 U.C.C. Rep. Serv. 2d 203 (Bankr. S.D.N.Y. 1988).

[230] 11 U.S.C. § 558.

[231] *In re* Wey, 827 F.2d 140 (7th Cir. 1987).

to attach to property acquired by the debtor after the bankruptcy petition date, this could significantly compromise the debtor's ability to reorganize its financial affairs. For example, suppose Bank holds a perfected floating lien upon Debtor's inventory and accounts. Debtor needs additional credit to reorganize successfully, but Bank does not wish to provide further financing to Debtor. Finance Company is willing to provide Debtor with a credit line, but only if Finance Company can be assured of a first priority lien upon Debtor's new inventory and accounts. Thus, if Bank's floating lien survived Debtor's bankruptcy filing, it could seriously compromise Debtor's ability to obtain the financing necessary to reorganize. For debtors to obtain a fresh start, Congress concluded that debtors needed the ability to negotiate for postpetition credit to be secured by assets acquired postpetition, without being limited by the terms of prepetition floating liens.[232] Congress accomplished this objective by enacting section 552(a), which provides that "property acquired by the estate or by the debtor after the commencement of the case [*i.e.*, the petition date] is not subject to any lien resulting from any security agreement entered into by the debtor before the commencement of the case."[233]

Note that section 552(a) has no effect on the creditor's security interest to the extent it had attached to property acquired by the debtor prior to the petition date; section 552(a) only cuts off the *prospective effect* of a creditor's floating lien as of the petition date. A useful way to recall the effect of section 552(a) is to analogize it to the chalk line that police draw around the body of an accident or murder victim. Bankruptcy declares Debtor "dead" in a financial sense, and section 552(a) draws a chalk line around Debtor's "body" (*i.e.*, Debtor's prepetition property). If Bank has a validly perfected and otherwise unavoidable security interest against any of the property within that chalk line (such as Debtor's prepetition inventory), Bank maintains its security interest in that property, notwithstanding Debtor's bankruptcy. But if Debtor acquires new inventory after the petition date, section 552(a) provides that Bank's security interest does not attach to that new inventory — even if Bank's security agreement contained an after-acquired property clause that would have been enforceable outside of bankruptcy under U.C.C. Article 9. The new inventory would remain "outside the chalk line," and thus could be used freely by Debtor in the course of its reorganization efforts.

[B] Proceeds of Prepetition Collateral — 11 U.S.C. § 552(b)

One must be careful to distinguish between (a) after-acquired property of the debtor and (b) proceeds of prepetition collateral that are received by the debtor postpetition. Although the debtor's after-acquired property is not subject to any prepetition security interest, the same is not true with respect to proceeds of prepetition collateral. For example, suppose that on the date Debtor files for bankruptcy protection, Debtor owns 100 units of inventory subject to Bank's validly perfected prepetition security interest. Suppose further that two weeks after bankruptcy, Debtor sells all 100 units for a total of $10,000. Outside of bankruptcy, Bank would have a validly perfected security interest in the $10,000, which constitutes identifiable proceeds of collateral in which Bank had

---

232 *In re* Bumper Sales, Inc., 907 F.2d 1430, 11 U.C.C. Rep. Serv. 2d 1044 (4th Cir. 1990); *In re* Photo Promotion Assocs., Inc., 53 B.R. 759 (Bankr. S.D.N.Y. 1985).

233 11 U.S.C. § 552(a).

a perfected security interest.[234] Moreover, sound policy suggests that Bank should maintain its security interest in the $10,000 despite Debtor's bankruptcy. Bank's prepetition security interest in the 100 units of inventory — which is not affected by section 552(a) — is worthless if Debtor can liquidate those units of inventory and use the proceeds without regard to Bank's lien. In order to provide meaningful protection for Bank's security interest in prepetition collateral, bankruptcy must protect not only Bank's interest in the collateral, but also the proceeds of that collateral.

To provide this protection, Congress enacted section 552(b), which provides that, if a prepetition security interest encumbers both prepetition collateral and its proceeds, any proceeds of that prepetition collateral remain subject to the security interest *even if they are not received until after the petition date.*[235] In the above example, Bank's prepetition security interest had validly attached to Debtor's prepetition inventory, and Bank's security interest in that inventory automatically continued into identifiable proceeds.[236] Bank thus would continue to hold an enforceable security interest in the $10,000 of inventory proceeds, notwithstanding section 552(a).

Now consider a more complicated scenario in which Debtor files for bankruptcy holding 100 units of inventory, subject to Bank's validly perfected prepetition floating lien. Two weeks after the petition date, Debtor sells all 100 units of inventory for $10,000, and uses the cash to purchase 100 new units of inventory from suppliers. Bank cannot claim a direct security interest in the new inventory by virtue of the after-acquired property clause in its prepetition security agreement; section 552(a) cuts off the prospective effect of that clause. The new inventory, however, constitutes identifiable second-generation proceeds of the prepetition inventory.[237] Can Bank successfully claim a security interest in the new inventory as proceeds of the prepetition inventory under section 552(b)?

As the Fourth Circuit noted in *In re Bumper Sales, Inc.*,[238] the answer is yes. In *Bumper Sales*, the secured party held a validly perfected prepetition floating lien against the debtor's inventory and accounts. The debtor continued operating in bankruptcy for nearly

---

[234] U.C.C. §§ 9-306(2), (3), **R9-315(a), (c)-(d).**

[235] 11 U.S.C. § 552(b)(1); *In re* Bumper Sales, Inc., 907 F.2d 1430, 11 U.C.C. Rep. Serv. 2d 1044 (4th Cir. 1990); *In re* Ludford Fruit Prods., Inc., 99 B.R. 18 (Bankr. C.D. Cal. 1989). The language of section 552(b)(1) covers not only "proceeds" of prepetition collateral, but also "profits," "products," or "offspring" of prepetition collateral. Smith v. Dairymen, Inc., 790 F.2d 1107, 1 U.C.C. Rep. Serv. 2d 543 (4th Cir. 1986) (creditor with prepetition lien upon cows and milk entitled to lien upon postpetition milk); *In re* Wobig, 73 B.R. 292 (Bankr. D. Neb. 1987) (creditor with prepetition lien upon sows and offspring entitled to lien upon feeder pigs born after bankruptcy petition).

Section 552(b)(2) provides similar protection for postpetition "rents" of prepetition collateral.

[236] Recall that proceeds coverage is automatic under Article 9 unless the security agreement provides otherwise. U.C.C. §§ 9-203(3), 9-306(2), **R9-203(f), R9-315(a).** *See* § 2.04[B] *supra.*

[237] Recall that proceeds of proceeds constitute "proceeds," U.C.C. §§ 9-306(1), **R9-102(a)(64),** and thus, the security interest in the original collateral continues in such proceeds so long as they are "identifiable," *i.e.,* so long as they can be traced precisely to the original collateral. U.C.C. §§ 9-306(2), **R9-315(a)-(b).**

[238] 907 F.2d 1430, 11 U.C.C. Rep. Serv. 2d 1044 (4th Cir. 1990).

six months before the secured party asked the court for adequate protection of its security interest. During that period, the debtor's inventory and accounts turned over at least twice, so that by the time of the secured party's motion, all of the debtor's existing inventory and accounts had been received or generated after the petition date. The debtor argued that section 552(a) had extinguished the secured party's lien altogether but the Fourth Circuit disagreed, holding that the new inventory was identifiable second-generation proceeds of the prepetition inventory and thus that the secured party's lien remained effective under section 552(b).[239]

There is a practical lesson lurking in the *Bumper Sales* -don't count on being as lucky as the secured creditor in that case. That secured party failed to act prudently to protect its secured position, but still ended up being protected anyway. Why was the secured party so lucky? Even under the U.C.C., a secured party only obtains a security interest in *identifiable* (*i.e.*, traceable) second-and third-generation proceeds.[240] Because the debtor in the case stipulated that all of the postpetition inventory was acquired using the proceeds of prepetition inventory and accounts, the secured party did not have to trace the postpetition inventory precisely back to the prepetition inventory; therefore, the Fourth Circuit had no choice but to conclude that the new inventory was identifiable proceeds of the prepetition inventory.

Most secured parties cannot count on such good fortune. If the *Bumper Sales* debtor had commingled any of the proceeds of prepetition inventory with other operating funds, and had then used those commingled funds to purchase new inventory postpetition, the secured party would have had a difficult (and perhaps impossible) tracing burden and, as a result, might have lost its security interest altogether under section 552(a). Rather than rely upon such uncommon good luck, the secured party in *Bumper Sales* should have filed a motion for adequate protection as soon as the debtor filed its bankruptcy petition. This motion should have sought an order requiring the debtor to sequester all proceeds of the secured party's collateral in a separate account containing only proceeds — thus enabling the secured party to trace the proceeds of its collateral with ease and preserving the secured party's ability to invoke the protection of section 552(b).

§ 16.07 The Debtor's Right to Claim Exempt Property

[A] Generally

The common law generally permits a creditor to enforce a judgment against any assets of the debtor that the creditor can locate. This general rule, however, is subject in every jurisdiction to constitutional or statutory *exemption* provisions, which allow an individual debtor to declare certain assets (or a portion of the debtor's equity in certain assets) to be exempt from seizure and sale by creditors. The goal of exemption laws is to avoid leaving an individual debtor destitute as a result of creditor collection activity. By providing the financially distressed debtor with some minimum amount of assets free of creditor claims, exemption laws enable the debtor to gain the financial foothold necessary to make a fresh financial start.[241]

---

239 *Bumper Sales*, 907 F.2d at 1439; *see also In re* Sherwood Ford, Inc., 125 B.R. 957 (Bankr. D. Md. 1991).

240 U.C.C. §§ 9-306(2), **R9-315(a)-(b).**

241 Woodward, *Exemptions, Opting Out, and Bankruptcy Reform*, 43 Ohio St. L.J. 335 (1982).

Bankruptcy law also incorporates the idea of exemptions for individual debtors. Section 522(d) provides a list of exemptions accorded to an individual debtor as a matter of bankruptcy law. These include, *inter alia*, $15,000 of equity in the debtor's residence, $2,400 of equity in one motor vehicle, $400 of equity in each item of the debtor's household goods (up to a total of $8,000), $1,000 of equity in the debtor's jewelry, and $1,500 of equity in the debtor's professional books or tools.[242] Under section 522(b), an individual debtor may declare certain of its assets as exempt from the claims of creditors pursuant to the foregoing federal exemptions[243] or may choose instead the exemptions available in their jurisdiction under nonbankruptcy law,[244] unless the debtor is located in a state that has opted to require debtors to rely only upon nonbankruptcy exemption laws.[245] In that case, the debtor has no option and is limited to whatever exemptions are provided under nonbankruptcy law.

Exemptions do not arise automatically; instead, the debtor must file with the court a list of the property that it claims as exempt.[246] The trustee and any creditor may then object and challenge any particular claim of exemption. Absent timely objection,[247] the property is exempted as claimed.[248] If there is a timely objection, the court must determine whether the debtor is entitled to the claimed exemption, with the objecting party bearing the burden of persuasion.[249] If the debtor is entitled to exempt an asset in its entirety (for example, the state's exemption law entitles the debtor to claim $2,000 of equity in one vehicle, and the debtor's car is worth only $1,500), the asset is returned to the debtor. If the asset is only partially exempt, the estate is entitled to the nonexempt portion of the asset; the trustee thus retains possession of the asset, and the debtor instead receives payment equal to the value of the exemption out of the proceeds of the asset.[250]

[B] The Debtor's Power to Avoid Liens Against Exempt Property

Suppose that Debtor's automobile is subject to three liens: a voluntary security interest granted to Bank to secure a $5,000 loan, a mechanic's lien held by Garage for unpaid repairs totaling $2,000, and an execution lien for a $10,000 judgment in favor of Defendant. If the applicable exemption law permits Debtor to exempt $4,000 of equity

---

[242] 11 U.S.C. § 522(d).

[243] *Id.* § 522(b)(1).

[244] *Id.* § 522(b)(2).

[245] Most states have opted out of the federal bankruptcy exemptions contained in section 522(d). Consequently, in most states, debtors are entitled to the same exemptions in bankruptcy as they would have received outside of bankruptcy.

[246] 11 U.S.C. § 522(*l*). In a voluntary bankruptcy case, the debtor must file its list of claimed exemption along with the petition or within 15 days thereafter. Bankr. Rules 1007, 4003(a).

[247] Generally, the trustee or any creditor must file any objection within 30 days after the initial meeting of creditors, unless the court grants additional time for objections. Bankr. Rule 4003(b).

[248] The Supreme Court has held that a Chapter 7 trustee could not contest the validity of a debtor's claimed exemption after the 30-day objection period had expired, even if debtor had no colorable basis for claiming the exemption. Taylor v. Freeland & Kronz, 503 U.S. 638 (1992).

[249] Bankr. Rule 4003(c).

[250] *In re* Salzer, 52 F.3d 708 (7th Cir. 1995), *cert. denied*, 516 U.S. 1177 (1996); *In re* Hyman, 123 B.R. 342 (9th Cir. Bankr. 1991), *aff'd*, 967 F.2d 1316 (9th Cir. 1992).

in one vehicle, to what extent do these liens affect Debtor's ability to claim the car as exempt property?

Outside of bankruptcy, a debtor's exemptions would not be of particular concern to a voluntary secured creditor like Bank. Exemptions generally are not effective against the holder of a valid security interest; as a practical matter, the granting of a consensual security interest in an asset is tantamount to a waiver of the right to assert the exemption against the secured party. The same is true in bankruptcy; as long as a security interest is valid and not otherwise avoidable in bankruptcy, the debtor's exemption rights are generally subordinate to the secured party's interest.[251] The same principle holds true for statutory lienholders like Garage: statutory liens generally take priority over the debtor's exemptions, on the theory that the debtor's assertion of the exemption would compromise the legislature's decision to accord special protection to the statutory lienholder.

In contrast, judicial liens are obtained by creditors through execution, levy, or the like — the very processes against which exemptions are intended to protect debtors.[252] If Defendant can freely enforce its execution lien without regard to Debtor's ability to claim an exemption in its car, Debtor's ability to obtain a fresh start is compromised. The Code thus provides debtors with a mechanism to preserve their exemptions, despite the actions of judicial lien creditors. Under section 522(f)(1)(A), the debtor can avoid a judicial lien against an asset "to the extent that such lien impairs an exemption to which the debtor would have been entitled"[253] — in other words, to the extent that the debtor would have been entitled to claim the asset as exempt under applicable exemption law *but for the effect of the lien.*[254] Accordingly, Debtor in the above example cannot avoid the liens of either Bank or Garage, regardless of the car's value. Debtor can avoid Defendant's execution lien under section 522(f)(1)(A), however, to the extent that Defendant's lien impairs Debtor's ability to claim an exemption in the car. If the car is worth $11,000 or less, enforcement of Defendant's execution lien against the car would completely impair Debtor's ability to claim an exemption in the car; Debtor could thus avoid Defendant's lien altogether.[255] If the car was worth $12,000, Debtor could not avoid

---

251 11 U.S.C. § 522(c)(2); H.R. Rep. No. 595, 95th Cong., 1st Sess. 361 (1977). This means, of course, that if the lien is so large that there is no equity in the property, the debtor effectively loses the exemption altogether.

252 *See* § 14.02 *supra.*

253 11 U.S.C. § 522(f)(1)(A). By its language, section 522(f)(1) allows the debtor to avoid "the fixing . . . [of a lien upon] an interest of the debtor in property." The Supreme Court has interpreted this language to mean that a debtor can avoid an exemption-impairing judicial lien against an asset that the debtor owned *before the judicial lien arose,* but not a judicial lien that arose before the debtor owned the asset or simultaneously with debtor's acquisition of the asset. Farrey v. Sanderfoot, 500 U.S. 291 (1991) (in divorce settlement, debtor received ex-wife's share of family home, subject to judicial lien in favor of ex-wife to secure debtor's monetary payment obligations; debtor could not avoid ex-wife's lien because it arose simultaneously to his acquisition of ex-wife's share of the home).

254 Owen v. Owen, 500 U.S. 305 (1991).

255 Under section 522(f)(2), a lien "impairs" an exemption to the extent that the value of the property is less than the sum of (a) the lien, (b) all other unavoidable liens on the asset, and (c)

Defendant's lien altogether, but could avoid the lien to the extent of the Debtor's exemptible equity in the car. The lien would remain effective, however, against the nonexempt portion of Debtor's equity in the car ($1,000).

The Code provides one significant exception to the general rule that exemptions are not effective to defeat the rights of a secured party. Under section 522(f)(1)(B), the debtor may avoid a *nonpossessory, nonpurchase-money* security interest to the extent it would impair the debtor's ability to claim an exemption in any of the following assets:

- household furnishings, household goods, clothes, appliances, books, animals, crops, musical instruments, or jewelry, so long as these assets are held for personal, family, or household use;

- implements, professional books, or tools of the trade; or

- professionally prescribed health aids. [256]

Section 522(f)(1)(B) permits the debtor to avoid exemption-impairing liens against these types of assets even if the debtor had earlier signed a waiver of its exemptions. [257] Congress allowed the debtor to avoid nonpossessory, nonpurchase-money liens against these kinds of assets out of concern for potential creditor overreaching. Congress was motivated by concerns that creditors lending money to consumer debtors were taking security interests in household goods and requiring debtors to waive the right to claim those goods as exempt. Although these types of assets generally have high replacement costs, they tend to have significantly smaller resale or forced sale values, and thus creditors are not likely to repossess these assets except as a last resort. Accordingly, Congress was concerned that creditors would use threats of repossession as a means of coercing unknowing debtors into making payments they could not otherwise afford to make. [258] By allowing the debtor to preserve his or her exemption in these assets, notwithstanding a waiver of exemptions, section 522(f)(1)(B) prevents this sort of creditor overreaching. [259]

---

the allowed amount of the exemption. In this example, the value of the car is $11,000, and the sum of (a), (b), and (c) is $21,000. The lien thus "impairs" the exemption to the full $10,000 extent of the lien, and is fully avoidable under section 522(f)(1)(A).

[256] 11 U.S.C. § 522(f)(1)(B). The debtor cannot avoid a security interest in furnishings, animals, or other such assets if they were acquired or used primarily for business or commercial purposes. *E.g., In re* Patterson, 825 F.2d 1140 (7th Cir. 1987) (livestock); *In re* Reid, 757 F.2d 230 (10th Cir. 1985) (paintings).

Although section 522(f)(1)(B) allows the debtor to avoid these exemption-impairing liens, section 522(f)(3) imposes a further maximum dollar limit with respect to certain items. Under section 522(f)(3), a debtor who takes the applicable state law exemptions cannot avoid a lien against implements, professional books, tools of the trade, farm animals, or crops, to the extent that the value of such items exceeds $5,000.

[257] 11 U.S.C. § 522(f)(1)(B).

[258] H.R. Rep. No. 595, 95th Cong., 1st Sess. 127.

[259] 11 U.S.C. § 522(f)(1)(B) is not the only federal law that prevents such creditor behavior. Federal Trade Commission and Federal Reserve Board regulations prohibit nonpurchase-money security interests in a consumer's household goods. *See, e.g.,* 16 C.F.R. § 444.2(4) (FTC); 12 C.F.R. § 227.13(d) (FRB).

(Matthew Bender & Co., Inc.)

The debtor may not use section 522(f)(1)(B) to avoid an exemption-impairing possessory security interest. According to the courts, whether the security interest is "nonpossessory" for purposes of section 522(f)(1)(B) depends upon the intent of the parties at the time the security interest attached. If the parties structured the transaction as a pledge, with the secured party holding the collateral, the security interest is not avoidable under section 522(f)(1)(B) even if it impairs the debtor's right to claim that item as exempt. In contrast, if the debtor retained possession prior to default, the security interest is nonpossessory, even if the secured party rightfully took possession of the collateral prior to bankruptcy in order to enforce its lien.[260] Likewise, to the extent that a lien qualifies as a purchase-money security interest under state law, the debtor may not use section 522(f)(1)(B) to avoid the lien.[261] This limitation reflects the solicitude that commercial law typically provides to purchase-money creditors.

Section 522(f)(1)(B) has generated a significant amount of litigation regarding whether the purchase-money character of a security interest survives the debtor's refinancing of the debt. For example, suppose Debtor purchases a television set from Seller, who retains a purchase-money security interest to secure the set's purchase price of $800, and that Seller subsequently assigns its interest to Finance Co. Suppose further that nine months later, after paying off one-half of the price of the set, Debtor signs a new promissory note to Finance Co. in the amount of $1,000 — representing both the refinancing of the $400 balance of the original contract and a new loan to Debtor of $600. Debtor then goes bankrupt without repaying anything to Finance Co., seeks to retain the television set as exempt, and further seeks to avoid Finance Co.'s security interest as an exemption-impairing lien.

A significant minority of courts have held that Debtor's refinancing of the original debt "transforms" the purchase-money security interest into a nonpurchase money security interest avoidable under section 522(f)(1)(B).[262] Most of these courts have reasoned that refinancing a purchase-money debt extinguishes the original debt and replaces it with a new obligation secured by a lien that cannot qualify as a PMSI under U.C.C. section 9-107(1972 text) because the debtor already owned the collateral at the time of the refinancing.[263] In contrast, the majority of courts have adopted the view that Debtor's refinancing does not *automatically* destroy the purchase-money character of Finance Co.'s

---

[260] *In re* Schultz, 101 B.R. 68 (Bankr. N.D. Iowa 1989).

[261] 11 U.S.C. § 522(f)(2); U.C.C. §§ 9-107, **R9-103**.

[262] This is often called the "transformation rule." *See In re* Matthews, 724 F.2d 798, 37 U.C.C. Rep. Serv. 1332 (9th Cir. 1984).

[263] A few courts have reasoned, incorrectly, that a security interest cannot constitute a PMSI under Article 9 if it secures more than the purchase price. *E.g., In re* Jones, 5 B.R. 655, 30 U.C.C. Rep. Serv. 1697 (Bankr. M.D.N.C. 1980); *In re* Scott, 5 B.R. 37, 29 U.C.C. Rep. Serv. 1038 (Bankr. M.D. Pa. 1980). This interpretation, however, is at odds with the language of Article 9 — which provides that a security interest is a PMSI "to the extent that" it secures the purchase price or an enabling loan, U.C.C. §§ 9-107, **R9-103(b)** — and has been rejected by most courts. *E.g.,* Geist v. Converse County Bank, 79 B.R. 939, 5 U.C.C. Rep. Serv. 2d 1267 (D. Wyo. 1987); *In re* Conn, 16 B.R. 454, 33 U.C.C. Rep. Serv. 701 (Bankr. W.D. Ky. 1982). This issue is discussed in detail in § 1.05 *supra.*

lien.[264] The majority view is preferable, as it looks to solve this question by reference to economic substance rather than form. As one bankruptcy court explained:

> Though in form the original note is cancelled, its balance is absorbed into the refinancing loan. To the extent of that balance, the purchase-money security interest taken under the original note likewise survives because what is owed on the original note is not eliminated, it is merely transferred to, and increased in amount by, another obligation. The refinancing changes the character of neither the balance due under the first loan nor the security interest taken under it.[265] Under this view, Finance Co.'s security interest would have a dual status: it would be a PMSI to the extent that it secures the unpaid balance attributable to the television set ($400), and a nonpurchase-money security interest to the extent of the remaining loan balance ($600). Debtor thus could not avoid Finance Co.'s lien to the extent that the lien secures the remaining $400 balance attributable to the television, but Debtor could use section 522(f)(1)(B) to avoid the lien to the extent it secures the remaining loan balance.[266]

In 1994, Congress amended section 522 by adding subsection 522(f)(3), which places a further limitation upon the debtor's power to avoid exemption-impairing liens under section 522(f)(1). Under section 522(f)(3), a debtor who claims exemptions under nonbankruptcy law cannot avoid the fixing of a nonpossessory, nonpurchase-money security interest in implements, professional books, tools of the trade, farm animals or crops, to the extent that the value of such items exceeds $5,000.[267]

§ 16.08 The Chapter 7 Debtor's Right of Redemption — 11 U.S.C. § 722

A debtor suffering from financial distress may wish to retain possession of certain important but encumbered assets (for example, the debtor's automobile). Outside of bankruptcy, however, a debtor in default can redeem the collateral and avoid foreclosure of a valid security interest only by paying the full amount of the debt (plus accrued but unpaid interest and reasonable costs of collection).[268] This may render it impossible for the debtor to retain possession of encumbered property, especially property in which the debtor has no equity.

In a Chapter 7 liquidation case, however, bankruptcy law, in certain circumstances, gives the debtor the right to redeem the collateral from a lien at a bargain price — the amount of the creditor's allowed secured claim. In the case of an undersecured creditor, this enables the debtor to redeem the collateral by paying the value of the collateral rather than the full balance of the debt. Section 722 provides the debtor with this right of redemption under the following circumstances:

---

[264] E.g., Pristas v. Landaus of Plymouth, Inc., 742 F.2d 797, 39 U.C.C. Rep. Serv. 1 (3d Cir. 1984).

[265] In re Conn, 16 B.R. 454, 33 U.C.C. Rep. Serv. 701 (Bankr. W.D. Ky. 1982).

[266] In re Parsley, 104 B.R. 72, 10 U.C.C. Rep. Serv. 2d 1398 (Bankr. S.D. Ind. 1988). Note that a creditor such as Finance Co. must prove the extent to which its security interest qualifies for purchase-money status, and the creditor's failure to meet this burden would enable the debtor to avoid the security interest altogether under section 522(f)(2). Geist v. Converse County Bank, 79 B.R. 939, 5 U.C.C. Rep. Serv. 2d 1267 (D. Wyo. 1987).

[267] 11 U.S.C. § 522(f)(3).

[268] U.C.C. §§ 9-506, **R9-623**.

- *The creditor's lien must secure a dischargeable consumer debt.* The debtor may not redeem collateral that secures a business indebtedness.[269] The debt must be one that is *capable of being discharged*; the debtor may exercise its right of redemption under section 722 even if a creditor later successfully challenges the debtor's right to discharge.[270]

- *The collateral sought to be redeemed must be tangible personal property intended primarily for personal, family or household use.* The asset sought to be redeemed must be "consumer goods" as defined by U.C.C. Article 9.[271]

- *The collateral sought to be redeemed must be exempted under section 522, or must have been abandoned by the trustee under section 554.* To the extent that the debtor has equity in an asset and that equity could benefit the estate, bankruptcy law should not permit redemption; in that case, the equity in that asset should remain with the estate for the benefit of general creditors. If the debtor has no equity in the collateral, however, the trustee likely will consider the collateral to be burdensome to the estate and abandon the collateral under section 554. In that case, the debtor can redeem the collateral by paying the amount of the secured claim to its holder. Alternatively, if the debtor has equity in the collateral but that equity is entirely exempt from general creditors, the estate has no interest in the collateral and redemption is also permitted.[272] If there is no applicable exemption law covering the asset and the trustee has not abandoned it, the debtor cannot redeem it.[273]

- *The debtor must have filed a timely statement of its intention to redeem the collateral.* The debtor must file this statement with the clerk of the bankruptcy court within 30 days following the petition date or, if the initial meeting of creditors[274] takes place during that 30 days, by the date of such meeting.[275]

- *The debtor must actually complete the redemption within 45 days after filing its statement of intent to redeem.*[276] Although section 722 does not

---

[269] *In re* Pipes, 78 B.R. 981 (Bankr. W.D. Mo. 1987) (debtor could not redeem pickup truck used for business purposes).

[270] 11 U.S.C. § 523(a)provides a list of certain debts -for example, liability for child support obligations, liability for willful or malicious injury, or liability for death or personal injury caused by drunk driving -that the debtor cannot discharge in bankruptcy.

[271] U.C.C. §§ 9-109(1), **R9-102(a)(23)**. *See also In re* Pipes, 78 B.R. 981 (Bankr. W.D. Mo. 1987) (debtor could not redeem pickup truck used for business purposes).

[272] *In re* Fitzgerald, 20 B.R. 27 (Bankr. N.D.N.Y. 1982).

[273] *In re* Zaicek, 29 B.R. 31 (Bankr. W.D. Ky. 1983).

[274] In every bankruptcy case, there is an initial meeting of creditors conducted pursuant to 11 U.S.C. § 341. At this meeting, the trustee and creditors may question the debtor under oath about the debtor's assets and financial affairs. 11 U.S.C. § 343.

[275] 11 U.S.C. § 521(2)(A).

[276] *Id.* § 521(2)(B).

specify the exact method by which the debtor must redeem, most courts have required the debtor to make a lump sum payment to the creditor equal to the amount of the creditor's allowed secured claim.[277]

Before the debtor can exercise its redemption right under section 722, the court must value the creditor's secured claim under section 506(a). Valuations for redemption purposes typically involve two principal issues. The first issue is the timing (*i.e.*, the effective date) of the valuation. For example, suppose that, on February 1, Debtor files for Chapter 7 bankruptcy and that Debtor's schedule of assets lists a 1988 Buick automobile worth $5,000, subject to a lien in favor of Bank to secure a $6,000 debt. On March 1, Debtor files a timely statement of intention to redeem. On April 1, Debtor tenders $3,500 to the Bank, claiming that depreciation and recent bad publicity about Buick safety had reduced the car's value by $1,500. Bank objects and a hearing is scheduled for April 10. As of what date should the court value the car for purposes of section 722? Should the court value the car as of the petition date (February 1), the time of the valuation hearing (April 10), or some other date?

The majority of courts have chosen to value the collateral for section 722 purposes as of the date of the valuation hearing rather than the petition date.[278] These courts have reasoned that Bank could not repossess and sell the collateral immediately once Debtor filed its petition; instead, there would be a delay while Bank sought relief from stay in order to foreclose. Accordingly, these courts have reasoned that valuing the collateral as of the time of redemption would more closely approximate what Bank could have obtained in foreclosure.[279] Although the timing of the majority rule will work to the detriment of the secured creditor in cases where the collateral has depreciated after the petition date, a secured creditor is not powerless to protect itself against this risk. As discussed earlier, a secured creditor can protect itself against the risk of postpetition depreciation of its collateral by filing a motion for adequate protection of its security interest as soon as it learns of the bankruptcy petition.[280]

---

[277] *In re* Edwards, 901 F.2d 1383 (7th Cir. 1990); *In re* Bell, 700 F.2d 1053 (6th Cir. 1983). A few courts have allowed the debtor to redeem by making installment payments over a period stretching beyond the 45-day period, *e.g.*, *In re* Berenguer, 77 B.R. 959 (Bankr. S.D. Fla. 1987), but this seems questionable. If the debtor wants to retain possession of the collateral and make installment payments to the creditor, the debtor has other alternatives for doing so, including (a) reaffirmation of the debt under section 524(c), *infra* § 16.09, and (b) filing a Chapter 13 petition and providing for installment payments to the creditor as part of the Chapter 13 plan. *See In re* Tucker, 158 B.R. 150 (Bankr. W.D. Mo. 1993) (debtor must redeem in lump-sum rather than installments).

[278] *In re* Lopez, 224 B.R. 439 (Bankr. C.D. Cal. 1998); *In re* King, 75 B.R. 287 (Bankr. S.D. Ohio. 1987). *But see* In re Kinser, 17 B.R. 468 (Bankr. N.D. Ga. 1981) (petition date).

[279] The reasoning behind the majority rule seems plainly wrong. Outside of bankruptcy, Bank could have repossessed the car and resold it under Article 9 with little delay and without the consequence of the automatic stay. Thus, a petition date valuation would more closely approximate the Bank's alternative foreclosure remedy. Nevertheless, the adverse consequences imposed by the majority rule are slight, and as explained in the text, creditors like Bank can protect themselves against even those minor consequences.

[280] *See* § 16.03[B][1][a][i] *supra*.

(Matthew Bender & Co., Inc.)

The second and more frequent valuation issue concerns the measure of value that courts should use for redemption purposes. For example, in the previous hypothetical, Debtor (who wants a low redemption price) likely will argue that the court should value the automobile at its wholesale value. Debtor will argue that this measure is appropriate because it best approximates the amount Bank would receive if it foreclosed; after all, banks are in the business of lending money, not selling cars, and most banks dispose of repossessed cars by reselling them at wholesale to persons in the business of selling used cars. In contrast, Bank (which wants a high redemption price) will argue that the court should value the automobile at its retail value, on the ground that after foreclosure, Debtor would have had to purchase another car at retail price.

Most courts faced with this question have decided to value the collateral at its wholesale value, on the ground that section 722 should leave the secured creditor in the same position as if it had repossessed and sold the collateral.[281] In reality, neither wholesale value nor retail value seems completely appropriate. Valuing the collateral at wholesale probably bestows a windfall upon the debtor (who would have to pay more for a replacement vehicle), whereas valuing the collateral at retail probably bestows a windfall upon the secured creditor (who likely could not obtain the retail value upon resale of the collateral unless the creditor was also in the business of selling cars). Consistent with this view, some recent courts and commentators have suggested "splitting the difference" and valuing the collateral at a value midway between its wholesale and retail values.[282]

§ 16.09 Reaffirmation by the Debtor

Where redemption is not feasible, the Bankruptcy Code provides the debtor with another option for retaining encumbered property — reaffirmation of the debt. Under limited circumstances, section 524(c) allows a debtor in bankruptcy to make a contract with a creditor under which it agrees to repay a debt to the creditor, even though that debt would otherwise be discharged in the debtor's bankruptcy. For example, suppose that Debtor owes Bank $5,000, secured by a consensual lien on Debtor's car. The car is worth only $4,000, and the Chapter 7 trustee has abandoned the car to Debtor. Debtor needs the car to get to and from work and desperately wants to retain possession of it. Unfortunately, Debtor does not have $4,000 in cash with which to redeem the car from Bank's lien under section 722, nor can Debtor likely obtain credit to acquire another, comparable car. Bank is willing, however, to allow Debtor to retain possession of the car if the Debtor will reaffirm its obligation to Bank (*i.e.*, if Debtor promises to resume and continue making monthly payments on the full $5,000 balance of the debt). To the extent that section 524(c) permits Debtor to enter into a reaffirmation agreement with

---

281 *In re* Waters, 122 B.R. 298 (Bankr. W.D. Tex. 1990); *In re* Van Holt, 28 B.R. 577 (Bankr. W.D. Mo. 1983). Note that the Supreme Court's decision in *In re Rash*, discussed in § 16.03[B][2][a] *supra*, focused only upon valuation in Chapter 13 reorganizations. Recent bankruptcy court decisions have concluded that *Rash*'s "replacement-value" standard does not apply to redemptions in Chapter 7 cases. *In re* Williams, 224 B.R. 873 (Bankr. S.D. Ohio 1998); *In re* Donley, 217 B.R. 1004 (Bankr. S.D. Ohio 1998).

282 *In re* Williams, 224 B.R. 873 (Bankr. S.D. Ohio 1998); David G. Epstein, Steve H. Nickles & James J. White, *Bankruptcy* § 7-49, at 447 (West Pract. Ed. 1992).

Bank, Debtor has an additional alternative for retaining possession of encumbered collateral.[283]

Although the Bankruptcy Code permits reaffirmation agreements, however, it does not encourage them. Discharge of indebtedness is one of the primary benefits that bankruptcy provides the individual debtor, and reaffirming a dischargeable debt often may not be in a debtor's best economic interest. Indeed, Congress was concerned that many reaffirmations were not economically sensible and resulted from threats or overreaching by creditors (*e.g.*, "Reaffirm this debt or we'll make sure that you never get credit from us or anybody else again.").[284]

In an attempt to reduce the frequency of unwarranted reaffirmations, Congress provided a series of prerequisites in section 524(c) that must be satisfied before a creditor legally may enforce a reaffirmation agreement:

- *The debtor and creditor must have entered into the reaffirmation agreement before the debtor was discharged.*[285] Section 524(a) generally operates to enjoin any act "to collect, recover, or offset" a discharged debt.[286] This injunction prevents the enforcement of any reaffirmation agreement entered into after discharge. Further, this injunction also reaches surreptitious attempts by creditors to obtain repayment or reaffirmation outside the scope of section 524(c). For example, suppose Debtor owed Bank a debt of $1,000 which was discharged in bankruptcy in 1994, and that Debtor approached Bank in 1997 to seek a $2,000 loan. In order to obtain repayment of the previously discharged debt, Bank agrees to loan Debtor $2,000, but only if Debtor will sign a promissory note for $3,000. Bank's actions violate section 524(a), and Bank could not enforce the promissory note in order to collect the additional $1,000.[287]

- *The debtor must not have validly rescinded the reaffirmation agreement.* Bankruptcy law permits the debtor to change its mind and rescind a reaffirmation agreement, but only if the debtor acts to rescind in prompt fashion. To rescind effectively, the debtor must give notice of rescission before the *later* of (a) the debtor's discharge or (b) the passage of more than 60 days after the entering of the reaffirmation agreement.[288] The rationale for this debtor opt-out provision is that a "cooling-off" period will allow debtors to reconsider and avoid the consequences of an imprudent decision to reaffirm a prepetition debt, especially in those cases

---

[283] Reaffirmation under section 524 is not limited to secured debts; theoretically, a debtor could choose to reaffirm an unsecured debt. In this text, discussion of reaffirmation is limited to its application to secured debts.

[284] H.R. Rep. No. 595, 95th Cong., 1st Sess. 162-164 (1977).

[285] 11 U.S.C. § 524(c)(1).

[286] *Id.* § 524(a)(2).

[287] Van Meter v. American State Bank, 89 B.R. 32 (W.D. Ark. 1988); *In re* Smurzynski, 72 B.R. 368 (Bankr. N.D. Ill. 1987).

[288] 11 U.S.C. § 524(c)(4).

where the decision to reaffirm may have resulted from significant pressure by the creditor whose debt was reaffirmed.

● *The agreement must contain the necessary "disclaimers."* The reaffirmation must include two statutorily required disclaimers. First, the agreement must advise the debtor of its right to rescind the agreement during the time period noted above.[289] Second, the agreement must advise the debtor that the debtor is not required to enter into any reaffirmation agreement.[290] Further, the agreement must state each of these disclaimers in "clear and conspicuous" fashion.[291]

● *The reaffirmation agreement must have been filed with the bankruptcy court.*[292]

● *If the debtor was not represented by an attorney at the time the agreement was negotiated, the bankruptcy court must have approved the agreement.* Where the debtor enters a reaffirmation agreement without legal advice, there is a justifiable concern that the debtor may not have fully understood the consequences of the agreement. By requiring approval of reaffirmation agreements entered into by uncounselled debtors, the Bankruptcy Code provides such debtors with protection from imprudent reaffirmation agreements. Where the debtor acts without legal advice, the Code provides several procedural safeguards before a creditor can enforce a reaffirmation agreement. *First,* the debtor must appear in person at a hearing, at which the court must (a) inform the debtor that it is not required to enter into a reaffirmation agreement and (b) explain the legal effect and consequences of entering into and defaulting under a reaffirmation agreement.[293] *Second,* the court cannot enforce the agreement unless the court determines that the agreement is in the "best interest of the debtor" and will not pose "undue hardship" to the debtor or a dependent.[294]

---

[289] *Id.* § 524(c)(2)(A).

[290] *Id.* § 524(c)(2)(B) (agreement must contain statement that "advises the debtor that such agreement is not required under this title, under nonbankruptcy law, or under any agreement not in accordance with the provisions of [§ 524(c)]").

[291] *Id.* § 524(c)(2)(A), (B). Bankruptcy courts have interpreted the words "clear and conspicuous" to impose two separate requirements — that the language be "clear" and that it also be "conspicuous." In *In re* Wallace, 102 B.R. 54 (Bankr. E.D.N.C. 1989), the reaffirmation contained a clear and express statement of the debtor's right to rescind but the statement appeared in paragraph 8 of the agreement, in type no larger than the previous seven paragraphs. The *Wallace* court held that the agreement violated the conspicuousness requirement and refused to enforce the reaffirmation agreement. *See also In re* Noble, 182 B.R. 854 (Bankr. W.D. Wash. 1995) (disclaimer printed in the same type face, format, size and color as remainder of agreement is not "conspicuous").

[292] 11 U.S.C. § 524(c)(3).

[293] *Id.* § 524(d)(1).

[294] *Id.* §§ 524(c)(6)(A), 524(d)(2). This determination is not required, however, if the debtor is seeking to reaffirm a consumer debt secured by real estate. *Id.* §§ 524(c)(6)(B), 524(d)(2). Courts have occasionally expressed significant doubt about the debtor's ability to make the payments specified in the reaffirmation agreement as grounds for disapproving the agreement as not being in the debtor's best interest. *In re* Bryant, 43 B.R. 189 (Bankr. E.D. Mich. 1984).

- *If the debtor was represented by an attorney at the time the agreement was negotiated, that attorney must have filed the required affidavit with the bankruptcy court.* The attorney's affidavit must declare that the debtor entered into the reaffirmation agreement voluntarily and with full information, that the agreement does not impose an undue hardship upon the debtor or a dependent, and that the attorney fully advised the debtor of the consequences of entering into and defaulting under a reaffirmation agreement.[295] The rationale for this provision is that if the debtor entered into the agreement with the advice of a competent attorney, the agreement probably reflects the debtor's best interests and thus should be freely enforced without the need for court approval.[296]

- *Finally, the agreement must be enforceable under applicable nonbankruptcy law.*[297] Under the common law, of course, the debtor's promise to pay a discharged debt does not require additional consideration; the original promise to pay constitutes sufficient "moral consideration" to enforce the reaffirmation. Nevertheless, nonbankruptcy law may provide the debtor with other defenses to the enforcement of the reaffirmation agreement, such as unconscionability, fraud, or duress.

Whereas redemption under section 722 is nonconsensual, reaffirmation under section 524(c) obviously requires an agreement between the debtor and the secured creditor.[298] Neither party can legally compel the other to accept reaffirmation. Thus, it is important to appreciate the circumstances under which a debtor is likely to reaffirm a secured debt.

For example, consider the hypothetical introduced at the beginning of this section, in which Debtor wishes to retain possession of its car but does not have the $4,000 cash necessary to redeem the vehicle. If Debtor is in Chapter 7 liquidation, Bank (which holds an undersecured claim) has little incentive to cooperate with Debtor's desire to retain possession of the car — unless Debtor is willing to negotiate an agreement that will make Bank better off than Bank would be if it repossessed and sold the car. If Debtor simply surrendered the car, Bank would receive $4,000 (less expenses of sale) from the car, but little or nothing on its unsecured deficiency claim. Here, each party has an incentive to reaffirm: reaffirmation is Debtor's only feasible means of maintaining a suitable car,

---

[295] 11 U.S.C. § 524(c)(3)(A)-(C).

[296] This requirement was added in 1984. Prior to 1984, the court had to approve *all* reaffirmation agreements, regardless of whether the debtor had the benefit of counsel.

One might argue that a sophisticated debtor who enters a reaffirmation agreement with the advice of counsel should be held to the agreement regardless of whether the agreement meets the other requirements of section 524(c). Courts have rejected this argument, however. *See In re Getzoff, 180 B.R. 572 (9th Cir. Bankr. 1995).*

[297] 11 U.S.C. § 524(c).

[298] If the debtor wishes to reaffirm a secured debt in order to retain the collateral, section 521 requires the debtor to file a statement of its intent with the clerk of the bankruptcy court within 30 days following the petition date (or, if the initial meeting of creditors takes place during that 30 days, by the date of such meeting). 11 U.S.C. § 521(2)(A). Further, section 521 obligates the debtor to carry out its intent and enter into a reaffirmation agreement within 45 days following its statement of intent. *Id.* § 521(2)(B).

and provides Bank with the possibility of a larger recovery than it might otherwise receive if Debtor surrendered the collateral.[299]

What if Debtor can neither redeem the car nor negotiate an acceptable reaffirmation agreement with Bank? Does Debtor have any other alternative for retaining possession of the car? If Debtor was in default at the time of its petition, the answer is no. But if Debtor was not in default at the time of its petition, the answer is: maybe, maybe not.

In *In re Edwards*,[300] a debtor attempted to retain possession of two cars, without redemption or reaffirmation, by continuing to make timely payments on the underlying debts during her Chapter 7 proceeding. The creditor moved to compel the debtor to either redeem the cars, surrender them, or reaffirm the debts, and the bankruptcy court granted this motion. The Seventh Circuit affirmed the bankruptcy court's order, holding that section 521(2) did not permit a Chapter 7 debtor to retain possession of collateral without either redeeming it or reaffirming the underlying debt.[301] The *Edwards* court interpreted section 521(2) to provide the Chapter 7 debtor with an exclusive set of options regarding the collateral — surrender, redemption, or reaffirmation of the underlying debt. In reaching this result, the *Edwards* court was clearly motivated by the concern that retention of possession without redemption or reaffirmation imposed unjustified financial risks upon the creditor — who could end up (if the debtor later defaulted) with depreciated collateral and no personal recourse against the debtor.[302]

In contrast to *Edwards* is the Fourth Circuit's decision in *In re Belanger*.[303] The debtors were current in repaying a debt secured by their mobile home at the time they filed a Chapter 7 bankruptcy petition. The debtors neither reaffirmed the debt nor redeemed the home, but simply continued making timely monthly payments to the creditor during the Chapter 7 proceeding. As in *Edwards*, the creditor argued that section 521 limited the Chapter 7 debtor to either redemption, reaffirmation, or surrender of the collateral. The Fourth Circuit disagreed and allowed the debtors to retain possession of the home as long as the debtors continued making timely installment payments under the original contract.[304] The *Belanger* court noted that nothing in the language of section

---

[299] Again, the comment in the text presumes that Debtor is in a Chapter 7 liquidation proceeding. While reaffirmation is not limited to Chapter 7, debtors in Chapter 11, 12, or 13 cases do not need reaffirmation to retain possession of collateral; those Chapters permit a debtor to retain possession of collateral while repaying undersecured prepetition claims under a reorganization plan.

[300] 901 F.2d 1383 (7th Cir. 1990).

[301] *Edwards*, 901 F.2d at 1386.

[302] *Id.* ("[Section 521(2)] speaks strongly against permitting debtors to improve their position dramatically against secured creditors by relieving them of personal liability. When a debtor is relieved of personal liability on loans secured by collateral, the debtor has little or no incentive to insure or maintain the property in which a creditor retains a security interest. The value of the collateral may fall below the level of the loan, leaving the creditor undersecured and driving up future costs of credit.").

The First, Fifth, and Eleventh Circuits have also adopted this view. *In re Burr*, 160 F.3d 843 (1st Cir. 1998); *In re Johnson*, 89 F.3d 249 (5th Cir. 1996); *In re Taylor*, 3 F.3d 1512 (11th Cir. 1993).

[303] 962 F.2d 345 (4th Cir. 1992).

[304] *Belanger*, 962 F.2d at 347. The Second, Ninth, and Tenth Circuits have reached a similar

521(2) "requires the debtor to choose redemption, reaffirmation or surrender of the property to the exclusion of all other alternatives";[305] thus, section 521(2) did not foreclose the possibility that the debtors could simply keep the original contract alive despite their Chapter 7 petition. The court also expressed concern that the *Edwards* approach would force the debtors to redeem or accept the creditor's terms of reaffirmation, thus giving the creditor too much bargaining leverage in reaffirmation negotiations.[306]

Obviously, the *Belanger* result provides the Chapter 7 debtor who was not in default on the petition date with little incentive to reaffirm a secured debt. Under *Belanger*, the debtor can retain possession of the collateral and obtain a discharge of the debt as long as the debtor continues making timely payments and does not violate the terms of its security agreement.[307] The creditor's lien survives the discharge, of course, and will sufficiently protect the creditor to the extent that the collateral maintains its value.[308] The debtor's discharge, however, will protect the debtor from liability in the event the collateral depreciates to a value below the remaining balance of the debt.

conclusion. *In re* Boodrow, 126 F.3d 43 (2d Cir. 1997), *cert. denied*, 118 S. Ct. 1055 (1998); *In re* Parker, 139 F.3d 668 (9th Cir.), *cert. denied*, 119 S. Ct. 592 (1998); Lowry Fed. Credit Union v. West, 882 F.2d 1543 (10th Cir. 1989).

[305] *Belanger*, 962 F.2d at 347-48.

[306] *Id.* at 348. The *Belanger* court also rejected the creditor's argument that "a debtor who wishes to retain the collateral and make installment payments as they come due should resort to Chapter 13. . . ." *Id.* at 349.

[307] What if the debtor's bankruptcy filing itself constitutes a default under the security agreement? Does this provision (often called an *ipso facto* clause) allow the creditor to declare a default and thus avoid the result in *Belanger*? The likely answer is no; the majority of courts have refused to enforce *ipso facto* clauses in bankruptcy. *E.g.*, Riggs Nat'l Bank v. Perry, 729 F.2d 982 (4th Cir. 1984); *In re* Nikokyrakis, 109 B.R. 260 (Bankr. N.D. Ohio 1989).

[308] Dewsnup v. Timm, 502 U.S. 410 (1992).

PART V:

DEFAULT

CHAPTER 17

DEFAULT AND ITS CONSEQUENCES

SYNOPSIS

§ 17.01　Importance of the Concept of Default

A security interest becomes enforceable when it has attached to the debtor's rights in the collateral.[1] Enforceability means that upon the debtor's "default," the secured party is entitled to the remedies set forth in the security agreement and in Article 9.[2] The existence of a default is thus critical to the availability of those remedies.

The U.C.C. does not define the term "default," generally leaving that to the parties themselves and to the common law. Most of the cases holding the debtor in default as a matter of common law involve a failure to make a payment when due.[3] While an occasional case holds that some other event constitutes a common-law default,[4] the

---

[1] U.C.C. §§ 9-203(2); **R9-203(a).**

[2] U.C.C. §§ 9-501(1); **R9-601(a).**

[3] *See, e.g.,* Cofield v. Randolph County Comm'n, 90 F.3d 468, 30 U.C.C. Rep. Serv. 2d 374 (11th Cir. 1996) (buyer purchased camper from secured party seller, trading in camper that was purportedly a 1987 model but was later found to be a 1978 model; court held that buyer failed to make payment and that failure constituted default under common law); Nationsbank v. Clegg, 29 U.C.C. Rep. Serv. 2d 1366 (Tenn. App. 1996).

[4] *See, e.g.,* Bentley v. Textile Banking Co., 26 A.D. 2d 112, 271 N.Y.S.2d 417 (App. Div. 1966) (debtor's bankruptcy constituted default).

secured party cannot rely upon the common law for sufficient protection. Accordingly, every well-drafted security agreement contains a section setting forth the various events that will constitute a default under the terms of the agreement. The list of events will be tailored to fit the special circumstances of the transaction, of course, but common events of default include the following:

- Failure to make a payment when due;

- Breach of any obligation imposed upon the debtor under another contract between the debtor and the secured party;

- Materially false representations made by the debtor in financial statements or other information furnished to the secured party in connection with any transaction between the parties;

- Breach of any warranty made by the debtor to the secured party, such as a warranty that the debtor has unencumbered title to the collateral;

- Breach of any promise made to the secured party by the debtor, such as a promise to use the collateral in a certain manner, keep the collateral in a certain location, insure the collateral, permit inspection of the collateral or of the debtor's records, etc.;

- Sale or other disposition of the collateral without the secured party's written consent (except for ordinary-course sales of inventory);

- Creation of a competing lien on the collateral, whether the lien arises voluntarily as a result of the debtor's agreement (*i.e.*, a competing security interest) or involuntarily as a result of a rule of law (*e.g.*, an artisan's lien, tax lien, lien arising through levy or the like, etc.);

- Death or bankruptcy of the debtor; dissolution, termination, insolvency or failure of the debtor's business; or an assignment for the benefit of creditors or other state debtor's relief proceeding;

- Theft, loss, substantial damage to or destruction of the collateral;

- Failure to account properly for proceeds of the collateral; and

- Any event which causes the secured party to feel insecure, such as a decline in the debtor's business fortunes or a depletion in the value of the collateral.[5]

The preceding list is certainly not exclusive, and other events should be added to the list depending upon the nature of the transaction.[6] In many commercial financing

---

[5] The secured party may declare a default and accelerate the maturity of the debt on grounds of insecurity only if the secured party "in good faith believes that the prospect of payment or performance is impaired," with the debtor bearing the burden to show the secured party's lack of good faith. U.C.C. § 1-208. For further discussion, *see* § 17.01[B] *infra.*

[6] State statutes sometimes limit the permissible events of default in consumer contracts, and a secured party's remedies under Article 9 are subject to such statutes. U.C.C. § 9-203(4); **R9-201(b), (c).** For example, § 408.552, R.S. Mo. 1994, provides that in certain credit transactions, primarily consumer in nature, an agreement concerning default "is enforceable only to the extent that: (1) The borrower fails to make a payment as required by agreement; or (2) The lender's

arrangements, for example, the debtor will be required to have on hand at all times collateral valued at a stipulated level in relation to the loan (the loan-to-value ratio),[7] and failure to maintain the necessary ratio will constitute an event of default. For another example, suppose that Secured Party sells goods to Debtor on credit, retaining a purchase-money security interest in them. If the goods prove to be defective, in breach of warranty, Debtor may unilaterally reduce its payments, relying upon an Article 2 provision that permits the buyer to notify the seller of breach and then deduct all or part of the damages from that portion of the price that is still due.[8] Secured Party, of course, will insist that the debtor's payment obligation is independent of its warranty obligation; a clause making any attempt at setoff an event of default, regardless of motivation, will achieve this result.

No attempt is made here to list all the events that might constitute a default. There is simply no substitute for the attorney's having a solid understanding of the transaction at issue and a good imagination to draft a document that protects the secured creditor against foreseeable risks. The security agreement should include as a default anything that foreseeably could impair the debtor's ability to pay or the secured party's interest in the collateral.

Any secured party that wrongfully repossesses collateral, whether intentionally or in the mistaken belief that a default has occurred, potentially faces significant liability. Repossession in the absence of default[9] typically constitutes a conversion that entitles the debtor to a credit equivalent to the fair market value of the collateral at the time of the repossession. Conversion is an intentional tort, which also opens the possibility of punitive damages against the secured party.[10]

[A]   Waiver of Default

The fact that the debtor is in default does not mean that the secured party *must* foreclose on its collateral. In some instances the security agreement may grant the secured party a remedy that is not as drastic as foreclosure. For example, if the debtor fails to keep the collateral insured, the security agreement may provide that the secured party can purchase insurance and add it to the principal balance of the obligation.[11] Even in the event of a default in payment, the secured party typically will attempt to work the problem out without resorting to its most drastic remedy. For example, suppose the debtor makes a late payment. The secured party may admonish the debtor or just do nothing, rather than declaring a default and accelerating the loan. After all, foreclosure is an expensive process that often leaves a deficiency unpaid, and (if carried out improperly) can expose the secured party to liability. In short, the secured party may choose to waive the default.

---

prospect of payment, performance, or ability to realize upon the collateral is significantly impaired; the burden of establishing significant impairment is on the lender."

[7] *See* § 3.04[B] *supra.*

[8] U.C.C. § 2-717.

[9] The secured party's right to take possession of the collateral is dependent upon default by the debtor. U.C.C. §§ 9-503; **R9-609(a).**

[10] Damages for wrongful repossession are discussed in § 19.01[B] *infra.*

[11] A secured party in possession of the collateral has the right to purchase insurance and add it to the debt, without a clause in the security agreement authorizing it to do so. *See* U.C.C. §§ 9-207(2)(a); **R9-207(b)(1).**

This attitude of leniency and compromise is one that courts should encourage, but in fact numerous court decisions have held that waiver of default may compromise the secured party's ability to enforce its rights in the event of future default. The problem typically arises when a secured party that has waived a default on prior occasions becomes fed up with the debtor's behavior and decides to accelerate the maturity of the indebtedness and foreclose its security interest. If the debtor attempts to resist foreclosure, the secured party may point to an "anti-waiver clause," a boilerplate provision contained in most security agreements stating that a waiver on one occasion does not operate as a blanket waiver of future defaults. Assertion of anti-waiver clauses, however, has met with mixed success in the courts.

For example, suppose that Debtor makes one late payment which Secured Party accepts. Suppose further that Debtor makes an additional late payment the following month, at which time the Secured Party accelerates the debt and repossesses the collateral. Debtor may argue that the waiver in the first instance operated also as a waiver in the second instance. On these facts, with just one prior waiver, courts generally have been unwilling to accept the debtor's argument.[12] If Secured Party has accepted late payments from Debtor on several previous occasions, however, Debtor's argument becomes much stronger. A number of courts have concluded that an established pattern of accepting late payments results in "waiver by estoppel" — in other words, the secured party is estopped from insisting upon the strict terms of the agreement (*i.e.*, timely payment) in the future. In most of these cases, the inclusion of an anti-waiver clause in the security agreement was not sufficient to preclude this result.

Many courts following the waiver-by-estoppel approach have borrowed the "course of performance" concept from Article 2.[13] For example, the secured party in *Moe v. John Deere Co.*[14] accepted a series of late payments and then declared a default without notifying the debtor that it had decided to enforce the payment due date in a strict fashion. The court held that the secured party had engaged in a course of performance that estopped it from insisting on timely payment and further estopped it from relying on the anti-waiver provision in the security agreement. The court noted that the secured party could revoke its waiver[15] by notifying the debtor that it would insist upon timely payments in the future.

Although this argument has some appeal in consumer cases, it loses some of its force in commercial contracts.[16] After all, the debtor is usually well aware of the fact that

---

[12] *See, e.g.*, Ash v. Peoples Bank of Greensboro, 500 So. 2d 5, 3 U.C.C. Rep. Serv. 2d 426 (Ala. 1986).

[13] U.C.C. § 2-208. Waiver by estoppel can also be predicated upon a course of dealing established during past loan transactions between the parties. *See, e.g.*, J.R. Hale Contracting Co. v. United N.M. Bank, 110 N.M. 712, 799 P.2d 581, 13 U.C.C. Rep. Serv. 2d 53 (1990).

[14] 516 N.W.2d 332, 25 U.C.C. Rep. Serv. 2d 997 (S.D. 1994). *See also* Mercedes-Benz Credit Corp. v. Morgan, 850 S.W.2d 297, 20 U.C.C. Rep. Serv. 2d 705 (Ark. 1993); Nevada Nat'l Bank v. Huff, 94 Nev. 506, 582 P.2d 364, 24 U.C.C. Rep. Serv. 1044 (Nev. 1978).

[15] U.C.C. § 2-209(5) permits revocation of a waiver affecting an executory portion of a contract unless revocation would be unjust because of reliance on the waiver.

[16] *See, e.g.*, B.P.G. Autoland Jeep-Eagle, Inc. v. Chrysler Credit Corp., 799 F. Supp. 1250, 19 U.C.C. Rep. Serv. 2d 649 (D. Mass. 1992).

it is making its payments late, and it is often relying on the fact that it is more trouble for the secured party to foreclose on the loan than it is to continue to accept late payments. As a result, a number of decisions have refused to apply the waiver doctrine in the commercial context.[17]

As discussed previously,[18] any repossession that is not predicated upon a default constitutes a conversion. Thus, a secured party who repossessed the collateral — only to have the debtor successfully raise the defense of waiver by estoppel — would be liable for conversion. When the facts have indicated that the creditor has simply tired of accepting late payments and chosen to accelerate the debt, however, courts have shown the creditor more leniency than in cases of knowing conversion. For example, the court in *Cobb v. Midwest Recovery Bureau Co.*[19] held that the secured creditor's repossession was wrongful because it had failed to notify the debtor that it would insist on timely payments in the future; however, the court refused to allow punitive damages.

Courts have not been equally forgiving when the secured party pursues its default remedies following an express waiver of default. For example, in *Alaska Statebank v. Fairco*,[20] the secured party told the defaulting debtor that it would not foreclose until after the holidays. When it later reneged and repossessed its collateral, effectively shutting down the debtor's business before it could reap the benefits of the holiday season, the court approved an award of punitive damages.

[B] Insecurity and Acceleration Clauses — § 1-208

When the debtor defaults, the secured party is entitled to invoke the remedies provided in Article 9 as well as any included in the security agreement. The agreement typically will contain an acceleration clause which, when invoked, renders the entire outstanding debt presently due and payable. The secured party will then repossess the collateral and proceed with foreclosure.[21]

When the secured party accelerates the maturity of the debt following one of the standard events of default, such as nonpayment or failure to protect the collateral, there is relatively little controversy. For example, suppose Secured Party accelerates the maturity of the debt after Debtor misses two monthly payments and fails to keep the collateral insured. Debtor may argue that acceleration is improper because Debtor's net worth is easily sufficient to ensure that Secured Party will eventually be paid; however, if the security agreement provides that nonpayment and failure to insure are events of default, Debtor's argument will almost certainly fail.[22] Problems can arise, however,

---

[17] *See, e.g.*, Lewis v. Nat'l City Bank, 814 F. Supp. 696, 21 U.C.C. Rep. Serv. 2d 380 (N.D. Ill. 1993), *aff'd*, 23 F.3d 410 (7th Cir. 1994); Wade v. Ford Motor Credit Co., 455 F. Supp. 147, 24 U.C.C. Rep. Serv. 1040 (E.D. Mo. 1978).

[18] *See* § 17.01 *supra*.

[19] 295 N.W.2d 232, 28 U.C.C. Rep. Serv. 941 (Minn. 1980).

[20] 674 P.2d 288, 37 U.C.C. Rep. Serv. 1782 (Alaska 1983).

[21] The secured party need not accelerate in order to foreclose, but if it fails to accelerate, the secured party cannot retain from the foreclosure sale any proceeds in excess of the amount due and unpaid at that time.

[22] Although the Code imposes a general obligation of good faith in the enforcement of a security

when the secured party accelerates[23] based upon a clause that entitles it to do so "at will" or when it "deems itself insecure." The U.C.C. permits such acceleration only when the secured party "in good faith believes that the prospect of payment or performance is impaired."[24] Even though the debtor bears the burden of establishing lack of good faith,[25] numerous lenders have incurred liability under this standard.

Much of the litigation in this area has turned on whether good faith is to be tested by a subjective or an objective standard. The Code's general definition of good faith clearly invokes a subjective test — whether the secured party is honest in its belief that its prospect of payment or performance has been impaired[26] — and the current Article 9 does not contain a special definition applicable to secured parties.[27] Under the purely subjective good faith standard, an honest lender invoking an insecurity clause would be immune from liability, even if most lenders would not have accelerated under the same circumstances. Indeed, under the subjective standard, a secured party can be deemed in good faith even though the facts upon which it acted are incorrect and further inquiry would have revealed the true circumstances.[28]

---

agreement, see U.C.C. § 1-203, this does not mean that a secured party can pursue its remedies only when its likelihood of payment or its security is threatened. The overwhelming majority of courts has held that the specific provisions of § 1-208 — which require likelihood of nonpayment or a threat to the creditor's security before the creditor may accelerate "at will" or for "insecurity" — do not apply following a traditional objective event of default defined in the security agreement. See, e.g., Bowen v. Danna, 276 Ark. 528, 637 S.W.2d 560, 34 U.C.C. Rep. Serv. 1095 (Ark. 1982); but see Brown v. AVEMCO Inv. Corp., 603 F.2d 1367 (9th Cir. 1979) (acceleration of debt and repossession and sale of plane, based upon debtor's lease and sale of plane, violated § 1-208 when plane's purchasers were prepared to redeem the plane and thus secured party had no reason to believe its prospect of payment was impaired).

Although the general duty of good faith applies, it is unlikely that a secured party would be held to have violated that duty by accelerating based upon an event that the parties agreed would constitute a default. Acceleration based upon such a default would be permissible unless the court concluded that the secured party was using the event of default as a pretext and was, in truth, motivated to accelerate the loan due to personal animus or some other illegitimate reason. See Freyermuth, Enforcement of Acceleration Provisions and the Rhetoric of Good Faith, 1998 B.Y.U. L. Rev. 1035.

23 Although most of the cases involve attempts to accelerate, the problems described in this section also arise when the secured party requires that the debtor provide additional collateral pursuant to a clause that allows it to demand so at will or when it deems itself insecure. U.C.C. § 1-208.

24 U.C.C. § 1-208.

25 Id. The effect is to create a presumption of good faith in the secured party's favor.

26 U.C.C. § 1-201(19).

27 Article 2, by contrast, defines good faith in the case of a merchant in dual terms, incorporating both subjective honesty and the observance of reasonable commercial standards of fair dealing. U.C.C. § 2-103(1)(b). There are similar provisions in other Articles [see, e.g., U.C.C. § 3-103(a)(4)], and revised Article 9 also redefines good faith to require both subjective honesty and the observance of reasonable commercial standards of fair dealing. § R9-102(a)(43).

28 See, e.g., Van Horn v. Van De Wol, Inc., 6 Wash. App. 959, 497 P.2d 252, 10 U.C.C. Rep. Serv. 1143 (Wash. App. 1972) (negligence in failing to investigate further is irrelevant to determination of good faith).

Despite the purely subjective standard in section 1-203, some authority favors an objective standard in this context; that is, a standard based on what a reasonable secured party would have done in the same or similar circumstances. Professor Grant Gilmore, one of the principal drafters of Article 9, has indicated that section 1-208 (concerning the option to accelerate at will) requires application of an objective standard, [29] and a number of courts have agreed. In *Sheppard Federal Credit Union v. Palmer*, [30] for example, the secured party, a credit union located on an Air Force base, accelerated and repossessed a vehicle because the debtor, an officer, was leaving the Air Force. The secured party accelerated even though every indication suggested that the debtor would quickly find other suitable employment, and the debtor in fact did obtain other employment. The court, citing Professor Gilmore, held that the secured party had acted in bad faith because it did not have an objective basis for believing that its debt was insecure.

In many cases, the same result would be reached under either an objective or a subjective test. [31] Even when good faith is tested subjectively, a lender who panics and terminates a transaction without any indication that the risk of default has actually increased will have a hard time convincing a factfinder that it acted honestly. [32] Generally, lenders have not fared well in litigation and an entire field of "lender liability" cases has developed in which courts have imposed substantial damages for conduct that may well have been subjectively honest. [33] Many of these cases involve unsecured loans and are therefore not directly on point, but their analysis of the problems associated with acceleration is relevant.

Revised Article 9 solves the split in the courts regarding whether good faith under section 1-208 is tested by an objective standard or a subjective standard. The revision redefines good faith under Article 9 to incorporate both an objective and a subjective

---

[29] 2 G. Gilmore, *Security Interests in Personal Property* § 43.4, at 1197 (1965). Professor Gilmore, however, does not discuss the definition of good faith in this context.

[30] 408 F.2d 1369, 6 U.C.C. Rep. Serv. 30 (5th Cir. 1969). *See also* Blaine v. General Motors Acceptance Corp., 82 Misc. 2d 653, 370 N.Y.S.2d 323, 17 U.C.C. Rep. Serv. 641 (Co. Ct. 1975) (applying objective standard to uphold creditor's acceleration for insecurity where creditor acted following debtor's arrest for drug transportation, based upon threat of forfeiture of collateral); Clayton v. Crossroads Equip. Co., 655 P.2d 1125, 34 U.C.C. Rep. Serv. 1448 (Utah 1982) (applying objective standard to impose liability on accelerating creditor, even though creditor had received information indicating that debtor's financial condition had deteriorated).

[31] The test selected is probably outcome-determinative when the secured party is operating on incorrect information and a reasonable secured party would have inquired further to determine the true facts. *See* Van Horn v. Van De Wol, Inc., 6 Wash. App. 959, 497 P.2d 252, 10 U.C.C. Rep. Serv. 1143 (Wash. App. 1972).

[32] For example, in Lane v. John Deere Co., 767 S.W.2d 138, 8 U.C.C. Rep. Serv. 2d 609 (Tenn. 1989), the court indicates that, though the test is subjective in nature, the acceleration must be based on an honest belief that the other party's ability to perform has deteriorated.

[33] The seminal case in this area is K.M.C. Co. v. Irving Trust Co., 757 F.2d 752 (6th Cir. 1985), in which the creditor refused to extend the debtor additional credit under an outstanding line of credit.

(Matthew Bender & Co., Inc.)

standard, requiring both "honesty in fact and the observance of reasonable commercial standards of fair dealing."[34]

§ 17.02 Remedies Available upon Default

[A] Types of Remedies

Provided that the debtor is in default, the secured party can avail itself of a variety of remedies. The core remedies are set forth in Article 9 and need not be reiterated in the security agreement (although the typical security agreement does so). The Code's remedial scheme permits the secured party to take possession of the collateral (through self-help if it can be done without breach of the peace, otherwise through judicial action) and then dispose of it in an attempt to satisfy the underlying obligation.[35] This process is generally known as the right of foreclosure.

Most secured parties establish a remedial regime that goes well beyond what the Code provides. The most important remedy not provided by operation of law, discussed in the preceding subsection, is the right to accelerate the debt. In addition, most well-drafted security agreements will provide for at least the following remedies:

- The right to call for additional collateral;[36]

- The right to recover attorneys' fees and costs of collection;

- The right to remedy a default (such as by purchasing insurance for collateral or paying off a competing lien) and add the cost of doing so to the principal balance of the debt;

- The right to require that the debtor assemble the collateral and make it available to the secured party at a place designated by the secured party (so long as it is reasonably convenient to the debtor);[37] and

- The right of the secured party to use collateral other than consumer goods pending disposition.[38]

---

[34] U.C.C. § R9-102(a)(43).

[35] If the collateral is intangible and not capable of repossession, Article 9 provides alternative methods for realizing upon its value. Foreclosure on intangible assets is discussed in § 18.03 *infra.*

[36] When this right is linked to an insecurity clause, the provisions of U.C.C. § 1-208 are applicable. *See* discussion in § 17.01[B] *supra.*

[37] U.C.C. §§ 9-503 and R9-609(c) explicitly authorize this remedy, but only if contained in the security agreement. The value of such a remedy is almost exclusively its "in terrorem" effect, although at least one court has issued a mandatory injunction requiring that the debtor comply with a mandatory-assembly clause. *See* Clark Equip. Co. v. Armstrong Equip. Co., 431 F.2d 54, 7 U.C.C. Rep. Serv. 1249 (5th Cir. 1970), *cert. denied,* 402 U.S. 909 (1971).

[38] U.C.C. §§ 9-207(4) and R9-207(b)(4) sanction this remedy. A secured party in possession of collateral has a statutory right to use or operate it for the purpose of preserving its value, even if this is not included in the security agreement. But if the secured party wishes to use the collateral to produce revenue (such as by leasing it to generate rent), the security agreement must permit this remedy or the secured party must get a court order authorizing such use. For a case in which an aircraft was leased to produce significant revenue pending disposition, *see* Contrail Leasing Partners, Ltd. v. Consolidated Airways, Inc., 742 F.2d 1095, 39 U.C.C. Rep. Serv. 9 (7th Cir. 1984).

Additional remedies may be called for depending upon the circumstances of the particular transaction or the law of the jurisdiction. In Missouri, for example, a secured party may include a clause in its security agreement allowing it to sell collateral upon fifteen days' notice following its replevy [39] by the sheriff but before the court has rendered a final judgment awarding possession to the secured party. [40]

The secured party need not pursue its remedies as an Article 9 secured party at all. It can instead ignore its collateral, sue to obtain an in personam judgment on the debt, and, after obtaining a judgment, use the ordinary judicial procedures available to any judgment creditor within the jurisdiction. [41] That is, the secured party can obtain a writ of execution pursuant to which the sheriff can levy on and sell any nonexempt assets of the debtor, real or personal. These assets can include, but are not limited to, the collateral. [42] There are some advantages for the secured party in following this procedure. Because the sheriff conducts the sale following procedures approved under non-Code state law, the secured party is insulated from liability for holding a commercially unreasonable sale. [43] Further, the secured party does not lose its priority by proceeding in this fashion, as any lien created by the levy relates back to the date of perfection of its security interest. [44] **Under revised Article 9, the lien created by the levy relates back to the earlier of the date of perfection of the security interest or the date that the secured party filed its financing statement covering the collateral.** [45]

There are serious drawbacks, however, to suing on the debt without first proceeding to repossess and foreclose on the collateral. Unless the secured party has some basis for pre-judgment attachment, [46] the secured party will have to wait until final judgment before

---

[39] Replevin is a judicial action in which the collateral is seized by the sheriff and then the court determines which party has the superior right of possession. If the debtor is in default, the secured party is statutorily entitled to possession [U.C.C. §§ 9-503 and **R9-609(a)**] and will ultimately obtain a judgment of possession from the court. The debtor, however, must have the opportunity to answer, and if the debtor does so, the issue must proceed to trial. In the meantime, the sheriff holds the asset *in custodia legis.*

[40] *See* B-W Acceptance Corp. v. Alexander, 494 S.W.2d 75 (Mo. 1973).

[41] U.C.C. §§ 9-501(1) and **R9-601(a)(1)** permit the secured party to reduce its claim to judgment, foreclose or otherwise enforce the security agreement by any available judicial procedure.

[42] *See* § 14.02 *supra.*

[43] *See, e.g.,* Dakota Bank & Trust Co. v. Reed, 402 N.W.2d 887, 3 U.C.C. Rep. Serv. 2d 1976 (N.D. 1987).

[44] U.C.C. §§ 9-501(1), **R9-601(e)**. Conceptually, the sheriff's levy and sale is a foreclosure of the original security interest. U.C.C. §§ 9-501(5); **R9-601(f)**. In most states, levy creates a lien that runs in favor of the judgment creditor. *See* § 14.02 *supra.* In the case of a secured party, this lien is not important unless the secured party failed to perfect its security interest. The fact that the sheriff's sale is a foreclosure of the original security interest offers protection against a claim that the levy and sale amount to a preferential transfer that is avoidable in bankruptcy. *See* discussion of preferential transfers in § 16.04[E] *supra.*

[45] U.C.C. § **R9-601(e)**.

[46] Although the grounds for attachment vary from state to state, the secured party typically must allege some type of fraud or evasion of process to obtain prejudgment attachment. A writ of attachment, when issued, orders the sheriff to seize assets of the debtor (including the collateral) and to hold them pending the outcome of the litigation. If the secured party ultimately obtains a judgment, the assets can be sold under a writ of execution.

it can obtain a writ of execution, and the collateral (which is still in the hands of the debtor) may diminish in value or disappear during the interim. Further, because most sheriff's sales are auction sales for ready cash, these sales typically bring very low prices — perhaps much lower than could be obtained in an ordinary course, arms-length sale. This latter disadvantage is offset by the fact that the secured party can bid at the sheriff's sale[47] and, because the amount bid by the purchaser at the sheriff's sale will be applied to reduce the judgment debt (after the costs of the sheriff's sale are paid), the secured party can bid up to the amount of its judgment without producing any cash. In other words, if the judgment is for $10,000 and the secured party is the successful bidder at $7,000, its judgment will be reduced in the court records to $3,000. The secured party then becomes the owner of the asset and can resell it in a more favorable market without having to worry about the Code's procedural requirements for foreclosure sales.[48]

The Code creates one additional remedy worth a brief mention. If the secured creditor has taken a security interest in both real and personal property as part of the same transaction,[49] it may be convenient to sell them together. Indeed, it may be financially advantageous to sell a business that owns the real estate on which it operates as a going concern rather than in a piecemeal fashion. In such cases, the Code permits the secured party to "proceed as to both the real and the personal property in accordance with his rights and remedies in respect of the real property."[50] This means that the secured party can sell the personal property as a part of the real estate foreclosure, and the secured party need not comply with the procedural rules governing Article 9 foreclosures.

[B] Cumulation of Remedies

Article 9 provides that the remedies available to the secured party — those available under the Code, the security agreement, and non-Code state law — are cumulative.[51] The secured party thus may exercise these various remedies simultaneously and need not make an election among its various remedies. It can sue to obtain an in personam judgment without losing its right to later repossess the collateral and commence an Article 9 foreclosure.[52] It can also, of course, go through the Article 9 foreclosure process and then sue to obtain a judgment for any remaining deficiency.[53] It can pursue guarantors

---

[47] U.C.C. §§ 9-501(5); **R9-601(f).**

[48] If it is proved that the secured party has resold the asset for more than it paid at the sheriff's sale but less than the judgment amount, its judgment should be reduced (with a credit for the costs of resale). If the asset is resold for more than the judgment, however, there is no need to turn the excess over to the debtor. After all, the secured party became the owner of the collateral, including any equity, at the sheriff's sale.

[49] This is common in corporate security issues.

[50] U.C.C. § 9-501(4). **Revised Article 9 provides a substantially identical provision. § R9-604(a).**

[51] U.C.C. §§ 9-501(1); **R9-601(c).**

[52] *See, e.g.,* Avco Fin. Servs. of Billings One, Inc. v. Christiaens, 201 Mont. 117, 652 P.2d 220, 34 U.C.C. Rep. Serv. 1445 (Mont. 1982); Fleming v. Carroll Publishing Co., 621 A.2d 829, 20 U.C.C. Rep. Serv. 2d 1141 (D.C. App. 1993).

[53] The secured party's right to a deficiency judgment may be precluded or limited because of its misconduct during the foreclosure process. This topic is discussed in § 19.02 *infra.*

first and then proceed against the collateral, or vice-versa.[54] It can exercise its common-law right of setoff against a bank account of the debtor and later proceed against the rest of its collateral.[55]

Perhaps the most extreme instance of the application of the cumulative remedies doctrine is *Kennedy v. Bank of Ephraim*,[56] in which the secured party held as collateral a certificate of deposit that it had issued to the debtor. Rather than cashing out the certificate, the secured party sued the debtor for an in personam judgment and then proceeded to levy against real estate owned by the debtor. The court held that the secured party was free to follow this rather unusual course under the cumulative-remedies doctrine.

The doctrine has some limitations. A few states have special consumer legislation that requires the secured party to make an election of remedies.[57] In addition, a few courts have held that a secured party may not simultaneously pursue two remedies against the debtor. The leading case to this effect is *Ayares-Eisenberg Perrine Datsun, Inc. v. Sun Bank of Miami*,[58] in which the court concluded that maintaining an action for an in personam judgment and simultaneously proceeding to foreclose against the collateral amounted to harassment of the debtor. Although Article 9 does not entirely displace common-law limitations on harassment of debtors,[59] it is difficult to understand why it is harassment for a secured party to do simultaneously what it could legitimately do sequentially, and a contrary (and appropriate) result was reached in *Glamorgan Coal Corp. v. Bowen*.[60] After all, the secured party has an obligation to proceed in good faith, and compliance with this duty should provide sufficient protection against debtor harassment.

In some circumstances, a secured party may be required to exhaust the value of specific collateral before proceeding against other assets in order to protect the rights of another creditor. This concept is called equitable marshaling and it arises when there are two potential assets available for satisfaction of competing creditors' claims but only one of the creditors has access to both funds. For example, suppose both SP-1 and SP-2 have perfected security interests in the debtor's equipment, with SP-1 having priority. SP-1

---

[54] If the secured party is going to defer action against guarantors, it should advise them that, by doing so, it is not abandoning its rights against them. Although such notice ought not be necessary under the doctrine of cumulative remedies, courts are solicitous of guarantors. Failure to give notice exposes a secured party to the argument that it abandoned its rights against a guarantor.

[55] *See, e.g.*, Jensen v. State Bank of Allison, 518 F.2d 1, 17 U.C.C. Rep. Serv. 286 (8th Cir. 1975).

[56] 594 P.2d 881, 26 U.C.C. Rep. Serv. 558 (Utah 1979).

[57] *See, e.g.*, California's Unruh Act, Cal. Civ. Code § 1801 *et seq.* (West 1985), pursuant to which parties enforcing retail installment sales contracts must make a binding election to pursue either the collateral or an in personam judgment.

[58] 455 So. 2d 525, 39 U.C.C. Rep. Serv. 360 (Fla. App. 1984).

[59] U.C.C. § 1-103("Unless displaced by the particular provisions of this Act, the principles of law and equity . . . shall supplement its provisions.").

[60] 742 F. Supp. 308, 13 U.C.C. Rep. Serv. 2d 596 (W.D. Va. 1990).

also has a mortgage on the debtor's real estate, but SP-2 has no interest in this real estate. Under the doctrine of marshaling, a court may require SP-1 to foreclose against the real estate before it proceeds against the equipment, in order to maximize SP-2's chances of being repaid.[61]

The equitable-marshaling doctrine is designed to protect competing creditors, and it cannot be used by the debtor or guarantors to undercut the cumulative-remedies doctrine. In other words, a guarantor cannot insist that a secured party proceed against the collateral before attempting to enforce the guaranty. If a guarantor wants to limit its liability, it should undertake to be a guarantor of collection rather than a guarantor of payment.[62] The secured party cannot enforce a guaranty of collection until it has exhausted its remedies against the debtor.

---

[61] One of the leading cases on equitable marshaling is Shedoudy v. Surgical Supply Co., 100 Cal. App. 3d 730, 161 Cal. Rptr. 164, 28 U.C.C. Rep. Serv. 1181 (1980).

[62] U.C.C. § 3-419(d) defines these terms for accommodation parties (parties who have incurred liability on a negotiable instrument for the purpose of accommodating another party obligated on the instrument). Similar language can be used in guaranties that are outside the scope of the U.C.C.

CHAPTER 18

THE FORECLOSURE PROCESS

---

§ 18.01   Repossession — §§ 9-503, R9-609

Once default occurs, the secured party has the right to repossess and dispose of its collateral. The right of repossession is established in section 9-503 of the 1972 text, which provides:

Unless otherwise agreed a secured party has on default the right to take possession of the collateral. In taking possession a secured party may proceed without judicial process if this can be done without breach of the peace or may proceed by action. If the security agreement so provides the secured party may require the debtor to assemble the collateral and make it available to the secured party at a place to be designated by the secured party which is reasonably convenient to both parties. Without removal a secured party may render equipment unusable, and may dispose of collateral on the debtor's premises under Section 9-504.[1]

In other words, the Code grants the secured party a limited right to use "self-help" in repossessing its collateral. If the secured party cannot repossess the collateral without breaching the peace, the secured party must abandon self-help. It can then proceed to repossess by judicial action, which is generally known as either replevin or claim and delivery.

A secured party that breaches the peace during an attempted self-help repossession exposes itself to considerable liability, including the possibility of punitive damages. For example, in *Big Three Motors, Inc. v. Rutherford,*[2] the secured party's agents forced the debtor's car off the highway and insisted that she return to their office, where they seized her car. Not surprisingly, the jury treated the seizure as a conversion and assessed significant punitive damages. Few repossessions are this dramatic, but every self-help repossession carries with it the possibility that the creditor's agents will miscalculate and expose their principal to liability.[3]

[A] Self-Help

Article 9 does not define the term "breach of the peace," but the Code drafters were well aware of its meaning based on pre-Code case law.[4] The secured party breaches the peace if it proceeds with its repossession under circumstances where there is a reasonable chance that violence may ensue. The goal is to avoid even potentially explosive situations. According to the overwhelming weight of authority, actual violence is not necessary for the secured party's conduct to amount to a breach of the peace.

Although the issue is one of fact and each case is different, one can extract some general guidelines from repeatedly recurring situations in the case law. If the debtor is present and consents to the repossession, the secured party is free to proceed.[5] If the debtor

---

[1] U.C.C. § 9-503. **Revised Article 9 provides a substantially identical provision on the secured party's right to repossess and dispose of its collateral. § R9-609(a)-(d).**

[2] 432 So. 2d 483, 36 U.C.C. Rep. Serv. 338 (Ala. 1983).

[3] Virtually all courts have held that repossession is a nondelegable duty and that the secured party cannot avoid liability by hiring an independent contractor to perform the repossession. *See, e.g.,* Mbank, El Paso, N.A. v. Sanchez, 836 S.W.2d 151, 17 U.C.C. Rep. Serv. 2d 1358 (Tex. 1992) (secured party liable for both actual damages caused by independent contractor and for punitive damages); Henderson v. Security Nat'l Bank, 72 Cal. App. 3d 764, 140 Cal. Rptr. 388, 22 U.C.C. Rep. Serv. 846 (1977) (secured party liable for actual but not punitive damages).

[4] *See, e.g.,* Girard v. Anderson, 219 Iowa 142, 257 N.W. 400 (1934) (leading pre-Code case holding that secured creditor's unauthorized entry into debtor's business premises to repossess collateral amounted to breach of the peace).

[5] The secured party is probably on safe ground when someone other than the debtor consents

protests, however, the secured party should cease its self-help efforts.[6] In effect, the debtor can force the secured party to judicialize the process. Although this will add somewhat to the cost of repossession and create some delay in the secured party's enforcement of its remedies, most replevin actions are fairly routine and the costs are not excessive. The rationale for this broad view of "breach of the peace" is that the advantage to society gained by forcing creditors in these situations to repossess through judicial means — that is, the avoidance of violent confrontation and potential injury that might have attended self-help repossession over the debtor's objection — outweigh these additional costs of collection. Furthermore, the secured party may recover the costs of judicial repossession following the disposition of the collateral (including the secured party's attorneys' fees, if the security agreement obligates the debtor to pay such fees).[7]

Not all decisions have taken such an enlightened view. For example, in *Chrysler Credit Corp. v. Koontz*,[8] the secured party sent its "repo" agent to the debtor's home, where it proceeded to take possession of a car in the debtor's front yard. The debtor, who had parked the car in the yard so that he could keep an eye on it, came racing out of the house in his underwear, shouting "Don't take it." The agent ignored the debtor and took the car, and the court held that there had been no breach of the peace. The court reasoned that, even though actual violence is not necessary to establish a breach of the peace, there must be some language or conduct that brings home to the repossessor the fact that violence is imminent. The court noted that the debtor had not held a weapon, clenched his fists, or even argued toe-to-toe with the repossessor.

The *Koontz* decision is wrong. In the first place, assessment of the volatility of a protesting debtor is difficult. The debtor's protests alone should have alerted the agent to the possibility of violence. Further, to the extent decisional law is designed to influence future conduct, the holding in *Koontz* establishes poor policy. Based on this decision, an attorney advising a client who is in default and fears repossession would have to suggest that the client express himself vehemently, perhaps even threatening physical violence, in order to stop the repossession. Surely this approach exacerbates the risk of violence and increases the likelihood that the repossession will result in injury to the debtor or third-party bystanders. The *Koontz* court stressed the efficiency of self-help, but efficiency is an insufficient rationale for a decision that increases the risk that repossessions will turn violent.

---

to the repossession. *See, e.g.*, Cottam v. Heppner, 777 P.2d 468, 9 U.C.C. Rep. Serv. 2d 805 (Utah 1989) (third-party's consent to removal of debtor's cattle from third-party's corral upheld). It would be unwise, however, to enter a closed area to remove collateral based on the consent of a small child or someone obviously lacking in mental capacity because of potential exposure to civil or even criminal liability. Society has recognized a strong interest in protecting these classes of individuals from dealings with strangers.

[6] *See, e.g.*, Morris v. First Nat'l Bank and Trust Co. of Ravenna, 21 Ohio St. 2d 25, 254 N.E.2d 683, 7 U.C.C. Rep. Serv. 131 (Ohio 1970); Dixon v. Ford Motor Credit Co., 72 Ill. App. 3d 903, 391 N.E.2d 493 (Ill. Ct. App. 1970); Hester v. Bandy, 627 So. 2d 833, 24 U.C.C. Rep. Serv. 2d 1344 (Miss. 1993).

[7] U.C.C. §§ 9-504(1)(a); **R9-608(a)(1)(A)**.

[8] 277 Ill. App. 3d 1078, 661 N.E.2d 1171, 29 U.C.C. Rep. Serv. 2d 1 (Ill. Ct. App. 1996).

The *Koontz* case raises another issue — whether a secured party can enter upon the debtor's premises to repossess the collateral. Most courts have held that the secured party has a limited privilege against trespass liability and can make minimally intrusive incursions onto the debtor's land. Numerous decisions allow the secured party to go onto the debtor's driveway or yard to remove an asset in plain sight.[9] Most courts, however, have refused to extend the privilege to assets located in an enclosed space, such as the debtor's home or garage. Several of the decisions permitting the removal of assets from the debtor's land stress that the repossession occurred without the secured party's entering any "gates, doors or other barricades."[10]

A secured party who chooses to enter a restricted space risks the assessment of punitive damages and, in extreme cases, criminal sanctions for trespass or for breaking and entering.[11] For example, in *Bloomquist v. First Nat'l Bank of Elk River*,[12] the secured party removed a pane of glass and entered the debtor's place of business to remove collateral. The court held that this was a breach of the peace and sustained an award of punitive damages. When the repossession is from the property of a third person, the secured party should exercise caution, even when the collateral is in plain sight. Although the debtor may have impliedly consented to minimal intrusions onto the debtor's own land, no comparable basis supports finding that the third party has done so. Although the cases in this area are mixed, the action is risky.[13]

Another common theme in the cases is the use of trickery to effect the repossession. Several decisions have held that bringing along a uniformed off-duty police officer to make it appear that the repossession is being carried out under color of law amounts to "constructive force" and thus breaches the peace.[14] The view can be supported on the theory that the debtor has the right to require the judicialization of the process by protesting, and the presence of the police officer strongly discourages the debtor from asserting this right (after all, most persons are strongly disinclined to resist the efforts of a police officer apparently acting within his or her authority). Yet courts occasionally

---

[9] *See, e.g.,* Oaklawn Bank v. Baldwin, 289 Ark. 79, 709 S.W.2d 91, 1 U.C.C. Rep. Serv. 2d 596 (1986) (removing car from debtor's driveway did not breach peace); Raffa v. Dania Bank, 321 So. 2d 83, 18 U.C.C. Rep. Serv. 263 (Fla. Dist. Ct. App. 1975) (car partially under carport in debtor's driveway removed without breach of the peace).

[10] *See, e.g.,* Oaklawn Bank v. Baldwin, *supra* n. 9; Ragde v. Peoples Bank, 53 Wash. App. 173, 767 P.2d 949, 7 U.C.C. Rep. Serv. 2d 1314 (Wash. Ct. App. 1989). When the collateral is located in an open garage, most courts have supported the repossessing creditor. *See, e.g.,* Pierce v. Leasing Int'l, Inc., 142 Ga. App. 371, 235 S.E.2d 752, 22 U.C.C. Rep. Serv. 269 (Ga. Ct. App. 1977).

[11] For further discussion of remedies for creditor misconduct, *see* § 19.01[B] *infra.*

[12] 378 N.W.2d 81, 42 U.C.C. Rep. Serv. 37 (Minn. Ct. App. 1985).

[13] *See, e.g.,* Census Fed. Credit Union v. Wann, 403 N.E.2d 348, 28 U.C.C. Rep. Serv. 1207 (Ind. Ct. App. 1980) (removal from apartment building's parking lot did not breach peace); Salisbury Livestock Co. v. Colorado Central Credit Union, 793 P.2d 470, 12 U.C.C. Rep. Serv. 2d 894 (Wyo. 1990) (removal of collateral from property of third party breached the peace).

[14] *See, e.g.,* Stone Machinery Co. v. Kessler, 1 Wash. App. 750, 463 P.2d 651, 7 U.C.C. Rep. Serv. 135 (Wash. Ct. App. 1970); First & Farmers Bank of Somerset v. Henderson, 763 S.W.2d 137, 7 U.C.C. Rep. Serv. 2d 1305 (Ky. Ct. App. 1988).

have upheld other types of trickery. For example, in *Thompson v. Ford Motor Credit Co.*,[15] the court upheld the secured party's repossession even though the secured party had falsely told a garage operator that it had the debtor's permission to take the debtor's car. As long as the trickery does not prevent the debtor from asserting a legal right or increase the risk that the repossession will turn violent, the courts should allow creditors a fair amount of latitude.

The foregoing comments must be taken only for what they are — mere generalizations. The cases tend to be extremely fact-specific and colorful, and authority can be found on both sides of almost every issue. In the face of this uncertainty, a creditor might be tempted to provide in the security agreement its own definition of "breach of the peace." After all, the 1972 text permits the parties to specify the standards by which their rights and duties are to be measured "if such standards are not manifestly unreasonable,"[16] and occasional decisions have upheld such an agreement.[17] Nevertheless, the courts are unlikely to grant the parties much leeway given the strong policy in favor of deterring violence. Because such a clause is unlikely to be enforced, its very existence is dangerous, as it might induce the secured party to engage in the described conduct. **Furthermore, revised Article 9 makes clear that the parties may not make an agreement authorizing the secured party to engage in conduct that would constitute a breach of the peace.**[18]

[B] Judicial Action

If the secured party cannot repossess peacefully, it must resort to a judicial action to gain possession of its collateral. An action in replevin[19] typically commences with the secured party filing a petition asking that the court find that its right to possession is superior to that of the debtor.[20] The secured party typically also asks for a writ of replevin, which is a court order directing the sheriff to take possession of the collateral. Because the sheriff handles the repossession, the risk of a violent confrontation is dramatically reduced; if violence does result, the sheriff is the appropriate person to deal with it. In many jurisdictions the sheriff turns the property over to the secured party for safekeeping while the action is pending; in others, the sheriff retains possession of the property during the pendency of the action. Once the secured party obtains a final judgment awarding

---

[15] 550 F.2d 256, 21 U.C.C. Rep. Serv. 907 (5th Cir. 1977).

[16] U.C.C. § 9-501(3). Section 9-501(3) provides a list of the rules that cannot be varied by agreement of the parties and section 9-503 is not included in that list. Limitations on freedom of contract are discussed generally in § 18.05 *infra.*

[17] *See, e.g.*, Sperry v. ITT Commercial Fin. Corp., 799 S.W.2d 871, 14 U.C.C. Rep. Serv. 2d 319 (Mo. Ct. App. 1990) (clause granting secured party right to peacefully enter debtor's store and remove collateral upheld).

[18] U.C.C. § R9-603(b).

[19] In some jurisdictions, replevin has been superseded by a statutory cause of action called claim and delivery.

[20] The secured party's right to possession must be predicated upon a default. *See* U.C.C. §§ 9-503, R9-609, and the discussion of default in Chapter 17 *supra.*

(Matthew Bender & Co., Inc.)

it permanent possession of the collateral,[21] it is free to proceed with its Article 9 disposition of the collateral.

Because replevin requires the involvement of a public actor, replevin actions impose an important constitutional overlay. In a series of cases that began with *Fuentes v. Shevin*[22] and culminated with *North Georgia Finishing, Inc. v. Di-Chem, Inc.*,[23] the Supreme Court defined the type of notice and hearing necessary to comply with the Constitution's requirement that persons not be deprived of their property without due process of law. In *Fuentes*, the Court held that, in consumer transactions, assets of the debtor could not be seized unless the debtor received notice and an opportunity for a pre-seizure hearing for the purpose of contesting the validity of the creditor's claim.

The most important of the cases is *Mitchell v. W.T. Grant Co.*,[24] in which the Court backed off somewhat from its holding in *Fuentes*. The *Mitchell* decision allows seizure without prior notice and an opportunity for a hearing so long as the replevin process contains the following safeguards:

- the writ of replevin must be signed by a judge rather than a clerk;
- the creditor must file an affidavit in support of its petition that contains specific factual allegations supporting its claim for possession;
- the debtor must have a right to a hearing soon after the seizure for the purpose of showing that it will probably prevail on the merits and that, therefore, the writ should be dissolved and the property returned;
- the debtor must have an alternative right to regain possession by posting a bond; and
- the creditor must post a bond indemnifying the debtor against loss.

If these procedures are in place, the court may enter a writ of replevin on an *ex parte* basis.

Replevin creates costs that the secured party can avoid using self-help repossession.[25] In addition to costs and attorney's fees, the secured party must post a bond to indemnify the debtor for its damages in the event the secured party's action proves wrongful.[26] There are also delays associated with replevin, because the debtor must receive time to answer the petition. In most cases, however, the costs and delays are minimal because the debtor fails to answer the petition and the secured party obtains a default judgment.

---

[21] Originally, a replevin action resulted only in a judgment for possession of the collateral, but many modern versions allow for an alternative judgment for the value of the collateral.

[22] 407 U.S. 67, *reh'g denied*, 409 U.S. 902 (1972).

[23] 419 U.S. 601 (1975) (extending the holding in *Mitchell*, note 24 *infra*, to nonconsumer transactions).

[24] 416 U.S. 600 (1974).

[25] The secured party can include in its security agreement a clause allowing it to add to the indebtedness its attorney's fees and legal expenses (to the extent that such clauses are generally permitted under state law). U.C.C. §§ 9-504(1)(a); **R9-608(a)(1)(A)**.

[26] The typical case involving damages is one in which the debtor convinces the court that there has been no default and thus that the repossession was wrongful.

§ 18.02   Disposition of Collateral — §§ 9-504, R9-610 -R9-615

Once the secured party is safely in possession of the collateral, through self-help or judicial action, it can proceed with its foreclosure.[27] This usually means that the secured party will dispose of the collateral, following the procedures set forth in Article 9 to govern such dispositions.[28] While disposition can consist of something like a lease rather than a sale,[29] virtually all secured parties hold foreclosure sales. A foreclosure sale of goods is subject to the provisions of Article 2,[30] and Article 2A is applicable if the disposition is by lease.[31]

Before exploring the specific procedures outlined in Article 9, it is important to understand the philosophy that underlies the provisions. The drafters' goal was for Article 9

---

[27] Technically, the secured party can foreclose without taking possession. U.C.C. §§ 9-504 and **R9-610** permit the secured party to dispose of the collateral after default, and U.C.C. §§ 9-503 and **R9-609(a)** allow the secured party to dispose of the collateral even though it is on the debtor's premises. This right is rarely invoked without the permission of the debtor, since the successful bidder at the foreclosure sale will then have to take the collateral from the debtor. This complication will inevitably drive down the price that buyers are willing to pay.

[28] The alternative is strict foreclosure (retention of title to the collateral by the secured party in lieu of sale), discussed in § 18.04 *infra.*

[29] *See, e.g.*, Canadian Community Bank v. Ascher Findley Co., 229 Cal. App. 3d 1139, 280 Cal. Rptr. 521, 14 U.C.C. Rep. Serv. 2d 958 (1991). Another variant, involving neither sale nor lease, arises when the collateral is a certificate of deposit issued by the secured creditor. The secured creditor can simply cancel the CD and retain its proceeds in satisfaction of the debt, a procedure that is akin to exercising the common law right of set off. Because the CD is worth a fixed amount of money, a sale is not needed to maximize its market value. *See, e.g.*, Smith v. Mark Twain Nat'l Bank, 805 F.2d 278, 2 U.C.C. Rep. Serv. 2d 1059 (8th Cir. 1986). Similarly, if insured collateral was totally wrecked by the debtor, the secured party should be free simply to convey title to the insurer in exchange for a settlement check.

[30] U.C.C. §§ 9-504(1); **R9-610 Cmt. 11.**

[31] The most important questions are whether the secured party is a merchant for purposes of §§ 2-314 and 2A-212 (the implied warranty of merchantability) and whether the secured party gives the buyer an implied warranty of title (§ 2-312) or quiet possession (§ 2A-211(1)). Resolution of the first question turns on the specific facts of the case. If the secured party is in the business of selling or leasing the type of asset which is the subject of the foreclosure — for example, if a car dealer conducted a foreclosure sale of a car — it may well qualify as a merchant.

Prior to revised Article 9, the Code generally answered the second question in the negative, at least as to sales. Under § 2-312(2), there is no implied warranty of title if "the circumstances give the buyer reason to know that the person selling does not claim title in himself . . . ." Formerly, the comments to § 2-312(2) suggested that the fact that the asset is being sold at a foreclosure sale gives the buyer reason to know that the secured party does not claim title for itself.

Revised Article 9, however, provides that a sale or other disposition by the secured party "includes the warranties relating to title, possession, quiet enjoyment, and the like which by operation of law accompany a voluntary disposition" of such goods, unless the secured party effectively disclaims such warranties. § R9-610(d). The secured party could disclaim any such warranties by means of "a record evidencing the contract for disposition and including an express disclaimer or modification" of the warranties. § R9-610(e). A record will constitute a sufficient disclaimer if it indicates "[t]here is no warranty relating to title, possession, quiet enjoyment, or the like" or uses similar language. § R9-610(f).

to produce higher sale prices than those typically obtained in real estate foreclosures. They were keenly aware that the procedures governing such foreclosures almost guarantee that the property will be sold for a price that is well below its fair market value. Specifically, real estate foreclosures are almost invariably conducted by auction rather than by placement with a qualified broker. Further, bidders must be prepared to pay cash when the hammer falls, which reduces the pool of potential buyers. Lastly, many states grant the debtor a right to redeem the property after the sale, further discouraging bidding.

Article 9, by contrast, does not permit post-sale redemption,[32] and its procedures governing sale are deliberately flexible. The secured party can sell by auction or by any other method so long as it is commercially reasonable, and it can sell for cash or on credit.[33] Article 9 does not require that the secured party sell the asset for its fair market value, but the secured party must adopt procedures that are designed to achieve that goal. Each of the foregoing points will be examined in detail in the ensuing material.

[A] The Standard of Commercial Reasonableness

Section 9-504(3) of the 1972 text and **revised section R9-610(b)**, which establish the standards that govern Article 9 dispositions, require that every aspect of the disposition of collateral — including the manner, method, time, place and other terms — must be "commercially reasonable." The advantage of this flexible standard is that it encourages secured parties to adopt procedures designed to bring a fair price for the collateral. The disadvantage, at least from a creditor's perspective, is that it allows courts, using 20/20 hindsight, to second-guess virtually every step that a creditor has taken in disposing of collateral. Courts have examined whether the chosen method of sale was adequate given the nature of the collateral, whether the sale was properly advertised, whether the time of sale was reasonable (both in absolute terms and in relation to the date on which the advertising appeared), and whether the terms of the sale were reasonable.

[1] Duty to Publicize

One of the most important elements of a commercially reasonable disposition — and one not mentioned directly in the Code — is the duty to publicize it adequately. Compliance with this duty requires the secured party to ensure that advertisement of the sale is sufficient to reach the proper audience for the type of asset being sold, that sufficient time is allowed between the advertising and the sale for potential buyers to respond, that the information contained in the advertising is adequate and accurate, and that the collateral is made available prior to the sale for inspection by potential buyers.

The most important of these issues is whether the advertising was sufficient to reach potential buyers for the type of asset involved. When the asset is highly specialized, targeted advertising may be needed — perhaps even in publications or trade magazines that have a nationwide circulation. For example, the case of *Contrail Leasing Partners, Ltd. v. Consolidated Airways, Inc.*,[34] involved the foreclosure sale of a corporate jet.

---

[32] It does provide a pre-sale right of redemption. See U.C.C. §§ 9-506 and **R9-623**, discussed in § 18.05 *infra*.

[33] U.C.C. §§ 9-504(3), **R9-610(b)**. This provision also allows the secured party to sell the collateral as a unit or to break it down into parcels that are sold separately.

[34] 742 F.2d 1095, 39 U.C.C. Rep. Serv. 9 (7th Cir. 1983).

The court held that the secured party's advertising, which consisted of one small ad in a trade publication, was not commercially reasonable. The court suggested that the ad should have been more conspicuous and that it should have been placed in additional trade journals. The key question was whether the ad was reasonably designed to reach major airplane buyers, and the secured party's duty is to explore the potential market so that its advertising will be effective.[35] As a result, a secured party with an interest in such specialized collateral would be well advised to consult a broker or dealer to help design its approach to advertising.

A few states have amended their versions of the Code to specify the manner in which advertising must occur. California's version of section 9-504(3), for example, requires that notice be given at least five days before the sale in a newspaper of general circulation published in the county where the sale is to take place. This provision can create a trap for the unwary creditor, as illustrated by the facts of *Ford & Vlahos v. ITT Commercial Finance Corp.*[36] The collateral in that case was a C-130A cargo plane, and the secured party advertised the sale in the local newspaper and nowhere else. The California Supreme Court held the sale to be commercially unreasonable since aircraft are ordinarily advertised in trade journals.[37] In other words, the requirement for local advertising was treated as a minimum requirement (or a "floor") and not as a safe harbor.

Advertising must do more than merely reach the proper audience. It must accurately describe the collateral,[38] and it must give correct information regarding the mechanics of the sale.[39] A number of courts have also held that the advertising must give sufficient information to allow prospective buyers to inspect the collateral prior to the sale.[40]

[2] Disposition Within a Reasonable Time

For most transactions, the Code does not specify the time-frame within which the secured party must dispose of the collateral after default, other than to state that the time of the disposition must be commercially reasonable. In other words, the secured party

---

[35] *See also, e.g.,* Key Bank of Me. v. Dunbar, 28 U.C.C. Rep. Serv. 2d 398 (E.D. Pa. 1995) (failure to take time necessary to explore and reach potential market for boat rendered sale commercially unreasonable); Smith v. Daniels, 634 S.W.2d 276, 34 U.C.C. Rep. Serv. 355 (Tenn. Ct. App. 1982) (advertising in county paper and calling local dealers was unreasonable for amusement equipment which was normally sold by advertising in major cities, in trade magazines, and by sending flyers to dealers).

[36] 8 Cal. 4th 1220, 36 Cal. Rptr. 2d 464, 885 P.2d 877, 25 U.C.C. Rep. Serv. 2d 630 (Cal. 1994).

[37] The Court relied on U.C.C. § 9-507(2), which insulates creditors who sell in conformity with the reasonable commercial practices of dealers.

[38] *See, e.g.,* ROC-Century Assoc. v. Giunta, 658 A.2d 223, 27 U.C.C. Rep. Serv. 2d 1091 (Me. 1995) (sale of partnership interest unreasonable because advertising mischaracterized nature of rights being sold).

[39] *See, e.g.,* Weiss v. Northwest Acceptance Corp., 274 Or. 343, 546 P.2d 1065, 19 U.C.C. Rep. Serv. 348 (Or. 1976) (advertising inaccurately stated that cash would be required).

[40] *See, e.g.,* Kobuk Eng'g & Contracting Servs., Inc. v. Superior Tank & Constr. Co. -Alaska, Inc., 568 P.2d 1007, 22 U.C.C. Rep. Serv. 854 (Alaska 1977); Connex Press, Inc. v. Int'l Airmotive, Inc., 436 F. Supp. 51, 22 U.C.C. Rep. Serv. 1310 (D.D.C. 1977).

must not act precipitously, such as by disposing of the collateral as a matter of convenience before its advertising has had time to be effective. Nor must the secured party delay so long that the collateral has depreciated significantly in value. The cases are highly fact-specific, and the time allowed will be longer for a motor vehicle than for perishable foodstuffs. Courts are also influenced by the conduct of the secured party during the delay. A creditor that is "sitting on its hands" will evoke less sympathy than one who takes time to fix up the collateral to enhance its sale value or to conduct a widespread advertising campaign in an attempt to attract additional bidders.

A number of decisions interpreting the 1972 text have penalized secured parties for unreasonable delay using a doctrine known as "constructive strict foreclosure." Under Article 9, strict foreclosure is a voluntary mechanism initiated by a secured party who intends to retain the collateral — including any equity to which the debtor (or a junior secured party) might otherwise be entitled — in lieu of conducting a sale or other disposition of the collateral.[41] The language of the 1972 text suggests that strict foreclosure can occur only when the secured party gives a written notice indicating its intent to seek this remedy. Nevertheless, some courts have treated the secured party's unreasonable delay in disposing of the collateral as being the "constructive" equivalent of written notice of the secured party's intent to retain title to the collateral.[42] The effect of this approach is to make the secured party the owner of the collateral in complete satisfaction of the debtor's obligation — leaving the secured party without any ability to seek a deficiency if the collateral is worth less than the balance of the secured obligation.

Despite the superficial appeal of this approach, it is wrong. When the secured party retains collateral too long but lacks the requisite intent to initiate a strict foreclosure, the proper approach is for the court to conclude that it has acted in a commercially unreasonable manner and then to impose whatever penalties are appropriate in the jurisdiction for such conduct. This is true even if the secured party *never* disposes of the collateral. Such an approach allows an adversely affected party to recover affirmatively if it can prove that the collateral would have generated a surplus had it been sold in a commercially reasonable manner. Constructive strict foreclosure precludes that possibility and, in fact, is nothing more than a fiction that allows a court to impose what is, in effect, an absolute bar on the secured party's right to a deficiency.[43] **Consistent with this critique, revised Article 9 abolishes the doctrine of constructive strict foreclosure.[44]**

---

41 If there is equity in the collateral, the debtor or junior secured party can object to strict foreclosure and force a disposition. If there is no timely objection, title to the collateral is vested in the secured party. Under the 1972 text, strict foreclosure results in the full satisfaction of the debtor's obligation, even if the value of the collateral is less than the outstanding balance of that obligation. U.C.C. § 9-505(2). **Under revised Article 9, a secured party may use strict foreclosure in partial satisfaction of the debtor's obligation. § R9-620(a).** Strict foreclosure is discussed in greater detail in § 18.04 *infra.*

42 *See, e.g.,* Haufler v. Ardinger, 28 U.C.C. Rep. Serv. 893 (Mass. Ct. App. 1979).

43 The consequences of commercially unreasonable conduct, including the absolute bar rule, are discussed in Chapter 19 *infra.*

44 U.C.C. § R9-620(b). *See also* § R9-620 Cmt. 5. **For further discussion of strict foreclosure under revised Article 9, see § 18.04 *infra.***

In one situation Article 9 dictates that the secured party dispose of the collateral within a time established by the Code. When the collateral is consumer goods, and the debtor has repaid 60% of the loan (or, in a purchase-money transaction, 60% of the cash price),[45] it is likely that the debtor may have built up some equity in the collateral. In such cases, the Code does not allow the secured party to initiate a strict foreclosure;[46] instead, under the 1972 text, the secured party must dispose of the collateral within 90 days after taking possession.[47] Doubts have persisted about the wisdom of this rule. Suppose, for example, the transaction is set in a northern state and the secured party repossesses a pleasure boat on November 1. Does it really make sense to force the secured party to sell the boat during the dead of winter? Although sale within 90 days is normally beneficial to consumers, there will be some circumstances in which the more flexible standard of commercial reasonableness would be preferable. **In recognition of this critique, revised Article 9 permits the secured party to take longer than 90 days if "the debtor and all secondary obligors have agreed in an agreement to that effect entered into and authenticated after default."[48]**

[3] The Method of Disposition: Public versus Private Sale

The secured party can sell the collateral at either a public or private sale so long as the method chosen is commercially reasonable.[49] As a rule, a public sale means an auction sale and a private sale refers to any other type of sale.[50] The distinction between public and private sales is relevant to the following issues: 1) whether the method chosen is commercially reasonable; 2) what information the required notice should contain; and 3) whether the secured party may purchase the collateral at the sale. Only the first issue is discussed in this section.[51]

---

[45] Article 9 differentiates between purchase-money and other transactions. §§ U.C.C. § 9-505(1), **R9-620(e)**. In a nonpurchase-money transaction, the debtor takes out a loan against a consumer asset that he or she already owns. Determining when 60% of the principal amount of the loan has been repaid is a straightforward matter.

The 60%-rule is applied to the "cash price" in the case of a purchase-money transaction, and the cash price is not necessarily the amount financed. It is, instead, the amount that the seller would have charged if the asset had been sold for cash rather than on credit. If, for example, the seller's price for a car is $20,000 and the buyer makes a $2,000 down payment and finances $18,000 (with the seller or with a lender), the secured party cannot use strict foreclosure after the debtor has paid a total of $12,000 (60% of the cash price of $20,000). The debtor gets credit for the down payment, and thus the rule is triggered when the debtor has reduced the principal by an additional $10,000.

[46] For discussion of strict foreclosure, *see* § 18.04 *infra.*

[47] U.C.C. § 9-505(1). The consequences to the secured party for failure to comply with this requirement are discussed in Chapter 19 *infra.*

[48] **U.C.C. § R9-620(f)(2).**

[49] U.C.C. §§ 9-504(3), **R9-610(b).**

[50] U.C.C. § 9-504 Cmt. 1 contains a cross-reference to § 2-706, which details the procedures that must be used by an aggrieved seller who wants to take advantage of the market/resale measure of damages. § 2-706 Cmt. 4 states that "public" sale means a sale by auction. A "private" sale may be effected by solicitation and negotiation conducted either directly or through a broker.

[51] Notice is discussed in § 18.02[B] *infra*, and the secured party's right to buy is discussed in § 18.02[C] *infra.*

Although the Comments to Article 2 indicate that a public sale means an auction sale, the word "public" suggests that the auction must be open to the general public. This issue has arisen in a number of cases involving dealers' auctions — auction sales open only to those who deal in the type of asset being sold. The typical dealer's auction involves automobiles. Most of the courts that have addressed this issue have concluded that such sales are private because they are not open to the general public,[52] but this result is debatable. By holding that the sale is private, the courts prevent the secured party from bidding at its own auction.[53] If the auction is competitive, the debtor is better served by letting the party with the most at stake — the secured party — bid.[54] The hallmark of a public sale should be the competitive nature of the sale, not whether the public is invited.

Occasionally with an auction sale, very few parties — sometimes, only the secured party — show up to bid. As a result, the lack of competitive bidding may result in the collateral being sold for a fraction of its value. Because the price received at the foreclosure sale is used to establish the amount of the deficiency that will be owed by the debtor, a debtor may attempt to argue that the low sale price demonstrates that the sale was not commercially reasonable. The paucity of bidders and/or a low sale price, standing alone, should *not* lead to the conclusion that the sale was commercially unreasonable. Instead, the proper inquiry is whether the *procedures* adopted by the secured party were reasonably designed to result in a competitive auction.

A paucity of bidders and/or a low sale price may serve as a "red flag" that justifies further investigation of the circumstances surrounding an auction sale. For example, the fact that the secured party was the only bidder may suggest inadequate advertising, that an auction was not a commercially reasonable method of sale, or that the time selected for the auction was not commercially reasonable. Although courts should be suspicious

---

[52] *See, e.g.*, John Derry Motors, Inc. v. Steinbronn, 383 N.W.2d 553, 42 U.C.C. Rep. Serv. 1855 (Iowa 1986) (auction limited to automobile dealers); Morrell Employees Credit Union v. Uselton, 28 U.C.C. Rep. Serv. 269 (Tenn. Ct. App. 1979) (auction limited to credit union members). *See also* Restatement of Security § 48 Cmt. c, indicating that a public sale must be open to the public.

The cases that find such sales to be private generally turn on whether the notice sent to the debtor was sufficient. Typically, the secured party will have sent a notice that states the date of the auction but not the time and place. This would be sufficient for a private sale, but not for a public sale. Because the debtor cannot bid at the sale, it may be that a private-sale type of notice is sufficient, and thus the decisions can be explained as an attempt by the courts to protect secured creditors who have sent such notices. Nevertheless, on balance, the debtor is better served by characterizing dealers' auctions as public sales. Requiring that the secured party state the date and time of the auction in its notice is not particularly burdensome.

[53] The secured party cannot purchase the collateral at a private sale unless the collateral is of a type customarily sold in a "recognized market" or is of a type for which there exist "widely distributed standard price quotations." U.C.C. §§ 9-504(3), **R9-610(c)(2). Section R9-610 Cmt. 9 defines a "recognized market" as "one in which the items sold are fungible and prices are not subject to individual negotiation." Thus, even under revised Article 9, the secured party could not bid if the dealer's auction is charactarized as a private sale.**

[54] The debtor might also argue that a sale at a dealer's auction ought not be approved because it resulted in a wholesale price being paid for the collateral rather than a retail price. This issue is discussed in § 18.02[A][5] *infra.*

in such cases and investigate such sales with care, the facts may indicate that every step taken by the secured party was commercially reasonable and that the lack of bidders was mere happenstance. In such cases, the court should not penalize the secured party for going ahead with the sale.[55] Nevertheless, a secured party whose auction sale attracts disappointingly few bidders should consider abandoning the effort and starting over with a private sale. In so doing, the secured party should take care to re-notify all parties entitled to notice and to tailor its advertising to its newly selected method.[56]

United States v. Willis[57] is a classic case disapproving of a public sale. The secured party in the case was aware of two offers to purchase the collateral privately but chose to go ahead with an auction sale that produced only one-fifth the amount expressed in the private offers. The court properly held that the secured party's decision to sell the collateral at auction was commercially unreasonable.[58] Although the secured party should be permitted significant latitude in choosing the method of sale, its range of discretion does have limits. The Comments support the result in *Willis*, stating that:

> Although public sale is recognized, it is hoped that private sale will be encouraged where, as is frequently the case, private sale through commercial channels will result in higher realization on collateral for the benefit of all parties. The only restriction placed on the secured party's method of disposition is that it must be commercially reasonable.[59]

Of course, the arguments set forth above apply equally when the results of a private sale prove disappointing. This fact may suggest that the collateral was of a type that should have been sold at auction. For example, in some parts of the country, livestock may bring higher prices at auctions than in private sales.

[4] Is There a Duty to Fix-up the Collateral?

The secured party is under a clear duty to use reasonable care in the "custody and preservation of collateral" in its possession.[60] Is there, however, a duty to fix-up the collateral so that it will command a higher price? Certainly, valid policy reasons support imposing at least minimal responsibilities on the secured party. For example, a car dealer

---

[55] *See, e.g., In re* Zsa Zsa, Ltd., 352 F. Supp. 665, 11 U.C.C. Rep. Serv. 1116 (S.D.N.Y. 1972), *aff'd*, 475 F.2d 1393 (2d Cir. 1973) (secured party did not bid, but sale at 10% of market value to sole bidder upheld). *See also* U.C.C. §§ 9-507(2) **and R9-627(a)**, which provide that the fact that the secured party could have obtained a better price by a sale at a different time or in a different manner is not, by itself, sufficient to establish that the sale was commercially unreasonable.

[56] *See, e.g.,* Gateway Aviation, Inc. v. Cessna Aircraft Co., 577 S.W.2d 860, 25 U.C.C. Rep. Serv. 901 (Mo. Ct. App. 1978) (debtor entitled to notice of private sale when secured party shifted to that method, even though notice of abandoned public sale had been sent). *See also* §§ 18.02[B][2] and [3] *infra.*

[57] 593 F.2d 247, 25 U.C.C. Rep. Serv. 1178 (6th Cir. 1979).

[58] *See also* United States v. Terrey, 554 F.2d 685, 21 U.C.C. Rep. Serv. 1488 (5th Cir. 1977) (sale of assets of electric sign-manufacturing enterprise at auction was commercially unreasonable).

[59] U.C.C. § 9-504 Cmt. 1. **A similar comment appears in § R9-610 Cmt. 2.**

[60] U.C.C. §§ 9-207(1), **R9-207(a)**. This provision is equally applicable to possessory security interests in the absence of default.

who is going to sell a repossessed car from its lot at retail should at least clean the car so that it is attractive to the dealer's customers. Perhaps the dealer should even have to send the car to its body shop (if it has one) to knock out minor collision damage or to its service department for a minor tune-up so that the car runs smoothly. Of course, the decision whether to commit major resources to repairing an item should be solely within the discretion of the secured party.

A duty to fix-up cannot be found in the text of the Code, which appears to leave all such decisions to the discretion of the secured party.[61] A few decisions, however, rely on the general concept of commercial reasonableness to impose on the secured party a minimal fix-up duty, and these decisions are to be applauded.[62] A court should not ratify a secured party's decision to drag a filthy car straight to the auction block without a detour through the carwash. Whether major cash outlays are a reasonable investment should be left to the discretion of the secured party.

[5] Price as an Indicator of Commercial Unreasonableness

A low price obtained at a foreclosure sale certainly provides a warning that there may have been something wrong with the sale. It may suggest that the sale was improperly advertised, that the secured party's method of sale was unreasonable, that the sale was held at an unreasonable time, or some other problem. A low price standing alone, however — uncoupled from any of these procedural flaws — should not be enough to invalidate a sale.[63] The standard of commercial reasonableness requires that the secured party adopt procedures *designed* — not *guaranteed* —to produce a reasonable price. Nevertheless, an exceptionally low price greatly increases the likelihood that a court will find that the

---

[61] Article 9 states explicitly that the secured party can sell the collateral in its existing condition or after any commercially reasonable preparation or processing. U.C.C. §§ 9-504(1), **R9-610(a)**. Further, the Code states that the secured party "may" make use of the collateral for the purpose of preserving its value. §§ 9-207(4), **R9-207(b)(4)**.

[62] *See, e.g.*, Weiss v. Northwest Acceptance Corp., 274 Or. 343, 546 P.2d 1065, 19 U.C.C. Rep. Serv. 348 (1976). *But see* C.I.T. Corp. v. Duncan Grading & Constr., Inc., 739 F.2d 359, 38 U.C.C. Rep. Serv. 1821 (8th Cir. 1984) (secured party not under duty to clean up construction equipment prior to sale).

The Code, to some extent, discourages secured parties from fixing up their collateral. After all, if a decision to invest in the collateral is not commercially reasonable, the secured party will be unable to recoup its investment from the proceeds of sale. *See* U.C.C. §§ 9-504(1), **R9-615(a)(1)**. Courts have somewhat ameliorated this constraint by showing general leniency in allowing secured parties to recover the expenses of preparing collateral for sale. *See* discussion in § 18.02[D] *infra*.

[63] The Code explicitly states that the fact that a better price could have been obtained by following other procedures is not *of itself* sufficient to hold that a sale was commercially unreasonable. U.C.C. §§ 9-507(2), **R9-627(a)**. *See also In re* Zsa Zsa, Ltd., 352 F. Supp. 665, 11 U.C.C. Rep. Serv. 1116 (S.D.N.Y. 1972), *aff'd*, 475 F.2d 1393 (2d Cir. 1973) (sale at 10% of market value to sole bidder upheld). *But see* F.D.I.C. v. Herald Square Fabrics Corp., 81 A.D.2d 168, 439 N.Y.S.2d 944, 32 U.C.C. Rep. Serv. 558 (N.Y. Sup. Ct. 1981) (low price alone proved commercial unreasonableness of sale).

secured party employed flawed procedures. In other words, low prices cause courts to scrutinize closely the secured party's disposition efforts. [64]

Suppose the secured party chooses to sell the collateral at wholesale. Can the debtor successfully claim that the sale was commercially unreasonable because the secured party made no attempt to obtain a retail price? The court in *Ford Motor Credit Co. v. Jackson* [65] answered this question in the affirmative. In *Jackson*, the secured party — a dealership that owned both retail and wholesale outlets — held a truck as collateral and chose to sell it at wholesale. The court noted that the truck needed no fixing up to prepare it for retail sale, and that the secured party received only about one-half the price it would have obtained through a retail sale. These factors persuaded the court that the decision to sell at wholesale rendered the foreclosure commercially unreasonable.

Despite the superficial appeal of decisions like *Jackson*, they are wrong. First, they run directly counter to the express language of the Code. The 1972 text provides that

[i]f the secured party either sells the collateral in the usual manner in *any* recognized market therefor or if he sells at the price current in such market at the time of his sale or if he has otherwise sold in conformity with reasonable commercial practices among dealers in the type of property sold he *has sold in a commercially reasonable manner.* [66]

Further, the fact that the secured party may have obtained a higher price at a retail sale does not mean that the retail price is more "fair" or "reasonable." Retail sales often involve higher costs (*e.g.*, retail sales commissions), and the price received at a retail sale must be adjusted to reflect those costs. Further, by selling at retail, the secured party may lose a sale that it otherwise would have made (*i.e.*, the secured party might have sold another unit from its own inventory to the same customer). Judge Posner gave perhaps the best analysis of the issue in *Contrail Leasing Partners, Ltd. v. Consolidated Airways, Inc.,* [67] when he stated:

Wholesale markets are recognized markets for most goods . . .. Although retail prices tend to be higher than wholesale prices, this is because it costs more to sell at retail. Not only can there be, therefor, no presumption that the net gains to the seller are different at the two levels, but economic theory implies that returns at the two levels will tend toward equality, since until they are equalized dealers will have incentives to enter at the level where the higher returns are being earned and by entering will bid those returns down. [68]

---

[64] *See, e.g.*, SNCB Corp. Fin., Ltd. v. Shuster, 877 F. Supp. 820, 26 U.C.C. Rep. Serv. 2d 953 (S.D.N.Y. 1994) (low price caused court to scrutinize procedures closely, but sale was upheld as commercially reasonable). *See also*, § **R9-610 Cmt. 10.**

[65] 466 N.E.2d 330, 39 U.C.C. Rep. Serv. 743 (Ill. Ct. App. 1984).

[66] U.C.C. § 9-507(2)(emphasis added). **Revised Article 9 contains a substantially identical provision. § R9-627(b).**

[67] 742 F.2d 1095, 39 U.C.C. Rep. Serv. 9 (7th Cir. 1983).

[68] 742 F.2d at 1101, 39 U.C.C. Rep. Serv. at 17.

[B] Notice of Sale

Unless they receive notice of a proposed foreclosure sale, parties with an interest in the collateral may be unable to protect those interests. With sufficient prior notice of a foreclosure sale, a debtor may be able to find additional financing to redeem the collateral from the foreclosing party's lien,[69] may be able to seek injunctive relief if there is any valid basis to challenge the secured party's conduct,[70] or may be able to attract additional bidders to the sale in an attempt to maximize the foreclosure sale price and thus limit the size of any deficiency. Likewise, with sufficient notice, a junior secured party could take steps to bid on the collateral at the sale, or to redeem the collateral by satisfying the foreclosing party's claim. To ensure that affected parties have an adequate opportunity to protect their interests from foreclosure, Article 9 provides a structure that generally requires the foreclosing secured party to give notice, prior to disposition, to certain persons most likely to be affected by that disposition.

The most common issues arising with respect to notice are: 1) those persons entitled to notice; 2) the amount of notice required; 3) the contents of the notice; and 4) the circumstances under which notice is excused altogether. These issues are discussed in the ensuing subsections.

[1] Those Entitled to Notice

Article 9 requires that the secured party give pre-disposition notice to the "debtor,"[71] but one should take care to appreciate that the 1972 text and the revision define the term "debtor" differently. Under the 1972 text, the term "debtor" includes not only a party with an interest in the collateral, but also anyone obligated on the debt.[72] **Under the revision, however, the term "debtor" is limited in this context to a person holding an interest in the collateral.[73] A person who is obligated on the debt but has no interest in the collateral is instead denominated as an "obligor."[74] Under the revision, the secured party must give notice to the "debtor" and any "secondary obligor,"[75] but not to any primary obligor.**

For example, suppose that Henning borrows $1,000 from Bank, that Lawrence grants a security interest in his automobile to secure Henning's obligation (but does not co-sign Henning's promissory note or otherwise guarantee Henning's obligation), and that Freyermuth agrees to be a surety for Henning's obligation to Bank. If Henning defaults and Bank repossesses the car from Lawrence, to whom would Bank have to give notice

---

[69] U.C.C. §§ 9-506, **R9-623**.

[70] Any party entitled to notice may want to police the sale to make certain that it is carried out in a commercially reasonable manner. Injunctive relief in furtherance of this goal may be obtained under U.C.C. §§ 9-507(1), **R9-625(a)**. *See* discussion of pre-disposition remedies in Chapter 19 *infra*.

[71] U.C.C. §§ 9-504(3), **R9-611(c)(1)**.

[72] U.C.C. § 9-105(1)(d).

[73] U.C.C. § **R9-102(a)(28)(A)**.

[74] U.C.C. § **R9-102(a)(59)**.

[75] U.C.C. § **R9-611(c)**. As discussed in § 1.10[C] *supra*, a "secondary obligor" is the term used by the revision to describe a surety. § **R9-102(a)(71)**.

prior to selling the car? Under the 1972 text, Henning, Lawrence, and Freyermuth are all "debtors" and Bank would have to notify each of them individually.[76] **Under the revision, Bank would have to give notice to Lawrence (the "debtor") and Freyermuth (a "secondary obligor"), but would have no obligation to notify Henning, who is the primary obligor but not a "debtor."[77] The rationale behind the revision is that notice to Lawrence (who, as debtor, will have a strong incentive to police the sale to protect his equity in the collateral) and Freyermuth (who, as secondary obligor, will have a strong incentive to police the sale to minimize the amount of any deficiency) should be sufficient to protect Henning's interest as primary obligor — minimizing his liability on the primary obligation — even if Henning does not receive notification of the sale. Nevertheless, for prudential reasons, Bank may elect to give Henning notice of the disposition anyway, either out of courtesy or in hope that Henning may also make additional efforts to satisfy the debt prior to the sale.**

The secured party should make certain that each such party is sent a copy of the notice.[78] If, for example, the debtors are husband and wife, the secured party should send a separate notice to each. If the notice is sent to "Mr. and Mrs." and the couple has separated or divorced, the secured party's notice to the debtor who no longer lives at the address may be insufficient.[79] The problem is not that the notice was sent to the wrong address — the secured party may rely on the debtor's original address if it has not received notice of a different address — but rather that the secured party cannot depend upon the debtor still living at the original address to forward the information to the other debtor.

---

[76] Under the 1972 text, most courts have construed the term "debtor" to include sureties. *See, e.g.,* May v. Women's Bank, 807 P.2d 1145 (Colo. 1991). This is a result that is consistent with the definition of the term "debtor," but somewhat inconsistent with normal concepts of suretyship law. As a matter of common law, sureties can waive almost any right, but under the 1972 text the "debtor" cannot waive the right to receive notice of a foreclosure sale prior to default. U.C.C. § 9-501(3)(b). As a result, the broad language of the term "debtor" has created some measure of confusion regarding whether guarantors may effectively waive the protections of § 9-504 prior to default. *Compare* May v. Women's Bank, *supra* (no) *with* Steinberg v. Cinema N' Drafthouse Sys., Inc., 28 F.3d 23 (5th Cir. 1994) (yes). Thus, under the 1972 text, a secured party who fails to send notice of default to a surety runs the risk that the surety will be discharged.

[77] *See* U.C.C. § R9-611 Cmt. 3.

[78] Under U.C.C. § 1-201(27), notice to an organization is effective "from the time when it is brought to the attention of the individual conducting that transaction, and in any event from the time when it would have been brought to his attention if the organization had exercised due diligence." "Organization" is broadly defined in § 1-201(28) to include, *inter alia,* partnerships and "two or more persons having a joint or common interest." This latter language often provides the best argument for a secured party who has sent notice to fewer than all the affected parties.

[79] *See, e.g.,* Huntington Nat'l Bank of Wash. Court House v. Stockwell, 10 Ohio App. 3d 30, 460 N.E.2d 303, 37 U.C.C. Rep. Serv. 1799 (Ohio Ct. App. 1983). When the couple resides together, most courts have found that notice to one spouse is notice to the other. In *In re* De Pasquale, 166 B.R. 663, 23 U.C.C. Rep. Serv. 2d 1022 (Bankr. N.D. Ill. 1994), the court justified this result on the basis that the other spouse was aware of the notice. The result could also be justified under a literal reading of U.C.C. § 1-201(26) and (28)(for notice purposes, an organization includes "two or more persons having a joint or common interest").

(Matthew Bender & Co., Inc.)

If the collateral is consumer goods, the secured party does not have to send notice to any other parties. For all other types of collateral, however, the secured party may have to provide notice to certain other secured parties. Junior secured parties, for example, have a significant interest in obtaining notice of a senior secured party's foreclosure sale, which would extinguish the junior security interest.[80] Further, a junior secured party will have an interest in generating a surplus at the foreclosure sale given that the Code allows it to share in that surplus.[81] Alternatively, a junior might want to redeem the collateral by paying off the senior and adding its expenditure to the debtor's principal obligation.[82]

Under the 1972 text, the foreclosing secured party must send notice to any other secured party that has previously advised the foreclosing secured party, in writing, that it claims an interest in the collateral.[83] The 1972 text, however, does not impose upon the secured party any duty to search the official filing records to discover other competing interests in the collateral. For example, suppose that Finance Company holds a security interest in Debtor's equipment, which it properly perfected by filing. Finance Company does not notify Bank, which holds a senior security interest against the same equipment, of its interest. Six months later, Debtor defaults to Bank, which repossesses the equipment and schedules an auction sale. Under the 1972 text, Bank is not obligated to provide notice to Finance Company. Finance Company was in a position to recognize that it possessed a subordinate lien and could have easily sent a letter to Bank requesting notice in the event of a foreclosure sale by Bank. **Under the revision, however, the foreclosing secured party also has a duty to search the filing records and provide notice to any other secured party who, as of ten days prior to the date of the notice, holds an interest in the same collateral that is perfected by filing or by notation on a certificate of title.[84] Thus, analyzing the above hypothetical under the revision, Bank would be obligated to provide notice to Finance Company prior to selling the equipment.**

---

[80] U.C.C. §§ 9-504(4), **R9-617(a)(3)**. The title of the purchaser at the foreclosure sale is discussed in § 18.02[E] *infra.*

[81] The junior must notify the senior in writing that it wants to share in the surplus before distribution of the proceeds of sale is complete. U.C.C. §§ 9-504(1), **R9-615(a)(3)**. *See* discussion at § 18.02[D] *infra.* In addition, notification to the senior will entitle the junior to damages if the senior's sale is commercially unreasonable and would, if properly conducted, have generated a surplus. U.C.C. §§ 9-507(1), **R9-625(b)**.

[82] Any competing secured party (junior or senior) may avoid a foreclosure sale by redeeming the collateral. U.C.C. §§ 9-506, **R9-623**.

[83] U.C.C. § 9-504(3). **§ R9-611(c)(3)(A) retains this requirement.**

[84] U.C.C. § **R9-611(c)(3)(B), (C). In Comment 4 to § R9-611, the drafters explained the rationale for this expanded search burden: "Many of the problems arising from dispositions of collateral encumbered by multiple security interests can be ameliorated or solved by informing all secured parties of an intended disposition and affording them the opportunity to work with one another."**

Revised Article 9 provides a "safe harbor" rule to help the foreclosing secured party satisfy its "search" obligations under § R9-611(c)(3)(B). To qualify for this safe harbor, the foreclosing secured party should file a "request for information" with the filing officer, seeking information about all financing statements indexed under the debtor's name. This request must be filed not less than 20 days nor more than 30 days prior to the date of the notice. After filing this request, the foreclosing secured party should receive from the filing officer

In some instances, the party holding a junior interest may not be a competing secured party, but instead a party holding some other interest in the collateral, such as a judgment lien. For example, suppose that in the above hypothetical, Creditor had obtained a judgment lien against the equipment and had notified Bank of its interest. Must Bank give notice to Creditor prior to disposing of the collateral? Under the 1972 text, Bank would not be obligated to provide notice to Creditor, because Creditor is not a "secured party."[85] **Under the revision, however, Bank would be obligated to notify Creditor, as the revision obligates the Bank to provide notification to "any other person from which the secured party has received . . . an authenticated notification of a claim of an interest in the collateral."[86]**

Although the drafters intended the notification provision primarily to benefit junior interests, a senior secured party who learns that a junior has acquired an interest in its collateral may wish to take advantage of the provision.[87] By advising the junior of its interest, the senior gains some protection if the debtor defaults to the junior and the junior commences foreclosure proceedings. Although that sale would not extinguish the senior's interest,[88] the senior will want to know if its collateral is about to be sold.[89] This will give it the option to redeem the collateral from the junior prior to sale or to take steps to have the buyer at the foreclosure sale redeem the collateral from the junior in order to avoid repossession. Another option (though seldom exercised) is for the senior whose debtor is in default to repossess the collateral from the junior before the junior's sale

---

copies of all effective financing statements indexed under the name of the debtor. The foreclosing secured party may then provide the necessary notification to any secured party that has filed a financing statement describing the collateral. If the foreclosing secured party provides these notices pursuant to a timely request for information, or if the secured party filed a timely request but did not receive a response from the filing officer, the secured party is deemed to have satisfied its obligations under § R9-611(c)(3)(B). U.C.C. § R9-611(e).

[85] U.C.C. § 9-504(3). Bank might choose to provide notice to Creditor, however, in an attempt to disseminate notice more widely and thereby generate greater interest in the sale.

[86] U.C.C. § R9-611(c)(3)(A).

[87] In most such cases, the senior will have the option of declaring a default and proceeding to foreclose on the collateral. Most security agreements make the creation of a competing security interest an event of default.

[88] See discussion in § 18.02[D] infra.

Even if the buyer at the foreclosure sale is a buyer in the ordinary course (which will be the case if the secured party is a seller who puts the collateral back into its inventory for resale), the buyer cannot take advantage of U.C.C. § 9-307(1) or § R9-320(a) because the senior's security interest will not have been created by the buyer's immediate seller (the junior secured party). Accordingly, the buyer at the foreclosure sale is at risk of having the collateral repossessed from it by the senior if the debtor is in default to the senior. Since the buyer may then have to redeem the collateral to protect its interest, it should pay no more at the junior's sale than the fair market value of the collateral less the amount of the senior's debt. Also, the buyer at the junior's sale should notify the senior of its interest to prevent the senior from making post-sale advances to the debtor that would increase the senior's interest in the collateral. See U.C.C. §§ 9-307(3), R9-323(d).

[89] The fact that the senior's interest survives foreclosure is of little good if its collateral has been sold to a third party who then disappears with it.

takes place.[90] As between the two secured parties, the senior should have the superior possessory interest and, by taking over the process and conducting its own foreclosure sale, the senior gains a significant level of protection.

One other party not mentioned in the Code must also receive notice of any proposed sale. If the United States government has filed a notice of tax lien more than 30 days before the foreclosure sale, its lien will survive the sale — even if that lien is junior to the secured party's interest — unless the secured party provides proper notice at least 25 days prior to the sale.[91]

In limited circumstances a party may be a debtor, secondary obligor or other party entitled to notice, and yet may be unknown to (and undiscoverable by) the foreclosing secured party. For example, suppose that Freyermuth holds a perfected security interest in Henning's equipment and that Freyermuth repossesses the equipment following default by Henning. Unknown to Freyermuth, however, Henning had sold the equipment two days earlier to Lawrence, who had not yet taken delivery of the equipment. Further, and also unknown to Freyermuth, Lawrence had granted a security interest in the equipment to Bank, which filed a financing statement covering the collateral and naming Lawrence as debtor. Must Freyermuth notify Lawrence and Bank of the sale, or would notice to Henning alone be sufficient? **Revised Article 9 addresses this "new debtor" problem, which the 1972 text did not address in a satisfactory fashion.[92] Under the revision, Freyermuth is excused from providing notice to Lawrence and Bank.[93]**

[2] Amount of Notice Necessary

The Code requires that the secured party send a "reasonable notification" of the foreclosure sale, which means that the secured party must send the notice so that a party receiving it in due course would have a reasonable opportunity prior to the sale to exercise its redemption rights or take other steps reasonably calculated to protect its interests.[94] A review of the cases decided under the 1972 text indicates that there will never be a problem if the notice is sent at least ten days before the date of the sale. **Furthermore, revised Article 9 provides the foreclosing secured party with an express "safe harbor" in nonconsumer transactions if the secured party sends the notice no later than ten days prior to the sale.[95]**

---

[90] *See, e.g.,* American Heritage & Trust Co. v. O. & E., Inc., 40 Colo. Ct. App. 306, 576 P.2d 566, 23 U.C.C. Rep. Serv. 1034 (Colo. Ct. App. 1978).

[91] 26 U.S.C. § 7425(b). The government has a post-sale right of redemption for real property, but not for personalty. *See* 26 U.S.C. § 7425(d). Tax liens are discussed generally in Chapter 13 *supra.*

[92] Under the 1972 text, Freyermuth would not have to notify Bank unless Bank had first given written notice to Freyermuth of its interest in the equipment. U.C.C. § 9-504(3). Section 9-504(3), however, requires notice to anyone who is a "debtor," and thus would appear to require Freyermuth to notify Lawrence even though Freyermuth does not know that Lawrence possesses any interest in the equipment. If Bank does give notice of its interest to Freyermuth, he would also know of Lawrence's interest as "debtor" and clearly would be obligated to give notice to Lawrence under § 9-504(3).

[93] U.C.C. § R9-605(1), (2).

[94] *See* U.C.C. § 9-504 Cmt. 5; § R9-612 Cmt. 2.

[95] U.C.C. § R9-612(b).

The foregoing does not suggest that the secured party must give at least 10 days notice in order to provide reasonable notification. Indeed, at least one court has approved of a notice that gave the debtor only three business days prior to the sale.[96] Such short notice is dangerous, however; even notices sent a week before the sale have occasionally been attacked because a weekend or holiday cut down on the amount of time available to the debtor to protect its interest.[97]

The careful secured party should never encounter a problem. Although the debtor cannot waive the right to notice in the security agreement, the security agreement can establish the standards by which the secured party's fulfillment of its duties are to be measured, so long as the standards selected are not "manifestly unreasonable."[98] Thus, a security agreement that specifies that notice will be deemed sufficient if it is sent a certain number of days before the sale should insulate the secured party as long as the secured party subsequently complies with the terms of the agreement. Of course, a one-day notice requirement would likely be stricken under the "manifestly unreasonable" standard, but a court should not strike down a clause giving a debtor three working days, particularly in a commercial transaction. Nevertheless, prudence dictates that the clause stipulate that the notice be sent ten days before the proposed sale date. Should the secured party or the debtor find a buyer willing to pay a fair price but not willing to wait ten days, the debtor can facilitate a sale by waiving its right to notice.[99]

The Code does not require that the debtor *receive* the notice, only that the secured party send it. This distinction is consistent with the Code's definition of "notify," which states that "[a] person 'notifies' or 'gives' a notice to another by taking such steps as may be reasonably required to inform the other in ordinary course *whether or not such other actually comes to know of it.*"[100] Thus, in most cases the secured party need only place the notice in the mail, properly addressed and with proper postage, to comply with the Code's requirements. Several caveats, however, are warranted here. If the secured party knows that the debtor has moved and is aware of the new address, some courts have held that the secured party must send a notice to that address.[101] If the secured party knows that the debtor has moved but does not have the new address, some courts have imposed a duty to take minimal steps to locate and notify the debtor, such as looking in the city directory or contacting a known relative or business associate of the debtor.[102]

---

[96] *See, e.g.,* Citizens State Bank v. Sparks, 202 Neb. 661, 276 N.W.2d 661, 26 U.C.C. Rep. Serv. 589 (1979). **The comments to revised Article 9 indicate clearly that the 10-day period mentioned in § R9-612(b) is a "safe harbor" and not a "minimum requirement." U.C.C. § R9-612 Cmt. 3.**

[97] *See, e.g.,* Levers v. Rio King Land & Inv. Co., 93 Nev. 95, 560 P.2d 917, 21 U.C.C. Rep. Serv. 344 (1977).

[98] U.C.C. §§ 9-501(3), **R9-603(a).**

[99] The right to notice can be waived after default — by a signed writing (under the 1972 text) **or by an authenticated agreement (under the revision).** *See* U.C.C. §§ 9-504(3), **R9-624(a),** and the discussion in § 18.02[B][4] *infra.*

[100] U.C.C. § 1-201(26)(emphasis added).

[101] *See, e.g., In re* Carter, 511 F.2d 1203, 16 U.C.C. Rep. Serv. 874 (9th Cir. 1975). Out of caution, the secured party should also send a notice to the address specified in the agreement.

[102] *See, e.g.,* Mallicoat v. Volunteer Fin. & Loan Corp., 57 Tenn. App. 106, 415 S.W.2d 347,

Many security agreements specify that notice is sufficient if sent to the debtor at a certain address, but secured parties who are aware that their debtor has moved would be well advised not to rely on such a provision. [103]

[3] Form and Content of Notice

The 1972 text requires that reasonable notification of the sale be "sent" by the secured party, but its language is not entirely clear as to whether that notice must be in writing. In connection with the term "notice," Article 1 defines "send" to mean "to deposit in the mail *or deliver for transmission by any other usual means of communication* with postage or cost of transmission provided for and properly addressed . . . ." [104] On the one hand, the italicized words can be read to suggest that the secured party may communicate notice by means other than a writing. Further, section 9-504(3) of the 1972 text does not use the word "writing" in connection with its notice requirement; the drafters frequently make explicit reference to a writing in other contexts throughout the 1972 text, [105] and one could argue that their omission of the term in section 9-504(3) indicated their willingness to sanction notice other than by writing. On the other hand, the Code sometimes refers to "giving" notice [106] rather than "sending" it; this could suggest that while notice can be "given" in any manner, including orally, one can only "send" notice in a tangible (written) form. Something about our normal usage of the word "send" suggests that a writing is necessary.

Not surprisingly, courts interpreting the 1972 text have split on this point. Although a majority of the decisions have approved of oral notifications, [107] a substantial number of decisions have rejected them. [108] **Partially in response to this split of authority, revised Article 9 requires the secured party to send an "authenticated" notification, [109] which effectively requires the secured party to send notice in a "record"**

---

3 U.C.C. Rep. Serv. 1035 (Tenn. Ct. App. 1966) (secured party who received notice back from post office marked "undeliverable" had duty to try to locate debtor). **The comments to revised Article 9 suggest that a secured party who sends a notification and later learns that the debtor did not receive it *may* have to attempt to locate the debtor and send another notice. *See* U.C.C. § R9-611, Cmt. 6 (leaving to "judicial resolution" whether requirement of reasonable notification requires "second try" by secured party).**

[103] The prudent secured party should send a notice to the address specified in the security agreement and an additional notice to any new address that comes to its attention.

[104] U.C.C. § 1-201(38)(emphasis added).

[105] Indeed, U.C.C. § 9-504(3), which contains the requirement that notice be sent, uses the word "writing" when referring to the method by which a debtor may waive the right to notice following default. Other Code sections refer to written notices. Of particular import is the fact that under § 9-505(2), a notice proposing strict foreclosure must be sent in writing.

[106] U.C.C. § 1-201(26)defines the point in time at which a party "gives" notice.

[107] *See, e.g., In re* Excello Press, Inc., 890 F.2d 896, 10 U.C.C. Rep. Serv. 2d 271 (7th Cir. 1989); *In re* De Pasquale, 166 B.R. 663, 23 U.C.C. Rep. Serv. 2d 1022 (Bankr. N.D. Ill. 1994).

[108] *See, e.g.,* Van Ness v. First State Bank of Ida Grove, 430 N.W.2d 109, 7 U.C.C. Rep. Serv. 2d 597 (Iowa 1988); *In re* Hull, 155 B.R. 515, 22 U.C.C. Rep. Serv. 2d 377 (Bankr. W.D. Mo. 1993).

[109] **U.C.C. § R9-611(c).**

— *i.e.*, either as a writing or as information that is "stored in an electronic or other medium and is retrievable in perceivable form."[110] Thus, under the revision, an oral notification will no longer satisfy the secured party's responsibility to provide presale notice.[111]

As discussed earlier, reasonable notification allows the recipient to protect its interest by redeeming the collateral, attending the sale (or causing others to attend) and bidding the price up to a fair level, or policing the proposed sale to make certain that it comports with the requirement of commercial reasonableness.[112] Unfortunately, the 1972 text provides only minimal guidance regarding the contents of a "reasonable" notification. Section 9-504(3) provides that for a public sale, the notice must state the time and place of the sale, whereas with a private sale the notice must provide the date after which the secured party may sell the collateral.[113] Section 9-504(3) provides no guidance to the secured party, however, regarding what other information (if any) to include in the notice.[114]

The revisions address this shortcoming by providing the secured party with a "safe harbor" rule applicable to most foreclosures. Except in the case of a consumer-goods transaction,[115] a secured party's notice will be deemed sufficient if it

- describes the debtor and the secured party;

- describes the collateral that is the subject of the intended disposition;

- states the method of the intended disposition;

- states that the debtor is entitled to an accounting of the unpaid indebtedness and states the charge, if any, for such an accounting; and

---

[110] U.C.C. § R9-102(a)(69).

[111] *See* U.C.C. § R9-611 Cmt. 5. As a matter of policy, one can question why oral notice should not be sufficient if such notice is commercially reasonable under the particular circumstances. As a matter of prudence, however, any secured lender should send a writing because the secured party will ordinarily bear the burden of proving compliance with the notice requirement, *see, e.g.*, Boatmen's Bank v. Dahmer, 716 S.W.2d 876, 2 U.C.C. Rep. Serv. 2d 754 (Mo. Ct. App. 1986), and a writing greatly simplifies that task.

[112] *See* U.C.C. § 9-507(1). *See also* Chrysler Credit Corp. v. B.J.M., Jr., Inc., 834 F. Supp. 813, 22 U.C.C. Rep. Serv. 2d 379 (E.D. Pa. 1993) (discussion of rationale for requiring notice).

[113] U.C.C. § 9-504(3). This distinction is justified because the secured party will likely be unable to predict the exact date and/or time that it will consummate a private sale.

[114] Some states have nonuniform amendments to the Code or separate consumer legislation requiring that additional information be provided, particularly when the secured party may later seek a deficiency judgment. For example, Nebraska's version of U.C.C. § 9-504 contains a subsection requiring that the debtor be advised that it may be liable for a deficiency following the foreclosure sale. **The revisions now require such notification in consumer-goods transactions. U.C.C. § R9-614(1).**

[115] U.C.C. § R9-102(a)(24). **Recall that revised Article 9 distinguishes between a "consumer transaction" and a "consumer-goods transaction." For discussion of the distinction,** *see* § 1.04[A][1] *infra.*

- states the time and place of the sale (for a public sale) or the time after which the secured party may sell the collateral (for a private sale).[116]

In a consumer-goods transaction, the above five elements are *mandatory* — in other words, the notification *will be deemed insufficient if it does not contain all of these elements.* Furthermore, a foreclosure notice in a consumer-goods transaction must also include

- a description of any liability that the recipient may have for a deficiency judgment following the sale;

- a telephone number from which the recipient may obtain information about the amount that must be paid to redeem the collateral; and

- a telephone number or mailing address from which the recipient may obtain information concerning the disposition of the collateral and the obligation secured.[117]

Secured parties should take special care to comply with the Code's stated requirements. Although a creditor could argue that less-than-perfect compliance should not necessarily render a notice unreasonable,[118] courts have shown a willingness to construe the Code's stated requirements very strictly. For example, in *Hayes v. Ring Power Corp.*,[119] the creditor held an auction sale but sent the debtor a notice that stated that the collateral would be disposed of "after June 12, 1981." Because the notice did not state the exact time and place of the auction, the court held the notice did not satisfy the creditor's duty to send notice. Likewise, in *Gateway Aviation, Inc. v. Cessna Aircraft Co.*,[120] the secured party sent proper notice of an auction sale, but withdrew the collateral when the bidding proved disappointing and instead sought a private buyer. The secured party later found a private buyer who purchased the collateral for several thousand dollars more than the top bid at the auction. In an action against the debtor for a deficiency, however, the court

---

[116] U.C.C. § R9-613(1). The secured party does not have to state the notification in the exact same words as appear in § R9-613(1). *See* § R9-613(4) ("A particular phrasing of the notification is not required."). Furthermore, a court may conclude that a secured party's notification is "reasonable" under the circumstances, even if it lacks one or more of the elements listed in the "safe harbor" provision. *See* § R9-613(2). Nevertheless, the secured party would be wise to track the suggested language closely. For convenience, the revisions also provide a suggested form of notice that, if complied with, would satisfy the reasonable notification requirement. § R9-613(5).

[117] U.C.C. § R9-614(1). Again, although no particular phrasing is required, the prudent secured party should track the language of § R9-614(1) as closely as possible. For convenience, the revisions also provide a suggested "safe harbor" form of notice, written in "plain english," that (if complied with) would satisfy the reasonable notification requirement. § R9-614(3).

[118] *See* U.C.C. § R9-613(2) (finder of fact may conclude that a notification is reasonable under the circumstances, even if it lacks some of the information specified in the "safe harbor" provision).

[119] 431 So. 2d 226, 36 U.C.C. Rep. Serv. 1452 (Fla. Ct. App. 1983).

[120] 577 S.W.2d 860, 25 U.C.C. Rep. Serv. 901 (Mo. Ct. App. 1978).

found that the private sale was defective because the secured party had failed properly to notify the debtor. [121]

Generally speaking, a secured party may include additional information in its notification, beyond the stated requirements of the Code, so long as the additional information is not seriously misleading. [122] For example, a notice may be defective if the secured party overstates the amount of the debt and thereby discourages the debtor from exercising its redemption right. [123] If the notice contains errors that are not misleading or prejudicial to the debtor, however, courts should be careful not to penalize the secured party, especially in transactions not involving consumers. [124] Overly rigorous policing of the foreclosure process (in this and other contexts) by the courts could have the unintended effect of causing more secured creditors to have their collateral sold through a judicial proceeding. [125] This approach would have the perverse effect of reducing the amounts realized through foreclosure, thereby increasing the deficiencies borne by debtors.

[4] When Notice is Excused

The Code specifies that the secured party need not give notice in the following situations: 1) when the collateral is perishable; 2) when it threatens to decline speedily in value; 3) when it is of a type that is customarily sold on a recognized market; and 4) when the debtor makes an effective waiver of the right to notice after default. [126]

The first two situations are fairly obvious. If the collateral is a crop of harvested tomatoes sitting in a truck in the heat of summer when repossession occurs, the secured party should not have to give notice. The collateral is perishable and the debtor will suffer positive harm if the secured party waits until it has complied with a notice requirement. Cases involving truly perishable assets are rare, however, and secured parties have had little success in attempting to use this provision. Several cases involve cattle — which must be fed and watered or they will perish — but the courts are nearly uniform in holding

---

[121] Although strict, the result in *Gateway Aviation* can be justified. The debtor should have had an opportunity to police the private sale to make certain that it was conducted fairly; further, with additional notice of the private sale, the debtor might have come up with the money to redeem the collateral after the date of the auction but before the private sale actually occurred.

[122] **Revised Article 9 makes explicit that minor errors that are not "seriously misleading" will not defeat the sufficiency of a presale notification that otherwise complies with the "safe harbor" provision for nonconsumer-goods transactions. U.C.C. § R9-613(3)(B).**

[123] *See, e.g.,* Wilmington Trust Co. v. Conner, 415 A.2d 773, 28 U.C.C. Rep. Serv. 900 (Del. 1980); Travis v. Boulevard Bank, 880 F. Supp. 1226, 28 U.C.C. Rep. Serv. 2d 410 (N.D. Ill. 1995).

Whether the notice must advise the debtor of redemption rights is discussed in § 18.05 *infra.*

[124] **Revised Article 9 holds the secured party to a higher standard with regard to consumer-goods transactions. Errors in the information required by § R9-614(1) will render the notice defective. Assuming that the secured party has used the "safe harbor" form specified in § R9-614(3), errors in additional information that the secured party chooses to provide will not render the notice defective unless that information is misleading with respect to the recipient's rights under Article 9. U.C.C. § R9-614(5).**

[125] Foreclosing through a sheriff's sale is discussed in § 17.02[A] *supra.*

[126] U.C.C. §§ 9-504(3), **R9-611(d), R9-624(a).**

that a secured party selling cattle must give notice.[127] This result is appropriate since nothing intrinsic about the cattle makes them perishable — they simply need to be cared for and it is the secured party's statutory responsibility to do so following repossession.[128]

The most common examples of collateral that threatens to decline speedily in value are stocks and commodities. In *Moutray v. Perry State Bank*,[129] the secured party failed to send notice of sale of the debtor's milo crop, but was excused because the evidence showed that the market for milo was likely to drop precipitously. In contrast, in *Chittenden Trust Co. v. Andre Noel Sports*,[130] the secured party failed to give notice of its sale of high-fashion ski and sports apparel. The court properly refused to excuse the failure because the ski season ended long before the sale occurred. Had repossession occurred toward the end of the ski season, however, the secured party might have prevailed by convincing the court that such seasonal goods had to be sold before the season ended.

Courts have limited the third exception — for collateral customarily sold on a recognized market — to assets that are sold without negotiation.[131] If, for example, the collateral consists of shares of a commonly traded stock, there is no plausible rationale for requiring notice.[132] If the debtor has the money to redeem the stock, the same money will buy an equivalent number of shares on the market. Furthermore, the debtor would not need to police the sale of a commonly traded stock for fairness. If the secured party sells the stock for its prevailing market price, the sale is, by definition, commercially reasonable; if it is not sold for that price, the secured party's misconduct will stick out like a sore thumb.[133]

In a number of cases, the secured party has tried to use this exception when it failed to give notice in connection with the sale of a used car or similar asset that has a "bluebook" price quotation. The courts have almost uniformly rejected such arguments,[134] because bluebook quotes simply provide a starting point for negotiating a price. With other assets, the issue is murkier. For example, even with a prevailing market price for cattle, in a particular area, they may be sold at an auction by competitive bidding.

---

[127] *See, e.g.*, Boatmen's Bank of Nev. v. Dahmer, 716 S.W.2d 876, 2 U.C.C. Rep. Serv. 2d 754 (Mo. Ct. App. 1986). *Cf.* City Bank & Trust Co. v. Van Andel, 220 Neb. 152, 368 N.W.2d 789, 41 U.C.C. Rep. Serv. 282 (1985) (whether cattle were perishable was question of fact for jury).

[128] U.C.C. §§ 9-207(1), **R9-207(a).**

[129] 748 S.W.2d 749, 7 U.C.C. Rep. Serv. 2d 1340 (Mo. Ct. App. 1988).

[130] 159 Vt. 307, 621 A.2d 215, 20 U.C.C. Rep. Serv. 2d 710 (1992).

[131] *See* **U.C.C. § R9-610 Cmt. 9.**

[132] *See, e.g.*, Finch v. Auburn Nat'l Bank of Auburn, 646 So. 2d 64, 25 U.C.C. Rep. Serv. 2d 1300 (Ala. Ct. App. 1995) (notice not required for stock traded on Midwest Stock Exchange).

[133] The same rationale underlies the policy permitting the secured party to buy such assets at a private sale. U.C.C. §§ 9-504(3); **R9-610(c)(2).** *See* discussion in § 18.02[C] *infra.*

[134] *See, e.g.*, Beneficial Fin. Co. of Black Hawk County v. Reed, 212 N.W.2d 454, 13 U.C.C. Rep. Serv. 974 (Iowa 1973). This phrase ("type sold on a recognized market") is discussed further in the context of the secured party's right to buy the collateral at a private foreclosure sale. *See* discussion in § 18.02[C] *infra.*

In such cases, whether the collateral falls within the exception is an issue of fact for the jury.[135]

Finally, the debtor can waive the notice requirement after default by a signed writing (under the 1972 text) **or an authenticated agreement (under the revision).**[136] The debtor may not waive the notice requirement in advance,[137] but allowing the debtor to waive it once default occurs makes sense. If the secured party finds a potential buyer who is willing to pay a reasonable price for the collateral but is unwilling to wait while the secured party notifies the debtor and a "commercially reasonable" time passes, it may well be in the debtor's interest to waive the notice requirement so that the secured party can make the sale. After default, there should be little concern that the waiver is the product of overreaching by the secured party.

[C] Whether Secured Party Can Purchase at Sale

The secured party is free to purchase the collateral at a public sale, but may not purchase the collateral at a private sale unless it is of a type customarily sold on a "recognized market" or is the subject of "widely distributed standard price quotations."[138] This distinction between public and private sales is sound. A public sale features competitive bidding,[139] and as a matter of policy and fairness the secured party should be able to join the competition. The debtor can only benefit from the participation of an extra bidder. In contrast, private sales provide too great an opportunity and temptation for secured parties to purchase the collateral and then later resell it for their own account at a higher price. If the collateral is something like a commonly traded stock or a commodity that sells without negotiation on a recognized market, however, there is no reason to prevent the secured party from buying at a private sale. If the secured party pays less than the prevailing price, it will be easy for the debtor to prove that the transaction was not commercially reasonable.[140]

The more difficult problem involves the meaning of the phrase "widely distributed standard price quotations." Because the Code uses the companion phrase "customarily sold on a recognized market" to describe one of the situations in which notice is excused,[141] the additional phrase "widely distributed standard price quotations" — which is not used in the notice context — arguably refers to something other than a sale on a recognized market. But what? The most obvious example would be the used-car type of situation, where the asset is the subject of "bluebook" price quotations. Surprisingly,

---

[135] *See, e.g.*, Havins v. First Nat'l Bank of Paducah, 919 S.W.2d 177, 29 U.C.C. Rep. Serv. 2d 1053 (Tex. Ct. App. 1996) (cattle auction); Aspen Enters., Inc. v. Bodge, 37 Cal. App. 4th 1811, 44 Cal. Rptr. 2d 763, 27 U.C.C. Rep. Serv. 2d 681 (1995) (used tires).

[136] U.C.C. §§ 9-504(3), **R9-624(a).**

[137] U.C.C. §§ 9-501(3)(b), **R9-602(7).**

[138] U.C.C. §§ 9-504(3), **R9-610(c).**

[139] Whether auctions that are not open qualify as public sales so that a secured party can compete is discussed in § 18.02[A][3] *supra.*

[140] The same phrase ("customarily sold on a recognized market") is used to describe situations in which the secured party need not give notice of sale. *See* discussion in § 18.02[B][4] *supra.*

[141] *Id.*

few decisions are directly on point; the dicta in several cases, however, suggest that the secured party should not be allowed to purchase such assets privately because the bluebook price is only the starting point for negotiations and the actual price that is paid depends upon the individual characteristics of the particular asset.[142] A few decisions, however, rule to the contrary.[143] Although the language of the Code invites the courts to allow the secured party to purchase "bluebook" assets privately, policy considerations dictate otherwise. Such an interpretation would allow the secured party to "cherry pick" — that is, to buy those assets that were in better than average condition for their bluebook price and then resell them at a higher price. Because the price at the foreclosure sale establishes the amount of the debtor's deficiency, such a result would be patently unfair. Courts should discourage this type of activity, even if it means effectively collapsing the definition of "standard price quotations" into that used for "recognized markets."

[D] Disposition of Proceeds of Sale

Article 9 establishes a four-step process to govern the manner in which the foreclosing secured party must distribute the proceeds of its foreclosure sale. First, the secured party can reimburse itself for the reasonable expenses incurred to repossess the collateral and dispose of the collateral.[144] The secured party may also recover its attorney's fees and other legal expenses from the proceeds of the collateral, if the security agreement so provides and the law of the jurisdiction does not otherwise preclude this.[145]

Second, the foreclosing secured party reimburses itself for the balance of the secured indebtedness being foreclosed upon.[146] Third, if there remain additional proceeds after satisfaction of its claim, the foreclosing secured party must distribute those proceeds to junior secured parties who have provided the foreclosing secured party with a timely demand for payment.[147] **Under revised Article 9, other junior lienholders (such as**

---

[142] *See, e.g.*, Northern Commercial Co. v. Cobb, 778 P.2d 205, 10 U.C.C. Rep. Serv. 2d 197 (Alaska 1989) (construction equipment did not fit within exception even though there were nationally published retail and wholesale prices available); M.P. Crum Co. v. First Southwest Savings & Loan Ass'n, 704 S.W.2d 925, 1 U.C.C. Rep. Serv. 2d 332 (Tex. Ct. App. 1986) (sale of home mortgages).

[143] *See, e.g.*, Dischner v. United Bank of Ala., 631 P.2d 107, 33 U.C.C. Rep. Serv. 796 (Alaska 1981). *Cf.* L.C. Arthur Trucking, Inc. v. Evans, 13 U.C.C. Rep. Serv. 2d 623 (Va. Cir. Ct. 1990) (tractor trailer was of type customarily sold in recognized market).

[144] These expenses include: the cost of repossession; the cost of holding or storing the collateral pending disposition; the cost of preparing the collateral for disposition, including any commercially reasonable expenses incurred in fixing the collateral so that it commands a higher sale price (*see* discussion in § 18.02[A][4] *supra*); and the cost of conducting the sale, including any reasonable auctioneer's charges. U.C.C. §§ 9-501(1)(a); **R9-615(a)(1).** Courts have also allowed the secured party to recover expenses incurred in paying off other liens in order to clear the title to the collateral prior to resale. *See, e.g.*, Contrail Leasing Partners, Ltd. v. Consolidated Airways, Inc., 742 F.2d 1095, 39 U.C.C. Rep. Serv. 9 (7th Cir. 1983).

[145] U.C.C. §§ 9-501(1)(a); **R9-615(a)(1).**

[146] U.C.C. §§ 9-501(1)(b); **R9-615(a)(2).**

[147] U.C.C. §§ 9-501(1)(c); **R9-615(a)(3).** To be entitled to payment, any subordinate party must make its demand before the foreclosing secured party has completed distribution of the sale proceeds. This demand must be in writing (under the 1972 text) **or be authenticated (under the**

subordinate judgment lien creditors) may also obtain a distribution of remaining proceeds following a timely demand. [148] Fourth, the secured party must turn over any remaining surplus to the owner of the collateral. [149]

Occasionally, courts have become confused regarding the proper distribution of proceeds under a sale conducted by a junior secured party when a senior secured party asserts a claim to the proceeds. An example is useful to explain this confusion. Suppose that Henning owns equipment subject to two security interests held by Lawrence and Freyermuth, respectively, with Lawrence holding the senior interest. Henning defaults to Freyermuth, and Freyermuth repossesses the equipment and conducts an auction sale. Does Lawrence have a claim to the proceeds from Freyermuth's foreclosure sale?

The correct answer is no. When a senior secured party like Lawrence takes a security interest in an asset owned by the debtor, its interest in the asset is limited. The debtor retains title to the collateral and, in a nonpossessory security arrangement, the right to possess the collateral. Should default and repossession occur, the debtor retains a right of redemption. Most importantly, the debtor has a right to any equity that it has built up in the collateral, a right that is vindicated in foreclosure proceedings by the secured party's duty to turn over to the debtor any surplus generated by the sale. [150] Thus, when a junior secured party like Freyermuth acquires an interest in collateral already subject to a senior's lien, the junior's security interest does not technically interfere with the existing rights of the senior. Conceptually, the junior's interest is best understood as attaching only to the debtor's equity in the collateral. Even if the senior's security agreement makes it an event of default for the debtor to alienate that equity, the debtor has the *power* to do so. [151]

Thus, although Freyermuth, as the junior secured party, has a right to repossess the equipment and foreclose upon it, all he can sell is his right to Henning's equity (and Henning's title and right to possession). As a result, whoever buys the equipment at the foreclosure sale takes title subject to Lawrence's senior security interest, and is at risk

---

revision). If the foreclosing secured party requests reasonable proof of the junior's claimant's interest and the junior claimant fails to provide it, the foreclosing secured party can ignore the demand. U.C.C. §§ 9-504(1), **R9-615(b).**

[148] U.C.C. § **R9-615(a)(3).**

[149] U.C.C. §§ 9-504(2), **R9-615(d)(1).** This disposition requirement assumes that the security interest secures an indebtedness. When the secured party is a buyer of accounts or chattel paper **(or, under the revision, payment intangibles or promissory notes)**, it owns the equity and need not account to the debtor for it.

The Code actually requires the secured party to distribute the surplus to the "debtor." Recall that under the 1972 text, however, the term "debtor" described both the owner of the collateral and any person obligated on the secured indebtedness. In those cases, where the owner of the collateral was not obligated on the debt, U.C.C. § 9-112of the 1972 text dictated that the secured party was to pay any surplus to the owner of the collateral. **Under the revision, the term "debtor" refers to the owner of the collateral, regardless of whether that person is obligated on the debt.** See § 1.10[C] *supra.*

[150] The debtor's right to the surplus, and the circumstances in which a junior secured party is entitled to participate in its distribution, are discussed *infra* this subsection.

[151] U.C.C. §§ 9-311; **R9-401(b).**

(Matthew Bender & Co., Inc.)

of having Lawrence repossess the equipment if Henning also defaults to Lawrence.[152] This also means, conceptually, that the proceeds of Freyermuth's sale are not "proceeds" of Lawrence's security interest, because the sale did not transfer the rights to which Lawrence's security interest attached.[153] As a result, Article 9 does not entitle Lawrence to any distribution of the proceeds of Freyermuth's sale.[154] To reach those proceeds, Lawrence must employ an extra-Code process such as garnishment.

Unfortunately, not every court has understood this point. A few cases use a standard "proceeds" analysis[155] to give the senior secured party priority in the proceeds of resale. According to these cases, Freyermuth's failure to turn the proceeds over to Lawrence upon demand would constitute a conversion.[156] These decisions are incorrect; requiring the foreclosing junior to turn over the proceeds of its sale to the senior eviscerates the conceptual underpinnings of the Code. In the hypothetical, Lawrence's security interest remains intact and he can continue to look to the equipment for satisfaction.

Revised Article 9 places an additional duty upon the foreclosing secured party in a consumer-goods transaction.[157] If the sale of the collateral produces a surplus belonging to the debtor, the secured party must provide the debtor with a written explanation of how the secured party calculated that surplus. Likewise, if the sale leaves a deficiency for which a consumer obligor would be liable, the secured party must provide any such consumer obligor with a written explanation of how the secured party calculated the deficiency amount.[158] The secured party must provide

---

[152] See related discussion in § 18.02[B][1] supra. Since the Code authorizes the junior's sale, the buyer is not a converter. It becomes liable for conversion, however, if it later resists the senior's proper demand to turn over possession. Because security agreements often define repossession as an event of default, the prospect of the debtor's default to the senior secured party is high.

[153] See, e.g., Consolidated Equip. Sales, Inc. v. First State Bank & Trust Co. of Guthrie, 627 P.2d 432, 31 U.C.C. Rep. Serv. 677 (Okla. 1981); Delaware Truck Sales, Inc. v. Wilson, 618 A.2d 303, 20 U.C.C. Rep. Serv. 2d 1420 (N.J. 1993).

[154] See, e.g., Continental Bank of Buffalo Grove, N.A. v. Krebs, 184 Ill. App. 3d 693, 540 N.E.2d 1023, 10 U.C.C. Rep. Serv. 2d 246 (Ill. Ct. App. 1989) (relying on U.C.C. § 9-311 to hold that senior secured party is not entitled to proceeds of junior's foreclosure sale).

[155] If the proceeds of the junior's sale were "proceeds" of the senior's security interest, the senior would have priority to them under U.C.C. §§ 9-312(6) and **R9-322(c)**.

[156] See, e.g., Consolidated Equipment Sales, Inc. v. First State Bank & Trust Co. of Guthrie, 627 P.2d 432, 31 U.C.C. Rep. Serv. 677 (Okla. 1981); Delaware Truck Sales, Inc. v. Wilson, 618 A.2d 303, 20 U.C.C. Rep. Serv. 2d 1420 (N.J. 1993).

[157] **For a definition of the term "consumer-goods transaction" and how that term differs from the term "consumer transaction," see § 1.10[B] supra.**

[158] **U.C.C. § R9-616(b). The "explanation" is a writing that states the amount of the surplus or deficiency, explains how the secured party calculated it, states whether "future debits, credits, charges . . . and expenses may affect the amount of the surplus or deficiency," and provides a phone number or mailing address from which the recipient could obtain additional information about the transaction. § R9-616(a)(1). Further, § R9-616(c) requires that the explanation of the secured party's calculation is sufficient only if it includes the following information in the following order: the aggregate amount of the secured obligation(s); the amount of proceeds of the disposition; the aggregate amount of the secured obligation(s) after the application of the proceeds; the amount and types of expenses of repossession and**

this explanation no later than when it accounts for any surplus or when it makes its first written demand for payment of the deficiency.[159]

[E]   Title of Purchaser at Sale

When the secured party disposes of collateral after default to a transferee who pays value, the disposition has the effect of passing the debtor's rights in the collateral to that transferee,[160] thereby extinguishing the debtor's right of redemption (which exists only prior to disposition of the collateral).[161] The disposition also discharges both the security interest being foreclosed and any subordinate liens or security interests.[162] This discharge is an application of the doctrine of derivative title, pursuant to which a transferee acquires whatever rights were held by the transferor. When a senior secured party transfers collateral to a buyer at a foreclosure sale, the buyer acquires the senior's rights and this results in the discharge of junior liens.[163] The buyer, however, takes subject to any liens that are senior to the interest of the foreclosing secured party. A foreclosure-sale buyer thus should pay no more than the fair market value of the collateral less the value of senior liens.[164]

Generally speaking, a transferee for value at a foreclosure sale acquires these rights even if the secured party has breached the peace in its repossession efforts, conducted a commercially unreasonable sale, or failed to give all necessary notices. In other words, the secured party's failure to comply with its responsibilities under Article 9 does not give the debtor a basis to seek collateral attack of the sale through judicial proceedings. The debtor's remedy for this misbehavior is against the foreclosing secured party, not

---

disposition; the amounts of credits (if any) to which any obligor is known to be entitled; and the amount of the surplus or deficiency.

[159] U.C.C. § R9-616(b)(1)(A). A debtor or secondary obligor does not have to wait until the secured party makes a written demand for payment in order to receive an explanation of how the secured party calculated the surplus or deficiency. Instead, § R9-616 authorizes the debtor or secondary obligor, after disposition of the collateral, to make an authenticated request to receive an explanation of how the secured party calculated the surplus or deficiency; following such a request, within 14 days the secured party must provide an explanation or a record waiving its right to pursue a deficiency judgment. § R9-616(b)(1)(B), (2).

[160] U.C.C. §§ 9-504(4), R9-617(a)(1). Section 9-504(4) of the 1972 text uses the term "purchaser," while § R9-617 uses the term "transferee" because the revision characterizes the foreclosure as an involuntary transaction. Both terms include a foreclosure-sale buyer, including the secured party when it buys at its own foreclosure sale.

[161] U.C.C. §§ 9-506, R9-623(c).

[162] U.C.C. §§ 9-504(4), R9-617(a)(2), (3).

[163] The junior secured party's right to notice of the sale so that it can protect its interests is discussed in § 18.02[B][1] supra, and the junior's right to participate in the distribution of the proceeds of sale is discussed in § 18.02[D].

[164] A prudent purchaser will contact the senior secured party before or at the time of the sale and make arrangements to pay off the lien. At a minimum, the purchaser should notify the senior of its purchase to ensure that the senior does not acquire priority for future advances that it might make to the debtor. See U.C.C. §§ 9-307(3); R9-323(d).

the foreclosure-sale buyer.[165] This rule promotes the finality of rights acquired through foreclosure sales — thereby hoping to encourage widespread participation in foreclosure sales, on the assumption that widespread participation should result in a higher sale price that will redound to the benefit of debtors generally.

Under limited circumstances, however, Article 9 permits a debtor to seek judicial invalidation of a foreclosure sale. Under the 1972 text, the buyer does not acquire "clear title" (*i.e.*, the debtor's rights in the collateral, free of the interest foreclosed and subordinate interests) if the buyer bought the collateral at a public sale either with knowledge[166] of defects in the sale or in collusion with the secured party, other bidders, or the agent conducting the sale.[167] In the case of a private sale, the 1972 text provides that the buyer acquires clear title if the buyer acted in good faith.[168] Thus, for example, if secured party's auction sale was collusive, the debtor and/or any junior secured party can bring an action to set aside the buyer's title and can then either redeem the collateral[169] or force the senior secured party to foreclose a second time.[170] Even unsecured parties (or their representative, the trustee in bankruptcy) may be able to set aside the sale if it constituted a fraudulent conveyance.[171] The court will typically order that restitution of the purchase price be made to the buyer as a condition to granting relief.[172]

---

[165] Remedies for creditor misbehavior are discussed generally in Chapter 19 *infra*.

[166] The term "knowledge" means *actual* knowledge. U.C.C. § 1-201(25). The purchaser does not have a duty to investigate to determine whether the sale was defective. § 9-504, Cmt. 4.

[167] U.C.C. § 9-504(4)(a).

[168] Under the 1972 text, "good faith" means subjective honesty in the case of a nonmerchant. U.C.C. § 1-201(19). Because Article 2 applies to the sales aspects of the foreclosure of goods [§ 9-504(1)], good faith in the case of a merchant means subjective honesty coupled with an observance of reasonable commercial standards of fair dealing in the trade. § 2-103(1)(b).

[169] The secured party's interest reattaches when the sale is set aside, so redemption is an appropriate remedy.

[170] Injunctive relief to force the secured party to conduct a commercially reasonable sale is available under U.C.C. §§ 9-507(1) and **R9-625(a)**. A properly conducted second sale would not excuse the secured party from any liability that it might have incurred as a result of its first sale.

[171] If the trustee sets aside the sale and is then able to avoid the security interest, it can make a distribution to unsecured creditors. *See, e.g.*, Sheffield Progressive, Inc. v. Kingston Tool Co., 10 Mass. App. Ct. 47, 405 N.E.2d 985, 29 U.C.C. Rep. Serv. 292 (Mass. Ct. App. 1980). *Cf.* Bezanson v. Fleet Bank -NH, 29 F.3d 16, 24 U.C.C. Rep. Serv. 2d 399 (1st Cir. 1994) (facts suggested fraudulent conveyance but debtor's action was brought against secured party for holding commercially unreasonable sale that failed to produce surplus). The subject of fraudulent conveyances in bankruptcy is discussed in detail in § 16.04[F] *supra*.

[172] If the secured party is joined in the action, the court should order that it make the restitutionary payment. If it is not joined, the party setting aside the sale should be entitled to restitution from the secured party for the payment made to the purchaser.

Under the 1972 text, restitution is likely the buyer's only remedy against the secured party, because there would be no implied warranty of title extended in connection with the foreclosure sale. *See* U.C.C. § 2-312(2). **Under the revision, however, the foreclosure sale would include an implied warranty of title unless the secured party effectively disclaimed that warranty.** *See* § **R9-610(d), (e).** In any event, the secured party will be liable to the buyer for breach of

By using different terminology — "good faith" as opposed to "knowledge" of defects or "collusion" — the 1972 text perhaps misleadingly suggests that entirely different standards govern public sales and private sales. **Revised Article 9 clarifies any uncertainty by adopting a unitary standard, stating that the transferee at a foreclosure sale acquires clear title despite defects in the sale if the transferee acts in good faith.**[173] **One might attempt to argue that the revision's omission of the "knowledge" and "collusion" standards found in the 1972 text suggests that, under the revision, a buyer could claim to act in "good faith" even though the buyer knew of defects in the sale or acted in collusion with other bidders. The comments to the revision, however, clearly reject this view:**

> [T]his change from former Section 9-504(4) should not be interpreted to mean that a transferee acts in good faith even though it has knowledge of defects or buys in collusion, standards applicable to public dispositions under the former section. *Properly understood, those standards were specific examples of the absence of good faith.*[174]

Because revised Article 9 expands the scope of the duty of "good faith" beyond the purely subjective "honesty in fact" definition contained in the 1972 text, the revisions may have an unintended chilling effect upon prospective foreclosure sale bidders. Under the 1972 text, buyers at auction sales had no duty to investigate the secured party's compliance with the requirements of Article 9 or to inquire into the circumstances surrounding the sale.[175] **Under revised Article 9, however, an auction sale buyer must act in good faith, which includes "the observance of reasonable commercial standards of fair dealing."**[176] **Would "observance of reasonable commercial standards of fair dealing" obligate the auction sale buyer to conduct an inquiry into the character of the sale? It is doubtful that the drafters so intended, and such an inquiry could easily discourage bidding, leading to lower prices at foreclosure sales and higher deficiency judgments for debtors. Nevertheless, courts have often demonstrated a willingness to apply the duty of "good faith" in sweeping terms when presented with compelling facts.**

§ 18.03   Foreclosure on Intangible Assets — §§ 9-502, R9-607

When a foreclosure involves intangible collateral such as accounts or chattel paper, the secured party may have to take steps that are unnecessary in the typical foreclosure involving tangible assets.[177] The secured party must first choose whether to sell the

---

any express warranties it makes in connection with the sale (§ 2-313), and it will be liable for any breach of the implied warranty of merchantability if it is a merchant with respect to goods of the type being sold (§ 2-314). If the disposition is by lease, there are parallel provisions in Article 2A. *See* note 31 *supra.*

[173] U.C.C. § R9-617(b). Under the revision, "good faith" means both honesty in fact and the observance of reasonable commercial standards of fair dealing. § R9-102(a)(43).

[174] U.C.C. § R9-617 Cmt. 3 (emphasis added).

[175] *See* U.C.C. § 9-504 Cmt. 4.

[176] U.C.C. § R9-102(a)(43).

[177] Full treatment of this topic is beyond the scope of this book. The text provides only a basic summary of Article 9's guidelines.

collateral as a package to a factor[178] or attempt to collect from the various account debtors. If the secured party sells the collateral to a factor *en masse*, the normal provisions governing Article 9 foreclosures will govern the sale. If instead the secured party chooses collection, the secured party will have to notify each account debtor to make payment to it;[179] further, the secured party will then have to collect the accounts in a commercially reasonable manner. This means that the secured party must exercise reasonable judgment in deciding whether to expend resources in pursuit of financially strapped account debtors, and it must act reasonably in compromising claims against account debtors who assert defenses or counterclaims that might have been valid if the debtor had attempted to collect the account.[180]

If the secured party is a buyer of accounts or chattel paper **(or, under the revision, payment intangibles or promissory notes)**, it ordinarily need not worry about collecting them in a commercially reasonable manner, because the debtor will not be liable for any deficiency and the secured party need not account for any surplus.[181] But if the secured party has a right of recourse or charge-back against the debtor in the event it cannot collect from an account debtor, then the secured party's collection efforts must be commercially reasonable.[182] When a secured party takes an assignment of accounts or chattel

---

[178] The term "factor" describes a party who purchases accounts or chattel paper. *See* § 3.04[A] *supra*. After making its purchase, the factor will proceed to collect from the individual account debtors. Having bought the assets outright, the factor will not be under a duty to remit any surplus to the debtor. Any surplus value should have been realized through the secured party's commercially reasonable sale to the factor.

[179] Article 9 permits the secured party, at any time there is a default, to notify account debtors of the assignment and to direct them to make payment to the secured party. U.C.C. §§ 9-502(1), **R9-607(a)(1)**. Article 9 also permits the secured party to give notice to account debtors, even prior to default, that the account has been assigned and that the account debtor should make payment to the secured party. §§ 9-318(3), **R9-406(a)**. After receiving notice of such an assignment, the account debtor thereafter may discharge its obligation only by payment to the secured party. Certain notification financing arrangements follow this pattern; in those transactions, because the secured party will already have notified the account debtors to make payment to it, the secured party need provide no further notification following the debtor's default.

[180] The most common example would be a breach of warranty claim against the debtor. For example, suppose Henning purchased equipment on account from Seller/Debtor, who assigned the account to Bank. Bank would take the account subject to any claim Henning might have that the equipment breached any express or implied warranties of quality or fitness, unless Henning had entered into an enforceable agreement not to assert claims against any assignee of Seller/Debtor. U.C.C. §§ 9-318(1), **R9-404(a)**. In attempting to collect the account from Henning, Bank could enforce Henning's agreement to waive claims and defenses in order to defeat any breach of warranty claim, provided that Bank took its assignment of the account for value, in good faith, and without notice of any such claim. §§ 9-206, **R9-403(a)**.

[181] If the assignee simply buys accounts or chattel paper outright, there is no underlying loan; thus, concepts like deficiency and surplus are inapt. Thus, if the underlying transaction is a sale of accounts or chattel paper **(or, under the revision, a sale of payment intangibles or promissory notes)**, the debtor is neither entitled to a surplus nor liable for any deficiency unless the debtor's agreement provides otherwise. U.C.C. §§ 9-502(2), **R9-608(b)**. *See also* § **R9-608 Cmt. 3.**

[182] U.C.C. §§ 9-502(2), **R9-607(c)**.

paper, its contract with the debtor typically gives it a right of recourse in the event an account debtor asserts a contract defense or counterclaim against it. In such situations, the secured party must take care that any compromise between it and an account debtor can be defended as a commercially-reasonable exercise of judgment.

If the collateral is a negotiable instrument, the secured party can either present it for collection to any party that is liable on it[183] or sell it at a normal foreclosure sale.[184] If the collateral is a document, the secured party can sell the document, or use it to obtain the goods and then sell the goods. With certain general intangibles, the secured party may need the consent of a third party for their sale. For example, the right to be a franchisee is a valuable right and, if the secured party wants to sell the debtor's rights as a franchisee, the purchaser will ordinarily have to meet with the franchisor's approval.[185]

---

[183] The mechanics of collection and the obligations of parties to the instrument are governed by Articles 3 and 4. The secured party will have an easier time of collection if the secured party is a holder, which means that as a matter of prudence, the secured party should have the debtor indorse the instrument to the secured party when its security interest first attaches. Having the status of holder is a necessary first step for the secured party to later assert that it is a "holder in due course" entitled to collect the instrument free from claims and defenses.

After default, the secured party may notify the obligor on an instrument to make payment to the secured party. U.C.C. §§ 9-502(1), **R9-607(a)(1)**. These provisions in no way vitiate any obligation that the party seeking to enforce the instrument may have to present it for payment or to surrender it when payment is received. Under the 1972 text, a secured party can collect a negotiable note that is part of chattel paper using the notification procedures described earlier in this subsection. **The revision provides that the obligor on such an instrument is not an account debtor. U.C.C. § R9-102(a)(3). Thus, the rules of Article 3 would govern collection.**

[184] Of course, any foreclosure sale of an intangible must meet the normal rules governing fore-closure sales generally (*e.g.*, notice and commercial reasonableness).

[185] Some franchise agreements preclude assignment entirely, which makes them unavailable as collateral under the 1972 text. Similar problems arise with government licenses. If the law governing a license precludes assignment, it cannot be used as collateral. Many licenses are assignable, however, but the licensing agency commonly must approve of the assignee. For example, in some states, a liquor license may be assigned if the licensing agency approves of the assignee. In such states, the secured party can privately sell the license to an approved purchaser.

Under revised Article 9, the fact that a franchise or license agreement prohibits the debtor from creating a security interest in the franchise or license (or makes such a transfer an event of default) does not prevent the security interest from having legal effect. U.C.C. § R9-408(a). Likewise, the fact that a statute or other rule of law purports to prohibit or restrict the debtor from creating a security interest in a license or permit, or requires government consent for such a transfer, does not prevent the security interest from taking effect. § R9-408(c). Nevertheless, the secured party is not entitled of right to enforce that security interest. § R9-408(d)(6). For example, Henning purchases a license for business software from Macrosoft, which license is nontransferrable without the prior written consent of Macrosoft. Henning later grants a security interest in all of its assets to Bank. Bank obtains a security interest in the software, despite the nontransferrability provision in the license; nevertheless, Bank cannot enforce the security interest against the software without the prior written consent of Macrosoft. Thus, Bank would be unable to enforce its security interest against Henning's computers (without risking liability to Macrosoft for conversion) without first removing the software from those computers.

§ 18.04 Strict Foreclosure — §§ 9-505, R9-620 -R9-622

Strict foreclosure is a straightforward method of foreclosure that can, in appropriate circumstances, benefit both the secured party and the debtor. A strict foreclosure is essentially a trade under which the secured party becomes the owner of the collateral without having to go through the normal sale processes.[186] In exchange, the obligation of the debtor — **or, under revised Article 9, perhaps some portion of that obligation** — is forgiven. The secured party is then free to resell the collateral, display it in the living room, or burn it on the back lot.

Under the 1972 text, strict foreclosure results in the complete satisfaction of the debtor's obligation.[187] Thus, if the secured party believes that a significant deficiency would remain after a foreclosure sale, and is willing to spend the resources necessary to pursue that deficiency, the secured party should opt to dispose of the collateral by sale. If, however, the secured party thinks that the collateral is worth as much as the debt (or more), or it has no intention of pursuing the debtor once the foreclosure is complete, strict foreclosure is an attractive alternative. This process releases the secured party from the procedural hassles that accompany an ordinary foreclosure and from any potential liability for failing to hold a commercially reasonable sale. **Under revised Article 9, the secured party in nonconsumer transactions may propose strict foreclosure of collateral in partial satisfaction of the obligation.[188] If the debtor effectively accepts**

---

[186] The normal foreclosure sale processes are discussed in § 18.02 *supra.*

[187] U.C.C. § 9-505(2)(secured party may retain collateral "in satisfaction of the obligation). Under the real property law of most states, a mortgagor and mortgagee can agree on the value of the property and the mortgagor can then give the mortgagee a deed in lieu of foreclosure. The mortgagee becomes the owner of the property and can then pursue the mortgagor for the amount of the debt less the agreed value of the property. The 1972 text does not appear to recognize "partial strict foreclosure." *See, e.g.,* U.C.C. § 9-505, Cmt. 1 (strict foreclosure involves "abandoning any claim for a deficiency").

Section 9-505(2) of the 1972 text does state that "notice [of a proposed strict foreclosure] shall be sent to the debtor if he has not signed after default a statement renouncing or modifying his rights *under this subsection*" (emphasis added). Although the most plausible construction of this provision is that the right to renounce or modify applies only to the notice requirement, one could argue that *any right* under the subsection, including the right to a full discharge, can be modified. Perhaps in reliance upon this language, a few courts have enforced freely negotiated partial strict foreclosures. *See, e.g.,* Northwest Acceptance Corp. v. Hesco Constr., Inc., 26 Wash. App. 823, 614 P.2d 1302, 30 U.C.C. Rep. Serv. 1487 (Wash. Ct. App. 1980); S.M. Flickinger Co., Inc. v. 18 Genesee Corp., 423 N.Y.S.2d 73, 71 A.D.2d 382, 27 U.C.C. Rep. Serv. 1232 (N.Y. 1979). Indeed, partial strict foreclosures should be approved, particularly in commercial settings. Once a default occurs and the secured party has repossessed, the parties are in a sufficiently adversarial relationship that any bargaining advantage that the secured party might otherwise have had is largely dissipated. If the secured party then offers a fair price for the collateral in lieu of foreclosure, the debtor should be able to accept it — after all, the alternative is a foreclosure sale, which may result in a sale price that is below the collateral's fair market value.

[188] U.C.C. § R9-620(a), (g). **In this case, the secured party's proposal should specify the amount of the secured obligation to be satisfied, or at least a means of calculating that amount.** *See* U.C.C. § R9-620 Cmt. 4. **Partial strict foreclosure is not available in consumer transactions. § R9-620(g).**

the secured party's proposal for partial strict foreclosure, the secured party may thereafter seek a deficiency judgment for the balance of the debtor's obligation. [189]

The secured party initiates strict foreclosure by making a "proposal" [190] to those parties who would have been entitled to notice of a foreclosure sale. [191] Under the 1972 text, if the secured party receives objection in writing from any of those parties within twenty-one days after the notice was sent, the secured party must dispose of the collateral by sale; absent such written objection, the secured party may keep the collateral in satisfaction of the debtor's obligation. [192] **Under the revision, if the secured party receives a timely authenticated notice of objection from any recipient of its proposal, or any other party holding a subordinate interest in the collateral, the secured party must dispose of the collateral by sale.** [193] A debtor should object if it believes that a foreclosure sale would generate a surplus for it. A successful strict foreclosure will also extinguish the lien of a junior secured party or lienholder, and thus the holder of

---

[189] U.C.C. § R9-620(c). **The debtor may accept the secured party's proposal for partial strict foreclosure only in a record authenticated after default.**

[190] Under the 1972 text, "proposal" is not defined; section 9-505(2) merely states that the secured party may "propose" to retain the collateral in satisfaction of the debt and must provide "written notice" of that proposal. U.C.C. § 9-505(2). **Under the revision, the term "proposal" is defined as an authenticated record that includes the terms upon which the secured party will accept the collateral in full or partial satisfaction of the debt. § R9-102(a)(66).**

[191] The parties entitled to notice are discussed in § 18.02[B][1] *supra*. Under the 1972 text, the secured party must notify the debtor (which includes both the owner of the collateral and anyone obligated on the debt) and, if the collateral is not consumer goods, any other secured parties that have previously given written notice of their interests. U.C.C. § 9-504(3). **Under the revision, the secured party must also search the public records and notify all secured parties or lienholders with perfected security interests in the collateral who had previously filed financing statements describing the collateral. § R9-611(c)(3)(B). In the event that the secured party proposes partial strict foreclosure, the secured party must also notify any secondary obligors on the debt. § R9-621(b).**

The decision to seek strict foreclosure rests with the secured party; the debtor cannot force the secured party to use strict foreclosure.

[192] U.C.C. §§ 9-505(2).

[193] U.C.C. § R9-620(a)(2). **Under § R9-620(d)(1), any party entitled to notice of the secured party's proposal must notify the secured party of its objection within 20 days after notice of the proposal was sent to it. Under § R9-620(d)(2), any other party entitled to object — such as a creditor holding a subordinate judgment lien — must notify the secured party of its objection within 20 days of the last notification given by the secured party or, if no such notifications were given, before the debtor consents to the proposal. For example, suppose Henning owns an automobile subject to a first priority security interest in favor of Freyermuth, a second priority security interest in favor of Lawrence, and a judgment lien in favor of Bruno. On February 1, Henning defaults to Freyermuth. On February 2, Freyermuth proposes in writing to accept the car in full satisfaction of Henning's obligation, sending notification of the proposal to Henning. Freyermuth sends notice of the proposal to Lawrence on February 5. Henning may object to Freyermuth's proposal until February 22. Lawrence and Bruno may object to the proposal until February 25. Even if Henning and Lawrence consent to the proposal, Freyermuth must still dispose of the collateral by sale if Bruno provides a timely objection.**

(Matthew Bender & Co., Inc.)

a junior interest should also object if a foreclosure sale could reasonably result in a surplus.[194]

The Code precludes the secured party from initiating strict foreclosure in certain cases involving consumer goods. The provision is predicated on the assumption that when the debtor has repaid 60% of the loan in a nonpurchase-money transaction or 60% of the cash price in a purchase-money transaction, the debtor likely has acquired sufficient equity to justify sale of the collateral in order to preserve that equity for the debtor's benefit.[195] A debtor who believes that this assumption is false and would prefer a strict foreclosure can waive this compulsory disposition requirement after default.[196]

Occasionally, a secured party that has no intention of initiating strict foreclosure holds the collateral for such an extended period of time that the debtor is able to claim that this conduct amounts to a "constructive strict foreclosure." In other words, the debtor argues that the secured party should be treated as having accepted the collateral in satisfaction of the debt. Constructive strict foreclosure is a fiction the courts interpreting the 1972 text have used from time to time to preclude the secured party from pursuing a deficiency judgment in particular cases. The doctrine is theoretically unsound, however, and less desirable than other methods of protecting the debtor from such creditor misconduct.[197] **Revised Article 9 abolishes constructive strict foreclosure.[198]**

The 1972 text requires that the secured party must be in possession of the collateral before it can initiate a strict foreclosure.[199] No convincing rationale underlies this requirement.[200] A secured party cannot "possess" intangible collateral like accounts and general intangibles, for example, yet the parties might desire strict foreclosure of such collateral in appropriate cases. The requirement seems misplaced even with tangible collateral. If the secured party becomes the owner of tangible collateral through strict foreclosure and the party in possession will not give it up, a replevin action is available. **In recognition of this critique, revised Article 9 has abolished the requirement that**

---

[194] The 1972 text did not explicitly state that strict foreclosure extinguished subordinate liens. Courts uniformly held that strict foreclosure did extinguish subordinate liens, however, either by analogizing strict foreclosure to a disposition by sale (which extinguished subordinate liens under § 9-504(4)) or by suggesting that the requirement to notify certain subordinate secured parties made sense only if their interests were at risk of extinguishment. **Revised Article 9 makes clear that strict foreclosure extinguishes the security interest being enforced and all subordinate interests in the collateral. U.C.C. § R9-622(a). Under the revision, strict foreclosure will extinguish subordinate interests even when the secured party fails to comply with its notification requirements; any party who was entitled to notification but did not receive it may seek damages caused by the secured party's noncompliance. §§ R9-622(b), R9-625(b).**

[195] U.C.C. §§ 9-505(1), **R9-620(e)**. *See* discussion in § 18.02[B][2] *supra.*

[196] U.C.C. §§ 9-505(1), **R9-624(b)**.

[197] The concept of constructive strict foreclosure is discussed in more detail in § 18.02[A][2] *supra.*

[198] *See* **U.C.C. § R9-620 Cmt. 5.**

[199] U.C.C. § 9-505(2).

[200] *See, e.g.*, II G. Gilmore, *Security Interests in Personal Property* § 44.3 at 1223 (1965) (one of reporters for original Article 9 unable to explain logic behind possession requirement).

the secured party have possession of the collateral before seeking strict foreclosure.[201]

§ 18.05   Redemption — §§ 9-506, R9-623

Under the 1972 text, any debtor (broadly defined)[202] and any secured party (senior or junior) with an interest in the collateral has the right to redeem the collateral.[203] **Under the revision, the right of redemption also extends to persons secondarily obligated on the debt and any party holding any junior or senior interest in the collateral (such as a judgment creditor).**[204] The U.C.C. does not allow post-sale redemption,[205] and therefore the party must exercise its right before the secured party has disposed of collateral, entered into a contract for its disposition, or acquired title by means of strict foreclosure.[206] To redeem the collateral, the party must tender "fulfillment of all obligations secured by the collateral" (including expenses reasonably incurred by the secured party in repossessing the collateral and preparing for disposition)[207] and, to the extent provided in the agreement and not prohibited by law, the secured party's reasonable attorney's fees and legal expenses.[208] The fact that the redeeming party must satisfy the entire indebtedness[209] plus costs makes the redemption provision of limited usefulness to debtors who are in default and usually in financial distress. The reality is that the right is more helpful to other secured parties than it is to debtors.

One of the major purposes underlying the Code's notice requirements is protection of the debtor's right of redemption, yet curiously the 1972 text does not require this right to be spelled out in the notice.[210] Other secured parties that receive a foreclosure notice should realize that the disposition will terminate their redemption rights, but the debtor is not as likely to be aware of this. A few courts have, therefore, read into the Code a requirement that the foreclosure notice advise the debtor of the right of redemption.[211] **Under the revision, the secured party in a consumer-goods transaction must include in the presale notification a telephone number from which the recipient may obtain**

---

[201] U.C.C. § R9-620 Cmt. 7. **If the collateral is consumer goods, however, the debtor may not effectively consent to the secured party's proposal while the collateral remains in the possession of the debtor. § R9-620(a)(3).**

[202] *See* discussion in § 18.02[B][1] *supra.*

[203] U.C.C. § 9-506.

[204] U.C.C. § R9-623(a); *see also* **§ R9-623 Cmt. 1.**

[205] The right to set aside a bad faith sale and then redeem the collateral from the purchaser is discussed in § 18.02[E] *supra.*

[206] U.C.C. §§ 9-506, **R9-623(c).**

[207] U.C.C. §§ 9-506, **R9-623(b)(1).**

[208] U.C.C. §§ 9-506, **R9-623(b)(2).**

[209] This full amount is based on the assumption that upon default, the secured party accelerated the maturity of future installments.

[210] The contents of the notice are set forth in § 18.02[B][3] *supra.*

[211] *See, e.g.,* Foster v. Knutson, 84 Wash. 2d 538, 527 P.2d 1108, 15 U.C.C. Rep. Serv. 1127 (1974). For a contrary decision, *see* Gaynor v. Union Trust Co., 216 Conn. 458, 582 A.2d 190, 13 U.C.C. Rep. Serv. 2d 1 (1990) (dictum indicating that secured party would have been liable had it voluntarily given incorrect information regarding the right of redemption).

information from the secured party regarding the amount necessary to redeem the collateral.[212]

Whether required to or not, many secured parties routinely advise debtors of their redemption rights, but doing so can create a trap for the careless creditor. In several cases, secured parties have provided inaccurate redemption information, and courts responded by concluding that the inaccuracy rendered the entire notice invalid. In *Moore v. Fidelity Financial Services, Inc.*,[213] for example, the secured party sent the debtor a notice of private sale that properly indicated the date *after which* the collateral would be sold. Unfortunately for the secured party, the notice went on to state that the collateral could be redeemed *until the specified date*. The correct rule is that the debtor can redeem until the disposition has actually occurred or the secured party has entered into a contract to dispose of the collateral; thus, the court felt that the notice could have misled the debtor into believing that he had less time to redeem than he actually had. This type of careful scrutiny by courts is understandable, as inaccurate information regarding redemption may have the effect of discouraging the debtor from seeking redemption. As a result, a creditor that chooses (or is required) to advise its debtor of the right of redemption must be sure to do so in an accurate manner.[214]

Generally speaking, any party with a right of redemption can waive that right after default in a signed writing **(or, under revised Article 9, by an authenticated agreement)**.[215] The only reason for doing so would be to facilitate an early sale of the collateral, and a secured party seeking a waiver of the right of redemption should make certain that the waiver also covers the debtor's right to be notified of the disposition.[216] **Revised Article 9 does not permit waiver of the right to redemption in a consumer-goods transaction.**[217]

---

[212] U.C.C. § **R9-614(1)**.

[213] 869 F. Supp. 557, 25 U.C.C. Rep. Serv. 2d 1306 (N.D. Ill. 1994).

[214] *See also* DiDominico v. First Nat'l Bank of Md., 57 Md. App. 62, 468 A.2d 1046, 37 U.C.C. Rep. Serv. 1427 (Md. Ct. App. 1984) (notice inaccurately informed debtor that redemption was limited to fifteen days).

[215] The right of redemption cannot be waived prior to default. *See* U.C.C. §§ 9-501(3)(d), **R9-602(11)**. *See also* Data Security, Inc. v. Plessman, 1 Neb. App. 659, 510 N.W.2d 361, 23 U.C.C. Rep. Serv. 2d 989 (Neb. Ct. App. 1993).

[216] The right to notice can also be waived after default in a signed writing **or authenticated agreement**. *See* U.C.C. §§ 9-504(3), 9-505(2), **R9-624(a), R9-624(b)**. A secured party that wants to consummate a quick sale should seek a waiver of both the right to notice and the right to redemption.

[217] U.C.C. § **R9-624(c)**.

CHAPTER 19

THE CONSEQUENCES OF CREDITOR MISBEHAVIOR

SYNOPSIS

§ 19.01　Overview

The preceding chapter dealt primarily with the rights and duties of secured parties during the foreclosure process. The focus of this chapter shifts to the consequences that befall a secured party when it fails to conform its conduct to the Code's requirements. Creditor misbehavior takes many forms, among them:

- Repossessing collateral even though there has not been an event of default;

- Repossessing collateral in a manner that constitutes a breach of the peace;[1]

---

[1] See § 18.01[A] supra.

- Failing to take one or more of the many steps necessary to ensure a commercially reasonable disposition of the collateral;[2]

- Failing to give proper notice of disposition (sometimes characterized as an aspect of commercial reasonableness);[3]

- Purchasing improperly at a private sale;[4]

- Failing to allow redemption;[5]

- Failing to use reasonable care to preserve collateral in its possession;[6]

- Failing to file a termination statement when required by the Code;[7] and

- Failing to respond to the debtor's request for a statement confirming the balance of the indebtedness or identifying the collateral.[8]

The most common complaints allege a failure to effect a commercially reasonable disposition (with all its myriad facets) and/or a failure to give proper notice. When the secured party fails to conform its conduct to the Code's requirements, Article 9 provides a variety of pre-and post-disposition remedies, each of which will be discussed below.

[A] Pre-Disposition Remedies

If the secured party was about to conduct a sale in a commercially unreasonable manner — for example, if the secured party gave notice of its intention to sell the collateral at an auction sale at 2:00 a.m. on a Sunday morning — the debtor might wish to seek a court order requiring the secured party to conduct the sale in a reasonable manner. The Comments to the 1972 text indicate that the drafters considered it critical for interested parties to have such pre-disposition remedies. The Comments state that when a secured party is about to proceed in a manner that is inconsistent with the Code's duties of good faith and commercial reasonableness,

it is vital both to the debtor and other creditors to provide a remedy for the failure to comply with the statutory duty. This remedy will be of particular importance when it is applied prospectively before the unreasonable disposition has been concluded. This section [section 9-507(1) of the 1972 text] therefore provides that a secured party proposing to dispose of collateral in an unreasonable manner, may, by court order, be restrained from doing so, and such an order might appropriately provide either that he proceed with the sale or other disposition under specified terms and conditions, or that the sale be made by a representative of creditors where insolvency proceedings have been instituted.[9]

---

2 *See* § 18.02[A] *supra.*

3 *See* § 18.02[B] *supra.*

4 *See* § 18.02[C] *supra.*

5 *See* § 18.05 *supra.*

6 *See* § 19.01[B][3] *infra.*

7 *See* § 19.01[B][4]; *infra.*

8 *See* § 19.01[B][5]; *infra.*

9 U.C.C. § 9-507 Cmt. 1; **see also** § R9-625 Cmt. 2.

To effectuate this concern, both section 9-507(1) of the 1972 text and **section R9-625(a) of the revision** authorize injunctive pre-disposition remedies. These remedies may be useful in the following situations:

1. When the secured party is planning a commercially unreasonable sale, such as a public auction of an asset that is so specialized that only a private sale will suffice, a court can issue a mandatory injunction requiring that the sale be conducted in accordance with terms and conditions dictated by the judge;

2. When the secured party has failed to give proper notice of sale, a court can issue a temporary restraining order prohibiting sale for a time that is sufficient to allow an aggrieved party (the debtor or another secured party) either to redeem or to prepare to protect its interests at the sale; and

3. When the secured party's repossession is wrongful because the debtor is not in default, the debtor should be able to recover the collateral through a replevin action.

In the first two situations, [10] the question arises whether the party seeking relief must demonstrate the presence of the normal equitable requirements for obtaining injunctive relief, most notably the requirement of showing irreparable injury if the relief is not granted. [11] Because most secured parties are financially solvent, the cases are rare in which the party seeking relief can make such a showing. Although the courts have split on the point, some authority supports the proposition that the party seeking relief need not meet the normal conditions for obtaining injunctive relief when the relief is authorized by statute. [12] Because of the importance that the drafters placed on the pre-disposition remedies and the limited intrusiveness of those remedies, the better-reasoned position is that the Code displaces the conditions normally found in equity. [13]

When there has been a default and the debtor's complaint is that the secured party's repossession breached the peace, replevin should not be available, [14] as the secured party still has the superior possessory interest even if it gained possession in an inappropriate manner. Returning the collateral to the debtor would not cure the default, and the secured party would simply repossess again. Damages are readily available to compensate the debtor in this situation.

---

[10] With regard to the third situation, the laws governing replevin actions typically specify the type of showing that the party seeking relief must make and the security it must provide.

[11] The other common requirements are that the party seeking relief post security for any harm caused by the court's order and demonstrate a probability of success on the merits.

[12] *See generally* D. Dobbs, *Law of Remedies* (2d ed.) § 2.10 (tendency is for courts to view statutory authorization of injunctive relief as substitute for irreparable injury rule).

[13] *See* U.C.C. § 1-103(unless displaced by particular Code provisions, Code is supplemented by principles of law and equity).

[14] *See, e.g.*, Clark v. Associates Commercial Corp., 820 F. Supp. 562, 21 U.C.C. Rep. Serv. 2d 860 (D. Kan. 1993) (temporary restraining order pending replevin inappropriate where debtor was in default but repossession breached the peace).

[B] Monetary Damages

What theories support a monetary recovery when a secured party engages in creditor misconduct? As a practical matter, the answer depends upon the type of misconduct involved.

[1] Wrongful Repossession

Section 9-507(1) of the 1972 text states that the secured party is liable for "any loss caused by a failure to comply with the provisions of this Part." This language authorizes the court to award damages in an amount sufficient to place the injured party in the position that it would have occupied had no violation occurred. In section 9-507(1), however, this language is part of a broader sentence that deals with problems arising during the "disposition" of collateral. A wrongful repossession is not a disposition [15] and thus is not governed by section 9-507(1).

If the secured party repossesses collateral in the mistaken belief that the debtor has defaulted, the debtor may choose to seek recovery of the goods *in specie* and sue for the tort of trespass to chattels. In such an action, the debtor may recover possession of the collateral, as well as damages for any harm done to the collateral and for the loss of its use while the collateral remains in the secured party's possession. [16] Alternatively, if the debtor does not want the collateral returned *in specie*, the debtor may allow the secured party to retain it and instead assert a claim for the intentional tort of conversion. [17] The standard measure of damages for conversion is the fair market value of the asset at the time of the conversion. [18] For example, suppose Freyermuth holds a security interest in Henning's automobile to secure a personal loan to Henning in the amount of $10,000. Wrongfully (but in good faith) believing Henning is in default, Freyermuth repossesses the car and conducts a commercially reasonable sale at which Lawrence purchases the car for $8,000 — $3,000 less than its actual fair market value of $11,000. Henning could sue to set aside the foreclosure sale and recover the automobile from Lawrence, [19] and could also sue Freyermuth for damages for any harm done to the automobile and for the loss of the automobile's use following repossession (*e.g.*, the amount required to lease a comparable vehicle). Alternatively, Henning could simply choose to sue Freyermuth for damages for conversion, and could recover damages from Freyermuth in the amount

---

[15] U.C.C. § 9-504(1)'s reference to "sale, lease or other disposition" suggests that disposition does not include the act of repossessing. Section 9-505(1) is even more direct, stating that "a secured party who has *taken possession* must *dispose*" of collateral (emphasis supplied). The clear inference is that taking possession and disposing are different concepts. For a case supporting this analysis, *see* Lee County Bank v. Winson, 444 So. 2d 459, 38 U.C.C. Rep. Serv. 682 (Fla. Dist. Ct. App. 1983).

[16] *See* Restatement (Second) of Torts § 222 Cmt. a.

[17] *See, e.g.*, Warren v. Ford Motor Credit Co., 693 F.2d 1373, 35 U.C.C. Rep. Serv. 306 (11th Cir. 1982).

[18] *See, e.g.*, Chemlease Worldwide, Inc. v. Brace, Inc., 338 N.W.2d 428, 37 U.C.C. Rep. Serv. 647 (Minn. 1983); Restatement (Second) of Torts § 222A Cmt. c (providing for recovery of "full value" of converted asset).

[19] If the debtor is not in default, the secured party cannot pass the debtor's rights in the collateral to the purchaser. U.C.C. §§ 9-504(4), **R9-617(a).**

of $1,000 — the $11,000 fair market value of the automobile less the $10,000 balance owed to Freyermuth.[20] In contrast, if the fair market value of the car had been only $9,000, Henning likely would raise the claim for conversion as a counterclaim to Freyermuth's suit for a deficiency judgment.[21]

Even though conversion is an intentional tort, courts typically refuse to allow a jury to assess punitive damages if a secured party acted in the mistaken but good faith belief that a default had occurred.[22] Although the standards vary somewhat from state to state, an award of punitive damages must be predicated on some type of egregious conduct by the secured party — either actual malicious conduct, or what courts have often called "constructive malice." Constructive malice typically consists of conduct that is reckless or grossly negligent. A case that comes close to the line is *Mitchell v. Ford Motor Credit Co.*,[23] in which the court approved an award of punitive damages following a wrongful repossession. The court concluded that the secured party was guilty of gross negligence because its records were in such a shambles that such incidents were bound to occur.

A debtor who claims wrongful repossession because the secured party committed a breach of the peace does not have a right to return of the goods *in specie*;[24] in such cases, the debtor may recover only monetary damages. In determining the theoretical basis for assessing damages, most courts simply treat the situation as analogous to a wrongful repossession without default and hold the secured party liable in conversion.[25] This is entirely appropriate and has the advantage of providing a uniform approach to all aspects of wrongful repossession. Courts may award punitive damages in cases of egregious conduct by the secured party.

Another situation in which courts have commonly used the concept of conversion is when a secured party refuses to accept a tender of the proper amount necessary to redeem the collateral.[26] The conversion approach is appropriate in this situation, because the secured party winds up in the same position it would have occupied had it repossessed in the absence of a default. A related problem occurs when the secured party miscalculates the amount necessary to redeem and demands an amount larger than that to which it is entitled. Again, damages in this situation are appropriately based upon conversion.[27]

---

[20] While the price received at a commercially reasonable sale is evidence of an asset's fair market value, it is not conclusive in that regard. *See* § 18.02 *supra.*

[21] *See* § 19.02 *infra.*

[22] *See, e.g.*, Oaklawn Bank v. Baldwin, 709 S.W.2d 91, 1 U.C.C. Rep. Serv. 2d 596 (Ark. 1986).

[23] 688 P.2d 42, 38 U.C.C. Rep. Serv. 1812 (Okla. 1984).

[24] *See, e.g.*, Clark v. Associates Commercial Corp., 820 F. Supp. 562, 21 U.C.C. Rep. Serv. 2d 860 (D. Kan. 1993).

[25] *See, e.g.*, Kinetics Technology Int'l Corp. v. Fourth Nat'l Bank of Tulsa, 705 F.2d 396, 36 U.C.C. Rep. Serv. 292 (10th Cir. 1983); Henderson v. Security Nat'l Bank, 72 Cal. App. 3d 764, 140 Cal. Rptr. 388, 22 U.C.C. Rep. Serv. 846 (1977). *But see* Nez v. Forney, 783 P.2d 471, 10 U.C.C. Rep. Serv. 2d 289 (N.M. 1989) (debtor's action for wrongful repossession sounded in contract).

[26] Redemption is discussed in § 18.05 *supra.*

[27] *See, e.g.*, Owens v. Automobile Recovery Bureau, Inc., 544 S.W.2d 26, 20 U.C.C. Rep. Serv. 820 (Mo. Ct. App. 1976).

Depending upon the nature of the secured party's conduct, liability may accrue for torts other than conversion, and the secured party may even face criminal sanctions in extreme cases. The cases are replete with instances of overbearing creditors who wrongfully entered another's property or roughed up someone who resisted repossession. On the civil side, this conduct may constitute trespass, assault, battery, or intentional infliction of emotional distress. On the criminal side, the secured party may be guilty of trespass, breach of the peace, assault, or battery.

As discussed above, section 9-507(1)'s damages remedy did not by its terms apply to wrongful repossession,[28] thus leaving the debtor to turn to tort law for relief. Revised Article 9, by contrast, provides that a secured party is liable for damages "in the amount of any loss caused by a failure to comply" with *any of its obligations under Article 9.*[29] Thus, a debtor injured by a wrongful repossession could seek to recover damages under section R9-625(b), and could recover the amount necessary to place the debtor in the position it would have occupied had no violation occurred.[30] Section R9-625(b) does not preclude the debtor from claiming a different measure of damages under tort law, however.[31]

For example, suppose that Freyermuth holds a security interest in Henning's car and repossesses the car by self-help following Henning's default. Freyermuth repossesses the car over Henning's objection, however, thereby breaching the peace. This conduct enables Freyermuth to obtain possession of the car one month sooner than he would have obtained it in a judicial proceeding. At the time of the repossession, Henning owes Freyermuth $10,000 and the car's fair market value is $15,000. Freyermuth proceeds to conduct a commercially reasonable foreclosure sale at which Lawrence purchases the car for $10,000. On what theories can Henning recover damages, and in what amount?

If Henning chooses to proceed under section R9-625, the appropriate measure of damages would be the amount reasonably calculated to put Henning in the position he would have occupied had Freyermuth complied with Article 9 and sought judicial repossession — *i.e.*, Henning would have had possession and use of the car for another month. Thus, under R9-625, Henning could recover the value of one month's use of the car, which may be no more than a few hundred dollars. As a result, on these facts Henning should instead raise a conversion claim, upon which he could recover damages in the amount of $5,000 (the car's fair market value less the balance of the debt owed to Freyermuth). In contrast, if the fair market value of the car had been only $10,000 at the time of repossession, Henning might instead choose to proceed under section R9-625(b), thereby allowing him to recover the lost value of one month's use of the car. Under either approach, the court could award

---

[28] *See* note 15 and accompanying text *supra.*

[29] U.C.C. § R9-625(b).

[30] *See* U.C.C. § 1-106; *see also* U.C.C. § R9-625 Cmt. 3.

[31] *Id. See also* U.C.C. § 1-103(unless specifically displaced, principles of law and equity supplement the Code's provisions).

punitive damages, if appropriate, for Freyermuth's willful refusal to honor Henning's objection.[32]

[2]   Wrongful Disposition of the Collateral

When an aggrieved party seeks damages on account of the secured party's conduct in disposing of the collateral, section 9-507(1) **and revised section R9-625(b)** directly apply, authorizing the aggrieved party to recover the damages that flow from the secured party's conduct.[33] In measuring the aggrieved party's damages, one must look to the Code's general damages provision, which states that "[t]he remedies provided by this Act shall be liberally administered to the end that the aggrieved party may be put in as good a position as if the other party had fully performed but neither consequential or special nor penal damages may be had except as specifically provided in this Act or by other rule of law."[34] When the aggrieved party seeks damages under this provision, recovery of consequential damages (such as damages for emotional distress) is limited by the high foreseeability standards of general contract law. Furthermore, the aggrieved party typically cannot recover punitive damages unless it can state a tort claim for trespass, conversion, intentional infliction of emotional distress or the like.[35]

A number of courts interpreting the 1972 text have concluded that section 9-507(1) sounds in tort; that is, it is predicated on the concept of conversion.[36] This conclusion is undercut by the Code's general remedial scheme as set forth above. It is also inconsistent with the plain language of section 9-505(2) of the 1972 text, which states that, in some circumstances, a secured party that fails to dispose of consumer collateral within 90 days is liable, at the debtor's option, "in conversion or under Section 9-507(1) on secured party's liability." **The comments to revised Article 9 also reject the view that the Code's remedial provisions sound in tort.**[37]

The fact that the Code's remedial provision does not sound in tort does not mean that it displaces the availability of conversion as an alternative remedy.[38] There are sound policy reasons for permitting recovery using a conversion measure in certain situations, especially in cases where the misconduct involves a failure to give proper notice to the debtor. Debtors rarely redeem collateral or take steps to protect their interests at foreclosure sales; thus, a failure to give notice is not likely to have an impact on the price received at the sale. Allowing only the Code's remedial provision (section 9-507(1) **or revised**

---

[32] U.C.C. § 1-106(1) generally does not permit punitive damages, but the court may award punitive damages where they are authorized by another rule of law, such as the law of conversion. **The comments to section R9-625 make clear that underlying principles of tort law, such as the law of conversion, supplement the remedies provided in section R9-625. § R9-625 Cmt. 3.**

[33] U.C.C. §§ 9-507(1), **R9-625(b).**

[34] U.C.C. § 1-106(1). **See also § R9-625 Cmt. 3.**

[35] *See* note 32 *supra.*

[36] *See, e.g.,* Chemical Sales Co. v. Diamond Chem. Co., 766 F.2d 364 (8th Cir. 1985).

[37] **U.C.C. § R9-625 Cmt. 3.**

[38] U.C.C. § 1-106(1). *See also* **§ R9-625 Cmt. 3** (debtor is not precluded from claiming a different measure of damages in tort).

section R9-625(b)) as a basis for recovery would, in such circumstances, yield no damages. Such a result would provide secured parties with relatively little incentive to make systematic efforts to comply with their obligations under Article 9.[39] Allowing debtors the alternative remedy of conversion, however, presents secured parties with a more meaningful risk that a court might award damages and thus may have a more significant *in terrorem* effect upon secured parties.[40]

The difference between damages based upon conversion and damages based upon the Code's remedial provision is illustrated neatly by the facts of *Schrock v. Citizens Valley Bank*,[41] in which the secured party conducted an auction sale in a commercially unreasonable manner. The auction produced only $143,000, but expert testimony indicated that a commercially reasonable auction would have produced $170,000 — roughly 85% of the collateral's $200,000 fair market value. Using the Code's remedial provision, the court should place the debtor "in as good a position as if the [secured] party had fully performed," and full performance in this context means a commercially reasonable auction. Thus, assuming that the debt in *Schrock* was $150,000, the Code's remedial scheme would entitle the debtor to recover damages of $20,000 — the surplus that would have been produced by a commercially reasonable sale. If the debtor proceeded in conversion, however, the debtor could recover damages of $50,000 — the fair market value of the collateral less the balance of the secured debt.[42]

[3] Failure to Use Reasonable Care Regarding Collateral in Secured Party's Possession

Both the 1972 text **and the revision** obligate the secured party to use reasonable care in the custody and preservation of collateral in its possession.[43] If the secured party fails to satisfy this obligation, any aggrieved party may recover damages for "any loss" caused by such failure.[44]

[4] Failure to File or Send Termination Statement

The Code permits the debtor to request that the secured party send to the debtor for filing (or, in the case of consumer goods, file) a termination statement terminating the effectiveness of a financing statement in any case when there remains no outstanding obligation and no commitment by the secured party to make subsequent advances, incur obligations, or otherwise give value to be secured by the collateral described in that

---

[39] Even if it does not lead to measurable damages, failure to give notice can have a profound effect on the secured party's right to a deficiency judgment. *See* discussion in § 19.02 *infra.*

[40] *But see* Kennedy v. Fournie, 898 S.W.2d 672, 26 U.C.C. Rep. Serv. 2d 640 (Mo. Ct. App. 1995) (debtor was not entitled to conversion damages for failure to give proper notice since secured party was entitled to possession).

[41] 49 Or. App. 1083, 621 P.2d 96, 30 U.C.C. Rep. Serv. 1169 (Or. Ct. App. 1980).

[42] The effect of such misconduct on a secured party's claim for a deficiency is discussed in § 19.02 *infra.*

[43] U.C.C. §§ 9-207(1), **R9-207(a).** The debtor and secured party may define in the security agreement what shall constitute "reasonable care," so long as the standards are not "manifestly unreasonable." §§ 9-501(3), **R9-603(a).**

[44] U.C.C. §§ 9-207(3), **R9-625(b).**

financing statement.[45] When the collateral is consumer goods, the Code obligates the secured party to file such a termination statement within one month even without the debtor's request.[46] If the secured party fails to satisfy its obligation in a timely fashion, the secured party is liable for any loss caused by its failure, *plus* a minimum statutory penalty in the amount of $100 (**increased by the revision to $500**).[47]

[5] Failure to Provide Statement of Account or List of Collateral

Article 9 permits the debtor to request that the secured party issue a statement setting forth or confirming the outstanding balance of the debtor's unpaid obligation to the secured party. In addition, Article 9 permits the debtor to request that the secured party approve or correct a list of the secured party's collateral.[48] Such statements are important to the debtor's ability to obtain subsequent financing or its ability to refinance the secured obligations, as future secured parties likely will seek to confirm the extent of encumbrances against the debtor's assets. Article 9 obligates the secured party to respond to the debtor's request in a timely fashion;[49] if the secured party fails to comply, the secured party is liable for any resulting loss.[50] Such loss could include, for example, the debtor's inability to obtain alternative financing or the increased costs of such financing.[51] **Furthermore, under revised Article 9, the debtor may recover (in addition to its actual damages) statutory damages of $500 if the secured party fails to comply with such a request without reasonable cause.**[52]

§ 19.02 Secured Party's Right to Deficiency Judgment

[A] The 1972 Text

Claims of creditor misconduct commonly arise when a secured party whose foreclosure failed to satisfy its debt seeks a judgment for the remaining deficiency. The secured party's right to recover a deficiency arises from section 9-504(2), which states that the secured party must account to the debtor for any surplus and "is liable for any deficiency."[53] The secured party's failure to observe Article 9's disposition rules, however, renders the secured party liable for any resulting loss under section 9-507(1). Reading these two provisions together, the Code scheme under the 1972 text seems straightforward — the secured party may recover any deficiency, subject to the amount

---

[45] U.C.C. §§ 9-404(1)(ten days following written demand), **R9-513(c) (twenty days following receipt of authenticated demand)**.

[46] U.C.C. §§ 9-404(1), **R9-513(a)**.

[47] U.C.C. §§ 9-404(1), **R9-625(e)(4)**.

[48] U.C.C. §§ 9-208(1), **R9-210(b)**.

[49] U.C.C. §§ 9-208(2)(secured party must respond within "two weeks"), **R9-210(b) (secured party must respond within "fourteen days")**.

[50] U.C.C. §§ 9-208(2), **R9-625(b)**.

[51] U.C.C. § **R9-625(b)makes this point explicitly.**

[52] U.C.C. § **R9-625(f). If the recipient of a request never claimed any interest in the collateral or the obligations referenced in the request, the recipient has reasonable cause for its failure to comply.** *Id.*

[53] U.C.C. § 9-504(2).

of that deficiency being reduced by any actual losses attributable to the secured party's misconduct. A court following this approach would calculate independently the amount due to each party and then "net out" the results, leaving a judgment in favor of one of the litigants. Under this approach, a secured party's misbehavior neither bars a deficiency nor creates a presumption of harm to the debtor. The secured party bears the burden of proving the facts that support its claim, whereas the debtor bears the burden of proving that the misconduct has caused it to suffer a loss.[54]

Using a variant on the facts of the *Schrock* case discussed in the previous subsection,[55] suppose that the outstanding debt is $225,000, that the secured party's commercially unreasonable auction yields $150,000, that a reasonable auction would have produced $170,000, and that the collateral's fair market value is $200,000. The secured party is entitled to a judgment on its claim for a $75,000 deficiency, calculated as its debt ($225,000) less the proceeds of its sale ($150,000). In turn, if the debtor raises a counterclaim under section 9-507(1), the debtor may recover damages of $20,000 — the amount that secured party would have received had it conducted a commercially reasonable sale ($170,000) less the actual sale proceeds ($150,000). When the claims are netted out, the secured party may recover a judgment for $55,000. If the debtor instead raises a counterclaim based on the theory of conversion,[56] it would be entitled to recover damages of $50,000 — the collateral's fair market value ($200,000) less the amount actually received ($150,000). Thus, after netting the claims, the secured party could recover a deficiency judgment for $25,000.[57]

Despite this straightforwardness of this "netting" approach and its consistency with the language of sections 9-504(2) and 9-507(1), very few courts have adopted it. Instead, courts interpreting the 1972 text generally have applied one of two other rules of decision — the "absolute bar" rule or the "rebuttable presumption" rule. These approaches are discussed in the following subsections.

[1] The Absolute Bar Rule

A number of courts have concluded that a secured party that violates its obligations in disposing of the collateral may not recover a deficiency judgment. This approach — generally known as the "absolute bar" rule — has two primary advantages. First, the rule is very simple and courts can apply it easily; there is no need for courts to make difficult factual judgments about what sale price the secured party might have obtained at a commercially reasonable sale. Second, the rule has significant *in terrorem* effect upon secured parties, for whom it provides a clear message: Comply with Article 9's obligations or lose your right to a deficiency judgment. To the extent that compliance

---

54 *See, e.g.,* Boender v. Chicago N. Clubhouse Ass'n, Inc., 608 N.E.2d 207, 20 U.C.C. Rep. Serv. 2d 687 (Ill. Ct. App. 1992).

55 *See* text accompanying note 41 *supra.* The numbers have been changed to make the math easier (like many students, the authors did not go to law school because of their proficiency in math).

56 *See* discussion in § 19.02[B] *infra.*

57 If the value of the debtor's claim exceeded the value of the secured party's claim, using whatever measure the court deemed appropriate, the debtor would be entitled to an affirmative recovery.

with Article 9 results in reasonable sales that generate higher sale prices, one might argue that an absolute bar rule is consistent with the best interest of debtors generally.

Despite its simplicity, however, many have argued that the absolute bar rule is misguided as a matter of commercial policy. In many cases, application of the absolute bar rule provides debtors with inappropriate windfalls. For example, suppose that a secured party deliberately makes an undersecured loan — that is, the collateral is insufficient to satisfy the debt. In this situation, the parties undoubtedly realize that the debtor would likely face a deficiency judgment even if the secured party complied perfectly with Article 9. Nevertheless, application of the absolute bar rule in this situation would wipe out even the *unsecured* portion of the debt.

Another example of the rule's inequity appears in *Gateway Aviation, Inc. v. Cessna Aircraft Co.*[58] In *Gateway Aviation*, an undersecured creditor (owed roughly $225,000) scheduled and properly noticed an auction sale that brought a high bid of $130,000. The secured party could have accepted this bid and recovered a $95,000 deficiency, but instead chose to abandon the sale because it felt that the bid was too low. The secured party then sought out a private buyer who agreed to pay $134,000. Unfortunately, the secured party failed to send the debtor notice of the private sale. The Missouri Court of Appeals held that the secured party could not recover a deficiency judgment because it had not strictly complied with the Code's notice rules. Thus, even though the secured party acted in good faith and its conduct actually had the effect of increasing the sale price of the collateral, its deficiency claim was entirely wiped out.

Further, some have argued that the absolute bar rule's consequences may have the effect of causing secured parties to be *excessively* cautious in conducting foreclosure sales. For example, a secured party that anticipates a significant deficiency may choose to run twelve notices advertising the sale, although six would be sufficient under the circumstances — in order to make its conduct look more "reasonable" and thus protect its right to recover a deficiency following the sale. Because the secured party typically adds these expenses to the balance of the debt, such expenses could actually have the effect of increasing the deficiency judgment if the additional expenses were not offset by a greater increase in the eventual sale price.[59] Thus, some have argued that the absolute bar rule, although a boon to the individual debtor entitled to raise it, may not be in the best interest of debtors as a class.[60]

Ultimately, the absolute bar rule finds no support in the 1972 text.[61] Further, it is inconsistent with the policy of placing an aggrieved party in the same economic position

---

[58] 577 S.W.2d 860, 25 U.C.C. Rep. Serv. 901 (Mo. Ct. App. 1978).

[59] The Code only allows the secured party to deduct the expenses of sale, such as the costs of advertising the sale, if those expenses are "reasonable." U.C.C. §§ 9-504(1), **R9-615(a)(1)**. Theoretically, then, a court could disallow the secured party any deduction for the cost of the additional advertisments. Except in the most egregious circumstances, however, courts would be hesitant to disallow a deduction for the cost of advertisements. If courts routinely disallowed such expenses, that could have the negative effect of discouraging secured parties from aggressively advertising foreclosure sales.

[60] *See* Robert M. Lloyd, *The Absolute Bar Rule in UCC Foreclosure Cases: A Prescription for Waste*, 40 UCLA L. Rev. 695 (1993).

[61] Although the absolute bar rule finds no support in the 1972 text, it was a common remedy

it would have occupied absent misbehavior. The rule is punitive in nature,[62] yet section 1-106(1) states that a party may not recover punitive damages except as provided in the Code or other rule of law.[63] The drafters were well aware of the absolute bar rule and chose not to adopt it. As a result, courts should respect that choice.

[2] The Rebuttable Presumption Rule

Many courts (perhaps a slight majority) have refused to follow the absolute bar rule, but have also refused to require that the debtor bear the burden of going forward with evidence that the secured party's misconduct caused a loss. These courts have employed a rule known as the "rebuttable presumption" rule.[64] Under this rule, once the debtor shows that the secured party violated Article 9's requirements in disposing of the collateral, the court draws a presumption that the collateral's value equals the outstanding debt. In other words, the court establishes a presumption that a proper disposition would have generated sale proceeds exactly sufficient to satisfy the debt. Effectively, this presumption places upon the secured party the burden of going forward with evidence to the contrary — *i.e.*, the secured party must produce evidence that even a sale in compliance with all of Article 9's requirements would still have resulted in a deficiency judgment. If the secured party cannot rebut the presumption, it cannot recover a judgment for the deficiency. If the secured party successfully rebuts the presumption, the secured party may recover a judgment unless the debtor successfully refutes the secured party's evidence.[65]

---

under one of the Code's predecessors, the Uniform Conditional Sales Act (UCSA). Commentators have argued convincingly, however, that cases decided under the UCSA do not support a modern absolute bar rule because they were predicated upon specific language in the UCSA. *See* R. Hillman, J. McDonald & S. Nickles, *Common Law and Equity Under the UCC*, ¶ 26.02[4][a], at 26-18 to 26-27.

[62] *See, e.g.*, All Valley Acceptance Co. v. Durfey, 800 S.W.2d 672, 13 U.C.C. Rep. Serv. 2d 1376 (Tex. Ct. App. 1991) (fact that absolute bar rule is punitive does not render it unconstitutional). *But see* Wilmington Trust Co. v. Conner, 415 A.2d 773, 28 U.C.C. Rep. Serv. 900 (Del. 1980) (absolute bar rule not punitive; compliance with foreclosure rules operates as condition precedent to recovery of deficiency).

[63] As indicated in § 19.01[B] *supra*, an argument can be made that U.C.C. § 9-507(1) co-exists with a remedy grounded in the independent tort of conversion. Though this analysis may provide a theoretical justification for the absolute bar rule in that punitive damages can be predicated on a conversion, applying an absolute bar rule is the equivalent of assessing punitive damages *in every case* in which a deficiency is sought. This is inconsistent with the normal approach to punitive damages, in which the fact-finder assesses whether the misconduct occurred in good faith or was, instead, actually or constructively malicious. *See* § 19.01[B] *supra.*

[64] The rebuttable presumption rule is sometimes called the "*Norton* presumption" because the seminal case in this area was Norton v. National Bank of Commerce of Pine Bluff, 240 Ark. 143, 398 S.W.2d 538, 3 U.C.C. Rep. Serv. 119 (1966). *See also* First Fla. Bank, N.A. v. Howard, 604 So. 2d 1286, 19 U.C.C. Rep. Serv. 2d 681 (Fla. Dist. Ct. App. 1992).

The rebuttable presumption rule derives from a corollary to the normal rule that a party pleading a fact has the burden of establishing that fact. *See* McCormick's Handbook on the Law of Evidence § 337 (3d ed. E. Cleary 1984). The corollary is that "where the facts with regard to an issue lie peculiarly within the knowledge of a party, that party has the burden of proving the issue." *Id.* at 950.

[65] The debtor bears the ultimate burden of persuasion on the issue of loss.

The mechanics of the rebuttable presumption rule can be seen by considering again the (modified) facts of the *Schrock* case.[66] Again, assume that the secured party conducts a commercially unreasonable auction that produces a $150,000 sale price to be applied against an outstanding debt of $225,000. Under the absolute bar rule, the secured party could not recover any deficiency. Under the rebuttable presumption rule, however, the debtor would start with the benefit of a presumption that the collateral was worth $225,000 (the full amount of the debt). The secured party would have to produce evidence to rebut the presumption. If the court applied the Code's remedial provisions, the secured party must present evidence tending to prove that a commercially reasonable auction still would have resulted in a deficiency. Thus, if the secured party presents expert testimony that a commercially reasonable sale would have produced a price of $170,000, and the factfinder determines this testimony sufficiently credible, the secured party may recover a judgment in the amount of $55,000. If the court instead proceeded upon a conversion theory, the secured party would have to produce evidence tending to prove that the fair market value of the collateral was less than the amount of the debt. Thus, if the secured party proved that the fair market value of the collateral was only $200,000, the secured party could recover a $25,000 deficiency judgment.

A few courts have concluded that they may address creditor misconduct under either the absolute bar rule or the rebuttable presumption rule, depending upon the circumstances. In Iowa, for example, courts may determine whether to use the absolute bar rule or the rebuttable presumption rule based on the facts and circumstances of each case.[67] In Maine, courts have applied the absolute bar rule in cases involving a secured party's failure to give notice, but have adopted the rebuttable presumption rule for other types of misconduct.[68]

[B]   Revised Article 9

In response to widespread criticism of the absolute bar rule, revised Article 9 expressly adopts the rebuttable presumption rule *for all nonconsumer transactions.* When the secured party seeks a deficiency judgment, it does not have to establish compliance with the Code's requirements as part of its prima facie case.[69] If the debtor or secondary obligor raises the secured party's noncompliance as an issue, the secured party must prove that the disposition complied with the Code's requirements.[70] If the secured party fails to carry this burden, then a presumption arises that a sale in compliance with the Code's requirements would have produced a sale price sufficient to satisfy the outstanding debt. The secured party may not recover a deficiency unless it proves that a sale in compliance with the Code's requirements would have produced a sale price less than the balance of the debt.[71]

---

[66] *See* discussion in §§ 19.01[B] and 19.02 *supra.*

[67] *See, e.g.*, Knierem v. First State Bank, 488 N.W.2d 454, 19 U.C.C. Rep. Serv. 2d 683 (Iowa Ct. App. 1992).

[68] ROC-Century Assocs. v. Giunta, 658 A.2d 223, 27 U.C.C. Rep. Serv. 2d 1091 (Me. 1995).

[69] U.C.C. § R9-626(a)(1).

[70] U.C.C. § R9-626(a)(2).

[71] U.C.C. § R9-626(a)(3), (4).

In *consumer transactions*, however, revised Article 9 does not provide a specific rule to govern the consequences of a secured party's noncompliance. Section R9-626(b) provides that Article 9 "is intended to leave to the court the determination of the proper rules in consumer transactions" and permits courts in consumer transactions "to apply established approaches."[72] Thus, courts would retain the discretion to choose to apply either the "netting out" rule, the absolute bar rule, or the rebuttable presumption rule in consumer transactions.

§ 19.03 The Consumer Penalty — §§ 9-507(1), R9-625(c)

In addition to authorizing pre-and post-disposition remedies, the Code contains a provision that is sometimes called the "consumer penalty." When a secured party fails to comply with Article 9 in disposing of consumer goods, the Code permits the debtor **or a secondary obligor** to recover "in any event an amount not less than the credit service charge plus 10 percent of the principal amount of the debt or the time price differential plus 10 percent of the cash price."[73] Because this provision is appended onto Article 9's basic damages provision and establishes an amount recoverable "in any event," one should read the consumer penalty as a substitute for ordinary monetary damages. If the consumer cannot establish loss in the ordinary manner, or if the amount of that loss is less than the consumer penalty, the consumer may recover the penalty *rather than* ordinary damages. In other words, the section functions to a certain extent as a liquidated damages provision;[74] the consumer could not recover both actual damages and the full amount of the consumer penalty.

Calculating the amount of the consumer penalty can be tricky because there are two basic formulas. Understanding which formula to use requires an appreciation for the difference between a credit service charge (which is the equivalent of interest on a loan) and a time-price differential.

At the time the Code was first adopted, several jurisdictions had statutes or constitutional provisions establishing restrictive usury laws. For example, suppose that a state's law allowed for a maximum interest rate of 10%. If a debtor went to a bank to borrow money to buy a car, the bank could not charge interest at a higher rate. Though these restrictions were popular in many states, they had a negative impact upon some sectors of the economy in those states. For example, if a national automotive concern that sold cars to consumers on secured credit could not obtain a competitive interest rate in a particular state, it might choose to do business in another state. Recognizing this economic reality, some courts came up with the fiction of the time-price differential. If, in our 10% state, a seller was willing to sell an asset for $10,000 today but had to be repaid $11,500 in installments over the course of a year, these courts reasoned that the $1,500 difference

---

[72] U.C.C. § R9-626(b).

[73] U.C.C. §§ 9-507(1), **R9-625(c)(2)**. Other aggrieved parties (such as a junior secured party) may recover damages under the Code's general remedial provision [§§ 9-507(1) **or R9-625(b)**], but may not rely upon the consumer penalty.

[74] Indeed, the provision appears to serve both a punitive and a liquidated damages function, concepts that are antithetical in normal contract law. The term "consumer penalty" is thus something of a misnomer.

was not interest and therefore was not subject to the usury laws. It was, instead, a time-price differential. In other words, the time-price differential was simply a means to avoid the impact of the usury laws.

The following hypothetical situations illustrate the differences in the formulas contained in the consumer penalty. Suppose Henning, a consumer, decides to purchase a car priced at $25,000. Henning intends to pay $5,000 down and finance $20,000, and has a choice of having Dealer or Bank handle the financing. If Henning borrows $20,000 from Bank to be repaid over four years and the total interest Bank will receive over the life of the loan is $4,000, the consumer penalty that Bank must pay if it engages in misconduct will be $6,000 — the sum of $2,000 (ten percent of the principal amount of the debt) and $4,000 (the credit service charge).

If Henning had decided to finance the $20,000 with Dealer and had agreed to repay a total of $24,000 over four years, the consumer penalty would be $4,000 (the time-price differential) plus ten percent of the cash price. But would the "cash price" be the cash amount that Henning had to pay Dealer to buy the car without any financing ($25,000), or the amount financed ($20,000)? It is tempting to say that $20,000 is the proper amount, because this equates the penalties for sellers and lenders. The problem is that the Code also uses the term "cash price" in its strict foreclosure provision [75] and, in that context, it almost certainly means the full price that would have been paid on the date of sale (in the example, $25,000). [76]

After grasping the basic formula, one may apply the consumer penalty as the drafters envisioned it in a relatively straightforward fashion. For example, suppose that in the above hypothetical, Henning chose to finance the car from Bank. Suppose further that Bank conducts a commercially unreasonable sale, bringing a price of $8,000 and leaving a deficiency of $8,000. As discussed above, Bank would incur a $6,000 penalty because of its misconduct. Henning could assert a counterclaim for his actual damages or, in the alternative, base his counterclaim on the consumer penalty. If the actual damages, however calculated, are less than $6,000, Henning will choose the penalty, resulting in a $2,000 deficiency for Bank. If instead the unreasonable sale had brought a price of $11,000, leaving a deficiency of $5,000, Henning could recover a judgment for $1,000.

This straightforward approach becomes more complex in jurisdictions that have adopted either the absolute bar rule or the rebuttable presumption rule. [77] For example, suppose that the above transaction occurs in a rebuttable-presumption state and Bank's unreasonable sale produces $8,000, leaving a deficiency of $8,000. If Bank cannot overcome the presumption that the car was worth the same amount as the debt, Bank cannot recover a deficiency judgment. Should Henning be allowed to obtain a judgment for the

---

[75] U.C.C. §§ 9-505(1), **R9-620(e)**.

[76] Because the purpose of the limitation on strict foreclosure is to protect the debtor's equity, whereas the purpose of the consumer penalty is (at least in part) to penalize creditor misbehavior, one might argue that it is appropriate to assign different meanings to the same term in these different contexts. This argument is subject to criticism, however — the consumer penalty also serves to protect the equity of consumer debtors generally, by encouraging consumer creditors to conduct reasonable sales.

[77] These approaches are discussed in § 19.02[A] and [B] *supra.*

$6,000 consumer penalty? The answer should be no. The effect of the presumption is to establish the loss flowing from the misconduct; on our facts, the loss is presumed to be $8,000. Because the consumer penalty is an alternative to damages, allowing Henning to recover it would violate the spirit of the Code.[78]

The same approach holds true for jurisdictions that have adopted the absolute bar rule. The debtor should not be able to avoid a deficiency entirely and then recover the consumer penalty, since this would be adding a penalty on top of a penalty. The debtor should be required to elect between the absolute bar rule and the result that would be reached by netting out the claimed deficiency against the consumer penalty. Unfortunately, not all courts have understood that the consumer penalty should be viewed only as an alternative method of measuring damages. In *Wilmington Trust Co. v. Conner*,[79] for example, the court applied the absolute bar rule to deny the secured party's deficiency claim and then allowed the debtor to recover the consumer penalty. The case is wrongly decided.[80]

In the revision, the drafters could have clarified the proper role of the consumer penalty in consumer-goods transactions. Unfortunately, the drafters failed to resolve the confusion fostered by cases like *Wilmington Trust Co. v. Conner*; the comments to section R9-625 "[Section R9-625(c)(2)] leaves the treatment of statutory damages as it was under former Article 9."[81] Although the drafters did not intend this language to reflect their approval of cases like *Wilmington Trust Co. v. Conner*, some courts may use the comments to justify allowing debtors in consumer-goods transactions to recover both actual damages and the consumer penalty (or to assert the benefit of the absolute bar rule and still recover the consumer penalty).[82]

---

[78] If Bank's unreasonable sale produced a price of $11,000, leaving a deficiency of $5,000, and Bank could not overcome the presumption, Henning would have a choice of taking the presumed $5,000 in damages (wiping out the deficiency) or the $6,000 consumer penalty. Obviously, Henning would select the consumer penalty, but the court should net this out against the full deficiency. In other words, Henning should recover $1,000.

[79] 415 A.2d 773, 28 U.C.C. Rep. Serv. 900 (Del. 1980).

[80] For a case that gets the issue right, *see* First City Bank-Farmers Branch v. Guex, 659 S.W.2d 734, 37 U.C.C. Rep. Serv. 1008 (Tex. Ct. App. 1983).

[81] U.C.C. § R9-625 Cmt. 4.

[82] Recall that under section R9-626(b), a court may (but is not required to) choose to apply the absolute bar rule in consumer transactions.

CHAPTER 20

THE TRANSITION TO REVISED ARTICLE 9

SYNOPSIS

§ 20.01   Introduction

Given the breadth of the changes wrought by the revision, the drafters were concerned that if the 1972 text remained in effect in some jurisdictions while the 1998 text took effect in others, "horrendous complications" might arise.[1] Accordingly, the states are being asked to enact section R9-701, which contains a deferred effective date of July 1, 2001. The hope is that virtually all states will have adopted the revision by then and that the entire system can come "on line" at one time. The Comments express the concern that "[a]ny one State's failure to adopt the uniform effective date will greatly increase the cost and uncertainty surrounding the transition."[2]

---

[1] U.C.C. § R9-701 Cmt.

[2] *Id.*

Even if revised Article 9 becomes effective in every state at the same time there will be difficult transitional problems. For example, the revision expands the scope of Article 9 to cover transactions that previously were left to other law. How will the revision affect such a transaction that is already in effect on July 1, 2001? Further, how will the revision affect transactions entered into under the 1972 text? If the perfection rules for such transactions are changed by the revision, will secured parties have to reperfect under the revision's rules or will they remain perfected if they complied with current law? Changes in priority rules and in choice-of-law rules will create similar problems. Part 7 of the 1998 text addresses issues that will inevitably arise from the transition. Its provisions are discussed in the ensuing subsections. The discussion assumes that the revision will become effective in every state on its deferred effective date of July 1, 2001.

§ 20.02 Application of Revised Article 9 to Pre-Effective-Date Transactions and Liens — § R9-702

Revised Article 9's expanded scope provision covers transactions that were not within the scope of the 1972 text. Examples include agricultural liens, sales of payment intangibles and promissory notes, and security interests in commercial tort claims. If such a transaction is in effect on July 1, 2001, will it continue to be governed by the law under which it was created or will it be governed by the revision? The answer is that both laws will apply.

The general rule is that revised Article 9 will apply to a transaction or lien within its scope even if the transaction or lien was created before July 1, 2001.[3] However, section R9-702(b) contains a savings clause for transactions and liens that arose under law other than the 1972 text of Article 9. That section states in its entirety:

(b) Except as otherwise provided in subsection (c) and Sections [R]9-703 through [R]9-708:

(1) transactions and liens that were not governed by former Article 9, were validly entered into or created before this Act takes effect, and would be subject to this Act if they had been entered into or created after this Act takes effect, and the rights, duties, and interests flowing from those transactions and liens remain valid after this Act takes effect; and

(2) the transactions and liens may be terminated, completed, consummated, and enforced as required or permitted by this Act or by the law that otherwise would apply if this Act had not taken effect.

For example, suppose that on May 1, 2001 a lessor obtains a nonpossessory lien on crops being grown by the lessee. The lien arises under non-Code state law, but on July 1, 2001, the lien becomes an agricultural lien and falls within the scope of the revision. If the lessee thereafter fails to pay rent as it comes due, the lessor can foreclose on the crops using the method provided by the law under which the lien arose, or it can foreclose using the procedures contained in the revision.

Notwithstanding the general applicability of the revision to pre-transition transactions and liens, its provisions will have no effect on litigation that is pending on the

---

[3] U.C.C. § R9-702(a).

transition date.[4] The law that governed the transaction at the time of its creation will govern the outcome of the litigation.

§ 20.03 The Effect of the Transition on Perfected Security Interests — § R9-703

Section R9-703 deals with the effect of revised Article 9 on security interests that are enforceable and perfected[5] under current Article 9 at the time the revision takes effect. As might be expected, if the steps taken by the secured party would also have created an enforceable, perfected security interest under the revision, no further action is necessary after the transition date for the security interest to maintain its enforceable, perfected status.[6] For example, a security interest in goods perfected by possession before July 1, 2001 remains perfected after that date.

Suppose, however, that the steps taken by the secured party would not have been sufficient to create an enforceable security interest under the revision, or would not have been sufficient for perfection to occur under the revision. For example, suppose that on March 1, 2001 Bank lends money to Debtor for a consumer purpose and takes as collateral a security interest in "all securities accounts." Bank also takes control of the accounts, thereby perfecting its interest. Under the revision, the transaction qualifies as a consumer transaction, and a generic description of securities accounts is insufficient to create an enforceable security interest in a consumer transaction. Section R9-703(b) provides that the secured party's interest remains enforceable for one year after July 1, 2001, but at the expiration of the one-year period it becomes unenforceable if the secured party has not within that year obtained a new security agreement that contains a specific description of each securities account.[7] Reperfection is not required because control remains the appropriate method under the revision for perfecting a security interest in a securities account.

The one-year period also applies to changes in the rules governing perfection by a method other than filing. For example, suppose a secured party has an enforceable security interest in an instrument in the hands of a bailee that became perfected under the 1972 text when the bailee received notice of the interest. Under the revision, receipt of notice is insufficient for the purpose of obtaining constructive possession; the bailee must instead authenticate a record acknowledging that it holds the instrument for the secured party's benefit. To remain perfected beyond the one-year period, the secured party must perfect properly under the revision. It can obtain an authenticated record from the bailee, obtain actual possession of the

---

[4] U.C.C. § R9-702(c).

[5] Perfection is defined functionally as the point in time at which the security interest attains priority over the rights of a lien creditor. U.C.C. § R9-703(a).

[6] *Id.* The mechanisms that can be used to continue perfection beyond the time when it would otherwise lapse under current law are discussed in § 20.06 *infra.*

[7] *See* U.C.C. § R9-703 Cmt. 2, example 1. § R9-703(b)(2) requires that the new security agreement comply with the requirements of § R9-203.

instrument, or file a financing statement. If it takes none of these steps, its security interest remains enforceable but becomes unperfected.[8]

The foregoing rule is subject to section R9-705, which provides a different result when perfection under current law results from the proper filing of a financing statement. The financing statement remains effective until the earlier of its normal lapse date or June 30, 2006.[9] Section R9-705 is discussed in more detail below.[10]

A transition problem can arise because the definitions of certain terms in the 1972 text are changed in the revision. For example, the right of payment held by a person who has sold land under an installment land contract is a general intangible under current law but is an account in the revision. If a secured party acquires an interest in such a right on August 1, 2000 and properly describes its collateral as a general intangible in the security agreement and financing statement, it will have both an enforcement problem and a perfection problem when the revision takes effect. It can avoid the enforcement problem by obtaining a new security agreement[11] covering accounts within the one-year period. It can avoid the perfection problem by filing[12] as to accounts.[13] The time period for making a new filing as to accounts, however, is not governed by the one-year rule. As indicated above, a properly filed financing statement remains effective until the earlier of its normal lapse date or June 30, 2006.

§ 20.04 The Effect of the Transition on Unperfected Security Interests — § R9-704

What is the effect of the transition on security interests that are enforceable but unperfected on the revision's effective date? As to enforcement issues, the rule is the same as that set forth in the preceding subsection with respect to perfected security interests. That is, if the security interest was enforceable under current law but would be unenforceable under the revision, the secured party has one year to take whatever steps are necessary to make it enforceable under the revision.[14]

If the steps taken by the secured party would have been effective to perfect its security interest under the revision but were ineffective under the 1972 text, the security interest becomes perfected when the revision takes effect.[15] For example, suppose a secured party takes a nonpossessory security interest in an instrument under current Article 9 and attempts to perfect by filing a financing statement. Security interests in instruments cannot be perfected by filing under current law, and thus the secured party is unperfected. The revision permits filing for instruments, however, and if the financing statement was filed in the proper office as

---

[8] *See* U.C.C. § R9-703 Cmt. 2, example 2.

[9] U.C.C. § R9-705(c).

[10] *See* § 20.05 *infra.*

[11] The security agreement must be sufficient under the revision's rules. U.C.C. § R9-702(b)(2).

[12] The filing must be sufficient under the revision's rules. U.C.C. § R9-702(b)(3).

[13] *See* U.C.C. § R9-703 Cmt. 3, example 3.

[14] U.C.C. §§ R9-704(1), (2).

[15] U.C.C. § R9-704(3)(A).

designated by the revision (and its contents are sufficient for perfection under the revision) the secured party will awaken on July 1, 2001 to find itself perfected. If, however, a security interest was unperfected under the 1972 text and remains unperfected under the revision, it becomes perfected only upon completion of the steps designated by the revision.[16] In the prior example, if the secured party had neither filed as to the instrument nor taken possession, it would remain unperfected after July 1, 2001. It could become perfected thereafter only by satisfying the revision's perfection requirements.

§ 20.05   Effectiveness of Action to Perfect Taken Before Revision's Effective Date — § R9-705

Section R9-705 deals with the effectiveness under the revision of an action to perfect taken prior to July 1, 2001. The section differentiates between perfection by filing and perfection by any other method. With regard to perfection by a method other than filing, the section deals only with situations where the action to perfect is taken before the transition date but attachment occurs after that date. Situations where attachment occurs before July 1, 2001 are governed by the rules discussed in the preceding subsections.[17]

For example, assume that Bank takes a security interest in "all Debtor's instruments, including after-acquired instruments" before July 1, 2001. Bank and Debtor agree that as instruments are generated by Debtor they will be turned over to Bailee, and Bailee is notified that Bank claims a security interest in all instruments that Bailee receives from Debtor. Receipt of this notice is sufficient under the 1972 text to perfect Bank's interest as to each instrument that comes into Bailee's possession. Assume further that Bailee does not authenticate a record acknowledging that it holds the instruments for the benefit of Bank, an act that would be necessary to perfect Bank's interest under the revision. The receipt-of-notification method continues to perfect Bank as to after-acquired instruments that are turned over to Bailee after July 1, 2001, but Bank's interest becomes unperfected one year after that date if it has not obtained the requisite authenticated acknowledgment. This result is consistent with the result for the instruments that were received by the Bailee prior to July 1, 2001.[18]

Section R9-705(b), which deals with the effectiveness of pre-revision filings, is not expressly limited to cases of post-revision attachment, but such a limitation is nevertheless implicit.[19] Section R9-703 deals with security interests that are

---

[16] U.C.C. § R9-704(3)(B).

[17] If attachment occurs before July 1, 2001 and the action (other than filing) to perfect is sufficient under current law, its effect after that date is determined under U.C.C. § R9-703(b). See § 20.03 supra. If the action is insufficient under current law, its post-revision effect is determined by § R9-704. See § 20.04 supra.

[18] See § 20.03 supra.

[19] See Comment 1 to U.C.C. § R9-705, which refers to the section generally and states that it "addresses primarily, the situation in which the perfection step is taken under former Article 9 or other applicable law before the effective date of this Article, but the security interest does not attach until after that date."

perfected before the transition date and provides that such interests *remain* perfected without further action if "the applicable requirements for enforceability and perfection under this Act are satisfied."[20] Section R9-704 deals with security interests that are unperfected before the transition date and provides that such interests *become* perfected without further action "when this Act takes effect if the applicable requirements for perfection under this Act are satisfied before or at that time . . . ."[21] Thus, section R9-705(b), which states that a pre-revision filing "is effective to perfect a security interest to the extent the filing would satisfy the applicable requirements for perfection under this Act," is necessary only in cases of post-revision attachment.

A pre-revision filing may be effective with regard to collateral acquired after the transition date because the appropriate filing office (*i.e.*, the proper office within the proper state) has not been changed by the revision. In other cases, a pre-revision filing made in the wrong office under current law might become effective as to after-acquired collateral because of the revision.[22] For example, assume Bank takes a security interest under current law in all Debtor's present and after-acquired farm equipment and files in the central filing office in the state where the equipment is located. The state has adopted Alternative 2 to section 9-401 of the 1972 text, and Debtor is a corporation organized under the laws of that same state. The filing is in the proper state because the law where the collateral is located dictates the proper jurisdiction for filing under current law. It is not, however, in the proper office within that state because Alternative 2 mandates local filing for farm equipment. Thus, Bank's security interest is unperfected under the 1972 text. Under the revision, the proper state of filing when the debtor is a registered organization is the state of registration, but in this case that state happens to be the same as the state where Bank filed. The central filing office is the proper place for filing under the revision to perfect all security interests (other than interests in certain land-related collateral), and again that happens to be where Bank filed. Section R9-704(3)(A) provides that Bank's formerly unperfected interest becomes perfected as to existing collateral on the transition date, and section R9-705(b) yields the same result for collateral acquired after that date.[23]

Suppose a filing is effective under the 1972 text but does not satisfy the revision's requirements. Had perfection been predicated on an action other than filing, the action's effectiveness as to both collateral in existence on the transition date and collateral acquired thereafter would be limited to one year after that date.[24] When perfection is predicated on filing, however, the transition rules yield a different result. Section R9-705(c) continues the effectiveness of a properly filed financing

---

[20] U.C.C. § R9-703(a).

[21] U.C.C. § R9-704(3)(A).

[22] If the filing is sufficient to perfect the secured party's interest under both current law and the revision, its effectiveness is continued under the rule set forth in U.C.C. § R9-703(a). *See* § 20.03 *supra.*

[23] This analysis assumes that the financing statement's contents are sufficient under the revision to perfect Bank's interest.

[24] U.C.C. § R9-703(b)(existing collateral), R9-705(a)(collateral acquired after transition date).

statement until the earlier of its normal lapse date or June 30, 2006.[25] In other words, secured parties who have properly filed under current law need not be concerned until their financing statement is about to lapse under current law or June 30, 2006 is approaching.

For example, suppose Bank takes a security interest in Debtor's present and after-acquired nonfarm equipment, the equipment does not qualify as mobile goods, Bank files in the central office of the state where the collateral is located, and Debtor's state of incorporation is a different state. Bank's security interest is perfected under current law since central filing is appropriate under all three alternatives to section 9-401 (although an additional, local filing might be required under the Third Alternative). The filing would not be in the proper state under the revision, but it would continue to be effective until the earlier of its normal lapse date or June 30, 2006.[26]

§ 20.06   Continuation Statements (Including Initial Financing Statements as Continuation Statements) — §§ R9-705, R9-706

The general rule under the revision is that the filing of a continuation statement after July 1, 2001 "does not continue the effectiveness of the financing statement filed before this Act takes effect."[27] If the financing statement was filed in the proper state and office as designated by the revision, however, the timely filing of a continuation statement after the transition date continues perfection for the period of time provided by the revision.[28] Such a continuation statement must comply with the revision's content requirements,[29] and the financing statement[30] that results from the combination of the financing statement[31] and the continuation statement must satisfy the revision's requirements for an initial financing statement.[32]

This last requirement is intended to deal with cases in which the filing was sufficient to perfect the security interest under current law and was filed in the proper state and office as designated by the revision, but the description (although adequate when filed) is inadequate under the revision. For example, the right of

---

[25] "The June 30, 2006, limitation addresses some nonuniform versions of former Article 9 that extended the effectiveness of a financing statement beyond five years." U.C.C. § R9-705 Cmt. 4.

[26] The mechanisms that can be used to continue Bank's perfected status beyond the applicable date are discussed in § 20.06 *infra.*

[27] U.C.C. § R9-705(d).

[28] *Id.*

[29] *Id.*

[30] Under the revision, "financing statement" means "a record or records composed of an initial financing statement and any filed record relating to the initial financing statement." U.C.C. § R9-102(a)(39).

[31] In this context, the term "financing statement" has the meaning set forth in current Article 9, that is "the original financing statement and any amendments." U.C.C. § 9-402(4). A continuation statement is not an amendment under the 1972 text, although it is an amendment in the revision. U.C.C. § R9-102(a)(27).

[32] U.C.C. § R9-705(f).

payment held by a person who has sold land under an installment land contract is a general intangible under current law but is an account in the revision. Suppose a secured party acquires an interest in such a right on August 1, 2000, describes its collateral as a general intangible in the financing statement, and files in the proper office on August 5, 2000. Although the financing statement is misleading after the revision takes effect, its effectiveness continues until its normal lapse date in August 2005. If secured party wishes to file a continuation statement in July 2005 to continue the effectiveness of its August 2000 financing statement, that continuation statement must accurately indicate that the collateral is an account.[33]

When a financing statement that is properly filed under current law is not in the proper state under the revision, or is in the proper state but not the proper office under the revision, a continuation statement will not extend its effectiveness beyond its normal lapse date or June 30, 2006, whichever comes earlier. In such cases, the secured party must file an initial financing statement in the proper state and office as designated by the revision,[34] and it must also make certain that its initial financing statement serves to continue the effectiveness of its original filing. Otherwise a gap in perfection will result that can be exploited by a third-party claimant. To serve as a continuation statement, the initial financing statement must: 1) satisfy the revision's requirements for initial financing statements generally;[35] 2) "identify the pre-effective-date financing statement by indicating the office in which the financing statement was filed and providing the dates of filing and file numbers, if any, of the financing statement and of the most recent continuation statement filed with respect to the financing statement;"[36] and 3) "indicate that the pre-effective-date financing statement remains effective."[37] The debtor need not authorize the filing of an initial financing statement that is filed for the purpose of continuing the effectiveness of a pre-transition filing.[38]

§ 20.07 Priority Rules — § R9-708

The transition to revised Article 9 will inevitably present courts with unusual priority issues, and section R9-708 is designed to provide answers. The basic rule is that current law governs priority contests if the relative priorities of the parties are fixed before the revision's effective date; otherwise the revision governs.[39]

---

[33] See U.C.C. § R9-705 Cmt. 6, example 5. Curiously, although the financing statement remains effective until 2005, the security agreement would have to be revised to cover accounts within one year after the revision's effective date. See U.C.C. § R9-703 Cmt. 3, example 3, discussed in § 20.03 *supra.*

[34] U.C.C. § R9-706(a).

[35] U.C.C. § R9-706(c)(i).

[36] U.C.C. § R9-706(c)(2).

[37] U.C.C. § R9-706(c)(3).

[38] U.C.C. § R9-707 (only secured party of record need authorize continuation statements or initial financing statements filed to continue effectiveness of pre-effective-date financing statement).

[39] U.C.C. § R9-708(a).

Section R9-708(b) deals with cases in which the secured party's interest is unperfected under current law but becomes perfected by virtue of the revision taking effect. For example, suppose that in 1999 Bank takes a security interest in all Debtor's accounts and general intangibles. Bank's security agreement accurately describes the collateral but Bank inadvertently omits general intangibles from its financing statement. Among Debtor's assets is a right to payment under an installment land contract — a general intangible under the 1972 text but an account under the revision — and Bank's security interest in this right is unperfected. In 2000, Finance Company takes and by filing perfects a security interest in all Debtor's accounts and general intangibles. When the revision takes effect, Bank becomes perfected as to Debtor's right under the installment land contract.[40] For purposes of the revision's general priority rule governing the priority contest between Bank and Finance Company,[41] however, Bank's filing and perfection as to the right to payment under the installment contract date only from July 1, 2001.[42] Finance Company has priority.

Section R9-708(c) provides a similar rule for cases in which a filing that occurs before the transition date is ineffective under current law but effective under the revision. For example, suppose that in 1999 Bank takes a security interest in Debtor's existing and after-acquired instruments and files as to "instruments." A financing statement will not perfect a security interest in instruments under the 1972 text but is sufficient under the revision. In 2000 Debtor grants a security interest in its existing and after-acquired accounts to Finance Company. After the transition date, one of Debtor's account debtors gives Debtor a negotiable note to evidence its obligation. Under the revision's normal first-to-file-or-perfect rule, Bank would have priority.[43] However, because Bank's financing statement did not become effective until July 1, 2001, its filing and perfection date from that time only.[44] Finance Company has priority as to the negotiable note.

---

[40] U.C.C. § R9-704(3)(A). The hypothetical assumes that the filing satisfies the revision's requirements as to the contents of the financing statement and the proper filing office.

[41] U.C.C. § R9-322(a)(1)(as between perfected secured parties, first to file or perfect prevails).

[42] See U.C.C. § R9-708 Cmt. 1, example 1. Bank would have priority as to all of Debtor's other accounts (as defined under the 1972 text), and Finance Company would have priority as to all of Debtor's general intangibles. § R9-708(b) provides that this rule does not apply if the interests of both parties become perfected on the transition date by virtue of § R9-704.

[43] U.C.C. § R9-322(a)(1).

[44] See U.C.C. § R9-708 Cmt. 2, example 3. § R9-708(c) provides that this rule does not apply to conflicting security interests each of which is perfected by a financing statement that is ineffective under current law but effective under the revision.

TABLE OF CASES

[References are to sections and footnotes.]

[References are to sections and footnotes.]

C

[References are to sections and footnotes.]

[References are to sections and footnotes.]

[References are to sections and footnotes.]

[References are to sections and footnotes.]

[References are to sections and footnotes.]

[References are to sections and footnotes.]

[References are to sections and footnotes.]

[References are to sections and footnotes.]

[References are to sections and footnotes.]

X

Y

Z

TABLE OF STATUTES AND AUTHORITIES

[References are to sections and footnotes.]

TS–1

(Matthew Bender & Co., Inc.)

(Pub.587)

[References are to sections and footnotes.]

[References are to sections and footnotes.]

[References are to sections and footnotes.]

[References are to sections and footnotes.]

[References are to sections and footnotes.]

[References are to sections and footnotes.]

[References are to sections and footnotes.]

INDEX

[References are to page numbers]

[References are to page numbers]

[References are to page numbers]

[References are to page numbers]

[References are to page numbers]

D

[References are to page numbers]

[References are to page numbers]

[References are to page numbers]

[References are to page numbers]

[References are to page numbers]

[References are to page numbers]

[References are to page numbers]

R

[References are to page numbers]

S

[References are to page numbers]